Guide to
Network Defense and Countermeasures

Greg Holden

Australia • Canada • Mexico • Singapore • Spain • United Kingdom • United States

Guide to Network Defense and Countermeasures
is published by Course Technology

Senior Editor:
William Pitkin III

Senior Editor:
Lisa Egan

Product Manager:
Amy M. Lyon

Developmental Editor:
Jill Batistick

Production Editor:
Elena Montillo

Technical Editor:
Ron Milione

Manufacturing Coordinator:
Trevor Kallop

MQA Technical Leader:
Nicole Ashton

Product Marketing Manager:
Jason Sakos

Associate Product Manager:
Nick Lombardi

Editorial Assistant:
Christy Urban

Cover Design:
Julie Malone

Text Designer:
GEX Publishing Services

Compositor:
GEX Publishing Services

Printed in Canada

1 2 3 4 5 6 7 8 9 WC 07 06 05 04 03

For more information, contact Course Technology, 25 Thomson Place, Boston, Massachusetts, 02210.

Or find us on the World Wide Web at: www.course.com

ISBN 0-619-13124-1

BRIEF

Contents

TABLE OF

Contents

Chapter 2

Chapter 3

Chapter 10

Chapter 11

Preface

This book is an introduction to one of the most important and urgent concepts associated with protecting computers and networks in the twenty-first century: intrusion detection.

In a narrow sense, intrusion detection is the ability of hardware and software to alert users to suspicious connection attempts that may represent attempts to gain unauthorized access to a computer and/or the resources on it. This specific function is covered extensively throughout several chapters of this book.

However, in a wider sense, the practice of intrusion detection encompasses virtually all aspects of network security, and these activities—such as risk analysis, security policies, damage assessment, intrusion response, anticipating future attacks, and prosecuting intruders—are also examined throughout the book.

This book was written toward two goals. The first goal is to provide students with a solid foundation in network security fundamentals; while the primary emphasis is on intrusion detection, the book also covers such essential practices as developing a security policy and then implementing that policy by performing Network Address Translation (NAT) and packet filtering and by installing proxy servers, firewalls, and virtual private networks (VPNs). The second goal is to prepare students to take the Network Defense and Countermeasures exam, which is the second exam for the Security Certified Network Professional certification.

Where Should You Start?

Guide to Network Defense and Countermeasures is intended for students and professionals who need hands-on introductory experience with installing firewalls and intrusion detection systems. The text assumes that the reader has some familiarity with the Internet and basic networking concepts such as TCP/IP, gateways, routers, and Ethernet. It also assumes that the student has fulfilled the prerequisites for exam SC0-402, which include IP troubleshooting; subnetting, subnet masking, IP datagram structure, routing, Web security, and common attack techniques.

Chapters 1 and 2 of this book should be a review for the student. They cover IP addressing, subnetting, routing, IP packet structure, and the different types of network attacks that a perimeter security configuring should defend against. Chapters 3 through 11 cover the development of a well-defined security policy, as well as encryption, authentication, VPNs, firewalls, and other security concepts that contribute to intrusion detection and countermeasures.

This book does not need to be studied in sequence. The first two chapters do, however, provide you with a solid introduction to network security, so it's highly recommended that you start there. However, if you need to focus on intrusion detection, skip ahead to Chapters 8 through 11. For a focus on firewalls, turn to Chapters 4 through 6; for VPNs, turn to Chapter 7. More detailed descriptions of each chapter are presented in the following section.

Chapter Descriptions

The chapters in this book discuss the following topics:

Chapter 1, "Foundations of Network Security," discusses the reasons for developing a network security program, including hackers, viruses, and disgruntled employees. It also examines the goals of a network security program, which balances the need for connectivity and access with the need to maintain privacy and integrity. Basic TCP/IP networking concepts that play a role in thwarting intrusions and attacks are also covered, including IP addressing, subnetting, IP packet structure, DNS, and routing and access control. The chapter rounds out with techniques for securing individual workstations and with maintaining security on the World Wide Web.

Chapter 2, "Designing a Network Defense," explores common security threats and vulnerabilities that need to be addressed by intrusion detection systems and other security devices. It also provides an introductory overview of the basic tools used to block those threats, including packet filters, anti-virus software, log files and software to analyze them, and intrusion detection systems.

Chapter 3, "Risk Analysis and Security Policy Design," examines an essential and often overlooked topic: the development of a security policy that tells members of an organization how to protect critical resources and how to respond in case an intrusion occurs. The policy grows out of a comprehensive risk analysis and risk assessment, and the chapter also examines the concept of risk analysis in regard to computer resources and security.

Chapter 4, "Choosing and Designing Firewalls," begins by discussing how to configure a bastion host, a highly secured computer that runs firewall or intrusion detection software. The chapter also provides you with an overview of the different kinds of firewalls and their primary functions so that you can choose the right one to meet your needs.

Chapter 5, "Configuring Firewalls," introduces you to the basic firewall security function—packet filtering. You also learn about other common security functions performed by firewalls, including NAT, authentication, and encryption.

Chapter 6, "Strengthening and Managing Firewalls," discusses how proxy servers work to shield individual hosts on the internal network by acting on their behalf. You also learn how to manage and customize the often-voluminous log files that firewalls accumulate, and how to improve firewall performance. Finally, you learn how to install and initiate the configuration of three popular firewalls: CheckPoint NG, Microsoft ISA Server, and iptables.

Chapter 7, "Setting Up a Virtual Private Network," discusses the establishment of VPNs, which provide corporations with a cost-effective means for conducting secure communications over the public Internet. Because VPNs use encryption and authentication, it's a good idea to read chapter 5 before you get to this chapter.

Chapter 8, "Intrusion Detection: An Overview," introduces the concept of intrusion detection, and provides an overview of the components that make up a typical network intrusion detection system (IDS). You follow the process of intrusion detection step-by-step, and you learn the features of network-based, host-based, and hybrid IDS implementations. Finally, you examine some of the most popular IDS packages available, ranging from freeware software to expensive hardware systems that employ multiple network sensors to detect suspicious traffic.

Chapter 9, "Intrusion Detection: Preventive Measures," delves into the approaches actually used by IDS hardware and software to detect unauthorized access attempts and block them. In particular, you examine different types of intrusion detection signatures—sets of characteristics that identify known suspicious packets. You learn how to capture packets and how to compare normal traffic signatures to suspicious ones. You also examine how to develop filters based on the unique characteristics of those signatures.

Chapter 10, "Intrusion Detection: Incident Response," explores the development and activities of a group of individuals who are assigned to respond to security incidents and minimize any damage that might occur. You learn the various options for assembling such a team, and how to deal with false alarms as they occur. Finally, you learn about computer forensics, and how to handle evidence of an intrusion so that it can be used in court to prosecute offenders.

Chapter 11, "Strengthening Defense through Ongoing Management," discusses issues associated with the efficient management of an existing IDS so that it not only continues to operate efficiently, but also continues to block new attacks as they occur. You learn about real-time event monitoring and evolving the IDS to keep pace with a growing network by adding memory, software, and hardware. You learn how to keep pace with the rapidly evolving challenges in the field of network security by strengthening your own personal knowledge base as well.

Appendix A, "SC0-402 Objectives," maps the objectives specified in Security Certified Professional's (SCP's) SC0-402 Network Defense and Countermeasures course to the corresponding chapter and section title where the objectives are covered in this book. If you need to brush up on a specific topic in preparation for the exam and you want to know where the topic is covered, use this section as a reference.

Appendix B, "Security Resources," provides a snapshot of the primary security-related organizations, groups, and information sources that were active when this book was written. If you're looking for up-to-the-minute news and views about virus attacks or security problems you are experiencing, turn to the resources listed in this section.

Readers are also encouraged to investigate the many pointers to online and printed sources of additional information that are cited throughout this book.

Features

To aid you in fully understanding networking security concepts, this book includes many features designed to enhance your learning expereince.

- *Chapter Objectives:* Each chapter in this book begins with a detailed list of the concepts to be mastered within that chapter. This list provides you with a quick reference to the contents of that chapter, as well as a useful study aid.
- *Illustrations, Tables, and Screenshots:* Numerous illustrations of networking configurations aid you in the visualization of common perimeter defense setups and architectures. In addition, many tables provide details and comparisons using both practical and theoretical information. Some tables provide specific examples of packet filtering rules you can use to build a firewall rule base. Because most campus laboratories use Microsoft operating systems, we use their products for screen shots and for most of the Hands-on Projects for this book.
- *Chapter Summaries:* Each chapter's text is followed by a summary of the concepts it has introduced. These summaries provide a helpful way to recap and revisit the ideas covered in each chapter.
- *Key Terms:* All of the terms within the chapter that were introduced with boldfaced text are gathered together in the Key Terms list at the end of the chapter. This provides you with a method of checking your understanding of all the terms introduced.
- *Review Questions:* The Key Terms list is followed by a set of review questions that reinforce the ideas introduced in each chapter. Answering these questions will ensure that you have mastered the important concepts.
- *Hands-on Projects:* Although it is important to understand the theory behind networking technology, nothing can improve upon real-world experience. With the exceptions of those chapters that are purely theoretical, each chapter provides a series of exercises aimed at providing you with hands-on implementation experience.
- *Case Projects:* Finally, each chapter closes with a section that proposes certain intrusion detection and security-related situations. You are asked to evaluate the situation and decide upon the course of action to be taken to remedy the problems described. This valuable tool will help you to sharpen decision-making and troubleshooting skills—important aspects of network security systems administration.

Text and Graphic Conventions

Wherever appropriate, additional information and exercises have been added to this book to help you better understand what is being discussed in the chapter. Icons throughout the text alert you to additional materials. The icons used in this textbook are described below.

The Note icon draws your attention to additional helpful material related to the subject being described.

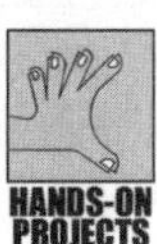

Each hands-on activity in this book is preceded by the Hands-On icon and a description of the exercise that follows.

Tips based on the author's experience provide extra information about how to attack a problem or what to do in real-world situations.

The Caution icon warns you about potential mistakes or problems and explains how to avoid them.

The Case Project icon marks case projects, which are more involved, scenario-based assignments. In these extensive case examples, you are asked to implement independently what you have learned.

Instructor's Materials

The following supplemental materials are available when this book is used in a classroom setting. All of the supplements available with this book are provided to the instructor on a single CD-ROM.

Electronic Instructor's Manual. The Instructor's Manual that accompanies this textbook includes additional instructional material to assist in class preparation, including suggestions for classroom activities, discussion topics, and additional projects.

Solutions. Solutions are included to all end-of-chapter material, including the Review Questions, and where applicable, Hands-on Projects and Case Project.

ExamView . This textbook is accompanied by ExamView, a powerful testing software package that allows instructors to create and administer printed, computer (LAN-based), and Internet exams. ExamView includes hundreds of questions that correspond to the topics covered in this text, enabling students to generate detailed study guides that include page references for further review. The computer-based and Internet testing components allow students to take exams at their computers, and also save the instructor time by grading each exam automatically.

PowerPoint Presentations. This book comes with Microsoft PowerPoint slides for each chapter. These are included as a teaching aid for classroom presentation, to make available to students on the network for chapter review, or to be printed for classroom distribution. Instructors, please feel at liberty to add your own slides for additional topics you introduce to the class.

Figure Files. All of the figures in the book are reproduced on the Instructor's Resources CD, in bit-mapped format. Similar to the PowerPoint presentations, these are included as a teaching aid for classroom presentation, to make available to students for review, or to be printed for classroom distribution.

Coping with Change on the Web

Sooner or later, all the specific Web-based resources mentioned throughout the rest of this book will go stale or be replaced by newer information. In some cases, the URLs you find here may lead you to their replacements; in other cases, the URLs will lead nowhere, leaving you with the dreaded 404 error message, "File not found."

When that happens, please don't give up! There's always a way to find what you want on the Web, if you're willing to invest some time and energy. To begin with, most large or complex Web sites offer a search engine. As long as you can get to the site itself, you can use this tool to help you find what you need.

Don't be afraid to use general search tools like *www.google.com*, *www.hotbot.com*, or *www.excite.com* to find related information. Although certain standards bodies may offer the most precise and specific information about their standards online, there are plenty of third-party sources of information, training, and assistance in this area as well. The bottom line is this: if you can't find something where the book says it lives, start looking around. It's got to be around there, somewhere!

Visit our World Wide Web Site

Additional materials designed especially for you might be available for your course on the World Wide Web. Go to *www.course.com* and search for this book title periodically for more details.

ACKNOWLEDGMENTS

I would like to thank the team at Course Technology for the opportunity to write this book on a topic of such value and interest, which is also my first book for them. This team includes, but is not limited to, Amy Lyon, Product Manager; Elena Montillo, Production Editor; the excellent copy editors; and the quality assurance folks, Sean Franey and Stephen

Connor. Thanks also to Jill Batistick, Development Editor, for her always-excellent edits, her words of encouragement, and her periodic reminders which kept me on track. Ron Milione, the Technical Editor, went above and beyond the call of duty to provide detailed suggestions based on his experience. I would also like to thank the reviewers, who guided me with excellent and helpful feedback on each chapter:

Timothy Culhane	New England Institute of Technology
Max Josquin	Spokane Falls Community College
Eileen Vidrine	Northern Virginia Community College

A special thanks goes to my best friend and faithful assistant Ann Lindner, and to my daughters Lucy and Zosia, whose patience and support made this project successful.

Read This Before You Begin

This book contains more than 65 hands-on projects, many of which require you to install and use different security-related software programs. You need to have access to a computer that is connected to the Internet and that can run the software programs. The suggested hardware and software requirements are described in the following sections.

Hardware Requirements

Your computer's CPU should be at least a Pentium II and running at 300MHz or faster. You also need to have a minimum of 128MB of RAM in order to operate Check Point NG; to run Web browsers, word processing programs, and other applications at the same time, you should have at least 192MB of RAM (ideally, 256MG or more of RAM) and a minimum of 75MB of available hard disk space.

Software Requirements

Most of the projects in this book can be completed using a computer that runs Windows 2000 or XP or Red Hat Linux 7.3 or later. Check Point NG is designed to run on Windows 2000; it will run with limited functionality on Windows XP.

Many of the programs used in this book's hands-on projects require you to download and install software. At the very least, your computer should be equipped with a Web browser and the archiving utility WinZip (available at *www.winzip.com*). You'll also need a word processing program or text editor to record answers from the hands-on projects. An e-mail application, such as Outlook Express or Netscape Messenger, is used in several of the projects as well.

CHAPTER

1

FOUNDATIONS OF NETWORK SECURITY

After reading this chapter and completing the exercises, you will be able to:

- Understand the individuals who might attempt to break into your network
- Set goals for developing a network security system
- Review the TCP/IP networking fundamentals that you'll need to secure a network
- Describe the elements of IP packets that can be misused by hackers
- Know the role routers play in a network security perimeter
- Secure workstations
- Understand aspects of Internet-based communications that present security risks

A recent survey conducted by the Computer Security Institute and the FBI reported that 90 percent of all respondents had detected intrusions in the previous year, and 80 percent reported financial losses of as much as $455 million as a result of those break-ins. (For the latest survey results, visit *www.gocsi.com*).

The increase in intrusions is only one reason why computer security is more important than ever. Another reason is terrorist attacks. As the reliance on information technology (IT) and the Internet grows, the amount of critical information left vulnerable to online access and the need to protect it grows.

This chapter introduces you to the fundamental network security challenges you need to know about. First, you learn about different kinds of intrusions and intruders. You then get a rundown of the goals of a network security project, including intrusion detection. You also get an overview of the TCP/IP networking issues that pertain most closely to setting up an IDS, and you become familiar with the structure of IP packets, which can be critical in blocking harmful communications. You learn about routing and access control and how to secure individual workstations. Finally, you get tips and pointers on how to secure Web servers and Web-based communications.

KNOWING YOUR ENEMIES

A variety of individuals may attempt to intrude on your network, causing loss of data, loss of privacy, and other consequences. The threat is one that concerns a growing number of corporate managers. A survey released by the Business Software Alliance in September 2002 found that nearly half of corporate administrators surveyed believed that U.S. businesses would be attacked in the coming year, but only 19 percent believed that their own companies were adequately protected against attacks.

This section of the chapter first provides a general overview of what drives some of these attacks. It then describes who might be doing it and what they might be trying to accomplish.

What Hackers Are Looking For and What You Should Protect

This section describes common motivations of hackers, including the desire to gain access to a remote system, revenge, financial gain, and theft of proprietary information and other data you want to keep private.

System Access

Some hackers attempt to take over computer systems just for the thrill of it. They like to keep count of how many systems they have access to as a sort of notch on their hacker's belt. Unfortunately, this rather benign situation is only one reason why hackers want to access other computer systems. The other reasons are more insidious, and they include theft of information as well as the ability to use the remote system as a staging area from which to launch attacks on other computers.

Revenge

Another motivation that impels individuals to attempt to break in to someone else's computer or network is revenge. Disgruntled current or former employees want to retaliate against an organization for policies or actions they consider wrong. They can sometimes gain entry to a database that is protected from outsiders through a **back door** —a way of gaining unauthorized access to a computer or other resource, usually through an opening in a computer program supposed to be known only to the program's author. A back door could also be an administrator password that an employee steals, a computer to which the employee has access, or another way into the system.

The point you need to keep in mind is that most computer attacks aren't completely random. The attackers seek to undo something they perceive as an injustice. Any employee you discipline or fire should be regarded as a potential security threat. Also, keep in mind that the policies your organization pursues may attract individuals who want to adversely affect your business. Where and with whom you do business could also be a catalyst. Many government and business leaders are concerned about the threat of cyber-terrorists launching coordinated attacks against U.S. business networks to make a political statement. More information on this internetnews.com article is available at *www.internet-news.com/stats/print.php/1448291*.

Financial Gain

While many hackers want to gain control of networks or remote computers, others have financial profit as their goal. A company can incur financial losses through computer-based security breaches in one of two ways:

- Financial losses through fraud or theft
- Financial losses due to the theft of proprietary information

Obviously, hackers who break in to a network can gain access to financial accounts. They can steal individual or corporate credit card numbers and use those numbers to make unauthorized purchases. In March 2002, CNET reported that hackers had broken into the user accounts of individuals who use the giant online auction service eBay (*www.ebay.com*). Many users had their accounts taken over in order to set up fraudulent auctions, and some bidders were even bilked out of money when they won the fake "auctions."

Just as often, hackers defraud people out of money with scams launched by e-mail or other means. In May 2002, six people were arrested in South Africa on suspicion of being involved in a Nigerian e-mail and letter scam in which thousands of e-mails were sent. The e-mails claimed they were trying to move a large sum of money and offered recipients a percentage of the cash if they let the money be deposited into their bank accounts—but only if they paid money to cover "expenses" first. Americans are reported to have been defrauded hundreds of thousands of dollars through this scam (*http://news.com.com/2110-1023-920452.html*).

One reason why there may be so many attackers and why computer intrusions are on the rise is the infrequency with which intrusions are actually reported and the perpetrators are pursued by police. According to the 2002 Computer Security and Crime Survey cited earlier, only 34 percent of the organizations surveyed actually reported the intrusions to law enforcement officials. While the report doesn't speculate as to why such incidents go unreported, the author's experience suggests that organizations are embarrassed to admit the loss of data to their stockholders or business partners, and they are afraid to let hackers know their networks have been violated.

Theft of Commercial Data

Credit card numbers, bank account numbers, or other financial information of individuals isn't always the most valuable commodity held in an organization's databases and **data warehouses**, which are central repositories where data is stored so that it can be accessed and analyzed as needed. Rather, the proprietary information gathered by many corporations as a result of the research and hard work of their employees is often valuable enough that it can be sold to unfriendly nations who want to upgrade their technological capabilities in some way.

Some of the more common kinds of attacks you need to guard against and the defensive strategies you can deploy to defeat them are described in Table 1-1.

Table 1-1 Hack attacks and the defenses you can employ

Attack	Description	Defense	Where Discussed In This Book
Denial of Service (DoS) attack	The traffic into and out of a network is blocked when servers are flooded with malformed packets (bits of digital information) that have false IP addresses or other data inserted into them or that contain other fake communications.	Keep your server OS up to date; log instances of frequent connection attempts against one service.	Chapter 2
SYN flood	A network is overloaded with packets that have the SYN flag set.	Keep your firewall and OS up-to-date so that such attacks are blocked by means of software patches and updates, and review your log files (files that record access attempts) to see if intrusion attempts have been made.	Chapter 2
Virus	The network computers are infected by viruses.	Install anti-virus software and keep virus definitions up-to-date.	Chapter 2
Trojan horse	A hacker delivers a malicious Trojan horse program through a "back door."	Install anti-virus software and keep virus definitions up-to-date.	Chapter 2
Social engineering	An employee is misled into giving out passwords or other sensitive information.	Educate employees about your security policy, which is a set of goals and procedures for making an organization's network secure.	Chapter 3

Attack	Description	Defense	Where Discussed In This Book
Malicious port scanning	A hacker looks for open ports to infiltrate a network.	Install and configure a firewall, which is hardware and/or software designed to filter out unwanted network traffic and protect authorized traffic.	Chapter 4
Internet Control Message Protocol (ICMP) message abuse	A network is flooded with a stream of ICMP echo requests to a target computer.	Packet filtering	Chapter 5
Finding vulnerable hosts on the internal network to attack	A hacker who gains access to one computer on a network can get IP addresses, hostnames, and passwords, which are then used to find other hosts to attack.	Proxy servers	Chapter 6
Man-in-the-middle	A hacker operates between two computers in a network and impersonates one computer to intercept communications.	VPN encryption	Chapter 7
New files being placed on the system	A virus or other program causes new files to proliferate on infected computers, using up system resources.	Install system auditing software such as Tripwire.	Chapter 8
Remote Procedure Call (RPC) attacks	The operating systems crash because they are unable to handle arbitrary data sent to an RPC port.	IDS system	Chapter 9

Who Are the Attackers?

When planning different intrusion detection methods, it is important to know the sorts of individuals who are likely to try to break into your system. Knowing something about who they are and what their motivations are can help you anticipate and set up detection systems, firewalls, and other defenses to repel them as effectively as possible. Being aware of hackers, disgruntled employees, criminals, and script kiddies will cover most of the incidents you are likely to face. We discuss each group of individuals next.

Hackers

A **hacker** is anyone who attempts to gain access to unauthorized resources on a network, usually by finding a way to circumvent passwords, firewalls, or other protective measures. The fact is that hackers aren't a monolithic group. They seek to break into computers for different reasons:

- The "old school" hackers consider themselves to be seekers of knowledge; they operate on the theory that knowledge is power, regardless of how they come by that knowledge. They are not out to destroy or harm; they want to discover how things work and open up any sources of knowledge that they can find. They believe the Internet was intended to be an open environment and anything online can and should be available to anyone.
- Other less "ethical" hackers pursue destructive aims such as the proliferation of viruses and e-mail bombs, much like vandals and graffiti artists.
- Some bored young people who are highly adept with computers try to gain control of as many systems as possible for the thrill of it. They enjoy disrupting systems and keeping them from working; they then tend to boast about their exploits online.
- Some are known as **crackers**, meaning they are attracted to the challenge of detecting passwords and removing copy protection from software.

The Hackers.com Web site (*www.hackers.com*) has the self-declared goal "to teach the world the ethics of true hackers and of hacking." Elsewhere on the home page, the site calls hacking an "industry." Can hacking—the practice of gaining access to networks and computers without authorization—have its own "ethics"? You be the judge.

What can you do to protect yourself against hackers? For starters, you can do the following:

- Make sure all users actually have passwords in place and don't simply press Return to log on to the network.
- Disable Guest accounts or other accounts that are not needed. Also, instruct employees to use passwords that are at least 6-8 characters long and that use both numbers and letters.
- Make an effort to change passwords periodically—every few weeks or months—rather than leaving them in place for months on end.

A good overview of the different motivations of hackers is available at The Learning Channel's Web site, *http://tlc.discovery.com/convergence/hackers/articles/psych.html*.

Disgruntled Employees

Who would be trying to access customer information, financial files, job records, or other sensitive information from *inside* the organization? Disgruntled employees would. These are employees who are unhappy over receiving termination notices, not receiving raises, and so on, and who want to exact revenge on their managers in particular or their place of employment in general by stealing information. Often, they provide the information to new employers. In some cases, information about sensitive computer programs or government agencies is in high demand by nations that are hostile to the U.S. and can be sold to those nations by employees seeking to profit. Whenever an employee is terminated, security measures should be taken to ensure that the former employee can no longer access the company network. Such measures should be included in the organization's security policy, as explained in Chapter 3.

You can read more about the 2002 Computer Crime and Security Survey, including the affects of the security breaches that were reported, by accessing *www.gocsi.com/press/20020407.html*.

Criminals

The reason why "old school" hackers emphasize that they are not out to destroy and that they observe their own set of ethical behaviors is because many hackers now are simply out to steal anything they can get their hands on. In the year 2000, a hacker named Maxim broke into the CD Universe Web site, allegedly stole thousands of credit card numbers, and demanded $100,000 to not post the numbers online.

Script Kiddies and Packet Monkeys

The term **script kiddie** is often used to describe young, immature computer programmers who spread viruses and other malicious scripts, and who use techniques to exploit weaknesses in computer systems. They lack the experience to create viruses or Trojan horses on their own, but they obtain such programs and spread them for their own aims. The assumption among the supposedly more sophisticated hackers is that the script kiddies seek only to break into as many computers as possible in order to gain attention and notoriety. Whatever the intention, script kiddies are dangerous individuals who can wreak havoc on unprotected systems.

Another type of mischievous hacker, a **packet monkey**, is primarily interested in blocking the activities of a Web site through a **Distributed Denial of Service (DDoS) attack**. A DDoS attack is an attack in which dozens or even hundreds of computers are hijacked by the hacker and used to flood a Web site with so many false requests that the site's server cannot process all of them, and normal traffic is blocked. A packet monkey may also want to **deface** Web sites by leaving messages on the sites that can be read by their friends. Their primary intention is simply to cause trouble rather than to see what information a site contains or how the site is structured.

Packet monkeys, script kiddies, and their exploits are explained in the Jargon File, an online version of the Hacker's Dictionary that you can research at *www.hack.gr/jargon*.

Goals of Network Security

The sections thus far have given you an overview of the threats faced by networks that want to permit access to trusted individuals but block unauthorized access. Such **risk analysis** (the analysis of the primary security risks faced by a network) gives you the foundation on which to build network security systems to defend against those risks.

In the sections that follow, you will learn what is needed to begin building secure systems. First, you must have a clear picture of the overriding goals of a network security effort, including privacy and data integrity. Next, you need to have a way to reliably authenticate authorized users. Finally, you need to enable partners, mobile workers, and contractors to connect securely to the main network.

Maintaining Privacy

Corporations, hospitals, and other organizations that hold databases full of personal and financial information need to maintain privacy not only to protect their customers, but also to maintain the integrity and credibility of their own companies.

One of the most important and effective ways to maintain the privacy of the information held on an organization's network resources is to educate rank-and-file employees about security dangers and policies. This sort of consciousness-raising isn't one of the duties that IT and network security students think about when they enter the corporate world, but it's an important task you should implement. Individual employees, after all, are the ones who are most likely to detect or even inadvertently cause security breaches through their own careless behavior. They are also able to monitor the activities of their fellow employees and may be aware of someone who stays after work to copy files, someone who accesses the corporate network from home using an insecure connection, or some other suspicious activity.

You may well be called upon to help develop a comprehensive security policy for a company and to inform employees about that policy and how it governs their behavior. (Chapter 3 discusses how to develop such policies in greater detail.) It may seem that it's not your job to educate employees about security issues, and that this sort of instruction was not in your job description when you are hired. However, if you take the time to make your coworkers aware of how the network can and cannot be used, you can help prevent data from being stolen by disgruntled employees. Ultimately, your efforts to protect the network and the information on it will help improve your company's bottom line.

Preserving Data Integrity

One of the things that hackers are able to do, and which you'll learn about in more detail in Chapter 2, is **spoofing**. Spoofing is entering false information into the packets of data that travel along the Internet or on any network that uses TCP/IP. Hackers are able to make e-mail messages look like they came from the person who is receiving them or from a trusted organization.

The e-mail message shown in Figure 1-1 was received by this book's author. It was made to look as though it was sent by the author and it contained an attachment that was identified by an anti-virus program as one of many variations on the notorious Klez virus.

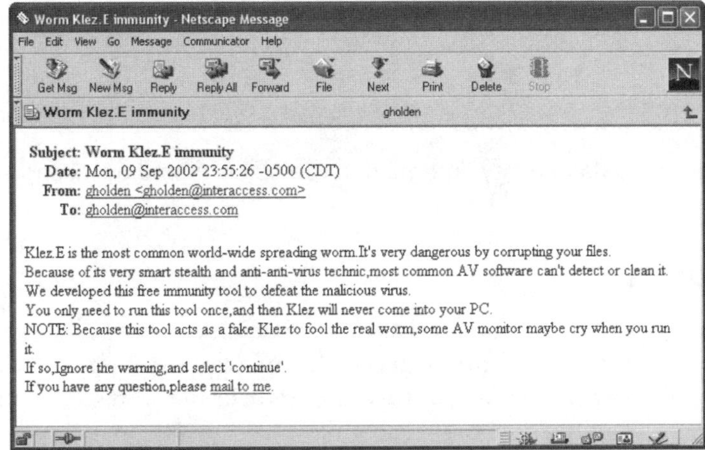

Figure 1-1 Hackers can falsify the source of TCP/IP communications like this e-mail message

Firewalls, anti-virus programs, and Intrusion Detection Systems (IDS) can all block mangled or falsified packets when they reach the perimeter of the network. A far more effective way to ensure network security, however, is to prevent network communications from being hacked or falsified in the first place—in other words, to preserve the integrity of such communications.

Data integrity can be preserved through any of the multiple encryption methods in use on the Internet. One of the most popular approaches is **public-key cryptography**, which encrypts communications through the use of long blocks of code called keys. Each user on the network can obtain one or more **keys**, which are generated by complex formulas called algorithms. The algorithms used by the freeware security program Pretty Good Privacy (PGP) are considered particularly strong. A user who obtains a program that uses PGP's algorithms obtains keys to encrypt files, folders, e-mail messages, and a variety of other data. A key generated with one of the two algorithms that can be used with PGP is shown in Figure 1-2.

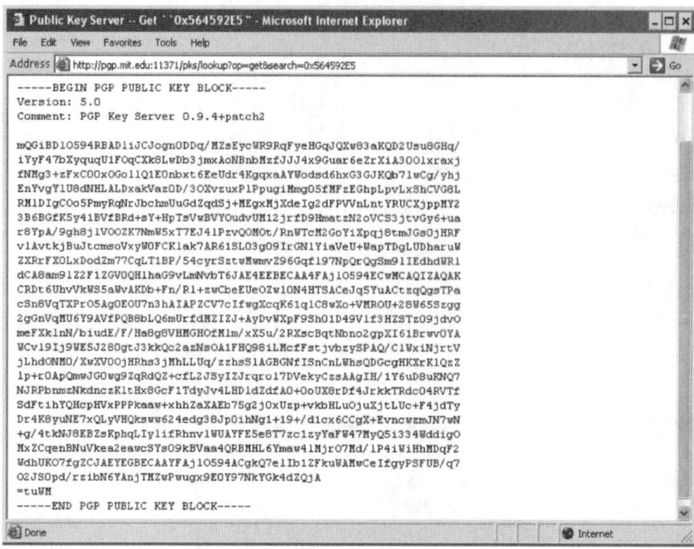

Figure 1-2 To preserve data integrity, information can be encrypted by means of keys like this

Authenticating Users

One of the most important and fundamental aspects of network security in the twenty-first century is the movement from **defended networks** (networks that put an emphasis on defensive measures and restricted access) to **trusted networks** (networks that permit access to trusted users whose identities they can reliably verify).

Firewalls, in particular, can be set up to force users to enter a username and password to gain access to networked services. The process of determining the identity of an authorized user through the matching of a username and password or by other means is known as **authentication**. A **proxy server** (a program that provides Web browsing, e-mail, and other services on behalf of networked users in order to conceal their identity from those outside the network) can sometimes be configured to require authentication before users can surf the Web or use other Internet-based services (see Figure 1-3).

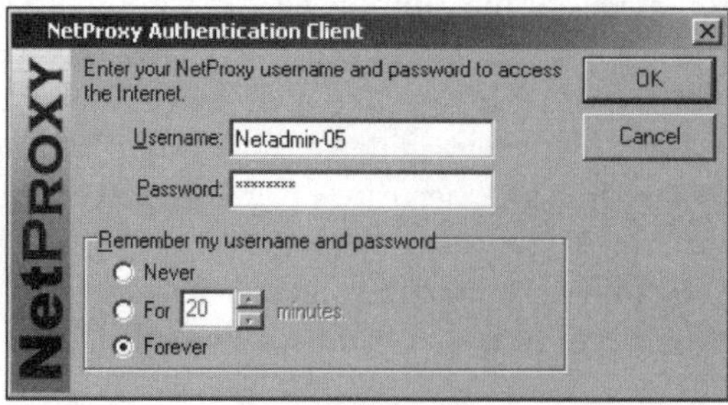

Figure 1-3 Authentication is designed to reliably identify authorized users

Enabling Connectivity

In the early days of the Internet, network security primarily emphasized blocking hackers and other unauthorized users from accessing the corporate network. These days, connectivity with trusted individuals and networks is needed most. Why? Because, as more businesses go online and obtain affordable high-speed connections, they are choosing to conduct more and more of their day-to-day operations through the Internet. Thus, these businesses (or their customers or clients) regularly do any number of activities that a hacker or criminal would seize upon:

- Place orders not by phone or fax, but by directly accessing the partner business's accounting system
- Pay bills by transferring funds through the Internet
- Access account information for budgeting purposes
- Look up personnel records
- Create passwords for employees who need to access the network

To provide security for such transactions, many businesses have traditionally set up **leased lines**, which are point-to-point frame relays or other connections established by the telecommunications companies that own the lines involved in making the connection. Leased lines are secure because they directly connect the two businesses, and no other companies can use the cables or connections involved. However, leased lines are expensive.

To cut costs, many businesses that already have high-speed connections to the Internet have set up virtual private networks (VPN), which use encryption, authentication, and **data encapsulation**, the latter of which is the process of protecting a packet of digital information by enclosing it within another packet. These VPNs are used to set up secure connections between computers or networks using the Internet. Data is transmitted from one VPN participant to another over the same Internet that the public uses. However, the data is highly protected by a variety of security measures:

- Firewalls can be used at either end of the VPN connection to block unauthorized communications.
- **AAA Servers** can perform authentication of users who dial in to the protected network through the VPN. They're called AAA Servers because they determine who the dial-in user is (authentication), determine what the user is allowed to do on the network (authorization), and keep a record of what the user actually does while connected (auditing).
- A VPN uses one of several encryption methods. These methods include the increasingly popular **Internet Protocol Security (IPSec)**, which enables data to be encrypted between computers, routers, and firewalls, and which uses encryption and authentication to securely transport data along a VPN. The data

is sent along the VPN in either transport mode or tunnel mode, both of which encrypt the data payload of Transmission Control Protocol/Internet Protocol (TCP/IP) packets.

The fact that the data is highly protected sets up a connection that is as secure as a virtual "tunnel." Such connections are shown in Figure 1-4.

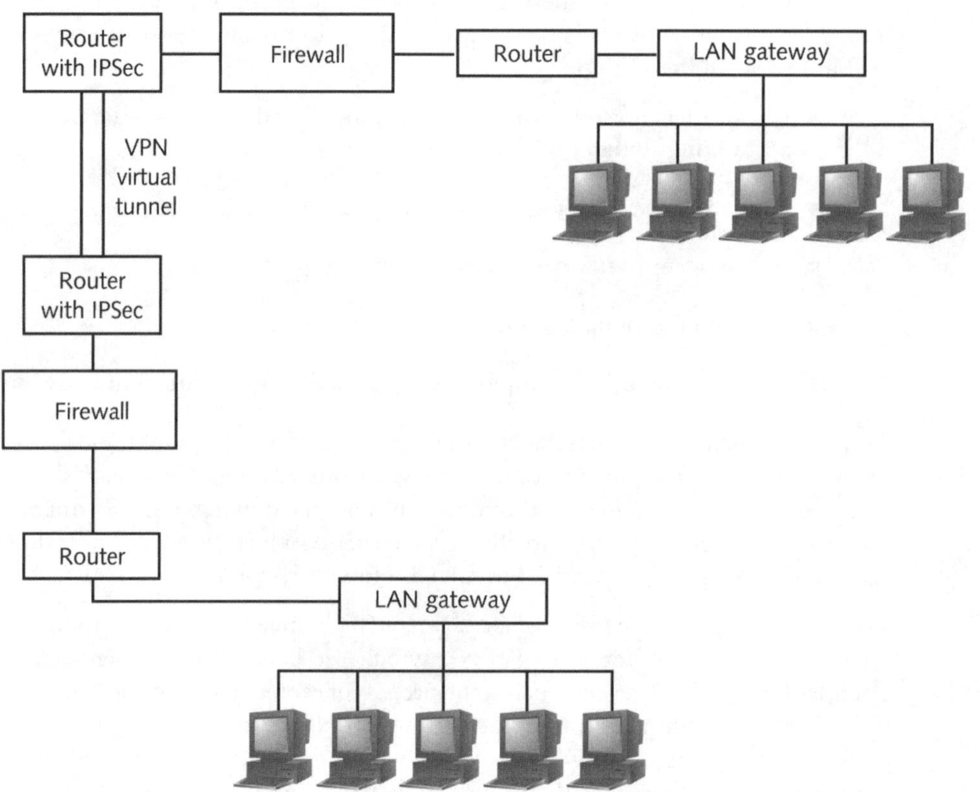

Figure 1-4 Many businesses provide secure connectivity through VPNs

VPNs are discussed in greater detail in Chapter 7.

Understanding TCP/IP Networking

One of the first and most important things you can do to secure your network is to understand its infrastructure. Take an inventory of your available equipment, and secure individual workstations. You should start with the communication medium that intruders will use (or rather, misuse) to try to get into your network: TCP/IP. TCP/IP is the combination of protocols, the most important of which are Transport Control Protocol and Internet Protocol, and it allows information to be transmitted from point to point on a network.

You are probably familiar with the Open Systems Interconnect (OSI) model of network communications, which breaks communications into seven separate layers. TCP/IP has its own stack of protocols that roughly corresponds to these layers. The two models are shown in Figure 1-5.

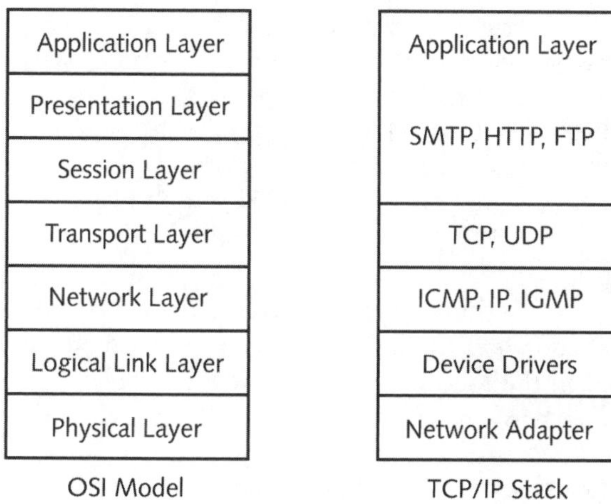

Figure 1-5 The OSI model and the TCP/IP stack

As you can see in Figure 1-5, at the Physical layer, TCP/IP makes use of network adapters such as Network Interface Cards (NICs). At the Logical Link layer, TCP/IP uses device drivers. At the Network Layer, you have protocols such as **Internet Control Message Protocol (ICMP)**, which reports network communications errors; Internet Protocol (IP), which handles network addressing; and **Internet Group Management Protocol (IGMP)**, which allows computers to identify their multicast group membership to routers on the network.

Understanding the fundamentals of TCP/IP networking, as described in the following sections on IP addressing and subnetting, will help you understand one of the ways an intruder can get into your network: through the IP addresses of the computers in it.

IP Addressing

One way hackers can gain access to your network is by determining the actual IP addresses of individual computers. After they have an address, they can take over the computer and use it to launch attacks on other computers in the network or access resources on the network. One of the fundamental goals of network security, then, is to understand IP addresses and other network addresses so that you can either conceal or change them to deter hackers.

IP addresses that are currently in use on the Internet conform to **Internet Protocol version 4 (IPv4)**, which calls for addresses with 32 bits or four bytes of data. Each of the four bytes in an IP address (which is also called an octet) has a value between 0 and 255, and each octet is separated by dots, as in 192.168.10.1. An IP address consists of two parts:

- The **network address**, the part of the address that it has in common with other computers in its **subdomain**, which is a set of IP addresses within a domain.
- The **station** (or host) **address**, which is unique to computers in its subdomain.

As you go through this part of the chapter, note that the four decimal numbers that make up an IP address have eight possible positions when viewed in binary form; for instance, the IP address 208.177.134.171 appears as 11010000.10110001.10000110. 10101011. Each of eight possible numbers in one of the segments of an IP address can have two values (0 or 1). Therefore, each of the segments of an IP address can have 2^8 or 256 possible values, in other words, values from 0 to 255.

These two values are combined with a third value, the **subnet mask**, which tells another computer which part of the IP address is the network address and which part represents the station address, as described in the following section. You can't really determine the exact IP address of a host without knowing the subnet mask.

The addressing system was developed with the belief that, with 4 billion possible addresses available, the amount of available address space would never run out. However, it has begun to run out, which is why **Internet Protocol version 6 (IPv6)** has been developed. IPv6 calls for 128-bit addresses. The 128 bits will be allocated as eight sets of four or fewer hexadecimal digits separated by colons; an example might look like this: ADCC:3FG::1566:DECC::75:88B:DEA7:90B4. The larger addresses will enable many more computer's to communicate via the Internet. In addition, because part of IPv6 addresses are derived from the MAC address of the computer's network interface, IPv6 addresses will be able to be allocated automatically and mobile IP networking will be possible as well.

IP addresses are valuable commodities. Not only is the number of available IPv4 addresses dwindling, but IP addresses are often used by hackers to locate computers they can attack. If a hacker can find a computer's IP address, a port scan can then be done to look for exploitable openings. If you can hide IP addresses, you can stop some hack attacks. How can you hide the addresses of the individual computers on your network? You can use Network Address Translation (NAT) to translate the non-routable internal addresses into the address of the external interface of the NAT server, thereby hiding the internal addresses. You can also use a proxy server, which makes all requests from internal computers look like they are actually coming from the proxy server, which effectively conceals the IP addresses of the internal machines, as shown in Figure 1-6.

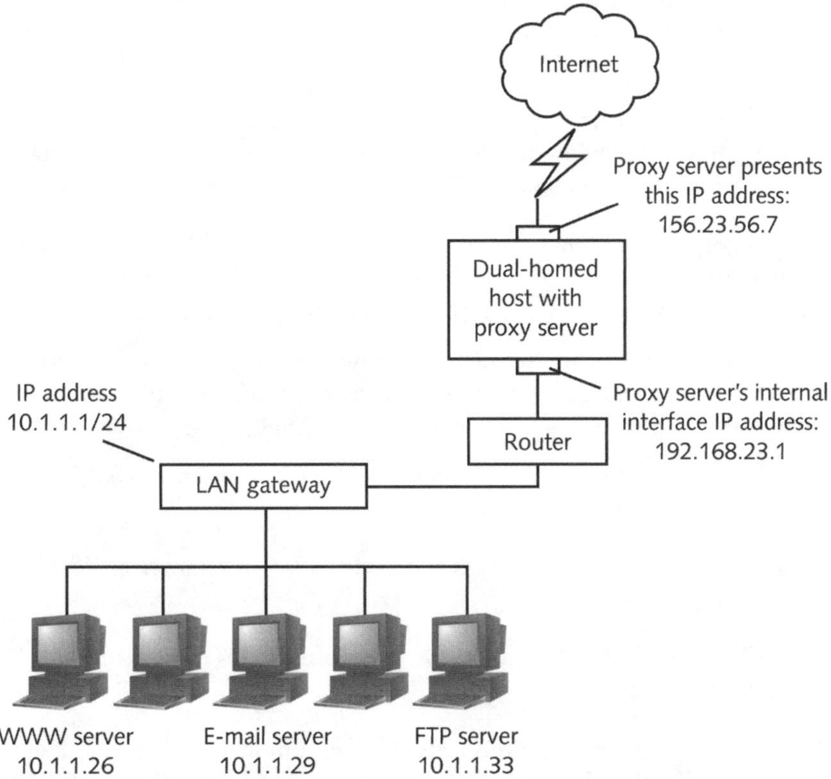

Figure 1-6 Proxy servers conceal IP addresses on the internal network

Proxy servers are discussed in Chapter 6. Chapter 5 has a section on NAT.

Subnetting

In IPv4, addresses are broken into one of the different address categories called *classes*. The class of an IP address is determined by the number of its networks compared to the number of its hosts. The class system of IP addressing is rapidly becoming a thing of the past, but it's worth understanding because it is still in use by both routable Internet computers and countless computers on internal Ethernet networks. The classes have been divided as follows:

- *Class A* —Originally, you could tell a Class A IP address by the first octet, which ranged from 1 to 127. There were only 125 of these networks; a Class A network can have more than 16 million stations. A Class A network address takes the form *network.host.host.host*; the first octet is the network address. The 127 address range is reserved as the "loopback" address and is used for testing the TCP/IP stack on the local interface by typing <ping 127.0.0.1> and pressing Enter.

- *Class B*—The first octet in a Class B address ranges from 128-191. These networks can have more than 65,000 stations. A Class B address takes the form *network.network.host.host*; the first two octets are the network address.

- *Class C*—The first octet in a Class C network ranges from 192-223. These networks can have up to 254 station addresses. A Class C address takes the form *network.network.network.host*; the first three octets are the network address.

A fourth category, Class D, has first octets that range from 224 to 239. Class D is reserved for **multicasting**, which is the process of sending packets to all of the IP addresses on a subnet rather than to a single IP address. The values 240-255 in Class E are experimental.

It's also worth noting that one set of IP addresses within each class is reserved for private networks; they can never be used on the public Internet. You can use them for test purposes or for addresses of hosts on your internal network. They are as follows:

- *10.0.0.0/8*—These Class A private addresses range from 10.0.0.1 to 10.255.255.254.

- *172.16.0.0/12*—These Class B private addresses range from 172.16.0.1 to 172.31.255.254.

- *192.168.0.0/16*—These Class C private addresses range from 192.168.0.1 to 192.168.255.254.

The class designation of an IP address is used to determine the subnet mask of that address, which is determined either by extracting the network number or by comparing the network number to a gateway's routing information to determine if a packet is used for a local address.

Calculating an IP Address with a Subnet Mask

IP addresses are scarce; the European Commission estimates that they will run out by the year 2005 (see *www.europemedia.net/shownews.asp?ArticleID=8614*). Subnetting is one way to take a single network address and divide it into multiple network addresses. You do this by "borrowing" bits from the host portion of the address and subdividing it. For example, consider the network address 146.118.105.204. Which part is the network address, and which is the host's address? Table 1-2 indicates how to determine it:

Table 1-2 Network addresses and host addresses

Address Component	Decimal Form
IP address	146.118.105.204
Subnet mask	255.255.255.184
Network address	146.118.105.136
Host address	68

You can find a number of IP address calculators on the Web; an excellent one is located at *www.telusplanet.net/public/sparkman/netcalc.htm.* For more on IP addresses and subnets, you can refer to *Guide to TCP/IP*, by Laura Chappell and Ed Tittel, published by Course Technology.

Variable-Length Subnet Masking

Subnet masks don't simply tell you what the components of an IP address are; you can also create a custom subnet mask to create a subnet—a subdivision of the IP addresses that are associated with a network address. Such a subnet mask tells you how many hosts can be on a physical segment.

Networks that don't have a large number of available IP addresses can employ **variable-length subnet masking (VLSM)**, which involves applying multiple masks of varying sizes to the same network. VLSM can help an organization that has a limited number of IP addresses and subnets of varying lengths use address space more efficiently. It's beyond the scope of this book to delve into the intricacies of determining custom subnet masks and variable-length subnet masks; the point you need to keep in mind is that IP addresses and their associated subnet masks need to be protected by security devices that perform NAT, by proxy servers, or by VPNs that encapsulate and encrypt IP packets.

You can follow an online tutorial that explains IP addresses and subnetting at *www.learntosubnet.com.* You can also refer to the Course Technology books *CCNA Guide to Cisco Networking Fundamentals* and *Microsoft Introduction to TCP/IP Internetworking* for more information.

Exploring IP Packet Structure

One of the reasons why TCP/IP has taken over the world and become a dominant network communications medium is the fact that it is packet-based: it gives computers of all sorts a relatively simple, easy-to-implement framework for transmitting information in small packages called packets.

Packet-based networks are easy to implement, which is why they have become so popular. Unfortunately, TCP/IP packets give hackers another way to gain entry into a network. They can intercept packets as they head from source to destination, and falsify the information within them in order to fool the computers receiving them into thinking they come from a legitimate host. They can also mangle the packets in a way that makes it impossible for the servers to receive them to respond, which then disables those servers and opens the network to attack.

Understanding the most important aspects of packets from a security standpoint is an essential network security objective. We discuss its elements in detail next.

IP Datagrams

As mentioned, TCP/IP enables data to be transmitted along networks in the form of discrete chunks called packets or datagrams. Each complete message is usually broken into multiple datagrams. In addition, each datagram contains information about the source and destination IP addresses, a variety of control settings, and the actual data that is intended to be exchanged by the client and the host.

Each IP datagram is divided into different sections. The primary subdivisions are the **header** (the part that contains source and destination information and general information about the datagram) and the **data** (the body of the message). They are described in the sections that follow.

NOTE

Besides the header and data sections, some packets have an additional segmented section at the end that is called either a **trailer** or **footer** and that contains data that indicates that this is the end of the packet. An error-checking procedure called a **Cyclical Redundancy Check (CRC)** might also be added.

IP Header Structure

The data within an IP packet may be the part that end users see, but the header is the part that computers use to communicate, and it plays an important role in terms of network security and intrusion detection. Why? An IP header (like a TCP header, which is described in a subsequent section) contains a number of components called flags. These flags can be used by firewalls or IDS systems to:

- Block packets that don't meet a predetermined set of rules
- Allow packets that have criteria that matches at least one rule
- Set off an intrusion alert if a particular flag or a set of criteria called a **signature** (a combination of flags, addresses, and other characteristics) is detected by a firewall or IDS system

These flags, unfortunately, can also be used by hackers to sneak through the network. This is called **IP spoofing**, and it's one way in which hackers try to sneak a packet into a network by making it seem legitimate. A set of IP options in the header (these are described in Chapter 5) can enable the source computer to perform **source routing**, which is the process of specifying the precise route a packet must take between computers to reach its destination. Hackers can abuse this process by specifying any IP address as the source but specifying their own computer as the destination, which ensures that they will be able to communicate with computers on the internal network.

A commonly used way of viewing the different sorts of information within an IP header is shown in Figure 1-7. The IP header shown contains 32 bits of information broken into different sections of layers.

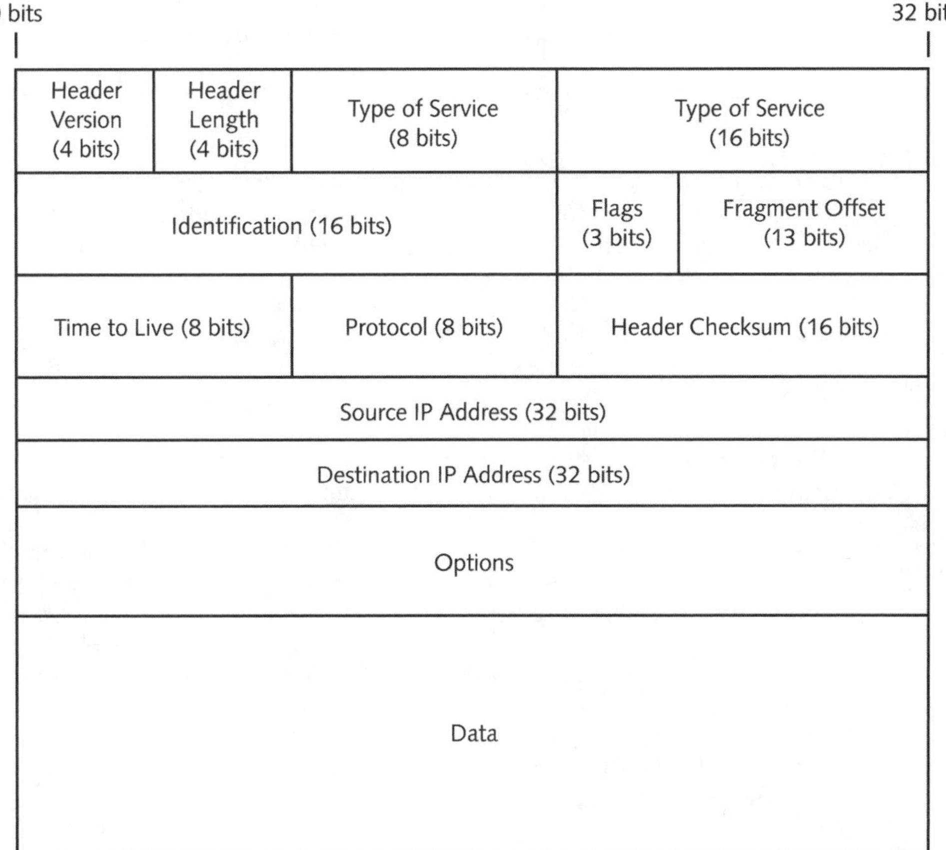

Figure 1-7 IP header structure

It's helpful to break the sections within a header into components because they have varying degrees of value when it comes to configuring packet filters. The elements at the top of the header structure diagram are less important than the components in the middle: the protocol, the source IP address, and destination IP address. A full explanation of the elements follows:

- *Header Version*— This identifies the version of IP that was used to generate the packet. At the time this was written, version 4 was still the most common. However, some ISPs have begun to deploy Ipv6.
- *Header Length*— This describes the length of the header in 32-bit words and is a 4-bit value. The default value is 20.
- *Type of Service*— This expresses the quality of service desired in the transmission of the packet through the network. Four options are available: minimize delay, maximize throughput, maximize reliability, and minimize cost. This field is of limited value, however, because most IP network setups don't enable an application

to set the Type of Service value. If high throughput or high reliability is specified in the header for this traffic, it can slow down traffic in another part of the network.

- *Total Length*— This 16-bit field gives the total length of the packet, to a maximum of 65,535 bytes.
- *Identification*— This is a 16-bit value that aids in the division of the data stream into packets of information. The identification number of each packet is used by the receiving computer (possibly a firewall) to reassemble the packets that make up the data stream in the correct order.
- *Flags*— This 3-bit value tells whether this packet is a **fragment** —one packet within a sequence of packets that makes up a whole communication—and, more specifically, whether it's the last fragment or whether more fragments are to follow.
- *Fragment Offset*— If the data received is a fragment, this value indicates where the fragment belongs in the sequence of fragments so that a packet can be reassembled.
- *Time to Live (TTL)*— This 8-bit value identifies the maximum time the packet can remain in the system before it is dropped. Each router or device through which the packet passes reduces the TTL by a value of one. Having a TTL prevents a packet from getting caught in loops because it is undeliverable. When the value reaches zero, the packet is destroyed and an ICMP message is transmitted to the sender.
- *Protocol*— This identifies the IP protocol that was used in the data portion of the packet and should receive the data at its destination (for example, TCP, UDP, or ICMP).
- *Header Checksum*— This is the sum of the 16-bit values in the packet header expressed as a single value.
- *Source Address*— This is the address of the computer or device that sent the IP packet.
- *Destination Address*— This is the address of the computer or device that is to receive the IP packet.
- *Options*— Various elements can exist in this category. They include a Security field, which enables the sender to assign a classification level to the packet (such as Secret, Top Secret, and so on). They also include several source routing fields by which the sender of the packet can supply routing information that gateways then can use to send the packet to its destination.

Programs that capture packets as they pass through a network interface give you another way to view packet header information. A program called Ethereal (which can be downloaded from *www.ethereal.com*) tracks packets and provides detailed information on each one (see Figure 1-8).

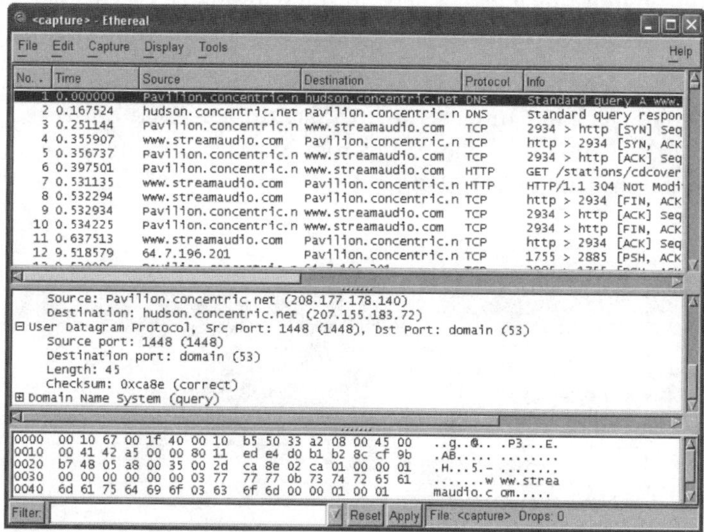

Figure 1-8 TCP/IP header information displayed by a packet "sniffer" called Ethereal

IP Data

The data part of a TCP/IP packet is the part that needs to be protected. Firewalls and virtual private networks (VPNs) have a number of ways in which they can protect the data within a packet. Firewalls primarily work by filtering out packets based on their header data, as detailed in the previous section. A VPN, in particular, can encapsulate the packet within another packet and encrypt its contents as well. A proxy server receives a packet from a host on the internal Local Area Network (LAN) that it is protecting and completely rebuilds the packet from scratch before sending it to its destination. The receiving computer then thinks the packet has come from the proxy server rather than the originating host.

Still, harmful objects such as viruses or harmful executables can be attached to e-mail messages or other files, and in this case, a firewall or IDS must work together with special third-party software that screens the content of network communications such as e-mail messages. Programs such as InterScan by Trend Micro (*www.opsec.com/solutions/partners/trend_micro.html*) or MAILsweeper by Clearswift (*www.opsec.com/solutions/partners/clearswift.html*) can be used with firewalls to scan the actual body of an e-mail message for harmful contents.

ICMP Messages

Internet Control Message Protocol (ICMP) is a protocol designed to assist TCP/IP networks with various communication problems. When used correctly, ICMP produces messages that tell a host if another host can be reached through a ping signal.

From a security standpoint, ICMP packets have a downside: they can be used by hackers to crash computers on your network. Because ICMP packets have no authentication method to verify the recipient of a packet, hackers can attempt man-in-the-middle attacks, in which they impersonate the intended recipient. They can also transmit packets that send the ICMP Redirect message type to direct traffic to a computer outside the protected network that they control.

Note that a firewall/packet filter must be able to determine, based on its message type, whether an ICMP packet should be allowed to pass. Some of the more common ICMP message type codes are shown in Table 1-3.

Table 1-3 ICMP message codes

ICMP Type	Name	Possible Cause
0	Echo Reply	Normal response to a ping
3	Destination Unreachable	Host is listed on the network but cannot be contacted
4	Source Quench	Router receiving too much traffic
5	Redirect	Faster route located
6	Destination Network Unknown	Network cannot be found
7	Destination Host Unknown	Host cannot be found on the network
8	Echo Request	Normal ping request
11	Time Exceeded	Too many hops to a destination
12	Parameter Problem	There is a problem with the IP header and the packet cannot be processed

You'll find a complete list of ICMP message types at *www.iana.org/assignments/icmp-parameters*.

In one kind of network protocol attack that takes advantage of the ICMP Echo Request message type, a hacker floods a target computer with a constant stream of ICMP echo requests. The receiving machine is so busy fielding requests that it can't process any other network traffic. If the computer that goes down is one that provides important services such as DNS, the hacker can gain access to internal hosts. An ICMP Redirect packet can be sent, pointing target computers to the hacker's computer where the hacker can attempt to access confidential information such as passwords. Reviewing firewall logs can tell you if a large number of echo messages is being received. You can configure your firewall to drop ICMP packets that change network behavior (such as ICMP Redirect) and that come from sources outside your own network.

TCP Headers

TCP/IP packets don't just contain IP header information. They also contain TCP headers, which provide hosts with a different set of flags—and hackers with a different set of elements they can mangle or misuse in an attempt to attack networks.

The most important element in a TCP header, from a security standpoint, is the Flags section because it's the one you can filter for when you create packet-filtering rules (see Chapter 5). The TCP header portion of a TCP packet that has an **Acknowledgement (ACK) Flag** set to 1 rather than 0 indicates that the destination computer has received the packets that were previously sent. IETF RFC 793 includes specifications for six such control flags in a TCP header:

- URG (Urgent)
- ACK (Acknowledgment)
- PSH (Push function)
- RST (Reset the connection)
- SYN (Synchronize sequence numbers)
- FIN (No more data from sender)

A hacker can craft a false TCP header that contains an ACK flag (and, presumably, a Trojan horse or other harmful software). A special kind of filter called a stateful packet filter allows such a packet to pass through, even though no connection has actually been established. See Chapter 5 for more about stateful filters.

UDP Headers

User Datagram Protocol (UDP) is a protocol that provides a datagram transport service for IP, but one that is considered unreliable because it is **connectionless**. In other words, it does not depend on an actual connection being established between a host and client in order for a UDP packet to be sent from host to client. This makes it easier for a hacker to send a malformed or dangerous UDP packet to a client.

UDP is often used for minor utilities such as Simple Network Management Protocol (SNMP) and Trivial File Transfer Protocol (TFTP). Hackers can scan for open UDP services they can exploit.

UDP packets have their own headers, as shown in Figure 1-9, as well as the data part of the packet beneath them.

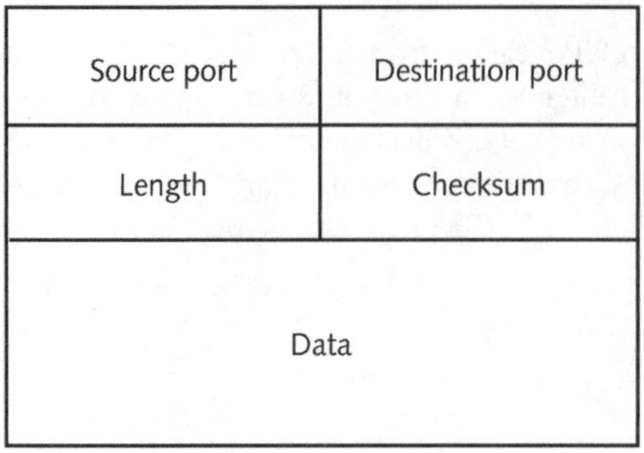

Source port	Destination port
Length	Checksum
Data	

Figure 1-9 A UDP packet header and data

The User Datagram Protocol UDP is described in detail in RFC 768.

IP Fragmentation

Fragmentation of IP packets was originally developed as a means of enabling large packets to pass through early routers that couldn't handle them due to frame size limitations. Routers were then able to divide packets into multiple fragments and send them along the network, where receiving routers would reassemble them in the correct order and pass them to their destination.

Fragmentation creates a number of security problems. One is that, because the TCP or UDP port number is provided only at the beginning of a packet, it will appear only in fragment number 0. Fragments numbered 1 or higher will simply be passed through the filter because they do not contain any port information. A hacker simply has to modify the IP header to start all fragment numbers of a packet at 1 or higher. All fragments would then go through the filter and be able to access internal resources.

To be safe, you should configure the firewall/packet filter to drop all fragmented packets—especially because fragmentation is seldom, if ever, used due to improvements in routers. Alternatively, you could have the firewall reassemble fragmented packets and allow only complete packets to pass through.

DNS and Network Security

The Domain Name System (DNS) is a general-purpose service used mainly on the Internet. DNS servers translate host names to IP addresses that are used to identify the host computer. In order to connect to Web sites, the employees in any organization need a DNS server that is able to resolve the **fully qualified domain names (FQDNs)** they enter, such as *course.com*, to their corresponding IP addresses so that the appropriate computers can connect to one another.

In terms of network security, DNS is important because it gives network administrators another tool to use to block unwanted communications. Firewalls, Web browsers, and proxy servers give administrators the ability to enter DNS names to block Web sites that contain content considered offensive or unsuitable. In addition, networks that use DNS servers need to enable traffic through the DNS servers when they are setting up packet filtering.

DNS can be exploited by hackers who perform buffer overflow or cache poisoning attacks. In a DNS buffer overflow attack, an overly-long DNS name is sent to the server. When the server is unable to process or interpret the DNS name, it is unable to process other requests. A DNS cache poisoning attack exploits the fact that every DNS packet contains a "Question" section and an "Answer" section. An older, more vulnerable server has stored answers that are sent in response to requests to connect to DNS addresses. Hackers can break into the cache to discover the DNS addresses of computers on the network. Most (though not all) DNS servers, however, have since been patched to eliminate this vulnerability.

Routing and Access Control

Another aspect of TCP/IP that has made it popular and practical (and, as you might expect, has subsequently provided hackers with potential vulnerabilities such as gaining access to routing tables or source routing) is the fact that it is routable. Routers are able to move TCP/IP packets from one LAN to another. IP does not require data to follow an exact, predefined path in order to get from point to point. Rather, as routers receive packets, the IP address information of each one is used to determine the best route the data needs to take in order to reach its destination. If one network resource becomes unavailable, the IP address information reroutes the data toward its destination.

Several security-related topics that pertain to routers and that you should know about—how routers can function as firewalls, how routers keep track of network addresses via routing tables, and how you can configure a router with an access control list of authorized computers—are described in the following sections.

Router-Based Firewalls

Some firewalls are software-based programs, while others (such as those made by Cisco Systems) come packaged in a hardware device that also functions as a **router**, a device that connects and directs traffic between networks. Routers are essential parts of any network, and by integrating a firewall with a hardware device that also functions as a router, it is easy to place the firewall on the perimeter of a network where it can be configured to perform packet filtering and other functions.

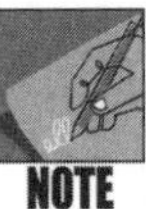

The Linksys EtherFast Cable/DSL Router comes with NAT functions that enable it to act as a firewall. Other Linksys routers enable users to set up VPNs and other gateways. Competitive pricing makes such products suitable for both home and business use.

Routing Tables

Every router makes use of a **routing table**, which is a list of network addresses and corresponding gateway IP addresses that a router uses to direct traffic. Routing tables are important because they give network administrators a list of IP addresses for the resources on the network as well as **default gateways**. If hackers can get their hands on such information, they can attack individual workstations and gateways by IP address. You can view a routing table for your own network by entering the netstat –r command in the Command Prompt window (see Figure 1-10).

```
Command Prompt
Route Table
===========================================================================
Interface List
0x1 ........................... MS TCP Loopback interface
0x2 ...00 10 b5 50 33 a2 ...... HP EN1207D-TX PCI 10/100 Fast Ethernet Adapter -
 SecuRemote Miniport
===========================================================================
===========================================================================
Active Routes:
Network Destination        Netmask          Gateway       Interface  Metric
          0.0.0.0          0.0.0.0    208.177.178.1  208.177.178.140     30
        127.0.0.0        255.0.0.0        127.0.0.1        127.0.0.1      1
    208.177.178.0    255.255.255.0  208.177.178.140  208.177.178.140     30
  208.177.178.140  255.255.255.255        127.0.0.1        127.0.0.1     30
  208.177.178.255  255.255.255.255  208.177.178.140  208.177.178.140     30
        224.0.0.0        240.0.0.0  208.177.178.140  208.177.178.140     30
  255.255.255.255  255.255.255.255  208.177.178.140  208.177.178.140      1
Default Gateway:     208.177.178.1
===========================================================================
Persistent Routes:
  None
```

Figure 1-10 A routing table

Access Control Lists

An **Access Control List (ACL)** does for users and groups what a routing table does for routers: it provides a host with a list of the users and groups that are authorized to use network resources, plus it details what level of authorization each user has. Typically, such privileges include the ability to read or write certain files or to execute different programs found in a directory. As you might expect, such lists also need to be protected against hackers. This requires assigning good passwords and disabling Guest accounts that hackers can exploit to gain access to resources. As an article on the SecurityFocus Web site (*http://online.securityfocus.com/news/268*) points out, routers that aren't secure can yield passwords and other sensitive information to hackers who are able to crack into them.

Securing Individual Workstations

The workstations that host security software are commonly placed on the perimeter of a network, which is a vulnerable spot that stands between the internal LAN and the external Internet (see Figure 1-11).

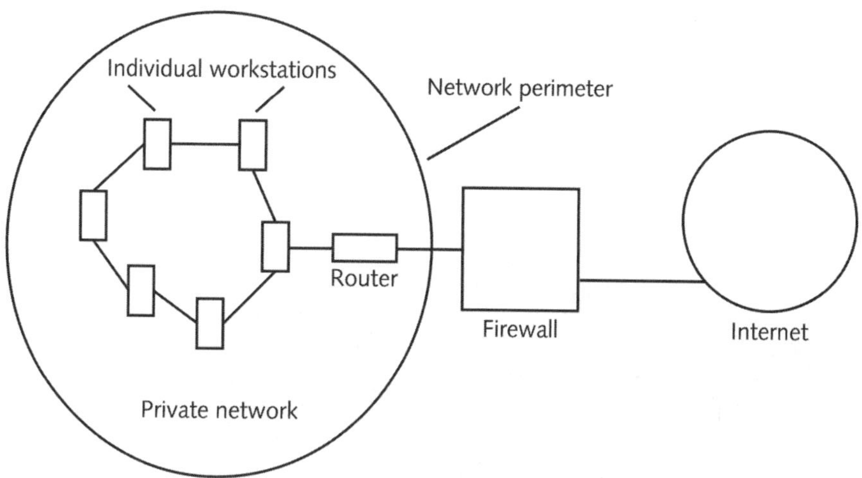

Figure 1-11 An IDS or firewall positioned on the perimeter of the network being protected

Some IDS systems are positioned on public servers that are placed outside the organization's internal LAN and that contain Web pages, FTP documents, and other materials. Such public servers are particularly vulnerable to attack because they are open to the public, so they are placed on an area called a **Demilitarized Zone (DMZ)** that is outside the LAN but still protected by the firewall (see Figure 1-12).

Because they are in vulnerable locations, many firewalls and intrusion detection systems make use of a **bastion host**, a machine that has been specially hardened (in other words, made secure and resistant to attack) by turning off all unneeded services except the bare essentials. Regardless of whether you want to create a bastion host, you can observe some general principles that apply to hardening workstations to make sure the machine that hosts your security software remains secure. We discuss those principles next.

General Principles When Securing a Workstation

One of the first principles in securing a workstation is that the choice of operating system isn't as important as the administrator's familiarity with it. Both the hardware and software that make up a bastion host should be familiar to the network administrator. This facilitates configuration as well as troubleshooting. The machine should present intruders with only a minimal set of resources and open ports; a bare bones configuration reduces the chances of attack and has the extra benefit of boosting efficiency. The fewer the resources and openings on the system, the more secure the host is.

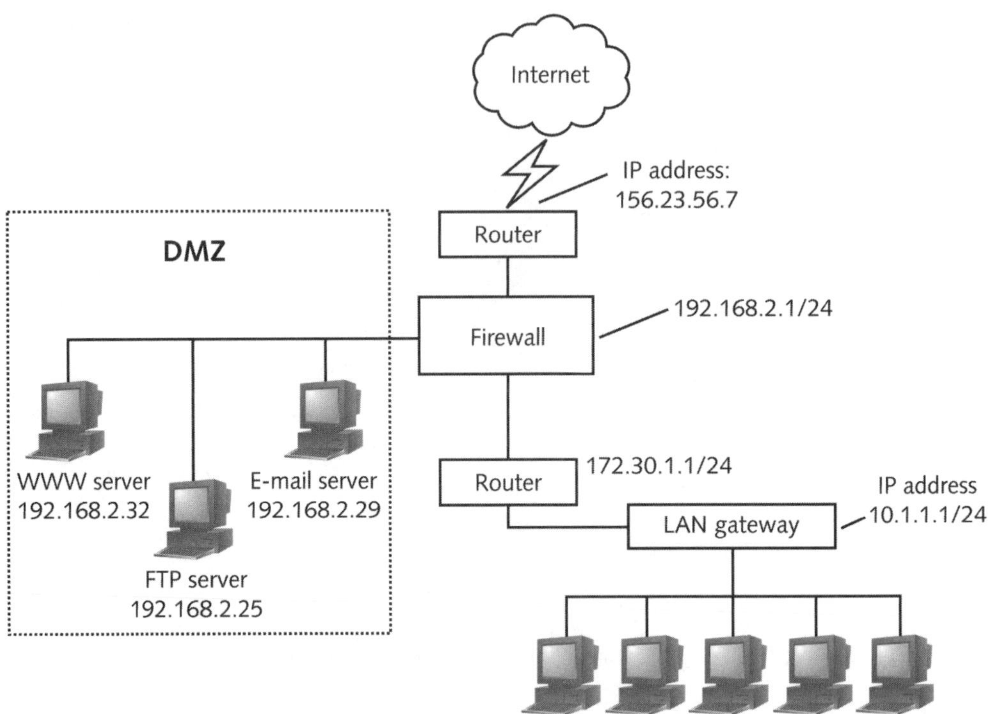

Figure 1-12 An IDS system placed on servers in the DMZ

When you're analyzing the cost of one or more bastion hosts, it's a good idea to conduct a comprehensive risk analysis of all the resources in your organization. Even if your company isn't able to lay out sizeable expenditures on separate hardware devices to protect every segment of your network topology, you should encourage them to at least conduct a risk assessment that identifies the most valuable information you have—the information that needs to be protected by the proper bastion host or other hardware. As described in Chapter 3, you compile a list of the resources you need to protect, and then determine which ones are the most critical. You'll have to perform the usual balancing act between cost-effectiveness and security by getting as many bastion hosts as you can afford to maximize security, and by combining two or more services on the bastion host if you need to save money.

Memory Considerations

Random Access Memory (RAM) is always important when operating a server, but because the host that operates your IDS and firewall may only be providing a single service on the network, you aren't likely to need multi-gigabytes worth of RAM. Hard disk storage space, on the other hand, should be in the multi-gigabyte category because you'll be accumulating vast quantities of records or log files detailing who accessed resources on the server and when the access attempts occurred. You also need some RAM to run log file analysis software that enables you to review and analyze this information on the host, unless you move the log file data to another workstation and manage it there.

Processor Speed

Because the firewall or IDS host is integral to network security, you should obtain a machine with the fastest processor you can afford. However, keep in mind that the speed of the machine doesn't depend solely on the type or number of processors within it. The speed of a computer's operation on a network is also a factor of available bandwidth: a fast computer won't be able to move traffic quickly if the speed of its own Internet connection is slow.

Some security administrators believe that a slower machine used as a bastion host actually helps to deter would-be attackers because when it's at work, it doesn't have as many resources sitting unused as a faster machine. If resources aren't available, a hacker cannot exploit them. In the real world, this doesn't mean that you should look for a slow, outdated computer to function as a bastion host. Rather, it means that in order to keep costs down or to be able to afford multiple bastion hosts, you don't necessarily have to look for the most expensive or full-featured box.

Whatever operating system you decide to use, be sure to pick a version of that system that is stable and secure. Check the operating system's development Web site for a list of updates.

Securing Windows 2000 and XP Computers

One of the most basic and time-consuming activities involved in securing a Windows operating system is installing the various patches and hotfixes that have been released for it. Such updates are issued by Microsoft on a regular basis as security concerns arise. By visiting the Windows 2000 Server site (*www.microsoft.com/windows2000/server/default.asp*) or the Windows XP Professional site (*www.microsoft.com/windowsxp/pro/default.asp*) on a regular basis you can obtain the latest updated software.

Windows 2000 and XP are also excellent choices for bastion host operating systems because of their reliability and widespread use as servers. If your network already uses Windows, the choice of Windows for the bastion host is a natural one.

If you plan to run Windows 2000 or XP on a bastion host that is intended to function solely as a Web server, you should disable the NetBIOS interface, Server service, and Workstation service as they are not needed. Also be sure to set up logging so that you can track any unauthorized attempts to perform the following actions: account logon and logoff, object access, policy changes, privilege use, and system events (restart and shutdown).

On a Windows 2000 or XP bastion host, create two partitions: one for the operating system (this should be the C: drive) and one for the Web server, DNS server, or other software you plan to run on the host (this could be the D: drive or another drive).

To create a partition, you need to have Administrator status on the computer and enough available free space. Open the Control Panel, and double-click Administrative Tools. Then double-click Computer Management, click Disk Management, right-click the disk drive you want to partition, and click New Partition. Then follow the steps shown in the New Partition Wizard.

If you are configuring a bastion host using a Windows 2000 or XP computer, you should make use of two utilities that Microsoft has provided to help harden the systems. The first is the Microsoft Baseline Security Analyzer (*www.microsoft.com/technet/treeview/default.asp?url=/technet/security/tools/Tools/MBSAhome.asp*). It performs an analysis of the current Windows 2000 or XP configuration. It identifies hotfixes and patches that are necessary and isolates vulnerabilities such as open Guest accounts and anonymous connections being enabled (see Figure 1-13).

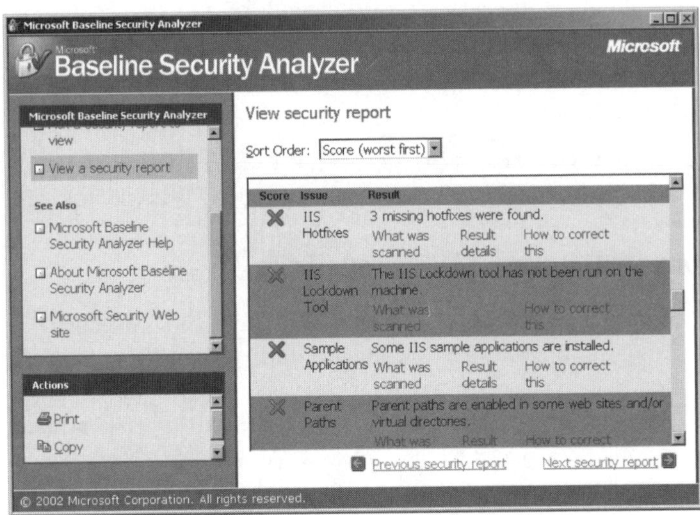

Figure 1-13 Microsoft Baseline Security Analyzer

Running the Baseline Security Analyzer after you do a clean install of the operating system on the bastion host is a good way to identify obvious vulnerabilities.

The second utility, the IIS Lockdown Tool, is intended to turn off the Windows 2000 or XP built-in Web server, Internet Information Server (IIS), and any services that depend on it.

Securing UNIX and Linux Computers

UNIX is the most popular operating system used to provide services on the World Wide Web (WWW), and one that is regarded by many network administrators as presenting fewer security holes than Windows. It contains an extensive set of software tools for development and auditing, and there is plenty of online documentation explaining how to configure the various types of UNIX. If the installation disk gives you the option of a stripped-down installation such as the HP-UX option "64-Bit Minimal HP-UX (English Only)", you should choose it. This option bypasses the installation of X-Windows and other unneeded items or services.

The security patches you install must correspond to the operating system you choose. If you are using HP-UX, install HP-UX security patches; for AIX, install AIX patches, and so on. Installing security patches is no small undertaking. You might have six, eight, or even a dozen to install. It can also be time-consuming and demanding to keep up with new patches as they come out. You should visit the operating system manufacturer's Web site on a periodic basis to check for the release of such patches. You may also want to install supplemental security software such as TCP Wrapper and **Secure Shell (SSH)**, a command interface that enables you to gain secure access to a remote computer.

You also need to do logging through the **syslog daemon**; be sure to configure syslog to record messages to files. It's useful to pick a version of UNIX that includes a utility called **chkconfig**, which reports on the services that are currently started—you can check the list of services to see if all of them are absolutely necessary, or whether they should be stopped.

UNIX makes use of a utility called security_patch_check, which automates the process of analyzing security patches that are already on the system and reporting on patches that should be added. On a UNIX host, run a Trusted Computing Base (TCB) check, which makes sure that any software you run is a trusted program.

Day-to-Day Security Maintenance

After you install the patches and service packs for your individual computers, the day-to-day responsibilities begin. You have to, on a daily basis, maintain the hotfixes, review security logs, and plug holes as they arise. How do you do it? Here are some suggestions:

- *Don't go it alone*—All the security responsibilities of a large-scale corporate network are too much for one security administrator to handle. Assemble a team, a security committee, and a delegate.
- *Follow a daily list*—Prepare a checklist of security tasks that your team should follow on a daily basis.
- *Gather weekly reports*—Have each systems group in the organization prepare a brief weekly report of its security activities and send it to the security committee.
- *Get individual users involved*—Encourage rank-and-file employees to get involved in the company's efforts to defeat hackers and be part of the security efforts of the

organization. They, after all, are your first line of defense as well as the most likely source of intrusion when clever hackers fool them into giving out information.

- *Establish and distribute your network's security policy* —All too often after an intrusion occurs, employees complain that they were never aware that a particular security policy or procedure was in place. Make sure you get a copy of the policy in everyone's hands so that they know what to do before trouble occurs.
- *Set up a network security perimeter* —Use firewalls, DMZs, and intrusion detection systems as well as VPNs to secure your network's perimeter. All of these tools can work together to provide a multilayered **Defense in Depth (DiD)** setup for the organization. This arrangement is a set of security layers that protect a network at many different levels using a variety of strategies and methodologies.

Web and Internet-Based Security Concerns

As you probably know from your study of basic networking and **Transport Control Protocol/Internet Protocol TCP/IP**, a port number combined with a computer's IP address constitutes a network connection called a **socket**. Software commonly used by hackers attempt to identify sockets that respond to connection requests. The sockets that respond can be targeted to see if they have been left open or have security vulnerabilities that can be exploited. **Hypertext Transport Protocol (HTTP)** Web services use port 80. HTTP, in fact, is among the most commonly exploited services.

The following sections briefly mention some of the aspects of using the Internet that you need to be aware of from a security standpoint. These sections cover e-mail vulnerabilities such as viruses; executable code that enters the network through e-mail or downloaded files; and broadband connections that enable computers to connect to the Internet with IP addresses that never change and that can easily be attacked by hackers.

E-Mail Vulnerabilities

For a home user who regularly surfs the Web, uses e-mail, and does Instant Messaging, a firewall's primary job is to keep viruses from infecting files and prevents **Trojan horses** from entering the system through hidden, often secret openings called back doors. Personal firewall programs such as Norton Internet Security, for instance, come with an anti-virus program that alerts users when an e-mail attachment or file containing a known virus is found.

Scripting

One of the most widespread kinds of intrusions into a network that is increasing in frequency and severity is the use of executable code attached to e-mail messages or downloaded files that infiltrates a system. It can be difficult for a firewall or IDS system by itself to block all such files; specialty firewalls and other programs should be integrated with existing security systems to keep scripts from infecting a network.

A specialty "e-mail firewall" can monitor and control a particular kind of content that passes into and out of a network. They can be configured to filter out pornographic content, junk e-mail, and malicious code. MailMarshal by Marshal Software (*www.mailmarshal.com*), for instance, unpacks and scans the content of each e-mail message before it reaches the recipient. This opens up obvious privacy issues that need to be balanced against an organization's need for protection—a trade-off that applies to virtually all aspects of network security, not just e-mail messages.

Problems with Always-On Connections

The proliferation of affordable, high-speed connections such as cable modem and DSL lines brings about special security concerns for network administrators . For one thing, computers that have such "always on" connections are easier to locate and attack because their IP address remains the same as long as they are connected to the Internet—which might be days at a time if computers are left on overnight or over a weekend. Some users pay extra to obtain static IP addresses that never change and that enable them to run Web servers or other services. The use of these static IP addresses makes it relatively easy for a hacker to locate a computer and scan it for open ports.

Another problem arises when users who are on the road, contractors who work at home, or business partners want to connect to your organization's internal network. In past years, such connections were primarily made through temporary, dial-up connections that used protocols such as Point-to-Point Protocol (PPP). Now, it's increasingly likely that such remote users connect to the network through an "always-on" DSL or cable modem connection, which means they might be connected to your network for hours at a time.

Such connections effectively extend the boundaries of your corporate network and you should secure them as you would any part of your network perimeter. At the very least, your network security policy should specify that remote users have their desktops equipped with firewall and anti-virus protection software. After all, if hackers are able to break in to the remote user's computer while that user is connected to your network through a VPN or other connection, your network becomes vulnerable as well. For more about securing VPN connections, see Chapter 7.

Chapter Summary

- You need to know the types of enemies you are up against, and what they are after, in order to defend against them. The individuals who might attempt to intrude on your network might simply be motivated by a desire to see what kinds of data you have and to gain control of your computer. Revenge by disgruntled current or former employees might be the primary motivation, however. Some hackers break into accounts and networks for financial gain. Others want to steal proprietary information either for their own use or for resale to other parties.
- You need to set goals for your network security program. These goals originate with an analysis of the risks you face and an assessment of the resources you want to protect. One

of the most important goals of any network security effort should be to maintain the privacy of the information related to customers and employees alike. Other goals include the preservation of data integrity, the authentication of approved users of network resources, and enabling remote users to connect securely to the internal network.

- Some basic knowledge of TCP/IP networking is important not only to configure the firewalls and routers that help form your Defense in Depth configuration, but also to be aware of vulnerabilities related to IP addresses. You may consider using proxy servers or NAT to shield the actual IP addresses of your internal hosts from external users.
- The IP and TCP header sections of IP packets were explored in some detail, because they contain a variety of settings that can be exploited by hackers. These include header information such as the fragmentation flag and the source or destination IP address. ICMP messages such as redirect and echo request can be misused by hackers to either intercept traffic and direct it to a server they control, or flood a server with so many requests that it can no longer handle other traffic.
- Routing and access control are important network concepts because the routers at the perimeter of a network are critical to the movement of all traffic into and out of the network, regardless of whether the traffic is legitimate or harmful. Because of their position on the perimeter of networks, routers can be equipped with their own firewall software so that they can perform packet filtering and other functions.
- It's also important to realize the various activities that go into securing the bastion hosts on which your firewall software or intrusion detection programs will be installed. These include obtaining the latest versions of operating system software and checking periodically for any new security patches or hot fixes that have been released. Computers that are expected to host firewall or IDS software or provide public services should be hardened as much as possible by reducing unnecessary software and accounts and by closing any open ports.
- Because the Internet and particularly the World Wide Web are playing increasingly important roles in the movement of business-related traffic from one corporate network to another, it's important to have some understanding of the network security concerns that pertain to e-commerce and online communications. E-mail is one of the most important services you can secure because of the possibility of malicious scripts being delivered in e-mail attachments. In addition, the "always-on" DSL and cable modem connections that are becoming increasingly popular present new security risks that need to be addressed with firewall and VPN solutions.

KEY TERMS

Access Control List (ACL) — A list of the users and groups that are authorized to use network resources, and the details about what level of authorization each user has.

Acknowledgement (ACK) Flag — If the ACK Flag is set to 1 rather than to 0, the destination computer has received the packets.

authentication — The process of determining the identity of an authorized user is through the matching of a username and password or by other means.

back door — A way of gaining unauthorized access to a computer or other resource, usually through an opening in a computer program supposed to be known only to the program's author.

bastion host — A machine that has been specially hardened by turning off all unneeded services except the bare essentials.

chkconfig — Short for configuration state checker, a UNIX utility that provides configuration listings for services being run on the computer.

connectionless — A feature of the UDP protocol, which does not depend on a connection actually having been established between a host and client for a UDP packet to be sent from host to client.

crackers — Individuals who are attracted to the challenge of detecting passwords and removing copy protection from software.

Cyclical Redundancy Check (CRC) — An error-checking procedure sometimes appended to the end of a TCP/IP packet.

data — The part of a datagram that contains the actual data being sent from client to server.

data encapsulation — The process of protecting a packet of digital information by enclosing it within another packet.

data warehouses — Central repositories where data is stored so it can be accessed and analyzed as needed.

deface — The hacker's act of breaking into a Web site and leaving publicly visible messages on the site's Web pages so friends of the hacker can see the hacker was there.

default gateway — The router or hub that the computers on a network use by default in order to gain access to resources either within or outside the network.

defended networks — Networks that put an emphasis on defensive measures and restricted access.

Defense in Depth (DiD) — A set of security layers that protect a network at many different levels using a variety of strategies and methodologies.

Demilitarized Zone (DMZ) — A subnetwork of publicly accessible Web, e-mail, and other servers that is outside the LAN but still protected by the firewall.

Distributed Denial of Service (DDoS) attack — An attack in hundreds or thousands of hijacked computers are used to launch an attack against a computer such as a Web site server.

footer — *See* trailer.

fragment — One packet within a sequence of TCP/IP packets that makes up a whole communication.

fully qualified domain name (FQDN) — The complete DNS name of a computer, including the computer name, domain name, and domain name extension, such as *www.course.com*.

hacker — An individual who attempts to gain access to unauthorized resources on a network, usually by finding a way to circumvent passwords, firewalls, or other protective measures.

header — The part of a datagram that contains source and destination information and general information about that datagram.

Hypertext Transport Protocol (HTTP) — A protocol used by Web services that communicates via a computer's TCP/IP port 80.

Internet Control Message Protocol (ICMP) — A protocol that reports network communications errors to support IP communications.

Internet Group Management Protocol (IGMP) — A protocol that allows computers to identify their multicast group membership to routers on the network.

Internet Protocol Security (IPSec) — A security system that enables data to be encrypted between computers, routers, and firewalls, and which uses encryption and authentication to securely transport data along a VPN in either transport mode or tunnel mode.

Internet Protocol version 4 (IPv4) — The addressing system currently in widespread use on the Internet, in which addresses are created with 32 bits or 4 bytes of data.

Internet Protocol version 6 (IPv6) — A new version of IP that is gaining support among software and hardware manufacturers and that will eventually replace IPv4; it calls for 128-bit IP addresses.

IP spoofing — One way in which hackers try to sneak a packet into a network by making it seem legitimate.

key — A long block of code that is generated by means of a mathematical formula called an algorithm. The longer the key, the harder it is to crack and the stronger the level of encryption involved.

leased lines — Point-to-point frame relay or other connections established by the telecommunications companies that own the lines involved in making the connection.

log files — Records detailing who accessed resources on the server and when the access attempts occurred.

multicasting — The process of sending packets to all of the IP addresses on a subnet rather than to a single IP address.

network address — The part of an IP address that a computer has in common with other computers in its subdomain.

packet monkey — A hacker who is primarily interested in blocking the activities of a Web site through a Distributed Denial of Service attack.

proxy server — A program that provides Web browsing, e-mail, and other services on behalf of networked users in order to conceal their identity from those outside the network.

public-key cryptography — Encrypts communications through the use of long blocks of code called keys.

risk analysis — The analysis of the primary security risks faced by a network.

router — A device that connects and directs traffic between networks.

routing table — A list of network addresses and corresponding gateway IP addresses that a router uses to direct traffic.

script kiddies — Individuals who spread viruses and other malicious scripts and use techniques to exploit weaknesses in computer systems.

Secure Shell (SSH) — A command interface that enables you to gain secure access to a remote computer.

signature — A combination of flags, addresses, and other characteristics that is detected by a firewall or IDS system.

socket — A network connection that uses a TCP/IP port number combined with a computer's IP address.

source routing — The process of specifying the precise route a packet must take between computers to reach its destination.

spoofing — Entering false information into the packets of data that travel along the Internet or on any network that uses TCP/IP.

station address — The part of an IP address that is unique to computers in its subdomain.

subdomain — A set of IP addresses within a domain.

subnet mask — A value that tells another computer which part of a computer's IP address is its network address and which part represents the station address.

syslog daemon — A UNIX utility that runs in the background, receiving, logging, and displaying messages from routers, switches, and other devices on the network.

trailer — An additional section that is added to a TCP/IP packet and that tells a computer that this is the end of the packet.

Transport Control Protocol/Internet Protocol (TCP/IP) — The combination of two protocols, Transport Control Protocol and Internet Protocol, that allow information to be transmitted from point to point on a network.

Trojan horses — A program that appears to be harmless but that actually introduces viruses or causes damage to a computer or system.

trusted networks — Networks that permit access to trusted users whose identities they can reliably verify.

variable-length subnet masking (VLSM) — A way of applying multiple masks of varying sizes to the same network.

Review Questions

1. Why is network security a more critical activity now than in the past? (Choose all that apply.)

   a. The threat of terrorist attack is increasing.

   b. Corporations are relying more heavily on the Internet to do business.

   c. More individuals and businesses are going online.

   d. More critical business and financial information is available online.

2. Which of the following is potentially more valuable than credit card numbers or other information held by a company on its network?

   a. budget and accounting files

   b. passwords

   c. proprietary information about products and research projects

   d. personal phone numbers, addresses, and other employee information

3. What sets "old school" hackers apart from other hackers? (Choose all that apply.)

   a. They don't seek to destroy.

   b. They don't seek knowledge.

   c. They don't need to know how systems work.

   d. They are concerned with open information on the Internet.

4. Which of the following types of hackers is primarily concerned with circumventing copyright protection on commercial software?

   a. script kiddies

   b. crackers

   c. packet monkeys

   d. old school hackers

5. Which of the following is a reason why IPv6 has been developed? (Choose all that apply.)

   a. IPv4 addresses are not secure.

   b. IPv4 addresses are running out.

   c. Dynamic address allocation is desired.

   d. Mobile IP networking is needed.

6. Which of the following is a way in which a TCP/IP packet can be tampered with by a hacker?

   a. Packet contents can be replaced with totally different packets.

   b. Packet contents can be duplicated.

   c. Packet contents can be falsified.

   d. Packet contents can be mangled.

7. Effective passwords should use __________. (Choose all that apply.)

   a. numerals

   b. at least 6-8 characters

   c. dots and other symbols

   d. names

8. Recent surveys have found that most intrusions originate from what location?

   a. inside the company

   b. foreign countries

   c. hacker Web sites

   d. computers based inside prisons

9. What happens when a Web site is defaced?

   a. The site is bombarded with e-mail messages.

   b. The site is flooded with requests for Web pages.

   c. A hacker leaves a message on a publicly visible Web page.

   d. A page is obliterated.

10. A network security specialist is typically called upon to perform what sort of tasks on a regular (perhaps even daily) basis?

    a. checking for connectivity

    b. reviewing logs

    c. maintaining hotfixes

    d. setting policies

11. A set of security layers that provide a variety of attack defenses for an internal network is called ____________.

    a a firewall configuration

    b a multilayered security system

    c. Defense in Depth (DiD)

    d. an Intrusion Detection System (IDS)

12. An attack in which a hacker impersonates the intended recipient of a message and uses the ICMP Redirect message to redirect traffic is called ________________.

    a. social engineering

    b. a denial of service (DoS) attack

    c. a SYN flood attack

    d. a man-in-the-middle attack

13. What kind of network communications requires a third-party program rather than a firewall or IDS to scan for viruses or harmful executables?

    a. e-mail message content

    b. e-mail message headers

    c. Web pages

    d. all of the above

14. What part of a TCP header can be manipulated by a hacker to falsely acknowledge that a connection has been made?

    a. the RST flag

    b. the ACK flag

    c. the Redirect flag

    d. the Header Checksum

15. Why is UDP a particularly vulnerable protocol?

    a. It is used for only minor protocols.

    b. It has a relatively simple header.

    c. It is connectionless.

    d. It is vulnerable to port scans.

16. Why is fragmentation considered a security risk?

    a. Fragments numbered 0 contain port information.

    b. Fragments numbered 1 or higher are passed through filters.

    c. Fragmented packets cannot be assembled.

    d. Fragmentation is frequently used.

17. Routers use what information to determine the best path for data to take to reach its destination?

    a. subnet masks

    b. routing tables

    c. access control lists

    d. IP address information

18. Which of the following gives hackers the IP addresses of computers on a network? (Choose all that apply.)

    a. a routing table

    b. fully qualified domain names

    c. an access control list

    d. a list of passwords

19. Public servers are often located where?

    a. on their own subnet

    b. on a DMZ

    c. on the internal LAN

    d. on the network perimeter

20. A machine that hosts a firewall or IDS should contain a limited set of what components? (Choose all that apply.)

    a. hard disks

    b. open ports

    c. resources

    d. processors

HANDS-ON PROJECTS

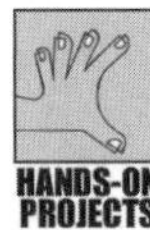

Project 1-1: Performing Risk Analysis

Risk analysis is one of the most fundamental network security activities. To know what kinds of attacks you are likely to face, you will review a recent security survey and prepare a list of the most frequently reported intrusions. This project requires you to have Adobe Acrobat Reader installed, either as a plug-in to your browser or as a stand-alone application.

1. Double-click the **Internet Explorer** icon on your desktop.
2. Type **http://www.gocsi.com/press/** into the Address box, and then press **Enter**.
3. Locate the most recent version of the Computer Crime and Security Survey, and click the link for the survey's press release.
4. Click the **Survey Request Form** link. The Request Survey page appears.
5. Fill out the form on this page. In the Company box, enter your school's name. Click **Submit Form**.
6. A page appears that thanks you and tells you your request is being processed. Click **Download the *current year* Survey** (where *current year* is the current year). The survey should appear in your browser window if your browser contains the Adobe Acrobat Reader plug-in; if it does not, you are prompted to download the file to your computer, where you will need the Adobe Acrobat Reader software to view it.
7. In your lab notebook or a word-processed document, list the top five types of attacks listed in the report. Which of the types of events is likely to occur to your school's network?

Project 1-2: Assessing Your Network Interface

For many of the projects in this book (including Project 1-3) you will need to know your computer's IP address, network interface name and address, and other basic information. You can use a built-in utility called netstat to analyze and record this information so that you can use it later on.

1. Click **Start**, point to **Programs** (**All Programs** on Windows XP), point to **Accessories**, and then click **Command Prompt** to open a Command Prompt window.
2. To begin, simply type **netstat**.
3. Press **Enter** to view the computer's current active connections.
4. Type **netstat –a**.

5. Press **Enter** to view not only the currently established connections, but also the ports on which your computer is listening for new connections.
6. Type **netstat –p TCP** and press **Enter** to view information about TCP connections.
7. Type **netstat –p UDP** and press **Enter** to view information about UDP connections.
8. To get a summary of all of Netstat's switches, type **netstat /?** and press **Enter**.
9. Type **exit** and press **Enter** to close the command prompt window.

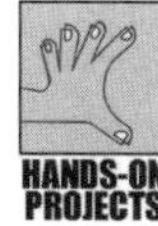

Project 1-3: Determining Your Computer's IP Address

Every computer that is connected to the Internet is assigned an IP address. Often the address is dynamically generated and changes from session to session. With some DSL connections and many T-1 or other connections, a static IP address is obtained. To determine the IP address of one of the computers to which you have access, follow these steps:

1. If your computer is not powered up, power it up now.
2. Click **Start**, point to **Programs** (or **All Programs** on Windows XP), point to **Accessories**, and then click **Command Prompt** to open a Command Prompt window.
3. To begin, type **ipconfig /all**. (Be sure to leave a single blank space between ipconfig and the forward-slash.)
4. Press **Enter**. The display that comes up will show you your IP address as well as other information. Your IP address will be four numbers separated by periods. In some cases you might have several addresses. The IP address assigned to your Ethernet adapter is the external address.
5. Write down the address in a lab book or word-processed document. Also write down your subnet mask and default gateway address. What other address is assigned to your Ethernet adapter?
6. Write down the name of your Ethernet adapter; you'll need it for Project 1-4.
7. Type **Exit** and press **Enter** to close the Command Prompt window.

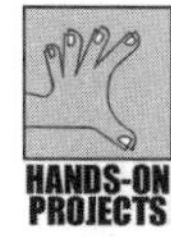

Project 1-4: Downloading and Installing a Network Traffic Analyzer

To get a better idea of what TCP/IP packet headers look like, it can be helpful to use a network traffic analyzer to capture individual packets as they enter or leave your network. In this project you will download and begin to use a program that lets you observe individual packets called Ethereal (*www.ethereal.com*). This project requires you to first download and install a packet capture utility called WinPcap that is needed to use Ethereal. It also requires you to stop any firewall programs you currently have running.

NOTE

You will need to complete Project 1-2 and Project 1-3 before working on Project 1-4.

1. Double-click the **Internet Explorer** icon on your desktop.
2. Enter the URL for the Pcap Web site (**http://winpcap.mirror.ethereal.com**), and then press **Enter**.
3. Click **Downloads**.
4. Start to download WinPcap by clicking the **WinPcap auto-installer (driver +DLLs)** link.
5. When the File Download dialog box appears, click **Open**. The file is downloaded to a temporary directory on your computer and the WinPcap setup utility opens automatically.
6. Click **Next** at the bottom of the first setup screen.
7. Click **Yes, I agree with all the terms of the license agreement** at the bottom of the next setup screen (entitled License Agreement), and then click **Next** twice to complete the setup. At the final Installation Complete screen, click **OK**.
8. Enter the URL for the Ethereal Web site (**http://www.ethereal.com**) in your browser's Address bar, and then press **Enter**.
9. Click **Download** to go to the Ethereal:Download page.
10. Click the **local archive** link next to Windows OT/NT. The Win32 Binary Distribution page appears.
11. Scroll down the page and click the latest **ethereal-setup-[*version number*].exe** file.
12. In the Select a Mirror for File page, click the icon in the Download column for the site that is closest to you geographically.
13. When the File Download dialog box appears, click **Open**.
14. When the Ethereal Setup: License screen appears, click **I Agree**.
15. When the Installation Options dialog box appears, leave the default components selected (Ethereal, Tetheral, Editcap, Text2Pcap, Mergecap, Plugins, and Start Menu Shortcuts), and then click **Next**.

16. In the Installation Directory dialog box, select the directory where you want to install the software, and click **Install**. The Installing Files dialog box appears, presenting you with a series of messages informing you of the installation progress. When the message Completed appears, click **Close**.
17. Click **Start**, point to **Programs** (**All Programs** on Windows XP), point to **Ethereal**, and click **Ethereal**. The Ethereal Network Analyzer window appears.
18. From the Ethereal menu bar, click **Capture**, and then click **Start**.
19. Click the **Interface** list arrow and select your network interface device from the drop-down list (see Project 1-3 for instructions on how to determine this). The Ethereal: Capture window appears with a series of 0% readings, reporting that no data has been captured yet.
20. Click **Start**, point to **Programs** (**All Programs** on Windows XP), point to **Accessories**, and click **Command Prompt** to open a command prompt window.
21. At the command prompt, type **ping *[IP address]*** , where *[IP address]* is the address of your own computer. (See Project 1-2 for instructions on how to obtain this address.)
22. Switch to the Ethereal: Capture window to make it active. What is the percentage of traffic that was just received? How much was TCP? How much was UDP?
23. Click **Stop** at the bottom of the Ethereal: Capture window. A wealth of information about the packets that have passed through your network gateway should appear in the main Ethereal window. The first line should contain information about your ping request. What is the protocol listed as? What do the initials stand for? (*Hint:* Look at the middle section of the Ethereal window, where detailed information about the packet is presented.)
24. Close the Command Prompt window.
25. Click **File**, and then click **Quit** to close the Ethereal window and return to the Windows desktop.

Project 1-5: Identifying Open Ports

It was mentioned in this chapter that a computer that is to be secured, particularly one that is to host firewall or IDS software, should have a minimal set of resources and open ports on it. How do you determine which ports are open on your computer? You can do so with a utility that is built in to both UNIX and Windows systems called netstat. The following steps apply to a Windows 2000 or XP computer, but you can also run the command netstat –a on UNIX to get the same information.

1. Click **Start**, point to **Programs** (**All Programs** on Windows XP), point to **Accessories**, and click **Command Prompt**.

2. When the command prompt window opens, type **netstat –a** (leave a blank space between netstat and the hyphen (-)). Press **Enter**.

3. In a few seconds, a set of information appears in the command prompt window. Netstat presents information in columns. The first column, Proto, gives you the protocol being used. The last column, State, tells you whether a connection has been established (ESTABLISHED) or the computer is listening for connections (LISTENING). How many TCP ports did you find that were reported in the State column as LISTENING? How many UDP ports? Write the results in a lab notebook or word-processed document.

4. Close the Command Prompt window.

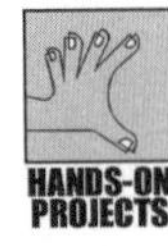

Project 1-6: Identify Existing Vulnerabilities

The Anonymizer.com Web site provides software that enables individuals to surf the Web while maintaining their privacy. This is done by hiding their IP address and other information. The site also enables visitors to take a test that reveals what information hackers or others can glean from their Web browser or their network. In this project, you go to the Authorizer.com site and run through what sorts of vulnerabilities you present to the outside world that need to be protected by firewalls, intrusion detection systems, and other defenses.

1. Double-click the **Internet Explorer** icon on your desktop to start your Web browser.

2. Enter the following URL in your browser's Address bar: **http://www.anonymizer.com**. Your browser should display the home page of the Anonymizer.com Web site.

3. Click the **SNOOP TEST** link.

4. The next page, entitled Test #1: Your Unique IP Address, should report your computer's IP address in a box at the top. Scroll down, if necessary, and click **Go**.

5. The next page, Test #2: Test Hidden Files (Cookies), reports on the cookies that the Anonymizer.com site can "see" on your machine and in your cache file. Scroll through the information presented at the top of the page to find out what information is vulnerable and record it in a lab notebook or workbook. Then click the **Test 4** link on the left side of the page.

6. Does the file win.ini appear in a separate window after clicking on the link for Test 4? Click the links for the Registry Editor and other critical applications shown in the box at the top of the Test 4: Hack and Exploit Vulnerability page. Can Anonymizer.com start your Registry Editor? Can it initiate an FTP connection from your computer? Write down any vulnerabilities you uncover. Then click the **Test 7** link on the left side of the page.

7. Wait a few minutes as Anonymizer attempts to trace a route from its server to your computer. After some time, the results of the trace appear in the box at the top of the page entitled Test #7: Your Network. Did the trace get all the way to your machine? Write the results in a lab notebook or workbook, and report back to your instructor on the vulnerabilities you found.

CASE PROJECTS

Case Project 1-1: Employee Awareness and Data Theft

A manager within your organization requests a set of technical specifications about a product line that he is not directly involved in and that he has not asked to see before. The individual is given access to the files on the project and acquires technical specifications for it. A week or two later the manager leaves the company and is hired by a competitor. The manager's employees report, after the fact, that they think he stole company information about the product line in order to give it to the competitor. What could you have done to prevent the theft from occurring?

Case Project 1-2: Making the Case for a Security Policy

Shortly after you are hired by a database software company to provide network security, you ask to revise the existing security policy. You are told to focus on network connectivity and "setting up firewalls and intrusion detection systems" instead. What could you say to argue for spending time on a security policy?

Case Project 1-3: Listing Good Password Procedures

You are asked to prepare a single set of recommendations for upgrading your network's passwords. What are four things you would tell your staff in a short e-mail message that remind them of good password security?

Case Project 1-4: Responding to Suspicious E-Mail

One of your employees sends you an e-mail reporting that he just received a message that appears to have come from his own e-mail address. The message urged him to install a new virus protection program to guard against the Klez virus. Before installing the program, the employee wanted to check to make sure it would not conflict with other virus protection programs already on his computer. What should you tell him?

CHAPTER

2

DESIGNING A NETWORK DEFENSE

After reading this chapter and completing the exercises, you will be able to:

- Understand covert channeling and other common attack threats you need to defend against
- Describe the network security components that make up a layered defense configuration
- List the essential activities that need to be performed in order to protect a network
- Integrate an intrusion detection system (IDS) into a network security configuration

Designing a network defense is not a matter of installing a single firewall and leaving the device to do its work. Rather, it's a matter of setting up layers of defense, configuring multiple security devices to work in a coordinated fashion, and keeping up with network traffic on an ongoing basis. This sort of effort is needed because a network defense needs to handle network attacks that can flood into a network at broadband speed, that can change as fast as hackers can develop them, and that can originate from multiple sources.

In this chapter, you will explore common threats and the technologies that can notify you when an attack is occurring. You'll then explore how to create layers of network defense, and essential security concept activities such as encryption, authentication, packet filtering, and virus protection. Finally, you'll see how intrusion detection systems help you anticipate attacks and respond to security alerts.

COMMON ATTACK THREATS

In Chapter 1, you learned about the kinds of individuals who might try to gain unauthorized access to your network. You also had a brief overview of the motivations behind the attacks those individuals might choose to launch. In this section, you'll get a more detailed description of the kinds of attacks you can face, including many that fall into the category of covert channeling.

A **covert channel** is a communications channel, such as a port on a computer or a network connection, that can be exploited in a way that compromises the security of a computer. Some of the hacker techniques mentioned in this section of the chapter are a way of covert channeling—in other words, a way to gain unauthorized access to a system by sending malformed or fragmented packets through a communications channel without the system administrator's knowledge.

Covert channeling can encompass any technique in which a host is prompted to give up information that enumerates open ports or other channels. Accordingly, in this section, you examine the following: vulnerable points of entry that your perimeter defense needs to close; Denial of Service (DoS) attacks that can effectively shut down a network; remote procedure call abuses that give hackers a way to use Windows networking services to gain access to other computers; viruses and Trojan horses that can enter the network through e-mail messages or downloaded files; man-in-the-middle attacks that can destroy the privacy of individual users; and fragmented IP packets that can be used to sneak malicious code into the network.

Network Vulnerabilities

To set up a defense, you need to know what kinds of attacks to expect, and what services and computers might present openings that can potentially be exploited. An attacker might attempt to access open points of entry that include:

- *Vulnerable services* —The hacker may be able to exploit known vulnerabilities in a server program.
- *E-mail gateways* —The hacker may be able to attach a virus payload to an e-mail message. If a recipient clicks the attachment to open it, the program executes and the virus installs itself on the user's system.
- *Porous borders* —Computers on the network may be listening (that is, waiting for connections) on a virtual channel called a port that is not being used. If a hacker discovers a port that the computer has left open and that is not yet being used, this open port can give the hacker access to the contents of that computer.

These kinds of vulnerable points of entry can be closed by packet filters, firewalls, and proxy servers, as well as by intrusion detection systems. Such defensive tools are described later in this chapter.

Another common way in which hackers gain access to an organization's resources is one that can't be defended with hardware or software. The vulnerability, in this case, is gullible employees who are fooled by the hacker into giving out a password or other access code. Attacks that involve personnel who don't observe accepted security practices (or who willfully abuse them) can best be defended with a strong security policy of the sort described in Chapter 3.

Sometimes the biggest vulnerabilities facing a company are the ones inside the firewall, not outside of it. In November 2002, the FBI broke up the largest identity theft ring in U.S. history. A help desk worker at a computer software company allegedly agreed to give the passwords and access codes for consumer credit reports to another individual, who was then able to make unauthorized purchases using the stolen information (the credit card numbers and other personal information of more than 30,000 individuals).

Denial of Service (DoS) Attacks

After a hacker has gained control of a computer, his or her ultimate goal may not be to actually steal the files within it. Rather, the compromised machine may be used as a launching point for a Denial of Service (DoS) attack against a network server. By gaining control of someone else's computer, the hacker protects his or her own identity from being traced. Note, however, that a DoS attack comes about only if a hacker is able to gain control of dozens or even hundreds of computers that then flood a targeted server with access requests.

In a DoS attack, a server is flooded with more requests to view Web pages and access files than it can handle at any one time. Such an attack can be likened to a telephone switchboard that is flooded with so many incoming calls at one time that no other calls can be handled. The server is so busy sending response messages to the requests that result from the DoS attack that it is unable to process legitimate requests and, as a result, the network is effectively blocked.

One of the most destructive outbreaks of DoS attacks occurred in early 2000, when some of the largest commercial Web sites, including Yahoo! (*www.yahoo.com*), eBay (*www.ebay.com*), Amazon.com (*www.amazon.com*), and eTrade (*www.etrade.com*) were rendered inaccessible to legitimate visitors after being flooded with traffic from hundreds of hijacked systems. A 15-year-old Canadian youth nicknamed MafiaBoy was later arrested and charged with the attacks. He was eventually sentenced to spend eight months in a juvenile detention center.

In another DoS attack a year later, the well-known Microsoft-owned Web sites *www.msn.com*, *www.expedia.com*, and *www.carpoint.com* sites were flooded with so much data that they were able to respond to as little as 2 percent of legitimate requests for one morning and part of the same afternoon. This example indicates that if DoS attacks can so dramatically effect such high-profile networks, they can do severe damage to the networks of smaller companies having less extensive security personnel on hand.

Numerous types of DoS attacks exist; the more common varieties—SYN floods and address spoofing—are discussed in the following sections.

SYN Flood Attacks

In a particular type of DoS attack called a SYN flood, the attacker, after determining the IP address of the server, sends a TCP packet to the host that has the SYN flag set. (See "TCP Headers" in Chapter 1 on SYN and other flags in the TCP header part of TCP/IP packets.) The server responds by sending a TCP SYN/ACK packet. Instead of responding to the SYN/ACK by sending an ACK back to the server (as it would in a normal communications session), the attacker never responds. The server waits for a response, and the resulting **half-open session** uses up server resources. The attacker then sends a flood of TCP SYN requests without responding. The server eventually runs out of resources, making it unable to service any other requests. This process is illustrated in Figure 2-1.

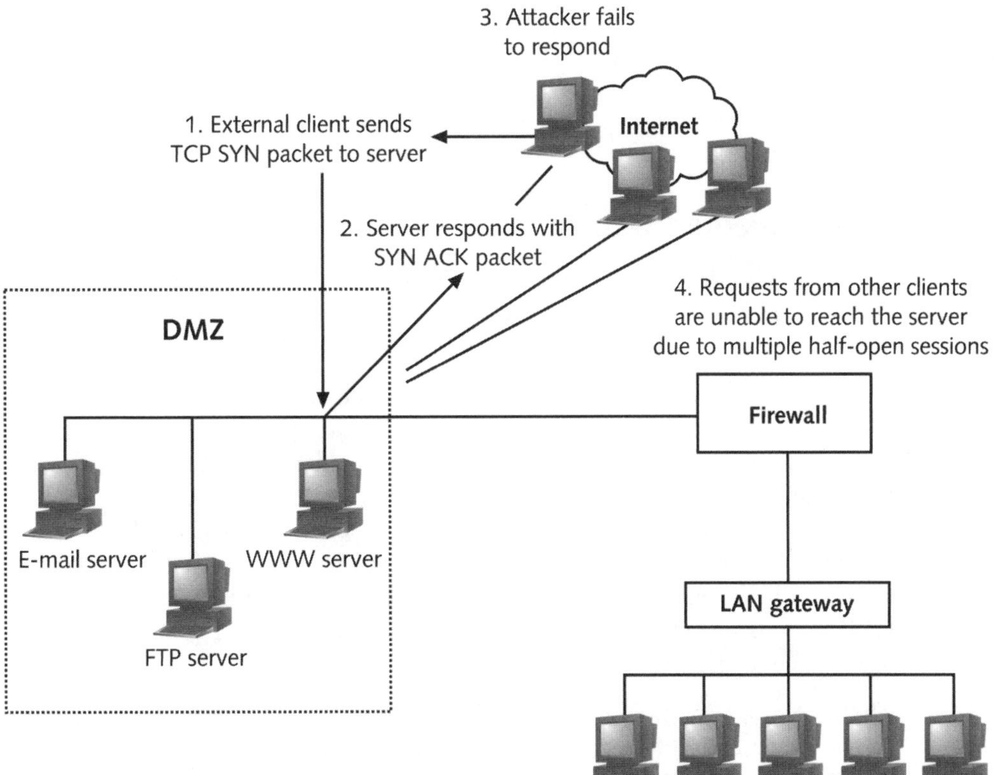

Figure 2-1 A SYN flood attack can cause a DoS

Address Spoofing

Another common type of DoS attack results from a **spoofed address** —an address that contains falsified information that is intended to comply with one of the firewall's packet filtering rules so that it can pass through the firewall and connect with a computer on the internal network. The attacker does a network scan to identify an open port on the server, and then sends a packet containing a spoofed address to the server. The packet contains the same source IP address and port as the server's own IP address and port. For example, if the server is at IP address 203.100.1.1, the source and destination addresses of the spoofed packet would be 203.100.1.1. The falsified—and technically impossible—set of information can crash some servers that don't have a sufficiently sophisticated set of filtering rules that enables them to simply drop such packets.

Sometimes, rather than a hacker using multiple computers to cause a DoS attack, the denial of service comes from software that has security vulnerabilities. In September 2002, as this book was being written, an updated version of Apache, the most popular Web server software in use on the Internet, had just been issued. The new version repaired or updated a number of features, including one that affected UNIX systems running Apache that use processes called **threads** to respond to requests for documents. The previous version contained a flaw that caused a single thread to terminate which then caused all other threads to terminate. This resulted in the server being unable to generate threads to handle subsequent requests, which had the same effect as a DoS attack. This scenario illustrates one way to combat DoS attacks or similar incidents: keeping abreast of patches and fixes and installing them as soon as they become available (and then testing the patches to make sure they work).

Remote Procedure Call Abuses

Remote Procedure Call (RPC) service is a fundamental component associated with Windows networking. It allows programs on computers to use resources on servers. It also enables UNIX computers to communicate, and as such, it's a magnet for hackers.

RPC uses UDP ports such as 111 or 135. In one type of RPC attack, RPC packets that contain spoofed addresses are sent to a server. The packets seem to come from one IP address, but they also contain information that points to another IP address as the source. When the RPC server is unable to interpret the IP address information to process the packet, it sends a message called an RPC REJECT packet that tells the other computer that there is a communications error. The end result is that REJECT packets are sent back and forth between server and client until the connection is dropped. If enough spoofed RPC packets are sent, the resulting proliferation of REJECT packets can drain the server of resources as well as available network bandwidth.

There's a quick solution for most RPC abuses: install a software patch. Microsoft released a software patch to protect against DoS attacks resulting from RPC traffic; you can read a report about the attacks and find a link to the patch at *www.microsoft.com/technet/treeview/default.asp?url=/technet/security/bulletin/MS98-014.asp*.

Viruses, Worms, and Trojan Horses

When managers and high-level administrators in the corporate and governmental sectors talk about security threats, they tend to focus on hackers and common attacks against the Domain Name System (DNS), file sharing systems, or administrator and user accounts.

They are also concerned with **buffer overflows** (attacks in which a hacker writes a piece of code that takes up more of a chunk of fixed-memory "buffer" space than a Web server or e-mail server allows, in such a way that the extra code can be executed on the server).

The Top Ten Most Critical Internet Security Threats maintained by the SANS Institute (*www.sans.org/topten.htm*) lists such attacks, and more. Note that as of this writing, there is now an appendix to the list. This appendix discusses viruses and malicious code that can be spread through e-mail attachments or downloaded files.

A **virus** is computer code that copies itself from one place to another surreptitiously and performs actions that range from benign to harmful. Some viruses simply spread themselves from one file to another; a type of virus called a **worm** creates files that copy themselves over and over and take up disk space. Others can destroy data on a hard disk. At this writing, for instance, news stories are being presented about a malicious program called W32BugBear@mm. Sometimes simply called Bugbear, it has the ability to scan a user's file system and send a list of files back to a hacker. It then mass mails itself to other computers using e-mail addresses stored in the address book of the infected user's computer. It also stops any anti-virus programs that are currently running on the infected computer. So far, a thousand computer systems have been infected around the world.

A **Trojan horse** is also a harmful computer program, and one that appears to be something useful, just as the wooden Trojan horse described in Greek legends. The difference between a virus and a Trojan horse is in how the malicious code is used. Viruses replicate themselves and can potentially cause damage when they execute on a user's computer. Trojan horses create a **back door** —an opening to a computer such as an unused port or terminal service that gives a hacker the ability to control a computer. In addition, the often hidden or obscure nature of the back door makes the hacker's activities difficult to detect.

Viruses, worms, and Trojan horses are a significant security threat. They can damage files, enable hackers to control computers, and cause applications to stop functioning correctly. In creating a network defense perimeter, you need to take them into consideration. Firewalls and intrusion detection systems don't block such malicious code on their own, however; you need to install anti-virus software or proxy servers that can be configured to filter them out and delete them before they cause harm.

Man-in-the-Middle Attacks

In a **man-in-the-middle attack**, a hacker intercepts part of an encrypted data session to gain control over the data being exchanged. Specifically, the hacker is able to intercept a log code called a public key that is exchanged during a public-private key encryption session. The hacker then substitutes his or her own public key for that of the intended recipient. As a result, the hacker can impersonate the intended recipient. Armed with a public key, the hacker can potentially gain the ability to read messages between the two individuals even though the messages are encrypted. The sequence of events in this type of attack is illustrated in more detail in Figure 2-2.

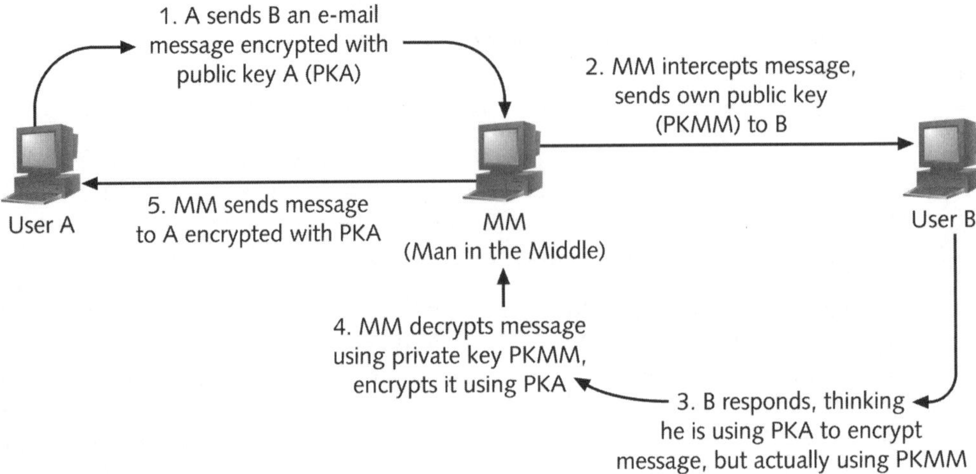

Figure 2-2 A man-in-the-middle attack

As you can see from Figure 2-2, one of the most insidious aspects of a man-in-the-middle attack is the fact that the participants may never realize that someone is reading their encrypted correspondence; they think they are sending and receiving messages using one another's public keys.

Fragmented IP Packets

Fragmentation refers to the division of a single IP packet into multiple packets. Fragmentation was originally developed as a means of enabling large packets to pass through early routers that couldn't handle them due to frame size limitations. Routers were then able to divide packets into multiple fragments and send them along the network, where receiving routers would reassemble them in the correct order and pass them to their destination.

By assigning a packet a false fragment number and embedding IP header information within it, a hacker can sometimes fool a host into letting the packet pass into the network, where it can infiltrate and potentially harm an internal host. By setting packet filter rules that block all packets that use fragmentation, such packets can be effectively blocked, however.

Providing Layers of Network Defense

No single security component or method can be expected to provide complete protection for a network—or even an individual host computer—working by itself. Rather, you need to assemble a group of components that work in coordinated fashion to provide protection against different threats.

The components and approaches that are described later in this chapter, and throughout the rest of this book, should be arranged in such a way that they provide layers of network defense. Each layer is discussed in more detail in the following sections.

Layer 1: Physical Security

The term "physical security" refers to measures taken to physically protect a computer or other network device from theft, fire, or environmental disaster. Each of these events can have an impact that is as great or greater than what a virus or a hacker can accomplish.

Along with installing computer locks that physically attach the device itself to a piece of furniture in your office, also consider placing critical servers in a room protected by a lock and/or a burglar alarm. In addition, Uninterruptible Power Supply (UPS) devices help maintain a steady level of electrical power and thus avoid the damage that can occur from voltage spikes—sudden and dramatic increases in power that can damage hardware.

Use an engraving tool to mark serial numbers, phone numbers, or other identifiers on portable devices such as laptops that can be easily lost or stolen. Specialized locks are available for PCs and laptops alike; many have alarms that go off if someone tries to take the device. You can also store portable computers in locked cabinets such as the ones sold by Datamation Systems (*http://pc-security.com/Newproducts/carts.html*).

Layer 2: Password Security

After you have physically secured your computers, you can begin to protect them "from the inside" as well. One simple but effective strategy is password security—having your employees select good passwords, keep them secure, and change them as needed. Simply choosing an administrator or root password that is *not* an obvious word in the dictionary or that is not blank closes a potential point of entry for password-crackers.

Using multiple passwords including screen savers and passwords that can be used to protect critical applications is also a good idea. (Task Lock by Posum.com, *http://posum.com/task-lock.html*, will even password-protect individual programs.) Screen saver and application passwords guard against unauthorized employees gaining control of computers while they are unattended.

In addition, password practices that might seem obvious to you probably need to be taught to employees and should be part of an organization's security policy (see Chapter 3). Instruct your coworkers to pick passwords that have at least seven characters, that use a mixture of characters and numerals, and that are not written down or shared with anyone.

You can provide an extra layer of protection for a laptop computer by setting the Basic Input-Output System (BIOS)—a password that keeps intruders from starting up a computer. However, such protection can easily be circumvented if the computer is booted from a floppy disk.

Layer 3: Operating System Security

Another way to secure computers and the data contained in them "from the inside" is by installing operating system patches that have been issued to address security flaws. It's your responsibility to keep up with such patches, hotfixes, or service packs and install them when they become available. In addition, stopping any unneeded services and disabling Guest accounts will help make an operating system more secure. (See "Securing Individual Workstations" in Chapter 1 for more information on this topic.)

Layer 4: Using Anti-Virus Protection

Virus scanning refers to the process of examining files or e-mail messages for filenames, filename extensions such as .exe (for executable code), or other indications that viruses are present. Anti-virus software is able to recognize the presence of viruses and either delete them from the file system or place them in a storage area called a **quarantine** where they cannot replicate themselves or do harm to other files.

Firewalls and IDSs, by themselves, are not equipped to scan for viruses and eliminate them. However, many enterprise-level firewalls come with anti-virus protection integrated into their feature set. For instance, Symantec Enterprise Firewall (*http://enterprisesecurity.symantec.com/products/products.cfm?ProductID=47*) includes a program called MIMEsweeper that can strip viruses out of e-mail attachments and downloaded files. Anti-virus software is a "must-have" for every computer in a network; if your firewall doesn't provide it, you need to install anti-virus software on the computer that hosts the firewall, and on your individual network computers as well.

Layer 5: Packet Filtering

Packet filters either block or allow the transmission of packets of information based on port, IP address, protocol, or other criteria. Think of a packet filter like a ticket-taker at the entrance gate of a baseball park. The employee's first task is to admit only those with valid tickets—and tickets for this day and not any other day. Having stripped off part of the ticket and handed the remainder back to the customer, the ticket-taker then provides directions on where to find the appropriate seats within the ballpark.

Of course, in the real world, you won't hear a client or manager approach you and ask, "Can you set up a packet filter for us?" Rather, you'll hear something like the following: "Is there a way to block this overseas site from sending us viruses or trying to break into our machines? Can we block that site and still give our suppliers a way to get in?" You also might get a request to "make the network more secure" and you'll think of packet filtering as one line of defense in a perimeter security system.

Different Types of Packet Filters

Packet filters, like firewalls and intrusion detection systems, come in many varieties. Some are hardware devices such as routers that are placed at a network gateway. Others are software programs that can either be installed on a gateway or an individual computer. Here are a few examples:

- *Routers* —These are probably the most common packet filters.
- *Operating systems* —Some systems, like Windows and Linux, have built-in utilities that can do packet filtering on the TCP/IP stack of the server software. Linux has a kernel-level packet filter called ipchains; Windows has TCP/IP Filtering.
- *Software firewalls* —Most enterprise-level programs, such as Check Point NG, do packet filtering; Check Point's product specializes in stateful filtering. Personal firewalls like ZoneAlarm and Sygate Personal Firewall do a less-sophisticated version called **stateless packet filtering**.

A router can keep unauthorized traffic from entering the protected network altogether. If a software filter is the only kind of packet filter being used, this means that an intentionally mangled, spoofed, or otherwise harmful packet has already reached a target machine. For that reason many security experts caution against using only software packet filters.

Whatever device is being used, the packet-filtering device evaluates the information in the header and compares the information to the rules that have been set up. If the information corresponds to one of the "Allow" rules, the packet is allowed to pass. On the other hand, if the information matches one of the "Deny" rules, the packet is dropped. Packet filters examine only the header of packets, in contrast to application proxies, which do their own kind of packet "filtering" by examining the data in the packet and then forwarding the packet to its destination on behalf of the originating host.

Stateless Versus Stateful Packet Filtering

There are two different approaches to filtering packets based on selected header contents. The simplest approach, stateless (also called static) packet filtering, reviews packet header contents and makes decisions on whether to allow or drop the packets based on whether a connection has actually been established between an external host and an internal one.

A more sophisticated and secure approach is stateful packet filtering. In this, the filter maintains a record of the state of a connection and can thus make "intelligent" decisions on whether traffic is a genuine reply to an established connection and should be allowed.

Stateless packet filters are useful when you need to completely block traffic from a subnet or other network. A stateless or static filter can be configured to use different types of header information to decide whether to allow or block a packet. The information includes the IP source or destination address; the TCP or UDP port number being used; the ICMP message type; and the TCP header flags, such as ACK and SYN.

Chapter 5 includes a more detailed examination of packet filtering that uses IP header information, port numbers, message types, and TCP header flags.

Stateful inspection takes the concept of packet filtering a step further than stateless filtering. A stateful filter can do everything a stateless filter can, but with one significant addition: it has the ability to maintain a record of the state of a connection. By "remembering" which packets are part of an active connection and which are not, the stateful filter can make "intelligent" decisions to allow traffic that is a true reply to an established connection and to deny traffic that represents "crafted" packets containing false information.

In addition to a rule base, a stateful filter has a **state table**, which is a list of current connections. The process of using the state table to "statefully" filter packets works as follows:

1. The packet filter receives a request to access a Web site.
2. The packet filter compares the packet to the state table. It sees that no connection exists as of yet, so the request is added to the state table and passed to the filter's rule base.
3. If a rule exists that enables internal hosts to access the Web using TCP port 80, the packet is allowed to pass.
4. When the packet is received, the Web server sends a reply with the TCP SYN and ACK flags set.
5. When the response reaches the packet filter, the filter references the state table and sees that an entry exists.
6. Entries that match criteria in both the state table and rule base are allowed to pass; all others are dropped.

Figure 2-3 illustrates steps involved in processing a single request from an internal host to access the Web site *www.course.com*.

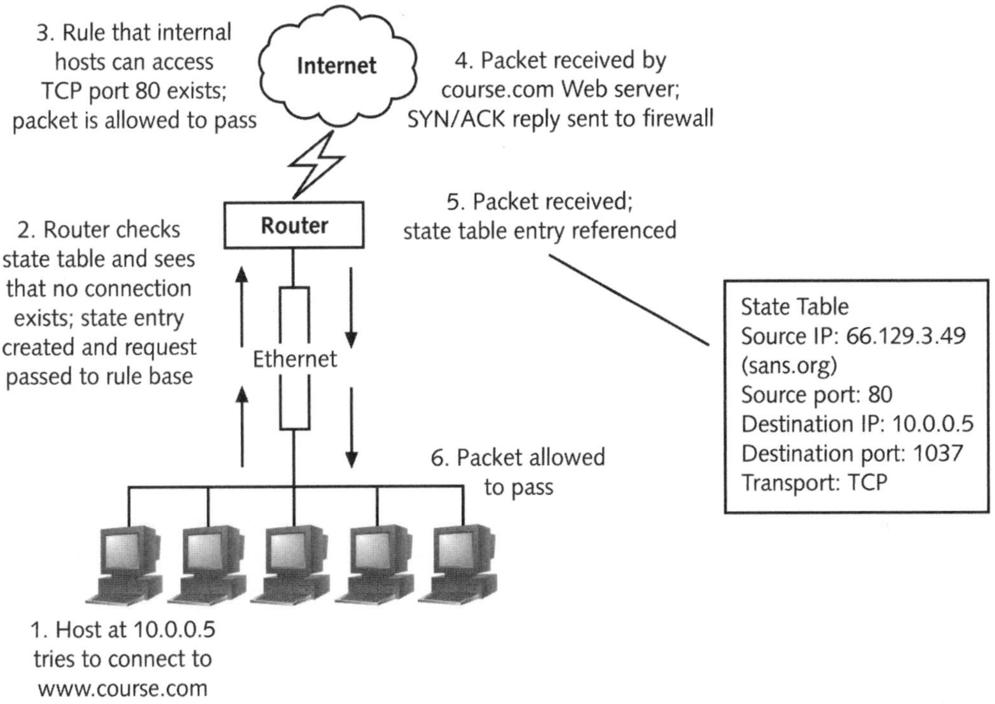

Figure 2-3 Stateful packet filtering

Layer 6: Firewalls

The foundation for installing a firewall to protect your network occurs even before you set up rules for packet filtering or other settings. You need to establish an overall security policy that governs how your firewall operates. After you have a policy in place, you implement it by creating a packet filtering rule base that reflects your overall approach to network security. You then set up Network Address Translation (NAT), encryption, and authentication, before moving on to more advanced functions like load balancing and intrusion alerts. You also set up a rule base and perform firewall administration using a Graphical User Interface (GUI) tool. The GUI also helps you create user accounts and set up remote users so that they can connect to your network using a VPN.

NOTE

Firewall configuration is only summarized briefly here because it is discussed in detail in Chapter 5.

Firewalls can be set up to protect a network in such a way that the overall approach to security specified by an organization's security policy is carried through into practice. Firewalls can be configured to control the amount of traffic the network receives and the ease with which internal users can access external networks. Firewalls can also control how internal hosts on the network are concealed.

The following sections describe two ways in which a firewall can control the amount of protection a network receives: permissive versus restrictive policies, and NAT.

Permissive Versus Restrictive Policies

A firewall, following the direction given in a security policy typically adopts a general approach to security such as a permissive or restrictive policy:

- *Permissive* —A permissive policy calls for a firewall and associated security components to allow all traffic through the network gateway by default, then block services on a case-by-case basis. Such an approach might be found in a setting such as a library or university campus where the primary orientation of a firewall is permissive—that is, permitting connectivity through the gateway.
- *Restrictive* —A restrictive policy calls for a firewall and associated network security components to deny all traffic by default. The first rule denies all traffic on any service and using any port. Subsequent rules in the rule base only specifically allow what services you need on a case-by-case basis. Such an approach might be suitable for a corporate environment, especially one that deals in sensitive information such as banking or other financial data.

These two approaches are illustrated in Figure 2-4:

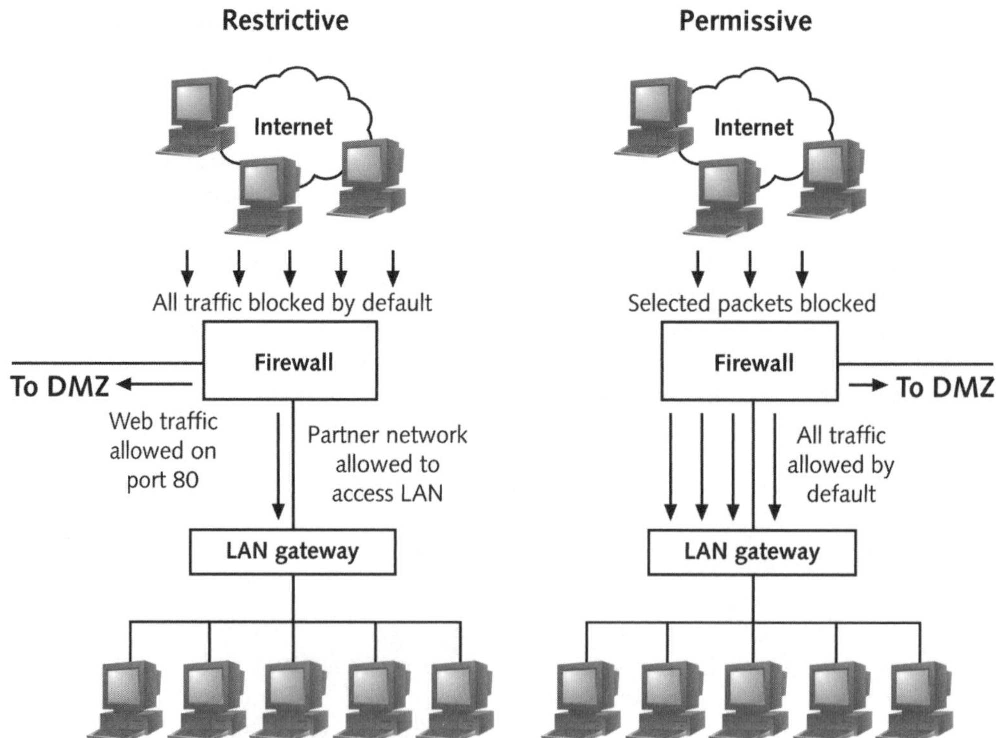

Figure 2-4 Permissive versus restrictive policies

A firewall should enforce the overall policy established by the administration of the organization being protected. Enforcement is handled primarily through setting up packet filtering rules, a set of which is contained in a **rule base**. The order of the rules contained in the rule base becomes important to how the firewall processes traffic, as is discussed in greater detail in Chapter 5.

Network Address Translation (NAT)

A function that virtually all firewalls are able to perform is **Network Address Translation (NAT)**, which converts the internal IP addresses of hosts on the LAN being protected into different IP addresses.

NAT comes in two forms: hide-mode NAT and one-to-one NAT. In **hide-mode NAT**, private IP addresses are turned into routable public IP addresses. Hosts on the internal network can thus be assigned addresses in one of the three ranges of non-routable IP addresses:

- 10.0.0.1 to 10.255.255.254
- 172.16.0.1 to 172.31.255.254
- 192.168.0.1 to 192.168.255.254

In the other form of NAT, **one-to-one NAT**, each workstation that has a private IP address is assigned an external IP address on an individual basis. This is sometimes called static NAT.

A router or firewall that performs NAT keeps external users from determining the IP addresses of computers on the protected network. Another benefit of hide-mode NAT is conservation of IP addresses, which are becoming scarce: each host on the internal network can be assigned an address in a private IP range, and the firewall can translate that address into an external, routable address when the host needs to communicate with the external Internet. The sequence of steps in a simple data transfer using NAT is shown in Figure 2-5.

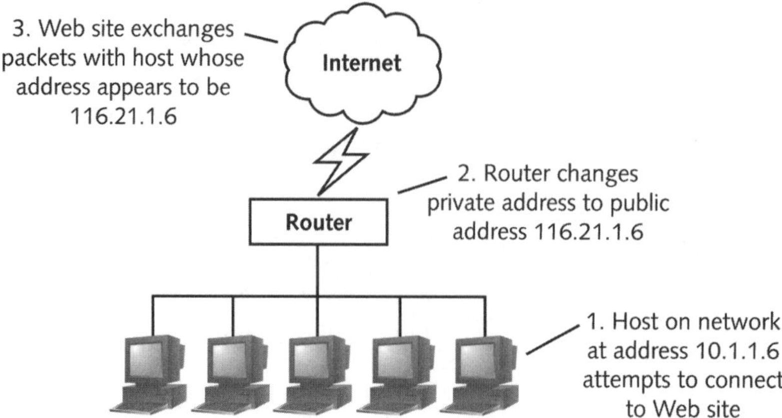

Figure 2-5 Simple data transfer using NAT

Layer 7: Proxy Servers

A **proxy server** is server software that, like firewalls or routers that perform NAT, can conceal the end users in a network. The benefit of concealing end users is that hackers cannot find individual computers on the internal network that they can target and try to attack.

Proxy servers function as a sort of software go-between, forwarding data between internal users and external hosts. Proxy servers go by many names, including proxy servers, proxy services, application-level gateways, or simply application proxies. This chapter uses the common designation "proxy servers."

Proxy servers were originally developed as a way to speed up communications on the Web by storing a site's most popular pages in cache. They can filter out undesirable Web sites, and they can block harmful content in much the same manner as packet filters. Today, most proxy servers function as firewalls at the boundary of a network, performing packet filtering and NAT in addition to HTTP Web proxy service and other proxy services.

Consider an assistant to the president of a corporation who is sent out to attend a meeting on the president's behalf. The assistant delivers the president's message to those attending the meeting, but translates the message into his or her own words. The assistant also keeps a record of what happened in the meeting. He or she will be functioning in much the same way as a proxy server. In other words, the assistant is to the proxy server as the message is to the packets of information that the proxy server processes.

How Proxy Servers Work

Similarly, proxies work by focusing on the port each service uses, screening all traffic into and out of each port and deciding whether to block or allow traffic based on rules set up by the proxy server administrator. Typically, a proxy server intercepts and then passes along a request from a computer on the internal network being protected. It then passes the request to a destination computer on the Internet. The process in which a proxy receives and processes a request, as described in the steps that follow, might seem complex and time-consuming, but collectively, they take only a matter of seconds:

1. An internal host makes a request to access a Web site.
2. The request goes to the application proxy, which examines the header and data of the packet against rules configured by the firewall administrator.
3. The proxy server recreates the packets in their entirety, with a different source IP address.
4. The proxy server sends the packet to its destination; the packet appears to be coming from the proxy server, not the original end-user who made the request.
5. The returned packets are sent to the proxy server, which inspects them again and compares them against its rule base.
6. The returned packets are rebuilt by the proxy server and sent to the originating computer; when received, the packets appear to have come from the external host, not the proxy server.

The preceding steps are illustrated in Figure 2-6.

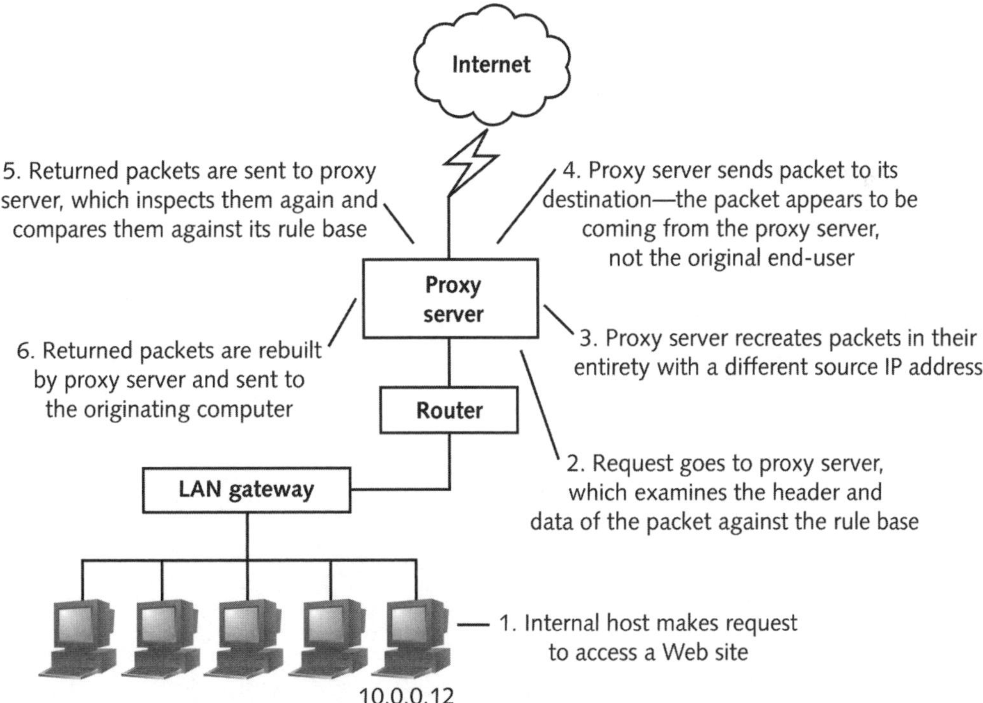

Figure 2-6 Steps involved in a typical proxy transaction

Strengths and Weaknesses of Proxy Servers

Proxy servers provide a network with some very powerful protection and monitoring activities. First and foremost, they conceal clients on the internal network by replacing source IP addresses with their own IP address. Second, they are able to inspect the data payload of a packet, which enables them to do filtering of viruses and other content (see Chapter 6). On the downside, proxy servers do add time to communications, and end-users might complain that it takes them a longer time to access Web sites with a proxy server than without one.

Ultimately, proxies and packet filters need to be used together in a firewall. Their respective strengths can complement one another in a way that provides a network with multiple layers of security. Both work at the Application layer, but they inspect different parts of IP packets and act on them in different ways. Proxy servers scan the entire data part of IP packets, and create much more detailed log file listings than packet filters.

Consider that packet filters log only header information, while application proxies can log much more. If a packet matches one of the packet filter's rules, the filter simply allows the packet to pass through as is and go to the destination computer. An application proxy completely rebuilds the packet with new source IP information, which shields internal users from those on the outside. Because the proxy rebuilds all packets that pass between them, attacks that can start with mangled packet data never reach the internal host.

On the downside, proxy servers are far more critical to network communications than packet filters are. If a packet filter fails to work for some reason, one possible result is that all packets might be allowed through to the internal network. If a proxy server crashes, all network communications cease.

Figure 2-7 shows how a proxy server and packet filters might be combined on a screened host at the perimeter of a network.

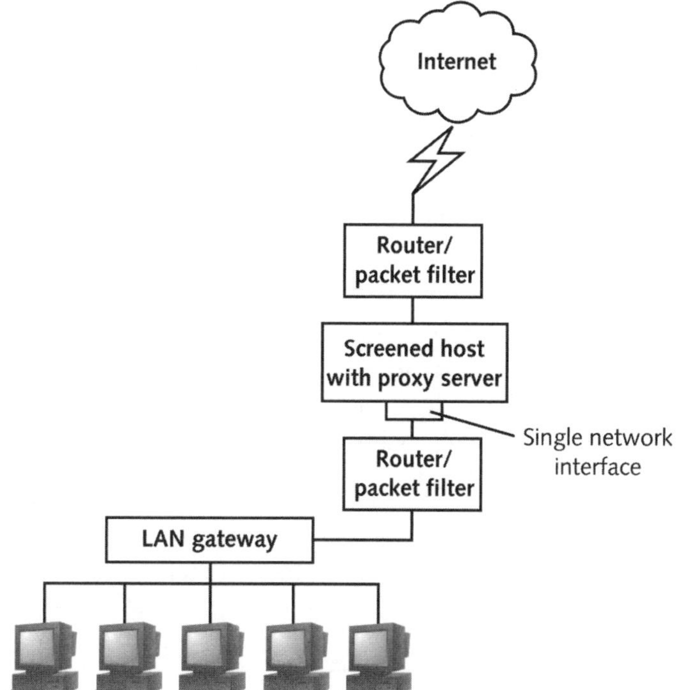

Figure 2-7 A proxy server on a screened host

In Figure 2-7, the proxy server is installed on a screened host, and routers that function as packet filters are positioned on either side. The packet filter that has an interface on the Internet is configured so that external traffic is allowed to pass only if it is destined for a service provided on the proxy server, which sits on the protected side of the perimeter.

It's important to note that in Figure 2-7, although the screened host/proxy server has a direct interface on the Internet, this isn't the optimal way to configure a proxy server. If you are able to use both a proxy server and a firewall, it's far better to use a proxy server behind a firewall. The firewall should have an interface to the Internet, and protect the proxy server behind it. The need for protection is critical because, if a hacker compromises the proxy, the hacker can make it look as though he or she is actually an internal client, and the results can be disastrous for the organization being protected.

Layer 8: DMZ

A subnet called a **Demilitarized Zone (DMZ)**, which is a network that sits outside the internal network but is connected to the firewall, makes services publicly available while protecting the internal LAN as well.

Why do we need DMZs? Well, e-commerce—particularly the type of e-commerce that occurs between companies and which is commonly called business-to-business (B2B) e-commerce—continues to be one of the most significant and widely used business uses of the Internet. Companies use the Internet to exchange files, place orders, and check on orders by viewing designated directories on one another's networks. In addition, consumers need to shop and place orders using Web-based catalogs, send e-mail inquiries, and possibly download programs or other files that a company provides on an FTP server. All of these situations require a DMZ to protect and ensure that successful electronic transactions can take place.

The following sections describe two aspects of DMZs: the fact that they are a screened subnet, and the fact that they aren't a perfect method of repelling hackers.

Screened Subnet

The most common type of DMZ is a **screened subnet**, which is created by adding servers that permit public services like a Web or FTP site and combining them with the firewall's subnet (see Figure 2-8). You might choose this setup when you need to provide services that are accessible to the public, such as an FTP server, Web server, or e-mail server. A DMZ might also contain a **Domain Name Server (DNS)**, which resolves easy-to-remember domain names to IP addresses, thus enabling internal employees to access the Internet more easily than if they had to enter IP addresses every time they wanted to connect to a Web page.

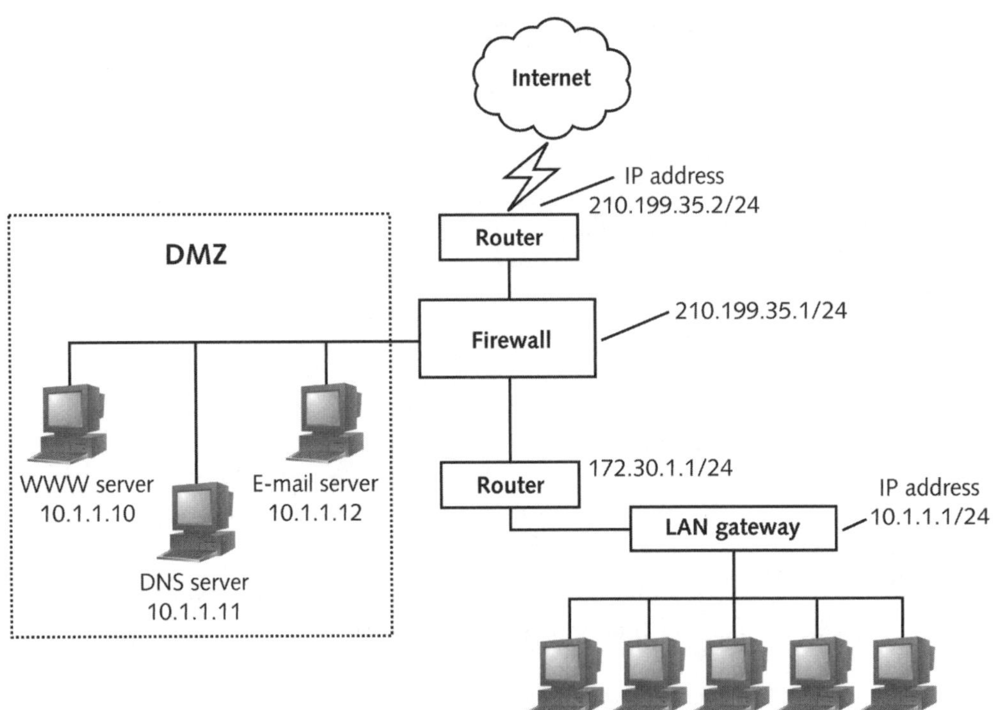

Figure 2-8 A screened subnet DMZ

The subnet attached to the firewall and contained in the DMZ is sometimes called a **service network** or **perimeter network** by those who dislike the military connotations of the term DMZ.

Hackers Can Still Get In

As you give individuals access to the outside world through the DMZ servers, you open up a way for hackers to connect to your network through the firewall. For this reason, many companies provide an extra level of security for their exposed public servers by adding a second firewall, as shown in Figure 2-9.

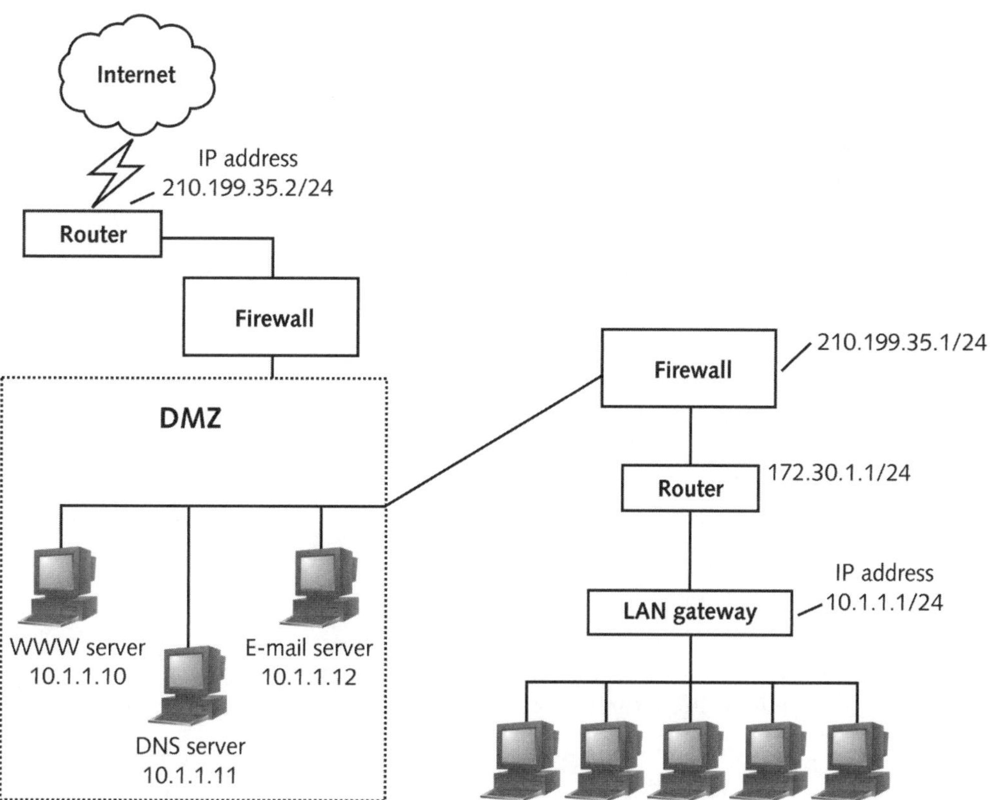

Figure 2-9 A multiple-firewall DMZ

End users might have to wait a few seconds before connecting to a Web site or downloading a file, but the added security makes it worthwhile. You will find this configuration used in business scenarios such as high-budget corporate networks that need to make information available to the public through a service network, but that put a premium on protecting their Web sites and other public information as well as the information on the internal network.

Layer 9: Intrusion Detection System (IDS)

Firewalls and proxy servers will ideally block intruders or malicious code from entering a network. However, an intrusion detection system (IDS) used in conjunction with such tools provides an additional layer of protection for a network. An IDS works by recognizing the signs of a possible attack and sending a notification to an administrator that such an attack is underway on a network. The signs of possible attacks are commonly called **signatures** —combinations of IP address, port number, and the frequency with which access attempts are made.

For IDS to work, the administrator has to define the signatures that constitute an intrusion attempt, as well as those that represent a "false-positive" (an access attempt that isn't really an attack). The method of notification also needs to be defined. Finally, the staff person or persons who will respond to the intrusion alert and what actions will be taken if the intrusion is found to be an attack are also defined.

Layer 10: Virtual Private Networks (VPNs)

When companies need to share files or exchange sensitive financial information, they will traditionally turn to expensive leased lines provided by telecommunications companies. Although these lines provide a point-to-point connection between the networks of the two companies involved and thus present a high level of security, the monthly costs are excessively high for many budget-conscious companies. A growing number of organizations are turning to **virtual private networks (VPNs)** to provide a relatively low-cost and secure connection between organizations that uses the public Internet.

VPNs are discussed in detail in Chapter 7, but for the purposes of this overview of fundamental network security components and layers of network defense, you need to know that VPNs represent a complex and powerful way to connect networks and individual computer users. Rather than stringing a cable between two companies or between a company's LAN and the home office of a contractor or at-home worker, VPNs do three fundamental activities:

- *Encrypt* —VPNs encrypt packets to preserve the integrity of information that is transmitted from point to point.
- *Authenticate* —VPNs use keys and certificates to ensure that the individuals who access the corporate network via the VPN are who they say they are.
- *Encapsulate* —VPNs encapsulate encrypted packets within other packets to protect information even more than conventional encryption.

The result of this combination of security schemes is a virtual "tunnel" between VPN participants through which information can pass securely. At the same time, VPNs extend the corporate LAN to other networks or to the laptops or PCs of remote employees. As a result, firewalls need to be installed at the endpoints of those VPN connections to keep viruses or other hack attacks from accessing the LAN through the VPN. This, too, is described in more detail in Chapter 7.

Layer 11: Logging and Administration

After a series of network defense layers is put into place, logging and administration are vital to their successful operation. Logging is the process of reviewing and analyzing the log files that firewalls and intrusion detection systems accumulate. Administrators scan the log files for intrusion attempts and respond by closing any vulnerable ports or computers that are the targets of those attempts.

Administration is a term that encompasses the activities required to maintain and keep a firewall, proxy server, IDS, or other tool up-to-date. Such activities include the updating of virus definitions and attack signatures. They also include the strengthening of the firewall's packet filtering rule base to work more efficiently and to address attacks that weren't anticipated when the rule base was originally created.

Essential Network Security Activities

Any network security configuration performs a set of basic security activities. Ultimately, those activities create a layered defense system for a network. The most common activities—encryption, authentication, packet filtering rules, virus protection, secure remote access, and log file management—are described briefly in the sections that follow.

Encryption

Packet filters, firewalls, and proxy servers all provide protection for packets of information that pass through a gateway at the perimeter of a network or subnet. However, corruption can also occur between the gateway and the gateway of the destination network. To protect a packet's contents from being intercepted, firewalls and other security components often encrypt the contents of packets leaving the network and are prepared to decrypt incoming packets.

Encryption is the process of concealing information to render it unreadable to all but the intended recipients. Encryption turns ordinary information into encoded **ciphertext** to preserve the authenticity, integrity, and privacy of the information that passes through the security perimeter.

Encryption protects the integrity, confidentiality, and authenticity of digital information. Encryption can also perform a business-related function called **non-repudiation**, which is the ability to prevent one participant in an electronic transaction from denying that it performed an action. Non-repudiation uses encryption to ensure that an electronic transaction occurred, that an action was performed by the legitimate originating party, and that the party that was supposed to receive something as a result of the transaction actually received that result.

Note that an encrypted code called a **digital signature** is attached to the files that are exchanged during the transaction so that each party can ensure the other's identity. Nonrepudiation is an important aspect of establishing trusted communications between corporations or other organizations that do business across a network rather than face-to-face.

Much of the encryption in use on the Internet today makes use of digital certificates—electronic documents that contain an encrypted series of numerals and characters called a digital signature, which authenticates the identity of the person sending the certificate. Certificates, in turn, make use of **keys**, which are long blocks of encoded text that are generated by complex mathematical formulas called algorithms.

An organization that wants to encrypt data often needs to set up a **Public-Key Infrastructure (PKI)**, which is needed to make digital certificates and public and private key distribution possible to its employees. The PKI framework is the foundation of some popular and highly trusted security schemes, including Pretty Good Privacy (PGP) and Secure Sockets Layer (SSL).

Encryption can be a very CPU-intensive process that can slow down network traffic. The bastion host that hosts your firewall should be robust enough to manage encryption, along with the other security functions you call on it to perform. The computer that hosts a firewall is called a bastion host because, like a medieval castle that functions as a bastion, it presents possible intruders with the fewest possible points of entry. (Bastion hosts are described in more detail in Chapter 4.) In addition, encrypted packets may need to be padded to uniform length to ensure that some algorithms work effectively.

NOTE

Because encryption is a fundamental activity of many firewalls, it is discussed further in Chapter 5; in addition, because it is central to VPNs, it is also discussed in Chapter 7.

Authentication

Firewalls, VPN devices, proxy servers, and intrusion detection systems all perform **authentication** —the act of reliably determining whether a person or entity is whom they claim to be. Authentication uses one of three methods: something the user knows, something the user possesses, and something the user is. Such authentication is critical because, for example, if an unauthorized individual is able to "fool" a firewall into thinking he or she is an employee or other authorized user, he or she can gain access to sensitive resources and thus circumvent the firewall.

In the field of network computing, authentication is performed in one of several ways. **Basic authentication** makes use of *something that the user knows* —such as a username/password pair to a server, which maintains a local file of usernames and passwords. In **challenge/response authentication**, the authenticating computer or firewall generates a random code or number (the challenge) and sends it to the user who wishes to be authenticated. The user re-submits the number or code and adds his or her secret PIN or password (the response), or uses *something that the user possesses*, such as a smart card that the user swipes through a card reader.

In large organizations, a centralized server typically handles authentication. The use of *something that the user is*—biometrics (retinal scans, voiceprints, fingerprints, and so on)—for authentication is also growing in popularity due to increasing concern over terrorist attacks and other criminal activities. Although computer operating systems and Web servers can perform authentication, having a firewall or other security component to also authenticate users adds an important level of security to an organization's overall defensive posture.

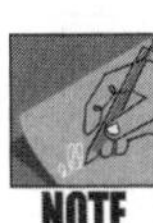
NOTE

Authentication is discussed in greater detail in Chapter 5.

Developing a Packet Filtering Rule Base

Packet filtering, which was described earlier in this chapter, might seem like the first and simplest line of defense in a Defense in Depth (DiD) configuration, which is a network defense configuration that makes use of multiple layers of protection (such as the 11 layers described earlier in this chapter). However, it's more accurate to look at the development of a rule base as the core activity of a firewall or intrusion detection device and as the way to put into practice an organization's security policy.

A packet filtering rule base is a set of individual rules that the filter reviews when it encounters a packet. Each rule contains a set of characteristics that the filter attempts to match to the characteristics of a packet. If a match is found, the filter performs an action (Allow or Deny) that is also part of the rule. Packet filtering rules can cover each of the activities that your employees are allowed to do, either on your internal network or on the Internet. If you want your employees to be able to send outgoing e-mail but not receive any incoming e-mail, you can set up packet filtering rules accordingly. You can also set up rules that prevent employees from accessing Web sites that present content that is considered unsuitable in some way. Such rules are discussed further in Chapter 4.

Virus Protection

Virus protection is also a central activity that needs to be performed to protect a network and its users, but it's not one that firewalls or other security components can perform on their own. To catch viruses, firewalls have to be integrated with anti-virus software that scans the content of e-mail messages rather than just the headers.

At the consumer level, the popular Norton Internet Security package combines a firewall program with Norton Anti-Virus software. At the enterprise level, a firewall program like Check Point NG uses a protocol it developed called Open Platform for Security (OPSEC) to integrate it with anti-virus protection and other software such as eSafe Protect, a product by Aladdin Systems (*www.esafe.com*). This product scans e-mail, Web pages, and FTP traffic for viruses.

Secure Remote Access

One of the biggest security challenges facing organizations that communicate via the Internet is the need to provide secure remote access for contractors and for employees who are traveling. A VPN, with its combination of encryption and authentication, provides an ideal solution.

In the days before cable modem, DSL, and other high-speed Internet connections became affordable enough for home and business use, remote users would dial in to the network with a temporary modem connection. Many still do, and you can configure your VPN to use protocols such as Point-to-Point Tunneling Protocol (PPTP), which uses Microsoft Point-to-Point Encryption (MPPE) to encrypt data that passes between the remote computer and the remote access server. A newer version of PPTP, Layer 2 Tunneling Protocol (L2TP), uses a sophisticated set of protocols called Internet Protocol Security (IPSec) to encrypt data sent over a dialup connection. In addition, if your network uses the UNIX operating system you can create a VPN connection "on the fly" using either Point-to-Point Protocol (PPP) over Secure Sockets Layer (SSL) and PPP over Secure Shell (SSH). Both combine an existing tunnel system (PPP) with a way of encrypting data in transport (SSL or SSH).

NOTE

SSL is a public key encryption system used to provide secure communications over the World Wide Web. SSH is the UNIX secure shell, which was developed when serious security flaws were identified in Telnet. SSH enables users to perform secure authenticated logons and encrypted communications between a client and host. SSH requires that both client and host have a secret key in advance, called a pre-shared key, in order to establish a connection.

Working with Log Files

One fundamental network security activity that tends to be overlooked by IT and other business managers who are preoccupied with configuring firewalls and intrusion detection systems is the detailed and periodic review of the log files that are generated by those same security devices.

By reviewing and maintaining log files, you can detect suspicious patterns of activity, such as regular and unsuccessful connection attempts that occur at the same time each day. You can identify—or at least gather enough information to begin to identify—the individuals who have attacked your network. You can set up rules to block attacks and keep your network defense systems up-to-date by adapting to attack attempts that have gotten by the firewalls and other components you have in place. Effective management of log files is an essential activity that goes hand-in-hand with any perimeter security configuration.

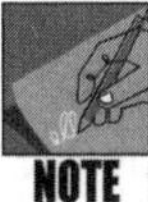

A 1989 book entitled *The Cuckoo's Egg: Tracking a Spy through the Maze of Computer Espionage*, provides an engrossing real-world example of how log files and other computer tools can be used to track down hackers. Author Clifford Stoll wanted to locate a computer password cracker after discovering a 75-cent accounting error in a computer log file at Lawrence Berkeley Laboratory. The trail led the author all the way to Germany and the discovery of a ring of computer hackers attempting to scour American computer systems for information they could sell to the KGB. You can find the book at *www.amazon.com/exec/obidos/ASIN/0743411463/ref%3Dnosim/sealarksgoodbook/102-4485290-9167306.*

Managing Log Files

Compiling, reviewing, and analyzing log files are among the most tedious and time-consuming tasks associated with network security. At its most basic level, the network administrator reads and analyzes log files to see who is accessing the network from the Internet. All connection attempts that were rejected should be recorded in the hope of identifying possible intruders or vulnerable points in the system.

For especially critical resources such as database files that hold customer profiles and job records, you can set up object auditing of the sort that is provided by Windows 2000, XP, or other operating systems. (Auditing is the process of recording which computers are accessing a network and what resources are being accessed, and recording the information in a log file.) One of the Windows security logs is shown in Figure 2-10.

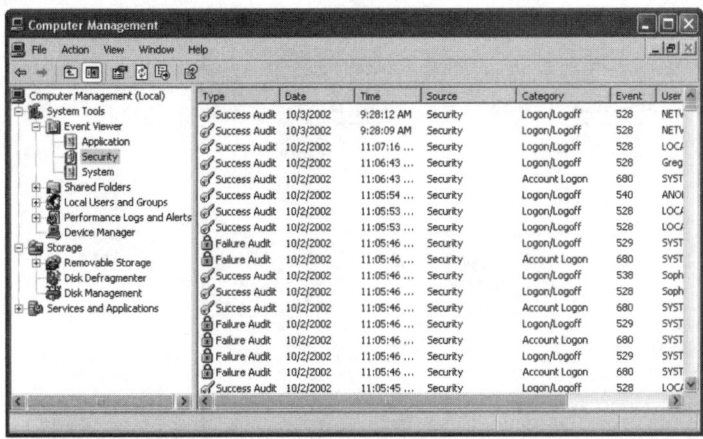

Figure 2-10 Windows security log

Object auditing not only tells a company who is trying to break into the system or run malicious code there, but who is accessing the Internet from inside the company. Often, security breaches come not from hackers in another country, but from an employee in one office trying to access files in another office.

Configuring Log Files

Typically, the log files compiled by firewalls or intrusion detection systems give you different options. You can view active data (data that is being compiled by the firewall as traffic moves through the gateway in real time) or data that has been recently recorded by the device. You can also usually view such information as:

- *System events* —These usually track the operations of the firewall or IDS itself, making a log entry whenever it starts up or shuts down.
- *Security events* —These are records of any alerts the firewall or IDS has issued.
- *Traffic* —This is the record of the traffic that passes through the firewall.
- *Packets* —Some programs let you view information about individual packets that pass through it.

Some more elaborate programs let you customize what you see in the log files, and help you search for specific items or events as well.

GUI Log Viewers

You can always view log files with a text editor, but if you have ever done so, you know how mind-numbing an experience this can be. You might want to use a graphical tool that organizes logged information into easy-to-read columns and lets you sort them by date, IP address, or other criteria. One such product is the Sygate Personal Firewall's log viewer, which is shown in Figure 2-11.

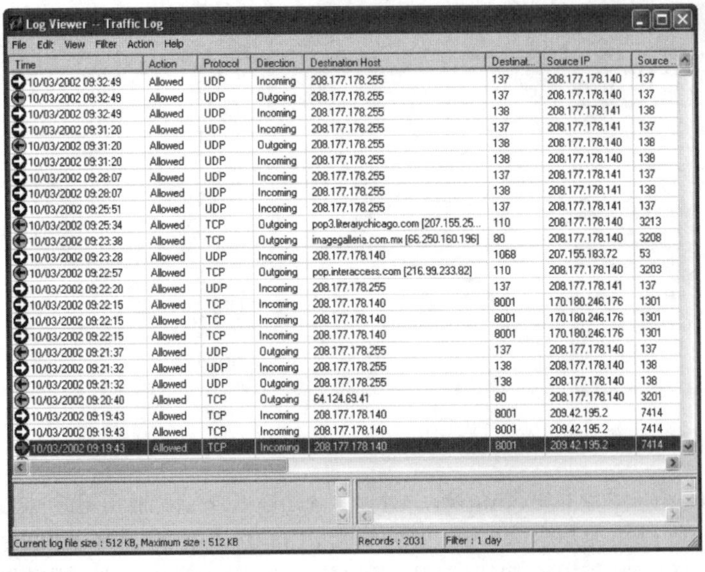

Log Viewer -- Traffic Log

File Edit View Filter Action Help

Time	Action	Protocol	Direction	Destination Host	Destinat...	Source IP	Source ...
10/03/2002 09:32:49	Allowed	UDP	Incoming	208.177.178.255	137	208.177.178.140	137
10/03/2002 09:32:49	Allowed	UDP	Outgoing	208.177.178.255	137	208.177.178.140	137
10/03/2002 09:32:49	Allowed	UDP	Incoming	208.177.178.255	138	208.177.178.141	138
10/03/2002 09:31:20	Allowed	UDP	Incoming	208.177.178.255	137	208.177.178.141	137
10/03/2002 09:31:20	Allowed	UDP	Outgoing	208.177.178.255	138	208.177.178.140	138
10/03/2002 09:31:20	Allowed	UDP	Incoming	208.177.178.255	138	208.177.178.140	138
10/03/2002 09:28:07	Allowed	UDP	Incoming	208.177.178.255	137	208.177.178.141	137
10/03/2002 09:28:07	Allowed	UDP	Incoming	208.177.178.255	138	208.177.178.141	138
10/03/2002 09:25:51	Allowed	UDP	Incoming	208.177.178.255	137	208.177.178.141	137
10/03/2002 09:25:34	Allowed	TCP	Outgoing	pop3.literarychicago.com [207.155.25...	110	208.177.178.140	3213
10/03/2002 09:23:38	Allowed	TCP	Outgoing	imagegalleria.com.mx [66.250.160.196]	80	208.177.178.140	3208
10/03/2002 09:23:28	Allowed	UDP	Incoming	208.177.178.140	1068	207.155.183.72	53
10/03/2002 09:22:57	Allowed	TCP	Outgoing	pop.interaccess.com [216.99.233.82]	110	208.177.178.140	3203
10/03/2002 09:22:20	Allowed	UDP	Incoming	208.177.178.255	137	208.177.178.141	137
10/03/2002 09:22:15	Allowed	TCP	Incoming	208.177.178.140	8001	170.180.246.176	1301
10/03/2002 09:22:15	Allowed	TCP	Incoming	208.177.178.140	8001	170.180.246.176	1301
10/03/2002 09:22:15	Allowed	TCP	Incoming	208.177.178.140	8001	170.180.246.176	1301
10/03/2002 09:21:37	Allowed	UDP	Outgoing	208.177.178.255	137	208.177.178.140	137
10/03/2002 09:21:32	Allowed	UDP	Incoming	208.177.178.255	138	208.177.178.140	138
10/03/2002 09:21:32	Allowed	UDP	Outgoing	208.177.178.255	138	208.177.178.140	138
10/03/2002 09:20:40	Allowed	TCP	Outgoing	64.124.69.41	80	208.177.178.140	3201
10/03/2002 09:19:43	Allowed	TCP	Incoming	208.177.178.140	8001	209.42.195.2	7414
10/03/2002 09:19:43	Allowed	TCP	Incoming	208.177.178.140	8001	209.42.195.2	7414
10/03/2002 09:19:43	Allowed	TCP	Incoming	208.177.178.140	8001	209.42.195.2	7414

Current log file size : 512 KB, Maximum size : 512 KB Records : 2031 Filter : 1 day

Figure 2-11 Sygate Personal Firewall's log viewer

Log File Analysis

When you first install intrusion detection or firewall hardware or software on your network, you'll probably be called upon to prepare reports that indicate how the network is being used and what kinds of filtering activities the device is performing. It's a good idea to sort the logs by time of day and per-hour. (Sorting the log files provides you with an organized way to approach them that is less intimidating than simply reviewing them as they are produced by the server, firewall, or other device.)

You should be sure to check the logs to learn when the peak traffic times are on your network, and try to identify the services that consume the largest part of your available bandwidth. If your firewall or IDS has the ability to graphically display log file entries (as shown in Figure 2-12), it's always a good idea to present management with such graphs, because they display trends with greater impact than lists of figures.

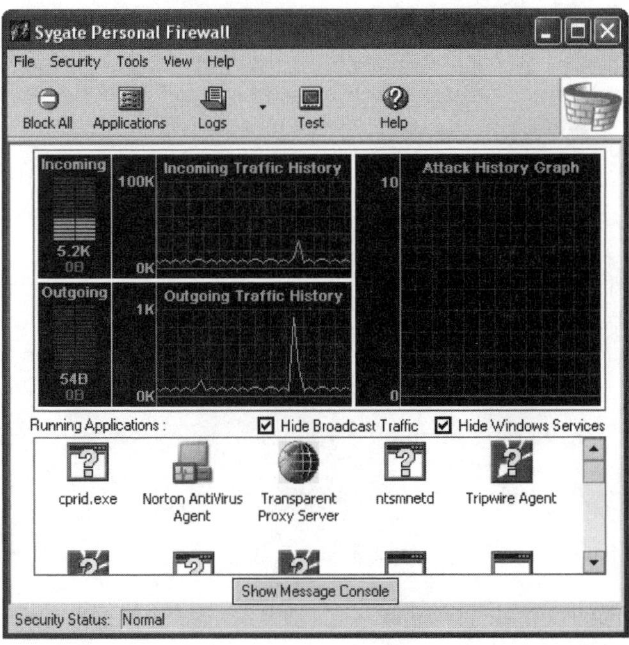

Figure 2-12 A graphical representation of log file traffic

Integrating Intrusion Detection Systems (IDSs)

An **intrusion detection system (IDS)** is software or hardware that detects whether a network or server has experienced an unauthorized access attempt and then sends notification to the appropriate network administrators so that the intrusion attempt can be analyzed, damage assessed, and responded to, if necessary. IDSs, like firewalls, don't work by themselves. They are ideally coordinated with packet filters, firewalls, proxy servers, and other security systems to provide a layered defense for a network.

The following sections give you an overview of how an IDS fits in an overall network security program. They discuss how IDSs can help you anticipate attacks, the notification options that you can use, what options you have for locating an IDS, and what you can do in response to security alerts sent to you by the IDS.

In the sections that follow, it might seem like an IDS is a stand-alone program. Many stand-alone IDS programs do exist. In fact, many firewalls have IDSs built into them; however, IDSs can also be added to an existing firewall configuration as software or hardware.

Anticipating Attacks

The best way to configure an IDS is to anticipate what attacks you are likely to encounter so that you can make sure the IDS has the appropriate signatures or rules available to it. In an ideal world, you'd be able to anticipate and prevent attacks before they even occur. An IDS, though, is an ideal product for real-world situations in which breaches can and do occur, and you only find out about them when the IDS informs you.

IDS Notification Options

A good IDS is more than just a "house alarm" that goes off when someone tries to break in. A good system also notifies the appropriate individuals and provides information about what type of event occurred and where in your network the intrusion attempt actually took place. Usually, you can tell your firewall or IDS to notify you in one of these ways:

- *E-mail* —You can have the system send you an e-mail message.
- *Alert* —The firewall or IDS can display a pop-up message.
- *Pager* —If your pager can accept e-mail, some IDSs can communicate with it.
- *Log* —You can have the IDS send an alert message to the log files.

An IDS can even point to the source of the intrusion if genuine (rather than "spoofed") source IP information has been provided. Some systems can provide an immediate response to an attack attempt, such as dropping the connection or blocking it for a predefined period of time.

A popular freeware IDS called Snort (*www.snort.org*), which is available for both UNIX-based and Windows systems, gives you several notification options. You can set up an audible alarm; you can view an alarm icon in the Windows system tray; or you can configure the IDS to send you an e-mail notification. A GUI for Snort called IDScenter makes e-mail notification easy, as shown in Figure 2-13.

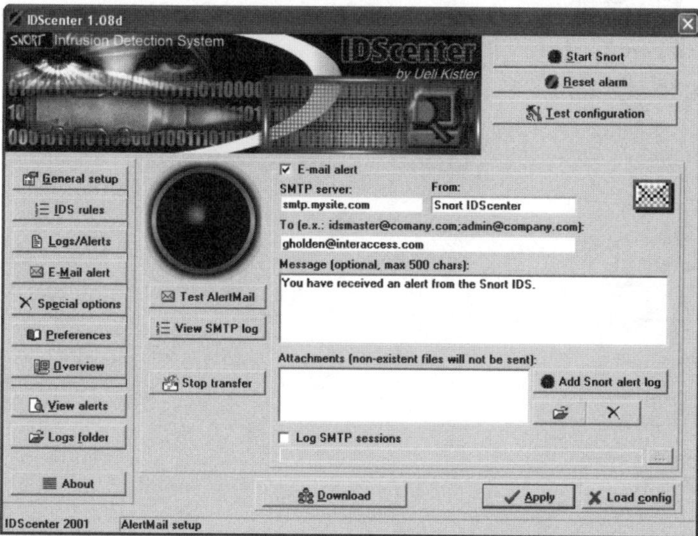

Figure 2-13 IDScenter's e-mail notification options

Locating the IDS

The logical place for locating a network-based IDS is near the point where the internal network has an interface with the external Internet. In the simplest network configuration, a router is placed at the perimeter of the network. The connection to the Internet is connected to the router's external interface; the connection to the internal network is the router's internal interface. The IDS is typically placed either between the router and the Internet (as denoted by A in Figure 2-14) or between the router and the LAN (as denoted by B in Figure 2-14).

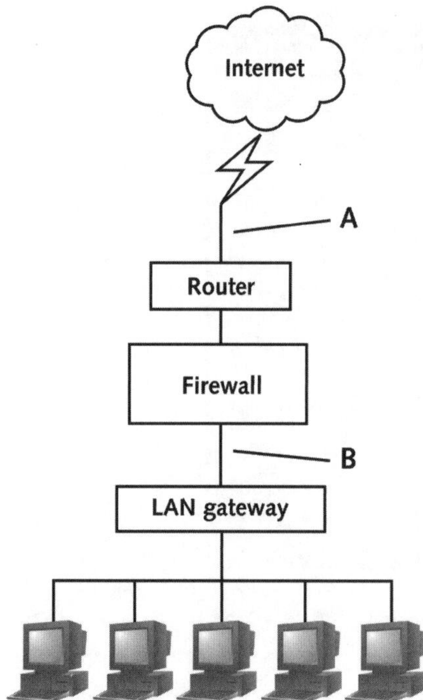

Figure 2-14 A simple IDS-router setup

If you locate the IDS outside the router at point A, the device will be able to detect all attacks against the network, but it will not show you which attacks actually get through the router and into the LAN. If you locate the IDS at point B, you will be able to see which attacks enter the LAN.

In a more typical network configuration that includes a DMZ and several bastion hosts that provide public services such as Web, FTP, and SMTP servers, the IDS can be located in one of several locations, which are indicated by A, B, and C in Figure 2-15.

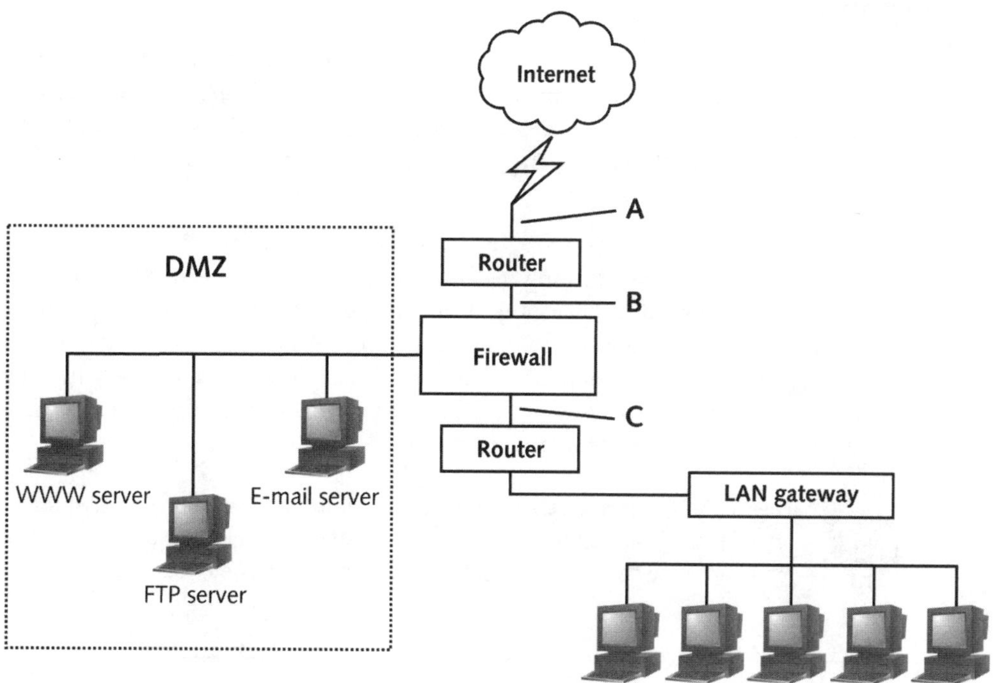

Figure 2-15 IDS placement in a network with a DMZ

If you place the IDS at point A, you will receive notification of any attacks against your network as a whole, but you won't know whether the attacks were aimed at your public servers or at hosts on the internal LAN.

If you place the IDS at point B, you will be notified of attacks that make it through your exterior router. If you are primarily interested in being notified of attacks against your bastion hosts, this is the optimal location. This location will also detect attacks targeted at your LAN, but not give you a hint of whether the attack was successful.

If you place the IDS at point C, you will be able to detect attacks that reach your LAN, but not attacks targeting your bastion hosts. In this type of configuration, multiple intrusion detection devices are advisable—at the very least, you should place them at points B and C.

How do you determine the right placement for the IDS? It depends on your network's layout, what you want to monitor, and where the sensor(s) should be placed. Remember that the sensor will detect all traffic on the physical wire. A standard hub repeats everything from one port to all its other ports. A switch will look for the MAC address of the destination and switch the packet to the proper port.

Most well-designed networks make use of a switch to connect a router to a LAN or bastion hosts. This is done to reduce broadcast traffic on the wire. By placing a hub between the router and the switch, you create a node that will allow you to easily move your sensor and accommodate security analysis.

Responding to Alerts

The fact that you have received an alert from an IDS system is not cause for alarm. In fact, you should get used to receiving false alarms from the IDS. When an intrusion is detected, it's important not to panic. Instead, react rationally. Use the alerts to begin to assess the situation. Ask yourself whether the hacker actually succeeded in breaking in. Is the hacker still present on your site?

Your next step is to analyze what resources were hit and what damage occurred, if any. You would do this by performing real-time analysis of network traffic to see if any unusual patterns are present. Also, check the ports on the machine that was attacked to see if any ports that are normally unused have been accessed. A network-auditing tool like Tripwire (*www.tripwire.com*) is invaluable in this instance because it reports on any new programs or files that were added to a system at a particular point in time. You can scan the list of files to see if any suspicious executable programs were added.

The CERT Coordination Center publishes an Intrusion Detection Checklist that provides suggestions for what to do in case an intrusion is detected. You can read it at *www.cert.org/tech_tips/intruder_detection_checklist.html.*

Chapter Summary

- This chapter gave you a rundown of the fundamental network security tools and approaches you need to design a defensive perimeter. An effective network security strategy involves many layers of defense working together to prevent many different kinds of threats.
- You began by reviewing the common security threats you need to guard against. These include Denial of Service attacks such as SYN floods and address spoofing; covert channeling attacks; virus attacks; and man-in-the-middle attacks.
- The following are the layers of network security that you can set up:
  - *Layer 1, or physical security* —Lock computers, provide environmental controls; use alarm systems.
  - *Layer 2, or password security* —Use good passwords and change them regularly.
  - *Layer 3, or operating system security* —Install operating system patches and updates to plug obvious holes such as unused ports.
  - *Layer 4, or use of anti-virus protection* —Set up anti-virus software and update virus definitions periodically.
  - *Layer 5, or packet filtering* —Set up a packet filtering rule base.
  - *Layer 6, or use of firewalls* —Set up a DMZ and firewall to protect your internal LAN while providing external clients with public services such as Web pages.

- *Layer 7, or use of proxy server*—Set up a proxy server to conceal the identity of internal hosts.
- *Layer 8, or use of DMZ* —Place proxy servers, Web servers, e-mail servers, and other servers in an area outside the internal network but still protected by the firewall called a DMZ.
- *Layer 9, use of Intrusion Detection System (IDS)* —Set up an IDS to notify you when security events occur.
- *Layer 10, or use of virtual private network (VPN)* —Set up a VPN and secure remote clients with firewalls and anti-virus software.
- *Layer 11, or use of logging and administration* —Keep reviewing your firewall, packet filtering, and IDS logs on an ongoing basis.

- Encryption protects data as it passes from one network to another, and authentication limits access to authorized users.
- Packet filtering to allow or block packets based on a set of rules, and virus protection helps prevent computer systems from being attacked.
- Secure remote access gives contractors and mobile workers a way to connect to the home network; log files give the network administrator the ability to analyze who is accessing the network from the Internet, as well as a way of detecting intrusion attempts based on patterns of suspicious activity.
- An IDS is an ideal tool for real-world situations in which security breaches occur. The IDS can notify you by e-mail, by log file alert messages, or even by sending a message to your pager. The IDS should be located on the perimeter of the network, but it can be located in any number of places—either on a server in the DMZ, between the external router and the Internet, or between the router and the LAN.
- When you receive an alert from an IDS, react rationally and use the alerts to assess whether the network has actually been breached or not, and to track what resources, if any, have been affected.

Key Terms

authentication — The act of reliably determining whether a person or entity is who they claim to be.

back door — An unused port, terminal service, or other entrance that makes the hacker's activities difficult to detect.

basic authentication — Authentication system in which a user submits a username/password pair to a server that maintains a local file of usernames and passwords.

buffer overflows — Attacks in which a hacker writes a piece of code that takes up more buffer space than a Web server or e-mail server allows, in such a way that the extra code can be executed on the server.

challenge/response authentication — Authentication system in which a computer or firewall generates a random code or number (the challenge) and sends it to the user who wishes to be authenticated. The user re-submits the number or code and adds his or her secret PIN or password (the response).

ciphertext — Ordinary text that has been rendered unreadable as a result of encryption.

covert channel — A communications channel, such as a port on a computer or a network connection, that can be exploited in a way that compromises the security of a computer.

Demilitarized Zone (DMZ) — A network that sits outside the internal network but is connected to the firewall, and makes publicly attainable services available while protecting an organization's internal LAN.

digital signature — A series of numerals and characters generated by an encryption process that is easily transportable, can be time-stamped, and is commonly used to authenticate the identify of the person who possesses it.

Domain Name Server (DNS) — A server that resolves IP addresses into easy-to-remember domain names.

encryption — The process of concealing information to render it unreadable to all but the intended recipients.

fragmentation — The division of a single IP packet into multiple packets, each of which is a fragment.

half-open session — A connection that is initiated, but not completed, between client and server.

hide-mode NAT — A form of NAT in which the actual IP addresses are turned into addresses in one of the three ranges of non-routable IP addresses, such as 10.0.0.1/8.

intrusion detection system (IDS) — Software or hardware that detects whether a network or server has experienced an unauthorized access attempt and sends notification to the appropriate network administrators.

keys — Values that can be processed by an algorithm to encrypt text, or to decrypt text that has already been encrypted.

man-in-the-middle attack — A type of attack in which an individual intercepts part of an encrypted data session in order to gain control over the data being exchanged.

Network Address Translation (NAT) — Converts the internal IP addresses of hosts being protected on the LAN into different IP addresses.

non-repudiation — The ability to prevent one participant in an electronic transaction from denying that it performed an action.

one-to-one NAT — A form of NAT in which each workstation that has a private IP address is assigned an external IP address on an individual basis.

perimeter network — *See* Demilitarized Zone (DMZ).

proxy server — Server software that monitors outbound and inbound traffic, caches Web pages to reduce the load on a network, filters content, and conceals the end users in a network.

Public-Key Infrastructure (PKI) — A system used to store, distribute, and manage public and private keys within an organization.

quarantine — An area of disk storage where viruses are placed when they cannot be deleted, and where they cannot replicate themselves or do harm to other files.

rule base — A set of rules maintained by a packet filter to determine whether packets should be allowed to pass through or should be dropped.

screened subnet — A network of servers or other computers that s shielded (or screened) by a router or firewall.

service network — *See* Demilitarized Zone (DMZ).

signatures — Combinations of IP addresses, port numbers, the frequency with which access attempts are made, and/or other characteristics.

spoofed address — An address that contains falsified information intended either to confuse or fool a server.

state table — A list of the current connections between internal hosts and hosts on the external network that is used by a stateful packet filter.

stateless packet filtering — Filtering that examines TCP/IP header information and blocks or allows packets based on that criteria, regardless of whether a connection has been established between server and client.

threads — Processes used on operating systems such as Windows that respond to requests for documents.

Trojan horse — A harmful computer program that initially appears to be something useful, but that creates an opening through which a hacker can potentially gain control of a computer.

virtual private network (VPN) — A relatively low-cost and secure connection between organizations that use the public Internet as well as sophisticated encryption and authentication methods.

virus — Computer code that copies itself from one place to another surreptitiously and performs actions that range from creating files to damaging information on a hard disk.

worm — A type of virus that creates files that copy themselves over and over and take up disk space.

Review Questions

1. Why does a hacker immediately patch an opening after gaining access to a system?

   a to keep the system administrator from noticing that the system has been breached

   b. to keep other hackers from exploiting the same vulnerabilities

   c. to keep the system from being damaged further

   d. to enable the hacker to search for other, more challenging points of entry

2. A SYN Flood attack is an example of what type of hacker attack?

   a. covert channeling

   b. remote procedure call

   c. spoofing

   d. Denial of Service (DoS)

3. Before you can begin to configure a firewall, what do you have to have in place?

   a. a network infrastructure

   b. a budget for a firewall and other components

   c. a rule base

   d. a security policy

4. Which of the following can perform packet filtering? (Choose all that apply.)

   a. a log file

   b. a router

   c. a firewall

   d. an operating system

5. What does stateful packet filtering do that stateless packet filtering does not?

   a. follows a rule base

   b. blocks or allows packets

   c. maintains a record of connection state

   d. reviews the packet header

6. Which of the following is a benefit of NAT? (Choose all that apply.)
   a. conservation of IP addresses
   b. creation of new IP addresses
   c. concealment of IP addresses
   d. making IP addresses understandable around the world
7. Which of the following is usually contained on a DMZ? (Choose all that apply.)
   a. DNS server
   b. Web server
   c. database server
   d. all of the above
8. What is the downside of using two or more firewalls to protect the DMZ?
   a. bandwidth
   b. memory
   c. speed
   d. accessibility
9. Why would a company choose to transfer sensitive information over the public Internet using a VPN tunnel rather than a direct leased line connection? (Choose all that apply.)
   a. VPNs are generally much less expensive than leased lines.
   b. VPNs are easy to implement.
   c. VPNs represent a more technically sophisticated option and work better than leased lines.
   d. Information sent through VPNs is highly protected through encryption and other security schemes.
10. Instead of a leased line connection, a VPN creates a virtual _______ between companies.
    a. network
    b. tunnel
    c. LAN
    d. firewall

11. What is a risk you need to keep in mind when considering whether to configure a VPN?

    a. man-in-the-middle attacks

    b. intrusions from home or remote computers

    c. Denial of Service (DoS) attacks

    d. all of the above

12. Which of the following is a port that is particularly susceptible to Denial of Service (DoS) attacks?

    a. TCP port 443

    b. TCP port 80

    c. UDP Port 53

    d. TCP port 143

13. To manage log files so that they do not consume excessive amounts of disk space, you should ______.

    a. rotate the files

    b. customize one or more of the files

    c. sort the files

    d. scan the files in detail

14. What kinds of data can you typically view with log files?

    a. network traffic

    b. packets

    c. alerts

    d. all of the above

15. Assume you have configured a small computer network protected by one router. What is the advantage of locating an IDS outside the router? What is the disadvantage? Would it be better to place the IDS inside the router? Make a case to support your answer.

16. Your network is protected by a firewall that lies between it and the Internet. In addition, a DMZ is connected to the firewall but is also outside the LAN. What would be the advantage of placing an IDS system outside the firewall? What would be the advantage of placing it inside the firewall?

17. How would you use alerts from an IDS system to help you assess the security situation on the network? (Choose all that apply.)
    a. You can inventory what hardware and software is still online.
    b. You can tell what resources were hit by the hacker.
    c. You can tell what damage actually occurred.
    d. You can see whether any files were added to the system.

18. What is the best way to configure an IDS system?
    a. anticipate attacks
    b. include all possible signatures
    c. include the fewest signatures possible
    d. create rules in response to actual attacks

19. A good IDS system goes beyond notification of an intrusion attempt and provides what additional information? (Choose all that apply.)
    a. what kind of event occurred
    b. whether the attacker is located inside or outside the network
    c. whether the attacker is still present on the network
    d. where the attempt occurred

20. Why can't you rely on the IDS to tell you with certainty where an attack originated?
    a. The IDS has no way of knowing.
    b. The IP address information may have been spoofed.
    c. The IDS may be in the wrong location.
    d. The hacker may have since moved to another location.

Hands-on Projects

Project 2-1: Designing a Layered Defense Configuration

In this project, you use what you learned earlier in this chapter to draw the configuration of a network. Show as many of the layers of protection as you think is necessary.

1. Draw a network that you wish to protect. Include at least 10 computers, a server, a gateway, a router, and a DMZ.

2. Arrange defenses around it in layers, as was discussed in the main part of the chapter.
3. Label each layer. Did you use less than 11 layers? Write the reason for your decision in a word-processed document.
4. Exchange your network diagram with a classmate and critique each other's work. Did you find something that you would add to your classmate's network defense? Did he or she find something that should be changed in your network defense?

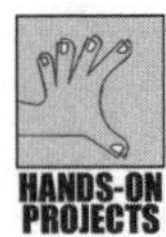

Project 2-2: Configuring a Denial of Service "Killer"

Zombie Zapper, a freeware utility by Razor Software, is configured to stop four common software agents that have been known to launch Denial of Service attacks: Trinoo, TFN, Shaft, and StachelDraht. (Such programs can turn a server into a "zombie" that fails to respond to other requests.)

You can easily install and configure the software to send out packets that "kill" such attacks. The program activates only if you are actually experiencing such an attack. Versions of Zombie Zapper are available for both Windows NT and UNIX-based systems; the software also works with Windows XP and 2000.

1. Double-click the **Internet Explorer** icon on your desktop.
2. Type **http://razor.bindview.com/tools/ZombieZapper_form.shtml** into the Address box, and then press **Enter**. (Note that this is a case-sensitive URL—copy it exactly as shown.)
3. Read the license agreement on the Zombie Zapper page, then scroll down and download the version for your operating system. This version assumes you are downloading the executable for Windows.
4. When the download is complete, the Zombie Zapper program window should open automatically on your computer screen. You need to specify the IP address of the machine that is likely to experience a Denial of Service (DoS) attack on your network. You can enter more than one IP address. You might enter the addresses of the servers on your DMZ, for instance. For this example, assume there's a single target IP: **203.167.168.1**.
5. Verify that **53** is entered as the number of the UDP source port in the UDP source box. Also verify that the **Trinoo**, **TFN**, and **StachelDraht** check boxes are checked.
6. You are now all set for an attack. Should you experience a DoS attack, you start up Zombie Zapper and click **Zap**. Packets would then be sent to kill the selected zombies.

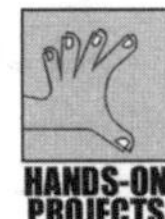

Project 2-3: Examine a Digital Certificate

A digital certificate, an electronic document that encrypts communications between networked computers, can be difficult to conceptualize. However, your Windows 2000 or XP computer already has a number of digital certificates that have been issued by various organizations called Certificate Authorities (CAs). You can view such certificates in order to get a better idea of the information they contain. In this project you will open the Microsoft Management Console and add the Certificates snap-in, then view the components of one of the certificates included with that snap-in.

1. Click **Start**, and then click **Run**.
2. Type **MMC** in the Open dialog box, and then click **OK**. The Microsoft Management Console (labeled Console1) opens.
3. Click **File**, and then click **Add/Remove Snap-in**.
4. In the Add/Remove Snap-in dialog box, click **Add**.
5. In the Add Standalone Snap-in dialog box, click **Certificates**, and then click **Add**.
6. In the Certificates snap-in dialog box, leave **My user account** selected, and then click **Finish**.
7. In the Add Standalone Snap-in dialog box, click **Close**.
8. Click **OK** to close Add/Remove Snap-in and return to Console1.
9. Click the **plus sign (+)** next to Certificates – Current User.
10. Click the **plus sign (+)** next to Trusted Root Certification Authorities.
11. Click **Certificates** beneath Trusted Root Certification Authorities.
12. Scroll down the list of certificates that appears in the right half of Console Root. Double-click the first certificate labeled **VeriSign Trust Network**.
13. In Certificate dialog box (which lists the components of the certificate), click **Details**.
14. Click **Public Key**. The public key associated with the digital signature appears in the bottom half of the Certificate dialog box.
15. Click **Enhanced key usage** to view the ways in which the digital certificate can be used.
16. Click **OK** to close Certificate.
17. Click **File** and click **Exit** to close Console1. When a dialog box appears asking if you want to save the settings to Console1, click **No**.

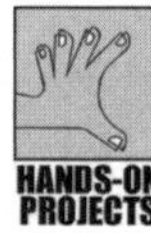

Project 2-4: Installing a Freeware IDS Program

Snort, a freeware IDS program developed by Brian Caswell and Martin Roesch, will give you some hands-on experience with setting up IDS systems. The program is available for both Linux and Windows systems; the following instructions show how to obtain and set up the program on Windows XP. You will not download the latest version, but a version that does not need to access a database program and that will work with a GUI front-end program for testing purposes.

1. Click **Start** and then click **Internet Explorer** to start your Web browser.
2. Enter the following URL in your browser's Address box: **http://www.silicondefense.com/techsupport/downloads.htm** and then press **Enter**.
3. Scroll down the list of files on the page, and click **Snort1.7Win32static:HERE** to download a simple version for Windows to your computer.
4. When the File Download dialog box appears, click **Save**. Create a folder called **Snort** at the top level of your disk drive (for example, C:\Snort or D:\Snort) where you can install the files and run them later. Then click **Save** to begin the download.
5. When downloading is complete, locate the icon for the file you downloaded in Windows Explorer and double-click it. The InstallShield wizard window opens.
6. In the next window, read the license agreement, and then click **Yes**.
7. In the Setup Type dialog box, leave the default option **Typical** selected, and then click **Next**.
8. The files are installed. When installation is complete, the InstallShield Wizard Complete screen appears. Click **Finish**.
9. To test that the installation worked, click **Start**, point to **All Programs**, point to **Accessories**, and click **Command Prompt**.
10. Enter the path that leads to the Snort.exe executable file at the command line, followed by a single blank space, followed then by **–V**. For instance, if you installed Snort in C:\Snort, you would enter **C:\Snort\Snort\snort.exe -V**.
11. Press **Enter**. If the installation is successful, you will see the following message:

    -*>Snort!<*- Version 1.7-WIN32 By Martin Roesch...”.

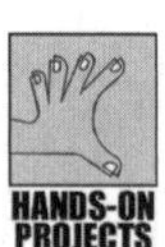

Project 2-5: Installing a GUI for Snort

Snort works well as a command-line program, but with a GUI it is far easier to configure. In this project, you will download and configure a GUI “front-end” interface designed especially for Snort called IDScenter. This project assumes you have Snort installed as described in Project 2-4, and that you have WinZip installed on your computer.

1. Click **Start** and then click **Internet Explorer** to start up your Web browser.
2. Enter the URL for a Web page that contains links to a number of GUIs for Snort: **http://www.snort.org/dl/contrib/front_ends**.
3. Click **ids_center/**.
4. Click the **idscenter.zip** link containing the IDS Center front end for Snort.
5. When the File Download dialog box appears, click **Open** to download the program.
6. The WinZip application on your computer automatically opens. Extract the setup.exe program to a folder where you can find it.
7. Locate and double-click the **setup.exe** program.
8. When the first Snort IDScenter 2001 screen appears, click **Next**.
9. Follow the instructions on subsequent setup screens to set up the program on your computer.
10. When a screen appears notifying you that setup is complete, leave the View info.txt box checked, and then click **Finish**.
11. Read the info.txt file, then click the **Close** box to close the file.
12. Double-click the **IDScente**r icon on your Windows desktop.
13. The IDScenter icon appears in the Windows system tray. Double-click this icon to start up the program.
14. When the IDScenter window opens, click **General setup** to make sure you are viewing the General setup window.
15. To begin configuring the program, click the button labeled with three dots (**...**) in the Snort setup section of the General setup window.
16. When the IDScenter 2001 dialog box appears, click the **Look in** drop-down arrow to locate the folder where you installed Snort. Open folders until you locate the Snort program file, snort.exe. Click **snort.exe**, and then click **Open**. The path leading to the Snort program file should appear in the Snort file box.
17. In the Home network box, enter the IP address for your computer.
18. In the Network interface box, enter the network interface number for your computer. (If you are working on a stand-alone computer, enter **1**. Otherwise, ask your network administrator for the network interface number.)
19. Click the IDS rules button on the left side of the IDScenter window.
20. In the Snort ruleset / Filters section of the window, click the button labeled with three dots (**...**).

21. In the IDScenter 2001 dialog box, locate the folder that contains the snort.exe program file. This same directory should also contain a number of predefined rules files for use with Snort. Select the file named **misc-lib**, and then click **Open**. The path leading to the attack-responses.rules file appears in the Snort IDS ruleset box.
22. Click **Load Config**.
23. Click **Save**. When a dialog box appears confirming if you want to save changes, click **Ja**.
24. Click **Apply**. The message "script successfully generated" should appear at the bottom of the window.
25. Click **Logs/Alerts**.
26. Click **Start**, point to **Programs** (**All Programs** on Windows XP), point to **Accessories**, and click **Windows Explorer**.
27. In the Windows Explorer window, create a new directory within the Snort directory called **log**.
28. In the Logs & Alerts section, click the button labeled with three dots next to **Set directory for Snort logfiles**.
29. In the Logs&Alerts dialog box, click the plus sign (+) next to the hard disk that contains Snort, and keep opening directories until you locate the log directory you just created. Click the **log** directory, and then click **OK**. The path leading to the log directory should appear in the box beneath Set directory for Snort logfiles.
30. Check each of the boxes beneath Specific packet infos and Other options.
31. Click **Apply**. The message "Script successfully generated" appears in the status bar.
32. Click **Start Snort**. The Start Snort button should change to Stop Snort; this indicates that the program is running.
33. Click the **Close** box to close the IDScenter window.

Project 2-6: Viewing Security Alert Options

Any IDS needs to alert a network administrator when an intrusion attempt is detected. Virtually all intrusion detection software gives you different options for notification: those options vary depending on the software being used. Although some programs can provide elaborate types of notification such as sending a message to your pager, the basic alert methods are e-mail, sound, and graphics. The following project assumes you have installed Snort and IDScenter on your Windows 2000 or XP workstation as described in Projects 2-4 and 2-5.

1. Right-click the **IDScenter** icon in the Windows system tray, and then click **Settings**.

2. Click **Special options**.
3. In the Alarm sound section, click the button next to one of the alarm sound options.
4. Notice that in the External program section, you can click the button labeled with three dots (**...**) to launch a program when an alert is received. (You might choose to launch your e-mail program so that you can e-mail other security personnel or staff that an intrusion has taken place.)
5. Click the **E-mail** alert button on the left side of the IDScenter window.
6. Check the **E-mail alert** check box.
7. In the SMTP server box, type **smtp. *myuniversity* .com**, where *myuniversity* is the name of your organization's e-mail server. In the From box, type the name you want to appear in the From section of the e-mail message. For this example, type the legitimate e-mail address of someone in your classroom.
8. In the To box, enter your own e-mail address.
9. In the Message box, you would type a standard alert message you want to receive; for this example, type **You have received an alert from the Snort IDS.**.
10. Click **Apply**.
11. Click **Stop Snort**, if necessary. Click **Test AlertMail**. In a few minutes, check your e-mail inbox to see if a message was received.
12. Click the **Close** box to close IDScenter.

Case Projects

Case Project 2-1: Business-to-Business Commerce

You work for a small manufacturer of aluminum cans, which has just begun conducting business-to-business e-commerce, making extensive use of the Internet. An estimated 120 of the company's 175 employees need to have Internet access. However, the company has given you a budget for Internet connectivity that will only enable you to obtain a block of 12 static IP addresses from an Internet Service Provider (ISP). Complicating the situation, two of the workstations in your internal network need to be connected to partner businesses using a VPN, and will thus have a separate external connection, one which does not go through the default gateway. How would you use Network Address Translation (NAT) to enable Internet connectivity in each of these situations?

Case Project 2-2: Adopting a Restrictive Packet Filtering Approach

You are hired as a security consultant for a twenty-person mortgage company whose members routinely receive e-mails and other files containing loan and salary information about their clients. When you check existing security systems, you find that e-mail messages containing viruses, ping and echo requests, and packets in which the source IP and destination IP are the same, are routinely being allowed through the stateless packet filter, which is a router at the perimeter of the network. One of your initial instructions was to make the network "as secure as possible." You were also told to "boost security to protect our clients' personal information." Describe the changes you would make to improve the packet filtering setup.

Case Project 2-3: Going a Step Beyond Packet Filtering

In the same office scenario described in Project 2-2, you have improved the packet filtering setup, but you are still receiving communications from hackers that have virus attachments (which, luckily, the existing antivirus software has so far been able to detect and block). In addition, one of the computers on your network has been targeted for port scans by someone who has apparently been able to obtain the IP address. What network security approach would you use that goes beyond packet filtering and hides internal IP addresses? When asking to purchase this item, what argument could you make to company managers to indicate that it is better than packet filtering?

Case Project 2-4: Tracking Intrusion Attempts

You have set up several firewalls and intrusion detection systems around the perimeter of your network. In addition, you have made sure that firewalls are installed on the desktops of remote users who need to gain access to your network. After setting up your system, you saved your log files for a week to establish a baseline for what constitutes "normal" use of the network. Upon coming to work a few days later, your intrusion detection system notifies you that several attempts were made to access a server on your network. Apparently, the attackers were able to circumvent at least one firewall on your system. What do you do to identify the apparent security flaw?

CHAPTER

3

RISK ANALYSIS AND SECURITY POLICY DESIGN

After reading this chapter and completing the exercises, you will be able to:

- Get started with basic concepts of risk analysis
- Decide how to minimize risk in your own network
- Explain what makes an effective security policy
- Formulate a network security policy
- Perform ongoing risk analysis

Computer crime is growing, and with it the risk to businesses of losing time, money, and credibility due to successful cyber-attacks. Computer Economics (*www.computereconomics.com*), a California-based Internet research organization, estimates that the economic impact of only four major malicious code attacks—Love Bug, SirCam, Code Red, and Nimda (all of which occurred in the year 2001)—was more than $13 million. The company is projecting that computer crime will continue to grow.

The CERT Coordination Center reports that attacks are growing in sophistication, speed, and threat level. That seems to be borne out by reports of major viruses such as Code Red, which managed to infect more than 359,000 computers in less than 14 hours in July of 2001, according to the Cooperative Association for Internet Data Analysis (CAIDA, *www.caida.org*).

Faced with such challenges, information security professionals and managers alike need to evaluate the risks their own organization faces. Armed with a detailed and accurate risk assessment, they should then develop a **security policy** —a statement that spells out exactly what defenses will be configured to block unauthorized access, how the organization will respond to attacks, and how employees should safely handle the organization's resources to discourage loss of data or damage to files.

Getting Started with Risk Analysis

The consensus among security professionals is that there is no zero-risk situation, or in other words, there is no situation in which security is perfect. Your first task, when undertaking the formulation of a security policy, is to assess the risk faced by your employees, your network, and your databases of customer, job-related, and personnel information. Your ultimate goal is not to reduce the risks to zero, but to devise ways to manage that risk in a reasonable fashion.

Because threats are changing all the time along with technology, the process of determining risks and developing a security policy to manage those risks is an ongoing process rather than a one-time operation. The ongoing process is illustrated in Figure 3-1.

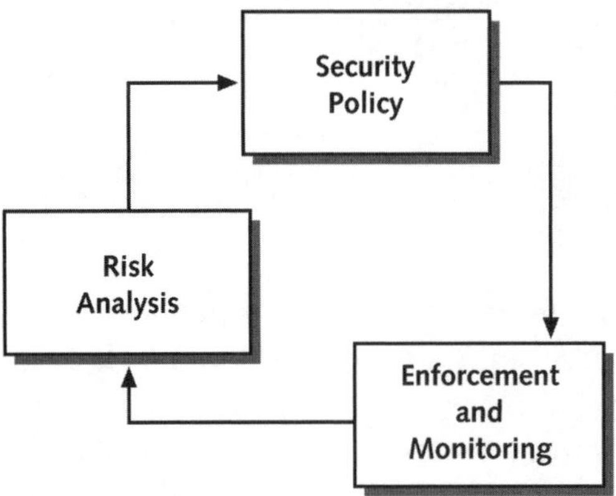

Figure 3-1 Risk analysis should be performed both before and after formulating a security policy

Of course, you're likely to encounter skepticism when you first report to work at the organization that hires you to manage its IT and/or security needs. Security policies and risk assessments are the overlooked factors in the process of developing network defenses and countermeasures for all too many companies. When you inquire as to whether a security policy is in place, don't be surprised to encounter remarks like " *What* security policy?" or "We started working on one three years ago but it never got anywhere." In the rush to cope with everyday business processes and amid the normal turnover of employees, security policies can easily be placed on the "back burner" and overlooked. One of your first tasks, then, may well be to sell managers and rank-and-file employees alike on the need to develop a risk analysis-security policy cycle for your organization.

The following sections lay the groundwork for a clear understanding of risk analysis, the first step in developing a network security policy. You'll learn about the fundamental concepts that underlie risk analysis, different approaches to conducting a risk analysis, principles to keep in mind to make risk analysis an ongoing process rather than an isolated occurrence, and ways to analyze the economic impacts of threats should they become realities.

If you're looking for statistics to back up your risk analysis and security policy drafts, visit SecurityStats.Com (*www.securitystats.com/webdeface.asp*), which maintains records of virus attacks and other security incidents.

Fundamental Concepts of Risk Analysis

Risk is defined as the possibility of damage or loss. **Risk analysis**, then, is the study of how great the possibility of damage or loss is in a particular situation, environment, or pertaining to an individual object or set of objects. In terms of a network of computers that is connected to the wider Internet, risk analysis should encompass the computer hardware and software within an organization plus its **data warehouses** —the storehouses of valuable customer, job-related, and personnel information that a company needs to safeguard.

People who conduct risk analysis for a living break the field into a group of related, fundamental concepts. The following sections describe a group of six concepts that go into creating a risk analysis.

Assets

The **assets** in an organization play a central role in a risk analysis—after all, they are the hardware, software, and informational resources you need to protect through the development and implementation of a comprehensive security policy. You are likely to encounter four different types of assets:

- *Physical assets* —These are the equipment and buildings in the organization.
- *Data* —These are the databases, job records, personnel records, customer or client information, and other data held by the organization.
- *Application software* —These are the server programs, security programs, and other applications that are used on a day-to-day basis to communicate and carry out the regular activities of the organization.
- *Personal assets* —These are the people who work in the organization as well as the customers, business partners, contractors, and freelance employees who make contributions to the organization.

Some assets are tangible objects that you can actually touch or work with. These objects include computers and the data they hold. Other assets are intangible; they include a company's reputation and the level of trust it inspires in its customers. In addition, you might also consider such essential business concepts as confidentiality, integrity of information, and availability of resources as assets. The most valuable information, such as a database whose contents need to be confidential and accurate, is what you should focus on first. In fact, it can be difficult to list every single asset you have. You may be able to analyze only the most important ones in great detail.

Threats

Threats are events and conditions that have not yet occurred but that can potentially occur, the presence of which increases risk. Some dangers are universal, such as weather-related disasters. Others are more specific to your own system, such as a server on which a customer database is stored. The obvious danger is the threat that a hacker will gain access to your system. Other threats include:

- *Power supply* —The power supply in your area might be unreliable, making your company subject to brownouts, blackouts, and sudden surges called voltage spikes.
- *Crime rate* —If you work in a high-crime area, or if other offices in your area have been broken into, your risk is increased.

The seriousness of a threat depends on the probability with which it will occur. This, in turn, depends on conditions such as your geographic location, the physical location of your organization, the existing security defenses you have in place (such as locks and alarm systems), and the degree to which your employees manage passwords and other sensitive information carefully.

Probabilities

Probabilities are geographic, physical, habitual, or other factors that affect the possibility that a threat will actually occur. If you live in a part of the country that frequently experiences earthquakes or floods, the threat of weather-related damage increases. If you have a group of disgruntled employees who have just been released from their jobs and who work with sensitive information, there is a greater probability that you will lose some of that information unless you take steps to protect it before they leave the premises. On the other hand, if your office has an alarm system wired to a security service, the probability of a burglary is reduced.

Make a list of the biggest threats to your own computer network, and rank them in order of probability. The Risk Management Standard developed by Standards Australia (*www.standards.com.au*) uses five steps to describe probability: Negligible, Very Low, Low, Medium, High, Very High, and Extreme. It can be helpful to rank the threats facing your own facility in the form found in Table 3-1.

Table 3-1 Threat probabilities

Threat	Probability
Earthquake	Medium
Fire	Low
Flood	High
Attack from the Internet	Very High
Virus infection	Very High
Employees giving out information	Low

NOTE

You can find out more about the Risk Management Standard at *www.riskmanagement.com.au/RISKMAN/INFO/RMSTANDARD/RMSTANDARD.HTM.*

Vulnerabilities

Vulnerabilities are situations or conditions that increase threat and that, in turn, increase risk. Examples include putting computers on the Internet, putting computers out in the open where anyone can use them, installing Web servers outside the corporate network in the vulnerable DMZ, and so on.

It doesn't take a lot of review to come up with examples of vulnerable situations that can affect networked hardware and software. Some of the most common flaws involve operating system software (particularly, the different versions of Windows, although Linux needs to be secured as well, and has fallen victim to specific attacks such as the Lion worm). They also involve application software (most notoriously, Internet Information Server, Internet Explorer, and Outlook Express), although the freeware Web server Apache has also fallen victim to security compromises as a result of software flaws. Opening up the network to remote users whose desktop computers are unprotected by anti-virus or firewall software can open the network up to intrusions and virus infections. Poorly configured firewalls or packet filters; passwords that are not protected; log files that aren't reviewed closely or on a regular basis; new threats to intrusion from networks that use wireless systems; and the complexity of modern computer networks means that any number of components can provide an attacker with an opening.

TIP

See "Choosing a Bastion Host" in Chapter 4 for more details on hardware and software vulnerabilities you need to address when installing firewall or intrusion detection software on a computer.

Consequences

Substantial consequences can result from a virus that forces staff to take your Web site offline for a week, or a fire that destroys all your computer equipment. You can extend the earlier identification of threats to include ratings that evaluate the consequences of those threats, as shown in Table 3-2.

Table 3-2 Probability and consequences of threats that occur

Threat	Probability	Consequences
Earthquake	Medium	Significant
Fire	Low	Significant
Flood	High	Minor
Attack from the Internet	Very High	Serious
Virus infection	Very High	Serious
Employees giving out information	Low	Significant

In Table 3-2, the probability of threats has been extended to a rating of the significance of their impact. It can be difficult to rank such items because the severity often depends on the particular virus you receive or your particular physical location. A flood won't have as great an impact on the computers stationed in an office on the 50th floor of an office tower as it does on the ground floor, for instance (although any electrical equipment located in the business would be devastated).

Besides the consequences associated with getting a system back online after an attack, there is a cost impact, as well as other impacts that can be more difficult to anticipate. These include insurance claims, police reports, shipping or delivery, and the time and effort to obtain and reinstall software or hardware. A software program, like the online ROI calculator provided by the PC security cable manufacturer Kensington Security, can help you calculate such losses, which can amount to far more than the actual price of the computer or other devices (see Figure 3-2).

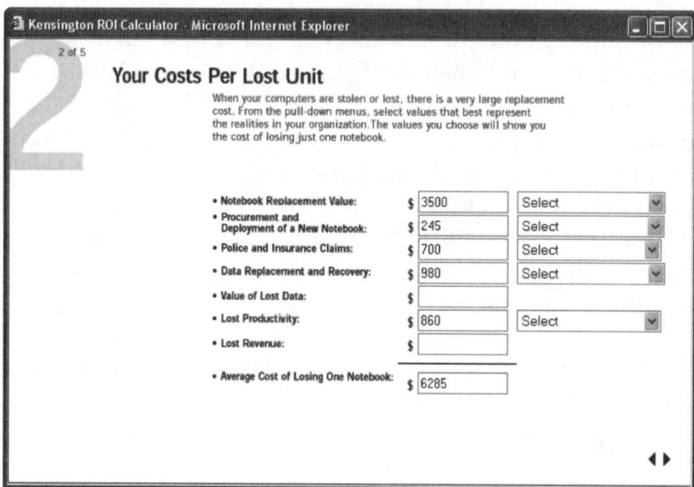

Figure 3-2 An online ROI calculator

As you can see from Figure 3-2, an individual piece of hardware that costs $3500 can actually cost much more to replace if you assign dollar values to the time, insurance costs, and other impacts that result from the loss.

Safeguards

Safeguards are measures you can take to reduce threats such as installing firewalls and intrusion detection systems, locking doors, and using passwords and/or encryption.

These aspects interact with one another to hopefully manage risk. An asset has an inherent amount of risk associated with it. Threat and vulnerability seek to make the risk bigger; countermeasures work to reduce risk. Residual risk is what is left over after countermeasures and defenses are implemented; risk never actually equals zero. You can visualize all of this as shown in Figure 3-3. 3

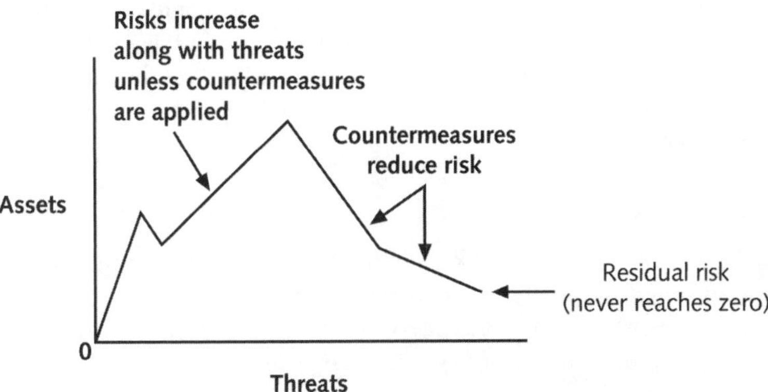

Figure 3-3 Countermeasures reduce, but never completely eliminate, risk

Approaches to Risk Analysis

After you have made a list of the assets you need to protect, the threats faced by those assets, the probability that they will occur, the consequences should they occur, and the safeguards you can take to protect them, you have the building blocks you need to prepare a risk analysis.

You can use different types of risk analysis to create a security policy to evaluate how well the policy is performing so that you can update and improve it. The following sections describe two of the approaches you are most likely to use.

Survivable Network Analysis

Survivable Network Analysis (SNA) is a security process developed by the CERT Coordination Center security group. SNA starts with the assumption that a computer system will be attacked. It leads you through a four-step process designed to ensure the **survivability** (the ability to continue functioning in the presence of attacks, system faults, accidents, or disasters) of a network should an attack actually occur.

Survivability focuses on the essential services/assets and the critical system capabilities of a system. Survivability also depends on three system capabilities:

- Resistance, which is the capability of a system to repel attacks
- Recognition, which is the capability to detect attacks as they occur, and to evaluate the extent of damage and compromise
- Recovery, which is the capability to maintain essential services during an attack and to restore all services following an attack

The study of the survivability of a network builds on other concepts related to risk analysis, including **fault tolerance** (the ability of an object or system to continue operations despite the presence of a fault), safety procedures, security systems, and ongoing testing. Most software products are not designed with survivability in mind. That's why survivability studies can be valuable. Rather, software is often designed to work for a certain number of users or a certain amount of information, until it is replaced by new and improved versions of the same or other software.

The steps involved in SNA are as follows:

1. *System definition* —First, you take a high-level overview of the requirements of the system organizationally. You analyze system architecture while taking into account its hardware components, software installations, and databases, servers, and other computers that store your information.
2. *Essential capability definition* —You identify the essential services and assets of the system—the assets that are critical to fulfilling your organization's missions and goals.
3. *Compromise capability definition* —You design scenarios in which intrusions to the system occur, and then trace the intrusion through your system architecture to identify what can be accessed and what sorts of damage can occur.
4. *Survivability analysis* —You identify the points of fault in the system—components that can be compromised and that are integral to the system. You then make recommendations for correcting the points of fault and suggest specific ways to improve the resistance of the system to intrusions and its ability to recover from attacks, accidents, and other disasters.

Often, the findings of the Survivable Network Analysis are summarized in the form of a Survivability Map, as shown in Table 3-3, which relates possible attacks and points of fault to architecture strategies to overcome them.

Table 3-3 Template for a survivability map

Intrusion Scenario	Points of Fault	Architecture Strategies for...	...Resistance	...Intrusion Detection	...Recovery
Scenario 1					
Scenario *(n)*					

The emphasis is on an ongoing process rather than a series of steps that ends in a report of a particular configuration that is regarded as secure and permanent. You might start with better password management, then upgrade the system to encrypt critical data, then install software that filters out potentially harmful e-mail messages, and so on, so that the system continually becomes more and more able to survive trouble.

Threat and Risk Assessment

Threat and Risk Assessment (TRA) approaches risk analysis from the standpoint of the threats and risks that confront an organization's assets and the consequences of those threats and risks should they occur. Like SNA, TRA is broken into four steps:

1. *Asset definition* —You identify software, hardware, and information you need to defend.
2. *Threat assessment* —You identify the kinds of threats that place the asset at risk. These include vandalism, fire, natural disasters such as floods, or attacks from the Internet. Threat assessment also includes an evaluation of the probability of each threat, and the consequences should one occur.
3. *Risk assessment* —You evaluate each asset with respect to any existing safeguards that are currently in place, the severity of the threats and risks facing those assets, and the consequences of the threat or risk actually taking place. The combination of these factors creates an assessment of the actual risk faced by each asset.
4. *Recommendations* —Based on the risks and current safeguards, you make recommendations to reduce the risk. These recommendations should then be made part of a security policy.

TRA is carried out in different ways by different security agencies all over the world. One of the clearest and most systematic statements of how TRA can be performed is by the Information Security Group of the Australian Government's Defense Signals Directorate. In a document entitled "Australian Communications – Electronic Security Instruction 33 (ACSI 33)," a variety of ratings systems are presented. Rather than assigning numeric values to risks and threat levels, these systems use terms such as "high," "low," and "medium." These can often be sufficient to assess risk and are easier to use than statistical tools. For instance, Table 3-4 presents ratings you can assign to describe the probability that threats will occur.

Table 3-4 Threat ratings system

Rating	What It Means
Negligible	Unlikely to occur
Very Low	Likely to occur only two or three times every five years
Low	Likely to occur within a year or less
Medium	Likely to occur every six months or less
High	Likely to occur after a month or less
Very High	Likely to occur multiple times per month or less
Extreme	Likely to occur multiple times each day

ASCI 33 is available online at *www.dsd.gov.au/infosec/acsi33/HB3.html*. If you want to research other governments' approaches to TRA, you'll find a set of links to TRA guidelines in Canada and other countries at *www.infosyssec.org/infosyssec/threat1.htm*.

After you have rated the severity of the threat or risk, you need to evaluate the consequences of the event should it actually occur. Here, too, a set of standard descriptors has been developed and published in ASCI 33. They are shown in Table 3-5.

Table 3-5 Describing consequences

Description	Consequences
Insignificant	If threat occurs there will be almost no impact
Minor	If threat occurs there will be minor effect on the value of the asset. No extra effort will be required to repair or reconfigure the system.
Significant	If the threat occurs there will be some tangible harm, albeit only small and perhaps only noted by a few individuals or agencies. Some expenditure of resources will be required to repair the damage.
Damaging	If the threat occurs, the reputation of system managers will occur, and/or notable loss of confidence in the system's resources or services. Significant resources will be required to repair the damage.
Serious	If the threat occurs there may be extended system outage, and/or loss of connected customers or business confidence. Compromise of large amounts of information or services may result.
Grave	As a result of the threat occurring, the system may be permanently closed and/or be subsumed by another network or organization. A complete compromise of the organization's resources may result.

After you have evaluated the threats faced by individual assets and described the consequences that would occur if the threats are realized, you can combine the two ratings (the level of threat and consequences of the threat occurring) to come up with an analysis of the risk faced by each asset, as described in the following section.

Risk Analysis: General Activities to Follow

Whatever specific method you use, risk analysis is not a single activity, but rather a group of related activities. They typically take this sequence:

1. *Initial tiger team sessions* —First, you need to get people together. Hold meetings to get groups of workers together in one place; hold individual interviews or hand out questionnaires to collect pertinent information. It's especially important to talk to all the managers in the organization to set the objectives and scope for the risk analysis, as well as a schedule of how long the project should take and who the important people are that you need to interview.
2. *Asset valuation* —After you get an overview of the scope of the risk analysis effort, you need to identify the assets you need to protect, and determine their value. This can be a subjective or speculative activity. If it is a subjective activity, you are assessing the impact of the loss of assets that might not be tangible, and you should either use your best judgment or solicit opinions from other qualified staffers. If it is a speculative activity, you are speculating on whether information might fall into the hands of unauthorized individuals, and if it does, what the cost would be to the company to recover such information. Personal interviews with managers will help you determine a realistic assessment.
3. *Evaluating vulnerability* —You investigate the levels of threat and vulnerability in relation to the value of the organization's assets. Ask IT staff to evaluate what they consider the threat of virus attack or other intrusions on a scale of one to five, for instance.
4. *Calculate risk* —After you have the asset value and an idea of the vulnerabilities threatening those assets, you can calculate risk. Usually, a numeric value is assigned: For instance, 1 is given to a low-level baseline security need and 7 to a very high security priority.

Risk Analysis: An Ongoing Process

Risk analysis is not a one-time activity that is used solely to create a security policy. Rather, risk analysis evolves to take into account the changing size and activities of an organization, the progression to larger and more complex computer systems, and new threats from both inside and outside the corporate network.

The initial risk analysis is used to formulate a security policy; the security policy is then enforced and security is monitored. New threats and intrusion attempts cause a reassessment of the risk faced by the organization.

So, what exactly do you do when you perform a risk analysis? If you are using the TRA method described in the previous section, you can combine ratings for each asset, following this formula:

(level of threat)   (seriousness of consequences) = Level of risk

The formulas you can use for such assessments are given in the Australian Communications-Electronic Security Instruction 33 (ASCI 33, *http://www.dsd.gov.au/infosec/acsi33/acsi_index.html*) and shown in Table 3-6.

Table 3-6 Risk assessment descriptions

Threat Levels	Insignificant	Minor	Significant	Damaging	Serious	Grave
Negligible	Negligible	Negligible	Negligible	Negligible	Negligible	Negligible
Very Low	Negligible	Low	Low	Low	Medium	Medium
Low	Negligible	Low	Medium	Medium	High	High
Medium	Negligible	Low	Medium	High	High	Critical
High	Negligible	Medium	High	High	Critical	Extreme
Very High	Negligible	Medium	High	Critical	Extreme	Extreme
Extreme	Negligible	Medium	High	Critical	Extreme	Extreme

The ratings in the far left column represent threat levels; the ones given in the top row are descriptions of consequences. The rest of the table cells provide ratings that cover the combination of threats consequences.

Analyzing Economic Impacts

An important part of conducting a risk analysis is preparing estimates of the financial impact of such losses. If you are familiar with statistics, you can use a number of different models for estimating the impacts. You can also use a software program to help you prepare reports that substantiate your estimates and give you charts and graphs to support your figures. A program called Project Risk Analysis by Katmar Software gives you a structure in which you can list the hardware and software assets in your organization (see Figure 3-4).

Project Risk Analysis gives you the chance to make cost estimates using a variety of statistical models. For those who are unfamiliar with statistics, the simplest model uses the following:

- *Likely Cost* —This is your best estimate of the money you'll have to spend to replace the item.
- *Low Cost* —This is lowest dollar amount you are likely to incur in replacing the item.
- *High Cost* —This is the highest dollar amount you might incur when replacing the item.

When you create a record of an asset in Project Risk Analysis and estimate its replacement cost, you enter these terms using the Normal distribution setting, as shown in Figure 3-5.

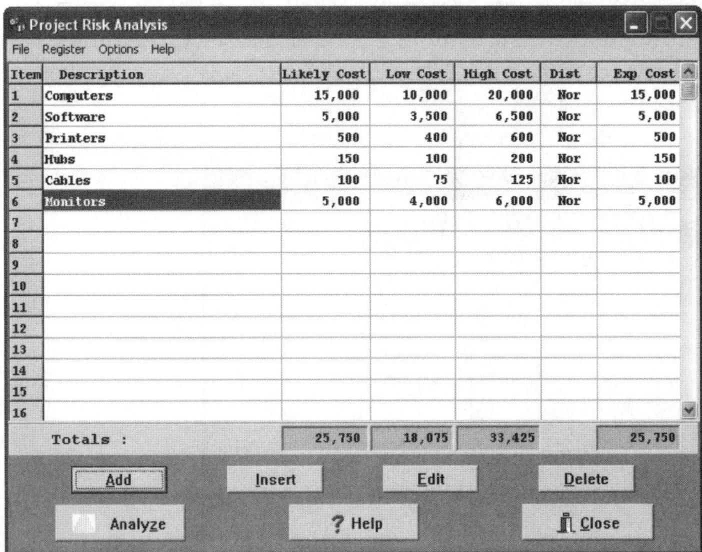

Figure 3-4 Project risk analysis gives you a structure for making cost estimates

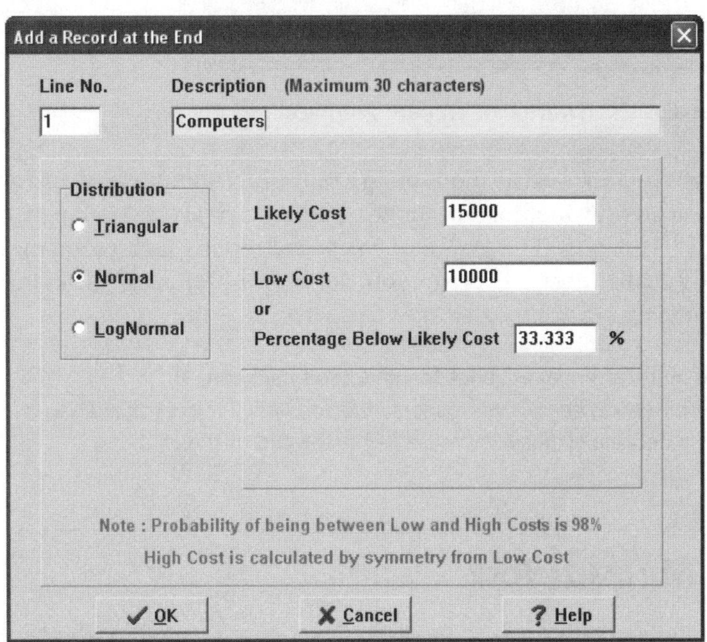

Figure 3-5 The simplest way to estimate replacement cost is to enter Likely Cost and Low Cost values

One desirable feature of a risk analysis program such as Project Risk Analysis is the ability to analyze cost estimates and present them in graphical format. In addition, such programs can quickly calculate the mean cost of replacing hardware, software, or other items in case a loss is incurred (see Figure 3-6).

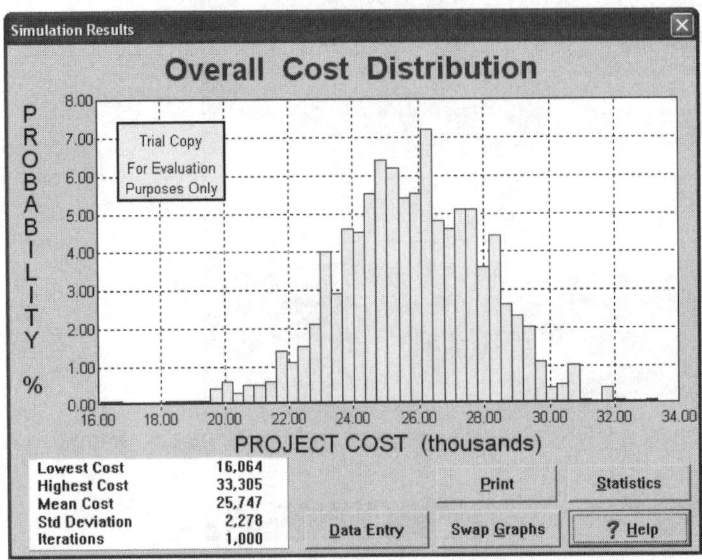

Figure 3-6 Risk analysis software can prepare graphical reports

Project Risk Analysis performs calculations using a statistical formula called a **Monte Carlo simulation** —an analytical method meant to simulate a real-life system by randomly generating values for variables. The graphical charts and reports such programs create can provide you with valuable documentation you can use in preparing a risk analysis; such visuals have great impact when presented to managers.

TIP

You'll find more information about Monte Carlo simulations at *www.decisioneering.com/monte-carlo-simulation.html*. Project risk analysis is examined in detail in Hands-On Project 3-3 at the end of this chapter.

Deciding How to Minimize Risk

After you have come up with an analysis of the level of risk faced by the hardware and software assets in your network, you can come up with recommendations of safeguards that will minimize the risk. **Risk management** , in fact, is the term that describes the process of identifying, choosing, and setting up countermeasures justified by the risks you identify. The countermeasures you describe are the statements that go into your security policy. In the following sections, you'll learn about important points to consider when deciding how to secure the hardware, how to secure information databases in your network, how to conduct routine analysis, and how to respond to security incidents when they occur.

Deciding How to Secure Hardware

Your company's physical computing assets—the actual hardware devices that keep data flowing throughout the network—are the most obvious objects that need to be identified. You have to decide how you're going to protect your hardware. First, think about obvious kinds of physical protection, such as environmental controls to keep machines cool in hot temperatures and the utilization of fire protection systems. Then consider whether you are going to lock up all the hardware in your organization, or whether you only want to provide theft protection for your database and other servers. (It's critical that you locate your servers in a room that can be locked with an alarm system, so unauthorized employees can't gain access to them, rather than leaving these computers out in the open.)

Be sure to pay special attention to all of the laptop computers in your organization. Such machines can be easily lost or stolen, and any proprietary information contained on them could be compromised. Such incidents happen regularly, and often with serious consequences. In August 2002, an audit performed by the U.S. Treasury Department discovered that approximately 2,200 laptops that had been issued by the Internal Revenue Service to volunteers in a tax assistance program were missing; they reportedly contained financial data belonging to individual taxpayers. In addition, government agencies, reported 400 laptops were lost between October 1999 and January 2002, according to *Government Executive* magazine (*www.govexec.com/dailyfed/0802/080502m1.htm*).

Lost laptops are only one problem; lost productivity can also result when employees misuse laptops in order to surf the Web or shop online. Be sure to install startup passwords as well as screen saver passwords; these can be circumvented by experienced thieves, of course, but at the very least they make it more difficult for files to be accessed. In addition, you can encrypt files on your laptop using a program such as Pretty Good Privacy (PGP), which is available at *www.pgp.com*.

Doing a Hardware Inventory

Make a list of servers, routers, cables, workstation PCs, printers, and all other pieces of hardware owned by the company. Be sure to include your company's **network assets** —the routers, cables, bastion hosts, servers, and firewall hardware and software that enable those within your organization to communicate with one another and other computers on the Internet. Make a topology map that shows how the devices are connected, along with an IP allocation register, such as the one shown in Figure 3-7.

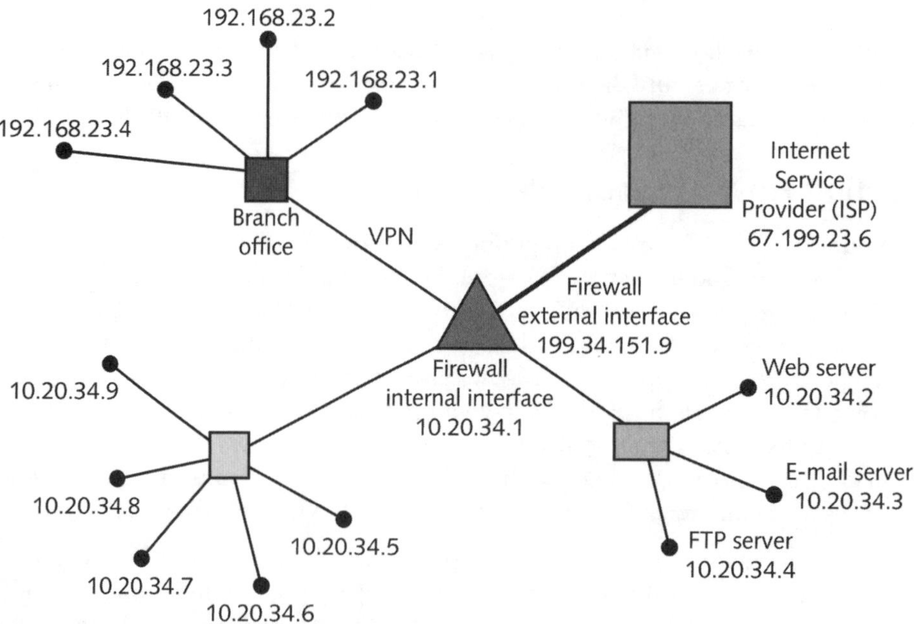

Figure 3-7 A topology map can supplement a hardware inventory

Ranking Resources to Be Protected

In listing physical, logical, network, and system assets, it is often helpful to assign a value to each object. The value can be an arbitrary number; what's important is to rank resources in order of importance, so that you can focus your security efforts on the most critical resources first. The team that helps you prepare your security policy will probably determine that data is more important than the digital devices in which they are stored.

The numbers you come up with might seem somewhat arbitrary; based on the author's own experience; you should derive your own rankings with the cooperation of your organization's higher management. Developing a lengthy list of resources and rankings on your own without input from managers is likely to result in extensive revisions. You'll get better results if you submit a list of the resources to your managers and ask them to develop their own rankings. Also ask them to consider the cost to replace both software and computers you have listed. Suggest that they rank the assets using a scale of 1 to 10.

Deciding How to Secure Information

After you have decided on safeguards for your hardware, you need to determine how best to protect your company's **logical assets** —the word processing, spreadsheet, Web page, and other documents contained on your network computers. Logical assets also include e-mail messages, any records of instant messaging conversations, and the log files that are compiled by your firewall and intrusion detection systems. It also includes personnel, customer, and financial information that your company needs to protect.

Maintaining Customer and Employee Privacy

Many companies now conduct all or part of their business operations on the Internet. If your organization conducts e-commerce, you need to strike a balance between making it easy to find goods for sale and completing electronic transactions, and keeping customer and business information confidential.

One way to protect the information your customers send you via the Internet is to isolate that information from the Internet so that hackers can't gain access to it. In many of the high-profile attacks that have plagued Web sites in recent years, hackers manage to break into a site and gain access to credit card numbers and other data stored on that site. You may well want to spell out, in your security policy, that to minimize the risk of critical customer data being stolen by hackers, your company needs to take such information from the directory where it is stored when it is submitted, and store it on a computer that is completely isolated from the Internet. You can configure backup software to save critical files in isolated locations automatically on a nightly or weekly basis. You can also use the following to protect information:

- *Encryption* —By encrypting data, you can protect it as it passes from one network to another so that it cannot be read if intercepted or captured.
- *Message filtering* —This keeps potentially harmful messages from entering the network from the outside.
- *Data encapsulation* —The data in individual packets can be encrypted in such a way that those packets are encapsulated (or "wrapped") for extra protection. Encapsulation is performed by virtual private network (VPN) software or hardware, as described in Chapter 7.
- *Redundancy* —By providing **redundancy** through backup systems, you ensure that databases and other stores of information remain accessible if the primary systems go offline.
- *Back ups* —Systematic and periodic back ups of information held on the network are one of the most basic and important ways to protect that information.

You can separate your customer databases from your Web servers using a hardware/software product called e-Gap by Whale Communications (*www.whalecommunications.com*). e-Gap uses a high-speed switch to keep data flowing between the external Web server and your internal database and other application servers. The switch means that at no time are the application servers actually connected to the Web servers—rather, they're only connected to the switch.

Protecting Corporate Information

Do workers at your organization handle information that is confidential, proprietary, or private? If so, the information they handle needs to be covered in the security policy as well. Safeguards are needed to inform these workers of their information protection duties, to tell them what they can and cannot do with respect to this sensitive information. You might decide to minimize risk by specifying the following measures in a security policy:

- Never leave company-owned laptops or palm devices unattended.
- Always password-protect information contained on corporate devices.
- Encrypt any financial information.
- Password-protect all job records and customer information.
- Restrict all personnel information to human resources staff and/or upper management.

You then need to make sure all employees read and understand the policy. You might consider distributing the policy in the form of a manual that is issued to all new employees upon hiring or during training, and that is published on the company Web site as well, so current employees can review it.

Deciding How to Conduct Routine Analysis

Risk analysis isn't an operation that is performed on a one-time basis. A company is constantly changing, in terms of the information it handles, the number of customers it receives, the size of the staff, and the number of computers on the network. Risk analysis should be done on a routine basis, despite obstacles that commonly arise, such as the indifference of IT staff and employees, the heavy workload in areas that are considered more critical (such as revenue generation), and lack of available personnel to do the evaluation.

Deciding how your organization will perform routine analysis starts with the following questions:

- How often will a risk analysis be performed? Every year, at budget time, is a logical and consistent level of frequency. Note, however, that monthly or weekly reassessment is more effective because it will enable you to keep up with new threats.
- Who will perform the risk analysis? The same professionals who manage security for the organization are the ones who should participate, along with accounting/bookkeeping staff.
- Do all hardware and software resources need to be reviewed every time? You may not need to conduct a new risk analysis for every asset you have; you may well decide that only the assets that have increased or changed substantially should be re-examined.

The calculations and evaluations associated with risk analysis require subjective evaluations of how much an asset is "worth" and how "valuable" it is. Because human emotions can influence such evaluations, many companies do not allow staff people to perform such calculations manually. Due to the often complex calculations (of levels of risk times assessed value, for instance) it can be easier to use risk analysis software.

One of the best-known software tools in the field is called CRAMM and is available from Insight Solutions in the UK (*www.insight.co.uk/cramm*).

Deciding How to Handle Security Incidents

It's important to use the security policy to define how you will respond to security break-ins. You may want to fill out a form specially intended to record what happens during a break-in. You don't have to prepare such a form from scratch; you can use one of the forms published on the Federal Agency Security Practices Web site of the National Institute of Standards and Technology. A sample form is shown in Figure 3-8.

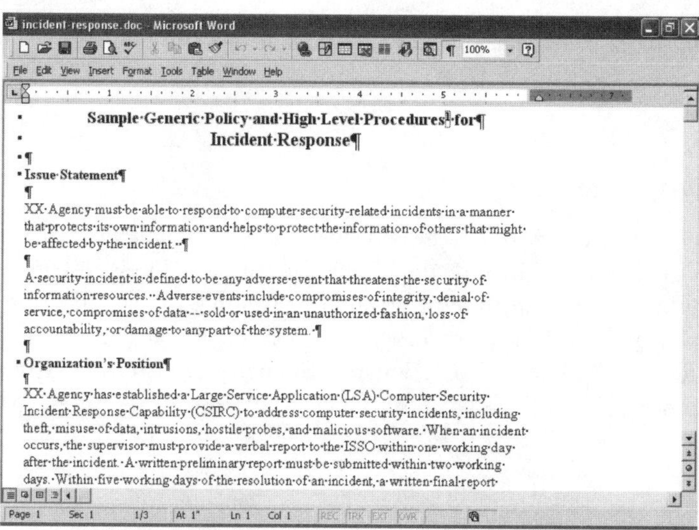

Sample Generic Policy and High Level Procedures for Incident Response

Issue Statement

XX Agency must be able to respond to computer security-related incidents in a manner that protects its own information and helps to protect the information of others that might be affected by the incident.

A security incident is defined to be any adverse event that threatens the security of information resources. Adverse events include compromises of integrity, denial of service, compromises of data --- sold or used in an unauthorized fashion, loss of accountability, or damage to any part of the system.

Organization's Position

XX Agency has established a Large Service Application (LSA) Computer Security Incident Response Capability (CSIRC) to address computer security incidents, including theft, misuse of data, intrusions, hostile probes, and malicious software. When an incident occurs, the supervisor must provide a verbal report to the ISSO within one working day after the incident. A written preliminary report must be submitted within two working days. Within five working days of the resolution of an incident, a written final report

Figure 3-8 Sample incident handling form

Describing Incident Handling Procedures

It pays to go into some detail, in the course of formulating a security policy, to describe exactly who will respond to security incidents, what needs to be done, and why such procedures need to happen at all.

You need to address the incident response section of a security policy. You should begin by describing the need for careful and expeditious handling of an intrusion if it occurs. You might also describe the kinds of incidents that need to be confronted, such as:

- Alarms sent by intrusion detection systems
- Repeated unsuccessful logon attempts
- New user accounts that suddenly appear without explanation
- New files that appear on system servers with unfamiliar file names
- Changes to data or deletion of records that go unexplained
- System crashes
- Poor system performance

The incident handling process to be followed should then be spelled out in the security policy. Tell employees to identify whether an intrusion has actually occurred. They can do this by auditing the system to see if new files have been added. If so, they next need to determine what resources have been compromised. The affected resources should then be contained, the viruses or any other files that have been introduced into the system should be eradicated, and resources should then be recovered.

See Chapter 10 for more details on how to respond to network intrusions.

Assembling a Response Team

If an incident occurs, the security policy should spell out exactly which security staff in the organization needs to be notified. Include the individual's e-mail address and phone number. Also specify a location where team members should assemble in case they are unable to communicate. Teamwork is essential in successfully responding to network security incidents, and it's common for an organization to designate a **Security Incident Response Team (SIRT)** —a group of staff people designated to take countermeasures when an incident is reported.

You might also see a SIRT referred to as a CERT—a Computer Emergency Response Team that can respond to any type of system failure, not just a security-related intrusion.

The SIRT is primarily intended to respond to security-related breaches, and typically includes in its mission functions such as:

- Reacting to security breaches that originate from outside as well as inside the organization
- Isolating, reviewing, and interpreting information about security incidents
- Assessing the extent of damage of a security incident

- Determining the causes of intrusions and other incidents, and recommending countermeasures to prevent them from reoccurring
- Monitoring the integrity of the organization's network on an ongoing basis

Typically, the SIRT contains IT operations and technical support staff, IT application staff, a chief security officer, and other information security specialists. In some large organizations, a special position called Incident Response Manager might be created; the designated individual would be primarily responsible for responding to incidents, doing an initial assessment, and summoning the SIRT and other staff people as needed. All of the staff people involved in the SIRT should be identified in the security policy; if the primary contact person cannot be contacted, one of the others on the list can then be summoned.

Describing Escalation Procedures

If an intrusion is found to have occurred and damage is more severe than originally thought—or if the intrusion is currently occurring and files are being accessed at the current time—the security policy should describe stages of response that escalate along with the consequences of the incident. An **escalation procedure**, then, is a set of roles, responsibilities, and measures taken in response to a security incident.

To determine how a response might escalate, you can come up with a system for ranking the severity of an incident (for instance, Low, Medium, High, and Severe). Each of the rankings could then be mapped to an escalation chain—a hierarchy of staff members who need to be involved in responding to incidents and making decisions. A possible mapping is shown in Table 3-7.

Table 3-7 Mapping escalation chain to incident severity

Incident Severity	Escalation Chain
Low	Network Administrator
Medium	SIRT
High	SIRT plus V-P of Security or V-P of Information Systems
Severe	SIRT plus all V-Ps, Department Heads, and President

Table 3-7 could be extended to spell out actions to be taken in response to incidents based on their severity. Incidents that have low to moderate severity might require a virus scan or log file review, while severe incidents might call for the disconnection of the local network from the Internet or from other network segments while the response is ongoing.

Including Worst Case Scenarios

Worst-case scenarios are descriptions of the worst consequences that befall an organization if a threat is realized. Such scenarios might be unlikely, but they can help you to determine the value of a resource that is at risk. Values are derived from reasonable consequences of files, computers, and databases being unavailable for specified periods of time. You might prepare scenarios that account for several time frames, such as a matter of minutes to a matter of several months.

This worst-case scenario approach to valuing assets is regarded as a shortcoming by some professionals in the field, because worst-case scenarios can be extremely unlikely in the real world and "can easily be used to distort a situation."

Another way to quantify the impact of financial loss or interruption of business activities is to assign a numeric value to an asset based on a range of dollar amounts. If the loss is estimated at $100 or less, the number 1 is assigned to that loss. If the loss is between $100 and $1,000, the number 2 is assigned, and so on.

What Makes a Good Security Policy?

"Do we really need a security policy?" Don't be surprised to be confronted with this question by your organization. You need to be prepared with a response to this question. You can begin by reminding your skeptical fellow employees that, indeed, you need a security policy if your company falls into one of the following categories:

- If your employees work with confidential or proprietary information
- If your organization holds "trade secrets" that are important to your goods or services
- If your employees regularly access the Internet
- If you have Internet connections to partner businesses or Application Service Providers (ASPs)—companies that provide Web-based services for a fee

To help your case, you can also convey stories that describe the sorts of public relations and human relations dilemmas that can occur if a clearly defined security policy is not in place. Here are some to consider:

- A copyeditor spent a great deal of time surfing the Internet while on the job, for both personal pursuits as well as work-related research. Management found itself unable to discipline the individual because no policy was in effect that stated what constituted excessive personal use. The employee's supervisor later discovered that the copyeditor had downloaded a substantial amount of pornography, and for this reason the employee was fired. However, the individual subsequently appealed the dismissal with the Civil Service Board, claiming that he couldn't be fired because he had never been told that he couldn't download pornography. After a hearing, the Board ordered him to be reinstated with back pay.
- A clerk who was laid off due to downsizing at an insurance company, was hired by a competing company. The former employer discovered that many of its customer files had been accessed and copied, and that a number of its clients had

switched to the competitor after they were offered lower insurance rates. The original company did not have a policy in place to protect its passwords or to switch passwords when employees are released. The laid-off employee was easily able to access his former employer's network and steal the files so his new employer could market itself aggressively to desirable customers.

The benefits of a security policy are wide-ranging. In general, though, the security policy provides a foundation for the overall security stance of the organization. A security policy not only gives employees guidelines on how they are to handle sensitive information, and IT staff with instructions on what defensive systems to configure, but also lowers the legal liability to the company and to its employees. It's very common for employees who are fired or laid-off to come back and sue their previous employer or file a grievance and, in such cases, the presence of a well-defined security policy can make the difference between the company having to pay substantial damages and not being liable at all. It's important to formulate a clear policy that states what rights the employee has and how the employee should responsibly handle company resources to protect overall security. That policy should be signed by each employee when he or she is first hired.

A good security policy is comprehensive and flexible; it is often not a single document, but a group of documents, each with its own specific emphasis. The following sections examine principles you need to keep in mind when designing a security policy, and that will result in an effective set of rules and procedures: the need to base the policy on a thoroughgoing risk assessment; the need to teach employees about acceptable use of network resources; the need to enable management to set priorities; the need to help administrators do their jobs; and the need to see the security policy as enabling subsequent risk analyses.

Developing Security Policies from Risk Assessment

"Where do we start with a security policy?" If you are faced with this question, you should be able to come up with an answer based on your review of the preceding sections on risk analysis. You start by identifying what needs to be protected. You then define the threats faced by the network, the probability that those threats will occur, and the respective consequences posed by each threat. You then propose safeguards and define how to respond to incidents.

The information you gather during the risk analysis phase should then go into the security policy, along with a statement of the overall goals of the report, and the importance of employees actually reading and following its guidelines. After the policy is implemented, the system is monitored. Based on any intrusions or incidents that occur, you can do a new risk analysis and update the policy as needed; the sequence of policy design, implementation, monitoring, and reassessment forms an ongoing cycle.

Teaching Employees about Acceptable Use

The issue of trust is an integral part of a security policy. The policy needs to define who to trust, and what level of trust should be placed within those individuals. It's easy to say that members of the organization should not be trusted at all. But you should spell out in writing all of the ways in which they should use system resources correctly so that acceptable use is no longer a matter of trust.

In reality, organizations have to achieve a balance between trust and issuing orders. You need to allow employees (or students or members) to use their computers to communicate and be productive. By placing too little trust in individuals and prescribing everything they should do in an excessively rigid fashion, you not only hamper their work, but you hurt morale and make it more likely that they'll circumvent your safeguards in some way.

The cornerstone of many security policies is the Acceptable Use Policy, which spells out how employees should make use of the organization's resources, including the Internet, e-mail, and the software programs they use every day.

Enabling Management to Set Priorities

Security policies give employees guidelines they can follow during everyday work activities. But they are also helpful to management. They also "cover" management in case disputes arise with employees, or in case employees complain about security tools the organization has in place.

Security policies do more than assist with dispute resolution, however. They provide a way for management to identify the most important security priorities facing the company. A security policy lists the network resources that managers find most valuable in the organization and that are most in need of protection. They spell out whether the priority of the organization will be to allow employees or members to access the Internet or to restrict access to both the Internet and the internal corporate network. In addition, they describe the measures the company will take if resources are misused or if information is compromised by individuals either outside or inside the company.

Helping Network Administrators Do Their Jobs

Network administrators tasked with instructing individual employees on how to access shared resources, change passwords, sort through e-mail, or other functions, can gain considerable assistance from security policies. A security policy can spell out mundane but important information that the administrator would otherwise have to convey personally, such as:

- Users are not allowed to share accounts with other employees or with visitors or family members.
- Users are allowed to install only software programs that are provided in the Downloadables directory on the Shared Project server. Any other software is subject to approval.

- Users are not allowed to make copies of office-owned software.
- Users are required to use password-protected screensavers during the day, and to shut down their computers each night.
- Only members of the IT staff are allowed to add hard drives or install networking devices into office computers.
- The network administrator first needs to assign a username and password to anyone who needs to connect to the office network from a remote location. In addition, any remote PCs that are used to connect to the network need to be protected with firewall and anti-virus software.

Administrators themselves can be covered by a specific part of a security policy called a Privileged Access Policy. Such a policy covers the access Administrators can have to network resources, and their ability to run network scanning tools, run password checking software, and have root or domain administrator access.

Using Security Policies to Enable Risk Analysis

Once a security policy is in place, the work doesn't end there. After employees and managers are educated to the policy's requirements and provisions, the safeguards it prescribes are put in place. Data can be generated after firewalls and other intrusion detection systems are installed. This data is used in further risk analysis.

It's up to you to determine how frequently to do another round of risk analysis. The first time you analyze the level of risk might be after a relatively short period, such as a month or six weeks. After you make any needed adjustments to the security configuration as a result of threats that have arisen, you might decide to perform ongoing risk analysis every three months or every six months; there isn't a hard-and-fast rule. It is important to perform the analysis after a significant change occurs, such as when new equipment is installed or there is significant staff turnover. The risk analysis that occurs after the security policy is implemented involves the same steps as the initial round of risk analysis. The difference is that now you have real-world data on which to base your evaluations of risk and their consequences, rather than being limited solely to "what if" situations.

Formulating a Security Policy

In the preceding sections you have learned that the formulation of a security policy begins with an analysis of the level of risk faced by the organization's assets. You also learned that a security policy isn't always a single document, but often contains many different component documents. After you know what assets are at risk and you've come up with suggestions for safeguards, you can put them together in the form of a security policy.

In this section, you'll get a rundown of the steps involved in creating a policy. You'll then get suggestions and examples of specific types of policies that you can create and that, taken together, make up a complete security policy.

Seven Steps to Creating a Security Policy

After you have conducted a risk analysis, you should summarize your findings in the form of a report. The report should call attention to the most urgent risks the company needs to address. You might do this in an introductory paragraph or section. After the introduction, you could then present a grid that lists the most important assets in the company and the level of risk you have determined. An example is shown in Table 3-8.

Table 3-8 Risk analysis example

Asset	Threat	Probability	Consequences	Risk Assessment
Physical Assets	Low	Low	Significant	Medium
Data	Medium	Medium	Damaging	High
Software	Negligible	Minor	Minor	Low
Personal Assets	Low	Low	Significant	Medium
Hardware	High	Medium	Damaging	High

If your report lists types or groups of assets (for example, "Physical Assets" rather than specific items like buildings, desks, telephones, and so on), include a set of definitions that explains what each group encompasses. Also be sure to list who prepared the report and when it was conducted, so readers can verify that the information within it is current.

In the example given, you would be well advised to explain why hardware and data assets are in a high-risk situation. This may not be obvious to the managers who read your analysis simply from looking at the grid. The hardware risk may be high because servers are left in openly accessible work areas that are not protected by locks or any special environmental controls, so they can be easily stolen or damaged. The data assets in the company may be in a state of high risk because of a lack of virus protection in some servers, for instance.

After you have completed your risk analysis and distributed it to the appropriate managers, you would follow these steps to actually create the policy:

1. Call for the formation of a group that will meet to formulate the security policy. Because of the political nature of security policies and the fact that they affect employees strongly, you should not do the formulation on your own. Be sure to include a senior administrator, a member of your legal staff, some IT staff, and a representative of rank-and-file employees.

2. Determine whether the organization's overall approach or slant toward security will be restrictive or permissive. A restrictive slant limits activity on the network to only a few authorized activities. A permissive approach allows traffic to flow freely and restricts only vulnerable ports, services, or computers.

3. Identify the assets you need to protect. You will have already done the groundwork for this in the risk analysis phase.
4. Determine which network communications need to be audited and how frequently the results should be reviewed. **Auditing** is the process of keeping records of the activities of computers on the network; these include who is connecting to a computer, what resources are being requested, and whether access was granted or blocked. Such information is typically recorded in a log file.
5. List the security risks that need to be addressed.
6. Define acceptable use of the Internet, office computers, passwords, and other network resources.
7. Create the policy. The risks specified in the policy can be translated as individual sections within one long security policy document, or as separate policies in their own right that, taken together, make up the organization's overall security policy.

Categories of Security Policies

After the security policy committee has determined what should go into the security policy, the contents need to be presented. Having a Security Policy Committee in place can help in this regard; specific members or groups within the committee can be assigned the task of preparing individual parts of the policy. A team approach ensures that all relevant points are covered. Many different kinds of policies can make up a policy; this section briefly describes the more common ones you are likely to need.

Acceptable Use

The Acceptable Use policy is usually listed first in a security policy because it most closely affects the largest number of employees in an organization, and it can generate the highest degree of controversy as well. The goal of the policy is to define acceptable—as well as unacceptable—uses of organizational resources.

Many companies require their employees to read and sign an Acceptable Use Policy before they are granted a user account, or when they are first hired.

An Acceptable Use statement might say the following:

"The following Acceptable Use statement covers the use of [*Company Name*] computers, network components, software applications, and other hardware. The term 'other hardware' includes personal computers, laptops, PDAs, floppy disks, CD-ROM drives and disks, servers, cables, routers, and tape backup systems. The term 'user' is defined as an individual who has an account to use [*Company Name*]'s network resources. All users of the [*Company Name*] network are expected to conduct themselves in a responsible, legal, non-threatening manner at all times. Specifically:

- Users are not allowed to make unauthorized copies of software that is copyrighted except with the permission of the copyright holder.
- Users are responsible for storing their personal data on their workstations. If you need assistance with storing data, consult the network administrator.
- Users are not permitted to engage in any activity, either online or offline, that harasses, threatens, or abuses other users.
- E-mail accounts are for business use only; personal e-mail messages as well as messages that may be judged obscene, harassing, or offensive shall not be sent from or stored on [*Company Name*] systems.

Users who violate the above policies will be reported to the security staff. Offenses may result in loss of network privileges. If the offense warrants, the company may press civil or criminal charges against the user.

I have read and understand the [*Company Name*] Acceptable Use statement and agree to abide by it."

The signature of the individual user follows; some companies also include the signature of a witness and the date the agreement was signed. The provisions given above are just a few examples of the kinds of provisions that can be included in an Acceptable Use agreement. Your own statement may go into far greater detail on the use of network resources.

User Account

By creating a policy that specifically spells out how user accounts are to be used, you gain flexibility in developing and enforcing the security policy because you don't limit yourself to actual employees who work on-site. User accounts include contractors who work at home and suppliers who connect to your network from their own facilities. Your security policy might specify user account policies such as the following:

- Users are not permitted to attempt to gain access to an unauthorized resource.
- Users cannot block the ability of an authorized user to gain access to an authorized resource.
- Users cannot give their account username and password to unauthorized users.
- Users must protect their username and password in a secure location not visible on their desktops.

Remote Access

More and more organizations are using freelancers and consultants who work with them via broadband connections to the Internet. In addition, mobile workers frequently need to connect to the home office while on the road or at home, and business partners often want to update their orders or view their account information by connecting directly to the company network.

Each of these cases represents an opportunity for increased productivity, but it raises security vulnerabilities as well. If the user who connects to the corporate network is working at a computer that is infected with a virus or that has been compromised by a hacker, that hacker or virus can potentially gain access to the corporate network while the individual is connected to it.

A Remote Access security policy spells out exactly what security measures need to be present on a remote desktop before the user or that desktop can connect to the organization's network. Such a policy spells out the use of **role-based authentication**, which gives users limited access based on what role they play in the company and what applications they need to use. The sensitivity of those applications determines the type of authentication to be used, and this can be spelled out in the Remote Access policy as well. Access to non-sensitive applications or data sources can be granted with a simple password, while access to sensitive resources can be secured with a smart card or token, a piece of hardware that is used along with a password to provide **two-factor authentication** —a type of authentication that combines something the owner possesses (the card or token) with something the owner knows (a password or PIN).

Password Protection

A Password Protection Policy or Statement can be included in the Acceptable Use agreement but it is worth discussing on its own because of its importance in an organization's overall security scheme.

Passwords represent a first line of defense (and possibly a second or even a third) for many organizations. Passwords not only allow users to gain access to e-mail messages, but they control access to the network from outside, to shared directories on servers, and much more. Often, companies require users to protect their computers or Web browsers by means of passwords so other staff people or visitors cannot use them after hours.

A password policy might state whether the network administrator should have the ability to run software that checks for passwords. It might prescribe that all passwords need to be, say, seven characters or more in length and that they should contain both alphanumeric characters and numbers; or that three incorrect logins will prevent the user from accessing the account.

Secure Use of the Internet

An Internet Use policy can also be integrated with an Acceptable Use statement or with the overall security policy. However, because Internet use is becoming so integral to the day-to-day work functions of many individuals, it's worth creating a stand-alone security policy section that covers how members of the organization can access and use the Internet.

If a clear policy governing the correct use of e-mail is not in place, the following type of incident might occur: an employee receives a virus hoax sent by e-mail. The message indicates that if other users receive a message with the heading "You're a Winner!" they should not read it, because such a message will erase all files on the user's hard disk. As a result, the employee broadcasts the e-mail to all other staffers in the company. Many of those staffers send the same e-mail to other parts of the organization, thinking that they are doing others a favor. Because no policy defined how they should handle these warnings, the company's mail servers are flooded with e-mail, and technical staff is called to diagnose the trouble, which wastes staff time and resources.

An Internet Use policy would prohibit broadcasting of any e-mail messages. Rather, users should be directed to contact the network administrator about the suspicious mail message. The policy would also spell out whether users are allowed to download software from the Internet or not, and if so, what the limits are on the size of files that can be downloaded. The policy could prohibit users from opening executable e-mail attachments that could contain viruses. It could also spell out whether any objectionable Web sites have been blocked by the company, and it could inform users of how the company will protect their privacy with regard to e-mail.

LAN Security Policy

A Local Area Network (LAN) security policy should clearly define and establish responsibility for the protection of information that is processed, stored and transmitted on the LAN, and for the LAN itself. Primary responsibility may be with the data owner—the manager of the organization that creates the data and processes it. Secondary responsibility is then assigned to the users and end-users within the organization who are given access to the information. LAN management should clearly define the role of the individuals responsible for maintaining the availability of the LAN.

Such a policy should describe:

- *Evaluations*— The value of the information stored on the LAN
- *Responsibilities*— Who is responsible for protecting the information on the LAN
- *Commitment*— The organization's commitment to protecting information and the LAN
- *Applicability*— What constitutes the LAN environment and what parts, if any, are exempted from the policy

The example LAN security policy that follows defines responsibilities for:

- *Functional managers*— Individuals who may have primary responsibility
- *Users*— Individuals who may have secondary responsibility
- *Local Administrators (LAs)*— Employees who are responsible for ensuring that end-users have access to needed LAN resources that reside on their respective servers
- *End-users*— Any employees who have access to the organization's LAN (They are responsible for using the LAN in accordance with the LAN security policy.)

All users of data are responsible for complying with the security policy established by those with the primary responsibility for the security of the data, and for reporting to management any suspected breach of security.

A Sample LAN Security Policy

The following is an example of a LAN security policy that was developed using the descriptions and defined responsibilities presented in the preceding section:

"A computer security incident is any adverse event whereby some aspect of computer security could be threatened: loss of data confidentiality, loss of data or system integrity, or disruption or denial of availability. In a LAN environment the concept of a computer security incident can be extended to all areas of the LAN (hardware, software, data, transmissions, etc.) including the LAN itself.

Contingency plans in a LAN environment should be developed so that any LAN security incident can be handled in a timely manner, with as minimal an impact as possible on the ability of the organization to process and transmit data. A contingency plan should consider (1) incident response, (2) back-up operations, and (3) recovery.

1. The purpose of incident response is to mitigate the potentially serious effects of a severe LAN security-related problem. It requires not only the capability to react to incidents, but the resources to alert and inform the users, if necessary. It requires the cooperation of all users to ensure that incidents are reported and resolved and that future incidents are prevented. It is recommended as guidance in developing an incident response capability.
2. Back-up Operations plans are prepared to ensure that essential tasks (as identified by a risk analysis) can be completed subsequent to disruption of the LAN environment and continuing until the LAN is sufficiently restored.
3. Recovery plans are made to permit smooth, rapid restoration of the LAN environment following interruption of LAN usage. Supporting documents should be developed and maintained that will minimize the time required for recovery. Priority should be given to those applications, services, etc. that are deemed critical to the functioning of the organization. Back-up operation procedures should ensure that these critical services and applications are available to users."

Performing Ongoing Risk Analysis

As stated, after the security policy has been in place for a period of time decided upon by the security policy committee, a routine reassessment of the risk faced by the company and its assets should be performed. You may or may not need to comprehensively examine every single asset in the company every time such a reassessment is done. Rather, you may decide to focus only on the most urgent security risks or on any new risks that have cropped up as a result of changes in the company.

The following sections examine what you should keep in mind when reevaluating the organization's security policy on an ongoing basis: the need to make such reviews routine; the need to work with management to accept the ongoing risk analysis/security policy cycle; the need to respond to security incidents as they occur; and the need to revise the security policy as a result of incidents and other risks that are identified.

Conducting Routine Security Reviews

An effective security policy not only describes the immediate steps to be taken when an intrusion is detected, but it can also look to the future and spell out how frequently risk analyses should be performed. A section of the policy that describes ongoing security reviews should begin by identifying the individuals who will do the analysis on an ongoing basis. It should then describe the circumstances under which a new risk analysis will be performed. For instance, whenever a substantial new purchase of equipment is made, these individuals can be notified so they can determine if new security policy statements need to be made or whether new measures should be taken.

Even though the security policy might state that a risk analysis should routinely be performed every six months or every year, the policy should also be flexible enough to allow such "emergency" reassessments as needed. For instance, any attacks to partner businesses or the offices of employees who work off-site should cause the team to reassess the risks facing the organization, as well as news of any major security attacks on Internet servers or viruses circulating widely on the Internet.

Working with Management

This section provides hints for working with management after you are hired and are in the workplace. When you prepare a project proposal for developing full-fledged security policies or for spending extensively on security-related hardware and software, you are likely to be asked what kind of return on investment (ROI) the company will realize.

Tell your colleagues that they should think about the issue not in terms of ROI, but in terms of the cost of doing nothing. Large organizations with employees who connect remotely from home or other locations are far more vulnerable to security breaches than other businesses. They need to consider three factors:

- How much their information systems and the data on them are worth

- Possible threats they've already encountered and will encounter
- The chances that those security threats will result in real losses of time and money

These days, security threats can originate from many different sources and have a wide variety of signatures, and no single solution will block all of them. A comprehensive security plan is not just a return on investment, but also a way of protecting your systems and your customers' personal information as well. Tell management to quantify the future revenue lost when customers' credit card numbers are stolen by a teenage hacker and posted on the Internet, which destroys their future credibility. In addition, ask them to estimate the cost to the business if such information is unavailable for weeks or months at a time.

Stay away from making quantitative statements, which can be difficult to fix with precision as equipment depreciates and an office's configuration changes. Rather, get people to consider the following aspects of a business's activities that can be affected adversely by intrusions:

- Costs related to financial loss and disruption
- Personal safety
- Personal information
- Legal and regulatory obligations
- Commercial and economic interests

It can be difficult to calculate ROI for security spending as it applies to lost data and staff time. However, Kensington provides a calculator that you can use to estimate the loss of PC hardware and software. See Hands-On Project 3-1.

Dealing with the Approval Process

The development of a security policy can take anywhere from several weeks to several months, depending on the organization. In the author's experience, a two to three week time period is possible under ideal circumstances—in other words, it is possible when you have cooperation by all relevant employees.

One fact that won't go away is the need for review and approval of the security policy, and this is a process that, by itself, can take anywhere from several weeks to several months. Don't be dismayed if the need to schedule and reschedule meetings, hold discussions, and get approvals takes longer than you think. For a security policy to work, rank-and-file employees need to accept it. You may encounter resistance, which is natural in any policy that affects an entire organization. A **Security User Awareness program**, in which employees are formally instructed about the organization's security strategy, can help.

Feeding Security Information to the Security Policy Team

Any changes made to the organization's security configuration should be conveyed to the security policy team. They, in turn, can suggest changes to the policy; the policy then dictates whether new security tools need to be purchased or new security measures need to be taken.

The participation and backing of top-level management can help the process of amending the security policy. Encourage managers to inform employees that the protection of company assets is everyone's responsibility. Provide training to the end-users to make them aware of security issues, and to explain why data collection and management should be conducted in a secure matter. Educate end-users so that they have the required knowledge to carry out their job in a secure manner. Listen to employees' concerns. Develop sensible security solutions that enable daily business while providing an acceptable level of protection against risks.

Responding to Security Incidents

Earlier in this chapter it was stated that a security policy should address the general steps to be followed when an intrusion is detected, and what security response team members should be notified.

The Incident Handling and Escalation Procedures section of a security policy spells out what happens when an alarm goes off. It also covers less dramatic situations that can, nevertheless, have serious implications, such as the steps the organization takes to respond when an employee loses a password, or when an employee's termination proceedings do not go smoothly.

Escalation Procedures

Escalation procedures describe how the organization increases its state of readiness when a threat arises or a security incident occurs. Levels of escalation within an organization are frequently divided into three levels:

- Level One incidents are the least severe and must typically be managed within one working day from when they occur.
- Level Two incidents are of moderate seriousness. They should be managed the same day the event takes place—ideally, within four hours.
- Level Three incidents are the most serious; they must be handled immediately.

Escalation procedures also spell out the staff members who will handle each level of incident. A larger organization may have a full-fledged department whose members are assigned only to maintaining security, and with titles such as Security Analyst, Security Architect, and Chief Security Officer. Many organizations assign technical staff to such roles, which have to be performed in addition to their other responsibilities. In either case, the Escalation Procedures part of the Security Policy will spell out who needs to respond in statements like the following:

- A Level One incident requires only that the on-duty Security Analyst be notified.
- A Level Two incident must be escalated to the Security Architect.
- A Level Three incident requires that the Chief Security Officer be notified.

In addition, Level Two or Level Three incidents might require the participation of outside security groups such as CIAC or CERT. Such highly regarded organizations keep records of serious security attacks; if your organization is hit by a new virus or an unusually strong Denial of Service attack, they should let others on the Internet be aware of it.

Security Incidents

To determine how incidents should be escalated, the Security Incidents part of the security policy should clearly define the types of incidents to watch out for and what level of escalation each one represents. Following are some examples.

Burglary or Other Illegal Building Access (Level Two Incident) — If an unauthorized individual is discovered on the premises, notify the police. The CSO should also be notified as soon as possible, as well as the Security Analyst on duty. The Security Analyst and/or the CSO will escort the individual outside the building. The Security Analyst will prepare an incident report.

Property Loss or Theft (Level Two or Level Three Incident) —If company property has been stolen, the Human Resources (HR) director should be notified. The HR director will escalate the incident to the CSO. If a company server has been lost, the CSO should be notified within 12 hours. If a company workstation has been lost, notify the on-duty SA within 24 hours.

Loss of Password (Level One Incident) —The on-duty SA should be notified within 24 hours. The on-duty SA should determine whether a change of password is necessary.

Updating the Security Policy

Based on the security incidents that are reported as a result of your ongoing security monitoring, and based on any new risks your company faces, you should update the security policy. Any changes to the policy should then be broadcast to the entire staff, either by e-mail or by posting the changes on the company's Web site or Intranet.

The ultimate goal of changing the security policy is to change individuals' habits so that they behave more responsibly. Ultimately, the security policy should result in actual physical changes to the organization's security configuration. A call for redundant systems in the security policy may result in the major expenditure of a new firewall and/or server to serve as a "failover" device, for instance. The need to review security logs on a daily basis, as prescribed in a security policy, may cause the company to invest in log file analysis software to make the jobs of IT professionals easier. Better protection will result in fewer intrusions and disputes, which ultimately enables the company to focus on its primary mission.

CHAPTER SUMMARY

- Risk analysis plays a central role in the formulation of one of the most essential (and yet most overlooked) elements in an organization's overall network defense configuration: a security policy. Risks need to be calculated and security policies amended on an ongoing basis as a network configuration evolves.
- Risk analysis covers a company's computer hardware, software and informational assets. It lists the threats those assets face, and the probability that those threats will actually occur. Vulnerabilities present in the system are described, as well as the consequences of a threat actually taking place. Your first task is to assess the level of risk faced by your network and its users. Risk analysis should be performed both before and after a security policy is created. The ultimate goal is not to reduce the risks to zero (which isn't possible), but to manage the risk at reasonable levels on an ongoing basis.
- After you have assessed the level of risk faced by the assets in your organization, you need to determine countermeasures that will minimize risk. You decide how to secure the physical computing assets in your company, the logical assets (your computer software, e-mail messages, and log file records), the data held in your databases, your application software, and the personal assets of those who work in the organization. You then come up with a plan for conducting risk analysis on a routine basis, and a plan for handling security incidents. You also assess the threats to your network such as hacker attacks, power outages, and environmental disasters. Next, you determine the probability that those threats might be realized, and the safeguards and countermeasures that can reduce the chances that they will occur. First, though, you use the data you have assembled to perform a risk analysis, using an approach such as Survivable Network Analysis (SNA) or Threat and Risk Assessment (TRA). A risk analysis describes the level of risk faced by each asset in the organization, as well as the economic impact should it be lost or damaged.
- Once you have determined the level of risk faced by your network assets, you need to develop safeguards that can manage that risk. You determine ways to secure your hardware assets, such as environmental controls, locks, or burglar alarms. The data contained on laptop computers can be protected through passwords and through file encryption. Logical assets such as word processing or other documents can be protected by backups and by isolation from the Internet. Corporate information can be protected by effective use of passwords. The countermeasures you describe will form the bases of your security policy. In addition, risk analysis includes some provision for regular updates. It also includes recommendations of measures to be taken in case security incidents occur.
- An effective network security policy should provide management with a way to express to all employees the overall security stance of the organization, and protects management in case of legal disputes. A good security policy is based on risk assessment, covers acceptable use of system resources, sets priorities for the most critical resources that need to be protected, and specifies the use of network resources by administrators and security staff as well.
- The actual formulation of a security policy may not be a single long document, but is often comprised of multiple specific policies. There are six steps to follow to create a

policy: the formulation of a security policy group; the determination of the overall security approach; the identification of assets to protect; the specification of auditing procedures; the listing of security risks and acceptable use, and the writing of specific policies themselves such as User Account, Password Protection, and Internet Use policies. Finally, you learned that security policies should be regularly updated as intrusion attempts or actual intrusions occur, and to account for personnel changes and acquisition of new equipment.

Key Terms

assets — The hardware, software, and informational resources you need to protect through the development and implementation of a comprehensive security policy.

auditing — The process of keeping records of the activities of computers on the network; these include who is connecting to a computer, what resources are being requested, and whether access was granted or blocked.

data warehouses — The storehouses of valuable customer, job-related, and personnel information within a company.

escalation procedure — A set of roles, responsibilities, and measures taken in response to a security incident.

fault tolerance — The ability of an object or system to continue operations despite a fault in its makeup or environment.

logical assets — The word processing, spreadsheet, Web page, and other documents contained on your network computers.

Monte Carlo simulation — An analytical method meant to simulate a real-life system by randomly generating values for variables.

network assets — The routers, cables, bastion hosts, servers, and firewall hardware and software that enable those within your organization to communicate with one another and other computers on the Internet.

redundancy — Back up systems that ensure that databases and other stores of information remain accessible if the primary systems go offline.

risk — The possibility of incurring damage or loss.

risk analysis — The study of how great the possibility of damage or loss is in a particular situation, environment, or pertaining to an individual object or set of objects.

Risk management — The process of identifying, choosing, and setting up of countermeasures justified by the risks you identify.

role-based authentication — A type of authentication that gives users limited access based on what role they play in the company and what applications they need to use.

safeguards — Measures you can take to reduce threats such as installing firewalls and intrusion detection systems, locking doors, and using passwords and/or encryption.

Security Incident Response Team (SIRT) — A group of staff people designated to take countermeasures when an incident is reported.

security policy — A statement that spells out exactly what defenses will be configured to block unauthorized access, what constitutes acceptable use of network resources, how the organization will respond to attacks, and how employees should safely handle the organization's resources in order to discourage loss of data or damage to files.

Security User Awareness program — A program in which employees are formally instructed about the organization's security strategy.

softspot component — A network component that is both essential and at risk of being compromised.

survivability — The ability to continue functioning in the presence of attacks or disasters.

Survivability wrappers — Message filters applied at the OS interface level through authentication or other means.

Survivable Network Analysis (SNA) — A security process that starts with the assumption that a computer system will be attacked and follows a set of steps to build a system that can survive such an attack.

Threat and Risk Assessment (TRA) — An approach to risk analysis that starts from the standpoint of the threats and accounts for risks that confront an organization's assets, and the consequences of those threats and risks should they occur.

threats — Events and conditions that have not yet occurred but that can potentially occur, the presence of which increases risk.

two-factor authentication — A type of authentication that combines something the owner possesses (a card or token) with something the owner knows (a password or PIN).

Vulnerabilities — Situations or conditions that increase threat and that, in turn, increase risk.

worst-case scenarios — Descriptions of the worst consequences that befall an organization if a threat is realized.

Review Questions

1. Which of the following should precede the formulation of a security policy? (Choose all that apply.)

   a. intrusion handling plan

   b. risk analysis

   c. security review

   d. list of assets

2. Personnel records fit into which category of asset?

   a. personal assets

   b. application software

   c. data

   d. physical assets

3. IT professionals need to overcome ___________ to develop a security policy. (Choose all that apply.)

   a. budget constraints

   b. conflicting security needs

   c. firewalls' poorly configured default security policies

   d. employees who regard security policies as unimportant

4. Survivable Network Analysis begins with what assumption?

   a. that you have laid the groundwork for a risk analysis

   b. that your network will be attacked

   c. that the probability of threats is continually increasing

   d. that an effective security policy can reduce risk to zero

5. Survivable Network Analysis looks for ___________ in a network.

   a. failure points

   b. bottlenecks

   c. collisions of data

   d. software incompatibilities

6. What is an escalation policy? (Choose all that apply.)

   a. It describes how network security can be improved in stages.

   b. It describes how a virus can multiply and affect more and more assets.

   c. It describes different levels of response based on incident severity.

   d. It describes different staff people who need to be involved in the response.

7. What can occur if a security policy is so rigidly formulated that too little trust is placed in individual network users? (Choose all that apply.)

   a Network resources can be compromised.

   b Productivity may be reduced.

   c Staff people might quit and go to other companies.

   d Staff people will find ways to circumvent your security systems.

8. Name three factors that can increase the cost of replacing a piece of hardware that has been damaged or stolen above and beyond the actual sticker price.

9. List the following four steps involved in a Survivable Network Analysis (SNA) in the order in which they should occur:

   a. calculation of risk

   b. initial meetings

   c. evaluation of vulnerability

   d. asset valuation

10. The hardware and software you need to protect can be more easily valued by following what approach?

    a. getting the latest prices online

    b. keeping records of purchase costs

    c. using your experience and expertise

    d. interviewing support personnel

11. The cornerstone of many security policies is the ___________.

    a. incident handling policy

    b. list of assets

    c. acceptable use policy

    d. remote access policy

12. If an organization does not have a full-fledged security staff on duty, what should it do?

    a. Hire a group such as CIAC or CERT.

    b. Designate IT staff to hold concurrent security positions.

    c. Designate managers to fulfill security functions.

    d. A stand-alone security staff is not needed.

13. How do security policies help management? (Choose all that apply.)
    a. They cover the management in case of disputes.
    b. They prevent employees from misusing company resources.
    c. They state the company's most important security priorities.
    d. They circumvent the need to hire security professionals.

14. When should an organization conduct a new round of risk analysis?
    a. once every six months
    b. once every three months
    c. as frequently as possible
    d. when equipment or staff change significantly

15. Which of the following policies would best contain this statement: "Network Administrators are the only staff people authorized to have root or domain administrator status"?
    a. User Account policy
    b. Acceptable Use policy
    c. Privileged Access policy
    d. Internet Usage policy

16. What is the primary difference between an initial security policy and an ongoing one?

17. A risk analysis report should call attention to ____________.
    a. all of the identified risks
    b. the most urgent risks
    c. the newest risks
    d. the risks that are easiest to manage

18. What fact may not be obvious from looking at a risk analysis report? (Choose all that apply.)
    a. what labels like "Personal Assets" mean
    b. the overall goals of the report
    c. the meaning of terms such as "users"
    d. why something is considered high risk

19. Why is an Acceptable Use Policy usually listed first in a Security Policy? (Choose all that apply.)
    a. It can generate controversy.
    b. It affects most employees.
    c. It can get employees in trouble.
    d. It is the basis for subsequent policies.

20. Why is it helpful to speak in terms of "user accounts" rather than "full-time employees" in a security policy?
    a. User accounts apply to all employees.
    b. User accounts include freelancers and partners.
    c. User accounts cover password usage.
    d. User accounts are the most important aspect of network security.

HANDS-ON PROJECTS

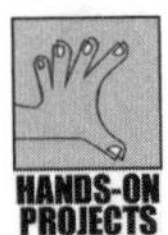

Project 3-1: Calculating Computer Loss

Part of risk analysis is estimating the value of lost data and the computers that store your data. Kensington, a company that manufacturers PC security cables, provides an online Return on Investment (ROI) calculator to calculate PC hardware losses. The calculator is intended to help customers justify the purchases of Kensington's own brand of security cables, but you can enter values for the computer equipment in your own lab as well as an estimate of the data on them. If you aren't in your computer lab or don't know about all the equipment in it, assume you are in a lab with 10 PCs, two printers, one network hub, and one removable disk drive. Also assume that each PC has a replacement value of $1500, and is equipped with an average of $1000 worth of software. Also assume that the data contained on each PC is valued at $500.

1. Double-click the **Internet Explorer** icon on your desktop.
2. Enter the address for the Kensington MicroSaver home page (**http://www.microsaver.com**), then press **Enter**.
3. When the home page appears, click **MicroSaver ROI calculator** on the right side of the page.
4. In the new browser window that pops up, click **Begin Calculator**.
5. On the first page, enter **10** for Your Notebook Population (or enter the actual number of PCs in your lab).

6. In the Your Average Annual Notebook Loss box, the value **1** is pre-entered. Leave the other values and click the right-pointing arrow at the bottom of the page to move to the next page.
7. In the Your Costs Per Lost Unit page, enter the values for the assumption given above. Leave the default values for Procurement and Deployment of a New Notebook, Police and Insurance Claims, and lost productivity pre-entered. What value is given at the bottom of the page as the Average Cost of Losing One Notebook? Note the answer in your lab notebook or in a word processing document. Since you have estimated that you would only lose one PC, this is your total annual expected computer loss. Click the **Close** box at the top of the screen to close the calculator, or click the left arrow to return to the first page of the calculator to do another calculation.

Project 3-2: Rewriting an Existing Security Policy

Security policies can and should be revised in order to address security breaches or new threats that arise. In this project, you evaluate an incident involving theft of proprietary information and some obvious deficiencies that are associated with it. Then you will rewrite a security policy in such a way that it prevents such incidents from occurring in the future.

Consider the following situation: A local branch office of a major national stock brokerage had no policy requiring the termination of user-ID and password privileges after an employee left. A senior trader left the brokerage and was immediately hired by a competing brokerage. Shortly thereafter, the first brokerage lost two clients who said they were moving to a competing firm and whose personal data files mysteriously disappeared from the company's databases. In addition, a year-end recommendations report that the employee had been preparing was released two weeks earlier by the same competing firm that the two clients had moved to. An investigation of the company's access logs revealed that the employee records file had been accessed by someone outside the company. But the job records did not reveal whether the report had been stolen because they had not been set up to record object accesses in a log.

The existing security policy states the following:

"On termination, employees shall surrender any laptops, disks, or computer manuals they have in their possession. They are no longer authorized to access the network, and they shall not take any hardware or software when they leave the office."

1. Rewrite the existing security policy so that it better handles security after employees are terminated.
2. Add a security policy clause that covers access of company records.
3. Add a security policy clause that will help to track when files are accessed.

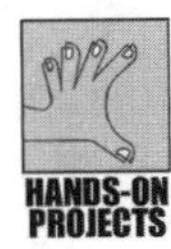

Project 3-3: Calculating Replacement Costs

Risk analysis can be a subjective practice when it's done by intuition, hunches, or "gut feelings." A software tool can help bring some consistency to the process. In this project you will download a trial version of a risk analysis tool for Windows called Project Risk Analysis (PRA) by Katmar Software. You'll then enter the characteristics of network resources in your own school's lab. You will then calculate the contingency funds needed to replace your lab equipment if a disaster struck. For this project, you'll need a computer running Windows 2000 or XP, as well as a file archive program such as WinZip. Use the same assumptions for this project that you used in Project 3-1: assume you are trying to estimate the cost associated with replacing the hardware and software in a computer lab with ten machines worth $1500 each, and so on.

1. Double-click the **Internet Explorer** icon on your desktop.
2. Enter the URL for the Project Risk Analysis and Contingency Analysis page (**http://www.katmarsoftware.com/pra.htm**), and then press **Enter**.
3. Read the description of the program as presented on this page, and then click the link **Download Now!**.
4. When you are prompted to either open or save the file **projrisk.zip**, click **Save** and save it to a directory on your file system.
5. When the file download is complete, click **Close** in the Download Complete dialog box. Then double-click the file to open it with WinZip. Extract the files to the same directory where you located the Zip file you downloaded.
6. Double-click the file **ProjRisk_Setup.exe** and follow the steps given in the setup program to install it on your computer.
7. Double-click the file **ProjRisk.exe** to start up the program. The first time you run the program, a Thank You for Installing PRA screen appears stating the terms under which the program can be run (it runs 30 times as an evaluation). Click **OK**, then **OK** when a second Shareware Reminder program appears.
8. Click **Add**. The Add a Record at the End dialog box opens. In the Description box, type **Computers**.
9. Under Distribution, click **Normal**.
10. In the Likely Cost box, type **15000** (don't use commas).
11. In the Low Cost box, type **10000**.
12. Click **OK**. The Add a Record at the End dialog box closes and you return to the main Project Risk Analysis window, where your estimate is entered in the first column.
13. Repeat Steps 8 through 12 for Software (likely cost 5000, low cost 3500), Printers (likely cost 500, low cost 400), hubs (likely cost 150, low cost 100), cables (likely cost 100, low cost 75), Monitors (likely cost 5000, low cost 4000).

14. Click **Analyze**. The Overall Cost Distribution graph appears. What are the Lowest Cost, Highest Cost, and Mean Cost figures as displayed on the Overall Cost Distribution screen? Record the answers in a lab notebook or word processing document.
15. Click **Statistics**. What is the Mean cost as listed in the Simulation Statistics Report dialog box? Record this answer as well.
16. Click the **Close** box at the top right-hand corner of the Simulation Results dialog box to close it, then click **Close** to close Project Risk Analysis and return to the Windows desktop.

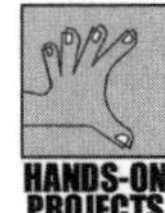

Project 3-4: Improving a Flawed Risk Analysis

One way to learn how to perform a task is to analyze an example of the task that is flawed and correct it. In this project you read a risk analysis and, applying some of the principles you have learned in this chapter, make the analysis stronger and more specific.

1. Analyze the following excerpts from a risk analysis:

   "The following risk analysis report was prepared in early 2004 for the Network Communications Group, a company of about 250 employees located in Kansas City, Missouri. The report examines various types of risks that are facing the company at this time and suggests better protections for them..."

   "Physical Location: The building is solidly built and located in a safe area on the banks of the Missouri River. Air conditioning systems should be well maintained due to excessive heat in summer."

   "Computers: The company's computer hardware is protected by computer locks; the servers are in a protected room that can be locked at night."

   "Software: We noticed that the company has anti-virus software installed on its e-mail server but not on individual workstations; we recommend that each user should have anti-virus software installed or substantial damage would result..."

2. List at least one way in which the introductory paragraph could be improved by making it more specific.
3. Describe some critical information that is missing from the Physical Location paragraph of the risk analysis.
4. How can the "Computers" paragraph be strengthened to be more direct about locking physical assets?
5. The risks from virus attacks mentioned in the "Software" paragraph could be more specific and presented in a more thorough way. Suggest how you would do this.

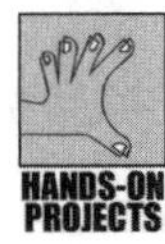

Project 3-5: Improving a Weak Security Policy

The following very brief and quickly prepared security policy came about as a result of the risk analysis described in the previous project. (Again, these are excerpts from the security policy introduction and Acceptable Use Agreement and not the entire document.) The security policy could be made stronger in a number of different ways. Examine it and suggest how you would improve the policy.

"Network Communications group has just designed and is in the process of manufacturing a new wireless hub that will enable up to 12 wireless devices to share information. The new wireless device has capabilities that are far above that which is currently on the market. This document establishes acceptable computer usage and network safety guidelines for Network Communication employees. The guidelines are intended to protect the company from loss of data, and customers from having unauthorized individuals access their proprietary information."

"All employees of Network Communications are expected to follow the guidelines as outlined in the Acceptable Use section of this document. Employers at Network Communications acknowledge that, in the course of performing their jobs, Network Communications Security staff require special access to company systems and resources. The Network Administration has responsibility for the overall management of network resources."

The following are excerpts from the "Acceptable Use Statement" section of the security policy.

"This section covers the use of Network Communications' networks, computers, and computing resources. Network, computer, and computing resources are defined as physical personal computers, servers, routers, switches, and network cables. Also included in this definition are floppy disks, CD-ROM disks and disk drives, DVD-ROM drives, and tape backup systems. All those considered "users" of the network are expected to conduct themselves in a respectful and legal manner..."

"Only authorized user accounts may access Network Communications resources. Unauthorized use may constitute grounds for civil or criminal prosecution."

"Users are responsible for the storage of their personal data on their own workstations. In addition, they shall not make copies of any software on the system."

"Users shall maintain themselves in a courteous and respectful manner to other users when they are using e-mail or company newsgroups."

1. Examine the introduction to the security policy, and name one aspect pertaining to employees that could be added.
2. Name a term that is used more than once in this excerpt and that should be defined.
3. Identify a statement pertaining to software usage that is too restrictive and that should more clearly state acceptable use of that software.
4. Describe how the statement about user behavior in the final excerpt can be made more specific and stronger as a result.

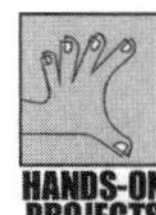

Project 3-6: Performing a Risk Analysis

Consider the following scenario: A business network has a firewall and DMZ installed as well as stateful packet filters. However, 10 percent of the individuals who access the network work off-site. On top of that, the office is located in an urban area that is plagued by high crime. This yields the threat ratings in Table 3-9.

Table 3-9 Threat ratings

Asset	Threat	Threat Level	Probability	Consequences
Hardware	Theft	High	High	Serious
Databases	Hacker attack	Medium	Medium	Significant (Medium)
Operating system software	Virus	High	High	Significant (High)

1. Calculate the risk for each of these assets.
2. Present the assets in rank order from highest to lowest risk.

Case Projects

Case Project 3-1: Defining Network Risk Analysis

You tell managers at a staff meeting that the company should perform an annual risk analysis of the company's IT resources. The managers respond that they are familiar with risk analysis that is performed in association with insurance coverage and health concerns. They ask you to explain what risk analysis means in regard to computer resources and security. You are asked to explain this concept "quickly—in one or two sentences." What would you say to them?

Case Project 3-2: Restricting Employee Access

The manager of data processing at ABC Stocks took a job with a competing stock brokerage firm. Because his former employer had nobody who could do the job that he did, ABC kept the individual on as a contractor. On a part-time basis, the individual would perform systems management tasks. To do these tasks he needed full privileges on the former employer's network. One day the manager at ABC learned that the data processing employee's new employer was opposing them in a high-visibility lawsuit. Could the former data processing manager gain access to the shared legal strategy files for this case on the network? The answer is yes, but the question for you is, what kinds of policies could be put in place to prevent such a situation?

Case Project 3-3: Creating Acceptable Use Policies

A construction company computer technician compiled a list of inappropriate jokes. Proud of his list, he broadcast this list on the Internet, adding his electronic mail address to the end, encouraging the recipients to send in any new ones. Management was able to have the posting deleted from several discussion groups, but was not able to control copies that had been made. Around the same time, the same technician had printed a copy of his list, and when distracted by something else, had left it in the hopper of a departmental printer. Women in the department objected that they had been subjected to inappropriate jokes via e-mail that they didn't want to hear. They pointed to the Internet postings and the printer output as examples. Two security policies would have prevented this situation: what are they?

Case Project 3-4: Mapping Risk Analysis to a Security Policy

Six months after a security policy has been formulated and put into place, your company decides to do a risk analysis. The data in Table 3-10 presents some of their findings. Suggest ways in which you would modify the security policy to cover the new threats.

Table 3-10 Modifying a security policy

Asset	Threat	Probability	Consequences	Risk Assessment	Change
Web server	High	Medium	Serious	Critical	Was medium; Web site went online during this period
Office workstations	Low	Low	Significant	Medium	Unchanged
Customer data	Medium	High	Damaging	High	Was medium; two employees in customer service were laid off and expressed anger
Job records	High	High	Serious	Critical	Was medium; one laptop was lost or stolen while V-P of marketing was in airport

CHAPTER

4

CHOOSING AND DESIGNING FIREWALLS

After reading this chapter and completing the exercises, you will be able to:

- List the requirements for and steps involved in setting up a bastion host
- Design common firewall configurations
- Choose the right firewall product for your organization's needs
- Establish a set of application rules and restrictions for a firewall

When you travel by air, you have to pass through a variety of security checkpoints. First, your bags are checked; then you go through a security checkpoint; then when you board the plane your tickets are checked and taken. The purpose of all this human "filtering" is to keep individuals who should not be on the plane from boarding. Your identity is verified by examination of the papers you are carrying; you are also checked for what you are carrying along with you personally.

In the same way, security devices placed at the perimeter of a computer network filter out packets of digital information. The arrangement of security devices is, together, called a firewall or firewall perimeter; in addition, at least one of the devices in the arrangement is a program or hardware device that is itself called a firewall. When you begin to design network defenses, one of the first decisions you have to make is what components you need to obtain to achieve your security goals, and how best to arrange those components.

This chapter discusses how to set up a firewall perimeter and determine which components you need. First, you learn how to secure the bastion host, which is the computer and operating system that hosts your firewall or intrusion detection software. Then, you learn about different ways in which firewalls can be arranged with routers or other firewalls. Next, the types of firewall hardware and software from which to choose are explained. Finally, this chapter covers what you need to get the firewall to function the way you want.

Choosing a Bastion Host

A firewall (or an intrusion detection system, proxy server, or other type of security software) doesn't operate on its own. You install it on a computer that runs on an operating system platform. Often, the computer also functions as a **server**, providing Web pages, e-mail, or other services to individuals both inside and outside the network being protected. Such a computer needs to be as secure as possible because of the importance of the security software on it, and its position on the perimeter of the network.

To protect the security software as well as the network, the computer needs to be turned into a **bastion host**, which sits on the perimeter of a network and that has been specially protected through operating system patches, authentication, and encryption. A computer that hosts a firewall and that is riddled with operating system vulnerabilities will be ineffective, and will also provide hackers with a way to compromise the entire network. They might even be able to disable the firewall software because, for instance, they are able to gain administrative privileges on the server, or they are able to crack passwords on the server.

This section of the chapter describes how to choose and configure a computer so that it serves as a bastion host that can safely host firewall or other security software: how to choose the machine; how to limit its functionality so that it discourages hackers; and how to handle backups and auditing.

General Requirements

In general, a bastion host should be a computer that runs an operating system (OS) that can be made secure. The OS should be one that is already secure, or that has been in release long enough that patches are available for download to plug potential security holes.

When the OS is made as secure as possible, the computer is said to be **hardened**, or made more secure than any others on the network by eliminating all unnecessary software, closing potential openings, and protecting the information on it with encryption and authentication.

In general, the steps involved in creating a bastion host are:

1. Select a machine with sufficient memory and processor speed.
2. Choose and install the operating system.
3. Determine where the host will fit in the network configuration, and put it in a safe and controlled physical environment.
4. Enable the host to defend itself.
5. Install the services you want to provide, or modify existing services.
6. Remove services and accounts that aren't needed.
7. Back up the system and all data on it, including log files.

8. Run a security audit.
9. Connect the machine to the network.

The following sections address the most important of these steps. The steps discussed were selected because they pertain directly to configuring a bastion host.

Selecting the Host Machine

You don't need to select the latest and greatest hardware and software combination that has just come out on the market to configure a bastion host. Rather, you should choose a combination of machine type and software that you are familiar with and can work on easily if you need to. You don't want to be repairing or rebuilding a machine under pressure and learning to operate it at the same time.

In an ideal situation, you'll be able to designate one host for each service you want to provide to the public: one FTP server/bastion host, one Web server/bastion host, one SMTP server/bastion host, and so on. However, it can be prohibitively expensive to purchase and install so much hardware. You may be forced by contingencies to combine two or more services on one bastion host. Here, a comprehensive risk analysis of the services and hardware you need to protect the most can be helpful; see Chapter 3 for more about risk analysis.

The following sections discuss essential components of a secure bastion host: the operating system; the memory and processor speed; and its location on the network.

Operating System

Bastion hosts don't need to contain the latest and most expensive processor/memory combinations. Rather, the most important requirements for a bastion host are your own level of comfort with the system, as well as its inherent security and reliability. Your managers aren't going to necessarily concern themselves with what operating system you install: their priority is that the machine protects the internal network and that you are able to get it up and running and maintain it smoothly.

Running a close second is the security level of the system itself. Whatever system you decide, be sure to pick a version of that system that is stable and secure. To ensure the security of the operating system, check the operating system's development Web site (as shown in the following list) for a list of patches, and update any that are available:

- The Windows XP Professional site (*www.microsoft.com/windowsxp/pro/default.asp*)
- The Red Hat Linux Web site (*www.redhat.com*)
- The Linux Home Page (*www.linux.org*)
- The FreeBSD Project (*www.freebsd.org*)

- The SANS Institute's list of Top Twenty Most Critical Internet Security Vulnerabilities, which includes subsections on UNIX and Windows vulnerabilities (*www.sans.org/top20.htm*)
- The U.S. Department of Energy's Computer Incident Advisory Capability (CIAC) site (*www.ciac.org/ciac*), which lists newly discovered security advisories right on its home page

Along with making sure your bastion host's operating system has the latest patches installed, also make sure your system of choice can reliably provide the services you want to make available on the public DMZ. It's a good idea to install a system patch that guards against an application that can be subject to **buffer overflow** : a situation that can result from a buffer overflow attack. In a buffer overflow, a program or process attempts to store more data than can be held in a temporary disk storage area called a buffer. In a buffer overflow attack, a computer is flooded with more information than it can handle, and some of it may contain instructions that could damage files on the computer or disclose information that is normally protected—or give the hacker root access to the system.

Memory and Processor Speed

Memory is always important when operating a server, but because the bastion host may be providing only a single service on the network, you aren't likely to need multi-gigabytes worth of RAM.

You will, on the other hand, need many gigabytes of hard disk storage space because you'll be accumulating vast quantities of **log files** —records detailing who accessed resources on the server and when the access attempts occurred. You'll need to review and analyze this information either manually or by making use of log file analysis software.

Don't forget that, in addition to the services you provide on the bastion host, you'll probably need to operate a program that manages log files. Such a program maintains, **rotates** (in other words, moves the current log file to a storage area and opens a new log file), and clears outdated log files that are accumulated by the firewall or intrusion detection system on the host.

Location on the Network

Bastion hosts are typically located outside the internal network being protected. They are frequently combined with packet filtering devices on either side, as shown in Figure 4-1.

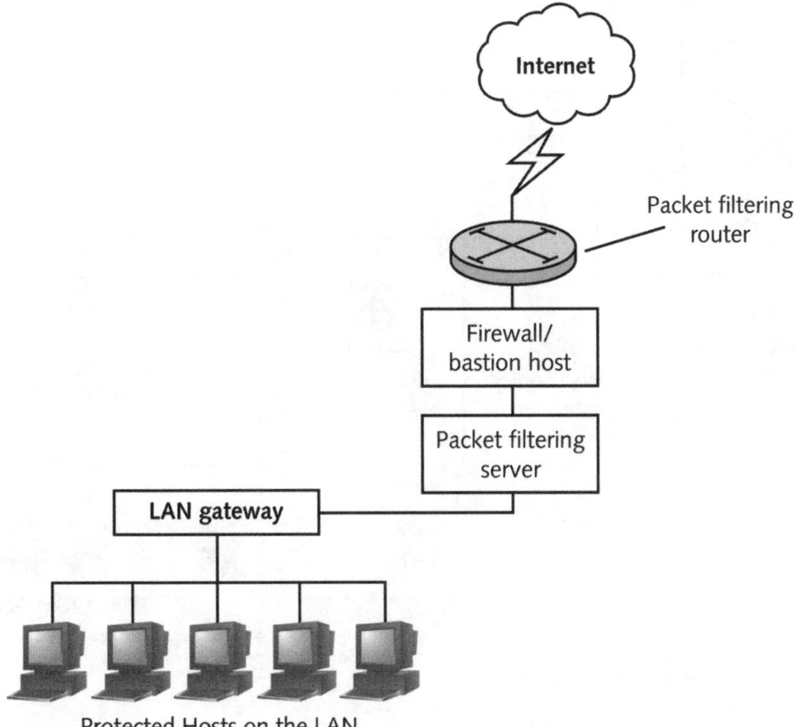

Figure 4-1 Bastion hosts are often combined with packet routers

Combining a bastion host with packet-filtering devices (such as routers and firewall appliances) on either side further protects the bastion host from attack: the router can filter out some of the tampered-with packets from reaching the bastion host in the first place. The packet-filtering server can filter out any suspicious packets that are coming from *inside* the internal network as a result of Trojan horses or viruses that may have circumvented existing network defenses on previous occasions.

More often, multiple bastion hosts are set up in the DMZ, where each machine provides a single service, such as Web services, to the public (see Figure 4-2).

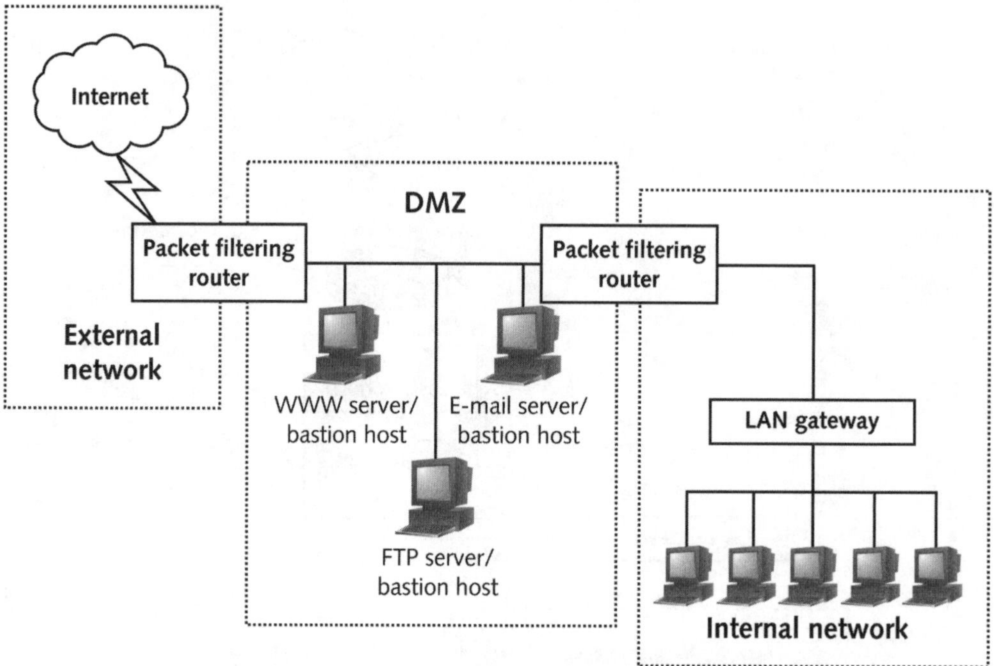

Figure 4-2 Bastion hosts in the DMZ

Deciding What the Bastion Host Will (and Will Not) Do

A bastion host can be any server that hosts a Web server, e-mail server, FTP server, or other network service. However, the more services that are offered on the bastion host, the greater the chance that a security vulnerability will occur on one of the services installed on the system.

One of the ways in which a bastion host is hardened, then, is by removing all unnecessary software, services, and user accounts from it. The simpler your bastion host is, the easier it is to secure. In addition, any service the bastion host offers could have software bugs or configuration errors in it, and any bugs or errors may lead to security problems. Only the minimal number of open ports should be provided on the network, and the bastion host then presents fewer security open ports that intruders can exploit.

Selecting Services to Be Provided

A bare bones configuration reduces the chances of attack and has the extra benefit of boosting efficiency. By closing off unneeded user accounts and ports, and by disabling services you don't plan to use, you give an attacker far fewer ways to gain access to the system.

Perhaps the most important services you should disable are those that enable the host to do routing or IP forwarding—unless, of course, the host is intended to function as a router. Disabling IP forwarding makes it more difficult for hackers to communicate with internal computers on your LAN.

When you are stopping or removing services, you should not disable any **dependency services** —services that the system needs to function correctly. In addition, it's advisable to stop services one at a time. You should also get in the habit of documenting every single change you make, and recording how the system reacts, so that you have a record to reference in case you're called upon to troubleshoot that same system at a later date.

A Note about Honeypots

A **honeypot** is a computer that is placed on the perimeter of the network to attract hackers. A honeypot server may or may not be a bastion host. Such a computer is equipped with software and possibly data files that look like they are used by the company but are not, in reality, used at all. A honeypot may also be purposely configured with some security holes so that it looks like it is vulnerable to known attacks. The goal of the honeypot is to attract attackers so that they stay away from actual servers on a network. A honeypot might be located between the bastion host and the internal network; if a hacker has managed to get past your external packet filter and enter your DMZ and is scanning for open ports, the honeypot could provide a place for the hacker to get "stuck" (in other words, diverted from your "real" files by being misdirected to some files that are of no value). See Figure 4-3.

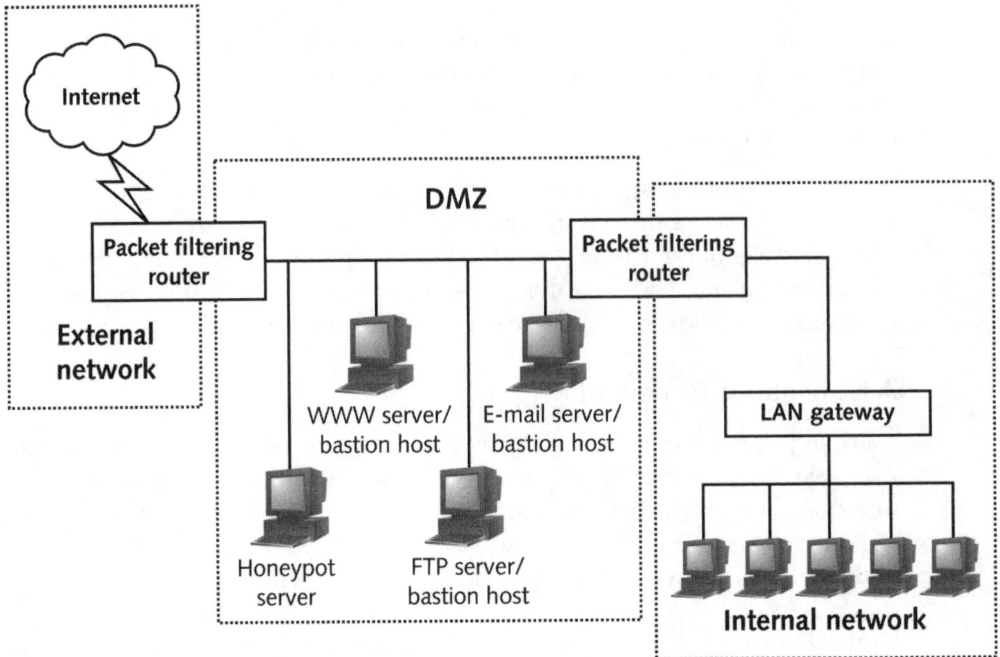

Figure 4-3 A honeypot located in the DMZ

Network security experts are divided over honeypots. Some think they have value; some think they are outdated and not worth implementing; some think they are unnecessary and even potentially dangerous if they contain actual information about your company and its individual hosts. Objections are sometimes raised regarding entrapment—whether, by overtly making an attempt to track a hacker, you would even then have legal grounds to actually prosecute the individual. In the author's opinion, honeypots are worth mentioning not only because you are likely to be asked about them in certification tests, but also because they are still discussed as options in a perimeter security configuration.

Another goal of a honeypot is logging. Because you have some expectation that the honeypot will be attacked by hackers who can't tell the difference between it and a legitimate target, you can configure the server to log every access carefully to identify who is trying to attack your network. A honeypot can also give you some indication of how hackers would try to attack your real network computers if they got the chance. By reviewing what operating system flaws, open ports, or other vulnerabilities are exploited on the honeypot, you can then take steps to close down such vulnerabilities on other machines.

Disabling User Accounts

As with most operating systems and application software, default accounts may be created during installation. Accordingly, you should delete all user accounts from the bastion host. They aren't needed, because individual users should not be able to connect to the host from their workstation. Each user account on the bastion host increases the chances of a security breach.

You should also rename the Administrator account as another way to thwart hackers. Many hackers are able to gain access to computers through Administrator accounts that use the default account name "Administrator" and that are never assigned a password. Renaming such accounts and using passwords that contain at least six or eight alphanumeric characters can prevent these obvious attacks.

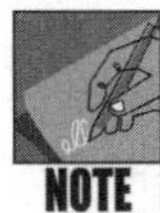

It's a good idea to assume that the bastion host will be compromised in some way and then proactively secure it. The bastion host is the machine most likely to be attacked because of its availability to external Internet users.

Handling Backups and Auditing

Setting up a bastion host requires you to be systematic and thorough to a higher degree than you may be used to: backups, detailed record-keeping, and auditing are essential steps to hardening a computer.

The bastion hosts generate log files and other data (such as alert messages). You need to copy this information to other computers inside your network on a regular basis. When you do perform such record keeping, keep in mind that the information will go through some of the layers of network defense that you have already implemented. Because of its high security configuration, your bastion host will likely be placed in a particularly vulnerable location on the DMZ and outside the internal LAN. Log files and system data, which needs to be backed up regularly, should go through the firewall that protects the internal LAN to screen it for viruses and other vulnerabilities, such as mangled packets. (Recall that mangled packets can enable hackers to access computers on the internal LAN by inserting falsified information into those packets.)

To avoid using network resources, be sure to get machines intended to function as bastion hosts that have CD-RW drives, removable disk drives, or tape drives so that you can make backups.

FIREWALL CONFIGURATIONS

As you learned in Chapter 1, a firewall is hardware or software that can be configured to block unauthorized access to a network. "Firewall" is frequently viewed as a catchall term that represents any device that can block hackers or viruses. Managers commonly assign their network administrators to "get a firewall and put it on the network so we have better security." This implies that the firewall is a single device and that it can single-handedly keep attackers off a network, both of which are incorrect assumptions. You will learn why these are incorrect assumptions as you progress through this section of the chapter.

This section explains what firewalls are and are not, so that you have a clearer idea of what they do. There are different ways in which firewalls can be deployed on a network: as part of a screening router, a dual-homed host, a screened host, a screened subnet DMZ, multiple DMZ, multiple firewall, or reverse firewall setup.

What Firewalls Are

First, you need to realize that the term "firewall" doesn't necessarily refer to a single router, computer, VPN gateway, or software program. Some firewalls are software programs. The earliest firewalls were, in fact, packet filters; a single packet-filtering router placed at the perimeter of a network can accurately function as a firewall for the network, though a rather weak one. Some firewall programs are designed for general consumer use, such as Norton Personal Firewall, ZoneAlarm, or Sygate Personal Firewall. These have relatively simple interfaces that give non-technical users a minimal set of decisions to make to configure the program, as shown in Figure 4-4.

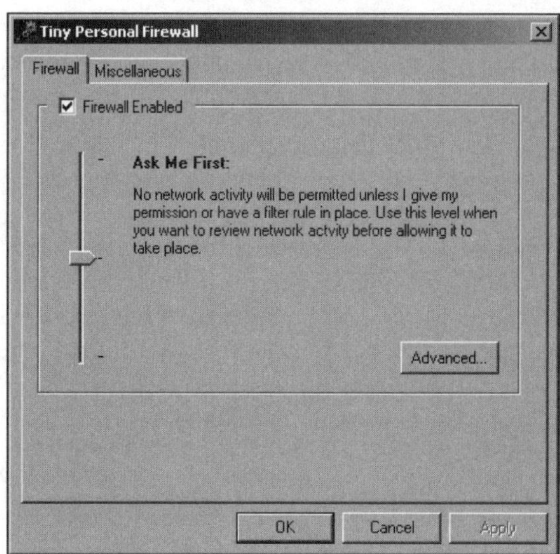

Figure 4-4 Tiny Personal Firewall, a general consumer firewall, has a simple interface

Much of the work involved to establish rules and block traffic is done on a case-by-case basis: when the firewall confronts a type of traffic it does not recognize, it prompts the user to decide whether the traffic should be blocked or allowed.

In Figure 4-5, Norton Personal Firewall is reporting that an ICMP Echo Request packet is being received from an unknown host (with IP address 64.91.96.108) on the Internet. The program provides simple decisions: Allow the traffic, block the traffic, or **customize**

access (that is, identify criteria under which this request would be allowed). In addition, as illustrated in Figure 4-5, the user is asked to decide whether the firewall should consider the decision into a rule to be applied automatically to any such traffic in the future.

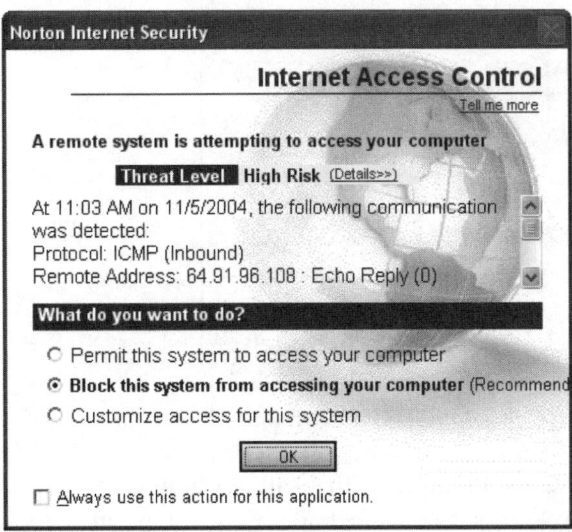

Figure 4-5 Personal firewalls establish rules on a case-by-case basis

Other firewall programs, such as Check Point Next Generation, are designed to protect and monitor large-scale networks. They come with a variety of Graphical User Interface (GUI) tools—programs that provide users with controls to configure and monitor network traffic. The range of options in such programs can be quite complex, as shown in Figure 4-6.

4

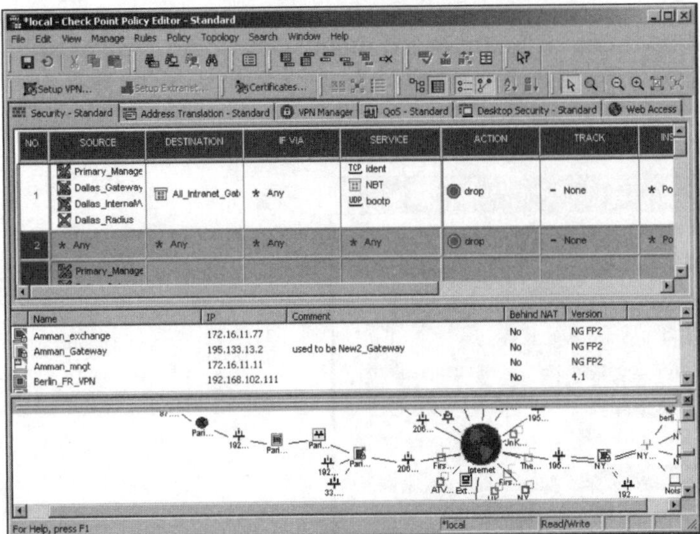

Figure 4-6 Check Point NG provides a more complex user interface

Still other firewalls, such as the Cisco PIX line of **firewall appliances** —hardware devices that have firewall functionality—are self-contained devices that you can add to a network rather than software you install. For a list of links to firewall appliances, you can check *http://directory.google.com/Top/Computers/Security/Firewalls/Products/Firewall_Appliances*. For more information on the Cisco PIX line of devices, you should visit *http://www.cisco.com/univercd/cc/td/doc/pcat/fw.htm*.

Whether they are hardware- or software-based, firewalls are only effective if they are correctly configured to block malicious or suspicious traffic. The most sophisticated firewalls are useless if they contain poorly configured rules that allow traffic in from untrusted sources. And the harsh truth is that, because new threats and modes of attack are being devised all the time, firewalls can be properly configured and still fail to block some harmful files from entering the system because the files' **signatures** —the characteristics that identify them—are not yet recognized by the firewall.

The second fact you need to understand is that any network firewall program is actually a combination of multiple software and hardware components. The term firewall may refer to all of the devices that are positioned on the perimeter of a network; in this case, the term "firewall perimeter" may be more descriptive.

What Firewalls Are *Not*

The third fact you need to realize about firewalls is that they are not a standalone solution. A firewall, by itself, should not be regarded as the only tool you need to protect a network. No firewall can protect a network from a disgruntled employee who has access to protected resources and wants to harm to the company, or from an employee who is able to circumvent security procedures by setting up a modem connection to the Internet using an office telephone. In both cases, a strong security policy and employee education become very important.

Ideally, a firewall should be combined with virus protection software and intrusion detection systems to provide a more comprehensive solution. Strong network security architecture encompasses many components, including intrusion detection systems, firewalls, anti-virus software, access control, and auditing.

Check Point's NG product integrates with products that provide anti-virus protection, intrusion detection, and other solutions through the use of its own protocol called **Open Platform for Security (OPSEC)** . Developers use OPSEC to create solutions that integrate well with Check Point NG to create a strong network security architecture. Examples of products you might integrate with the firewall include:

- eSafe Protect, a product by Aladdin Systems (*www.esafe.com*) that scans e-mail, Web pages, and FTP traffic for viruses
- StoneBeat, an event logging program by Stonesoft Corp. (*www.stonesoft.com*) (You can use third-party applications to send log data to the central firewall log database where it can be consolidated with other logs.)
- WebTrends, a program by NetIQ Corporation (*www.netiq.com/webtrends/default.asp*) that is well known for its ability to create graphical reports from log database information

The expense of purchasing and installing multiple software programs can be considerable, easily running into many thousands of dollars. The important consideration is the need for an integrated security system in which a firewall plays an important—but by no means solitary—role.

Firewalls cannot protect you against malicious insiders who are able to send proprietary information out of the organization through a network connection or by copying the data onto a disk. A firewall also cannot protect connections that don't go through it, such as the connections used by those who dial into the network from outside. Such dial-in connections require a virtual private network (VPN) for protection, as described in Chapter 7.

Screening Router

As stated earlier in this chapter, a single router that has been configured to filter packets is the simplest kind of firewall you can have. Such a device makes decisions on whether to allow or deny packets based on their source and destination IP addresses or other information in their headers (see Figure 4-7).

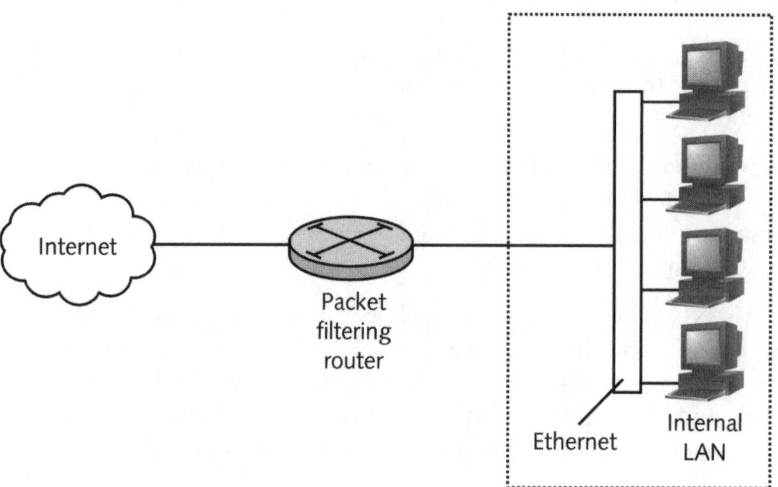

Figure 4-7 A packet-filtering router at the perimeter of a network

There's nothing wrong with having a router on the perimeter of a network to perform packet-filtering functions. The problem is that such a device alone will not stop many attacks, especially those that use spoofed or mangled IP address information. Such a router should be combined with a firewall or proxy server for added protection.

Dual-Homed Host

A very common arrangement is to install firewall or other security-related software (such as a proxy server) on a **dual-homed host**, a computer that has been configured with more than one network interface. The ability to forward packets is disabled on the computer itself. Thus, only the firewall software on the computer can forward traffic from one interface to another (see Figure 4-8). This type of setup is used by millions of individuals with personal computers that are connected to the Internet. Rules are established so that the firewall moves traffic between the Internet and the home workstation or network.

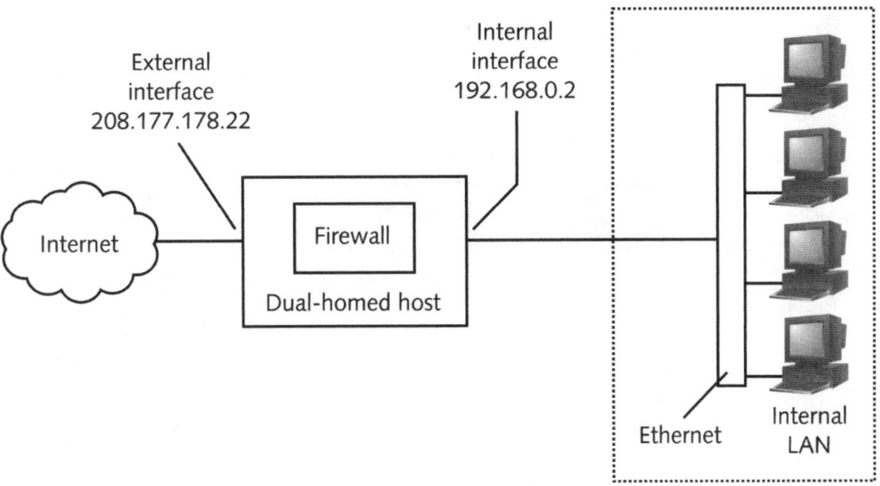

Figure 4-8 A firewall installed on a dual-homed host

Originally, the term "dual-homed host" was reserved for a computer equipped with two separate **network interface cards (NICs)** —cards that connect the computer to a network, with one NIC for each **interface** (the plug or socket that a device uses to connect with another device or with a network). Now this term is used to describe the scenario in Figure 4-8.

A dual-homed host is limited in the standpoint of security it can provide, because the firewall depends on the same computer system that is used for day-to-day communications. Any problem with the host machine weakens the firewall. The big disadvantage is the fact that the host serves as a single point of entry to the organization. Having a simple checkpoint means that a hacker has only one layer of protection to break through to infiltrate the local network. Thus, a multilayered Defense in Depth (DiD) arrangement proves to be even more important with this firewall architecture.

The machine that hosts the firewall software might well have more than two network interfaces. It might be connected to the DMZ, to the Internet, and to the internal LAN, for example. In that case it would be called a multi-homed host.

Screened Host

A screened host setup is similar to the dual-homed host, but the big difference is that a router is often added between the host and the Internet to do IP packet filtering. The router thus screens the host, which is also dedicated to perform security functions (see Figure 4-9).

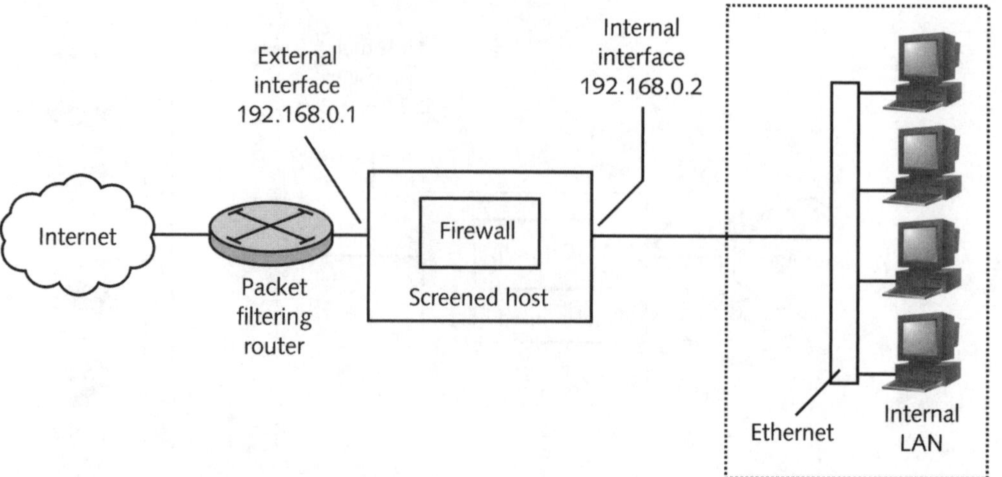

Figure 4-9 A screened host shielded by a packet-filtering router

You might choose this setup in situations such as perimeter security on a corporate network, for instance. A common enhancement is to have the screened host function as an application gateway or proxy server. The only network services that are allowed to pass through the proxy server are those for which proxy applications are already available.

Screened Subnet DMZ

As you learned in Chapter 1, a DMZ is a set of publicly accessible servers that is placed outside the internal LAN. Because this subnet contains a substantial amount of important information either owned by or related to the company, a packet filter or other security software should screen the DMZ. A common solution is to take the servers and make them a subnet of a firewall (see Figure 4-10).

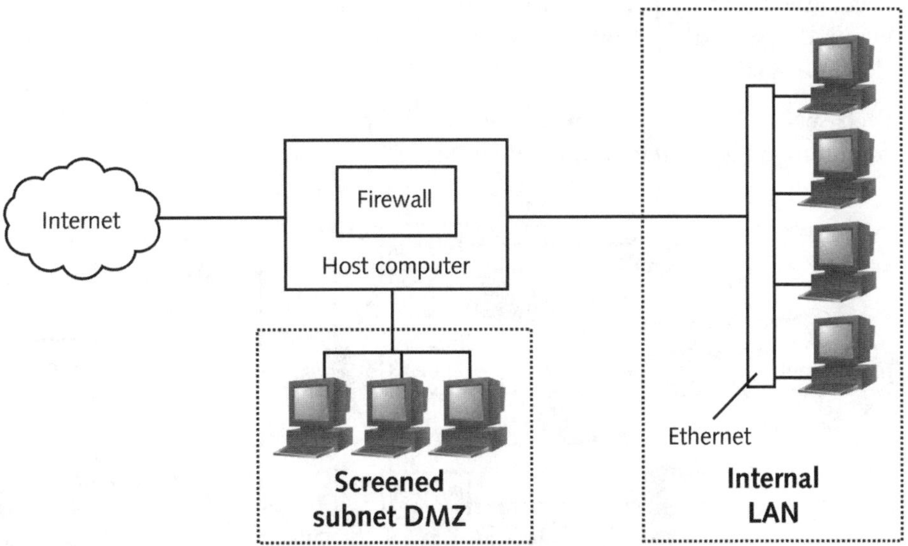

Figure 4-10 A firewall turns a DMZ into a screened subnet

Because the firewall that protects the DMZ is also connected to the Internet and may also be connected to the internal LAN, the firewall in this case is often called a **three-pronged firewall** . You might choose this setup when you need to provide services that are accessible to the public, such as an FTP server, Web server, or e-mail server, but want to make sure that hackers don't gain access to your Web site or FTP resources.

The subnet that's attached to the firewall and contained in the DMZ is sometimes called a **service network** or **perimeter network** by those who dislike the military connotations of the term DMZ. The services provided in the DMZ vary depending on the organization, but typically include a Web server, FTP server, and outgoing and incoming e-mail servers.

Multiple DMZ/Firewall Configurations

One DMZ provides insufficient security for many large-scale corporations that are connected to the Internet or that do business online. To handle a large demand from the Internet while keeping the response time of Web servers and other public servers as low as possible, set up multiple DMZs. Each DMZ is a **server farm** : a group of servers that are connected in their own subnet and that work together to receive requests with the help of **load balancing software** , which prioritizes and schedules requests and distributes them to servers based on each server's current load and processing power.

Installing clusters of servers in DMZs that are outside the internal network helps protect the internal network from becoming overloaded. Placing the company's Web server in the exposed subnet makes the server better equipped to handle heavy traffic. Consider a Web server that gets as many as 20,000 hits a minute. If the server is behind the firewall, that amount of traffic could crash or at least seriously slow down the firewall, as well as the other traffic that needs to pass through it. If the server is outside the protected network but in the

DMZ, the firewall's performance won't be compromised. To protect the local network, inbound connectivity from the Web server should be blocked, and accesses should be closely logged.

Each server farm/DMZ can and should be protected by its own firewall. A possible configuration is illustrated in Figure 4-11.

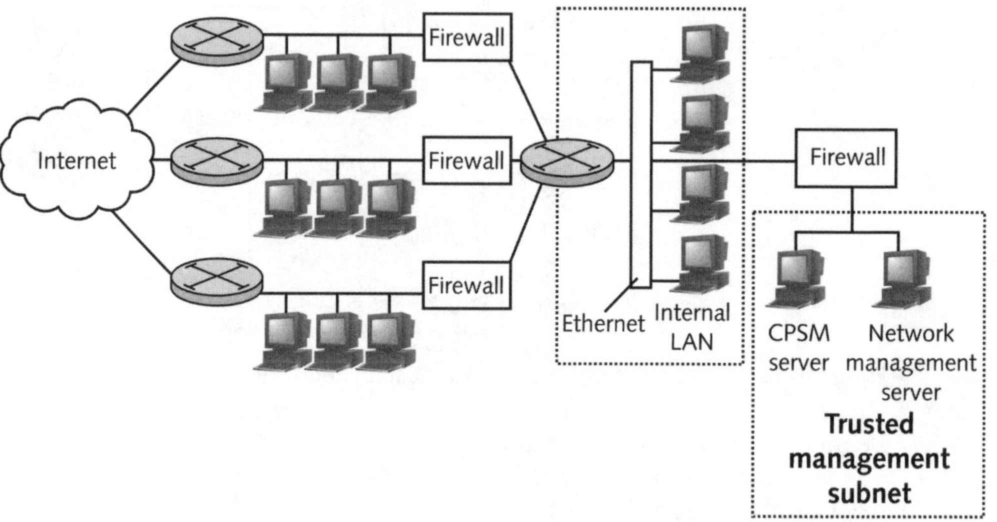

Figure 4-11 Multiple DMZs protected by multiple firewalls

As you can see in Figure 4-11, the server farms do not need to be protected from one another directly; rather, they all feed into a single router, which sends traffic into the internal network. In addition, the server farms aren't directly connected to the Internet; a packet-filtering router screens each. Finally, an additional firewall is placed inside the internal network to protect two management servers. One contains management software that enables the network administrator to manage the network as a whole. The other manages security policy settings for the firewalls.

In the example in Figure 4-11, one of the management computers contains Cisco's Security Policy Management (CSPM) software, which controls the Cisco PIX firewalls that protect the server farms and the management servers as well. The advantage of locating management software **out of band** —outside the internal network, on a protected subnet of its own—is that the management servers gain an extra level of protection from intruders. If the intruders gain control of either the firewall or network management software, they could potentially gain access to all hosts on the network.

A protected subnet within an already-protected internal LAN could be used to provide an extra layer of protection for other types of sensitive information such as customer or personnel data. The extra protection might protect the servers from disgruntled employees inside the organization, as well as hackers coming from the Internet.

Multiple Firewall Configurations

DiD is a term you'll hear throughout this book as well as in the field of network security, and it simply means this: multiple security devices configured to work together to provide protection. DiD makes use of many different layers of network security. To achieve the level of protection afforded by DiD, many organizations find that they need to implement more than one firewall, either throughout the network or on a particular subnet of it.

The following sections describe various ways in which two or more firewalls can be used to protect not only an internal network, but also one DMZ, two DMZs, and branch offices that need to connect to the main office's internal network. In addition, multiple firewalls can help you achieve load distribution that can keep heavy traffic flowing smoothly through the gateway.

Protecting a DMZ with Two or More Firewalls

When multiple firewalls are deployed around the perimeter of a network, they can work together to balance the traffic load in and out of the network. When two firewalls are used in tandem, they must be configured identically and use the same firewall software. That way, the traffic coming from the Internet can be balanced between them, using routers or switches on either side, as shown in Figure 4-12.

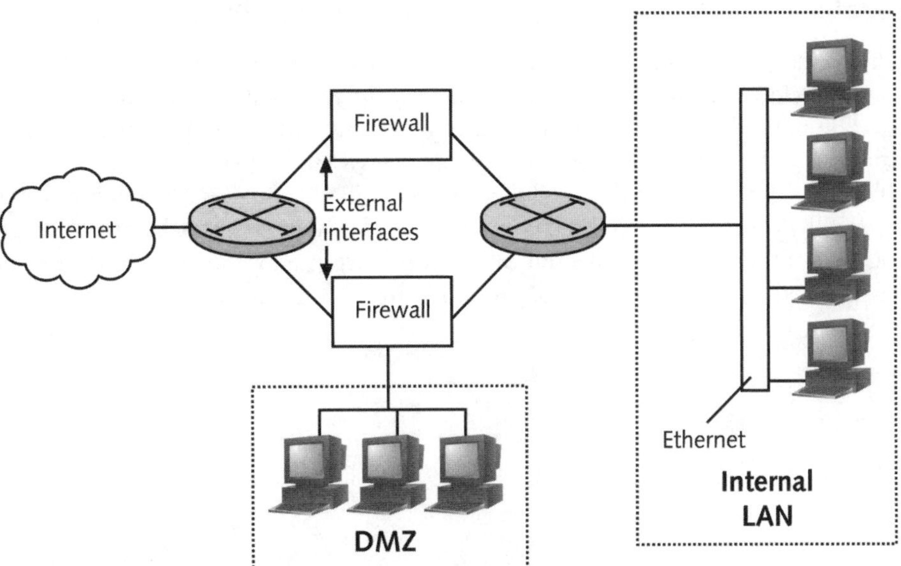

Figure 4-12 Two firewalls used for load balancing

In Figure 4-12, the two firewalls have an external interface on the Internet. You can also have a configuration in which one firewall has an interface on the Internet and the second has an interface on the internal LAN; the DMZ being protected would be positioned between them. In any case, using two firewalls helps in the following ways:

- One firewall can control traffic between the DMZ and the Internet, while the other can control traffic between the protected LAN and the DMZ.
- The second firewall can serve as a **failover firewall**. It is a backup that can be configured to switch on if the first one fails, thus providing uninterrupted service for the organization.

One of the biggest advantages of setting up a DMZ with two firewalls is that you can control where traffic goes in the three networks with which you're dealing: the external network outside the DMZ, the external network within the DMZ, and the internal network behind the DMZ. You can identify certain protocols, such as outbound HTTP port 80, that should go to the external network within the DMZ, while allowing other protocols to pass through to the internal network.

Using multiple interior routers to connect your DMZ subnet to multiple parts of your internal subnets can cause problems. For example, the routing software on an internal system could determine that the most direct route to another internal system is through the DMZ. As a result, sensitive internal traffic will flow across your DMZ, where it can be intercepted if a hacker manages to break into a bastion host. Having multiple interior routers in place makes overall network configuration more difficult as well.

Protecting Branch Offices with Multiple Firewalls

A multinational corporation that needs to share information among branch offices in outlying locations can communicate securely using a single security policy that is implemented by multiple firewalls. The central office has its own centralized firewall: a firewall that directs traffic for branch offices and their own individual firewalls. The central office develops the security policy and deploys the policy through its centralized firewall with its associated rules, on a dedicated computer called a **security workstation**. Each office has its own firewall, but the central office can develop and control the security policy. The policy is then copied on each of the other firewalls in the corporation. See Figure 4-13.

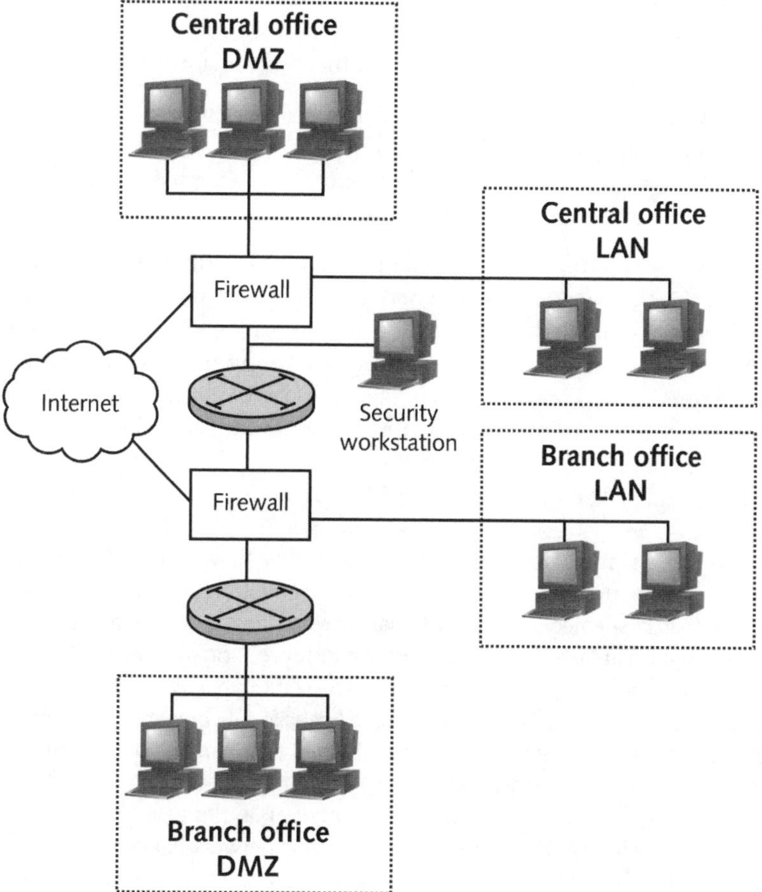

Figure 4-13 Multiple firewalls protecting branch offices

One notable aspect about Figure 4-13 is that the two firewalls have a path they can use to communicate with one another as well as a router to direct traffic to each firewall. However, traffic from the Internet or from the corporate LAN doesn't travel between the two firewalls; only traffic from the security workstation travels on the connection between the DMZs, carrying configuration information to the firewalls, and receiving log file data from them as well.

Reverse Firewall

Some forward-thinking companies have taken to installing a **reverse firewall** , a device that monitors connections headed out of a network, rather than trying to block what's coming in. Sometimes, the biggest threats facing an internal network come from users who are located on the internal network itself. Consider a university that makes selected applications available to researchers, but restricts access to those programs to the scientists who need access to them. Some clever computer science students might well try to break into the server that stores such applications so that they can download and use the programs for free. A reverse firewall would help by monitoring connection attempts out of a network that originate from internal users. It would then filter out unauthorized attempts.

Reverse firewalls have other purposes. A company that is concerned about how its employees use the Web and other Internet services can set up a reverse firewall to log connections to Web sites. It can then block sites that are accessed repeatedly and that are considered unsuitable for employees to visit during work hours.

In a Denial of Service (DoS) attack, information floods out of the network from the infected computer(s), thus overloading the network. A reverse firewall, such as the hardware device Reverse Firewall sold by Los Angeles-based company Cs3 (*www.cs3-inc.com/rfw.html*), inspects outgoing packets and tracks where they're coming from within the network. If a high number of unexpected packets are seen leaving the network, the firewall notifies the network administrator. Such functionality, in fact, could be part of any firewall, and could be programmed into a hardware or software firewall by a qualified engineer, alleviating the need to purchase a specialized reverse firewall.

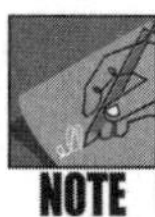

Much of this chapter assumes that you are building a firewall to protect your internal network from the Internet. However, in some situations, you may also want to protect segments of your internal network from other segments. You may want to isolate lab or test networks, for instance. You may also have networks that need to be more secure than the rest of your site—for instance, where projects are being developed or where financial data or grades are stored. In these cases, internal firewalls can be positioned between two parts of the same organization, or two separate organizations that share a network, rather than between a single organization and the Internet. In this case, you need to set up packet filtering rules that isolate the internal network being protected from the Internet and from your own bastion host—so if the bastion host is compromised it will not lead to a compromise of the internal firewall as well.

Proxy servers also monitor traffic moving in the outbound direction—that is, from the internal LAN to the Internet. However, proxy servers have the advantage of shielding information about internal computers. See Chapter 6 for more information about proxy servers.

Which firewall configuration is the best one for your needs? Each has its advantages and disadvantages. It's important to remember that firewall setups are not a matter of an either-or decision. You can combine a screened host setup with a multiple firewall setup, for instance; you can also have a reverse firewall in addition to a conventional forward firewall. The advantages and disadvantages of each setup are summarized in Table 4-1.

Table 4-1 Firewall configuration advantages and disadvantages

Configuration	Advantages	Disadvantages
Screening Router	Simplicity, cost; good for home applications if a stateful packet filter is used	Provides only minimal protection; viruses, Trojan horses, and some malformed packets may get through
Dual-homed host	Simple, economical; can provide effective protection if configured correctly	Provides a single point of entry (and fault); firewall depends entirely on the computer that hosts it
Screened host	Provides two layers of protection for home and small business networks	Provides a single point of entry (and fault); firewall depends on the computer that hosts it and on the router that protects it
Screened subnet DMZ	Protects public servers by isolating them from the internal LAN	Servers in the DMZ are highly vulnerable and need to be hardened
Multiple DMZ/firewalls	Provides layers of protection for a business network	Expensive
Single DMZ/two firewalls	Balances traffic load in heavy load situations	Expensive
Branch offices/multiple firewalls	Provides protection for all offices in a corporate network, as well as central administration	Firewalls must be purchased, installed, and configured at each office location
Reverse firewall	Monitors attack from inside the network; enables organizations to monitor user activity	Can slow down user access to external networks or other parts of the internal LAN

Firewall Software and Hardware

If you become a security specialist or network administrator whose responsibilities include security for your organization, you'll be called upon to evaluate the different kinds of firewall software and hardware packages and recommend the best choice for your company's needs.

Firewalls come in many varieties. They all do the core functions: filtering, proxying, and logging. Some of the expensive packages add "bells and whistles" like caching and address translation. However, don't let price rule your decision. Some freeware products like PGP let you perform some of the same functions as, say, Microsoft's Internet Security and Acceleration Server (which costs $1,999 to $5,999 per host processor).

This section shows how the basic strategies and concepts governing firewalls are implemented in a range of software and hardware combinations you are likely to encounter in the workplace. Having this overview should help you choose your own package when the time comes. The discussion is divided into two sections: software and hardware.

Network World conducted a test of several high-end firewall products to see how well they performed under especially high loads. The firewalls tested included Cisco's PIX 525; Check Point FireWall-1; CyberGuard's KnightStar, Enternet's Enternet Firewall, Secure Computing's SideWinder; SonicWall's SonicWall Pro VX; Symantec's Raptor; and WatchGuard's Firebox II. Results can be found at *www.nwfusion.com/reviews/2001/0312rev.html.*

Software-Based Firewalls

The kinds of firewalls that people think about most commonly consist solely of firewall software. They can be combined with various hardware devices to make an extra-secure security checkpoint.

The downside of software-based firewalls is that they require a good deal of administration, both to configure the software itself and to secure the operating system through patches or removal of vulnerable services. On the other hand, they also tend to be less expensive than hardware firewalls and thus easier to deploy in multiple locations. The question of whether software firewalls are more secure than hardware firewalls is a question that is frequently debated by security professionals. Many believe that the level of security depends on the skill with which the firewall is configured and the regularity with which it is maintained and updated rather than the specific program or device used.

Free Firewall Programs

Free firewall programs aren't perfect. Their logging capabilities aren't as robust as some commercial products, and configuring can be difficult; they usually don't include a way to monitor the traffic that passes through the firewall in real-time, or a way to manage firewall settings for a network of computers from a centralized location. Nonetheless, they have a place in small business networks and home networks because of the advantages of their convenience, simplicity, and unbeatable price (free!). Some of the more popular free firewall programs are:

- *Netfilter* —This firewall software, which comes with the Linux 2.4 Kernel, is a powerful (and freely available) solution for stateless and stateful packet filtering, NAT, and packet processing. Netfilter is very good at logging copious information about the traffic that passes through it in a way that is well-organized and easy to review.

- *ZoneAlarm* —The free version of this firewall program (the installation of which is described in Hands-On Project 4-4) is very effective—so much so that you may lose your Internet connectivity when you first set up the program. Correct configuration to allow just the software and IP addresses you want is critical to maintaining Internet connectivity; after that, the program is very effective. One big downside is that when questionable traffic is encountered, you don't get the choice to block or allow it: the packets are simply dropped.

- *Tiny Personal Firewall* —This is the most stripped-down of the freeware programs listed here. The software presents alerts as packets are received that it can't match to one of its existing rules, and you decide whether to block or allow, and then whether the action should be made into a rule.
- *Sygate Personal Firewall* —An excellent program for general home use; the program presents you with extensive logs that contain header information about packets. You also get the ability to configure packet-filtering rules.

The last three free firewall programs are all stripped-down versions of more elaborate products available commercially from the same companies. You can try out an evaluation version of these programs (ZoneAlarm Pro, Tiny Personal Firewall Pro, and Sygate Personal Firewall Pro) and then decide whether to purchase them.

Commercial Firewall Software: Personal Firewalls

Personal firewall products work by locating themselves between the Ethernet adapter driver of the machine on which they are installed and the TCP/IP stack, where they inspect traffic going between the driver and the stack. They include programs such as:

- *Norton Personal Firewall* —This is an excellent and easy-to-use program for home computing users that comes either as a standalone product or as part of the Norton Internet Security package with anti-virus software.
- *ZoneAlarm Pro* —Along with firewall software, you get anti-virus protection and the ability to block pop-up ads and cookies.
- *BlackICE PC Protection* —It combines intrusion detection with firewall functionality.
- *Sygate Personal Firewall Pro* —Along with firewall and intrusion detection, this program can do content filtering; it matches attack patterns to block possible intrusions.

Despite the features mentioned in the preceding bulleted list, the well-known personal firewall products are considered "lightweight" in terms of firewall protection. Some work with multiple protocols, while most guard only against IP threats. Some programs don't do outbound connection blocking, while others do. Some are inconvenient to configure because they don't work on a "configure as you compute" basis. Rather, you set a general security level (such as Cautious, Nervous, or Paranoid) and the software adjusts its security settings accordingly.

Commercial Firewall Software: Enterprise Firewalls

Enterprise firewalls are programs that come with a centralized management option as well as, in some cases, the capability to install multiple instances of the software from a centralized location. Following are some examples.

- PGP Desktop is a combined firewall and encryption package that makes use of Pretty Good Privacy (PGP) encryption; it is available from PGP Corporation (*www.pgp.com*). One disadvantage is pricing: a one-year license to use the software costs $80; a "perpetual license" costs $165 for a single user.

- CheckPoint NG is a suite of management and configuration tools that enable you to do real-time monitoring and remote administration as well as log file analysis.

- The RealSecure set of security packages (*www.iss.net/products_services/enterprise_protection/*) by Internet Security Systems, Inc. has all the features of other packages, but the emphasis is on centralized management.

- Novell's BorderManager (*www.novell.com/products/bordermanager*) uses a proxy server to not only protect employees but also to give employers a way to monitor their online activities.

Firewalls, which used to consist primarily of packet filtering tools, have added user authentication, Network Address Translation, encryption, and centralized management to their list of features to stay ahead in an increasingly competitive market.

Firewall Hardware

One advantage of hardware firewalls is that they do not depend on a conventional operating system like Windows, Solaris, or Linux, which can provide openings through bugs or other flaws. On the other hand, hardware firewalls *do* run on an operating system—some of Cisco's hardware firewalls run on Cisco's own IOS system, for instance—and these can be subject to the same sorts of flaws as computer operating systems. Hardware firewall devices are generally more **scalable** than software firewalls—that is, they can handle an increasing amount of traffic as an organization grows—and they can handle more data with faster throughput as well.

On the downside, hardware firewalls tend to be more expensive than software products. The Cisco PIX firewall, for example, ranges from $595 for the PIX 501 to $60,000 for the top-of-the-line PIX 535. Aladdin's eSafe Appliance costs about $2,800 for a 25-user license; Network Associates' WebShield e500 appliance can support thousands of users per device; a 500-user license costs nearly $15,000.

Hardware firewalls that run their own operating system can be more difficult to patch in the event of a security alert or software problem. There may not be a "patch" as such; you may need to download and install a complete image, or a complete copy, of the updated operating system.

Hybrid Firewalls

A **hybrid firewall** combines aspects of both firewall appliances and software firewalls in one package. As a hardware appliance, it can provide a network with high performance. However, it is also able to perform functions that are normally only provided by software firewalls, such as protection against DoS attacks or even integrated anti-virus scanning. A hybrid solution would be a good choice in a large-scale organization in which the appliance needs to protect hundreds or even thousands of users, while providing good throughput and virus protection as well.

TIP

Sidewinder, a firewall and VPN gateway produced by Secure Computing (*www.securecomputing.com*), is an example of a well-regarded hybrid firewall solution. The cost is comparable to that of other appliances: a 25-user license costs $2,755, and a 250-user license costs $9,395.

Which firewall product is best for your needs? That depends on the number of users you plan to protect, the amount of network traffic that needs to pass through the firewall, your budget, and your overall level of concern about security. Budget shouldn't always be the primary consideration. An inexpensive software program can quickly become inadequate as a network grows. It pays to buy the strongest program you can afford at the outset. Table 4-2 presents some advantages and disadvantages you should consider when determining whether to choose a hardware or software product, and if software, what kind you might purchase.

Table 4-2 Firewall software advantages and disadvantages

Type of Firewall	Advantages	Disadvantages
Software—freeware	Unbeatable price; small file size; ease of installation	Only a minimal set of features is offered; lack of technical support
Software—commercial personal firewalls	Simple to install; economical price; auto-configuration features help novice users	Not as full-featured as enterprise products; not as robust as appliances; tend to be installed on single-computer systems, which reduces security
Software—enterprise firewalls	Usually installed on dedicated host for maximum security; centralized administration available for large networks; real-time monitoring and other administrative features	Can be difficult to install and configure
Hardware appliances	More scalable than software firewalls, and can handle faster throughput	Can be very expensive, and difficult to patch if bugs or security alerts require it
Hybrid firewall	Provides throughput and security of an appliance with features of a software firewall	Just as expensive or more expensive than other appliances

Establishing Rules and Restrictions

Firewalls can be expensive and elaborate, and they come in many varieties, but most network security professionals would agree that even the most full-featured firewall depends on a good **rule base** , which is a set of rules that tell the firewall what action to take when a particular kind of traffic attempts to pass through it. A simple firewall with well-constructed rules stands to be more effective than a complex product with rules that don't block the intrusion attempts they need to stop.

What makes an effective firewall rule base? The following sections describe some points to consider: the firewall rule base should be as simple and short as possible; it should be based on a security policy; it should provide rules for how applications can access the Internet; and it should restrict access to ports and subnets on the internal network from the Internet.

NOTE

A set of packet filtering rules is frequently called an Access Control List (ACL) instead of a rule base.

Keep the Rule Base Simple

Keep the list of rules in your rule base as short as possible. The more complex the rule base is, the greater your chances of misconfiguring it. Some professionals suggest that your own rule base contains no more than 30 rules, and certainly no more than 50 rules. The shorter the rule base, the quicker your firewall can process requests, because it has fewer rules to review.

Rules are typically processed by a firewall in a particular order. The rules are usually numbered: 1, 2, 3, and so on. A list of firewall rules is usually presented in the form of a grid. The first cell in the grid is the rule number of the individual rule. The subsequent cells describe the attributes that the firewall should test for: an IP address, a protocol, and an action to be taken. The rule grid presented by Check Point NG is shown in Figure 4-14.

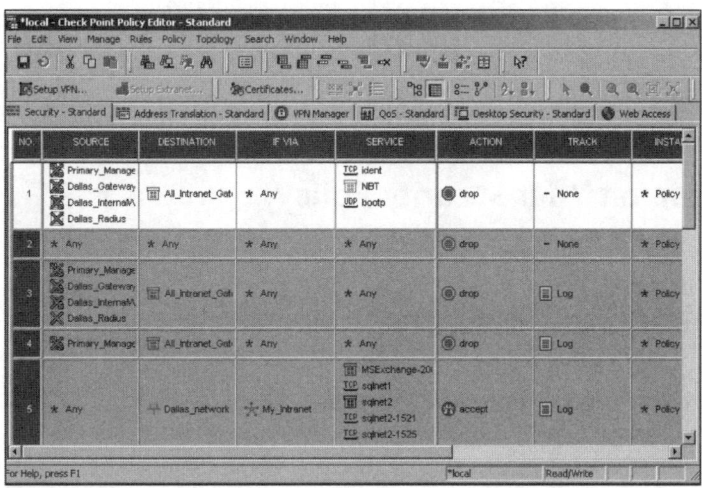

Figure 4-14 A firewall processes rules in order, from top to bottom

The fact that rules are processed in order means that the most important ones—the ones that need to be processed first—should be put at the top of the list. (All firewalls give you a way to reorder the rules in the rule base.) It's a good idea to make the last rule in the rule base a **cleanup rule** , which is a rule that covers any other packets that haven't been covered in preceding rules.

When a packet hits a firewall, it tests the rules one after another. As soon as a match is found, the action corresponding to the rule is followed: most often, there are two possible actions. The first is Allow (to allow the packet to proceed through the firewall to its destination either in the Internet or in the internal network). The second is Deny (to drop the packet altogether—usually, no notification is sent to the sender, because such notification might give clues to hackers about the characteristics of the network; the packet is simply dropped). The process by which the firewall reviews packets and decides whether to allow or deny them is shown in Figure 4-15.

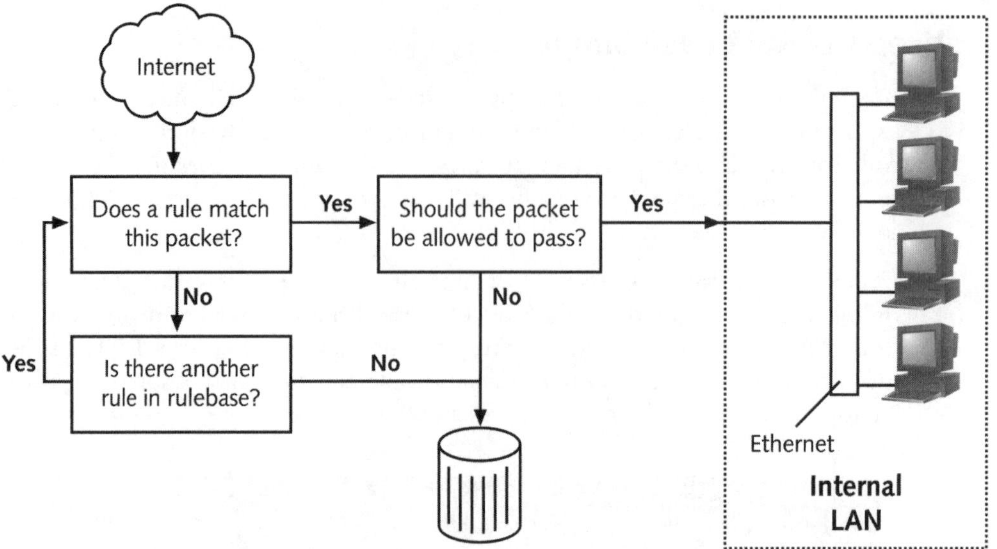

Figure 4-15 Firewalls process rules in order until a match is found

Base the Rule Base on Your Security Policy

When you're configuring the firewall rule base, you have the opportunity to put your organization's security policy rules and procedures into practice. Certain elements associated with filtering packets are especially important to configuring rules and thus implementing the organization's security policy:

- *Logging and auditing*—Most security policies require methods for detecting intrusions and other security problems such as viruses.
- *Tracking*—The Track column in each rule enables you to initiate notification so that you can follow response procedures in case of intrusion.
- *Filtering*—One of the primary objectives of the rule base is to filter communications based on complex rules so that only traffic that makes use of approved protocols, ports, and source and destination IP addresses is allowed.
- *Network Address Translation (NAT)*— The rule base should provide for internal names and addresses on the company LAN to be concealed from those outside the network.
- *Quality of Service (QoS)*—QoS rules can be set up to enable the firewall to maintain a baseline level of functionality, which may be specified in your organization's security policy.
- *Desktop Security Policy*—A Desktop Security Policy gives you the ability to specify the level of access remote users have when they log on to the network.

A rule base is a practical implementation of the policies adopted by the organization. Consider the following common policies that need to be reflected in the rule base:

- Employees can have unrestricted access to the Internet.
- The public can access the company's Web server and e-mail server.
- Only traffic that has been authenticated can access the internal LAN.
- Employees are not allowed to use instant messaging software.
- Traffic from the company's ISP should be allowed.
- Traffic that attempts to connect to one of the ports used by instant messaging software should be blocked except when it is coming from trusted sources.
- Only the network administrator should be able to access the internal network directly from the Internet for management purposes.

TIP

Note that Hands-on Project 4-4 leads you through the process of downloading and installing ZoneAlarm and beginning to use it. Project 4-5 shows you how to set up rules with the program.

Setting Up Application Rules

One of the ways in which firewalls let you control access to your computer or network is to control access to particular applications. Some Trojan horse programs work by gaining control of other applications (for instance, Microsoft Outlook Express), which then access the Internet. Sometimes, hackers try to access applications on your computer or the ports they use. If a computer on your network has an instant messaging application installed such as MSN Messenger or ICQ, such applications probably launch on startup; the computer listens for incoming connections on the ports used by those applications. Hackers can scan for such open ports.

Firewall software gives you a way to block applications from accessing the Internet so that such ports are not left open—or, if the application needs to be used, the application can be flagged so that the user must be prompted if it is to access the Internet. Typically, you are given three options:

- *Allow*—The application can access the Internet at any time. (You'll probably want to establish this rule for Web browsers, e-mail applications, and other software you normally use.)
- *Block*—The application is blocked from accessing the Internet.
- *Ask or Prompt*—The user is prompted when the application attempts to access the Internet.

In the set of security policies listed in the preceding section, you would set up rules that allow Web browsers to access the Internet through your firewall; you would also block instant messaging programs from accessing the Internet. Figure 4-16 shows MSN Messenger being blocked from accessing the Internet—using the firewall program ZoneAlarm.

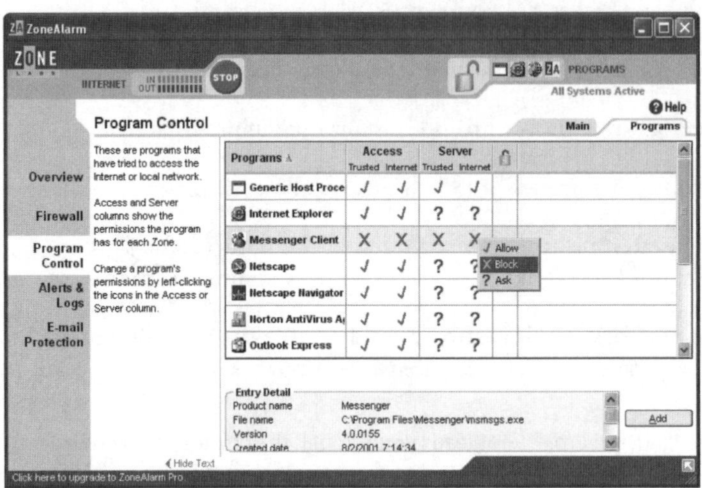

Figure 4-16 Firewalls let you block applications from inbound or outbound communications

Restricting or Allowing Subnets

Firewalls aren't intuitive. You need to tell them what traffic to allow or restrict. One of the ways you can identify traffic is by IP address range. Some traffic is legitimate; it comes from a network you trust, such as your own network or your ISP's servers, and should not be blocked by the firewall. However, most firewalls start from the sensible premise that all traffic should be blocked by default, and you need to identify the "trusted" networks whose communications should be allowed.

For instance, if your network subnet contains IP addresses in the range from 10.10.56.0 to 10.10.56.255, you would specify that those are to be regarded by the firewall as "trusted," as shown in one of ZoneAlarm's configuration dialog boxes (see Figure 4-17).

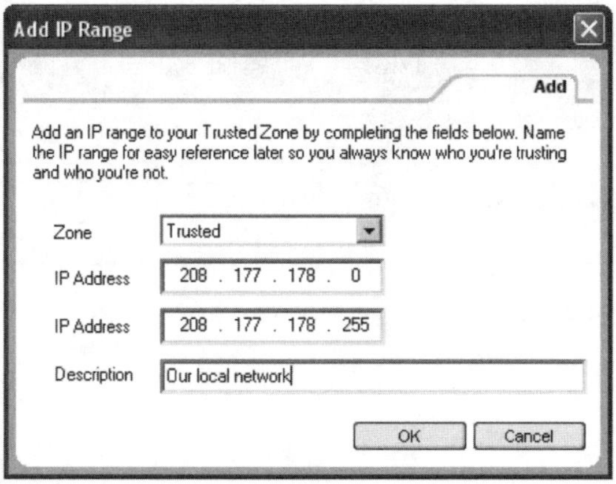

Add IP Range

Add

Add an IP range to your Trusted Zone by completing the fields below. Name the IP range for easy reference later so you always know who you're trusting and who you're not.

Zone: Trusted

IP Address: 208 . 177 . 178 . 0

IP Address: 208 . 177 . 178 . 255

Description: Our local network

OK Cancel

Figure 4-17 Identify which subnets or IP addresses are to be trusted

Restricting Ports and Protocols

The goal in coming up with packet filter rules is to account for all possible ports that a type of communication might use, or for all variations within a particular protocol (for instance, passive and active FTP, or standard HTTP and secure HTTP.) Some of this configuration comes by trial and error: an employee complains that he or she can't communicate with someone using MSN Messenger, and you adjust the packet filter's rule base accordingly (after consulting the security policy, of course). However, the better you understand the sorts of situations you're likely to encounter and the rules you can set up to cover them, the more time you'll save. You'll be able to review logs, install patches, and perform other security-related functions knowing that your actions are producing the desired effect.

Before you create the first rule in your rule base, it's a good idea to stop any traffic that the firewall already allows. Some firewalls allow UDP or other traffic by default; by specifically blocking all communications you can gradually specify the types of traffic you want to allow.

Controlling Internet Services

After you are sure that your firewall is starting from a "clean slate" and is not allowing any traffic in either direction, you can begin to allow the traffic you want. The following sections give some examples of rules that you might create to enable such connectivity; rules that restrict individual protocols are covered in Chapter 5. The rules are numbered in sequence from table to table because together they comprise a rule base for an organization.

World Wide Web

The first priority of the employees in the protected network is (not surprisingly) to be able to surf the Web and exchange e-mail messages. The rules for accessing the Web need to cover both standard HTTP traffic on TCP port 80, as well as Secure HTTP (HTTPS) traffic on TCP port 443. These are shown in Table 4-3.

Table 4-3 Outbound Web access

Rule	Protocol	Transport Protocol	Source IP	Source Port	Destination IP	Destination Port	Action
1	HTTP outbound	TCP	207.177.178.0/24	Any	Any	80	Allow
2	HTTPS outbound	TCP	208.177.178.0/24	Any	Any	443	Allow

These rules assume that the local network being protected has an IP address range of 207.177.178.0/24.

DNS

To connect to Web sites, the employees in our sample organization need to be able to resolve the **fully qualified domain names (FQDNs)** they enter, such as course.com, to their corresponding IP addresses using the Domain Name System (DNS). Internal users connect to external hosts using a DNS server located in the DMZ of the security perimeter. DNS uses either UDP port 53 or TCP port 53 for connection attempts. In addition, you need to set up rules that enable external clients to access computers in your own network using the same TCP and UDP ports, as shown in Table 4-4. (The rules in Table 4-4 assume that your organization's DNS server is located at IP address 208.177.178.31.)

Table 4-4 DNS resolution rules

Rule	Protocol	Transport Protocol	Source IP	Source Port	Destination IP	Destination Port	Action
3	DNS outbound	TCP	208.177.178.31	Any	Any	53	Allow
4	DNS outbound	UDP	208.177.178.31	Any	Any	53	Allow
5	DNS inbound	TCP	Any	Any	208.177.178.31	53	Allow
6	DNS inbound	UDP	Any	Any	208.177.178.31	53	Allow

E-Mail

To set up your own configuration rules, you need to assess whether your organization needs to accept incoming e-mail messages at all, whether internal users can access mail services outside your company (such as Hotmail), and what e-mail clients are supported by your company. By identifying the e-mail clients your company will support, you can provide the highest level of security without blocking e-mail access.

Yet, setting up firewall rules that permit the filtering of e-mail messages is not trivial. One reason is the variety of e-mail protocols that might be used:

- Post Office Protocol version 3 (POP3) and Internet E-mail Access Protocol version 4 (IMAP4) for inbound mail transport
- Simple Mail Transfer Protocol (SMTP) for outbound mail transport
- Lightweight Directory Access Protocol (LDAP) for looking up e-mail addresses
- Hypertext Transport Protocol (HTTP) for Web-based mail service

To keep things simple, consider a configuration that uses only POP3 and SMTP for inbound and outbound e-mail, respectively. However, SSL encryption (a form of encryption between Web server and client that is described in more detail in Chapter 7) should be used for additional security. Some sample rules are found in Table 4-5. (The rules assume that your SMTP mail server is located at 208.177.178.29.)

Table 4-5 E-mail rules

Rule	Protocol	Transport Protocol	Source IP	Source Port	Destination IP	Destination Port	Action
7	POP3 outbound	TCP	208.177.178.0/24	Any	Any	110	Allow
8	POP3/S outbound	TCP	208.177.178.0/24	Any	Any	995	Allow
9	POP inbound	TCP	Any	Any	208.177.178.0/24	110	Allow
10	POP3/S inbound	TCP	Any	Any	208.177.178.0/24	995	Allow
11	SMTP outbound	TCP	208.177.178.29	Any	Any	25	Allow
12	SMTP/S outbound	TCP	208.177.178.29	Any	Any	465	Allow
13	SMTP inbound	TCP	Any	Any	208.177.178.29	25	Allow
14	SMTP/S inbound	TCP	Any	Any	208.177.178.29	465	Allow

FTP

Two kinds of FTP transactions can take place on networks: active FTP or passive FTP. The rules you set up for FTP need to support two separate connections: TCP port 21, the FTP control port, and TCP 20, the FTP data port. If some clients in your network support active FTP, you can't specify a particular port, because the client can establish a connection with the FTP server at any port above 1023. Instead, you specify the IP address of your FTP server (in this example 208.177.178.25), as shown in Table 4-6.

Table 4-6 FTP rules

Rule	Protocol	Transport Protocol	Source IP	Source Port	Destination IP	Destination Port	Action
15	FTP control inbound	TCP	Any	Any	208.177.178.0/25	21	Allow
16	FTP Data inbound	TCP	208.177.178.0/25	20	Any	Any	Allow
17	FTP PASV	TCP	Any	Any	208.177.178.0/25	Any	Allow
18	FTP control outbound	TCP	208.177.178.0/25	Any	Any	21	Allow
19	FTP Data outbound	TCP	Any	20	208.177.178.25	Any	Allow

CHAPTER SUMMARY

- This chapter introduced you to general practices and configuration options that pertain to one of the most important elements in any network security effort—firewalls. First, you learned that the effectiveness of a firewall depends in part on the security of the computer or other device that hosts it. It's an excellent practice, especially in a corporate network, to install a firewall on a computer that has been hardened to function as a bastion host. Such a computer has had all available operating system patches applied, as well as unnecessary services removed.
- The requirements for the bastion host aren't extensive in terms of RAM, but they are in terms of hard disk storage space, because the firewall or intrusion detection system (IDS) on the system is likely to be accumulating large amounts of log file data. The operating system chosen for the bastion host should be one with which the administrator is familiar, as well as one that is inherently secure (or that can be secured through patches and updates).
- Once you have installed the firewall and located it on a bastion host at the perimeter of your network, you need to create a firewall configuration that will protect that network. You can set up a simple packet filtering router that screens your network, but such a screening router setup offers only minimal security. A dual-homed host that runs a firewall is more secure, but the combination of router and host will provide layers of security and be more effective. Multiple firewalls can be used for load balancing or for protecting different branch networks within a single organization. In addition, a reverse firewall can be used to monitor communications from the internal network to the Internet.
- One of your responsibilities as network administrator or security specialist will be to select the firewall hardware or software for your company's needs. Software firewalls come in many varieties: freeware, shareware, and enterprise. Hardware firewall "appliances" are more expensive, but they can handle a larger amount of traffic. Hybrid firewalls combine the scalability of hardware devices with content filtering that is normally provided only by software firewalls.

- When you have chosen the firewall you need, you need to construct a rule base that implements the security policy your organization has created. The firewall should first be configured to block traffic altogether; then rules can be set up that enable employees to access the Web and exchange e-mail messages, resolve DNS information, and use FTP. The final rule in the rule base should be a cleanup rule, which drops all packets that haven't been covered by preceding rules.

Key Terms

bastion host — A computer that sits on the perimeter of a network and that has been specially protected through operating system patches, authentication, and encryption.

buffer overflow — A type of attack in which a program or process attempts to store more data than can be held in a temporary disk storage area called a buffer; the host computer is flooded with more information than it can handle.

cleanup rule — A packet-filtering rule that comes last in a rule base, and that covers any other packets that haven't been covered in preceding rules.

customize access — Identify criteria under which a connection request would be allowed by a firewall, rather than allowing the firewall to automatically deny all or allow all instances of such requests.

dependency services — Services that an operating system needs to function correctly.

dual-homed host — A computer that has been configured with more than one network interface.

firewall appliances — Hardware devices that have firewall functionality.

fully qualified domain names (FQDN) — The complete domain name for a computer, including the server name and domain name in its URL, such as "computer.mycompany.com".

hardened — A term that describes a computer that is made more secure than any others on the network by eliminating all unnecessary software, closing potential openings, and protecting the information on it with encryption and authentication.

honeypot — A computer that is placed on the perimeter of the network in order to attract hackers.

hybrid firewall — A product that combines aspects of both firewall appliances and software firewalls in one package.

interface — The plug or socket that a device uses to connect with another device or with a network.

load balancing software — Software that prioritizes and schedules requests and distributes them to a group of servers based on each machine's current load and processing power.

log files — Records detailing who accessed resources on the server and when the access attempts occurred.

network interface cards (NICs) — Cards that connect a computer to a network and that enable the computer to communicate on a network.

Open Platform for Security (OPSEC) — A protocol developed by Check Point Technologies that enables its firewall products to integrate with software that provides anti-virus protection, intrusion detection, and other solutions.

out of band — A term that describes the practice of locating computers outside the internal network, on a protected subnet of their own.

perimeter network — The subnet that's attached to the firewall and contained in an organization's DMZ.

reverse firewall — A device that monitors information going out of a network rather than trying to block what's coming in.

rotate — The process of moving the current log file to a storage area and opening up a new log file.

rule base — A set of rules that tell the firewall what action to take when a particular kind of traffic attempts to pass through it.

scalable — A term that describes the ability of hardware or software to handle an increasing amount of throughput.

security workstation — A dedicated computer that deploys a security policy through a centralized firewall to other firewalls that protect branch offices or other networks within the organization.

server — A computer that provides Web pages, e-mail, or other services to individuals both inside and outside the network being protected.

server farm — A group of servers that are connected together in their own subnet and that work together to receive a large number of requests; the load is distributed among all of the servers in the "farm."

service network — *See* perimeter network.

signatures — The characteristics that identify a particular type of network traffic, such as source or destination IP address, protocol, or a combination of features.

three-pronged firewall — A firewall that has three separate interfaces—for example, one to a DMZ, one to the Internet, and one to the internal LAN.

Review Questions

1. Why does a computer that runs firewall software need to be especially secure? (Choose all that apply.)
   a. because it is on the perimeter of the network
   b. because the public will use the server and cannot have their information compromised
   c. because the software on the host is critical to network security
   d. because security problems can slow down the operation of the server
2. What are the most important requirements for a bastion host operating system? (Choose all that apply.)
   a. speed
   b. popularity
   c. ability to be secured
   d. the familiarity of the administrator with the OS
3. Which of the following is an advantage of setting up a honeypot server? (Choose all that apply.)
   a. It can be a bastion host.
   b. It can distract hackers from attacking real hosts.
   c. It can help with identifying and prosecuting hackers.
   d. It can help with certification tests.
4. In what way can a honeypot server discourage future network attacks?
   a. by keeping hackers too busy to do anything else
   b. by keeping hackers off the internal network
   c. by providing examples of what resources might be attacked
   d. by frustrating hackers and forcing them to turn to other networks

5. What is the primary difference between a screened host and dual-homed host setup?

   a A dual-homed host has dual network interface cards.

   b IP forwarding is disabled.

   c A packet filter shields the host.

   d The host is screened by a firewall.

6. A dual-homed host setup is frequently used in what computing environment?

   a. a DMZ

   b. a home computer or network

   c. a business computer or network

   d. a virtual private network connecting two LANs

7. What is the primary problem with a screening router setup?

   a. The router can be improperly configured.

   b. The router may not provide an adequate screen.

   c. The router cannot be used with a firewall.

   d. The router alone cannot stop many types of attacks.

8. Name three functions that most firewalls cannot handle by themselves and that need to be performed by additional software products.

9. What enables a server farm to work together to handle requests?

   a. a router

   b. a switch

   c. a network hub

   d. load balancing software

10. Why would a company consider going through the expense and extra work involved in purchasing and installing clusters of servers and creating multiple DMZs?

    a. The network can better handle high traffic.

    b. The company can put more information online.

    c. The company gains better security.

    d. The company gains another layer of defense.

11. Why create a protected subnet within an already-protected internal network? (Choose all that apply.)

    a. to protect Web servers

    b. to protect customer information

    c. to protect management servers

    d. to protect the company's reputation

12. What is the purpose of making a connection between DMZs that belong to the networks of separate companies?

    a. load balancing

    b. Defense in Depth

    c. configuration information

    d. honeypot information

13. A corporation that maintains multiple branch offices has decided to maintain multiple firewalls, one to protect each branch office's network. What is the most efficient way to maintain each of those firewalls?

    a. Use a centralized security workstation.

    b. Send security policy information to each network administrator.

    c. Set up remote desktop management software such as pcAnywhere.

    d. Broadcast configuration instructions periodically by e-mail.

14. Software or hardware that is configured to monitor traffic heading from the internal network to the Internet is called a ____________. (Choose all that apply.)

    a. stateful packet filter

    b. proxy server

    c. reverse firewall

    d. Network Address Translation (NAT)

15. Which of the following is an advantage of using a software firewall over a hardware firewall?

    a. throughput

    b. reliability

    c. cost

    d. availability

16. Which of the following is an advantage of using a hardware firewall over a software firewall? (Choose all that apply.)

    a. scalability

    b. cost

    c. ease of maintenance

    d. throughput

17. Virtually every type of firewall depends on what configurable feature for its effectiveness?

    a. network connection

    b. state table

    c. rule base

    d. management console

18. Given that many kinds of network traffic can pass through a network gateway, what is the problem with creating a long and complex rule base that is designed to handle every possible situation? (Choose all that apply.)

    a. disk space

    b. slower performance

    c. danger of misconfiguration

    d. danger of missing attack attempts

19. The most important rules in a rule base should go where?

    a. in the ACL

    b. at the bottom of the rule base

    c. in the state table

    d. at the top of the rule base

20. What works by using applications such as e-mail programs to spread information?

    a. spyware

    b. worm

    c. Trojan horses

    d. malformed packets

Hands-on Projects

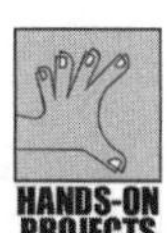

Project 4-1: Creating a Firewall Configuration Diagram

When you are called upon to create and install a firewall configuration for a network, you will need to be able to create a diagram showing how the system will be implemented. Such a diagram can be useful at the planning phase or if you are proposing a security setup for the network.

1. Draw a diagram depicting a screening router configuration. Use a simple circle or rectangle to represent the LAN being protected.
2. Draw a dual-homed host configuration. Be sure to label the external and internal interfaces of the dual-homed host.
3. Draw a screened host configuration. Again, be sure to label the external and internal interfaces of the screened host.

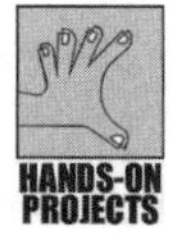

Project 4-2: Limiting Unnecessary Services

When it comes time for you to set up a bastion host, one of the most important tasks is to stop any services you have running on that machine. Often, an operating system by default has a number of services running that you do not really need; a Windows XP system with a typical setup might have as many as 80 services running at any one time. The following steps show you how to inventory and stop running services on a Windows XP or 2000 computer.

1. Click **Start** and then click **Control Panel**. Click **Start,** point to **Settings**, and then click **Control Panel** on Windows 2000.
2. Double-click **Administrative Tools**.
3. Double-click **Services**.
4. If necessary, click the **Standard** tab near the bottom of the Services window.
5. Scroll down the list of services and see if there are any you don't need. (You may want to refer to *www.blkviper.com/WinXP/servicecfg.htm* for a list of services you can safely eliminate.) For instance, check Routing and Remote Access. If this service is listed as Started in the Status column, double-click it.
6. In the Routing and Remote Access Properties dialog box, click **Stop** to stop the service.
7. Select **Disabled** in the Startup type drop-down list to stop the service from restarting automatically in the future.
8. Click **OK** to close Routing and Remote Access Properties and return to Services.

9. Repeat Steps 5 through 8 for other services you want to stop.
10. When you are done, close all open windows to return to the Windows desktop.

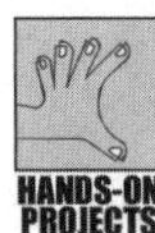

Project 4-3: Eliminating Unnecessary Accounts

Another important aspect of creating a bastion host is eliminating user accounts that you do not need, and that present hackers with possible vulnerable spots that they can exploit. Often, the Guest account on Windows systems gives them a way to get in. You should also have only one Administrator account. Your job is to eliminate or disable all unnecessary accounts except the ones you need for administration. The following steps show you how to do this on a Windows 2000 or XP computer.

On a Windows XP computer:

1. Click **Start** and click **Control Panel**.
2. Double-click **User Accounts**.
3. The user accounts are displayed. If you see the message "Guest account is on" under Guest, click **Guest**. The User Accounts dialog box for the Guest account opens on the screen. Click **Turn off the Guest account**. The account is turned off and you automatically return to the previous User Accounts dialog box.
4. If you see more than one account labeled Computer administrator, decide which administrator account you want to keep. Click each of the others in succession. In the next User Accounts screen that appears, either click **Delete the account** or **Change the account type** to reduce access privileges.

On a Windows 2000 computer:

1. Click **Start**, point to **Settings**, and click **Control Panel**.
2. Double-click **Users and Passwords**.
3. In the Users and Passwords dialog box, click **Guest**, and then **Delete**. What happens? Write the answer in a lab notebook or word processing document. Then click **Properties**.
4. In the Guest Properties dialog box, click **Restricted User**, and then click **OK**. Guest Properties closes and you return to Users and Passwords.
5. In the Users and Properties dialog box, check for multiple Administrator accounts you don't need. Click any unnecessary accounts, and then click **Remove**.
6. When you are done, click **OK** to close Users and Passwords.
7. Click the **Close** box to close the Control Panel window and return to the Windows desktop.

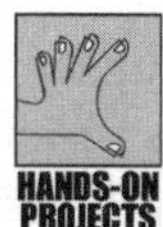

Project 4-4: Installing a Freeware Firewall Program

As stated in this chapter, freeware firewall programs are available on the Internet—programs that you can download and install for personal use without being charged a shareware or purchase fee. Such programs aren't as full-featured as commercial firewalls, but they're good for testing and learning how such programs work. In this project you need a Windows 2000 or XP computer to download and start to use the freeware version of a popular personal firewall, ZoneAlarm by Zone Labs.

1. Double-click the **Internet Explorer** icon on your desktop.
2. Enter the URL **download.com.com/** in your browser's Address bar and press **Enter** to go to CNET's Download.com home page.
3. In the Search box, type **ZoneAlarm** and click **Go!**. (Alternatively, you can type the following direct URL: **download.com.com/3000-2092-10039884 .html?part=zonealarm&subj= dlpage&tag=button**.)
4. Click the first **Download Now** link. A page notifying you that a third-party download site is being contacted. When the File Download dialog box appears, click **Open** to begin downloading.
5. The ZoneAlarm Installation wizard opens automatically after the download is completed. Follow the steps shown in the wizard to select a location for ZoneAlarm, enter your personal information, and accept the license agreement. When you are done, click **Install** to close the wizard and install the software.
6. When a User survey dialog box appears, choose options from the drop-down lists displayed, and then click **Finish**.
7. When the ZoneAlarm Setup dialog box asks if you want to start ZoneAlarm now, click **Yes**.
8. Click the **ZoneAlarm** button on the taskbar to open the Welcome window, if it does not appear already.
9. Click **Next**. Leave the default option (Alert me whenever ZoneAlarm blocks traffic) selected.
10. Click **Finish**. The Secure Programs window appears. (By clicking Yes, you enable the program to grant applications you normally use with access to the Internet.) In this case, to give you more control over the process, you should click **Advanced**, and then click **Next**.
11. When the next screen appears (it has the heading Secure Your Programs for Internet Access), click **Add**.
12. In the Add Program dialog box, locate the program you usually use to browse the Internet. If you use Internet Explorer, the program file is called **iexplore.exe**: click this file and then click **Open**. The program is added to the list of programs in the ZoneAlarm wizard.

13. Repeat Steps 11 and 12 for any other programs you want to access the Internet, such as your e-mail application(s), FTP programs, and so on. (For example, if you use Outlook Express for e-mail, the program's name is *msimn.exe*, and if you use Netscape Navigator, the program's name is *netscape.exe*.) When you are done, click **Finish**.
14. When the Congratulations! screen appears, click **Skip the tutorial and start ZoneAlarm**, and then click **Finish**.
15. A series of ZoneAlarm Alert dialog boxes may appear as the program starts up, depending on what your are currently accessing on the Internet. If a dialog box asks you whether you want Generic Host Process for Win32 to access the Internet, click **Yes**.

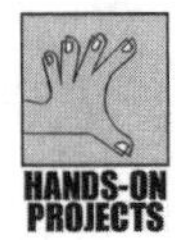

Project 4-5: Adding Computers to a Trusted Zone

If you work on a network, you need to allow other computers to communicate with yours. By default, ZoneAlarm blocks all connections until you identify the computers you want to be able to access your machine freely. The following steps add a computer to your trusted zone.

If you don't already have the information, you will need to determine the IP addresses of the other computers in your lab network. To do so, open a Command Prompt window, type ipconfig, and press Enter to determine the IP address.

1. Open the ZoneAlarm window if it is not open already.
2. Click **Firewall** in the list of program features.
3. Click the **Zones** tab. A list of computers in your "trusted zone" appears. If only one machine is listed, you probably need to add others to your zone.
4. Click **Add**, and then click **IP Range**.
5. In the Add IP Range dialog box, enter the starting address for the first IP address in your lab network or other local network in the first IP Address box. Enter the ending address in the second IP Address box. Then enter a name for the network, and then click **OK**.
6. Click **Apply**.

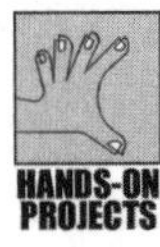

Project 4-6: Tracing a Blocked IP Address

ZoneAlarm will block all traffic from outside computers unless you specifically tell the program that a particular type of traffic is to be allowed. When you first start to use the program, you are likely to get a flood of Alert Messages, and corresponding log file entries for each type of connection attempt that is blocked. Some connections might be legitimate communications from your own ISP. However, many others are from hackers. You can use the program tracert, which is included with Windows 2000 and XP (as well as Linux and other versions of Windows) to determine whether the server from which the packet is originating is coming from your own ISP or your school, or from a server you don't recognize.

1. To use tracert to determine the origination of a packet, click **Start**, point to **Programs** (**All Programs** on Windows XP), point to **Accessories**, and then open a Command Prompt window: Type **tracert** followed by one blank space, type the IP address you want to investigate, and press **Enter**.
2. Using the information you gathered in Step 1, determine what IP addresses aren't suspicious: contact your school's network administrator or the office that manages Internet services, and ask what range of IP addresses are commonly used to give access to on-campus computers. If you use an ISP to connect to the Internet, contact the ISP and ask what IP address ranges it uses for its customers.
3. Double-click the **ZoneAlarm** icon in your system tray to start up the program.
4. First, make sure alerts are on. Click **Alerts & Logs** on the left side of the ZoneAlarm window.
5. Make sure that the Log viewer tab is selected. Keep track of the kinds of alert messages you receive. Do you receive any NetBIOS connection attempts from IP addresses that are not on your network? What could be the source of a NetBIOS scan? Write down the information in your lab book. Then view ZoneAlarm's Web page on NetBIOS scans at *http://fwalerts.zonelabs.com/cat-port/netbiosscan.shtml*.
6. Do you get any attempts to connect on ports such as 1243 or 53001? Write down the port numbers displayed in the Destination IP column after the IP addresses shown, and see if any match the list of ports that well-known Trojan horse programs attempt to use. (Review the list at *http://fwalerts.zonelabs.com/cat-mal/trojanports_num.shtml*.)
7. Do you get any attempts to connect on port 137? This port is commonly used by WINS registration. What could be the cause of this common connection attempt that is related to Windows?
8. When you are done evaluating alert messages, click **Alerts & Logs** in the ZoneAlarm window, click the **Main** tab, and click **Off** under Alert Events Shown to stop the program from showing you alert messages.

Case Projects

Case Project 4-1: Layers of Defense for High-Traffic Networks

You install a firewall at the perimeter of your company network, and create a DMZ that contains a Web server and FTP server, so that visitors can gain access to your Web site and download trial and commercial versions of software that you create. Over time, your company's products gain in popularity to the point where your Web server is receiving several thousand "hits" per hour. Diagram a setup that would enable your Web server to handle a steadily increasing amount of traffic while still providing security for the internal LAN.

Case Project 4-2: Trying to Attract Hackers

You have been experiencing intrusion attempts from a number of different sources, but you are unable to identify who might be attempting to hack into your network because they do not stay in your DMZ very long. They have not been able to access your internal LAN as yet, but you fear they will eventually be able to do so. What would you suggest for attracting intruders and getting them to stay on your site long enough to be traced? What are the pros and cons of such a strategy?

Case Project 4-3: A Failover Firewall Design

Your organization's security policy calls for your Web site to be online 95 to 100% of the time, even in case of a firewall failure due to a Denial of Service attack or other problem. You know that one way to ensure the availability of the Web server and other publicly accessible computers in your DMZ is to protect them with two firewalls. What are the requirements for such a setup? How might you configure the two firewalls?

Case Project 4-4: Tracking Connection Attempts

After installing a firewall program on your computer, you receive a number of connection alerts that tell you connection attempts are being made on your computer's UDP port 1027. You go to *www.seifried.org/security/ports/1000/1027.html*, where you learn that this port is used by the instant messaging program ICQ, and is commonly exploited by hackers (as well as port 1024). The firewall has successfully blocked the attempts, but you are concerned that repeated attempts will come at a moment when the firewall is not functioning. What can you do to prevent hackers from getting through on ICQ port 1027?

Case Project 4-5: Monitoring Outbound Network Traffic

Your company is concerned about the amount of staff time supposedly spent surfing entertainment and shopping sites on the Web during office hours. You are asked to come up with a way to monitor and track (and possibly, block) connections from hosts on the internal network trying to make outbound connections to the Internet. How could you do this with a firewall?

CHAPTER

5

CONFIGURING FIREWALLS

After reading this chapter and completing the exercises, you will be able to:

- Describe the difference between stateless and stateful packet filtering
- Create different packet filter rules for real-world situations
- Set up Network Address Translation (NAT)
- Decide when to use user, session, or client authentication

After you have determined the best firewall configuration for your network defense needs, you can get down to the nitty-gritty of actually configuring the firewall to do the things it needs to do to protect you.

Depending on the type of firewall you've installed, you can do much more than simple packet filtering. You may also be able to set up Network Address Translation (NAT) and user authentication as well. In fact, firewalls are doing more and more different types of security activities.

In this chapter, you examine the basic tasks that a firewall actually does. You deal with packet filtering, NAT, and authentication.

APPROACHES TO PACKET FILTERING

In Chapter 2, you were introduced to packet filtering. Chapter 3 discussed the importance of a security policy toward creating a network defense program. In Chapter 4, you began to examine some of the specific packet filtering rules that can enable network communications through a firewall. Now, you're going to put all these pieces together to develop a packet-filtering rule base. First, you'll learn about stateless and stateful packet filtering. Then, you'll learn how a packet filter's activities depend on the other security components it is intended to work with, and its position in your perimeter security configuration.

Stateless Packet Filtering

As you have learned in preceding chapters, packet filters work by filtering traffic that arrives on the perimeter of one network. Stateless packet filters decide whether to allow or block packets based on the information in the protocol headers. Most often, filtering is done on common IP protocol header features such as:

- *IP address*— Each packet filter rule specifies a source IP address and a destination IP address.
- *Ports and sockets*— Ports make filtering rules more granular: they give you a finer level of control over what is allowed and what is blocked. A socket is a software connection that enables an application to send and receive data using a network protocol.
- *ACK bits*— These are parts of TCP headers and they are discussed in the section "Filtering by ACK Bit" later in this chapter.

Consider the simple set of rules for a firewall located at 192.168.120.1, on computer network 192.168.120.0, as shown in Table 5.1.

Table 5-1 Stateless packet filter rules

Rule	Source IP	Source Port	Destination IP	Destination Port	Action
1	Any	Any	192.168.120.0	>1023	Allow
2	192.168.120.1	Any	Any	Any	Deny
3	Any	Any	192.168.120.1	Any	Deny
4	192.168.120.0	Any	Any	Any	Any
5	Any	Any	192.168.120.2	25	Allow
6	Any	Any	192.168.120.3	80	Allow
7	Any	Any	Any	Any	Deny

An explanation of each of these rules follows:

- *Rule 1* —Many external hosts that are contacted by a host on the internal network respond by connecting to TCP ports above 1023; this rule enables such connections.
- *Rule 2* —This rule prevents the firewall from connecting to any other hosts, either external or internal. The firewall is only supposed to monitor traffic, not to make connections itself. A hacker who manages to get control of the firewall might conceivably try to use it to make such a connection; this rule would block it.
- *Rule 3* —This rule would provide extra security for the firewall, in addition to Rule 2, by keeping external users from establishing a direct connection to the firewall.
- *Rule 4* —This rule enables internal hosts to make connections to computers outside the network.
- *Rule 5* —This rule enables external users to send e-mail into the network.
- *Rule 6* —This rule gives external users the ability to access the network's Web server.
- *Rule 7* —This cleanup rule denies any other traffic that has not been explicitly allowed by previous rules.

However, people can get around such defenses easily. For instance, consider the first rule: hosts that are responding to connections are allowed access to ports above 1023. The problem is that this rule will also enable connections that have been faked to seem like they are responding to connections to gain access as well.

Stateless packet filters do have their advantages. One advantage is cost; they tend to be inexpensive, and many are free. Some are included with routers or open source operating systems. On the other hand, stateless filters can be cumbersome to maintain in a complex network. They are vulnerable to IP spoofing attacks, and they offer no form of authentication.

Stateful Packet Filtering

Stateless packet filters aren't sufficient for most needs. They lack the ability to filter intrusions that occur when someone connects to a computer without the computer already having initiated a connection. Without a connection in place, a hacker can spoof the computer into creating one where one does not exist. Denial of Service (DoS) and other attacks can result. Another potential vulnerability is that a stateless filter handles every packet on an individual basis and has no recollection of what packets have already passed through the filter. Previously forwarded packets belonging to a connection have no bearing on the filter's decision to forward or drop a packet.

A stateful packet filter keeps a record of the connections that the host computer has made with other computers. Stateful packet filters maintain a file called a **state table** that contains a record of all current connections. The packet filter will allow incoming packets to pass through it only from external hosts that are already connected and that have a record in the state table.

Here is a more concrete example. Suppose a firewall has Rule 1 of Table 5-1 in its rule base, external connections are allowed on ports above 1023. One of the hosts on the internal network has specific connections underway, as recorded in a short sample from a state table shown in Table 5-2.

Table 5-2 State table example

Source IP	Source Port	Destination IP	Destination Port	Connection State
192.168.120.101	1037	209.233.19.22	80	Established
192.168.120.104	1022	165.66.28.22	80	Established
192.168.120.107	1010	65.66.122.101	25	Established
192.168.120.102	1035	213.136.87.88	79	Established
223.56.78.11	1899	192.168.120.101	80	Established
206.121.55.8	3558	192.168.120.101	80	Established
224.209.122.1	1079	192.168.120.105	80	Established

Ports numbered 1023 and lower are reserved for the use of specific protocols or other purposes. Therefore, when a Web page you originally request using your own port 80 is sent back to you, the Web server returns it using a TCP port higher than 1023. That's why it's important for a firewall to allow such connections.

In the state table, a number of internal hosts on the network that have the address range 192.168.120.0 to 192.168.120.255 have established connections with hosts on the external network. Some are using HTTP port 80 to connect via the World Wide Web. One has established a connection to an e-mail server on port 25. Near the bottom of the table, several external hosts have established connections to hosts on the internal network on port 80.

Suppose a hacker tries to connect to the network on port 10995 from IP address 201.202.100.1 by sending a packet that has the ACK TCP header set. The ACK header normally is sent at the end of a "handshake" between two networked computers and means that a connection is established. When the stateful firewall receives such a packet, it checks the state table to see if a connection between any host on the internal network and the computer at 201.202.100.1 exists. If such a connection is not found on the state table, the packet is dropped.

One of the simplest stateful packet filters you can use is built into Windows XP. You select a network connection that you want to protect, and activate the firewall by checking a box in the Advanced tab of the connection's Properties dialog box (see Figure 5-1).

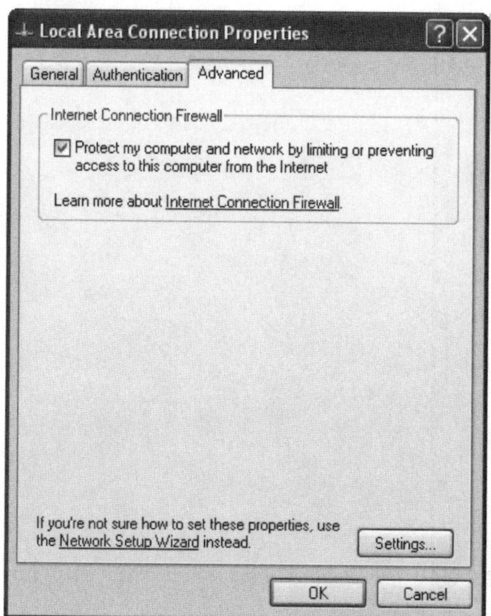

Figure 5-1 Windows XP's Internet Connection Firewall performs stateful filtering

The Internet Connection Firewall makes use of a state table to track connections based on source and destination IP address: it blocks any connections that the host computer has not already initiated, unless an entry has specifically been made in the program's Services tab (see Figure 5-2) to allow passage of such traffic.

The problem with Internet Connection Firewall is that its level of protection is not very **granular** —it doesn't allow you the very fine level of control that you need to limit the amount of traffic as much as possible. You cannot limit specific IP addresses or ports, for example. For that, you need a more full-featured firewall, such as Check Point NG.

Stateful packet filtering does not necessarily address all of the problems with static filtering. Authentication, for instance, may still not be addressed.

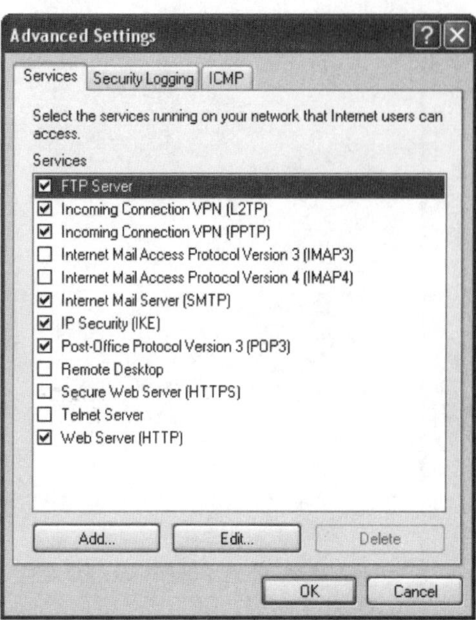

Figure 5-2 You can specify which services can gain access, but not specific IP addresses or ports

Packet Filtering Depends on Position

The type of filtering that a firewall, router, or other packet filtering device performs depends on its position in the firewall perimeter configuration, and on the other hardware or software with which its activities need to be coordinated. For instance, a packet filter that is positioned between the Internet and an individual host or a network, and that provides the only protection for that host or network, needs to be configured with a great deal of care: all of the inbound and outbound traffic needs to be accounted for in the packet filter's rule base.

In contrast, a packet filter that is placed between a proxy server and the Internet needs to help in shielding all internal users from external hosts. A company that is highly concerned about protecting the privacy of its individual employees and its **data warehouses** (storehouses of proprietary information) might install a proxy server on the perimeter of a network. A **proxy server** handles traffic on behalf of the individual computers on the network it protects, rebuilding both outbound and inbound requests from scratch in order to hide internal IP address information. A packet filter placed between the proxy server and the Internet would need to direct traffic to and from the proxy server. One of its primary goals would be to prevent any direct connections between the internal network and the Internet (see Figure 5-3).

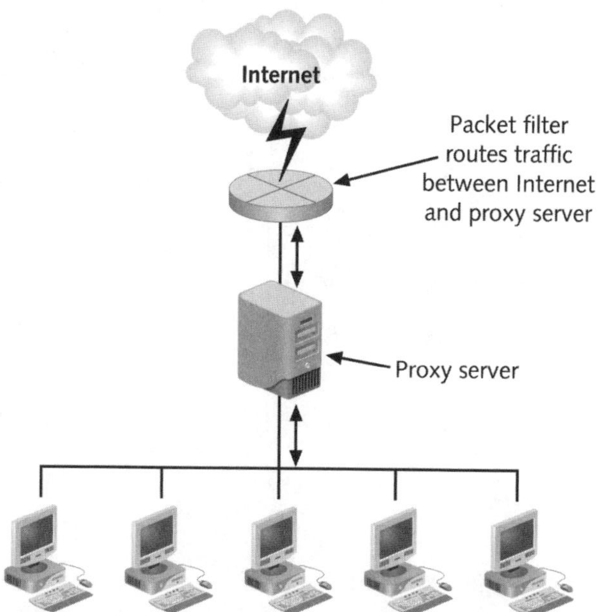

Figure 5-3 A packet filter connects a proxy server with the Internet

Proxy servers, in fact, can perform stateful packet filtering on their own. They operate at the Application layer of the OSI model of network communications and, as a result, they are able to make intelligent decisions about what traffic is allowed to pass. The tradeoff is the drop in performance that can result from the demand that proxy servers place on the host computer, which is significantly higher than those associated with a traditional firewall.

Another type of configuration would combine packet filtering with a DMZ. One common setup would be to place packet-filtering devices (routers or firewalls) at either end of the DMZ. The packet filter on the external interface of the DMZ would need to allow Internet users to gain access to the servers on the DMZ, but would need to block access to the internal LAN. The packet filter on the internal interface would perform a similar function, but for internal users: it would enable them to access the servers on the DMZ, but not connect directly to the Internet. Rather, they would connect to the Internet through a proxy server located on the DMZ (see Figure 5-4).

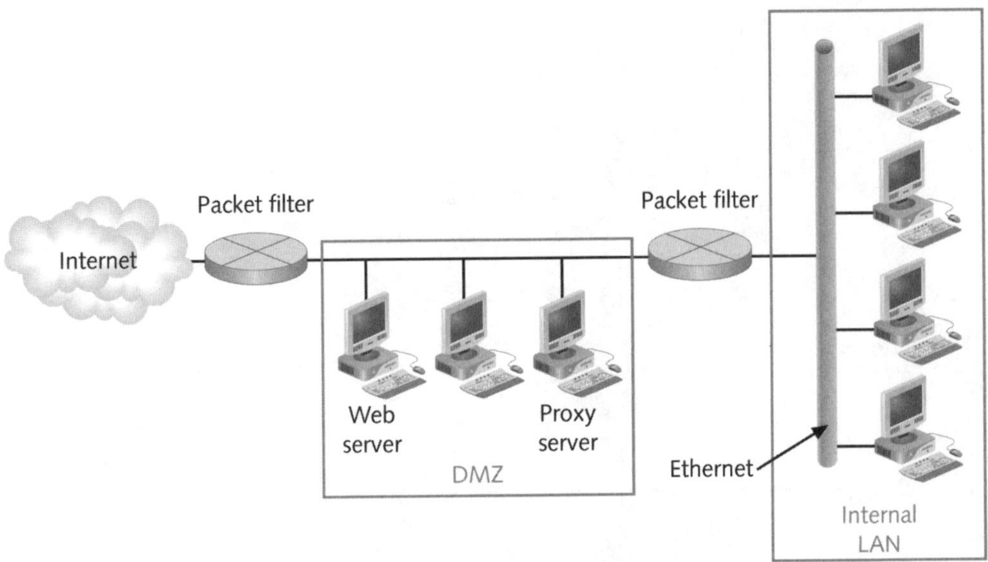

Figure 5-4 Packet filters routing traffic to and from a DMZ

The question of how many packet filters to use and where to place them depends on your needs. A simple home network might gain adequate protection from a single well-configured stateful packet filter. A small business network that needs to protect proprietary information can use a proxy server/packet filter combination to prevent any external users from "seeing" IP or port information associated with hosts on the internal network. If no IP address or ports are visible through port scans or other means, no attacks can be launched. For larger companies that run public Web servers and that have proprietary information to protect, placing packet filters on either side of a DMZ can provide effective multilayered protection for both public servers and employees.

Creating Packet Filter Rules

After you have determined where your packet filtering devices need to be positioned and what their functions will be on the network, you need to establish the rule base that enables them to function. The packet filtering rule base is the primary security tool employed by many routers; it is also the fundamental security function performed by virtually all firewalls. Packet filter rules can and should be tailored to meet a network's special needs. However, there are a few general practices that every rule base should follow:

- A firewall or packet filter that follows a "Deny All" security policy should start from a "clean slate"; in other words, it should begin by blocking all traffic of any sort, and then selectively allow services as needed.
- The rule base should keep everyone except the network administrators from connecting to the firewall. (Anyone who accesses the firewall can learn all the IP addresses on the internal network, and open up access to the internal network.)

- The rule base should block direct access from the Internet to any computers behind the firewall or packet filter. All inbound traffic, in other words, should be filtered first.
- In addition, the rule base should permit access to public servers in the DMZ, and should enable individual users in the organization to access the Internet.

A rule base, then, is a mixture of rules that denies access and allows access on a selective basis. Table 5-3 lists a typical set of such rules; the table assumes that the firewall is located at 192.168.120.1, the e-mail server at 192.168.120.2, the Web server at 192.168.120.3, and the DNS server at 192.168.120.4. The internal network is represented by 192.168.120.0.

Table 5-3 A typical packet filtering rule base

Rule	Source IP	Source Port	Destination IP	Destination Port	Action	What It Does
1	192.168.120.1	Any	Any	Any	Deny	Prevents the firewall itself from making any connections
2	Any	Any	192.168.120.1	Any	Deny	Prevents anyone from connecting to the firewall
3	192.168.120.0	Any	Any	Any	Allow	Allows internal users to access external computers
4	192.168.120.0	Any	192.168120.4	53	Allow	Enables internal users to connect to the DNS server
5	Any	Any	192.168.120.2	25	Allow	Allows external and internal users to access the e-mail server via SMTP port 25
6	192.168.120.0	Any	192.168.120.2	110	Allow	Enables internal users to connect to the e-mail server using POP3 port 110
7	Any	Any	192.168.120.3	80	Allow	Enables both external and internal users to connect to the Web server
8	Any	Any	Any	Any	Deny	Blocks all traffic not covered by previous rules

Packet filters can usually give you more fine-grained control over what traffic can be blocked or allowed. The more flexibility you have, the greater your ability to control specific types of traffic. The following sections provide an overview of the more common TCP or IP header elements you can identify in order to filter packets as they hit the firewall: TCP or UDP port number, ICMP message type, the name of the service being used, ACK bit, or IP option settings.

Filtering by TCP or UDP Port Number

TCP/IP and UDP both provide for the transmission of information by breaking it into segments of uniform length called **packets** (or, just as often, **datagrams**). Packets can vary in length from, say, 54 bits of information to 1054 bits; however, the important thing to remember is that a system that uses TCP or UDP will send packets in a particular transmission that are all the same length so that they are more easily sent and received by individual computers. An individual file might be broken into multiple packets, but those packets are all of the same length.

Ports Help Packets Reach their Destination

Packet filters work by reviewing the header information in packets and deciding whether to drop or allow the packets based on parts of that information. You already know about filtering packets on source and IP addresses. The IP address (which is provided by the IP part of the TCP/IP protocol) enables the information to reach the right computer. However, in order to reach their final destination—a server or client program within the computer that will process the information in the data portion—packets also need to specify a port number (which is provided for by the TCP part of the TCP/IP protocol). The term port, in this sense, does not refer to the plugs on the back of a computer; rather, a port is a logical concept that identifies the type of information in the packet and the program that should process it. A port number is like the apartment number in the address "1234 Anywhere St., Apt. 101." The address will get a message to the right building, but the apartment number is needed to direct that message to its ultimate destination within the building.

When packets arrive at a device such as a packet filter or firewall, they are passed between server or client by means of the port number, which appears not as the decimal number we recognize (such as port 21 for FTP), but as a binary equivalent (such as 10101, the binary equivalent of the decimal number 21).

If you're interested in converting common decimal port numbers to their binary equivalents or vice versa, try out the online Binary Decimal Converter Calculator at *http://mistupid.com/computers/binaryconv.htm.*

Filtering by TCP or UDP port numbers is commonly called either **port filtering** or **protocol filtering** . Using TCP or UDP port numbers can help you filter a wide variety of different types of information, including SMTP and POP e-mail messages, NetBIOS sessions, DNS requests, and Network News Transfer Protocol (NNTP) newsgroup sessions. You can filter out everything but TCP Port 80 for Web, TCP Port 25 for e-mail, or TCP Port 21 for FTP. The port filtering process is illustrated in Figure 5-5.

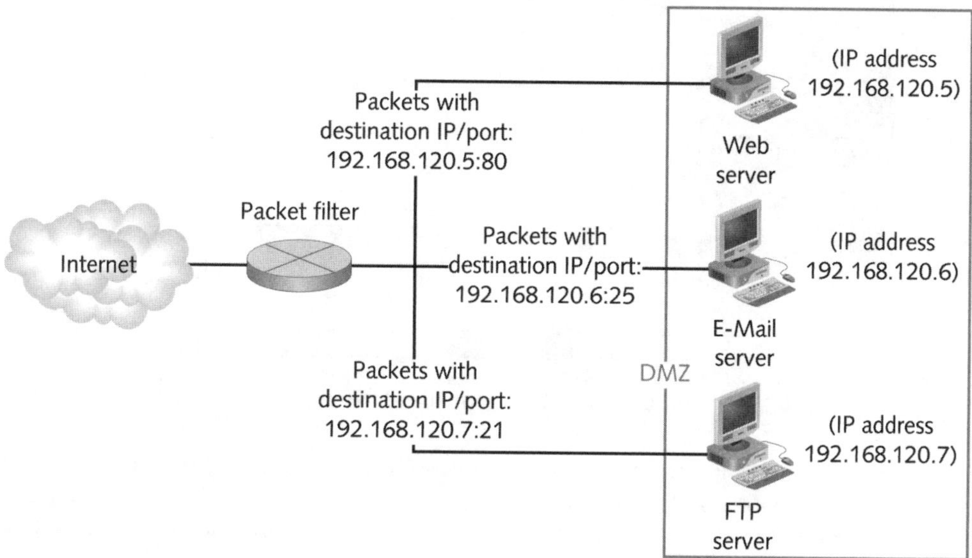

Figure 5-5 Port numbers direct packets to the client or server that needs them

Source and Destination Ports

Figure 5-5 indicates that ports are filtered by a router and directed to the appropriate combination of computer and software by their IP address and port number. The port numbers shown in Figure 5-5 are technically correct: port 80 is reserved for HTTP Web pages, port 25 for SMTP e-mail, and so on. However, in practice, when two computers exchange information, they use two different port numbers: the port from which data is sent out (the **source port**), and the port at which the response data is received (the **destination port**). You can see the two ports in action if you use the packet capture program Ethereal to connect to a Web site such as Course Technology's (*www.course.com*). Some of the packets sent back and forth during this request are shown in Figure 5-6.

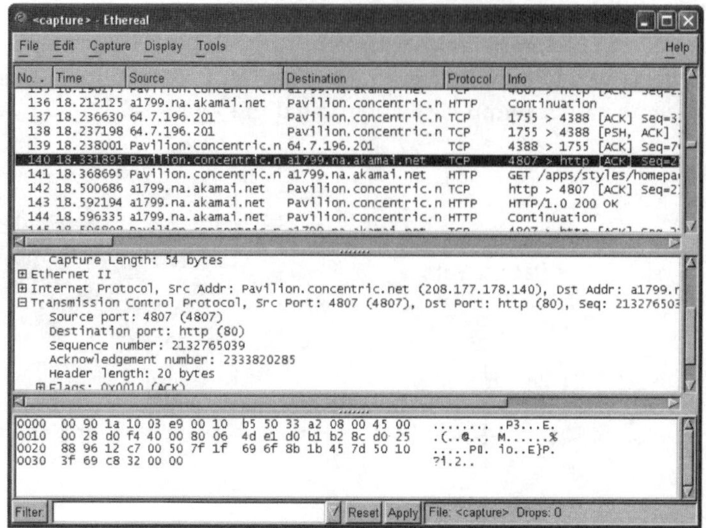

Figure 5-6 TCP and UDP transmissions use different source and destination ports

As you can see in the Transmission Control Protocol section of the Ethereal window shown in Figure 5-6, a packet 54 bytes in length is being sent from the remote server at *akamai.net* (a service that hosts image files for many business Web sites) to the author's computer (*pavilion.concentric.net*). The source port—the port being used by the computer that initiates the transmission—is 4807, which is different from the destination port, the usual HTTP port 80.

Ethereal is available for download at *www.ethereal.com*.

It's quite normal for network communications between two computers to use different source and destination ports (in fact, it's rare for the source and destination ports to be the same). However, the fact that ports are different and that the destination port is dynamically determined—that is, determined on a per-connection basis and therefore impossible to predict—makes filtering by port number complicated.

First, you need to understand how port numbers are allocated. The Internet Assigned Numbers Authority (IANA) has allocated a range of ports from 0 to 65535 for TCP/UDP communications. Ports from 0 to 1023 are called **well-known ports** —ports that have been reserved for use by common services ranging from Telnet to chat. **Dynamic port numbers** —numbers that applications assume for the length of a communications session—are supposed to be limited to the range 49152 through 65535. In practice, however, many applications use ports in the range from 1024 to 49152. Traditionally, network administrators would configure packet filters to filter packets that use ports below

1024. In fact, these days, the ports above 1024 are the ones that need to be monitored and that are commonly exploited by Trojan horse applications and Denial of Service (DoS) attacks from hackers.

There isn't a magic solution to filtering services based on port number when the ports are above 1023. You have to know what services you are running on your network and what ports are used by those services; you block the ports you don't need and allow the ones you do. For instance, if you are on a Windows-based network, your computers probably use NetBIOS name service to find one another on NetBIOS ports 137, 138, and 139. However, such traffic should originate inside your internal network and stay inside the firewall; any traffic coming from the Internet that attempts to use such ports should be dropped. You should block inbound traffic that attempts to use ports that are assigned to other Windows networking services as well. Table 5-4 provides some examples; note that this table adds a new element that is found in many firewalls or packet filters—the specification of the direction in which the traffic is flowing. In Table 5-4, the traffic is inbound and being received at the external interface (EXT, the interface that connects to the Internet). In Table 5-6, you will also see traffic that is outbound and being received at the internal interface (INT, the interface that connects to the internal LAN).

The Internet Security Services (ISS) Web site maintains a list of common Windows services and the ports they use at *www.iss.net/security_center/advice/Exploits/Ports/groups/Microsoft/default.htm.* ISS also maintains a list of UNIX services and ports at *www.iss.net/security_center/advice/Exploits/Ports/groups/UNIX/default.htm.*

UNIX, too, has its own set of services that should be blocked when coming inbound from the Internet. Some examples are shown in Table 5-5.

The problem with specifying a port number for filtering is that some applications don t use a fixed port number when they reply to a client. AOL instant messenger, as well as the messaging program ICQ, is known for this: it assigns itself dynamic port numbers, which are only used for the length of a particular communication. You have to filter such communications by IP address instead.

ICMP Message Type

Internet Control Message Protocol (ICMP) functions as a sort of housekeeping protocol for TCP/IP, helping networks to cope with various communication problems. From a security standpoint, ICMP packets have a downside: they can be used by hackers to crash computers on your network. Because ICMP packets have no authentication method to verify the recipient of a packet, hackers can attempt man-in-the-middle attacks, in which they impersonate the intended recipient; they can also send packets that send the ICMP Redirect message type to direct traffic to a computer they control that is outside the protected network. A firewall/packet filter must be able to determine, based on its message type, whether an ICMP packet should be allowed to pass. Some rules that you can use to block the more common ICMP message types are shown in Table 5-6.

Table 5-4 Windows services and ports

Rule	EXT	Protocol	Source IP	Source Port	Destination IP	Destination Port	Action	Service
1	X	TCP	Any	Any	Any	135	Deny	NetBIOS RPC
2	X	UDP	Any	Any	Any	135	Deny	NetBIOS RPC
3	X	TCP	Any	Any	Any	137	Deny	NetBIOS Name Service
4	X	UDP	Any	Any	Any	137	Deny	NetBIOS Name Service
5	X	TCP	Any	Any	Any	445	Deny	SMB/File Sharing
6	X	UDP	Any	Any	Any	445	Deny	SMB/File Sharing
7	X	TCP	Any	Any	Any	1720	Deny	Net Meeting
8	X	UDP	Any	Any	Any	1720	Deny	Net Meeting
9	X	TCP	Any	Any	Any	1755	Deny	Windows Media
10	X	UDP	Any	Any	Any	1755	Deny	Windows Media
11	X	TCP	Any	Any	Any	3389	Deny	Remote Desktop Protocol
12	X	UDP	Any	Any	Any	3389	Deny	Remote Desktop Protocol

Table 5-5 UNIX services and ports

Rule	Protocol	Source IP	Source Port	Destination IP	Destination Port	Action	Service
1	TCP	Any	Any	Any	17	Deny	QOTD
2	UDP	Any	Any	Any	17	Deny	QOTD
3	TCP	Any	Any	Any	111	Deny	Portmapper
4	UDP	Any	Any	Any	111	Deny	Portmapper
5	TCP	Any	Any	Any	513	Deny	Remote Login
6	TCP	Any	Any	Any	514	Deny	Syslog
7	UDP	Any	Any	Any	514	Deny	Syslog
8	TCP	Any	Any	Any	635	Deny	mountd (NFS Service)

Table 5-6 ICMP message types

Rule	INT	EXT	Protocol	ICMP Type	Source IP	Source Port	Destination IP	Destination Port	Action
1			ICMP	Source Quench	Any	Any	Any	Any	Deny
2	X		ICMP	Echo Request	Any	Any	Any	Any	Deny
3		X	ICMP	Echo Reply	Any	Any	Any	Any	Deny
4	X		ICMP	Destination Unreachable	Any	Any	Any	Any	Deny
5		X	ICMP	Redirect	Any	Any	Any	Any	Deny
6		X	ICMP	Destination Unreachable	Any	Any	Any	Any	Deny
7			ICMP		Any	Any	Any	Any	Deny

The INT and EXT columns are left empty for Rules 1 and 7 because that enables them to apply to both inbound and outbound traffic. Rule 7 in Table 5-6 is a cleanup rule that drops all ICMP packets that haven't been filtered by previous rules.

Filtering by Service

Some firewalls let you filter by naming the service you want to use. You don't have to specify a port number. Check Point NG does this in its rule base; the rules shown in the Service column in Figure 5-7, for instance, name Telnet, SMTP, and HTTP by name.

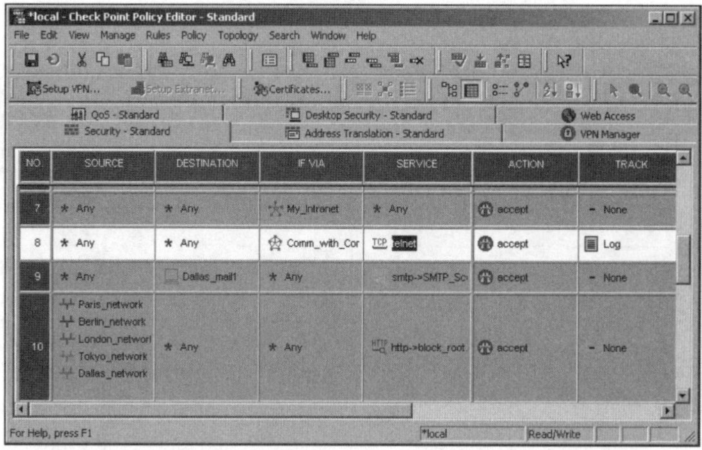

Figure 5-7 Some rule bases let you filter by service

Packets can also be filtered based on the IP protocol ID field in the header. The filter can use the data to allow or deny traffic of an entire type of service, including:

- TCP (Protocol number 6)
- UDP (Protocol number 17)
- IGMP (Protocol number 2)
- ICMP (Protocol number 1)

Internet Group Management Protocol (IGMP) enables a computer to identify its multicast group membership to routers so that it can receive a multicast (a broadcast of streaming media, newsletters, or other content) from another computer. You can find a complete list of protocol numbers at *www.iana.org/assignments/protocol-numbers*.

Filtering by ACK Bit

Transmission Control Protocol (TCP) is intended to enable packets to reach their ultimate destination. TCP provides reliable network communications by guaranteeing that the data will reach its destination in its entirety and in the correct order. Certain bits in the header of the TCP portion of a packet have been set aside to provide signals that indicate whether a packet has been received. IETF RFC 793 includes specifications for six control flags in a TCP header:

- URG (Urgent)
- ACK (Acknowledgment)
- PSH (Push Function)
- RST (Reset the connection)

- SYN (Synchronize sequence numbers)
- FIN (No more data from sender)

The most common control flags are SYN and ACK. They are activated by changing the bit that is allocated to each of them from 0 to 1. SYN is sent when two computers are attempting to make a connection. The first packet in the start of a connection between two computers is distinguished by the fact that it does not have an ACK flag; rather, it has a SYN flag. ACK is sent when the request is acknowledged. If the originating computer does not receive an ACK in a certain period of time, it sends its data again. Every packet that is sent must be responded to with a packet with the ACK bit set to 1 before another packet is sent. Consider a simple request from Computer 1 to Computer 2:

1. Computer 1 sends a packet with the SYN bit set to 1 in its TCP header to Computer 2.
2. Computer 2 responds by sending back a packet with both the SYN and ACK bits set to 1.
3. Computer 1 sends Computer 2 another packet with the ACK bit set to 1, which acknowledges that the connection has been established.

Denial of Service attacks occur when an external computer initiates a connection with a server but never completes the connection by sending the final packet with the ACK bit set to 1. You can prevent such attacks by allowing only packets from outside the network to pass through the firewall by setting up a packet filter rule that blocks all packets that do not have the ACK bit set to 1. In effect, you prevent any external hosts from initiating connections with your network's computers; you allow those external hosts to respond only to connections that have already been established.

IP Option Specifications

Options are a set of flags that can appear in an IP header and whose presence in the header is, as their name implies, optional. Options add information to a packet, as in these examples:

- *Security*— This option enables hosts to send security parameters, handling restrictions, and other information.
- *Loose Source and Record Routing*— This option enables the source computer that is sending the packet to specify the routers that should be used in forwarding the packet to its destination.
- *Strict Source and Record Route*— Same as Loose Source and Record Route, except that the host compute must send the packet directly to the next address in the source route.
- *Internet Timestamp*— Provides a timestamp indicating when the packet was sent.

Both hosts and routers can set the Options field in an IP header. Options, though, are rarely used. They might be of some use if you need to use the Traceroute utility to locate a host, but they are just as frequently abused as well. Source routing, for instance, is not required by any protocol or Internet Service provider. Yet, source routing is a tempting tool to hackers, who only need to enter their own IP address in the destination in order to have the packet returned to them.

NETWORK ADDRESS TRANSLATION (NAT)

If a port number is like the part of an address that helps a piece of mail arrive at the correct apartment in a building, **Network Address Translation (NAT)** is like a mailroom worker who receives mail and routes it to the correct location without the sender ever having to know the correct address. Consider the mail addressed to "Santa Claus, North Pole" or "Santa Claus, c/o the Post Office." The mailroom workers who receive such mail route them (hopefully) to individuals who have taken on the responsibility of responding to such mail, but whose exact locations and identities are kept secret.

NAT works in much the same way: computers outside the internal network being protected don't see the IP addresses of host computers on that internal network. The device that performs NAT (such as a firewall or router) acts as a go-between, receiving requests at its own IP address and forwarding them to the correct IP addresses inside the organization.

Using NAT means that you don't have to assign public IP addresses to each of the computers in your organization in order for those computers to send and receive information on the Internet. The NAT-enabled firewall or router is the only device that needs to have a public IP address (as mentioned in Chapter 1, such addresses are becoming scarce). The internal hosts can be assigned private IP addresses.

NAT is one of the essential functions performed by many firewalls or routers. The NAT device typically has a public, routable IP address. It is one that can be used on the Internet and that does not fall into one of the three private IP address ranges that are set aside for use on Local Area Networks (LANs). (The three private IP address ranges are listed in the section "Subnetting" in Chapter 1.)

The reason for NAT, from a security standpoint, doesn't have to do with conserving IP addresses, however. Rather, by shielding the IP addresses of internal host computers, the NAT-enabled device makes it that much more difficult for hackers to find specific computers to attack. Many attacks begin with a hacker locating a computer that has a static, public IP address; the hacker can then scan the machine for open ports to exploit. If the hacker cannot find the computer's IP address, such attacks might never start. NAT can be performed in two different ways—hide-mode mapping and static mapping—which are described in the sections that follow.

Hide-Mode Mapping

You may already be using a form of NAT called **hide-mode mapping** —the process of hiding multiple private IP addresses behind one public IP address—in your home or classroom network. Consider a computer that functions as a server for a network and that has a gateway to the Internet, and that uses Dynamic Host Control Protocol (DHCP), a protocol that enables IP addresses to be assigned dynamically among the hosts on a network. The server might have a public IP address such as 201.100.13.5, but the addresses on the internal network might be private ones such as 192.168.1.1, 192.168.1.2, 192.168.1.3, and so on. This enables the computers on your network to share the single Internet connection at 201.100.13.5.

Hide-mode NAT enables multiple computers to communicate with the Internet while having their individual IP addresses hidden from other computers on the Internet, as shown in Figure 5-8.

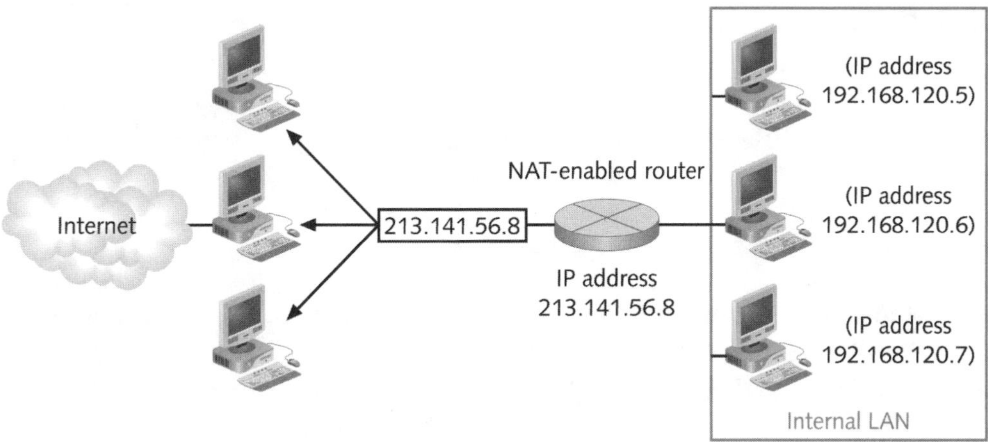

Figure 5-8 Hide-mode NAT

The computers on the Internet see only the IP address of the NAT device; the packets that actually originate from individual internal hosts all seem to be coming from the NAT device.

Hide-mode NAT has significant limitations as well. First, external hosts on the Internet might occasionally need to make connections with hosts on the internal network, using their "real" IP addresses. Second, NAT does not always work, such as if a VPN is in place. In that case, you need to use a static form of NAT.

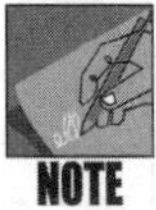

A single device such as a router that performs NAT essentially sets up a firewall for the internal network. In fact, any security scheme that shields one or more computers from external attack is called a firewall in a generic sense. That applies regardless of whether the hardware or software device actually contains the label "firewall."

Static Mapping

Static mapping is a form of NAT in which internal IP addresses are mapped to external, routable IP addresses on a one-to-one basis. The internal IP addresses are still hidden, but the computers that have those internal IP addresses appear to have public, routable IP addresses. Neither the public nor the private IP addresses change dynamically; rather, they are static. The static translation by the NAT device from private to public IP addresses is shown in Figure 5-9.

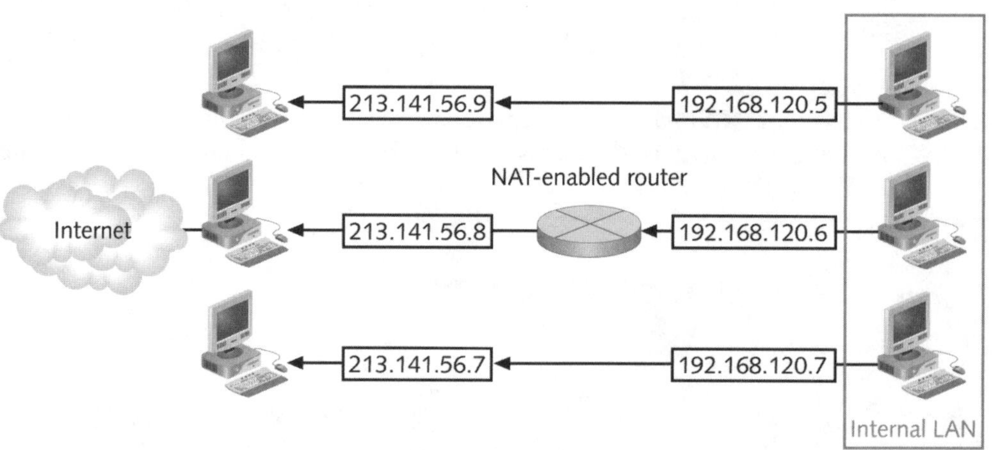

Figure 5-9 Static NAT translation

As you can see in Figure 5-9, each internal IP address has a corresponding public IP address that is visible to external hosts. The external hosts think they are making a direct connection to an internal computer, but in reality, they are still connecting directly to the NAT device, which forwards the request to the internal computer.

Because NAT devices function as a sort of digital "go-between" for internal and external computers, they can be confused with proxy servers. Proxy servers, too, shield internal hosts by forwarding requests from the Internet to individual computers, and vice versa. However, proxy servers completely rebuild packets from scratch before sending them on, while NAT simply forwards packets as is. Proxy filters also provide caching functions that speed up access to documents that need to be accessed repeatedly. You can find out more about proxy servers in Chapter 6.

AUTHENTICATING USERS

Authentication —the process of identifying individuals who are authorized to access the network resources they are requesting and verifying their level of authorization—is an important element in a network defense program, and one that is performed by many of the more full-featured firewalls and intrusion detection systems. It doesn't take too much analysis to identify a variety of ways in which authentication plays an important role in firewall or other security-related configurations.

- As network administrator, you need to log on securely to the firewall itself and make sure unauthorized users cannot use it and possibly gain control of other computers in the network.
- The participants in a virtual private network (VPN) can use a variety of authentication protocols to make sure they can connect to one another.
- In order to change the access control lists in a router you need to be able to log on as administrator.
- If you want to keep track of the Web sites visited by employees in your organization, you can have them authenticate themselves at the firewall so that you don't have to determine who they are from their IP address.

Without authentication, all of your security policies and implementations can be undone because you would not be able to tell who is an authorized user and who is an unauthorized user—and keeping unauthorized users out of your network is, after all, the primary goal of a network defense effort.

In general, authentication depends on the exchange of information that tells one entity that the other entity is recognized as an authorized user and can be trusted. That information can be a password; a long, encrypted block of code called a **key** ; a formula used to verify digital information called a checksum; a physical object such as a smart card; or physical information gained from biometrically reading fingerprints, retinas, or voiceprints.

This section describes the different kinds of authentication schemes you may have to put into use when configuring a firewall. First, you examine what can be authenticated: users, clients, or sessions. Next, you examine how the authentication is actually done, through, for instance, the exchange of passwords or keys (blocks of encrypted code that are generated by mathematical formulas called algorithms). Then you examine authentication methods that combine a variety of approaches to authenticate dial-in users (such as RADIUS) and users on the internal network (such as Internet Protocol Security combined with Internet Key Exchange).

Step 1: Deciding What to Authenticate

You're probably already familiar with the type of authentication you use to get your e-mail, gain access to a file server, or dial in to your Internet Service Provider. Authentication by a firewall would be another level of security in addition to those logins. Whenever a connection is made to the firewall, you can have the firewall authorize the connection by requesting a username and password or by exchanging information "behind the scenes" so that end-users don't have to log in at every session.

Of course, not all firewalls perform authentication, and the ones that do might only handle relatively simple user authentication. The Check Point NG firewall handles three different types of authentication—user, client, and session authentication—and will be used as the example in this section.

User Authentication

User authentication is the process of identifying an individual who has been authorized to access network resources. The user who presents the proper credentials can log on to the network from any location or any computer, which provides the user with great flexibility. You don't need to require users to log on every time they access the firewall; rather, you can configure the authentication to be transparent and based on the exchange of keys.

First, you have to define users. In Check Point NG, you assign a user to a user group; you can then set up access rules for that group. You not only provide a username, but you can identify source and destination subdomains, which allows you to restrict the resources to which they have access. If the user can have unrestricted access, you specify Any in the Source and Destination boxes in the Location tab of the User Properties dialog box (see Figure 5-10).

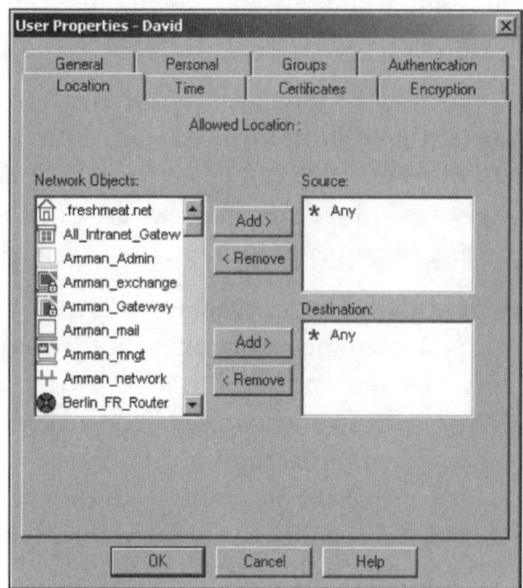

Figure 5-10 Restricting user access

In addition, you can specify time-based restrictions that control when a user is allowed to access the network. You can have the user access the network only on weekdays during daytime hours, as indicated in Figure 5-11.

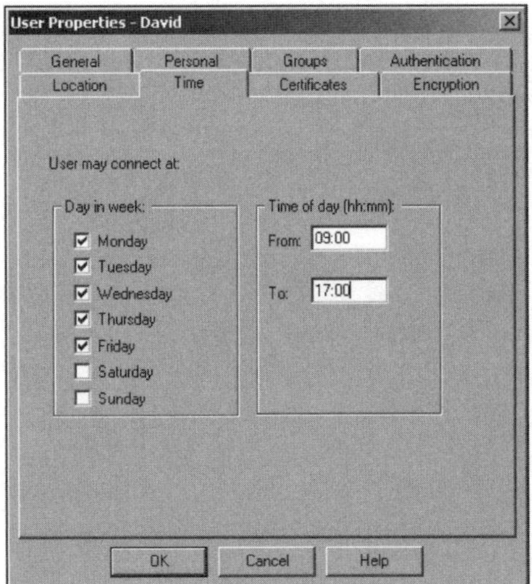

Figure 5-11 Time-based user access restrictions

Implementing time-based restrictions provides another level of security for your office, if you and IT staff cannot be on the premises during overnight hours to handle intrusion attempts should they occur. By blocking authorized access in the overnight hours, you make it that much more difficult for hackers to attack in the middle of the night.

If you prevent users from accessing the network on evenings or weekends, you may run into complaints from workers who need to work "after hours." Make sure employees don't need to work in off-hours before you implement such restrictions.

Client Authentication

Client authentication is the process of granting access to network resources based on a source IP address or computer name rather than user information. With client authentication, as with user authentication, the identification process can be either transparent or manual. If you require computers to manually authenticate themselves, their users have to enter a username or password. This makes them go through some extra effort to access the resources they want, but it provides you with extra security as well: you restrict access based on the source computer and username/password in one process.

If the IP addresses on your network are dynamically assigned and change frequently, enterprise-level firewalls like Check Point NG account for this by using computer names (such as "Email Server") to perform client authentication rather than IP addresses. On the other hand, you can also configure the client authentication process to be automatic. In Check Point NG, you do this by choosing an option from the Sign On Method section of the Client Authentication Action Properties dialog box (see Figure 5-12).

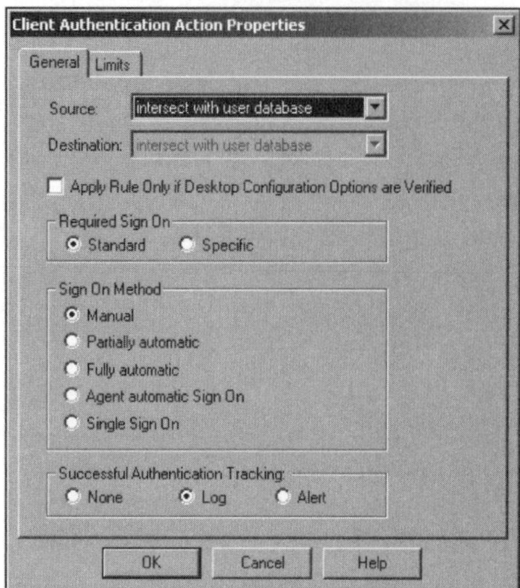

Figure 5-12 Client authentication can be either manual or transparent

Even if a hacker steals an individual user's username and/or password, having that user log on with client authentication means that access could be gained only by using the computer with the required IP address—or by spoofing the correct address, which the hacker would have to obtain as well.

Session Authentication

Session authentication is the process of authorizing a user or computer on a per-connection basis using special authentication software installed on the client computer that exchanges information with the firewall. Session authentication gives the user even greater flexibility than user or client authentication; it enables any user and any computer to access network resources of any sort. The connection between client computer and firewall is authorized rather than an individual or a machine name or address.

For session authentication to work with Check Point NG, you need to install an application called the Session Authentication Agent on any client computer on which authentication needs to be performed. The client computer and the firewall authenticate in the background; however, the user who is making the connection does need to enter a password. You can configure session authentication so that a user is asked to enter a password every time a file or other resource is requested, once per session, or after a specified number of minutes of inactivity. The third option prevents unauthorized users from working at a machine that the original user has abandoned and that is connected to a protected resource.

How do you decide which type of authentication is right for your needs? Table 5-7 compares the advantages and disadvantages of each of the three general authentication approaches.

Table 5-7 User, client, and session authentication

Method	Advantages	Disadvantages
User Authentication	Gives the user great flexibility in being able to access the network from any location	If username/password or other information is stolen, an unauthorized user can gain access
Client Authentication	Provides better security than user authentication; can be configured to work with all applications and services	User must work at a computer configured for client authentication
Session Authentication	Gives the user the highest amount of flexibility; provides both password and session authentication	Session Authentication Agent must be installed on each client computer

The type of general authentication you want your firewall to perform is only one aspect of authentication that you have to determine. Another is the type of information that will be exchanged in order for the authentication to work reliably, as described in the next section.

Step 2: Deciding How to Authenticate

The determination of the type of authentication to use depends, in part, on the level of security of that method. The level of security, in turn, depends to a great extent on the type of information that is exchanged in order to ensure the identity of the user or computer being authenticated. When you make a purchase at a retail store, you are often asked to present an identification card and to sign a receipt in order to ensure your identity. Over a network, computers or individuals present other types of digital information in order to declare who they are. This section examines many of the types of information firewalls can exchange with clients in order to authenticate themselves or their users.

Password Security

Password-based authentication, in which an individual enters a username and password that is compared against a database of approved users, is probably the simplest and most straightforward authentication a firewall can perform. However, it isn't always straightforward. Because passwords can easily be lost, cracked, or misappropriated by unauthorized users, some variations on the usual password system have been developed for greater security. Firewalls can use a number of password systems, including:

- *OS password* —The firewall refers to the user's password stored on the operating system of the host computer for authentication.
- *Firewall password* —Some firewalls provide their own system of user passwords.
- *S/Key password* —S-Key uses a special application to generate a one-time password that is then encrypted. The user is given the password and enters it once to authenticate. The password is not used again.

- *SecurID* —This is an example of **two-factor authentication** : a password (something the user knows) is combined with something the user has (a small electronic device called a **token** that generates a random number every 60 seconds). Combining the random number with the password provides a one-time combination with secure authentication.

The OS PASSWORD system is simple, but won't work if the firewall is hosted on a standalone computer because it's not likely that users will have an account on a computer that's only designated to run the firewall system. The S/Key one-time password system is far more secure and highly configurable; Check Point NG's configuration options for S/Key are shown in Figure 5-13.

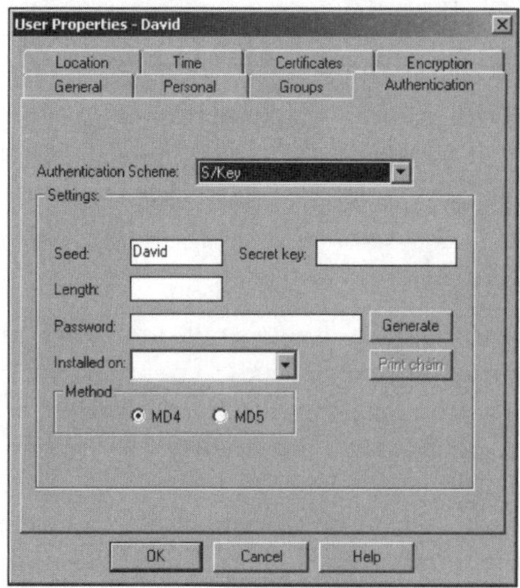

Figure 5-13 S/Key configuration options

As you can see from Figure 5-13, in order to use S/Key authentication you have to enter a **seed** —a random string that will be used to generate a one-time password. The Secret key: text box is used to specify the user's password—this secret password is used along with the seed to create the one-time password. The Length: text box enables you to specify the number of one-time passwords that will be generated by the seed and the secret password.

The Check Point NG S/Key one-time password system lets you generate a list of passwords that are used in succession. Such password lists are one of the two kinds of one-time passwords that can be used. In the other system, challenge-response, the user receives an identifier and then submits a challenge value. The server or firewall performing the authentication response with a password responds with a response value that the user submits to complete the authentication.

Smart Cards and Tokens

Objects that the user physically possesses can be combined with passwords to create secure two-factor authentication. The most common physical objects used in authentication are smart cards and tokens. You're probably familiar with smart cards because credit cards and ATM cards fall into this category: they are small plastic cards with a magnetic stripe on one side that stores information about the cardholder. For smart cards to work, the user's computer needs to have a card reader installed.

Any object that enables individuals to authenticate themselves with a network can also be called a token. A smart card is a form of token; other types are handheld or key fob electronic devices that generate random numbers. The numbers are changed periodically (perhaps every five minutes). The user authenticates by entering the current number from the token as well as a PIN number or password. Although smart cards and other tokens are easy to lose or have stolen, the fact that they require the PIN number or password makes it difficult for a thief to actually use them.

You can find out more about security tokens by visiting the RSA Security Web site (*www.rsasecurity.com*). RSA Security sells a variety of different tokens for use in its SecureID authentication system.

Exchanging Public and Private Keys

A password is a "code" you keep in your personal memory and that you use when you want to authenticate yourself on a network. Computers, too, can authenticate themselves to one another (or to software programs that use encryption such as enterprise-level firewalls) by exchanging codes. As you might expect, because of the power of computers to carry out calculations and store information, the codes exchanged by computers can be very long and complicated: the longer the code and the more complex the formula used to create it, the more secure the level of authentication.

The codes exchanged by computers to authenticate themselves to servers, firewalls, or other computers are called keys. Keys are blocks of encrypted code that are generated by mathematical formulas called algorithms; they are very long (1024, 2048, or 4096 bits in length or even longer) and thus difficult (perhaps nearly impossible) to crack. Keys can be issued not only to computers, but also to individuals. One of the most popular and secure forms of authentication in use on the Internet, **public key cryptography** , authenticates individuals through the exchange of public and private keys:

- A **private key** is a key that you generate after obtaining it from a Certificate Authority (CA) and that you never exchange with anyone else; rather, you use the private key to generate public keys. A CA is an entity that holds the right to use an encryption algorithm. Some firewalls function as CAs themselves. They issue keys to users so that they can connect to the firewall via a VPN connection—a highly secure connection that protects data through encryption and other methods, as described in Chapter 7.

- A **public key** is a key that you create with your private key and that you issue to individuals with whom you want to conduct secure communications.

How Public-Key Encryption Works

Data encrypted with your public key can be decrypted only with your private key. Figure 5-14 shows a simplified view of the way public-key encryption works.

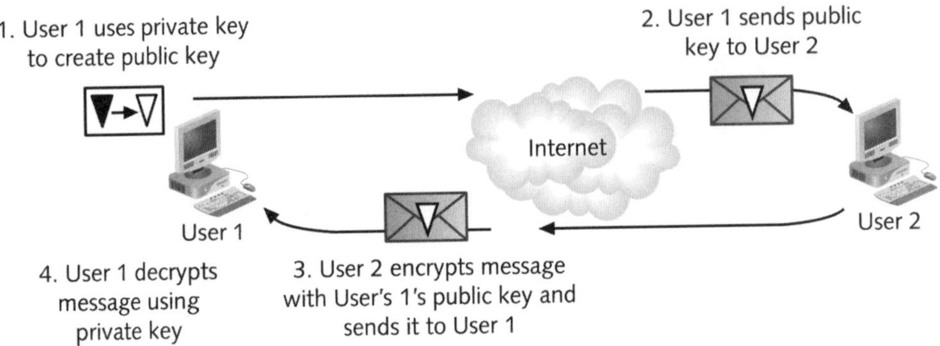

Figure 5-14 Public-key encryption involves the exchange of a public key that is created with a private key

The scheme shown in Figure 5-14 enables you to freely distribute a public key. Only you will be able to read data encrypted using this key. In general, to send encrypted data to someone, you encrypt the data with the recipient's public key, and the recipient decrypts the encrypted data by means of the corresponding private key. Compared with symmetric-key encryption (in which the same key is used rather than a pair of public and private keys), public-key encryption requires more computation and is therefore not always appropriate for large amounts of data.

As it happens, the reverse of the scheme shown in Figure 5-14 also works: data encrypted with your private key can be decrypted only with your public key. This would not be a desirable way to encrypt sensitive data, however, because it means that anyone with your public key, which is by definition published, could decrypt the data. Nevertheless, private-key encryption is useful because it means you can use your private key to sign data with your digital signature—an important requirement for electronic commerce and other commercial applications of cryptography. Client software such as Netscape Communicator or Microsoft Internet Explorer can then use your public key to confirm that the message was signed with your private key and that it hasn't been tampered with since being signed.

CheckPoint NG and Public-Key Cryptography

CheckPoint NG uses public key cryptography to authenticate users over a VPN connection as follows: During installation, you generate a series of random keystrokes that is used to generate an electronic file called a digital certificate. The digital certificate contains a public key as well as information about the server. A user connects to the firewall using Check-

Point's VPN client software, SecuRemote, which has its own public key. The firewall and client software exchange public keys. When information is sent to the firewall over the VPN connection, it is encrypted using the public key obtained from the firewall. When the encrypted information reaches the firewall, it is then decrypted using the private key that was originally used to generate the digital certificate and public key.

Digital Signatures

Encryption and decryption address the problem of eavesdropping. But encryption and decryption, by themselves, do not address the two other security issues: tampering and impersonation. A **digital signature** is an attachment to an e-mail or other message that enables the recipient of the message to authenticate the sender's identity. The digital signature provides tamper detection and authentication through a mathematical function called a **one-way hash**. A one-way hash is also known as a **message digest** (a code of fixed length that results from processing a message or other input through a mathematical function, usually resulting in a shortened version of the original input.) A one-way hash has the following characteristics:

- The value of the hash is unique for the hashed data. Any change in the data, even deleting or altering a single character, results in a different value.
- The content of the hashed data cannot, for all practical purposes, be deduced from the hash, which is why it is called "one-way."

As mentioned earlier, it's possible to use your private key for encryption and your public key for decryption. Although this is not desirable when you are encrypting sensitive information, it is a crucial part of digitally signing any data. Instead of encrypting the data itself, the signing software creates a one-way hash of the data. It then uses your private key to encrypt the hash. The encrypted hash, along with other information, such as the hashing algorithm, creates a digital signature.

To validate the integrity of the data, the receiving software first uses the signer s public key to decrypt the hash. It then uses the same hashing algorithm that generated the original hash to generate a new one-way hash of the same data. (Information about the hashing algorithm used is sent with the digital signature.) Finally, the receiving software compares the new hash against the original hash. If the two hashes match, the recipient can be certain that the public key used to decrypt the digital signature corresponds to the private key used to create the digital signature. If they don't match, the data may have been tampered with since it was signed, or the signature may have been created with a private key that doesn't correspond to the public key presented by the signer.

Some firewalls can generate digital signatures so that users on the network can identify themselves to one another. Look for a firewall that supports the MD4 and MD5 **hash functions** —common mathematical functions that create digest versions of messages.

Step 3: Putting It All Together

Passwords, tokens, keys, digital signatures, and certificates are being used with increasing frequency on the Internet to secure communications and to authenticate users. This naturally has an impact on firewalls because they stand at the perimeter of a network and provide a gateway for the communications between external computers on the Internet and internal computers on the LAN being protected. If any users on the internal network use encryption to authenticate themselves, those communications go through the firewall.

Firewalls, therefore, need to be able to recognize and process a variety of authentication methods to enable individuals to make purchases from Web sites, send and receive encrypted e-mail with others, or log on to databases. Three of the methods they will probably have to use are: Secure HyperText Transport Protocol (HTTPS); Internet Protocol Security with Internet Key Exchange (IPSec/IKE); and Remote Authentication Dial-in User Service (RADIUS).

TIP

You can find out more about Secure HyperText Transport Protocol by reading the original proposal for its creation at *www.ietf.org/rfc/rfc2660.txt*.

HTTPS

The term Secure HyperText Transport Protocol (HTTPS) refers to the use of a common security protocol like Secure Sockets Layer (SSL) or Transport Layer Security (TLS) to encrypt communications between a Web server and a Web browser. SSL, which is used more often than TLS, involves the exchange of public and private keys, and it uses a digital certificate to ensure the server's identity.

From the standpoint of a firewall, SSL doesn't present an inherent problem. In an SSL packet, the data portion is encrypted, but the IP and TCP/UDP headers are not, so the firewall can filter and route the packet as needed. The firewall cannot, however, scan or filter the data portion because of the encryption. Although SSL does provide a way to encrypt credit card numbers and other sensitive information when it is submitted to a Web site, it does not provide for authentication of users.

IPSec/IKE

Internet Protocol Security (IPSec) works by encrypting communications at the Network layer (layer 3) of the OSI model of network communications. This is beneath the level of the application-layer communications produced by a specific program such as a Web browser or Web server. IPSec is transparent to the end-user, and can automatically protect e-mail, Web traffic, and file transfers using FTP. IPSec has quickly become widely used because of its strong encryption algorithms and effective authentication methods. Firewalls that support IPSec can give employees or members of an organization a way to effectively secure their network communications.

IPSec isn't a single authentication or encryption method, but is a set of standards and software tools that work together to create secure network communications. It was created by the Internet Engineering Task Force (IETF) as a set of protocols that would function with both IP Version 4 and IP Version 6. IPSec provides secure tunnels between two devices, such as two routers. You define which packets are considered sensitive and should be sent through these secure tunnels, and you define the parameters that should be used to protect these sensitive packets, by specifying characteristics of these tunnels. When the IPSec-compliant device sees such a sensitive packet, it sets up the appropriate secure tunnel and sends the packet through the tunnel to the remote device.

Note that the IPSec tunnels are sets of security associations that are established between two IPSec-compliant devices. The security associations define which protocols and algorithms should be applied to sensitive packets. IPSec can make use of two different protocols for protecting packets. The first is **Authentication Header (AH)** , which adds a digital signature; to packets to protect against repeat attacks, spoofing, or other tampering. It is used to verify that parts of the packet headers, such as the source and destination IP addresses, have not been altered on the way from the client to the IPSec-enabled host. If the packet fails this verification test, it is dropped. The other protocol, **Encapsulating Security Payload (ESP)**, provides a higher level of security than AH because it encrypts the payload of a packet. (Actually, the data part of a packet is enclosed by a digital signature as well as an ESP header and trailer.) ESP does not encrypt the IP header of a packet, so a firewall can still filter it.

A firewall activity that was discussed earlier in this chapter, Network Address Translation (NAT), can interfere with some forms of IPSec and other encryption methods. If the firewall itself is used to configure rules for IPSec encryption, there should be no problem with NAT or filtering by the firewall. However, if IPSec is implemented by software inside the firewall and the IPSec communications are intended to pass through the firewall, some IPSec-protected packets won't be read by the firewall. Specifically, because the AH protocol encrypts the IP header portion of packets, firewalls that perform NAT won't be able to handle such traffic; they won't be able to read the encrypted headers, and thus, will be unable to translate them into other IP addresses. In addition, because the ESP protocol does not encrypt the IP header but does encrypt the TCP or UDP port number, firewalls won't be able to perform NAT on such packets either, because NAT changes port information as well as IP addresses.

In addition to its encryption schemes, IPSec includes a variety of software components, including **Internet Key Exchange (IKE)** , which provides for the exchange of public and private keys in order to authenticate users. Another IPSec protocol, **Internet Security Association Key Management Protocol (ISAKMP)** , enables two computers to reach agreed-upon security settings and securely exchange security keys so they can encrypt communications.

IPSec is discussed only briefly here; because it is used in connection with VPNs, it is examined in more detail in Chapter 7.

Dial-in Authentication: RADIUS and TACACS+

Workers in corporations and nonprofit organizations alike are growing increasingly mobile. Laptops, handheld devices, and tablet PCs mean that workers can stay connected to the office by working at home or during business trips. Each time a user dials in to the corporate network, a potential security breach arises: any hackers or unauthorized users who gain access to the remote user's system could also potentially gain access to files on the main office network.

Some special authentication systems designed especially for use with dial-in users can be used by firewalls. The two best-known systems are:

- Terminal Access Controller Access Control System (TACACS+)—commonly called "tac-plus" — is a set of authentication protocols developed by Cisco Systems. TACACS+ uses the MD5 algorithm to produce an encrypted digest version of transmitted data.

- **Remote Authentication Dial-In User Service (RADIUS)** is generally considered to provide a lower level of security than TACACS+, even though it's more widely supported. RADIUS transmits authentication packets unencrypted across the network, which means they are vulnerable to attacks from packet sniffers.

Such systems are perhaps becoming less critical because more and more remote contractors and business partners have direct connections to the Internet and can more easily establish connections through VPNs. However, they still play a role in many corporate networks' security schemes.

In the case of either TACACS+ or RADIUS, authentication is conducted by a server specially set up to perform authentication: A TACACS+ server or a RADIUS server is implemented in conjunction with the usual dial-in access server the network uses to receive connection requests from remote users. The dial-in server can usually be configured to configure requests to the TACACS+ or RADIUS server for authentication. The authentication server needs to have its own IP address and uses special ports for communications. This requires the network administrator to configure the authentication for filtering, proxying, and network address translation, as discussed in the following list.

- *Filtering characteristics*— TACACS+ uses TCP port 49; RADIUS uses UDP port 1812 for authentication and UDP port 1813 for accounting. You need to set up packet filtering rules that enable clients to exchange authorization packets with the TACACS+ or RADIUS server.

- *Proxy characteristics*— A RADIUS server can function as a proxy server (a server that monitors and relays outbound traffic). RADIUS doesn't work with generic proxy systems you might have implemented for Web access or other services, however. TACACS+, in contrast, does work with generic proxy systems.

- *NAT characteristics*— RADIUS simply isn't compatible with NAT. TACACS+ does work with NAT systems. However, static NAT works best because some TACACS+ systems use the source IP address to create the encryption key.

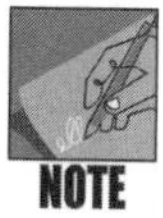

Wireless users who need to connect to the corporate network need to connect to a wireless LAN access point. Such users can be authenticated in a manner that conforms to the 802.11 standard created by the Institute of Electrical and Electronics Engineers (IEEE). VPNs should be used for such access, because of its high vulnerability: network traffic or Internet access can be gained by wireless users who manage to get close enough to a wireless access point and thus fall within one of the network's hot spots. You can read a paper on security and wireless access at *http://rr.sans.org/wireless/IEEE_80211.php*.

CHAPTER SUMMARY

- This chapter examined the various firewall components and functions that need to be configured in order to create a network defense perimeter. The basic function performed by firewalls is packet filtering, and much of this chapter was devoted to the establishment of a rule base. However, these days, firewalls are being called on to perform more and more security-related functions, and the most common ones were examined in this chapter as well.
- There are two general approaches to packet filtering: stateless and stateful filtering. Stateless packet filters decide whether to allow or deny packets based on the information in the TCP, IP, or UDP headers. Filtering is usually done by IP address, port number, or ACK flag. Stateless filtering does not take into account whether or not a connection has already been established between the external computer making the request and the internal computer listed as the destination of the request.
- Stateful packet filtering, in contrast to stateless filtering, keeps a record called a state table that maintains a record of the connections that have been made between internal and external computers. Such a packet filter only allows incoming packets to pass through the firewall from external hosts that are already connected and listed in the state table.
- Both stateless and stateful packet filters depend on a set of rules called a rule base that enables them to perform security functions. Although the exact rules in the rule base depend on the network being protected, some general practices should be observed: the firewall should be protected from all users except necessary administrators, and it should be blocked from making connections on its own; the rule base should block direct access from external computers to computers inside the firewall; it should enable internal users to access the Internet; and both external and internal users should be able to gain access to the servers in the DMZ.
- Packets can be filtered by TCP or UDP port numbers as well as IP addresses. Such port filtering can be used to block access by services that are not needed and that would not be used in the inbound direction. Keep in mind, though, that the source port and destination port are different when a connection is made. Services that are used by Windows and UNIX for internal communications should be blocked if connection attempts are made from the Internet using their ports. Inbound connection attempts using one of the ICMP message types should be blocked as well.

- Another basic firewall function, Network Address Translation (NAT), is performed by many firewalls. It is used to conceal the IP addresses of computers on the internal network so that hackers cannot locate them and initiate intrusion attempts. NAT also has the benefit of enabling network administrators to assign private IP addresses to computers inside the network, thus conserving scarce public IP addresses. Hide-mode NAT conceals multiple IP addresses behind a single IP address, while static NAT maps each internal IP address to a public IP address.
- Many firewalls also perform the essential function of authenticating individuals who are authorized to access requested network resources. Firewalls can perform user, client, or session authentication. They can authorize by accepting one-time or multiple-use passwords; by using two-factor authentication systems such as SecurID; by exchanging public and private keys; and by issuing digital signatures. Many enterprise-level firewalls can operate with encryption schemes such as Secure Sockets Layer (SSL) and Internet Protocol Security (IPSec). In addition, firewalls can work with a server configured to enable remote employees to dial in to the network and access the resources they need.

Key Terms

authentication — The process of identifying individuals who are authorized to access the network resources they are requesting and verifying their level of authorization.

Authentication Header (AH) — A method provided as an option with Internet Protocol Security (IPSec), in which an encrypted header is added to a packet in order to authenticate its source.

client authentication — The process of granting access to network resources based on a source IP address rather than user information.

data warehouses — Storehouses of proprietary information held by a company or other organization.

datagrams — *See* packets.

destination port — The port at which the data is received by a computer from another computer.

digital signature — An attachment to an e-mail or other message that enables the recipient of the message to authenticate the sender's identity.

dynamic port numbers — Numbers that applications assume for the length of a communications session and that are in the range 49152 through 65535.

Encapsulating Security Payload (ESP) — An encryption method provided as an option with Internet Protocol Security (IPSec), in which the data payload of a TCP/IP packet is encrypted.

granular — A very fine level of control that you need to limit the amount of traffic through a firewall as much as possible.

Hash function — A mathematical function (such as MD4 or MD5) that creates a digest version of a message.

hide-mode mapping — The process of hiding multiple private IP addresses behind one public IP address.

Internet Control Message Protocol (IMCP) — A protocol that functions as a housekeeping protocol for TCP/IP, helping networks to cope with various communication problems.

Internet Key Exchange (IKE) — A component of Internet Protocol Security (IPSec) that provides for the exchange of public and private keys in order to authenticate users.

Internet Protocol Security (IPSec) — A system of encrypting communications at the TCP/IP level rather than the communications produced by a specific program such as a Web browser or Web server.

Internet Security Association Key Management Protocol (ISAKMP) — A component protocol used by Internet Protocol Security (IPSec) that enables two computers to reach agreed-upon security settings and securely exchange security keys so they can encrypt communications.

key — A long, encrypted block of code used in public key cryptography, and generated by a mathematical formula called an algorithm.

message digest — A code that results from processing a message or other input through a mathematical function, usually resulting in a shortened version of the original input.

Network Address Translation (NAT) — The process of concealing the IP addresses on a network by translating them into another IP address used by a router, firewall, or system software that performs NAT.

one-way hash — *See* message digest.

packets — Segments of digital information that are of uniform length and that contain header information as well as a data payload; also called datagrams.

port filtering — The process of filtering packets of digital information by reviewing their TCP or UDP port numbers.

private key — A key that you generate after obtaining it from a Certificate Authority (CA) and that you never exchange with anyone else; rather, you use the private key to generate public keys.

protocol filtering — *See* port filtering.

proxy server — Security software that handles traffic on behalf of the individual computers on the network it is protecting, rebuilding both outbound and inbound requests from scratch in order to hide internal IP address information.

public key — A key that you create with your private key and that you issue to individuals with whom you want to conduct secure communications.

public key cryptography — A form of network authentication that identifies individuals through the exchange of public and private keys.

Remote Authentication Dial-In User Service (RADIUS) — An authentication method used to identify and verify the authorization of users who dial in to a central server in order to gain access to networked resources.

seed — A random string that will be used to generate a one-time password.

session authentication — The process of authorizing a user or computer on a per-connection basis using special authentication software installed on the client computer that exchanges information with the firewall.

source port — The port from which data is sent out to another computer.

state table — A file maintained by a firewall or other software that contains a record of all current connections or processes.

token — A small electronic device that generates a random number or password that can be used in authentication.

two-factor authentication — A form of authentication that combines a password or PIN number (something the user knows) with something the user physically possesses, such as a smart card or token.

user authentication — The process of identifying an individual who has been authorized to access network resources.

well-known ports — Ports that have been reserved for use by common TCP/IP services.

Review Questions

1. When you request a Web page, the Web server that holds the page would send it back to you using what port?

   a. 80

   b. 443

   c. one greater than 1023

   d. one less than 1023

2. What TCP header is normally sent at the end of a "handshake" between two networked computers?

   a. SYN

   b. FIN

   c. ACK

   d. CON

3. Which of the following is a limitation of Windows XP's built-in Internet Connection Firewall? (Choose all that apply.)

   a. You cannot block services.

   b. You cannot add services.

   c. You cannot block IP addresses.

   d. You cannot specify ports.

4. A packet filter located between a proxy server and the Internet needs to route traffic to and from the ___________. (Choose all that apply.)

   a. Internet

   b. internal network

   c. DMZ

   d. proxy server

5. Which of the following can hide internal IP addresses from the Internet?

   a. packet filters

   b. DMZs

   c. proxy servers

   d. state tables

6. Port numbers are provided for by which data transmission protocol?

   a. IP

   b. ICMP

   c. IGMP

   d. TCP

7. The fact that ________ makes filtering by port number complicated.

   a. source and destination ports are different

   b. ports can be dynamically assigned

   c. more than 65000 ports are available

   d. well-known ports are reserved

8. Inbound traffic from the Internet is often represented in the rule base by what designation?
   a Int
   b Src IP
   c. Ext
   d. Src Port

9. Built-in Windows or UNIX services should be blocked on the inbound direction at the external interface for what reason?
   a. Such services aren't generally needed.
   b. Inbound communications can interfere with internal network communications.
   c. Only outbound communications are needed.
   d. Inbound communications from the Internet are likely intrusion attempts.

10. The ability to ______ is a benefit of performing some form of NAT. (Choose all that apply.)
    a. rebuild packets from scratch
    b. store files in cache
    c. shield internal IP addresses from hackers
    d. use private rather than public IP addresses

11. Why would you use static rather than hide-mode mapping? (Choose all that apply.)
    a. It translates internal addresses to one IP address.
    b. Hide-mode mapping doesn't work with some VPNs.
    c. It dynamically assigns IP addresses.
    d. Some external users want to connect directly to individual internal hosts.

12. What do proxy servers do that NAT does not do?
    a. perform encryption
    b. rebuild packets from scratch
    c. packet filtering
    d. work with static IP addresses

13. Which of the following is a situation that would cause you to choose user authentication rather than the more secure client authentication?

a. Users move around a lot and need to log in from different locations.

b. Client IP addresses are dynamically assigned.

c. Client IP addresses are private.

d. Users work at the same location and do not move around frequently.

14. What kinds of restrictions can you impose in user authentication? (Choose all that apply.)

a. IP address

b. network resources being requested

c. time

d. user's physical location

15. What would a hacker have to do to gain access to an account protected with client authorization? (Choose all that apply.)

a. be physically present inside the company

b. obtain the correct username/password

c. log on at the correct time

d. obtain the correct IP address

16. For session authentication to work, you need to ___________. (Choose all that apply.)

a. identify the computer name

b. install a Session Authentication Agent

c. determine password prompt frequency

d. determine the username to be used during the session

17. Which of the following is an example of a one-time password? (Choose all that apply.)

a. S/Key

b. SecurID

c. firewall password

d. OS password

18. Which elements are used together to create two-factor authentication? (Choose the two answers that apply.)
    a. something the user requests
    b. something the user lacks
    c. something the user has
    d. something the user knows
19. Name three elements that some firewalls can use to incorporate encryption and to protect end users.
20. What does IPSec encrypt that SSL and public-key cryptography do not encrypt?
    a. networks
    b. computers
    c. data
    d. passwords

Hands-on Projects

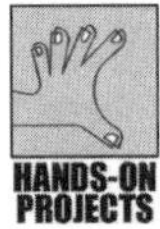

Project 5-1: Setting Up the Windows XP Built-In Firewall

As stated earlier in this chapter, you don't have to look far if you want to install your own stateful packet filter, at least if you have access to a computer that runs Windows XP. This version of Windows comes with a bare-bones security tool called Internet Connection Firewall (ICF). ICF can be activated to protect a particular connection to the Internet. However, it is not active by default; you need to tell Windows to use the program. You'll set up the program in this project, and you'll learn how to add a service that needs to pass through the firewall as well. By default, ICF does not specify that Network News Transport Protocol newsgroup traffic can pass through the firewall. To add newsgroup service to the ICF's settings, you'll need the IP address of your school's news server. You'll probably need to get this from your computer science department or the office that maintains Internet services for your school.

1. Click **Start**, and click **Control Panel**.
2. Double-click **Network Connections**. (If the Control Panel is in Category View rather than Classic View, click **Network and Internet Connections**, and then click **Network Connections**.)
3. Right-click the icon that represents your computer's connection to the Internet. If you have a direct connection that is used by one or more computers, chances are this is called Local Area Connection (in other words, you use your local Ethernet connection to connect to the Internet). Click **Properties**.

4. In the Properties dialog box for your connection, click the **Advanced** tab.
5. Click the **Protect my computer and network by limiting or preventing access to this computer...** check box to activate Internet Connection Firewall.
6. Click **Settings**. A "Please Wait" box appears, followed by the Advanced Settings dialog box. The items checked in the Services list are the services that you and other networked users can use to access the Internet through the firewall.
7. Click **Add**. The Service Settings dialog box appears.
8. In the Description of service box, type **Network News Transport Protocol**.
9. In the Name or IP address box, type the IP address of your local area network's news server. If you don't know the address or don't have such a server, type **172.16.1.121** for the purposes of this example.
10. In the External Port number for this service box, type **119**, which is the port assigned for NNTP communications.
11. In the Internal Port number for this service box, type **119**.
12. Leave TCP checked, and click **OK** to close Service Settings.
13. You return to Advanced Settings. Verify that Network News Transport Protocol appears in the Services list with a check mark next to it.
14. Click **OK** to close Advanced Settings, and then click **OK** to close the Properties dialog box.
15. Close all windows to return to the Windows desktop.

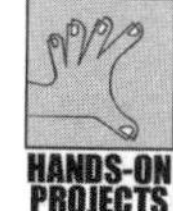

Project 5-2: Filtering UDP Traffic: Version 1

When you install and configure the freeware firewall program ZoneAlarm (as described in Project 4-4) to send you alert messages, you'll probably notice a large number of alerts from computers attempting to connect to yours on a User Datagram Protocol (UDP) port. Because UDP is less often used than TCP and is considered less secure than TCP, you might be inclined to block it altogether. However, UDP is commonly used by computers on your own network, as well as your DNS server and your ISP's servers, all trying to connect to yours. One way to selectively block UDP communications is to use Windows 2000 or XP's built-in TCP/IP filtering function.

In this project, you need to specify what services would be allowed to use specific UDP ports, rather than blocking UDP specifically. To enter such ports, you need to know what services to run. You can scan a list of ports at *www.iana.org/assignments/port-numbers*. For this project, you'll enable the common UDP ports for DNS service (port 53) and NetBIOS name service (port 137).

1. Click **Start**, and click **Control Panel**.

2. Double-click **Network Connections**. (If the Control Panel is in Category View rather than Classic View, click **Network and Internet Connections**, and then click **Network Connections**.)
3. Right-click the icon that represents your computer's connection to the Internet. If you have a direct connection that is used by one or more computers, chances are this is called Local Area Connection (in other words, you use your local Ethernet connection to connect to the Internet). Click **Properties**.
4. In the General tab of the Properties dialog box for your Internet connection, click **Internet Protocol (TCP/IP)**, and then click **Properties**.
5. Click **Advanced**.
6. Click the **Options** tab.
7. Click **TCP/IP filtering**, and then click **Properties**.
8. In the TCP/IP Filtering dialog box, check the **Enable TCP/IP Filtering (All adapters)** check box.
9. In the UDP Ports column, click the **Permit Only** option button.
10. Click **Add**.
11. In the Add Filter dialog box, type **53**, and then click **OK**. The Add Filter dialog box closes and a Microsoft TCP/IP dialog box appears. Click **OK** to close the Add Filter dialog box. The number 53 is listed under UDP Ports.
12. Click **Add**.
13. In the Add Filter dialog box, type **137**, then click **OK**. Click **OK** to close the Microsoft TCP/IP dialog box. The number 137 is added to the list under UDP ports.
14. Click **OK** to close TCP/IP Filtering, Advanced TCP/IP Settings, Internet Protocol (TCP/IP) Properties, and your connection's Properties dialog box.
15. Close all open windows to return to the Windows desktop. If a dialog box appears prompting you to restart your computer, click **No**.

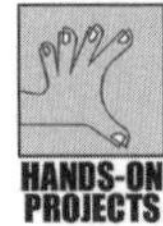

Project 5-3: Filtering UDP Traffic: Version 2

You set up ZoneAlarm as described in Hands-On Project 4-4. You are noticing a lot of alert messages seeking communication on User Datagram Protocol (UDP) ports. The TCP/IP Filtering feature described in the previous project isn't very easy to implement because it requires you to add UDP ports that you need to use, and looking up such ports can be tedious. It is easier to specifically allow UDP traffic that is obviously legitimate because it is coming from your DNS server or your ISP's servers. ZoneAlarm lets you do this by reviewing log file entries and adding them to your "trusted" zone. This project requires a Windows 2000 or XP computer that has ZoneAlarm installed. You'll also need to know the IP address of your network's DNS server.

1. If you already know your DNS server's IP address, skip ahead to Step 5. Otherwise, click **Start** and click **Control Panel** to begin the process of locating the address.
2. Double-click **Network Connections**. (If the Control Panel is in Category View rather than Classic View, click **Network and Internet Connections**, and then click **Network Connections**.)
3. Right-click the icon that represents your computer's connection to the Internet. If you have a direct connection that is used by one or more computers, chances are this is called Local Area Connection (in other words, you use your local Ethernet connection to connect to the Internet). Click **Properties**.
4. In the General tab of the Properties dialog box for your Internet connection, click **Internet Protocol (TCP/IP)**, and then click **Properties**.
5. From the Internet Protocol (TCP/IP) Properties dialog box, write down the IP addresses listed next to Preferred DNS server and Alternate DNS server, if you have DNS servers listed.
6. Click **OK** to close Internet Protocol (TCP/IP) Properties and your connection's Properties dialog box.
7. Start up ZoneAlarm by clicking the program's icon in the Windows system tray or by clicking the program itself (**zonealarm.exe**) in the directory where you originally installed it.
8. Click **Alerts & Logs** in the list on the left side of the ZoneAlarm window.
9. Click the **Log Viewer** tab to bring it to the front.
10. Scroll down the list of connection attempts in the Log Viewer. Click the listings that have UDP listed in the Protocol column. Make a note of any ports that are listed in the Entry Detail box at the bottom of the ZoneAlarm window.

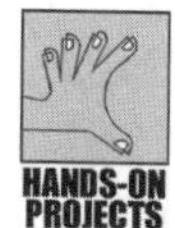

Project 5-4: Designing a Rule Base

Configure with your own set of basic rules for packet filtering for a network that has the following characteristics: The internal network is represented by 192.168.1.20.0; the firewall is hosted at 192.168.120.1; the e-mail server is at 192.168.120.2; the Web server is at 192.168.120.3; and the DNS server is at 192.168.120.4. Follow these steps:

1. Create a rule that allows internal hosts to access the external network.
2. Create a rule that prevents any access to the firewall itself.
3. Create a rule that allows internal and external access to the e-mail server and Web server.
4. Create a rule that allows internal access to the DNS server.
5. For "extra credit," what additional rule could you specify that involves the firewall itself?

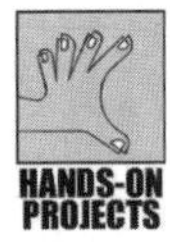

Project 5-5: Troubleshooting a Rule Base

One of the tasks you may be called on to perform as a security professional is the editing of packet filtering rule bases. Sometimes, you may be called on to improve a rule base that actually opens up security holes rather than closes them up. Analyze the following rule base:

Table 5-8 Rule Base

Rule	Source IP	Source Port	Destination IP	Destination Port	Action
1	Any	Any	192.168.120.0	>1023	Allow
2	192.168.120.1	Any	Any	Any	Deny
3	Any	Any	192.168.120.1	Any	Deny
4	192.168.120.0	Any	Any	Any	Any
5	Any	Any	192.168.120.2	25	Allow
6	Any	Any	192.168.120.3	80	Allow
7	Any	Any	Any	Any	Allow

1. Examine Rule 1 and state what security risk it poses in its current configuration. Describe how this rule could be improved.
2. Look for a problem with the "cleanup rule" in the rule base.

Project 5-6: Testing Your User Passwords

Effective authentication depends on user passwords that cannot easily be cracked. Such passwords avoid obvious weaknesses: they don't use the username as the password; they don't leave the password blank; they don't use recognizable English words. You can test the "crackability" of your passwords by downloading and installing a 15-day trial version of a password-cracking tool. Such a tool gives you an idea how easy it is for hackers to crack passwords that aren't encrypted or not sufficiently complex. You need to be logged in as Administrator on a Windows 2000 or XP computer to install and use the program described in this project.

1. Double-click the **Internet Explorer** icon on your desktop to start your Web browser.
2. Enter the following URL in your browser's Address box: **http://www.atstake.com/ research/lc/download.html**, and then press **Enter**. Your browser goes to the Web page for LC4, a password-cracking tool that you can download and try with limited functionality.
3. Click the link **Download LC4 for Win95/Win98/NT/2000/XP**.
4. When the File Download dialog box appears, click **Open** to download the file to your computer.

5. When downloading is complete, the installation program opens automatically. Follow the steps in the installation program to install LC4 in a directory on your computer.
6. When installation is complete, open LC4, either from the Start menu or by double-clicking the program icon **lc4.exe** in the directory where you installed it.
7. When the LC4 Trial Version dialog box appears, click **Trial**.
8. In the first screen of the LC4 Wizard, click **Next**.
9. Click the option that indicates where your network passwords are stored: if in doubt, leave the option button next to **Retrieve from the local machine** selected, and then click **Next**.
10. In the next screen, entitled Choose Auditing Method, click the type of password audit you want to perform. For this project, click **Common Password Audit,** and then click **Next**.
11. In the next screen, entitled Pick Reporting Style, leave all check boxes checked, and then click **Next**.
12. Click **Finish** in the next screen to begin the audit.
13. In the Dictionary Status box on the right side of the @stake LC4 window, you can track the progress of the audit. Any passwords that are found are listed in the LM Password or NTLM Password column. When you are done, a dialog box stating that the auditing session has been completed appears. Click **OK**.
14. Optionally, you can click the **Audit NTLM Hashes** button in the LC4 toolbar and then click **Session** and **Begin Audit** to do a new check. Were any found on your computer? Are any user accounts listed that you didn't know you had?

5

Case Projects

Case Project 5-1: Converting Binary to Decimal Port Numbers

In reading the log files generated during an intrusion attempt, you review the raw packet data and see the port number listed as 110111011. What is this in decimal form? How could you quickly calculate the answer?

Case Project 5-2: Blocking Suspicious UDP Traffic

In the process of scanning your firewall log files, you notice that many of the packets that reach your firewall use the UDP protocol and attempt to connect to a variety of ports on your computer. A check with your ISP reveals that many of the UDP packets are coming from your own DNS servers and from the ISP servers themselves. However, many others are coming from unknown IP addresses or domains, and are attempting to access ports that don't run any services you have in place—specifically, the ports 18890 and 1332. What could you do to determine whether such traffic is suspicious or not? What kind of rule would you add to your firewall's rule base to block such traffic?

Case Project 5-3: Providing Detailed Packet Filtering Criteria

You receive a number of alerts from external hosts that appear to have mangled or hard-to-understand DNS names, such as w008.z297145146.inISP.net. It's difficult to filter such traffic because they come from a variety of IP addresses. What other criteria could you use to filter such traffic?

Case Project 5-4: Blocking Packets with Suspicious TCP Headers

In reviewing your firewall log files, you notice a high number of packets with the S (for SYN) and A (for ACK) flags set. You check the origins of such packets and, while many of them are from your own DNS servers, others are from IP addresses or domain names you don't recognize. A high percentage of such packets are from the IP addresses 61.23.204.12 and 204.22.13.4. Write two packet-filtering rules that would block such access attempts. Remember that in order to filter for SYN packets, you specify that the ACK bit is cleared (C); in order to filter for the ACK flag, specify that the ACK bit is set (S).

CHAPTER

6

STRENGTHENING AND MANAGING FIREWALLS

After reading this chapter and completing the exercises, you will be able to:

- Understand how to work with a proxy server to supplement a firewall with a proxy server
- Describe the most important issues to be faced when managing a firewall
- Know how to install and configure Check Point NG
- Know how to install and configure Microsoft ISA Server 2000
- Know how to manage and configure iptables for Linux

Firewalls can go a long way toward blocking traffic that attempts to access your network from external networks such as the Internet. However, when you actually implement a firewall at the perimeter of your network, a number of issues arise. One is the fact that the basic purpose of firewalls is not to monitor traffic heading from your network in the outbound direction, but rather to filter attacks coming from the Internet or other external networks. The focus on inbound traffic means that you may become vulnerable to malicious programs such as Trojan horses, which often work by installing themselves on an internal host and then attempting to connect to an external location. Your best defense is to manage the firewall so that it runs efficiently and in such a way that you are able to track possible intrusions and respond to them quickly.

This chapter examines different ways in which you can strengthen and manage your firewall configurations. First, you examine how you can work with proxy servers to make a network defense more effective by understanding their goals, knowing how they work, knowing how to choose proxy servers, and knowing how they filter content. You then learn how to make a firewall's packet filtering rule base more efficient, including editing the rule base and managing the log files that are generated during the filtering. The next step is to put these principles into practice by working with three popular firewall applications: Check Point NG, Microsoft ISA Server 2000, and iptables.

Working with Proxy Servers

Security policies call for perimeter security devices to provide maximum protection for internal hosts and to monitor how employees use the Internet. Such policies can call for the installation of a **proxy server** —software that forwards packets to and from the network being protected and that caches Web pages to speed up network performance. This section describes the goals of setting up a proxy server and explains how proxy servers work, how to choose a proxy server, and how proxy servers can filter content for your network.

Proxy servers provide effective protection because they work at the Application layer of the seven-layer OSI model of network communications. They are able to interpret what application is being used to make a request, and they can forward the request on behalf of that application. In contrast, firewalls primarily interpret IP and TCP header information, working at the Transport layer instead of the Application layer.

Goals of Proxy Servers

Speeding up network communications was originally the primary goal of proxy servers. As Web pages were requested from the company's Web server, the proxy server would receive the Web pages and forward them to the computer making the request. At the same time, it would cache the page's text and image files—in other words, store those files on disk so they could be retrieved later if needed. Computers that requested the same Web page more than once would have their requests received by the proxy server rather than the Web server. The proxy server would check its cache for the Web page being requested and compare the page's contents against the contents of the page currently published on the Web server. If no changes were found, the files would be retrieved from the cache rather than from the original Web server. Storing documents in disk cache reduces the load placed on the Web server and also speeds up network traffic in general. This process is illustrated in Figure 6-1.

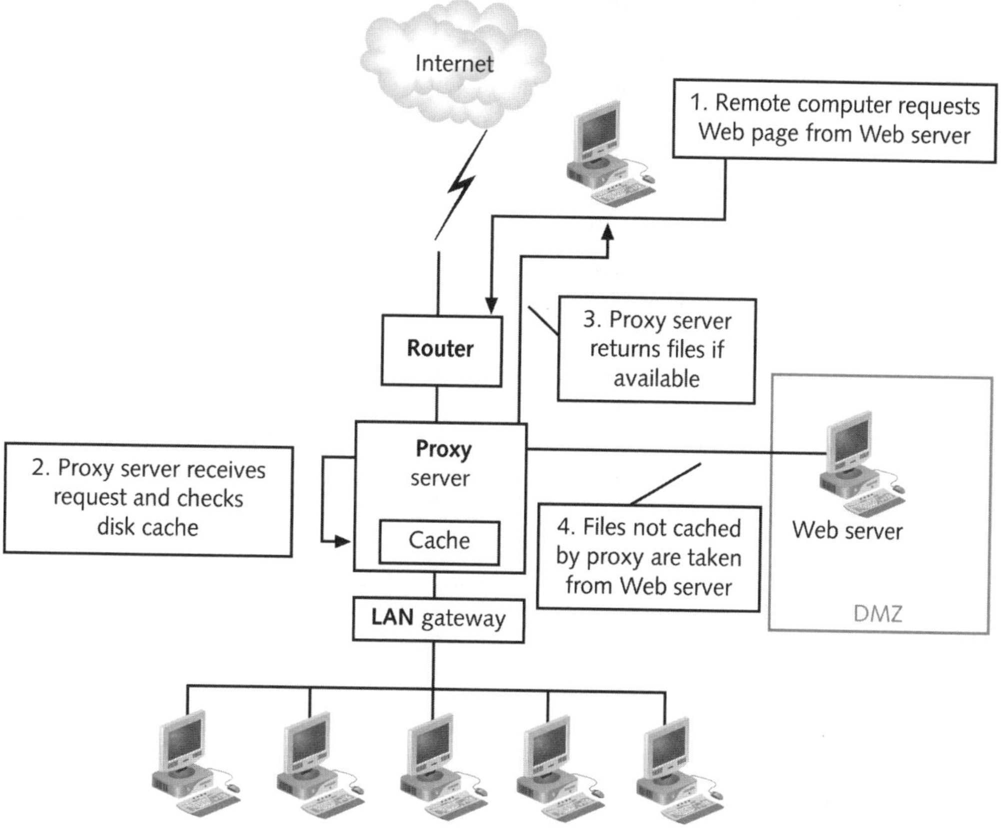

Figure 6-1 Proxy servers cache Web pages and other files

Microsoft Internet Security and Acceleration (ISA) Server 2000 also caches documents to speed up network performance and is discussed later in this chapter.

The primary goal of proxy servers these days is to provide security at the Application layer and shield hosts on the internal network. A secondary goal is the logging of traffic headed outbound from the internal network to the Internet so that the activities of employees who surf the Web, exchange e-mail, and use other services can be monitored. How those goals are accomplished is described in the following section.

Many proxy servers come with default configurations that enable users to access the Internet using multiple services. However, the default configurations can open up security holes. They may be set up to enable Telnet access, for example, or come configured to enable Web access on a 24/7 basis, which most users don't need. For better security, you might want to disable services that most end users won't need.

How Proxy Servers Work

Examining how packet filters work will help you understand how proxy servers work because the two types of security devices process individual packets in dramatically different ways. Packet filters look only at the header part of a TCP/IP packet. Their goal is to block unauthorized packets and to allow only authorized packets to reach their destination. If packets are authorized, the packet filter enables the host and client computers to communicate with one another directly.

In contrast, the goal of proxy servers is to prevent a direct connection between an external computer and an internal computer from ever occurring. One way proxy servers do this is by working at the Application layer. When a request is received, either from an internal or an external computer, the proxy server opens the packet and looks at the data. If, for example, the request is for a Web page and uses the standard GET method, the proxy server will reconstruct the packet and forward it to the requested Web server, acting as a proxy Web browser. By acting at the Application layer, the proxy server can interpret which application was originally used to make a request and which application is needed to forward that request.

What does it mean to "reconstruct" a packet? It means that when a proxy server receives a request, it opens the packet, examines the contents, and replaces the original header with a new header containing its own IP address rather than that of the original client's. An example is shown in Figure 6-2.

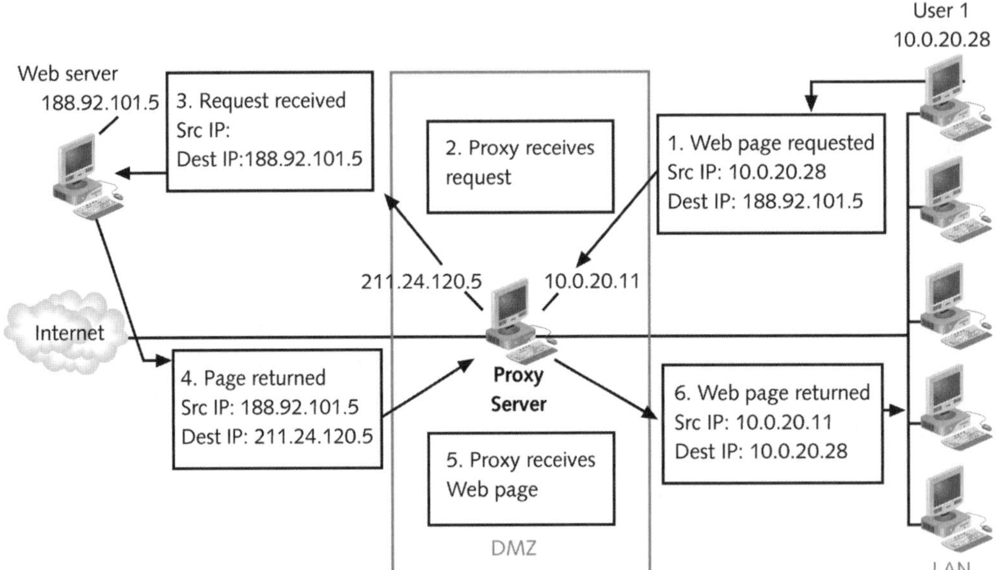

Figure 6-2 Proxy servers replace source IP addresses with their own address

As you can see in Figure 6-2, the proxy server is located in the DMZ along with the Web server and other publicly accessible Web servers. The following sequence occurs:

1. The proxy server receives the request from User 1's individual Web browser inside the internal LAN.
2. The proxy server examines the request, stripping off the header.
3. The proxy server replaces the header with its own public source IP address before sending the packet on its way.
4. The Web server that receives the request interprets it as coming from the IP address of the proxy server rather than from User 1's computer. In fact, the server (or a hacker who intercepts the request) has no way of knowing that User 1's computer exists. The Web server sends its response to the proxy server.
5. When the response is returned to User 1's computer it goes through the proxy server. The IP header sent by the server is replaced.
6. The requested Web page is sent to User 1's computer where it is displayed by the browser.

The proxy server is configured to receive traffic first before it goes to the Internet; client programs such as Web browsers and e-mail applications are configured to connect to the proxy rather than the Internet. A typical browser configuration is shown in Figure 6-3.

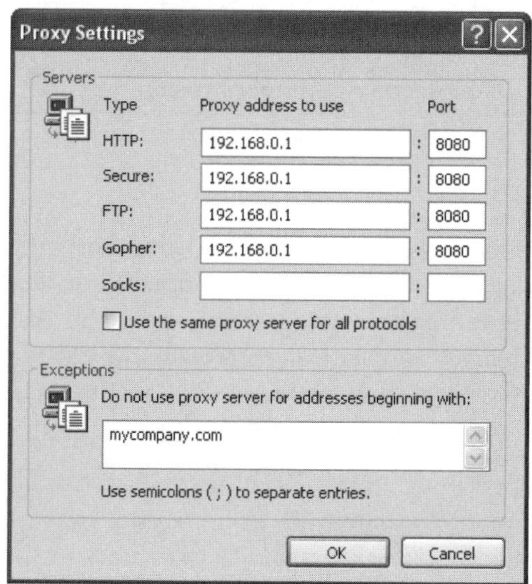

Figure 6-3 Each client program needs to be configured to connect to the proxy server rather than to the Internet

In Figure 6-3, the proxy server's IP address of 192.168.0.1 has been specified in the Proxy address to use box. Port 8080, which is normally used for proxy services, is also specified. Such a configuration results in the proxy server forwarding requests to external hosts over port 8080 while using a source IP address of 192.168.0.1. The SOCKS box is empty because (as explained below in "The SOCKS Protocol") it is used only for applications that proxy servers don't normally support; in this case HTTP, Secure HTTP, FTP, and Gopher services are the only ones that need to use the proxy. It should be noted that proxy servers require all users on a network to configure client programs accordingly. Depending on the number of users on your network, configuration can be time-consuming. If you are unable to complete a high number of configurations yourself, you can prepare a set of instructions that end users can follow to configure their own software so that you only have to deal with problems as they arise.

Note that many proxy server programs come with an auto-configuration script that enables client programs to automatically be set with the address and port number of the proxy server. You need only provide the URL for the auto-configuration script and instruct end-users to download the script to configure their browsers or other programs.

Some advantages and disadvantages of using proxy servers are summarized in Table 6-1.

Table 6-1 Proxy server advantages and disadvantages

Advantages	Disadvantages
Examines contents of packets and filters based on contents	Can be weak
Shields internal host IP address	Can slow down network access
Caches Web pages for faster access	Requires configuration of client programs in order to use proxy server
Provides a single point of logging	Provides a single point of failure

Choosing a Proxy Server

Different proxy servers perform different functions. Each of these functions can strengthen your existing firewall configuration. The type of proxy server you install depends on your individual needs. You can install a simple freeware proxy server if you are satisfied with the level of protection already provided by your existing firewall and you want to add functions that the firewall cannot perform (such as filtering out pop-up ads, executable codes, or other types of content).

On the other hand, if you are dissatisfied with your existing firewall, a standalone proxy server program can perform many functions that make your overall network security configuration stronger, including a single point of logging and the ability to hide internal IP addresses. If you need to save installation time and want to have only one program to manage, an enterprise-level firewall that performs proxy server functions along with packet filtering and other functions is a good choice. The basic types of proxy servers you can choose—freeware proxy servers, commercial proxy servers, or a firewall that can perform proxy server functions—are described in the following sections. The SOCKS protocol for proxy servers is also discussed.

Freeware Proxy Servers

The term "freeware" means the application is made freely available without charging a fee for its use. Freeware proxy servers tend to provide a particular function rather than the full range of proxy server functions. As such, they might go by an entirely different descriptor, such as "content filter." One such free program, Proxomitron, is examined in the section "Filtering Content" later in this chapter.

Commercial Proxy Servers

The many benefits of using commercial proxy servers become evident when you install a program like Microsoft Internet Security and Acceleration (ISA) Server 2000, as described later in this chapter. This commercial program combines the ability to cache Web pages and translate IP source and destination IP addresses with content filtering and traditional firewall functions such as packet filtering and Network Address Translation (NAT). To compete with other security programs, most proxy servers aren't advertised as such. Instead, they are presented as part of a more comprehensive firewall package.

A commercial proxy server is a good choice if you need the program for a business network and you plan to upgrade the software as new versions become available. Any commercial program should provide you with technical support to help with installation and configuration issues should they arise. Examples include Permeo Technologies' Application Security Platform (*www.permeo.com/Products/ApplicationSecurity.asp*) and Linkbytes' ComTun server (*www.linkbyte.com/*).

Firewalls That Can Perform Proxy Server Functions

Some firewalls are set up to act as proxy servers (in addition to performing other duties). Having an all-in-one program simplifies the amount of installation, product updating, and day-to-day management you have to do. On the other hand, it puts all of your network security needs in the hands of a single program. If something goes wrong with your firewall, your proxy server goes down as well.

It's a good idea to use multiple software and hardware programs in a coordinated network defense layer, such as those described in Chapter 2.

The SOCKS Protocol

Suppose you want to provide proxy services for applications that are not normally supported by proxies. These applications include RealAudio or instant messaging. Fortunately, a standalone proxy server will give you access to the SOCKS protocol so that you can use it to provide proxy services.

SOCKS isn't a proxy server itself. It's a communication protocol that sets up a secure channel by which two computers can exchange data. It also authenticates (ensures the correct identity of) the user who wishes to send data using SOCKS through the simple, unencrypted exchange of a username and password. The SOCKS package includes the following components:

- The SOCKS server, which must run on a UNIX system, although it has been ported to many different variants of UNIX
- The SOCKS client library for UNIX machines
- Versions of several standard UNIX client programs that support SOCKS, such as FTP and Telnet

Because SOCKS is widely used, server implementations and versions of programs such as FTP and Telnet (that have already been converted to use SOCKS) are commonly available, and help is easy to find. (This can be a double-edged sword; cases have been reported in which intruders to firewall-protected sites have installed their own SOCKS-knowledgeable clients.) In addition, client libraries for Macintosh and Windows systems are available as separate packages.

You can find out more about SOCKS by reading a set of Frequently Asked Questions at *www.socks.permeo.com/TechnicalResources/SOCKSFAQ/SOCKSGeneralFAQ/index.asp*.

The popularity of SOCKS counts as one of the biggest advantages. Virtually all proxy servers support SOCKS, which is intended to provide proxy server filtering for applications that aren't otherwise supported by proxy servers. These days, however, such applications are increasingly rare because proxy servers are increasingly common and support a wide range of applications. SOCKS support is something you should look for in a proxy server, if only because the protocol also supports Windows, UNIX, and the Macintosh. SOCKS enables applications that are specific to those platforms and that aren't normally supported by proxy servers to be proxied.

Filtering Content

One of the most useful applications of proxy servers comes from their ability to open up TCP/IP packets, inspect the data portion of those packets, and take action based on their contents. This capability enables proxy servers to filter out contents that would otherwise appear in a user's Web browser window during everyday Web surfing. In a business environment, proxy servers can be configured to block Web sites that are found to contain content that employees should not be allowed to view. They can also drop any executable programs such as Java applets or ActiveX controls that are sometimes embedded in Web pages and that can potentially damage files or replicate files when they execute themselves on a user's computer.

NOTE

The vast majority of Web pages do not have executable code embedded in them. However, hackers have attempted to distribute malicious code by adding executable code to Web pages. An example is the well-known W32/Nimda worm that, according to a security alert issued by the CERT Coordination Center (*www.cert.org/advisories/CA-2001-26.html*), can propagate itself when Web browsers open Web pages or when e-mail programs receive certain e-mail attachments.

Filtering Web Content

Simple proxy applications have been developed for both business and personal environments that are intended to filter out various kinds of Web content that the user finds undesirable. Programs such as Cookie Pal (*www.kburra.com/cpal.html*) and Cookie Cop (*www.pcmag.com/article2/0,4149,6244,00.asp*) are designed to give the user the option to block some or all of the **HTTP cookies** (short segments of HTML code that a Web server places on a visitor's Web browser to identify that browser on subsequent visits) sent by many Web sites.

Other applications filter out pop-up ads, background music, or other contents to which the user does not want to be exposed while surfing. Such applications are proxy servers; after they are installed, the administrator needs to configure a Web browser to connect to the proxy server rather than directly to the Internet. All Web content is routed through the proxy before it goes to the browser, and specified contents are stripped out before the page is viewed (see Figure 6-4).

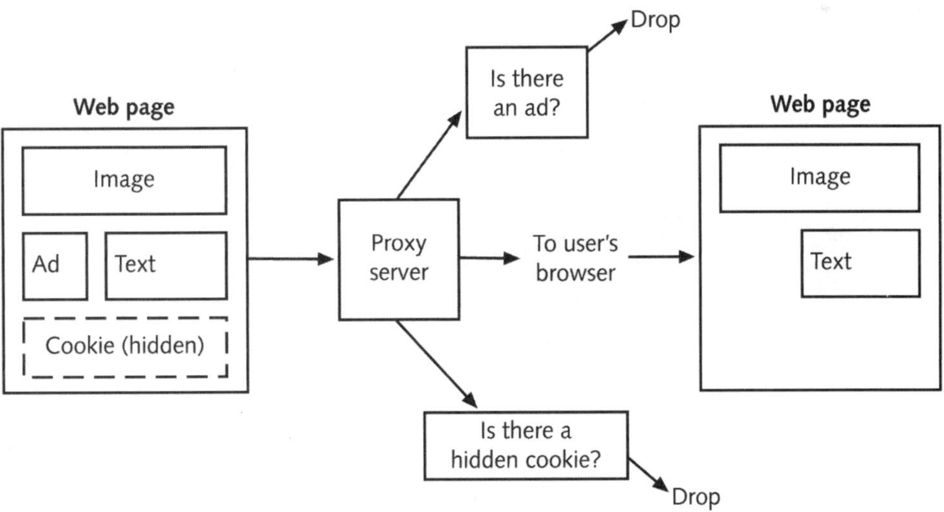

Figure 6-4 Proxy servers can filter out Web page or other content

Creating Filter Rules

Proxy servers give administrators the ability to set rules identifying the types of content they want to filter out before they reach their Web browser window. One simple freeware program, Proxomitron, lets you filter out a variety of contents, including:

- Pop-up windows
- Background music or other sounds
- Embedded Java applets or other scripts
- Advertising banners
- Scrolling messages that appear in the browser's status bar
- Blinking text (it is converted to bold type)
- Background images

The Proxomitron's filtering settings are easy to use. The program lets you develop a list of Web sites to block, as shown in Figure 6-5.

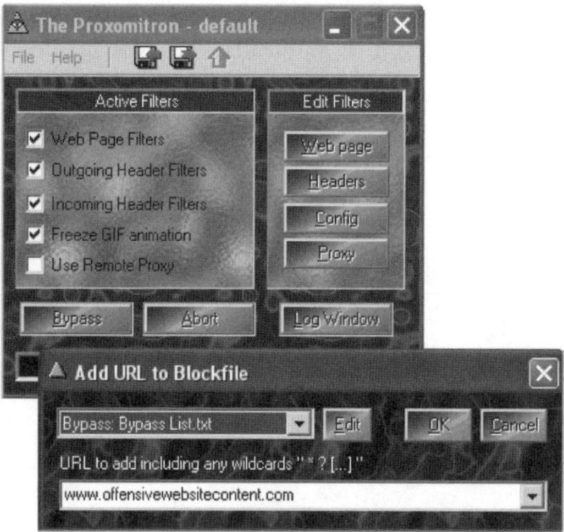

Figure 6-5 This free proxy server lets you create lists of Web sites to block

The Proxomitron also permits the user to filter layers (containers within a Web page that can be freely moved around and that can be used to arrange elements precisely), and to block Dynamic HTML (Web page markup that enables special effects such as images that appear to roll over or change when a mouse is passed over them).

The danger with such extensive content filtering is that the content that the Web page's author has created to convey a legitimate message can also be blocked. Such content adds to the experience of a Web site, and use of it is not necessarily harmful. If you block such content, you may make a Web page more difficult to read; be sure to use such filtering selectively.

Proxomitron is available as freeware at *http://proxomitron.org*. The program's installation and configuration options are described in Hands-On Project 6-2.

MANAGING FIREWALLS TO IMPROVE SECURITY

A firewall's effectiveness depends on the ongoing attention its administrator devotes to it. All too often, firewalls are installed and left to do their job without any adjustments. This means that, while new types of attack and new attackers are constantly making their presence felt, the firewall is not reconfigured to keep them away. Intrusion attempts are undetected in the log files, and the attacker eventually succeeds in gaining access to a supposedly protected computer.

Firewall maintenance can be a difficult task in the light of other duties that might seem more urgent. However, because of its importance as a gateway for the network, managing the firewall in a way that improves security is essential. Effective management impacts the network in the following important ways:

- *Security* —A firewall that isn't protecting the network the way it should leaves everyone in the organization in danger of having their privacy violated and their files damaged. Managing the firewall enables the organization to cope with new threats and continue to effectively block attacks.
- *Throughput* —The term "throughput" refers to the capacity of a device or connection to move data in a specific period of time. A firewall that is configured with too many filtering rules reduces network traffic throughput as it processes packets against each of those rules one by one. Adjusting the firewall so that it performs better will speed up the performance of your entire network.
- *Disaster recovery* —Should an environmental or other disaster occur, you need to get your firewall up and running again to restore secure network communications. Restoring the firewall's security policy and configuration is an essential administrative task; by saving backups of the current configuration in a secure location, you make such recovery possible.

The following sections examine some tasks you and the other members of your administrative team (if you are lucky enough to have one) can perform on a regular basis to keep your firewall performing effectively. These tasks include editing the rule base to conform to your organization's security policy; managing the firewall log files; improving firewall performance; and configuring advanced firewall functions that can keep the entire network running more smoothly.

Editing the Rule Base

Editing the rules in your firewall's rule base is one of the best ways to improve security and performance. Making the rule base more effective also has the benefit of enabling the firewall to more effectively implement your organization's security policies. Improving the rule base can include a number of administrative activities:

- Making sure the most important rules are near the top of the rule base
- Making sure you don't make the firewall do any more logging than it has to
- Reducing the number of **domain objects** (objects that exist within your organization's own domain) in the rule base (see the following note)
- Keeping rules that cover domain objects near the bottom of the rule base

NOTE

The problem with using domain objects in the rule base is that it could lead to a security breach. When the firewall encounters a rule in the rule base that includes a computer or other domain object as either the source or the destination, it will attempt to look up the domain name of the object from its IP address. Through a type of hacker attack called **DNS spoofing** or **DNS poisoning**, such an object could give a hacker who has gained control of the network's DNS server the ability to identify a specific computer on the internal network that can then be targeted for attack.

Reducing Rules

One of the simplest and most effective ways to improve the rule base is to see if there are any rules in it that aren't needed. You want the rules to be as relevant and as few as possible. How many rules should you have, exactly? There isn't any hard-and-fast rule covering the number of rules; it's most effective to scan the rules and make sure there aren't any duplicates or unnecessary listings.

Consider a rule base that is for a network with IP addresses in the range 210.101.101.0–210.100.101.255. The firewall is at 210.100.101.1, and the Web server is at 210.100.101.2. Suppose your organization's security policy calls for users on the internal LAN to be able to use Hypertext Transport Protocol (HTTP) to access any Web sites, and to use Secure HTTP (HTTPS) on the Internet, but not on the Web server in the organization's own DMZ. You could write the rules as shown in Table 6-2:

Table 6-2 Too many firewall rules

Rule	Source IP	Destination IP	Protocol	Action	Track	Comments
1	Any	210.100.101.1	Any	Deny	Alert	Block access to firewall
2	210.100.101.0-210.100.101.255	210.100.101.2	HTTPS	Deny	None	Block LAN access to Web server using HTTPS
3	210.100.101.0-210.100.101.255	Any	HTTP, HTTPS	Allow	None	Allow LAN access to all Web sites
4	Any	210.100.101.2	HTTP	Allow	Log	Allow all computers to access the Web server using HTTP
5	Any	Any	Any	Deny	Log	Cleanup rule

6

This brief rule base uses three rules to allow internal and external users to connect to the Web server using HTTP but not using HTTPS. A much more efficient way would be to consolidate three of the rules (2, 3, and 4 in Table 6-2) into two rules (3 and 4 in Table 6-3).

Table 6-3 More efficient firewall rules

Rule	Source IP	Destination IP	Protocol	Action	Track	Comments
1	Any	210.100.101.1	Any	Deny	Alert	Block access to firewall
2	Any	210.100.101.2	HTTP	Allow	None	Allow full access to Web server using HTTP
3	210.100.101.0-210.100.101.255	All except 210.100.101.2	HTTP, HTTPS	Allow	None	Enable LAN access to Web using HTTP and HTTPS but not to DMZ Web server
4	Any	Any	Any	Deny	Log	Cleanup rule

NOTE

Tables 6-2 and 6-3 include a rule base column called Track. This column is used by some firewalls (such as Check Point NG, which is described later in this chapter) to determine whether the firewall should record the action it performs when a match is found to a particular rule. Typical options available in the Track column are Alert (which causes the firewall to send an alert message in response to a match), Log (which tells the firewall to log the event), and None (which tells the firewall not to track the event).

Reordering and Editing Rules

Another way to improve your firewall rule base is to make sure the rules that are most frequently matched appear near the top rather than the bottom. Such ordering is beneficial because a firewall checks the rules in top-to-bottom order until a match is found. If the firewall continually has to proceed from rule 1 to rule 11 before finding the first match at rule 12, it will spend unnecessary time and processing power moving from rule 1 to 11. However, moving the rule closer to the top will make the match occur more quickly and allow the traffic through with less delay.

To reorder your rules, scan the log files. They will indicate the most popular services, which are those with the highest number of log file entries. You need only move such rules closer to the top of the rule base than the bottom.

As an example of the reordering possibilities, consider that one of the most popular services in many organizations is Simple Mail Transport Protocol (SMTP) for outgoing e-mail. (This is followed closely by Post Office Protocol version 3 or POP3 for incoming e-mail, and HTTP for the Web.) A rule base that allows internal users to connect to the SMTP server in the DMZ should not be number 12, 15, or 20 in the rule base, but should probably be in the "top five" rules instead. Any traffic to or from your network's DNS server should probably go right at the top of the rule base, after the rule that prevents access to your firewall.

Your goal should be to reduce the number of rules that have Log as the action to the bare minimum. In doing so, you improve firewall rule base efficiency even further. You should log only those events that occur as a result of attempts to access resources that you have restricted (such as the firewall itself) or that occur on resources whose activities you really want to track (such as your external Web server's level of activity).

Managing Log Files

You already know that the log files that are generated by firewalls and other security devices provide you with critical information about network traffic and attempts to attack hosts on your internal network. You can control exactly what the firewall records in the log files and how those files are stored. Doing so improves the firewall's performance while maintaining network security.

This section discusses ways in which you can administer a firewall to more efficiently generate its log files. You can control what the firewall logs; configure the log file format; prepare log file summaries; and generate reports that, in turn, help you make changes to the firewall so that it operates more effectively.

Assembling a team of administrators to manage tasks ensures that they are completed quickly. However, be aware that having too many administrators making changes on a firewall can result in confusion, as well as misconfiguration of the firewall. Make sure team members keep a record of every change they make to the firewall that includes the time the change was made and the reason for the adjustment.

Deciding What to Log

Every firewall includes default settings for different events that it will log. By default, some firewalls (like Microsoft ISA Server 2000, which is described later in this chapter) log only packets that are subject to a rule with a Deny action. This makes sense, because it enables the administrator to keep track of attempts to access the network that prove unsuccessful. However, you can also select to log all packets, including those that have been allowed, but this will dramatically slow the operation of the firewall/proxy server/IDS.

Many firewalls give you not one, but many different kinds of log files. These might include one or more of the following:

- *Security log* —This log records any specific security events that have been detected by the firewall, such as Denial of Service attempts or port scans.
- *System log* —This log records when the firewall was started and stopped, so that you can keep track of who attempts to use or configure it.
- *Traffic log* —This log captures each packet that enters or leaves the firewall. You can use it for preparing reports that describe when traffic is heaviest, lightest, and so on.
- *Active log (Check Point)* —This log displays the connections that are currently active and is used for real-time traffic monitoring.
- *Audit log (Check Point)* —This log enables you to keep track of who accesses the firewall and what actions were performed on it.

6

In addition, you can choose exactly which elements are to be included in the log files. A typical set of options is shown in Check Point NG's Log Viewer (see Figure 6-6).

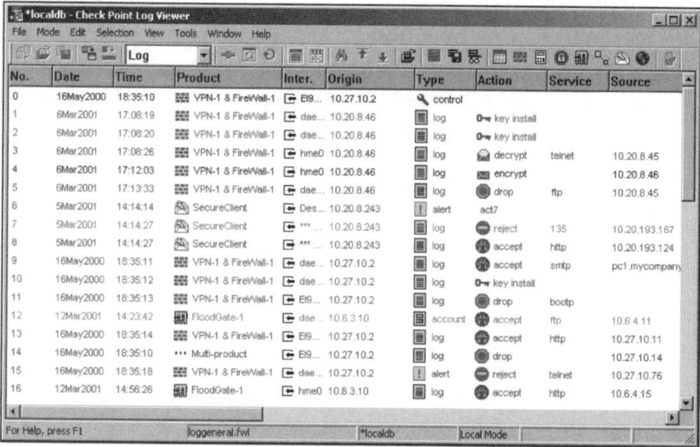

No.	Date	Time	Product	Inter.	Origin	Type	Action	Service	Source
0	16May2000	18:35:10	VPN-1 & FireWall-1	El9...	10.27.10.2	control			
1	6Mar2001	17:08:19	VPN-1 & FireWall-1	dae...	10.20.8.46	log	key install		
2	6Mar2001	17:08:20	VPN-1 & FireWall-1	dae...	10.20.8.46	log	key install		
3	6Mar2001	17:08:26	VPN-1 & FireWall-1	hme0	10.20.8.46	log	decrypt	telnet	10.20.8.45
4	6Mar2001	17:12:03	VPN-1 & FireWall-1	hme0	10.20.8.46	log	encrypt		10.20.8.46
5	6Mar2001	17:13:33	VPN-1 & FireWall-1	dae...	10.20.8.46	log	drop	ftp	10.20.8.45
6	5Mar2001	14:14:14	SecureClient	Des...	10.20.8.243	alert	act7		
7	5Mar2001	14:14:27	SecureClient	*** ...	10.20.8.243	log	reject	135	10.20.193.167
8	5Mar2001	14:14:27	SecureClient	*** ...	10.20.8.243	log	accept	http	10.20.193.124
9	16May2000	18:35:11	VPN-1 & FireWall-1	dae...	10.27.10.2	log	accept	smtp	pc1.mycompany
10	16May2000	18:35:12	VPN-1 & FireWall-1	dae...	10.27.10.2	log	key install		
11	16May2000	18:35:13	VPN-1 & FireWall-1	El9...	10.27.10.2	log	drop	bootp	
12	12Mar2001	14:23:42	FloodGate-1	dae...	10.6.3.10	account	accept	ftp	10.6.4.11
13	16May2000	18:35:14	VPN-1 & FireWall-1	El9...	10.27.10.2	log	accept	http	10.27.10.11
14	16May2000	18:35:10	Multi-product	El9...	10.27.10.2	log	drop		10.27.10.14
15	16May2000	18:35:18	VPN-1 & FireWall-1	dae...	10.27.10.2	alert	reject	telnet	10.27.10.76
16	12Mar2001	14:56:26	FloodGate-1	hme0	10.6.3.10	log	accept	http	10.6.4.15

Figure 6-6 Log Viewer presents you with columns of data that you can rearrange to make information easier to read

Sometimes, firewalls come with so many types of logging data that including them all would make the files unwieldy. On the other hand, some options that can give you useful information can be easily overlooked, simply because they would make the log file entries difficult to view without scrolling across a computer screen, or because they won't fit on a standard sheet of paper. Table 6-4 lists some log file data you might find useful. The first seven are "must-have" log file data; the remaining data are useful, but not essential.

Table 6-4 Types of log file data

Log File Data	What It Records
Date	The date when the event occurred
Time	The time when the event occurred, usually in Greenwich Mean Time (GMT)
Source IP	The IP address of the computer that made the request
Destination IP	The IP address of the computer that is being asked to provide a service to the requesting computer
Protocol	The name of the application protocol used to make the connection
Source Port	The port number being used on the source computer to make the request
Destination Port	The port number being used to provide the requested service to the requesting computer
Authentication status	Whether the client making the request has been authenticated
Interface	The firewall interface on which the request was received (such as INT for internal interface or EXT for external interface)
Service	The name of the service (such as DNS, HTTP, or FTP) that was used to make the request or connection
Rule	The number of the rule that was used to process the request
Processing time	The time, in milliseconds, that was required to process the request
Bytes sent	The number of bytes sent from the internal host to the external computer as a result of the connection
Cache info	Indicates whether the requested object was cached

Firewalls that enable you to manipulate the log file presentation with a GUI program usually allow you to customize which fields are included in the log. Check Point NG gives you a wide range of data fields from which you can choose (see Figure 6-7).

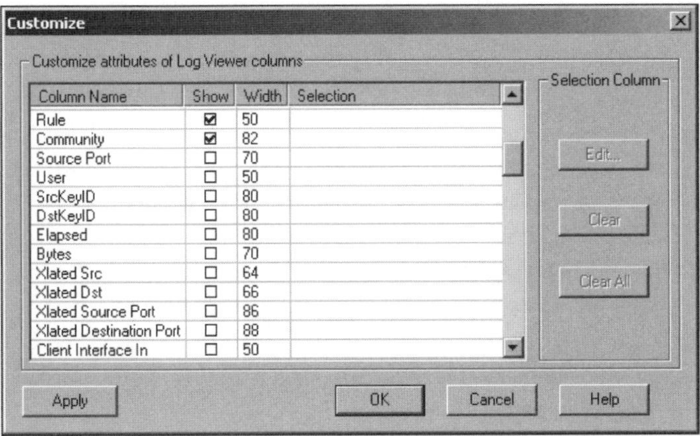

Figure 6-7 Many firewalls make it easy for you to customize log files by adding extra information

Configuring the Log File Format

Many firewalls and intrusion detection systems generate log files that are formatted in plain text. They can be viewed with Notepad or another text editor. The more sophisticated firewalls, like Microsoft ISA Server 2000, give you the option to save log files in different formats, such as:

- *Native format* —You view the log files using the firewall program itself.
- *Open Database Connectivity (ODBC) format* —Log files saved in this format can be viewed with Microsoft SQL Server or another ODBC-compliant database program, which makes it easy to run reports on the data or pull out individual elements for study.
- *W3C format* —This format, which was developed by the World Wide Web consortium (W3C), doesn't mean you can view it with a Web browser; rather, it means that you view it with a text editor.

Log files can be edited and reconfigured as a first step to improving firewall efficiency. They can and should also be reviewed, and the firewall rules should then be edited to improve security. The sequence of events proceeds as follows:

1. You open up your log viewing software and review the summary of recent log file events.
2. You present the raw data in the form of a report. You might create a report of all the traffic in the previous data, or one that sorts access attempts by source IP address so that you can see who's been attempting to connect to your network recently.
3. You review the data and identify traffic patterns that point to problems with the firewall rules. For instance, log files that have multiple duplicated entries provide evidence of rules that can be reconfigured to eliminate repetition.

4. You adjust the rules accordingly.
5. You review subsequent log file data to make sure the changes to the rules reduced the number of unnecessary log file entries.

Log files can also provide you with "signatures" of attack attempts such as port scans. As an example of a signature, consider that a sequence of log file entries in which one computer makes connection attempts to a sequence of consecutive ports on a single computer (such as 192.168.0.1:234, 192.168.0.1:235, 192.168.0.1:236, and so on) is scanning that computer for open ports. You should respond by blocking all connection attempts from the source computer and making sure no open ports exist on the targeted computer or others on the internal network.

Preparing Log File Summaries

A log file summary presents the major events that generated log file entries over a particular period, such as a day, a week, or a month. Such summaries aren't reports. Rather, they provide totals of how many events occurred and what type they were, and they can be used to prepare reports. Before you create a report with ISA Server 2000, for instance, you need to have a summary on hand. If you use daily summaries, this means you have to wait until the time of day when the summary is generated before you generate a report. If you choose a weekly summary, you have to wait a week before creating the report, and so on.

Some firewall programs provide you with log file analysis tools that prepare summaries of the raw data over a particular period and then give you options for organizing the information in the form of reports. Other programs require you to use an add-on log analyzer. The freeware firewall Zone Alarm by Zone Labs is popular enough that another company, MCS (*http://zonelog.co.uk*) has created a log file analysis tool for it. First, you open ZoneLog Analyser. Then you decide what data to import into the tool—the default log file or another one located elsewhere on your network. See Figure 6-8.

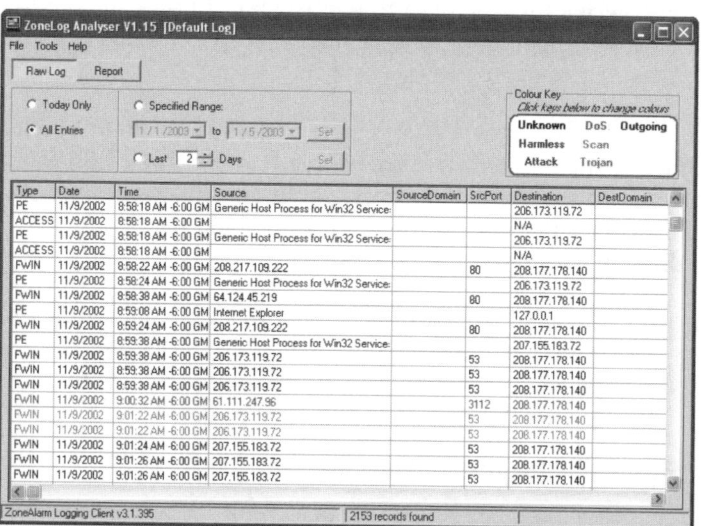

Figure 6-8 A log file analysis tool gives you a summary from which you can prepare reports

By clicking the Report button shown to the right of the Raw Log button in the ZoneLog Analyser window, you are presented with a variety of reports you can assemble from the summary data.

Generating Reports

After you have a log file summary available, you can generate a report. A **report** is an analysis of a set of firewall data that is then presented in a format that is easy to read and interpret. Formats include the use of graphs and columns.

A comprehensive firewall program gives you the ability to present statistics such as the number of visitors your Web site received, the types of browsers that the visitors used, and the most popular pages that were accessed. The reports aren't much different from those presented by a Web server, with one exception: the firewall will also be able to report on security-related events such as attack attempts. A Web server couldn't do this because it doesn't have a way of determining what constitutes a suspicious packet or an intrusion attempt. The Web server's job is simply to serve Web page files and receive data submitted by clients.

Improving Firewall Performance

After you install your firewall, you may notice that it takes longer to get on the Internet or receive files from external hosts. The problem may be that the firewall's default settings are causing the firewall to perform unnecessary lookups and unnecessary operations. Here are some examples:

- *Host lookups* —Make sure the firewall uses the list of host names in the host computer to look up computers rather than having to resolve a domain name to an IP address every time a request is received.
- *Decryption* —Check Point FireWall-1 (part of the Check Point NG security suite described later in this chapter) decrypts packets that arrive at the firewall—regardless of whether they are encrypted. By unchecking the "Enable decryption on accept" option in the firewall's Global Properties dialog box (see Figure 6-9), you can speed up the firewall's operation considerably.
- *Logging* —Many firewalls are set up by default to log events multiple times or to log events that aren't critical. By changing the default settings, you can save the firewall some work and reduce the disk space consumed by your log files as well.

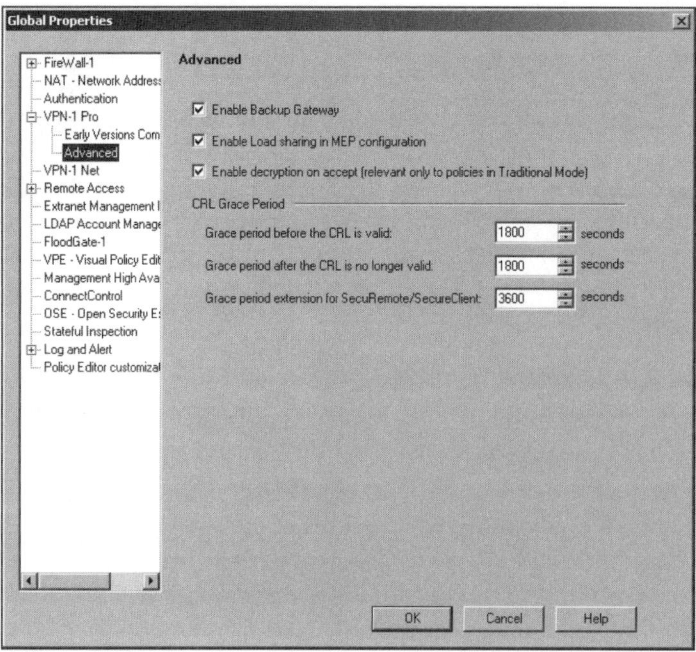

Figure 6-9 FireWall-1 attempts to decrypt all packets by default

The speed of the host computer's Central Processing Unit (CPU) has the greatest impact on firewall performance. Choose a machine with the fastest CPU available. A host that uses two or more CPUs in a symmetric processing configuration will be able to maintain a near-constant performance level when the network traffic level grows.

Calculating Memory Requirements of Firewalls

For the firewall to operate smoothly, it must have at least the minimum amount of Random Access Memory (RAM) required, if not more. The system requirements for the firewall are listed on the manual that comes with the software and on the manufacturer's Web site. For instance, a proxy server like ISA Server 2000 needs a minimum of 256MB of RAM, as mentioned at *www.microsoft.com/isaserver/evaluation/sysreqs/default.asp*. In most cases, though, 512MB to 1GB of available RAM is preferred. It also requires storage space to cache Web pages and other files. A standard formula for determining cache memory is [100MB + (0.5MB   number of users)]. If the program is intended to serve 500 users, you would need, at minimum, 100MB + (0.5   500)=350MB of cache space.

Testing the Firewall

After you have configured the firewall, testing it both before and after it goes online ensures that users won't run into access problems. Ideally, you should test the firewall before you put it in place on the network, so that you can shut down the software if needed and make changes without interrupting traffic on the network. An ideal environment for testing would be a lab with two client computers: one connected to the external interface (to simulate a machine on the Internet) and another on the internal interface (to simulate a computer on the internal LAN). It's an especially good idea to equip one of the client computers with a network vulnerability scanner such as SAINT (see Chapter 10 for more information) to scan it for open ports services you don't need and that might present a hacker with a means to circumvent the firewall.

If you don't have two computers, you can use one test machine and connect it to the internal interface and then connect to the firewall's external interface through a dial-up modem connection.

Configuring Advanced Firewall Functions

After you have the basic functions in place, you can improve the firewall by adding on more advanced features. These can include:

- *Data caching*—The storing of Web pages in cache has already been discussed in connection with ISA Server 2000, but other firewalls can cache Web pages as well.
- *Remote management*—You can install remote management software, if your firewall provides it, on one or more remote workstations so that you can more easily monitor the program and make configuration changes.

In addition, you might also want to set up a form of load balancing such as **load sharing**—the practice of configuring two or more firewalls to share the total traffic load. Each firewall in a load sharing setup is active at the same time, using a specialized protocol such as Open Shortest Path First (OSPF) or Border Gateway Protocol (BGP).

INSTALLING AND CONFIGURING CHECK POINT NG

Check Point NG is one of a number of enterprise-level firewalls that combine all of the security functions described earlier in this chapter and in Chapter 5. In this section, you examine the decisions you need to make to install and configure this powerful software. A high-level overview of the installation and configuration procedure indicates how the component activities of such a security program can work together to protect a network.

With Check Point NG, as with the other firewall applications such as Microsoft Internet Security and Acceleration Server, and iptables, you start by reviewing your organization's security policy. The policy describes the goals of the firewall. The goals, in turn, tell you what rules should be configured. The placement of the firewall is also important: a firewall that is the sole gateway for a network should be configured different from one that shares a DMZ with a second firewall, or that is just one of multiple firewalls on a network.

To finish planning, you need to answer questions such as the following:

- Is the firewall on the outside of the DMZ or does it protect one part of the internal network from another part of the network?
- How important is it to monitor the activities of employees on the network?

After you are fully aware of the security stance the firewall is to perform and its position in the network, you can begin to install and configure it. We discuss these steps next.

Installing Check Point Modules

You can install Check Point NG on a computer running Windows 2000 Professional or Server, Windows NT with Service Pack 4 or above installed, Sun Solaris 7 or 8, or Red Hat Linux 6.2 or later. You can also install it on a dedicated hardware appliance such as the Nokia IP series.

A component is an application that performs a specific range of functions within a larger software package. Check Point NG contains a variety of components that you can install. The various security components work together to create an overall security architecture for the network. The Check Point NG CD-ROM gives you the option to select the components you need early in the installation process. They include the following:

- *Check Point Management NG*—You use this module to enter your license information and generate a public and private key pair.
- *Policy Editor NG*—You'll probably use this module most often; it enables you to create filter rules and identify network objects to protect.
- *Status Manager NG*—You use this module to track the current operation of the firewall in case you need to improve performance.

- *Log Viewer NG*—You configure and organize the log files that the firewall generates using this module.
- *Traffic Monitoring NG*—You use this module to do real-time monitoring of traffic as it passes into and out of the firewall.

Note that Check Point NG product integrates with products that provide anti-virus protection and other solutions through the use of Check Point's own protocol called Open Platform for Security (OPSEC). Developers use OPSEC to create solutions that integrate well with Check Point NG to create a strong network security architecture. Examples of products you might integrate with the firewall include eSafe Protect (*www.esafe.com*), a program that scans e-mail, Web pages, and FTP traffic for viruses, and WebTrends (*www.netiq.com/ webtrends/default.asp*), a program that is well known for its ability to create graphical reports from log database information.

Preparing to Install Check Point NG

Before you install Check Point NG, you need to determine where the program will be installed; you also need to prepare the host computer. You should not install the program on the same directory as the operating system. Rather, you should use an NTFS partition. Pick a directory on a standalone server if possible. Eliminate all unnecessary services as described in the section on creating a bastion host in Chapter 4. Install all service packs and patches. You also need to enable IP forwarding on the computer.

After you have the host computer prepared, you need to go to the Check Point User Center (*http://usercenter.checkpoint.com*) to obtain a license to use the software. You then need to add it by clicking Add in the License tab of the Check Point Configuration Tool shown in Figure 6-10.

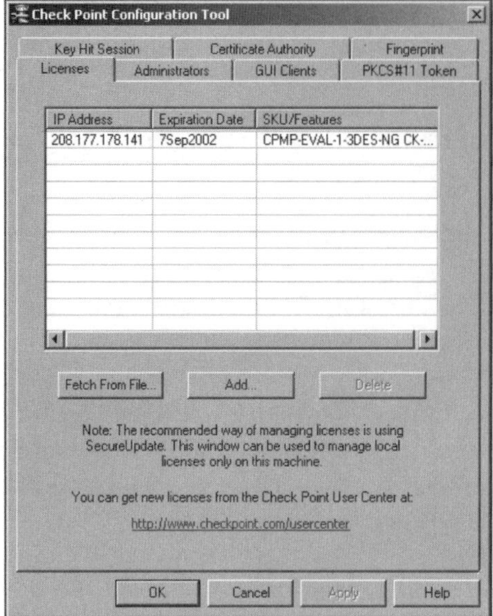

Figure 6-10 You need a license key to install and use Check Point NG

Remember that the type of license key you obtain determines how long you can use the software and the IP address on which the software has been installed. Be sure to obtain a license that covers the length of time you plan to use Check Point NG before you renew or update the license.

Using the Management Module

The Management Module is the first component you use during installation; it enables you to create a password that is used for secure communications between the Management Server and the other Check Point NG components.

You have to determine whether the Management Server will be on the same computer as the policy server or whether you are going to use a remote management server. The Management Module consists of the Management Server and the GUI Client. These components can all be on one computer or on different computers. Figure 6-11 shows the GUI Client and Management Server all on different machines, but they can be on one machine if you do not have enough computers available.

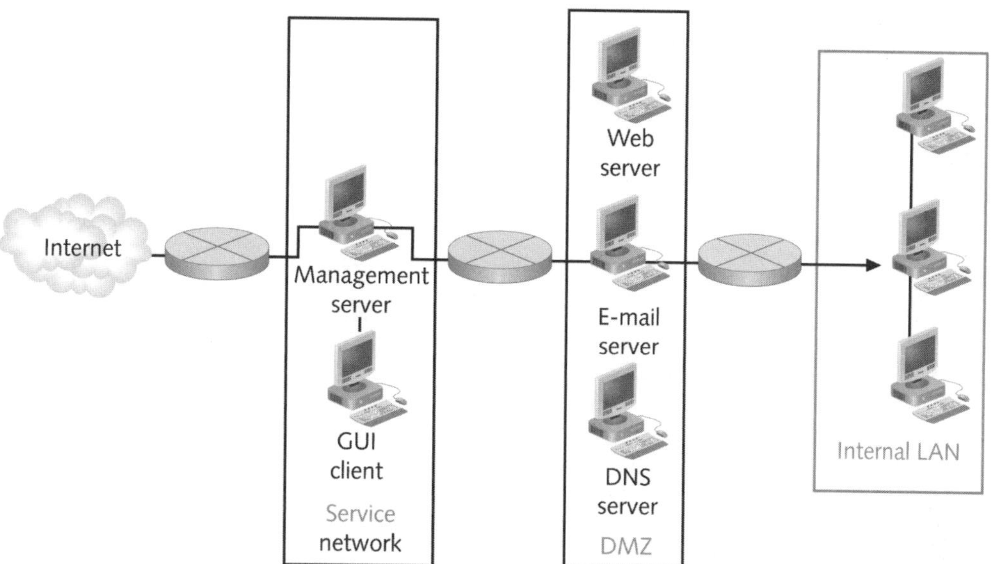

Figure 6-11 A possible configuration for Check Point NG

After you have your license and have created your key pair, the installation program installs the modules you have selected.

Configuring Network Objects

After you have installed the software, you can begin to define the objects on the network that the firewall needs to protect. Start up the Policy Editor, and log on using the username and password you created during the installation process. Then you define the gateway and computers that the firewall needs to protect, which the program interface calls Network Objects.

When you start up the Policy Editor, you are presented with a substantial amount of information and configuration options. The main program window is broken into these sections:

- *Objects Tree*— This is a hierarchically ordered list of the objects in your network. A network object can be a gateway, a workstation or node, a domain, a service, or individual device.
- *Rule Base* —This is a list of rules in the rule base. These rules make up the current network security policy.
- *Objects List* —This pane, which is found beneath Rule Base by default, provides an alternative to Objects Tree. The Objects List network objects can be sorted by name, IP address, or comments you add about each object.

- *Topology Map* —This is a visual and interactive view of all the objects being protected on your network.

The easiest way to define objects is to use a GUI tool that is part of the Policy Editor. This GUI tool is the Network Objects Manager. You open the Network Objects Manager by choosing Manage from the Policy Editor menu bar and then choosing Network Objects. The objects you'll most likely use are Check Point Gateway (a gateway managed by the Management Server) and Check Point Node (a host computer on the network). A **node** can be a single workstation, a VPN appliance, a gateway, a host, or any combination of these.

Creating Filter Rules

After you have defined the essential objects in your network, you can begin to develop a security policy. In the context of a Check Point firewall, a security policy is a set of packet filtering rules. The program calls a rule base a "Policy Package." This set of rules can be applied to a specific part of your network, such as your VPN.

To create a new Policy Package, click File from the Policy Editor menu bar and click New. A dialog box opens prompting you to save your work to this point. Click OK, and the New Policy Package dialog box opens. Assign a name to the Policy Package and click OK. The Select Installation Targets dialog box appears so that you can identify the network objects to which the rules will apply. When you select the objects and click OK, a new, blank version of the Rules pane opens in the Policy Editor so that you can begin to create rules.

INSTALLING AND CONFIGURING MICROSOFT ISA SERVER 2000

Microsoft ISA Server 2000 is a firewall designed to protect the networks of businesses. ISA Server 2000 is notable for its ability to perform a variety of proxy server functions in addition to packet filtering, Network Address Translation, and other traditional firewall functions. The proxy server features include the ability to screen communications at the application level and the caching of Web pages to reduce network server load and improve the speed with which users access Web server pages.

Your first step to installation is to select the version of ISA Server 2000 that you want. The program comes in two editions, Standard and Enterprise. Table 6-5 indicates the primary differences between the two.

Table 6-5 ISA Server 2000: Standard versus Enterprise

Feature	Standard	Enterprise
Server	Standalone	Multiple
Processors	One	Up to Four
Policy	Simple	Multilevel

Microsoft ISA Server 2000 runs only on Windows 2000 Server, Advanced Server, or Datacenter Server, not on Windows XP or 2000 Professional.

The following sections describe the stages you follow in installing and configuring ISA Server 2000: licensing, installing the program itself, creating a security policy, and monitoring the program.

Licensing ISA Server 2000

You need to obtain a license to use ISA Server 2000 on a permanent basis. The program is licensed on a "per-processor" basis: you need to purchase one license for each processor on the host on which ISA Server 2000 will be installed. You can then use as many clients as you need to connect to the server. However, if you aren't sure you want a license, you can install a 120-day trial version from Microsoft's Web site (*www.microsoft.com/isaserver*).

Installation Issues

Installation of ISA Server 2000 is simplified by the use of a wizard that guides you through the various installation stages. However, after you begin to install the program, Windows 2000's built-in Web server, Internet Information Server (IIS), is stopped. After ISA Server 2000 is installed, you'll have to either uninstall IIS or reconfigure it to work with ISA Server 2000.

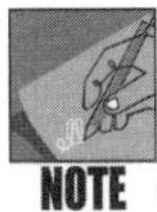

If you choose to install the Enterprise Edition of ISA Server 2000, you need to run additional software called the ISA Server Enterprise Initialization Tool, which modifies the Windows 2000 Active Directory so that ISA Server 2000 can use it.

The following sections describe the steps to follow during the installation of ISA Server 2000. During the installation, you'll need to choose a server mode, configure cache locations, and then set addresses.

Make sure you have the latest Windows 2000 Server Pack installed before you install ISA Server 2000. You can find the current Server Pack at *www.microsoft.com/windows2000/downloads/servicepacks*.

Choosing a Server Mode

One of the first decisions you need to make during the installation process is the mode in which the server will operate: in other words, the set of features that the firewall will provide. The options are:

- *Multi-Layer Firewall mode* —In this mode, ISA Server 2000 can perform stateful packet filtering at multiple layers of the OSI model of network communications: packet-level, circuit-level, and application-level.

- *Web-Cache mode* —In this mode, ISA Server 2000 stores Web pages in cache.
- *Integrated mode* —This mode alleviates the need to choose between the Multi-Layer Firewall mode or Web-Cache mode: ISA Server 2000 performs the functions associated with both modes.

Integrated mode seems an obvious choice because it gives you the highest level of functionality. However, you might choose Multi-Layer Firewall mode if you already have a proxy server on the network that stores Web pages in cache, or if you don't want to cache Web pages. You might choose Web-Cache mode if you already have a stateful packet filter in place.

Configuring Cache and Setting Addresses

If you specified that the server will run in Web-Cache or Integrated mode, the installation wizard prompts you to select the location where you want to install cached files. Cached Web pages need to be stored on an NTFS-formatted drive. You also specify the amount of disk storage space set aside for cache; the amount you choose depends on the number of users who will be protected by ISA Server 2000 (see "Calculating Memory Requirements" earlier in this chapter).

After configuring the disk cache space, you create a **Local Address Table** that defines the internal addressing scheme of your network. You tell the installation wizard the range of IP addresses that span the address space of your internal network. You also identify the network adapter of the host computer. After you have completed the Local Address Table, the wizard completes the installation of ISA Server 2000 and automatically launches a Getting Started Wizard so that you can begin to configure the program.

Creating a Security Policy

ISA Server 2000's Getting Started Wizard leads you through the steps involved in creating the security policy. This wizard makes ISA Server 2000 especially easy to configure because it helps you create the filtering rules that govern Internet access for your organization. The Getting Started Wizard runs within the ISA Management Console, which gives you a way to change the configuration after the program is up and running. The following sections describe the most important stages in the configuration process: selecting policy elements, configuring clients, and configuring protocol rules.

ISA Server 2000 comes with a pair of built-in application filters designed to defeat two of the most common types of hacker attacks. The first type is the DNS host name overflow (in which very long host names are sent to the DNS server, which can cause some DNS servers to stop running and thus open them to the hacker's control). The second type is the POP buffer overflow (in which the attacker sends more data than the buffer of a POP server can handle, thus overflowing it so the hacker can gain access to the root level of the server).

Selecting Policy Elements

One of the first steps in configuring ISA Server 2000 (or any firewall) is the identification of the policy elements you want the program to filter and/or protect. You select four types of elements that you want ISA Server 2000 to work with: users and groups; computer names or IP addresses; a schedule that enables you to grant or deny access based on time restrictions; and **destination sets** —groups of destination computers that can be named and handled together to make rules easier to configure. (You can name a group of computers DMZ, for instance, rather than having to enter the IP addresses of each computer in the DMZ to create a rule.)

Configuring Clients

One advantage of using ISA Server 2000 over its predecessor (Microsoft Proxy Server 2.0) or other proxy servers is the minimal need to configure clients to use the program. Web browsers or other clients can connect to ISA Server 2000 through a system called SecureNAT. This means that client software running many different types of systems can access ISA Server 2000.

The Getting Started Wizard also gives you the ability to define **client sets**: groups of client computers that you can group together by IP address so that you can identify them by name when you create rules.

Configuring Protocol Rules

When it comes to configuring individual protocol rules, the Getting Started Wizard leads you through the process in a user-friendly way. A series of screens asks you to name a rule, choose an action such as Allow or Deny, identify the protocols to which the rule will apply, and set a schedule during which the rule will apply. To create a new rule, you click Create a Protocol Rule in the Getting Started Wizard and repeat the process. You can return to the Getting Started Wizard whenever you need to revise the rules or add new ones.

Monitoring the Server

After you have created a set of filtering rules for ISA Server 2000, you restart your computer and log on as Administrator so that you can manage the program. You reopen the ISA Management console, click Configure Firewall Protection, and then click Configure Packet Filtering and Intrusion Detection so that you can set up intrusion detection and packet filtering options.

The ISA Management Console also enables you to perform real-time monitoring of the server, including the ability to view alerts as soon as they are issued. You can set up **counters** —utilities that keep track of the number of active TCP, UDP, or other connections currently forwarding data on the network.

MANAGING AND CONFIGURING IPTABLES

iptables enables the user to configure packet filter rules for the Linux firewall Netfilter. iptables comes built-in with version 2.4.x or later of the Linux kernel. It replaces an earlier program called ipchains (which, in turn, was developed from a Linux firewall called ipfwadm). Unlike ipchains, iptables enables Netfilter to perform stateful rather than static packet filtering. It also enables you to filter packets based on a full set of TCP options flags such as ACK, rather than just the SYN flag, which was covered by ipchains.

iptables, unlike Check Point NG and Microsoft ISA Server 2000, is a command-line tool. It can be used to set up logging, Network Address Translation, and forwarding packets from one port to another.

Like other programs that do packet filtering, iptables works with sets of rules. Unlike other programs, however, the rules are grouped together in the form of **chains**. Because you are already familiar with the idea of a rule base—a set of packet filtering rules used by a firewall or router—you might think of a chain as being similar to a rule base. The differences are that Linux makes use of multiple rule bases/chains, and a rule in one chain can have, as the effect of its action, the activation of a specific rule in another chain.

Built-In Chains

When a packet is received by the system, the chains are reviewed. The system comes with three built-in chains:

- *Output* —This chain of rules is reviewed when packets are received that originate from inside a LAN with a destination on an external network.
- *Input* —This chain of rules is for packets that originate from an external network destined for a location on the internal network.
- *Forward* —This chain is used when a packet needs to be routed to another location.

The packet then moves through all of the rules in a chain until a match is found. If a match is found, one of four decisions is made on how to handle it:

- *Accept* —The packet is accepted.
- *Drop* —The packet is dropped without any error message which provides effective security because it doesn't let outside users know anything about the system that received and processed the request.
- *Queue* —The packet is queued for processing by a specific application.
- *Return* —Tells iptables to stop checking rules in the chain and return to the original chain.

The chains of rules work together, as illustrated in Figure 6-12.

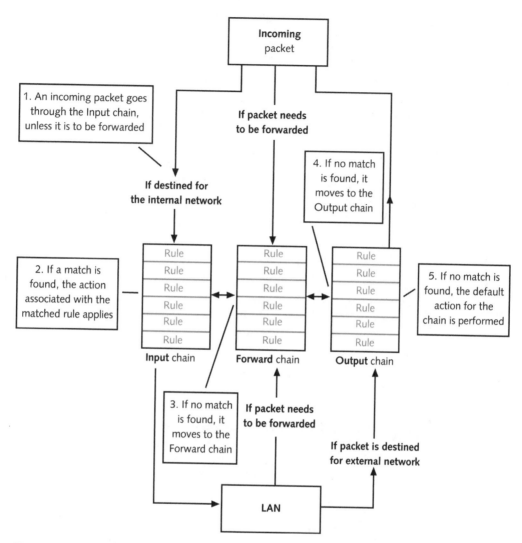

Figure 6-12 iptables makes use of three built-in chains of packet filtering rules

An incoming packet goes through the Input chain, unless it is to be forwarded.

As you can see from Figure 6-12:

1. If a match is found, the action associated with the matched rule applies.
2. If no match is found, it moves to the Forward chain.
3. If no match is found, it moves to the Output chain.
4. If no match is found, the default action for the chain is performed.

You can configure the default action for a chain with the use of the –P command, which sets the default policy for one of the built-in chains. The command is written like this:

```
iptables –P OUTPUT ACCEPT
```

This command sets the default action Accept for any packets that originate from the internal network destined for the Internet. It's an optional starting point for more restrictive rules to follow for outbound packets—as is this default action for inbound packets. The command is written like this:

```
iptables –P INPUT DENY
```

The preceding command blocks all incoming connection attempts by default. After you set this default action, you can configure more specific actions on a case-by-case basis. Another default command rejects all forwarded packets by default. The command is written like this:

```
iptables –P FORWARD DROP
```

This command blocks, by default, any packets that are to be forwarded by the firewall to a destination computer. Blocking such forwarding by default prevents external users from being able to access internal computers in case a user activates a service on a port by accident, and then the hacker can exploit the opening.

The –P command is one of the built-in commands for use with iptables. To see the others, type iptables –h at the command prompt to access the program's Help file, which is shown in Figure 6-13.

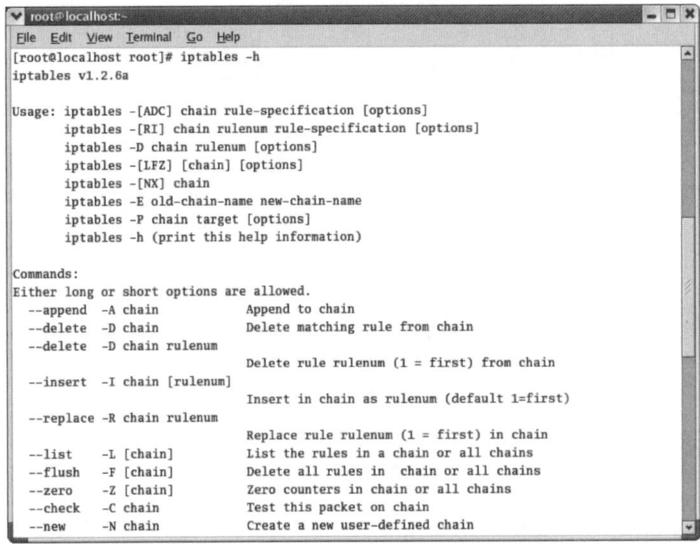

Figure 6-13 You can view and print out a list of the commands for the chains used by iptables

After you set the default rules, you can create more specific rules using the more specific commands described in the following section.

One advantage of using iptables rather than an add-on firewall is that because iptables is part of the Linux kernel, it runs through its packet filtering rule base and makes decisions very quickly.

User-Defined Chains

In addition to the built-in chains, user-defined chains can also be established. You create these using the commands set aside for configuring individual rules, in which [*chain*] is the name of the chain to which the rule belongs:

6

- *-A [chain] rule* —This adds a new rule to the chain.
- *-I [chain] [rule-number] rule* —This enables you to place a new rule in a specific location in the chain as specified by rule number.
- *-R [chain] [rule-number] rule* —This enables you to replace a rule with a new one in the location specified by [rule-number].
- *-D [chain] [rule-number]* —This deletes the rule at the position specified by [rule-number].
- *-D [chain] rule* —This deletes a rule.

Commands that are used to create rules include the following:

- *-s source* —This identifies the source IP address.
- *-d destination* —This identifies the destination IP address.
- *-p protocol* —This identifies the protocol to be used in the rule (such as TCP, UDP, ICMP).
- *-i interface* —This identifies the network interface used by the rule.
- *-j target* —This identifies the action (or **target**) associated with the rule; the target can be an action such as ALLOW or DROP, a network, or a subnet.
- *!* —The exclamation mark (!) negates whatever follows it, such as an IP address you want to exclude.
- *-l* —This switch activates logging if a packet matches the rule.

Some examples should make these commands clearer. For example, refer back to the set of rules presented in Table 6-3 earlier in this chapter. The following commands would create the same rules:

```
iptables -A output -s any -d 210.100.101.1 -p any -t DROP
iptables -A output -s any-d 210.100.101.2 -p HTTP -t ALLOW
iptables -A output -s 210.100.101.0-210.100.101.255 -d any !
   210.100.101.2 HTTP,HTTPS -t ALLOW
iptables -A output -s any -d any -p any -t DROP -l
```

In addition, you can identify a service rather than a protocol: www for the World Wide Web, smtp for outgoing e-mail, and pop3 for incoming e-mail. The following rule enables all users on the network 10.0.20.0/24 to access the company Web server at 10.0.20.2 using the service www:

```
iptables -A output -s 10.0.20.0/24 -d 10.0.20.2 www -j ACCEPT
```

The configuration of iptables is complex; this overview is only intended to provide a starting point. For more information, see the main pages for iptables in the Red Hat Linux Help files, as well as Hands-On Project 6-6.

At this writing, the domain requirements for the Security Certified Professional exam on which this book is based cover the installation of ipchains. However, iptables is covered in this book because it has replaced ipchains and because the two programs share similar configurations. If you are curious about the differences between the two Linux firewall programs, you can view a comparison on Josh Ballard's Oofle.com Security site (*www.oofle.com/iptables/comparison.html*).

CHAPTER SUMMARY

- This chapter discussed issues and techniques used to manage firewalls in a way that improves their performance and reinforces the effectiveness with which they protect a network. Sometimes, improving a firewall configuration involves the installation of a new component such as a proxy server. Firewall management can also be realized by adjusting resources already in place, such as the rule base and log files.
- A proxy server is software that processes traffic to and from the internal network, and that stores Web pages in cache to speed up performance. Unlike packet filters, proxy servers can filter data at the application level by inspecting the contents of packets. They also shield hosts on the internal network, and log traffic headed outbound from internal hosts so that the activities of end-users within the organization can be tracked. Proxy servers provide a high level of security because they prevent a direct connection between an external and an internal computer from ever occurring. One of their most powerful attributes is the ability to open up TCP/IP packets and make decisions based not just on their headers but on the data those packets contain. This gives proxies the ability to filter out pop-up windows, offensive text, advertising banners, or Java applets or other scripts that are embedded in Web pages.
- Firewall performance can also be strengthened through ongoing management. Tightening and rearranging the rule base can speed up performance, as can managing log files in a way that reduces the load on the server and detects intrusion attempts. The rule base

should be as short as possible and have the most important rules near the top of the list so the firewall processes data in the most efficient way.

- A firewall's performance can also be improved by logging only the traffic that represents the most serious security concerns and by rotating log files before they consume too much disk space and slow down the host on which they reside. Log files that are saved in ODBC format can be viewed with an ODBC-compliant database so you can run reports on the data or study individual elements. It's also useful to prepare log file summaries—reports of log file activity for a specified period such as a day or a week—so you can share the information with your colleagues in a format that is easy to read and interpret.
- Check Point NG is a suite of firewall modules that allow you to implement a security policy through stateful packet filtering, Network Address Translation, and authentication. Log file analysis, real-time monitoring, and remote management are also provided.
- Microsoft ISA Server 2000 has several goals: the improvement of network security through traditional firewall filtering and NAT, and faster network performance through the caching of Web pages.
- iptables is a built-in tool for creating packet filter rules. The program includes three built-in "chains" of filter rules that monitor inbound and outbound packets as well as packets that the firewall needs to forward to specific destinations.

6

KEY TERMS

cache — Store data on disk so those files can be retrieved later on if needed; an area of a hard disk where files are stored.

Chains — Sets of packet filtering rules used by the Linux tool iptables.

client sets — Groups of client computers that you can group together by IP address so you can identify them by name when you create rules.

counters — Utilities that keep track of the number of active TCP, UDP or other connections currently forwarding data on the network.

destination sets — Groups of destination computers that can be named and handled together to make rules easier to configure.

DNS poisoning — *See* DNS spoofing.

DNS spoofing — A type of attack against a DNS server that enables a hacker to gain control over it; the hacker submits false information that causes a DNS server to behave as if a domain has a different IP address range then it actually does.

domain objects — Objects that exist within your organization's own domain.

HTTP cookies — Short segments of HTML code that a Web server places on a visitor's Web browser to identify that browser on subsequent visits.

iptables — A packet filtering program that comes with version 2.4.x or later of the Linux kernel. Also called Netfilter.

load sharing — The practice of configuring two or more firewalls to share the total traffic load.

Local Address Table — A set of IP addresses that defines the internal addressing scheme of your network for a firewall or proxy server.

node — A single workstation, a VPN appliance, a gateway, a host, or any combination of these.

proxy server — Software that forwards packets to and from the network being protected and that caches Web pages to speed up network performance.

report — An analysis of a set of firewall data that is then presented in a format that is easy to read and interpret, such as a graph.

target — In the Linux packet filtering application iptables, this term denotes the action (such as drop, accept, queue, or reject) associated with a rule.

Review Questions

1. In what way does a proxy server enhance the security of a network already protected by a packet filter? (Choose all that apply.)

   a. caching of files

   b. logging

   c. content filtering

   d. monitoring of inbound traffic

2. A proxy server works at the ____________ layer of the OSI model of network communications.

   a. Network

   b. Transport

   c. Application

   d. Data Link

3. A proxy server works by opening and examining what object?

   a. disk cache

   b. a log file entry

   c. request header

   d. a TCP/IP packet

4. Proxy servers are able to function as filters for ______.
   a. IP addresses
   b. data portions of packets
   c. protocols
   d. port numbers

5. Which of the following is a security-related benefit of implementing a proxy server's logging capabilities?
   a. single point of logging
   b. intrusion detection
   c. employee monitoring
   d. faster network access

6. A security policy that prohibits employees from accessing offensive material on the Web could be implemented by means of what security tool?
   a. packet filter
   b. firewall
   c. proxy server
   d. router

7. Which of the following is a type of content that can be filtered out by a proxy server to improve network security? (Choose all that apply.)
   a. Web sites
   b. background music
   c. executable code
   d. pop-up ads

8. How can effective firewall administration play a role in disaster recovery?
   a. by keeping the rule base simple
   b. by keeping backups of the current configuration
   c. by keeping copies of the most recent log files
   d. by testing the firewall on a regular basis

9. What is the advantage gained by firewall logs saved in Open Database Connectivity (ODBC) format?

   a to read them using the firewall itself

   b. to present them in a graphical format

   c. to open them in a web browser

   d. to open them using a database application

10. Having multiple administrators available to configure a firewall can ___________. (Choose all that apply.)

    a. make developing contact filters easier

    b. create multiple packet filter rules

    c. speed up periodic firewall maintenance

    d. cause confusion

11. Why do so many firewalls, by default, log packets that are denied?

    a. to keep log file size to a minimum

    b. to track unsuccessful access attempts

    c. to have a record on file in case users complain

    d. to be able to correct rules to allow access to the same packets

12. If the firewall does not look up hostnames on the host computer, what happens?

    a. performance slows

    b. The firewall has to resolve domain names.

    c. The firewall drops all packets.

    d. The firewall can potentially crash.

13. To generate a report, Microsoft ISA Server 2000 requires you to first create ________.

    a. active log files

    b. W3C-formatted log files

    c. log file summaries

    d. backups of log files

14. Which program decrypts incoming packets by default?

    a. Microsoft ISA Server 2000

    b. iptables

    c. Proxomitron

    d. Check Point NG

15. Which of the following programs can be managed from a remote location? (Choose all that apply.)

    a. Check Point NG

    b. iptables

    c. Microsoft ISA Server 2000

    d. Snort

16. The Check Point NG Management module consists of which two programs?

    a. Policy Server

    b. Management Server

    c. GUI Client

    d. System Status

17. Microsoft ISA Server 2000 is notable for its ability to perform ______.

    a. real-time monitoring

    b. IP forwarding

    c. packet filtering

    d. proxy services

18. Which mode lets you perform the widest range of security functions on Microsoft ISA Server 2000?

    a. Web-Cache

    b. Multi-Layer Firewall

    c. Integrated

    d. Permissive

19. An attack in which a hacker transmits a greater amount of data than a server's fixed-memory unit can handle is called a ___________.
    a Denial of Service (DoS)
    b buffer overflow
    c. port scan
    d SYN flood

20. What are the "chains" that iptables uses?
    a. IP addresses
    b. packet filter rules
    c. log file listings
    d encrypted packets

HANDS-ON PROJECTS

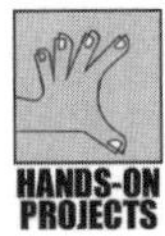

Project 6-1: Analyzing How Proxy Servers Handle Packets

As you learned in this chapter, one of the basic functions performed by proxy servers is the shielding of internal computers by rebuilding packets and changing IP addresses. In this project, you will improve your understanding of how proxy servers process IP addresses by analyzing the process step by step. Figure 6-14 shows a Web browser, a proxy server, and a Web server and how they interact in a typical situation. Use this diagram to guide you through this project.

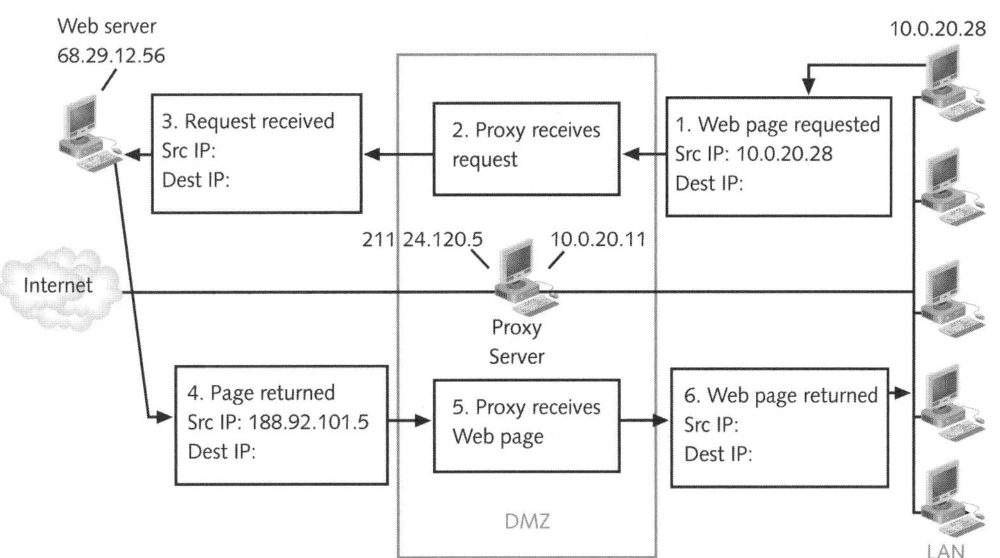

Figure 6-14 Interaction of the elements in a transaction

You will list the source and IP addresses for each step in the transaction, to show how the IP addresses change as they go through the proxy. In each case, write your answers in a lab booklet or word-processed document so that you can check them later.

1. A computer on the internal network with the source IP address 10.0.20.28 makes a request to view a Web page from the server shown in the upper left corner of the diagram. Fill in the destination IP address in box number 1 that would appear in the packet received by the proxy server.
2. In box number 3, fill in the source and destination IP addresses that would appear in the packet sent by the proxy server to the external Web server.
3. In box number 4, fill in the destination IP address that the proxy server would receive in the response sent to it by the external Web server.
4. In box number 6, fill in the source and destination IP addresses in the packet sent by the proxy server to the original host after processing the response from the Web server.

Project 6-2: Monitoring Outbound Traffic with Proxomitron

The freeware application called the Proxomitron by Scott R. Lemmon isn't a full-fledged proxy server in the sense that it doesn't sit on the perimeter of a network, forwarding requests from multiple services. However, it does provide a practical application of one of a proxy server's most important functions: the ability to look inside a packet and filter its contents. The Proxomitron is intended to look at the HTML markup code that makes up Web pages and filter out types of content that the user finds undesirable, such as pop-up ads. The program can also be configured to rewrite or redirect URLs that the user identifies as undesirable. The Proxomitron will work with Windows 2000 or XP. Note that after you configure your browser to use a proxy server as described in the following steps, you'll need to have the Proxomitron running to access Web pages. (You can always undo the proxy settings to surf without the Proxomitron again.)

1. Double-click the **Internet Explorer** icon on your desktop.
2. Enter the URL for the Proxomitron's home page (**http://proxomitron.org**) in your browser's Address box, and then press **Enter**.
3. Read about the Proxomitron to get an idea of what the program can filter, and then click **Downloads**.
4. On the download page that appears, click one of the download files that includes an installer: **Download the Proxomitron with Installer (Site #1)** or **Download the Proxomitron with Installer (Site #2).**
5. When the File Download dialog box appears, click **Open** to begin downloading.
6. When a Setup dialog box appears asking to confirm that you want to install the Proxomitron, click **Yes**.
7. When the first Setup screen appears, click **Next**. Follow through the subsequent screens as indicated by the setup program. Click **Finish** when installation is complete.
8. Start the Proxomitron from the Start menu or double-click the icon that was created on your desktop during installation.
9. Read the Welcome page that opens in your browser window when you open the Proxomitron. (If for some reason the Welcome page does not appear, you can open it directly by entering the path that leads to the directory where you installed Proxomitron. For example, you can type **C:\Program Files *[name of Proxomitron folder]* \help\Welcome.html** in the Address box and then press **Enter**.)
10. Click **Tools** and click **Internet Options** from the Internet Explorer menu bar.
11. Click **Connections**.
12. Click **LAN Settings**. (This assumes you are in a computer lab that uses a direct connection to the Internet via Ethernet. If you are on a dial-up connection, click the connection's name and then click **Settings**.)
13. Check the **Use a proxy server for your LAN** check box. In the Address box, type **localhost**. In the Port box, type **8080**.
14. Click **Advanced**. The Proxy Settings dialog box appears.
15. Uncheck the **Use the same server for all protocols** check box if it is checked.
16. Click **OK** to close Proxy Settings, click **OK** to close Local Area Network (LAN) Settings, and click **OK** to close Internet Options.

17. Now that you have configured your Web browser to use the Promomitron, click The Proxomitron taskbar button to make it the active application. Then click **Log Window** to open a separate logging window.
18. Switch back to your browser, and enter the following URL in the Address box (**http://www.google.com**), and then press **Enter**.
19. Click the **HTTP Message Log** button on the taskbar.
20. In the log, review the HTTP headers exchanged by your computer and the Google server (your computer's outbound headers are shown in green; the responding server's headers are shown in purple). What Web server program is being used by the Google server? Also look for any default filter rules at the bottom of the message log. Were any of the Proxomitron's default filter rules matched simply by visiting the Google home page? Write your answers in a lab notebook or word-processed document.
21. From the Log Window's menu bar, click **Edit** and then **Reset** to clear the log. Click **Edit** and then click **View Posted Data**.
22. Switch back to your browser. In the search box on the Google home page, type **proxy server**, and then click **Google Search**.
23. Switch back to the Log Window. Scroll up to the top of the log file listings. What is the header that indicates how your search request was submitted to Google? Write the answer in a lab notebook or word-processed document.
24. If you don't plan to move on to Project 6-3 right away, click **File** and then click **Exit** to close the Log Window. Do the same for the Proxomitron itself, and then do the same for Internet Explorer. Otherwise, leave both applications open for Project 6-3.

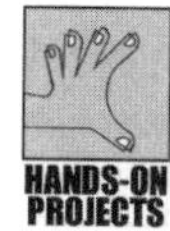

Project 6-3: Configuring Content Filters with The Proxomitron

As you learned in this chapter, one of the features that distinguishes proxy servers from packet filters is their ability to interpret the data part of a TCP/IP packet and act on the contents. The Proxomitron's primary feature, in fact, is the ability to filter Web content such as advertisements in just this way. In this project you will use this simple freeware program on a Windows 2000 or XP computer to filter out content that represents a security risk—executable file attachments—as well as fictitious Web sites that you or your employers might find objectionable.

1. If necessary, start up the Proxomitron by double-clicking the program icon.
2. In the Proxomitron window, under Edit Filters, click **Web Page**.
3. In the HTML Web Page Filters dialog box, scroll down and check the **Kill specific Java applets** check box. Then click to highlight the line **Kill specific Java applets**, and click **Edit**.

4. In the HTML Web Page Filter Editor, in the Matching Expression section, examine the default code: `*code=$AV((scroll|NavigatorTicker|movie|WSSApplet|hyper)*)*`.

5. Click to position the text cursor just after the term "movie" shown in the Matching Expression section. Type **BackOrifice**, press the spacebar once to add a blank space, and then press the | key. This adds the name of a harmful Java, Java.BackOrifice, to the list.

6. Make the line of text in the Matching Expresson section read as follows: **`*code=$AV((scroll|NavigatorTicker|movie|BackOrifice|WSSApplet|hyper)`** .

7. Click **OK**.

8. Right-click the **Proxomitron** icon in the Windows system tray, point to **Add to Blockfile**, and click **Bypass**.

9. In the Add URL to Blockfile dialog box, in the box labeled URL to add including any wildcards, add the name of a fictitious site you want the Proxomitron to block. For the purposes of this example, enter **http://www.offensivesite.com**, and then click **OK**.

10. Click **OK** to close HTML Web Page Filters, and then close the Proxomitron's window.

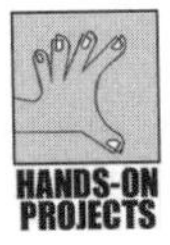

Project 6-4: Improving a Rule Base

Reviewing and rewriting your firewall's packet filtering rule base can speed up your firewall's performance and improve security as well. Consider the example rule base shown in Table 6-5, which has some rules that could be edited and rearranged. The LAN has IP addresses from 210.100.101.0 to 210.100.101.255; the firewall is at 210.100.101.1, the Web server at 210.100.101.2, the DNS server at 210.100.101.3, the SMTP server at 210.100.101.4; and the POP3 server at 210.100.101.5. The firewall that has such a rule base will operate properly, but some simple changes will improve its performance dramatically.

Table 6-6 Sample firewall rule base

Rule	Source IP	Destination IP	Protocol	Action	Track	Comments
1	Any	210.100.101.1	Any	Any	Alert	Block access to firewall
2	210.100.101.0-210.100.101.255	210.100.101.2	HTTPS	Deny	None	Block LAN access to Web server using HTTPS
3	210.100.101.0-210.100.101.255	Any	HTTP, HTTPS	Allow	None	Allow LAN access to all Web sites
4	Any	210.100.101.2	HTTP	Allow	Log	Allow all computers to access the Web server using HTTP
5	210.100.101.0 to 210.100.101.255	210.100.101.3	UDP	Allow	Log	Enable LAN to make queries to DNS server
6	210.100.101.3	Any except 210.100.101.0 to 210.100.101.255	TCP	Allow	Log	Enable DNS server to make lookups on the Web but not in LAN
7	210.100.101.0 to 210.100.101.255	210.100.101.5	TCP	Allow	None	Allow LAN access to POP3 server
8	Any	210.100.101.4	TCP	Allow	None	Allow any computer to access the SMTP server
9	Any	Any	Any	Deny	Log	Cleanup rule

6

1. Look at three rules that cover the same sort of communications. Which ones are they? Rewrite them so they take fewer rules.
2. Look for a rule that is too far down the list and should be moved up.
3. Look for rule bases that give the firewall more work to do than is necessary. Which rules would you change? (*Hint:* Look in the Track column.)

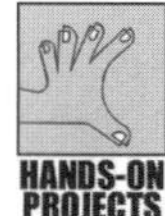

Project 6-5: Analyzing a Log File

In this chapter, you learned that log files can be customized and configured to provide you with the information you need, and to detect attack attempts as well. Consider the simplified set of log file entries in Table 6-7 and analyze it so that you can identify intrusion attacks that need to be blocked, thus improving firewall efficiency and security. The LAN has IP addresses from 210.100.101.0 to 210.100.101.255; the firewall is at 210.100.101.1, the Web server is at 210.100.101.2, the DNS server at 210.100.101.3, the SMTP server at 210.100.101.4; and the POP3 server at 210.100.101.5.

Table 6-7 Sample log file entries

No.	Date	Source	Destination	Destination Port	Action	Type	Protocol
1	21Mar2004	67.23.89.9	210.100.101.23	137	Deny	Log	UDP
2	21Mar2004	67.23.89.9	210.100.101.23	137	Deny	Log	UDP
3	21Mar2004	189.101.10.88	210/100.101.151	114	Deny	Log	TCP
4	21Mar2004	189.101.10.88	210/100.101.151	115	Deny	Log	TCP
5	21Mar2004	210.100.101.3	155.201.8.83	37	Allow	Log	TCP
6	21Mar2004	67.23.89.9	210.100.101.23	137	Deny	Log	UDP
7	21Mar2004	210.100.101.35	210.100.101.3	137	Allow	Log	TCP
8	21Mar2004	189.101.10.88	210/100.101.151	116	Deny	Log	TCP
9	21Mar2004	189.101.10.88	210/100.101.151	117	Deny	Log	TCP
10	21Mar2004	210.100.101.126	210.100.101.2	80	Allow	Log	TCP
11	21Mar2004	225.23.202.5	210.100.101.2	80	Allow	Log	TCP
12	21Mar2004	189.101.10.88	210/100.101.151	118	Deny	Log	TCP

1. Look for any duplicate log file entries. Where are they? What do they indicate, and how could you cut back on such duplication?
2. Look for any events that do not need to be logged.
3. Identify any attack attempts.
4. Identify any types of information that are missing from the log files and that need to be there.

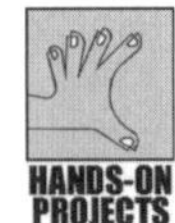

Project 6-6: Configuring iptables

iptables is a packet filtering configuration program that allows an application called Netfilter to perform stateful packet filtering, Network Address Translation, logging, and other security functions for the Linux kernel. In this project you will activate iptables and begin to configure the program. You need a computer equipped with Red Hat Linux 8.0 or later to perform this project. Assume the following about the network you are to configure: the network is at 10.0.20.0/24; the firewall is at 10.0.20.1; the e-mail server is at 10.0.20.2; and the Web server is at 10.0.20.3.

1. Click the **Red Hat** icon, point to **System Tools**, and click **Terminal**.
2. At the command prompt, enter the following to configure iptables to run whenever you boot up your computer: **chkconfig --level 345 iptables on**. Then press **Enter**.
3. If necessary, turn off any other security programs you have running by entering the following: **service ipchains off service ip6tables off**
4. Type **iptables –L**, then press **Enter** to view the default chains and their policies. What do you notice about the default actions?

5. Type the following commands to set the default policies for each of the built-in chains. After each line, press **Enter**:
   - **iptables –P OUTPUT ACCEPT**
   - **iptables –P INPUT DROP**
   - **iptables –P FORWARD DROP**
6. Type **iptables –L** to verify the policy changes.
7. Create a rule that implements the following security policy statement: anyone on the internal network can access the Web server on the DMZ as well as external Web sites.
8. Create a rule that prevents hosts on the Internet from accessing internal hosts directly using the www (World Wide Web) service.
9. Create two rules that enable anyone on the internal network from connecting to the company e-mail server but not to any external e-mail servers using smtp.
10. Type the following so you can save your changes: **service iptables save**, and then press **Enter**.

Case Projects

Case Project 6-1: Proxy Servers and Network Access

Several months before you were hired by Midwest Medical Supply Corporation, the company's network went offline for two days due to a Denial of Service attack and the time it took to reconfigure the network's single firewall to prevent subsequent attacks. Now that you are on board, one of the first assignments you are given is to install a proxy server to keep track of how employees use the Internet. You have concerns: what would you say to your new employers?

Case Project 6-2: Content Filtering

The management of Midwest Medical Supply discovers that employees have been circulating revealing photos of movie stars as well as potentially offensive jokes that have been downloaded from the Internet. You are asked to suggest how such material can be blocked and whether the employees who obtained it can be identified. What would you say to them?

Case Project 6-3: Advantages and Disadvantages of Proxy Servers

The management of Midwest Medical Supply enthusiastically embraces the idea of installing a proxy server to filter content and log employee activity. They are anxious to get such a system underway and ask if it can be done within the week. You are also asked if the server will "speed up" access to the Internet. You are placed in the uncomfortable position of having to state concerns of using a proxy server and provide reasons why its implementation can be time-consuming. What are three reasons you would give?

Case Project 6-4: Improving Your Rule Base

You have a remote user who has a Linux workstation and who connects to the central office using a VPN. You receive some access attempts from this user's computer at ports ranging from 31337 to 31340, which are commonly used by Trojan horses. The user has no knowledge of attempting to access the network at the times when the attempts were recorded on the firewall log. You are instructed by your superiors in the IT department to "install a firewall on that user's computer immediately." Name three things you could do (or help the end user to do) to defend against this security threat.

CHAPTER

7

SETTING UP A VIRTUAL PRIVATE NETWORK

After reading this chapter and completing the exercises, you will be able to:

- Explain the "what, why, and how" of virtual private networks (VPNs)
- Understand the tunneling protocols that enable secure VPN connections
- Describe the encryption schemes used by VPNs
- Know how to adjust packet filtering rules for VPNs

A virtual private network (VPN) combines two qualities that represent essential elements of a network defense strategy: security and connectivity. VPNs play increasingly important roles among businesses that rely on the Internet for critical communications. As travel and other costs of doing business rise, companies need to reduce costs while maintaining productivity.

In the past, companies that wanted to conduct secure electronic transactions would use **leased lines** —private connections rented from telecommunications companies, using technologies such as frame relay or Integrated Services Digital Network (ISDN). Such lines form a secure connection between two networks, but the cost to rent them can quickly reach thousands of dollars per month. A **virtual private network (VPN)** provides a cost-effective way for two or more networks to make a secure connection through the public Internet.

A VPN is said to be "virtual" because the connection between networks isn't really proprietary. Rather, it uses the same public Internet connections used by millions of other individuals. Users who make VPN connections gain privacy by means of a variety of technologies, such as encryption and authentication. In this chapter, you'll learn what VPNs are, why they are growing in popularity, and how they ensure private communications between networks; you'll understand the different protocols that create a secure "tunnel" between computers; you'll learn about encryption methods that are integral to maintaining the privacy and integrity of VPN communications; finally, you'll also learn how packet filtering rules need to be adjusted to enable VPNs to function efficiently on a network.

Exploring VPNs: What, Why, and How

A VPN provides a way for two computers or computer networks to communicate securely using the same public communications channels available on the Internet, where millions of computers and networks exchange data at any one time. To better understand what VPNs do, imagine that you are on the crowded trading floor of a stock exchange, where many individuals are calling out instructions to one another simultaneously. Suppose you want to communicate some private financial information to one other trader on the floor. In the midst of the crowd, you identify one another by your ID badges. You then write messages on paper and exchange them, making sure no one is looking over your shoulders as you write. You could even take further precautions by writing the messages in a code, such as shorthand, that those around you will probably not be able to understand.

This analogy begins to describe what VPNs do: they enable computers to exchange private encrypted messages that others can't decipher. The following sections give you an overview of how VPNs work: you'll learn what VPNs are, why your organization might establish a VPN, and how to configure VPNs.

What VPNs Are

To understand what VPNs are, we can break the "virtual private network" into its three components. First, a virtual private network is virtual. Rather than a direct network connection between computers in a LAN that is established by a permanent cable connection, it uses a combination of Internet-based routers and network segments. Second, it is private. Specified computers, users, or network gateways are identified as endpoints of the VPN connection, which is called a **tunnel** , and only those designated computers, users, or gateways can participate in the VPN. Finally, the VPN itself is a network because it connects one group of computers to another and it extends the existing organizations' networks beyond their current boundaries.

A VPN, then, is a virtual network connection that uses the Internet to establish a connection that is secure. The following sections describe the VPN components that enable the connection to be made and the VPN core activities that ensure security.

The VPN endpoints represent extensions of the participating networks. Those endpoints must be secured by firewall software or they could potentially give intruders a way to access the network. Some VPN software products (like CheckPoint's SecuRemote program, which enables remote users to connect to a network protected with CheckPoint's VPN-1 program) incorporate a built-in firewall. Unless your VPN client software incorporates its own firewall, you need to make sure that any remote users' computers that connect to your organization's VPN are equipped with their own desktop firewalls.

VPN Components

VPNs can be assembled using a variety of different components. However, they all contain a set of essential elements that enable the data to be transmitted securely from one point to another. These include:

- ***VPN server*** *or host* — This computer is configured to accept connections from clients who either dial in or connect directly using a broadband Internet connection.
- ***VPN client*** *or guest* — This can be a router that serves as the endpoint of a **gateway-to-gateway VPN connection** , which uses hardware to connect two networks. It can also be a computer operating system that can be configured to function as an endpoint in a VPN, such as Windows XP or 2000.
- *Tunnel* — This is the connection through which the data is sent.
- ***VPN protocols*** — These are sets of standardized communication settings that computer software and hardware uses to encrypt data that is sent along the VPN. They include Internet Protocol Security (IPSec), Point-to-Point Tunneling Protocol (PPTP), or Layer 2 Tunneling Protocol (L2TP).

The number of elements in a VPN depends on the number of networks included in its configuration. For instance, if four networks are contained in a VPN, it will have at least four separate servers and four tunnels; multiple clients may participate as well.

In general, you can set up two different types of VPNs. The first type links two or more networks and is called a **site-to-site** (or gateway to gateway) **VPN**. The second type makes a network accessible to remote users who need dial-in access and is called a **client-to-site VPN** . The two types of VPNs are not mutually exclusive—many large corporations link the central office to one or more branch locations using site-to-site VPNs, and they also provide dial-in access to the central office by means of a client-to-site VPN.

Hardware Versus Software VPNs

The components you choose to establish a VPN depend on whether you want to use existing hardware or software. If you want to create a VPN using new components, this is likely to increase your IT costs, but will also have the benefit of reducing the load on the other network security components (such as firewalls).

Hardware-based VPNs connect one gateway to another. Typically, the VPN hardware used is a router at each network gateway that encrypts outbound packets and decrypts inbound ones. Another hardware option involves the purchase of a **VPN appliance** , a hardware device specially designed to terminate VPNs and join multiple LANs (see Figure 7-1).

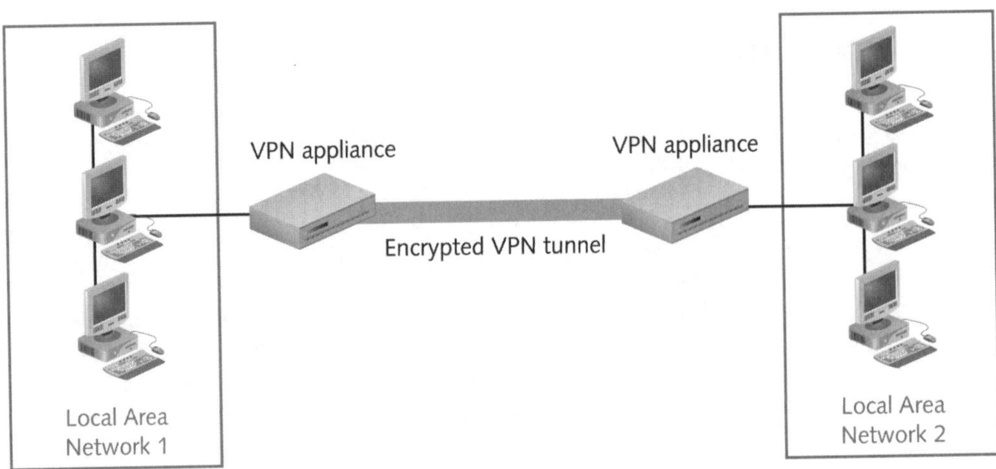

Figure 7-1 VPN appliances create secure connections between two or more LANs

VPN appliances can permit connections between large numbers of users or multiple networks, but they don't provide other services such as file sharing and printing.

In general, hardware products such as routers that are dedicated to the operation of VPNs tend to handle more network traffic than software products. As a result, they are more **scalable** (able to maintain a consistent level of functionality as a network grows) than software VPNs. They can also be more secure than software VPNs because they do not depend on an underlying operating system that might have security flaws. Hardware VPNs should be chosen for fast-growing networks that need all traffic that passes through the VPN device to be encrypted. They also represent a good choice when the endpoints of the VPN use the same routers and are controlled by the same organizations. Some examples of hardware VPN devices are presented in Table 7-1.

Table 7-1 Hardware VPN products

Manufacturer	Product Name	Web Site
Cisco Systems	7100, 7200, 7400 Series routers *VPN 3000 series* Concentrators	*www.cisco.com*
NetScreen Technologies	NetScreen Appliances	*www.netscreen.com*
Nokia	Nokia Firewall/VPN Appliance	*www.nokia.com*
SonicWALL	SonicWALL PRO 100, 200, 300	*www.sonicwall.com*
WatchGuard Technologies	WatchGuard Firebox	*www.watchguard.com*

Most software-based VPNs are integrated with firewalls. They are more cost-effective and convenient to configure than hardware VPN devices. They also increase network security because they are integrated with functions that the firewall already performs, such as packet filtering and Network Address Translation (NAT). Software-based VPNs are appropriate when the networks participating in the VPN use different routers and firewalls, or when the endpoints are controlled by totally different organizations and network administrators. The reason for using software VPNs to link networks is that software VPN solutions offer maximum flexibility. They can, for instance, be configured to enable traffic based on domain name, protocol, or IP address. Such restrictions prove useful when only some, but not all, of the traffic passing through the VPN is meant to be encrypted and sent through the tunnel. Some examples of VPN software solutions are shown in Table 7-2.

Another kind of hardware device audits inbound connections that pass through the VPN appliance before they reach the internal network to verify that they conform with the organization's security policy: CyberGatekeeper Remote Policy Enforcer by InfoExpress, Inc. ensures that you won't receive viruses or intrusions from your own remote access VPN users. The product functions as its own host computer and it contains policy manager software. Find out more about it at *www.infoexpress.com*.

7

Table 7-2 Software VPN products

Manufacturer	Product Name	Web Site
3Com Corporation	3Com OfficeConnect Upgrade for Internet Firewall	*www.3com.com*
Borderware Technologies	Borderware Firewall Server	*www.borderware.com*
CheckPoint Technologies	VPN-1/FireWall-1 SmallOffice	*www.checkpoint.com*
Lucent Technologies	Firewall Brick Series	*www.lucent.com*
Symantec Corporation	Symantec Enterprise VPN	*www.symantec.com*

VPN Combinations

VPN installations need to be flexible to keep up with changing network needs. By combining VPN hardware or software with other hardware or software, you add layers of network security. One useful combination is a VPN that is bundled with a firewall. VPNs do not eliminate the need for firewalls. In fact, firewalls are essential to ensure that VPN traffic passes through the network gateway to the desired destination and non-VPN traffic is filtered according to the organization's security policy.

Cisco Systems, in a study by the research group Cahners In-Stat (*www.instat.com/panels/lan_security.pdf*), led the market in VPN/Firewall combo devices with its PIX line of appliances.

A VPN combination makes use of VPN hardware and software in the same device. The Cisco 3002 VPN device, for instance, gives users the choice of operating in one of two modes: client mode and network extension mode. In client mode, the VPN 3002 acts as a software client, enabling users to connect to another remote network via a VPN. In network extension mode, the VPN 3002 provides a secure site-to-site VPN connection. Both modes are able to scale to hundreds or even thousands of VPN users.

VPN Core Activity #1: Encapsulation

VPNs can use public Internet connections and still provide a high level of security because they perform a core set of activities. Together, these activities tunnel data from one network to another using the infrastructure of the Internet.

First, VPNs perform **encapsulation** of data: they enclose a packet within another one that has different IP source and destination information to provide a high degree of protection. Encapsulation protects the integrity of the data sent along the VPN tunnel: the source and destination information of the actual data packets (the ones being encapsulated) are completely hidden. The VPN encapsulates the actual data packets within packets that use the source and destination addresses of the VPN gateway, as shown in Figure 7-2. The gateway might be a router that uses IPSec, or a VPN appliance, or a firewall that functions as a VPN and that has a gateway set up.

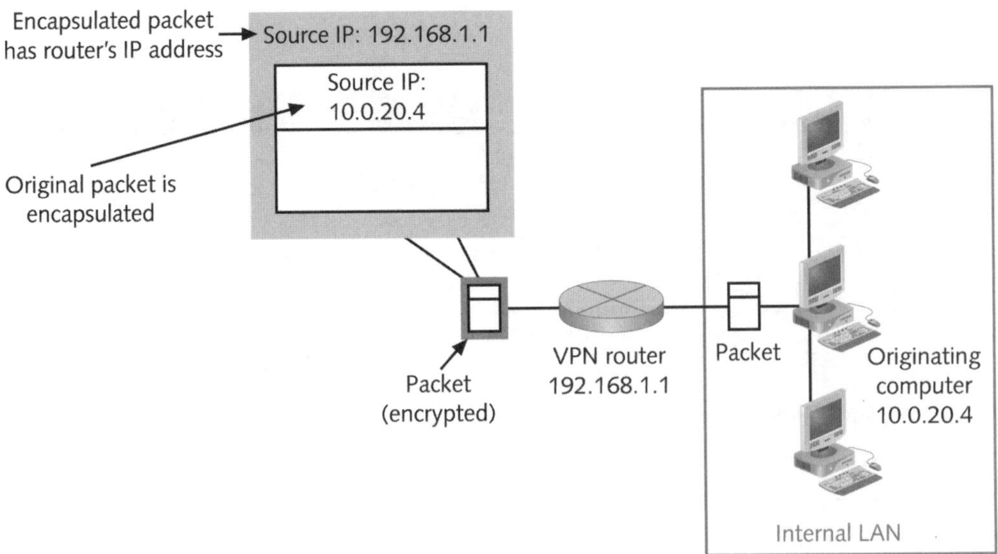

Figure 7-2 VPNs encapsulate data to conceal source and destination information

When a VPN tunnel is in place, the source and destination IP addresses of the actual data packets (the ones that have been encapsulated) can be in the private reserved blocks that are not routable over the Internet, such as the 10.0.0.0/8 addresses or the 192.168.0.0/16 reserved network blocks.

VPN Core Activity #2: Encryption

Encryption is the process of rendering information unreadable by all but the intended recipient. The process of encryption is performed by means of a mathematical formula called an algorithm, which is used to generate an encoded block of data called a **key**. The key is part of an electronic document called a **digital certificate**, which is obtained from a **certificate authority (CA)**, a trusted organization that issues keys. The key is then used to process the data that the VPN transmits from one point to another—to encrypt it at the originating endpoint and to decrypt it at its destination endpoint, as shown in Figure 7-3.

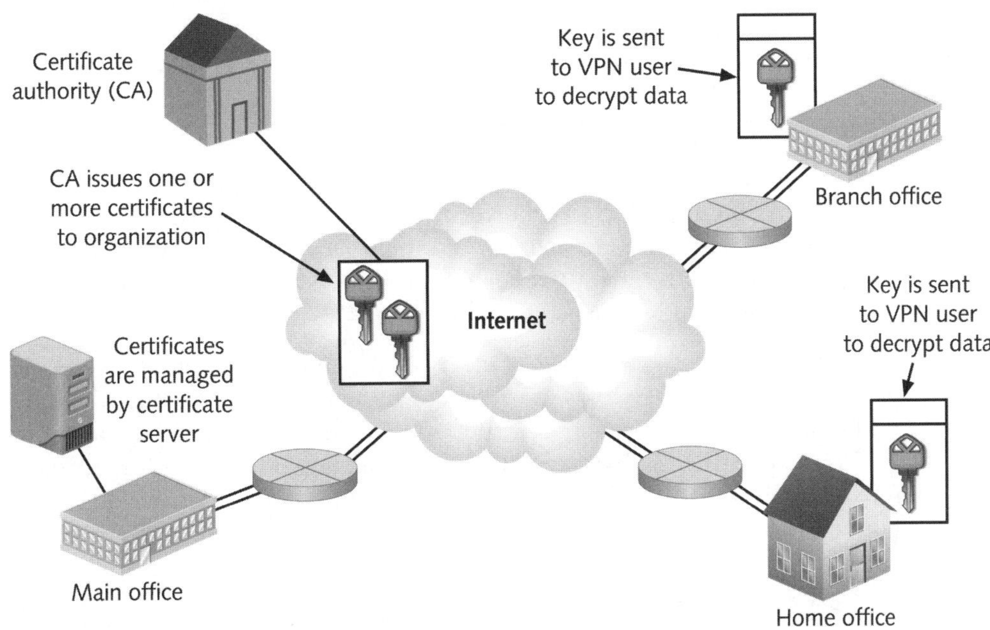

Figure 7-3 VPN endpoints encrypt and decrypt data by exchanging keys

To perform the encryption at both endpoints of the VPN, the keys must be exchanged by participants who have a **Security Association (SA)**. The exchange can be performed using a variety of encryption methods. In one such method, **symmetric cryptography**, the same key is exchanged by sender and recipient. In **asymmetric cryptography** (also called **public key cryptography**), two different keys are used—a public key and a private key. When an individual or organization obtains a digital certificate from a CA, an encryption algorithm is used to generate a private key. This key is never exchanged but is maintained securely by the certificate holder. The private key is used to generate a public key, which is freely exchanged among VPN participants.

For a more detailed discussion of public key encryption, see "Exchanging Public and Private Keys" in Chapter 5.

Another type of key exchange method, **Internet Key Exchange (IKE)**, employs **tunnel method encryption** to encrypt both the header and data parts of a packet and encapsulate the packet within a new packet that has a different header. IKE is increasingly popular because it provides a high level of security, which offsets the degradation in network performance that results from such complex encryption.

Other key exchange methods, such as FWZ, a proprietary protocol developed by CheckPoint for its CheckPoint NG firewall, use **transport method encryption**, in which only the data portion of a packet is encrypted, not the header. Because the packet's original TCP/IP headers are left in place, performance is improved. However, transport method encryption does not provide as high a level of security as tunnel method: the original IP header source and destination addresses can potentially be intercepted, which could reveal information about the organization's internal arrangement to a hacker.

VPN Core Activity #3: Authentication

The third core activity performed by VPNs to ensure the security of tunneled communications is **authentication** —the process of identifying a user or computer as being authorized to access and use network resources. Authentication is essential because hosts in the network that receive VPN communications need to know that the host originating the communications is an approved user of the VPN.

The type of authentication used in the VPN depends on the tunneling protocol used. A growing number of networks use IPSec to authenticate users: the participants in a VPN establish a Security Association (SA) and exchange keys to authenticate one another. **Point-to-Point Tunneling Protocol (PPTP)** , which is used for dial-in access to a remote server, uses Microsoft Challenge/Response Authentication Protocol (MS-CHAP), in which both computers exchange authentication packets and authenticate one another.

VPNs use digital certificates (electronic documents that contain encoded blocks and that ensure the owner's identity) to authenticate users. They then use encryption to ensure that, even if the communications are intercepted in transit, they cannot be read.

The VPN core activities of encapsulation, encryption, and authentication are illustrated together in Figure 7-4.

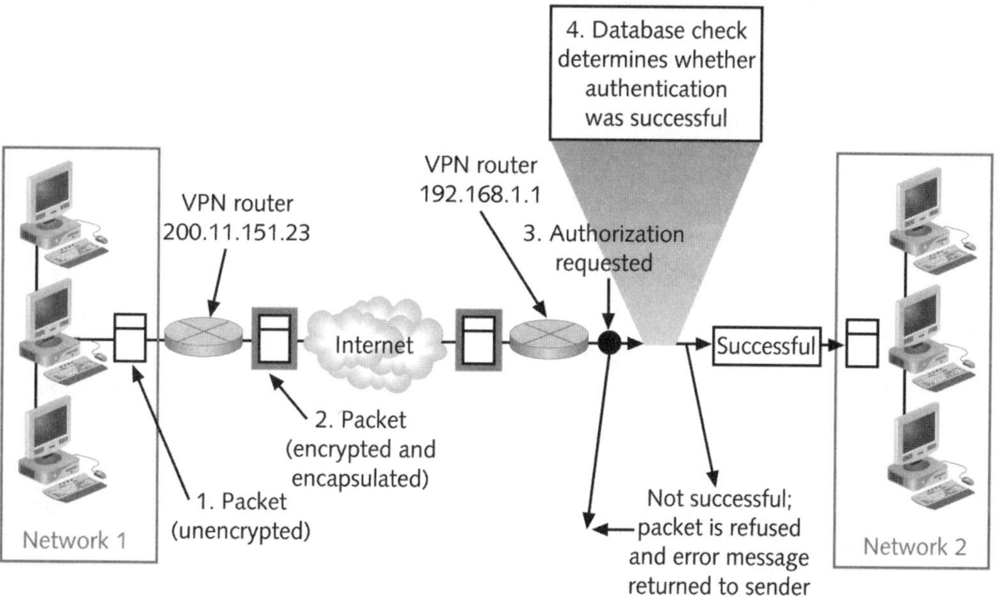

Figure 7-4 VPN core activities

Figure 7-4 illustrates the basic steps in the authentication process:

1. The unencrypted packet is transmitted by the source computer on internal network 1.
2. The packet, after being encrypted and encapsulated by the VPN router at 200.11.151.23, passes through the gateway into the Internet.
3. Authentication is requested by the VPN router at internal network 2.
4. A database check determines whether authentication is successful. If successful, the packet is allowed to reach its destination. If not successful, an error message is returned.

Why Establish a VPN?

The need to keep business transactions private drives an increasing number of organizations to adopt VPNs. The popularity of e-commerce provides an incentive as well. In addition, government and military agencies need to share information more than ever to provide effective homeland security (the protection of U.S. citizens from terrorist attacks and the damage they cause). A VPN provides an excellent solution for an agency that needs to stick to a budget while maintaining security. The following sections examine the business incentives driving VPN adoption and the advantages and disadvantages of using VPNs.

Business Incentives Driving VPN Adoption

Budgetary considerations have always made VPNs an attractive business proposition. When you implement a VPN, you are essentially spreading the cost of its operation over many users, which makes it very cost effective.

In addition, many companies employ remote contractors who need to access the corporate network from their respective homes or offices. Employees who travel for business reasons need to check e-mail and transfer files with colleagues in the central office. Accordingly, secure remote access represents an essential requirement for businesses and provides an important incentive for establishing a VPN.

Another incentive for creating a VPN is the need to establish a high level of security in an **extranet** —a wide area network in which one local area network is connected to another—as illustrated in Figure 7-5.

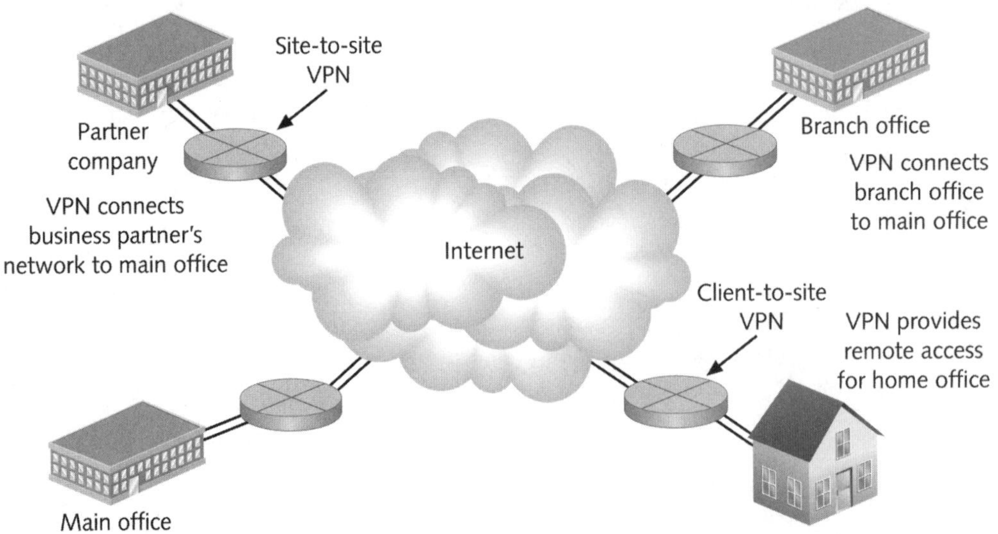

Figure 7-5 A VPN enables an organization to establish extranet and remote access connections

As you can see in Figure 7-5, the public "cloud" of the Internet is used to extend VPN tunnels so that main offices can be connected to branch offices, partner business's networks, and remote workers' home-offices.

Advantages and Disadvantages of VPNs

VPNs provide a high level of security—provided the administrator meets the challenges they present. For instance, if a VPN device is poorly configured or a remote user at the endpoint of a VPN disables his or her firewall by mistake and lets in a hacker, the protection the VPN normally provides can be undone. In addition, VPNs can be complex to configure and the hardware and software involved can represent a substantial investment. You should be aware of the advantages and disadvantages of VPNs, some of the more important of which are summarized in Table 7-3.

Table 7-3 Some advantages and disadvantages of VPNs

Advantages	Disadvantages
Far less expensive than leased lines	Can be complex to configure
Many elements working together provide strong security	Can result in slower data transfer rates than a leased line
Standards and protocols used in VPNs are well-developed and widely used	Depends on the often unpredictable Internet: if your ISP or other parts of the Internet go down, your VPN goes down
Can result in less overall complexity in an organization's network	Requires administrator to install VPN client software on remote computers
Can make use of a company's existing broadband connection	VPN hardware and software from different vendors may prove incompatible because they use different protocols

By focusing on Internet-based technologies, VPNs simplify a network overall. You have only one Internet connection to manage rather than an Internet connection plus one or more leased lines. In addition, running a VPN means you have even more reason to maximize your **network uptime** (the amount of time you are connected to a network, such as the Internet). If your network is up and running smoothly, you don't need to be spending your time troubleshooting and making repairs.

Some companies that maintain VPNs with partner organizations benefit by using the same ISP as those partners for their Internet connection. Positioning the participants in the VPN on the same part of the Internet backbone can make the VPN run more smoothly and reliably.

How to Configure VPNs

To set up the VPN, you define a **VPN domain** : a set of one or more computers that is handled by the VPN hardware and software as a single entity, and that uses the VPN to communicate with another domain. With a firewall program like CheckPoint NG, a domain might be a set of networked computers that is grouped together under a name such as Local_Net or Office_Net. If you set up Windows to function as a VPN host (as described in Hands-On Project 7-2 at the end of this chapter), you can designate a set of IP addresses that can be used to access that host (see Figure 7-6).

7

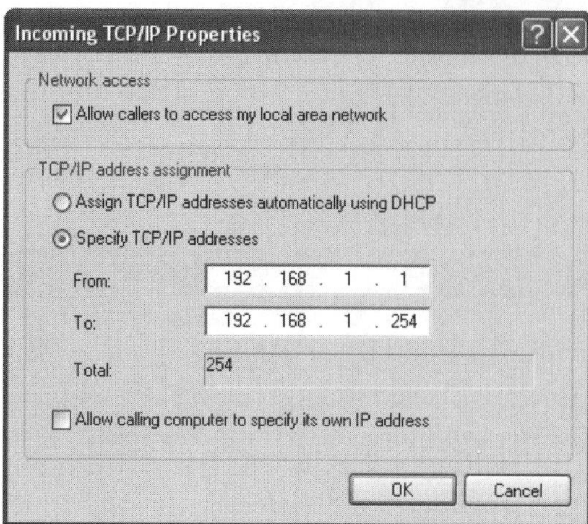

Figure 7-6 Enabling a Windows-based VPN host to work with a set of IP addresses

Besides defining a VPN domain, you also need to determine whether the network gateway will be included in that domain. That, in turn, depends on whether your network has a site-to-site or client-to-site VPN configuration. (Both types of connections, in fact, are illustrated in Figure 7- 4, which appears earlier in this chapter.)

Single and Multiple-Entry Point Configurations

Smaller networks that use VPNs often have **single entry point configurations** : all traffic to and from the network passes through a single gateway such as a router or firewall (or both). In this single entry point configuration, the gateway itself must be a member of the VPN domain (see Figure 7-7).

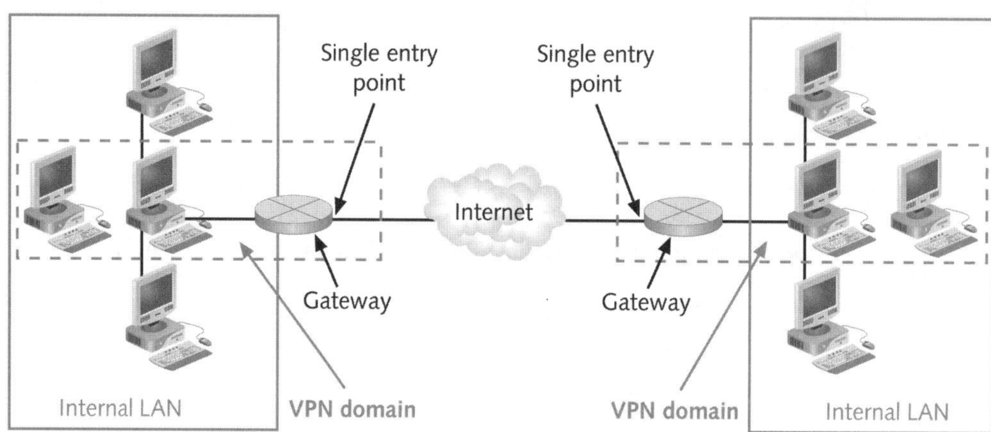

Figure 7-7 Single entry point configuration

In the single entry point configuration illustrated in Figure 7-7, a group of computers within the internal LAN is included in the VPN domain, as well as the gateway itself. In contrast, many large organizations have networks that require **multiple-entry point configurations**, in which multiple gateways are used, each with a VPN tunnel connecting a different location (see Figure 7-8).

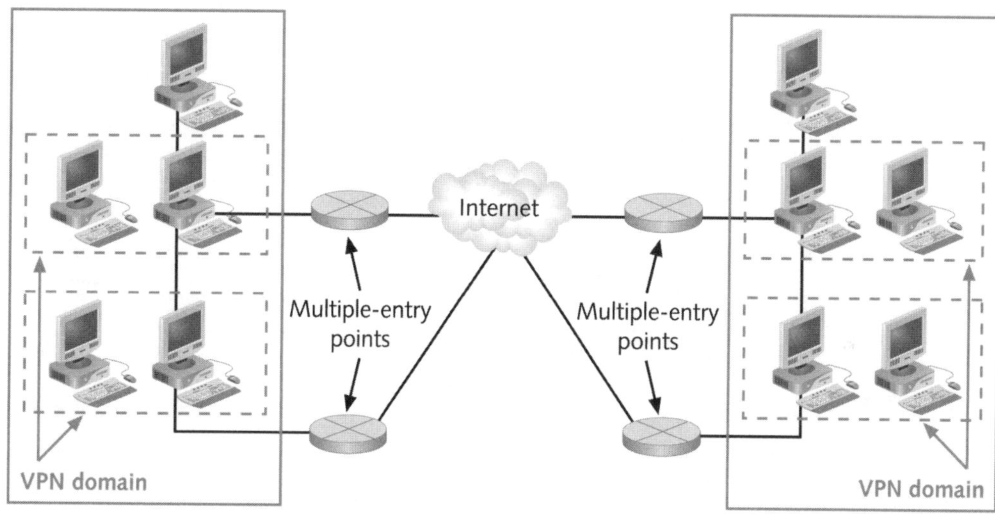

Figure 7-8 Multiple-entry point configuration

7

In a multiple-entry point configuration, it is important to exclude the gateway itself from the VPN domain. If you do not exclude the gateway, all traffic to and from each gateway will be encrypted. It is also important to prevent VPN domains from overlapping, or some traffic may be routed incorrectly or not at all due to repeated IP addresses—the router will have two options for directing packets and may not respond correctly.

VPN Topology Configurations

A VPN's **topology** —the way the participants in a network are connected to one another—determines how the gateways, networks, and clients are related to each other. The three basic configurations are a mesh VPN, a star (or hub-and-spoke), and a hybrid.

In a **mesh** topology, all participants in the VPN have Security Associations (SAs) with one another. (SAs are states of authentication that exist between two computers that have exchanged keys and encryption protocols.) Two types of mesh arrangements are possible:

- *Full mesh* — Every subnetwork is connected to all other subnets in the VPN (see Figure 7-9). Such a network is very complex to manage, and is best used with smaller VPNs.

- *Partial mesh* — Any subnet in the VPN may or may not be connected to the other subnets. This configuration offers more flexibility than a full mesh arrangement.

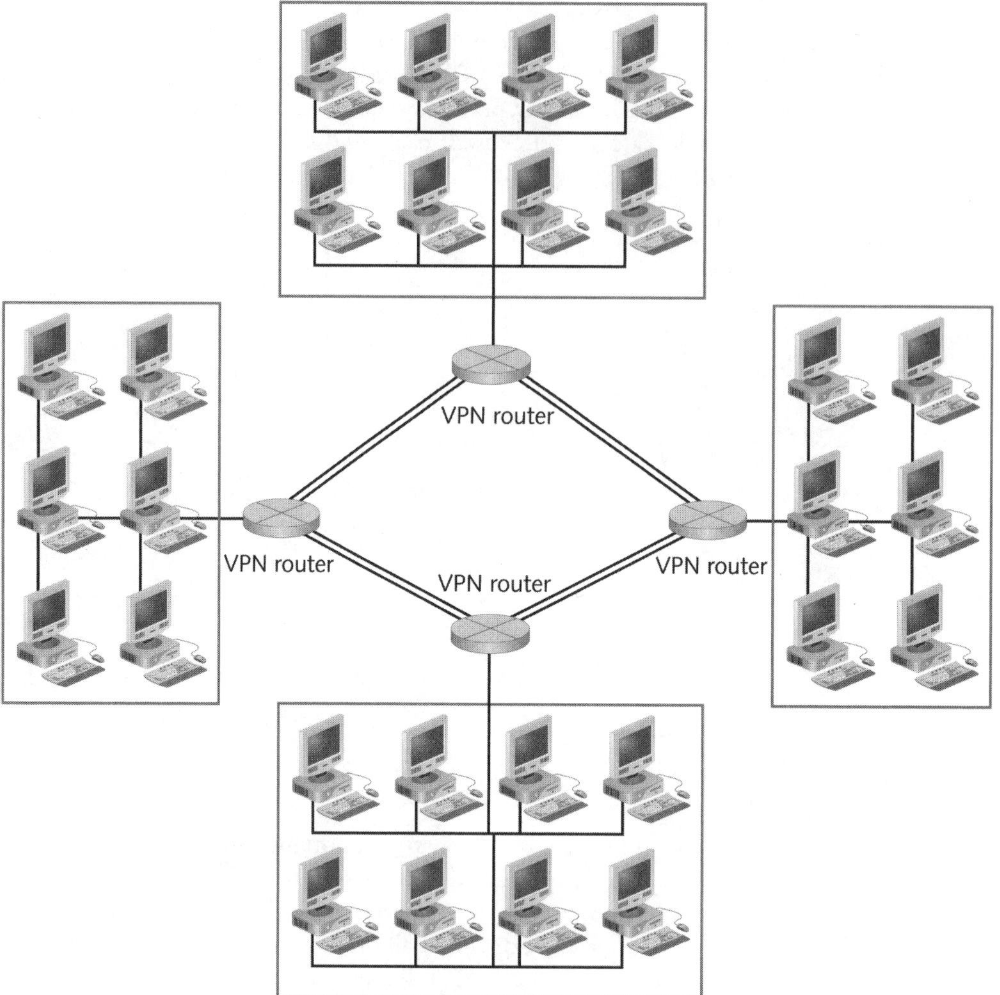

Figure 7-9 A full mesh VPN configuration

The advantage of a mesh configuration is that each participant has the ability to establish VPN communications with all of the other participants. However, if a new LAN is added to the VPN, all other VPN devices will have to be updated to include information about the new users in the LAN. The problem with mesh VPNs is the difficulty associated with expanding the network and updating every VPN device whenever a host is added.

In a **star** configuration (also known as a hub-and-spoke configuration), the VPN gateway is the hub, and other networks that participate in the VPN are called rim subnetworks (see Figure 7-10).

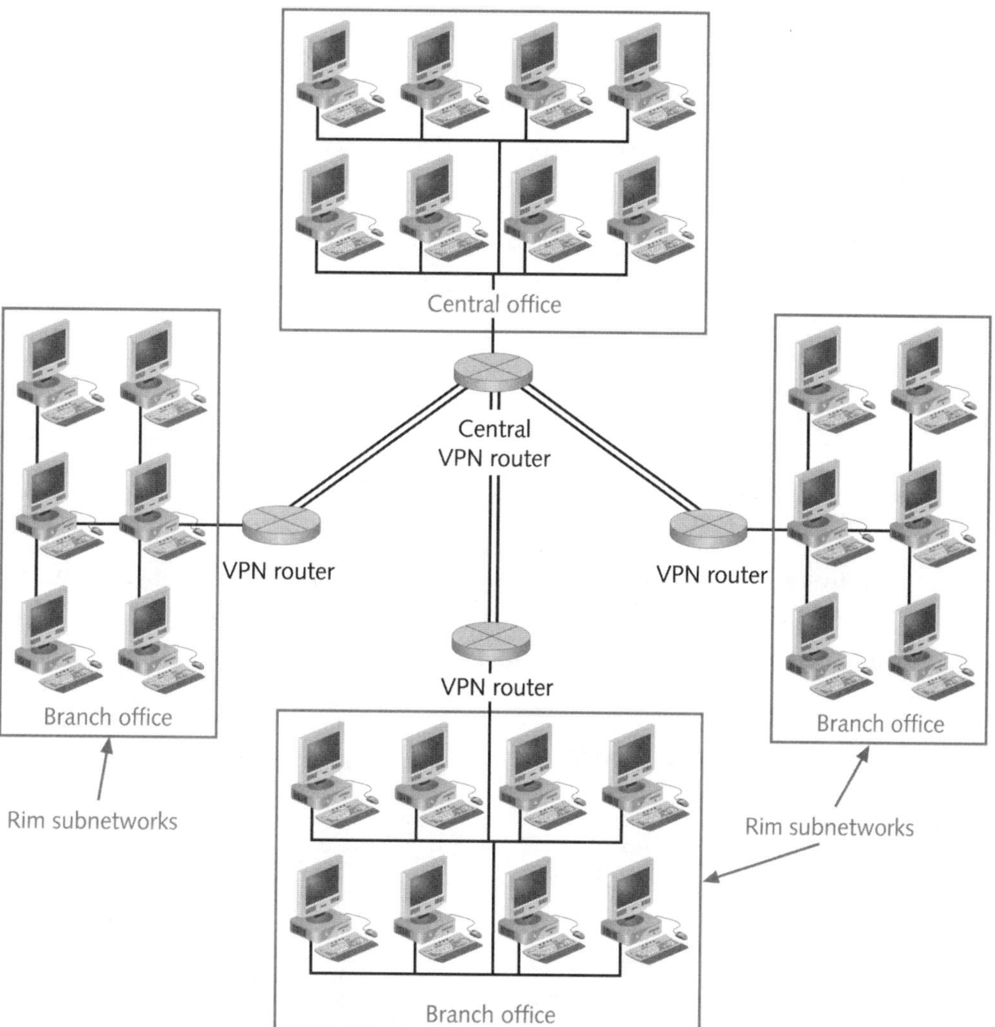

Figure 7-10 A star VPN configuration

Separate SAs are made between the hubs of each of the rim subnetworks in the star configuration. The central VPN router resides at the organization's central office because that is the most common configuration for a hub-and-spoke VPN to have all communications go through the central office where the main IT staff resides. Any LANs or computers that want to participate in the VPN need only connect to the central server, not to any other machines in the VPN. This setup makes it easy to increase the size of the VPN as more branch offices or computers are added. On the other hand, in hub-and-spoke configurations, all communications flow into and out of the central router. This creates a single point of failure at the central router. This flow can also slow communications, especially if branch offices are located on different continents around the world.

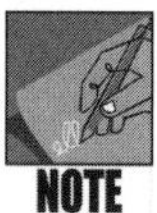

The terms *star* and *hub-and-spoke* aren't exclusive to VPNs, but they are used to configure computer networks in general.

As organizations with VPNs grow to include new computers and new branch offices, they naturally evolve from a mesh or hub-and-spoke configuration into a hybrid configuration that combines the two. Because mesh configurations tend to operate more efficiently, the central core linking the most important branches of the network should probably be a mesh configuration. However, as branch offices are added they can be added as spokes that connect to a central VPN router at the central office. A hybrid setup that combines the two configurations benefits from the strengths of each one—the scalability of the hub-and-spoke option and the speed of the mesh option.

UNDERSTANDING TUNNELING PROTOCOLS

Because VPNs link networks and gateways that might have different operating systems or hardware platforms, standard sets of instructions called protocols need to be established so that communications can take place.

When you configure a device to function as a VPN host, you need to choose the protocol you want to use. For instance, Internet Security Protocol with Internet Key Exchange (IPSec/IKE) is fast becoming the protocol of choice among VPNs. However, if you need to enable remote users to dial in to your main office network you'll need to use a dial-in protocol such as PPTP or L2TP.

A variety of VPN protocols—IPSec/IKE, Secure Shell, Socks v. 5, PPTP, and L2TP—are discussed in the sections that follow.

IPSec/IKE

Internet Protocol Security (IPSec) is a set of standard procedures that was developed by the Internet Engineering Task Force (IETF) for enabling secure communications on the Internet. IPSec has become the de facto set of protocols for VPN security for a number of reasons:

- IPSec works at Layer 3 (the Network layer) of the OSI model of network communications, and thus provides a type of security not given by other protocols, which work at Layer 2 (the Data Link layer).
- IPSec has the ability to encrypt an entire TCP/IP packet—the data portion as well as the source and destination IP addresses in the header. Other protocols only encrypt the data portion of a packet.
- IPSec was originally developed for use with the next version of Internet Protocol, IPv6, though it can also work with the current version, IPv4. Other protocols can work only with IPv4.

- IPSec provides for the authentication of source and destination computers before the data is encrypted or transmitted. In other words, its various components combine authentication, strong encryption, and key management. Other protocols provide for authentication or encryption, not both.

Perhaps the biggest advantage of using IPSec is the fact that it has gone through the process of standardization and is supported by a wide variety of VPN hardware and software devices. Operating systems such as Windows 2000 and XP enable you to set up an IPSec connection with another Windows computer that has IPSec enabled. In fact, you add IPSec security policy support as a snap-in to the Microsoft Management Console (see Figure 7-11).

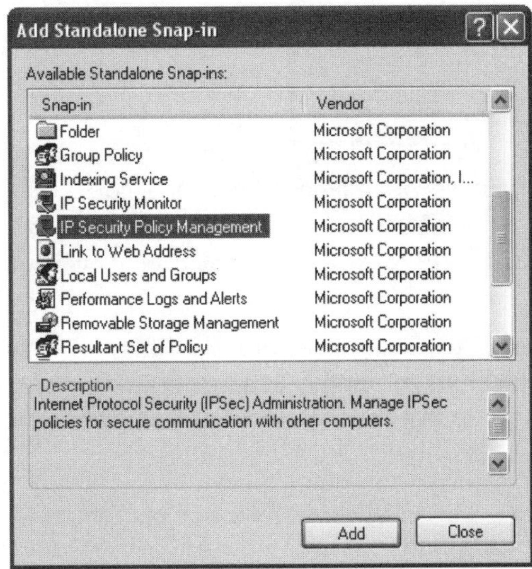

Figure 7-11 Operating systems such as Windows enable you to add IPSec security policy support

If you want more background on IPSec and its related technologies, you'll find links to the original Request for Comment (RFC) papers for those technologies on the IETF Web site (*www.ietf.org/html.charters/ipsec-charter.html*).

When an IPSec connection is established between two computers, they authenticate one another and then establish the SA settings they will use to communicate. Such transactions take place in the background and are transparent to the end user. However, in an operating system environment you do need to decide whether IPSec will be required for all connections to the host machine, or whether the host will request an IPSec connection for computers or other devices that support it. If IPSec is not supported on the client machine, it won't be used. You also have the option of requiring a secure connection to another computer over a VPN. If you want to connect to another computer while requiring IPSec, you need to adjust the packet filtering rules, as shown in Figure 7-12; otherwise, your IPSec-enabled computer will block all other connections by default.

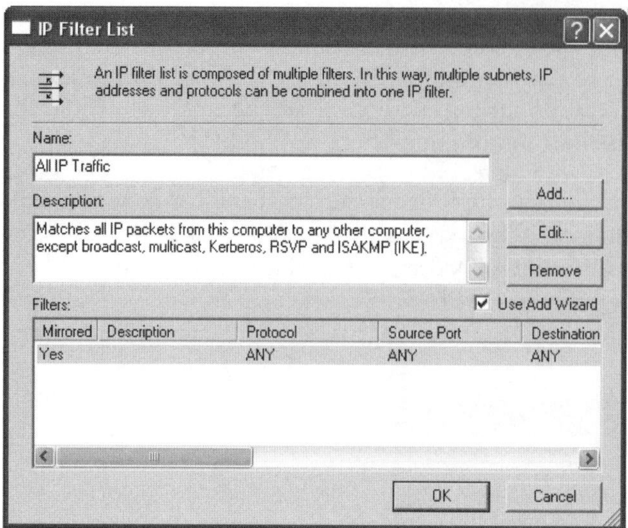

Figure 7-12 Adjusting packet filtering rules for an IPSec VPN connection

IPSec's many components provide for encryption, encapsulation, key exchange, and authentication. They include:

- ***Internet Security Association Key Management Protocol (ISAKMP)*** — This IPSec-related protocol enables two computers to agree on security settings and establish a Security Association so that they can then exchange keys using Internet Key Exchange.
- *Internet Key Exchange (IKE)* — This protocol enables two computers that establish an IPSec connection to exchange keys to make a Security Association. IKE uses UDP port 500 on both the client and server computers.
- *Oakley* — This protocol enables IPSec to use the Diffie-Hellman encryption algorithm to create keys. (You can find out more about Diffie-Hellman encryption at *www.ietf.org/rfc/rfc2631.txt*.)
- *IPSecurity Policy Management* — This is a service that runs on Windows computers. It retrieves IPSec security policy settings from the Active Directory and applies them to the computers in the domain that use IPSec.
- ***IPSec Driver*** — This software handles the actual tasks of encrypting, authenticating, decrypting, and checking packets.

Suppose you have configured a VPN connection between two computers and you want that connection to make use of IPSec. When one IPSec-compliant computer connects to the other, the following events occur:

1. The IPSec driver and the ISAKMP retrieve the IPSec policy settings.

2. ISAKMP negotiates between hosts, based on their policy settings, and builds a Security Association (SA) between them.
3. The Oakley protocol generates a master key that is used to secure IPSec communications.
4. Based on the security policy established for the session, the IPSec driver monitors, filters, and secures the network traffic.

IPSec isn't foolproof. For instance, if the machine that runs IPSec-compliant software has already been compromised, none of the communications that come from that machine, including IPSec communications, can be trusted. IPSec isn't a substitute for firewall, anti-virus, and intrusion detection software.

The two IPSec components that are best known and most frequently examined are the ones that protect the TCP/IP packets exchanged in the VPN: Authentication Header (AH) and Encapsulating Security Payload (ESP). We discuss each of them next.

Hands-On Project 7-5 shows you how to activate IPSec and set up filtering rules for IPSec connections.

Authentication Header (AH)

As its name suggests, **Authentication Header (AH)** is an IPSec component that provides for the authentication of TCP/IP packets to ensure data integrity. AH causes packets to be signed with a block of encoded data called a digital signature. The fact that the signature is present communicates to the other IPSec-compliant device that "this packet contains accurate IP header information because it originated from this computer, which is using IPSec." Digitally signing a packet indicates that it hasn't been tampered with or that the IP information in the header has not been spoofed. It preserves integrity but doesn't ensure confidentiality.

Encapsulating Security Payload (ESP)

The confidentiality of data transmitted through a VPN tunnel using IPSec is ensured by means of **Encapsulating Security Payload (ESP)** . ESP encrypts different parts of a TCP/IP packet depending on whether IPSec is being used in transport mode or tunnel mode.

In tunnel mode, ESP encrypts both the header and data parts of each packet. Such encryption protects data but, because the IP header is encrypted, the data will not be able to pass through a firewall that uses Network Address Translation (NAT). The data won't pass because the firewall won't know how to interpret the IP source and destination information in its encrypted form.

In transport mode, only the data portion of the packet is encrypted. As a result, if the VPN is to be used with a firewall that performs NAT, IPSec should be configured to work in transport mode.

You don't need to use AH and ESP together. The two used in conjunction provide additional security, but you might not want to use ESP if encryption is already provided by another device or application. ESP, like other forms of encryption, requires a substantial amount of processing resources and can slow down the rate of data transfer through the VPN.

Secure Shell (SSH)

Like IPSec, **Secure Shell (SSH)** provides for authentication and encryption of TCP/IP packets over a VPN or other connection. SSH works with UNIX-based systems such as Red Hat Linux. SSH creates a secure Transport layer connection between participating computers, and makes use of public key cryptography.

When a client initiates an SSH connection, the two computers exchange keys and negotiate the algorithms to be used for authentication and encryption to create a secure connection at the Transport layer. The username and password transmitted to the server are encrypted. All data that is subsequently sent is also encrypted. SSH is freely available by means of the OpenSSH package of applications, which are available at *www.openssh.org*.

Socks V. 5

The **Socks** protocol, which was mentioned in Chapter 6, is normally handled as a way to provide proxy services for applications that don't normally support proxying. Socks Version 5 adds encrypted authentication and support for User Datagram Protocol (UDP). The new features help Version 5 of Socks enable applications to set up a secure tunnel using encryption and authentication.

Both SSH and Socks v. 5 are not widely supported by VPNs.

Point-to-Point Protocol Tunneling (PPTP)

IPSec and SSH provide VPN security in many circumstances but they are not appropriate for every application. Users who need to dial in to a server using a modem connection on a computer running an older operating system may need to connect to VPN servers that have been configured to use Point-to-Point Protocol Tunneling (PPTP).

PPTP encapsulates a TCP/IP packet. The header information that encloses the packet and that appears on the network contains only the information needed to route the data from the VPN client to the VPN server, or vice versa. PPTP uses a proprietary technology called Microsoft Point-to-Point Encryption (MPPE) to encrypt data that passes between the remote computer and the remote access server. In contrast, the newer L2TP protocol uses

IPSec encryption, which is more secure and more widely supported. PPTP is useful, however, if your dial-in users need to connect from computers running Windows 95, 98, or NT 4.0.

Vulnerabilities related to MPPE as well as Microsoft's Challenge/Response Authentication Protocol make PPTP a poor choice for high-performance networks with a large number of hosts. Only use PPTP for a small-scale VPN that needs to support mobile users.

Layer 2 Tunneling Protocol (L2TP)

As mentioned in the preceding section, Layer 2 Tunneling Protocol (L2TP) provides a higher level of security through its support for IPSec. IPSec enables L2TP to perform authentication and encapsulation as well as encryption. Using L2TP, a host machine can make a connection to a modem and then have its PPP data packets forwarded to another, separate remote access server. When the data reaches the remote access server, its payload is unpacked and forwarded to the destination host on the internal network. Table 7-4 indicates which protocols are supported by which operating systems:

7

Table 7-4 Support for PPTP and L2TP

Protocol	Windows 95	Windows 98	Windows NT 4.0	Windows 2000	Windows XP	Red Hat Linux
PPTP	Yes	Yes	Yes	Yes	Yes	Yes
L2TP	No	No	No	Yes	Yes	Yes

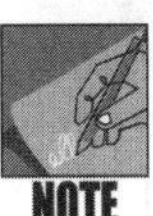

L2TP also works with non-VPN connections such as frame relay or Asynchronous Transfer Mode (ATM) networks.

Encryption Schemes Used by VPNs

One of the great advantages of a VPN is the ability to extend a Wide Area Network (WAN) to multiple locations using the Internet. However, the very openness of the Internet creates security risks that need to be addressed by encryption. Encryption is one of the most important aspects of a firewall because this is what achieves the VPNs primary goal of protecting the data payload from being read by unauthorized users.

Encryption schemes do not provide a uniform level of security. Some provide strong encryption—encryption that makes use of very long (for instance, 128-bit) keys, or multiple keys. The following sections describe encryption methods frequently used by VPNs: Data Encryption Standard (DES), Secure Sockets Layer (SSL), and Kerberos.

Triple-Data Encryption Standard (Triple-DES)

Most VPN software or hardware makes use of Triple-Data Encryption Standard (Triple-DES) encryption. Triple-DES is a variation on **Data Encryption Standard (DES)**, which was developed by IBM in the mid-1970s and was adopted as an encryption standard in 1977. DES is a relatively insecure encryption method; it has been cracked, though it requires multiple computers working solidly on the problem for many hours. Triple-DES is a far more secure protocol.

Triple-DES is strong because it uses three separate 64-bit keys to process data. The same bit of unencrypted text is processed by the three keys in turn: the first key encrypts it, the second key decrypts it, and the third key encrypts it again, as illustrated in Figure 7-13.

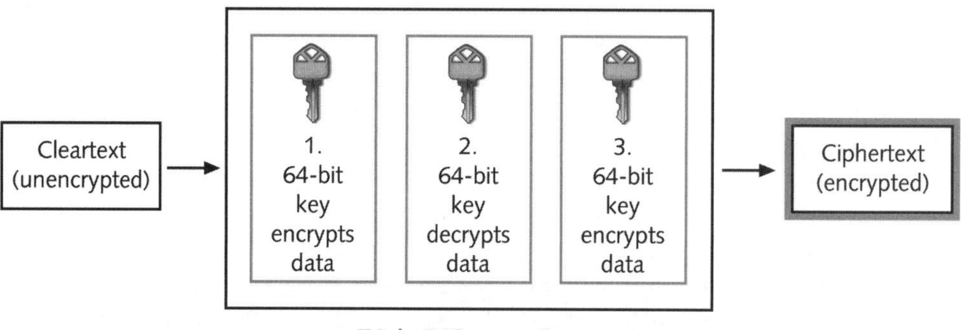

Figure 7-13 Most VPNs use Triple-DES encryption

Although the use of three keys in Figure 7-13 makes for a very strong level of encryption, the problem is the time involved to encrypt the information: it takes three times as long compared to using the original or "regular" version of DES, which only uses a single key.

The National Institute of Standards and Technology (NIST) is working to develop a new encryption standard, Advanced Encryption Standard (AES), to replace Triple-DES. AES is expected to be comparable in strength to Triple-DES and have the advantage of working much faster.

Secure Sockets Layer (SSL)

A growing number of VPNs are using Secure Sockets Layer (SSL) to encrypt tunneled information via the World Wide Web. SSL was developed by Netscape Communications Corporation as a way of enabling Web servers and browsers to exchange encrypted information. SSL gets its name because:

- It uses public and private key encryption to create secure communications.
- It uses the sockets method of communication between servers and clients.

- It operates at the Network layer, Layer 3 of the seven-layer Open Systems Interconnect (OSI) model of network communications. However, it is still able to provide a level of security that works between TCP and Hypertext Transfer Protocol (HTTP).

SSL is widely used on the Web, and in fact, VPNs that use SSL can support only data that is exchanged by Web-enabled applications. For this reason, SSL is unlikely to replace IPSec as a security standard for VPNs, but it can be a useful adjunct to IPSec when Web browsers and Web servers need to connect securely.

An SSL session makes use of both symmetric and asymmetric keys. The asymmetric keys are used to start an SSL session, but symmetric keys are then dynamically generated for the bulk of the transfer. It works like this:

1. The client connects to Web server using SSL protocol.
2. The two machines arrange a "handshake" during which they authenticate each other and determine what formulas and protocols will be used to encrypt and exchange information. The client sends the server its preferences for "cipher settings," the SSL version number, and a randomly generated number to be used later.
3. The server responds with the SSL version number and its own cipher preferences along with its digital certificate. The digital certificate tells the client who issued it, a data range, and the public key of the server. The server may ask the client for its own digital certificate at this point.
4. The client verifies that the date and other information on the digital certificate are valid. The domain name on the digital certificate is checked to verify whether it matches the domain name of the server. If it matches, the client generates a "pre-master" code and sends it to the server using the server's public key. The client's digital certificate is also sent, if one was requested by the server.
5. The server uses its private key to decode the pre-master code sent by the client. The server generates a "master secret" which will be used by both client and server to generate session keys—symmetric keys that will be used only for the duration of the session because of their efficiency.
6. The session keys are generated and used to encrypt the data going from client to server.

SSL is a secure way to transmit data on the Web, such as the personal information associated with a consumer who makes a purchase on a retail Web site. Note that SSL can cause problems for firewalls that can't interpret SSL data in much the same way that firewalls can have trouble interpreting IPSec data that uses tunnel mode encryption.

Kerberos

Kerberos is a system for authentication that was developed at the Massachusetts Institute of Technology (MIT). The name refers to the three-headed dog in Greek mythology that was said to guard the gates of Hades. Kerberos authenticates the identity of individual network users. It uses a simple authentication method called authentication by assertion: the computer that connects to a server and requests services asserts that it is acting on behalf of an approved user of those services.

Although the general authentication by assertion approach sounds simple, the method by which computers communicate the assertion and response is not. Kerberos uses encryption and authentication applied through credentials issued by a third party. The system resembles the issuance of digital certificates by CAs. In the case of Kerberos, the trusted third party is known as a Key Distribution Center (KDC). Instead of digital certificates, a Kerberos KDC issues "tickets." To access an application that is protected by Kerberos, a ticket is required.

Kerberos is an excellent choice for the authentication of computers that need to access resources on internal networks on a regular basis. It's a good choice because Kerberos tickets typically only last for short periods of time, such as hours or days, in contrast to digital certificates, which might last one or more years. An employee can log in to a network one day and use a Kerberos ticket for that day. After the day's usage is over, the ticket expires so that an unauthorized user can't steal it. The following day login will be required once again, along with a new ticket.

Kerberos has a lower "network overhead" than a Public Key Infrastructure (PKI). This means that Kerberos doesn't require you to necessarily install a central server and perform as many management tasks as a PKI. This is especially true in a small internal network where a limited number of individuals need access to shared resources. Kerberos is, in fact, the authentication scheme used in the VPN implementations built into Windows 2000 and XP.

Kerberos authentication is highly secure because it employs an elaborate system for granting tickets.

ADJUSTING PACKET FILTERING RULES FOR VPNS

VPNs need to be used in conjunction with firewalls. The VPN can be located in front of an existing firewall, in the public network outside the LAN. It can also be placed in the DMZ in parallel to an existing firewall. There are advantages and disadvantages to each configuration option. If you terminate the VPN connection in front of the firewall, VPN traffic will be on the unprotected external network for a brief period of time before it passes through the firewall. On the other hand, placing a VPN in the DMZ opens up two connections to your LAN. You need to block all non-VPN transmissions to prevent security risks.

Whatever way you choose to configure your VPN and firewall combination, you need to set up packet filtering rules that allow the VPN traffic to pass through as needed. Packet filtering makes use of three IP packet header fields in particular:

- The source address is the 32-bit IP address of the host that sent the packet and generated the information in it.
- The destination address is the 32-bit IP address of the intended destination host expected to receive the packet and the information the packet carries.
- The Protocol Identifier (Protocol ID) is the identifier of the protocol information the IP packet carries.

You can conduct packet filtering based on any or all of these fields. Using the source or destination address, for example, you can block all packets from an address or set of addresses, and you can route to a set of addresses those packets you let enter. The Protocol ID field can be used to refer to many protocols, including:

- Internet Control Message Protocol (ICMP), Protocol ID 1
- TCP, Protocol ID 6
- UDP, which provides connectionless, unreliable host-to-host connections, Protocol ID 17
- Generic Routing Encapsulation (GRE), an encapsulation protocol commonly used in VPNs Protocol ID 47
- Encapsulating Security Payload (ESP), Protocol ID 50
- Authentication Header (AH), Protocol ID 51

TIP

The Internet Assigned Numbers Authority (IANA) maintains a list of all protocol numbers at *www.iana.org/assignments/protocol-numbers*. See "Establishing Rules and Restrictions" in Chapter 4 for more about setting up packet filtering rules.

PPTP Filters

PPTP frequently comes into play when older clients need to connect to a network through a VPN or when a tunnel must pass through a firewall that performs NAT. For PPTP traffic to pass through the firewall, you need to set up packet filtering rules that permit such communications. PPTP uses two protocols: TCP and Generic Routing Encapsulation (GRE). A VPN server that has been configured to receive PPTP traffic listens for incoming connections arriving on TCP port 1723. It also needs to receive Generic Routing Encapsulating (GRE) packets that are identified by protocol identification number ID 47. Table 7-5 shows the filtering rules that you would use for your own gateway, if it had an IP address of 205.43.1.78 and a remote gateway with an IP address of 77.127.39.2.

Table 7-5 PPTP packet filtering rules

Rule	Source IP	Destination IP	Protocol	Source Port	Destination Port	Action
1	Any	205.43.1.78	TCP	Any	1723	Allow
2	Any	205.43.1.78	IP 47			Allow

In Table 7-5, two rules are established. Rule number 1 allows incoming PPTP connections from any computer to be received at the VPN server at 205.43.1.78 via port 1723. Rule 2 allows incoming traffic that uses IP 47. This rule allows incoming traffic that consists of GRE packets.

For a greater level of security, in the Action column, you could specify an option such as "Drop all packets except those that meet this criteria" or something similar, if your firewall allows you to make such distinctions.

L2TP and IPSec Filters

If you use L2TP, you need to set up rules that permit IPSec traffic. You have to account for the fact that IKE uses IP 171 and UDP on port 500. ESP uses IP 50, and AH uses IP 51. Table 7-6 shows the filter rules that you would use for your own gateway, if it had an IP address of 205.43.1.78 and a remote gateway with an IP address of 77.127.39.2.

Table 7-6 L2TP packet filtering rules

Rule	Source IP	Destination IP	Protocol	Transport Protocol	Source Port	Destination Port	Action
1	Any	205.43.1.78	IKE	UDP	500	500	Allow
2	Any	205.43.1.78	ESP	IP 50			Allow
3	Any	205.43.1.78	AH	IP 51			

In Table 7-6, Rule 1 covers inbound IKE traffic, which uses UDP port 500. Rule 2 enables traffic if you decide to use ESP, which requires a filter rule that enables IP 50 packets. Rule 3 enables traffic if you use AH, which requires a rule for IP 51. As with the filters for PPTP, you will achieve a higher level of security if, in the Action column, you could specify an option such as "Drop all packets except those that meet this criteria" or something similar, if your firewall allows you to make such distinctions.

Chapter Summary

- This chapter discussed issues involved in configuring a Virtual Private Network (VPN) and the role that the VPN plays in a network defense strategy.
- VPNs are virtual in that they do not make use of proprietary leased lines. Rather, they connect computers and networks through the public Internet. VPNs are private because they send data through a secure tunnel that leads from one endpoint to another. Each endpoint is terminated by VPN hardware or software that encrypts and encapsulates the data. VPNs are networks that connect one network to one or more networks, one computer to another, or one computer to a network.
- VPNs consist of various components. These include VPN servers, which are configured to accept connections from client computers; VPN clients; the tunnels through which data passes, and protocols that determine how the tunneled data is to be encrypted, such as Internet Protocol Security (IPSec). A site-to-site VPN uses such components to connect to networks. A client-to-site VPN connects a remote user to a network. VPN endpoints can be terminated by VPN hardware, VPN software, or a combination of both.
- VPNs perform three core activities. Encapsulation encloses one packet of digital information within another one to conceal the original packet's source and destination IP address and to protect the contents. Encryption makes the contents of the packet—not only its data, but its header information as well—unreadable by all but the intended recipient. Authentication ensures that the computers participating in a VPN are authorized users.
- Because VPNs can be complex to configure, the reasons for establishing them should be understood. The need to keep critical business communications private and secure drives the adoption of VPNs. The cost-effectiveness of using the Internet for VPN communications also makes VPNs attractive. On the other hand, the encryption performed by VPNs can slow down data transfer rates. Reliance on the Internet, which is often unpredictable, can result in the VPN going down along with ISP connections.
- A VPN is often configured by establishing a VPN domain, a group of computers that are handled as one entity. Networks that use VPNs can have single entry point configurations, in which all traffic to and from the network passes through a single gateway. Some VPNs are part of multiple entry point configurations, in which more than one gateway is used. Whether single or multiple entry points are in place in one network, that network can then be connected to other VPN participants using a mesh or star configuration, or a combination of both.
- VPNs make use of standard sets of instructions called protocols that secure tunneled communications between endpoints. Internet Protocol Security (IPSec) combined with Internet Key Exchange (IKE) is one of the most popular protocols because of its wide support in the industry and high degree of security through Authentication Header (AH) authentication and Encapsulating Security Payload (ESP) encryption. Secure Shell is a protocol used to authenticate and encrypt packets in a UNIX-based environment. Version 5 of the Socks protocol can also provide security for VPN transactions, though it is not widely used. Point-to-Point Protocol Tunneling (PPTP) and Layer 2 Tunneling Protocol (L2TP) enable remote users to dial in to a computer over a secure VPN connection.

- Encryption is one of the technologies that make VPNs possible. Most VPNs today use Triple-DES encryption, a variation of Data Encryption Standard (DES) in which three separate keys are used to process information. However, some VPNs use Secure Sockets Layer (SSL) encryption when Web-based applications need to be connected securely. Another strong authentication/encryption system, Kerberos, is used in Windows and other operating systems to give employees access to network resources for relatively short periods of time through the issuance of "tickets."
- VPNs need to be used in conjunction with firewalls. For the two devices to work together, packet filtering rules need to be set up. The rules cover such protocols as PPTP, L2TP, and IPSec. They have as their ultimate goal the filtering of packets so that only traffic to and from VPN endpoints passes through the VPN, and other traffic is filtered by the firewall to reach specific destinations on the network.

Key Terms

asymmetric cryptography — A type of encryption in which two different keys are used. A private key is kept by the certificate holder and never shared, while a public key is shared among users to encrypt and decrypt communications.

authentication — The process of identifying a user or computer as being authorized to access and use network resources.

Authentication Header (AH) — An IPSec protocol that provides for the authentication of TCP/IP packets to ensure data integrity.

certificate authority(CA) — A trusted organization that issues digital certificates that can be used to generate keys.

client-to-site VPN — A type of VPN connection that makes a network accessible to remote users requiring dial-in access.

Data Encryption Standard (DES) — An encryption scheme developed by IBM in the mid-1970s that was adopted as an encryption standard in 1977.

digital certificate — An electronic document issued by a certificate authority that contains information about the certificate holder and that can be used to exchange public and private keys.

Encapsulating Security Payload (ESP) — An IPSec protocol that encrypts both the header and data parts of each TCP/IP packet.

encapsulation — The process of enclosing a packet within another one that has different IP source and destination information to provide a high degree of protection.

encryption — The process of rendering information unreadable by all those but the intended recipient.

extranet — A network that uses Internet technologies and consists of one or more networks connected to one another.

gateway-to-gateway VPN connection — A VPN that uses hardware devices such as routers to connect two networks.

Internet Key Exchange (IKE) — A form of key exchange used to encrypt and decrypt data as it passes through a VPN tunnel. IKE uses tunnel method encryption to encrypt and then encapsulate packets for extra security.

Internet Security Association Key Management Protocol (ISAKMP) — An IPSec-related protocol that enables two computers to agree on security settings and establish a Security Association so that they can then exchange keys using Internet Key Exchange.

IPSec driver — Software that handles the actual tasks of encrypting, authenticating, decrypting, and checking packets in an IPSec connection.

key — An encoded block of data that is generated by an algorithm and that is used to encrypt and decrypt data.

leased lines — Private connections rented from telecommunications companies and using technologies such as frame relay.

mesh — A configuration in which all participants in the VPN are connected to one another.

multiple-entry point configuration — A type of VPN configuration in which multiple gateways are used, each with a VPN tunnel connecting a different location.

network uptime — The amount of time you are connected to a network, such as the Internet.

Point-to-Point Tunneling Protocol (PPTP) — A tunneling protocol that is used for dial-in access to a remote server.

public key cryptography — *See* asymmetric cryptography.

scalable — Being able to maintain a consistent level of functionality as a network grows.

Secure Shell (SSH) — A VPN authentication that works with UNIX-based systems that creates a secure Transport layer connection between participating computers and makes use of public key cryptography.

Security Association (SA) — A designation used to describe users, computers, or gateways that can participate in a VPN and encrypt and decrypt data using keys.

single entry point configuration — A VPN configuration in which all traffic to and from the network passes through a single gateway such as a router or firewall.

Socks — A communications protocol that provides proxy services for applications that don't normally support proxying and that enables applications to set up a secure tunnel using encryption and authentication.

star — A VPN configuration in which a single gateway is the "hub" and other networks that participate in the VPN are considered "rim" networks.

symmetric cryptography — A type of encryption in which the same key is exchanged by sender and recipient.

topology — The way in which the participants in a network are connected to one another.

transport method encryption — A type of VPN encryption in which only the data portion of a packet is encrypted, not the header.

tunnel — The connection between two endpoints in a VPN.

tunnel method encryption — A method of key exchange that encrypts both the header and data parts of a packet and encapsulates the packet within a new packet that has a different header.

virtual private network (VPN) — A set of technologies that provides a cost-effective way for two or more networks to make a secure connection, not through a proprietary line, but through the public Internet.

VPN appliance — A hardware device specially designed to terminate VPNs and join multiple LANs.

VPN client — A router or operating system that initiates a connection to a VPN server.

VPN domain — A set of one or more computers that is handled by the VPN hardware and software as a single entity, and that uses the VPN to communicate with another domain.

VPN protocols — Sets of standardized communication settings that computer software and hardware use to encrypt data that is sent along a VPN.

VPN server — A computer that is configured to accept VPN connections from clients.

Review Questions

1. Before establishing a virtual private network connection, a business would typically lease a line from a telecommunications company using what sort of technology? (Choose all that apply.)

   a. Frame relay

   b. DSL

   c. ISDN

   d. T-1

2. VPNs differ from leased lines in that they use ______________ to make connections.

   a. either hardware or software

   b. routers

   c. operating systems

   d. the public Internet

3. The VPN connection through which data passes from one endpoint to another is called a(n) ________________.
   a. gateway
   b. extranet
   c. tunnel
   d. transport
4. Under what circumstances does a firewall need to be installed at the endpoint of a VPN connection, and why?
5. A VPN that uses hardware to connect two networks is called a ______________. (Choose all that apply.)
   a. gateway-to-gateway VPN connection
   b. hub-and-spoke arrangement
   c. tunnel
   d. site-to-site VPN

6. What term is used to describe a set of procedures that enables a VPN to encrypt traffic?
   a. public key cryptography
   b. protocol
   c. encapsulation
   d. digital certificate
7. Place the following elements involved in encryption in the order in which they occur in the encryption process: digital certificate, private key, algorithm, certificate authority, and public key.
8. How does asymmetric cryptography differ from symmetric cryptography?
   a. It uses two keys.
   b. It exchanges keys.
   c. It does not require a key exchange.
   d. It uses an algorithm.

9. Because transport method encryption encrypts only the data portion of a TCP/IP packet, why would it be used in place of tunnel method encryption, which encrypts the entire packet? (Choose all that apply.)

   a compatibility with NAT

   b It is more widely supported than tunnel method encryption.

   c. improved performance

   d. Encrypting the data portion of a packet provides better security.

10. What type of VPN is used to provide remote users with dial-in access to a central office?

    a. client-to-site

    b. site-to-site

    c. gateway-to-gateway

    d. mesh configuration

11. A group of authentication and encryption settings that two computers negotiate to set up a secure VPN connection is called a ______________.

    a. protocol

    b. Security Association (SA)

    c. handshake

    d. key exchange

12. Computers in a VPN authenticate one another by means of what encryption-related component?

    a. public key

    b. challenge/response

    c. digital certificate

    d. username/password

13. What makes a VPN such a cost-effective option?

    a. Computers can use the same hardware and software.

    b. Cost is spread over multiple users.

    c. Many VPN applications are available as shareware or freeware.

    d. VPNs use the public Internet and ISP connections.

14. What term describes a network that uses Internet technologies and that is used by an organization?

    a. subnet

    b. intranet

    c. tunnel

    d. extranet

15. Companies that maintain VPNs with business partners often benefit by using the same ______________. (Choose all that apply.)

    a. VPN hardware

    b. IP address range

    c. Internet Service Provider (ISP)

    d. Certificate Authority (CA)

16. A VPN domain is a group of computers ________.

    a. that shares the same domain name

    b. in the same subnet

    c. that is handled as a single entity

    d. that makes up a VPN

17. In what kind of VPN configuration must a router belong to the VPN domain?

    a. gateway-to-gateway VPN

    b. multiple entry point

    c. single entry point

    d. partial mesh

18. Which of the following is an advantage of using a mesh VPN configuration?

    a. You only need to configure the main office VPN server.

    b. All participants can communicate securely with all other participants.

    c. All participants can exchange encrypted communications.

    d. The VPN is able to scale along with the organization.

19. Which of the following is an advantage of using a star VPN configuration?
    a Fewer connections need to be made with ISPs.
    b Fewer VPN hardware or software devices need to be used.
    c Only the VPN server at the center or "hub" needs to be updated.
    d. All participants can communicate with all other participants.

20. IPSec provides for what security activity to take place before data is encrypted or transmitted?
    a. encapsulation
    b. authentication
    c. establishment of a Security Association (SA)
    d. application of security policy settings

HANDS-ON PROJECTS

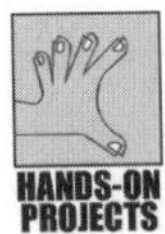

Project 7-1: Direct Connecting Two Lab Computers

In this project, you will direct connect two computers in your lab so you can then create a virtual private network between them in subsequent projects. You will need two computers that use Windows for this project. However, you can also connect a laptop or other computer running Windows 95, 98, or ME as the client computer to a server computer that runs Windows 2000 or XP. Or, you could connect two Windows 2000 or Windows XP computers to one another.

In this project, one that functions as the VPN host will be running Windows XP and one that functions as the VPN guest will be running Windows 2000.

1. Obtain a crossover, null modem, or direct connection cable. This is a specially designed cable with a 25-pin connector at each end. (A 9-pin null modem cable also works.)
2. The connectors at the end of the cable look the same, but they are not. Inspect them and explain the difference. Also explain the purpose of such a cable. Write the answers in a lab notebook or a word processing document. (Hint: Double-click the **Internet Explorer** icon on your desktop, enter the URL **http://www.nullmodem.com/NullModem.htm** in the Address box, and press **Enter**. Read the Web page that appears for more information on how null modem cables work.)
3. Make sure the computers are physically close to one another so that the cable can reach easily.
4. Plug the cable into the serial port of each computer you want to connect.

5. On both Windows XP and Windows 2000 computers, open the Control Panel. (On Windows XP, click **Start** and then click **Control Panel**; on Windows 2000, either double-click the **Control Panel** icon in My Computer or click **Start**, point to **Settings**, and click **Control Panel**.)
6. Double-click **Phone and Modem Options**. When the Phone and Modem Options dialog box appears, click the **Modems** tab.
7. Click **Add**.
8. Click **Don't detect my modem; I will detect it from a list**.
9. Click **Next**.
10. In the Manufacturers list, verify that **Standard Modem Types** is selected. In the Model list, click **Communications cable between two computers**. Then click **Next**.
11. Select **COM1** or **COM2**, and then click **Next**.
12. Click **Finish**.
13. Click **OK** to close Phone and Modem Options.

Project 7-2: Setting Up a Remote Access Server

In this project, you will configure Routing and Remote Access on one of the two computers you connected directly (the one running Windows XP) so it can accept incoming VPN connections. Once it is a remote access server you can use it to set up a direct VPN connection or a dial-in connection using PPTP or L2TP. This project requires you to have set up a direct connection between two computers as described in Project 7-1.

1. Click **Start**, and then click **Control Panel**.
2. Double-click the **Network Connections** icon.
3. Under Network Tasks, click **Create a New Connection**.
4. When the New Connection Wizard appears, click **Next**.
5. Click **Set up an advanced connection**, and then click **Next**.
6. Verify that **Accept Incoming Connections** is clicked, and then click **Next**.
7. Click **Communications cable between two computers,** and then click **Next**.
8. Verify that **Allow virtual private connections** is clicked, and then click **Next**.
9. In the User Permissions dialog box, click the box next to the user(s) you want to grant access to your computer. If your lab partner doesn't have a username, click **Add** and create a username and password in the Add User dialog box. When you are done, click **Next**.

10. In the Networking Software dialog box, verify that **Internet Protocol (TCP/IP)** and **File and printer sharing for Microsoft Networks** are clicked. Click **Internet Protocol (TCP/IP)** and then click **Properties**.
11. Verify that the **Allow callers to access my local area network** check box is checked.
12. Click **Specify TCP/IP addresses**.
13. In the From and To boxes, specify a range of IP addresses to be allocated by the VPN server. For this example, enter **192.168.1.1** in the From box and **192.168.1.254** in the To box. Click **OK**.
14. Click **Next**, and then click **Finish**.

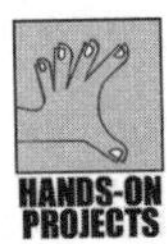

Project 7-3: Setting Up a Direct Client Connection

After installing a null modem cable between two computers, you can configure the second computer to function as the client. You need to disable the current network interface so that the client can use the null modem cable as the network interface. You then determine the IP address of the cable's interface. Use a Windows 2000 computer for this project. This project assumes you have installed a null modem cable as described in Project 7-1.

1. Double-click **My Computer**.
2. Click **Network and Dial-up Connections**.
3. When the first screen of the Network Connection Wizard appears, click **Make a New Connection**, and then click **Next**.
4. Click **Connect directly to another computer**, and then click **Next**.
5. Click **Guest**, and then click **Next**.
6. From the Select a device drop-down list, select the port where you installed your null modem cable in Project 7-1, and then click **Next**.
7. Click **For all users**, and then click **Next**.
8. Click **Finish**. The Direct Cable Connection dialog box appears.
9. In the User Logon dialog box, enter the User Name and Password you created in Project 7-2. Then click **Connect**.
10. A dialog box appears stating that the connection is being made. In a few seconds, a second dialog box should appear, stating that the connection has been established. Verify this by switching to the Windows XP computer and opening the Network Connections dialog box. An icon labeled <user name> should appear.

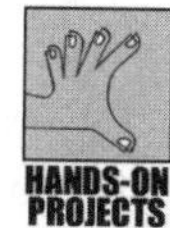

Project 7-4: Establishing a VPN Connection

After you have established a direct connection between your two lab computers, you can then establish a VPN connection on top of the direct connection: the VPN connection uses the direct connection you already established and adds authentication and encryption. This project assumes you have completed Projects 7-1, 7-2, and 7-3.

1. On the Windows XP host computer, click **Start**, point to **All Programs**, point to **Accessories**, and click **Command Prompt**.
2. When the Command Prompt window opens, type **ipconfig** and then press **Enter**. Details about your computer's IP addresses appear. How many connections do you have listed? What is the IP address for the first connection listed? Write down the IP addresses in a lab notebook or word processed document.
3. Switch to the Windows 2000 client computer. If necessary, open Network and Dial-up Connections by double-clicking **My Computer** and then double-clicking **Network and Dial-up Connections.** Make note of the name of the icon that represents the direct connection you made to the other lab computer (it will probably be the generic name Direct Connection unless you changed it to something else).
4. Right-click any other network connections that might be active (such as Local Area Connection, if you use it to connect to the Internet) and click **Disable**.
5. Double-click **Make New Connection**. When the Network Connection Wizard appears, click **Next**.
6. Click **Connect to a private network through the Internet**, and then click **Next**.
7. In the Public Network screen, click **Automatically dial this initial connection.**
8. From the drop-list, click the direct connection you made to the other lab computer. Then click **Next**.
9. In the Destination Address dialog box, type the RAS IP address of the Windows XP host computer that you entered in Step 2. Then click **Next**.
10. In the next screen, verify that **For all users** is clicked, and then click **Next**.
11. In the final screen of the Wizard, change the default name of the connection (Virtual Private Connection) if you want to, and then click **Finish**.
12. When the Connect Virtual Private Network dialog box appears, enter the network username and password you created in Project 7-2, and then click **Connect**. A dialog box appears notifying you of the progress of the connection. After a few seconds, a second dialog box should appear, notifying you that you are connected.

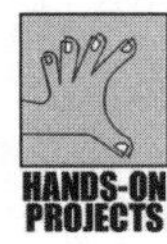

Project 7-5: Activating IPSec and Specifying a Policy

Once you have two computers connected via a VPN, you can configure them to use IPSec to talk to one another. You can also set up a tunnel using L2TP or PPTP as the tunneling protocol. Follow these steps on the Windows XP computer that serves as the host for your VPN connection. This project requires you to have established a virtual private connection as described in Project 7-4.

1. Click **Start** and click **Run**.
2. In the Open box of the Run dialog box, type **MMC**, then click **OK**.
3. A Microsoft Management Console opens, labeled Console1. Click **File** and click **Add/Remove Snap-in**.
4. In the Add/Remove Snap-in dialog box, click **Add**.
5. Click **IP Security Policy Management**, and then click **Add**.
6. When the Security Policy Management dialog box appears, verify that **Local Computer** is clicked, and then click **Finish.**
7. Click **IP Security Monitor** in the Add standalone snap-in window, and then click **Add**.
8. Click **Close**, and then click **OK** to close Add Standalone Snap-in.
9. In the left pane of the management console, click **IP Security Policies on Local Computer.**
10. In the right pane of the management console, right-click **Secure Server (Require Security)**. Click **Assign**.
11. Right-click **Secure Server (Require Security)** a second time, and click **Properties**.
12. In the Secure Server (Require Security) Properties dialog box, click **All ICMP Traffic**, and then click **Edit**.
13. Click **All IP Traffic**. In the Description field, you can read that the rule blocks all IP traffic to and from the local computer that does not use IP security. You need to create a less restrictive rule—one that sets up a tunnel between the host computer and your VPN guest.
14. Click **Edit**. The IP Filter List dialog box appears. Click **Edit**.
15. In the Filter Properties dialog box, click **A specific IP Address** from the Destination address drop-down list, and then enter the IP address of the client computer that is directly connected to this host computer.
16. Click **OK**.
17. Click **OK** to close IP Filter List.
18. Click **All ICMP Traffic**, and then click **Edit**.

19. Repeat Steps 14 through 16 one time to set up an ICMP traffic rule for the same IP address you specified in Step 15.
20. Click **Apply** or **OK**.
21. Click **OK** to close Edit Rule Properties, and then click **Close** to close Secure Server (Require Security) Properties.
22. Click **File** and then click **Exit** to close Console1. When prompted to save your changes, click **Yes**.

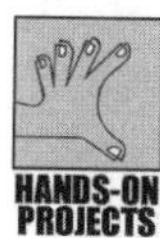

Project 7-6: Configuring the Client VPN Tunnel Using IPSec

After you have set up the host computer in your VPN connection to require IPSec, you need to configure the client computer to use IPSec as well. This project assumes that you have directly connected two lab computers as described in Projects 7-1 and 7-2, and that you have configured a VPN client connection as described in Project 7-3, and set up IPSec on the host computer as described in Project 7-4. It requires that you use a Windows 2000 computer as the client.

1. Double-click **My Computer**.
2. Double-click the **Network and Dial-up Connections** icon.
3. Right-click the **VPN** icon, and then click **Properties**.
4. In the Virtual Private Connection Properties dialog box, click the **Networking** tab.
5. In the Type of VPN server I am calling drop-down list, click **Layer-2 Tunneling Protocol (L2TP)**.
6. Click **Internet Protocol (TCP/IP),** and then click **Properties**.
7. Click **Advanced**.
8. Click **Options**.
9. Click **IP security**, and then click **Properties**.
10. Click **Use this IP security policy**. Verify that Client (Respond Only) is selected from the drop-down list.
11. Click **OK** to close IP Security, **OK** to close Advanced TCP/IP Settings, **OK** to close Internet Protocol (TCP/IP) Properties, and **OK** to close Virtual Private Connection Properties.
12. Right-click the **Virtual Private Connection** icon and click **Connect**. A dialog box appears notifying you that something is needed to make the connection. What is it?

Project 7-7: Configuring L2TP Packet Filtering Rules

Draw up a set of packet filtering rules that would enable a remote user to connect to your VPN gateway at 101.26.111.8 from the user's gateway, which would be dynamically assigned an IP address and would use the L2TP protocol. The packet filtering rules would enable the VPN traffic to pass through your firewall.

1. Write down the UDP source and destination ports used by L2TP. (*Hint:* Refer to the section "L2TP and IPSec Filters" earlier in this chapter.)
2. Write two rules for inbound traffic. What are the two options you could specify as the Action for these rules?
3. Write two rules for outbound traffic.

Case Projects

Case Project 7-1: Adjusting the VPN for Scalability

Your security policy calls for your network defenses to provide maximum security, as well as compatibility with other systems. Accordingly, you configure your organization's VPN to use both AH authentication and ESP encryption. You perform a network audit after a week. You notice that performance has slowed down dramatically, and you have received user complaints about it. You need to make adjustments. What are your options?

Case Project 7-2: Combining the VPN with a Firewall

You configured a VPN to use IPSec in its most secure mode—using ESP with tunnel mode. However, you encounter problems with the firewall, which is positioned between the VPN and the internal LAN. The firewall ends up dropping a substantial percentage of the packets that are terminated by the VPN device. Troubleshoot the situation: What could be causing the firewall to fail to process VPN traffic? How could you solve the problem?

Case Project 7-3: Designing a VPN Topology

You manage a network that connects via a VPN to a combination of branch offices and remote workers. The branch offices all need to communicate with one another securely to transfer files, especially sensitive budgeting data. At the same time, you have three remote workers who also need to communicate with the network using a VPN, but who don't need to talk to one another because they work in different areas of the company. Describe a VPN configuration that would serve all parts of the extended corporate network.

Case Project 7-4: Recommending VPN Procurement

You manage all parts of an extranet that comprises several different subnets. Because you are the administrator for these subnets, you are able to exercise control over what equipment each part of the network uses. You are expecting to have heavy traffic needs, especially during an important contract your company has arranged to fulfill for the government. You are assigned to recommend VPN equipment. What kind of VPN components would make sense in this situation? Additionally, what kind of topology would be the easiest for you to configure and maintain?

Case Project 7-5: Firewalls and VPNs (optional)

You need to determine whether you should put the VPN server in front of the firewall and exposed to the Internet connection, or in the DMZ behind the firewall. Your organization's security policy calls for the firewall to implement NAT. In addition, the VPN only needs to connect to a single gateway. Members of the IT staff are in disagreement about where the firewall should be placed. One group argues that there is a security risk associated with putting the VPN in the DMZ because it creates two points of entry to the LAN (the firewall and the VPN device). Another argues that placing the VPN in front of the firewall means that the firewall needs to be configured with great care to let traffic through from the VPN without giving hackers a point of attack. You are asked to resolve the disagreement. What argument would you make?

CHAPTER

8

INTRUSION DETECTION: AN OVERVIEW

After reading this chapter and completing the exercises, you will be able to:

- Describe intrusion detection system components
- Follow the intrusion detection process step-by-step
- Understand options for configuring intrusion detection systems
- Know the issues involved in choosing an intrusion detection system

Firewalls and anti-virus software form the first measure of defense for an organization's network, and an intrusion detection system (IDS) provides a powerful supplementary level of defense. Like a burglar alarm in your home or apartment, an IDS incorporates sensors to detect when unauthorized individuals attempt to gain access. Both a burglar alarm and an IDS notify you if someone is attempting to break in so that you can take appropriate countermeasures. Unlike a burglar alarm, however, some IDS devices can be configured to respond in a way that can actually stop an attack.

A network **intrusion** is an attempt to gain unauthorized access to network resources and compromise the integrity and confidentiality of the data contained on the network or the privacy of its users. **Intrusion detection** involves monitoring network traffic, detecting attempts to gain unauthorized access to a system or resource, and notifying the appropriate professionals so that countermeasures can be taken.

This chapter introduces the subject of intrusion detection by first discussing the components of an IDS. It then gives a step-by-step examination of how those components operate together to protect a network. Next, you learn about the options for designing an IDS by distributing its components at critical locations. Finally, you get descriptions of real-world IDS products that take different approaches to intrusion detection.

Intrusion Detection System Components

An intrusion detection system consists of more than one application or hardware device. It also incorporates more than just detection. Intrusion detection involves three core activities—prevention, detection, and response—which are illustrated in Figure 8-1.

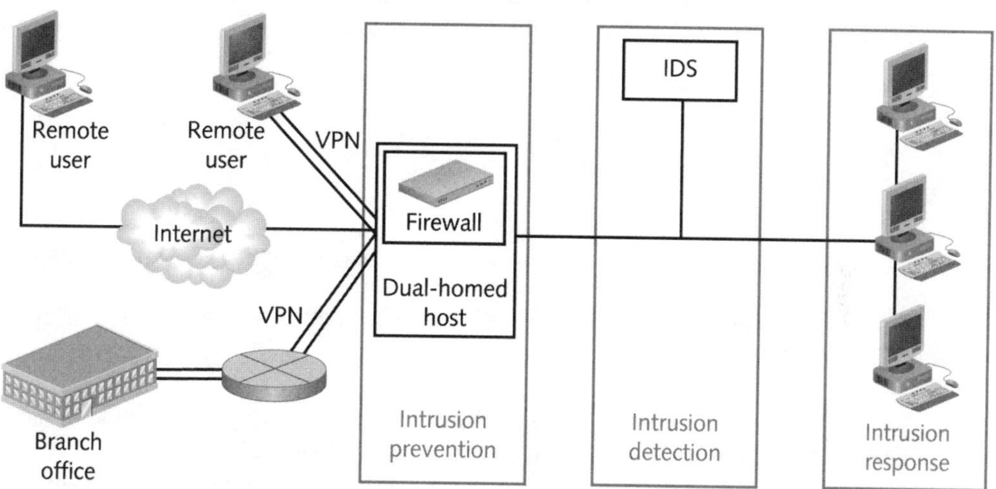

Figure 8-1 The role of intrusion detection in an overall network defense configuration

Figure 8-1 illustrates three network defense functions. Firewalls perform the first function: prevention. Intrusion detection systems provide the next function: detection. The network administrators perform the final function: response.

In the following sections you read about the components that make up an IDS: the network sensors that detect suspicious packets; the alert systems that notify you of those packets; the command console on which you read the alerts; the response system that can automatically take countermeasures when possible intrusions occur; and the database of attack signatures or behaviors that the IDS uses to identify traffic against which to take those countermeasures.

Network Sensor

A sensor functions as the electronic "eyes" of an intrusion detection system. In the case of the burglar alarm analogy mentioned earlier, a sensor is a switch that is attached to a door or metal tape that adheres to a glass window. When the door is opened or the glass breaks, the alarm goes off (unless the owner has disabled the system or turned it off).

In terms of a network intrusion detection system, a network sensor is hardware or software that monitors traffic passing into and out of the network in real time. When the sensor detects an event it considers suspicious, an alarm is triggered. Attacks detected by an IDS sensor can take one of two forms:

- Single-session attacks in which the intruder makes a single isolated attempt to locate a computer on the internal network or gain access by other means
- Multiple-session attacks such as port scans or network scans that take place over a period of time and that comprise multiple events

An IDS that is installed on an individual host computer (which is called a host-based IDS) has its sensor built into the IDS software. An IDS that checks for intrusions on a network (which is called a network-based IDS) might have one or more hardware sensors placed at strategic locations. Sensors should be placed at common entry points into the network, such as:

- Internet gateways
- Connections between one LAN and another, or one part of a LAN and another part
- A remote access server that receives dial-in connections from remote users
- Virtual private network (VPN) devices that connect the LAN to the LAN or a business partner

In some IDS configurations, software called a network sensor is software that collects data from a hardware device called a network tap. The network tap actually collects data from network traffic, and the sensor determines if an event is suspicious by comparing the characteristics of the event to a set of user behaviors or rules, or a database of known attack characteristics.

In the case of a sophisticated security product such as the Cisco Secure IDS system, a management program called the Secure IDS Director controls one or more sensors. The options for sensor placement are shown in Figure 8-2.

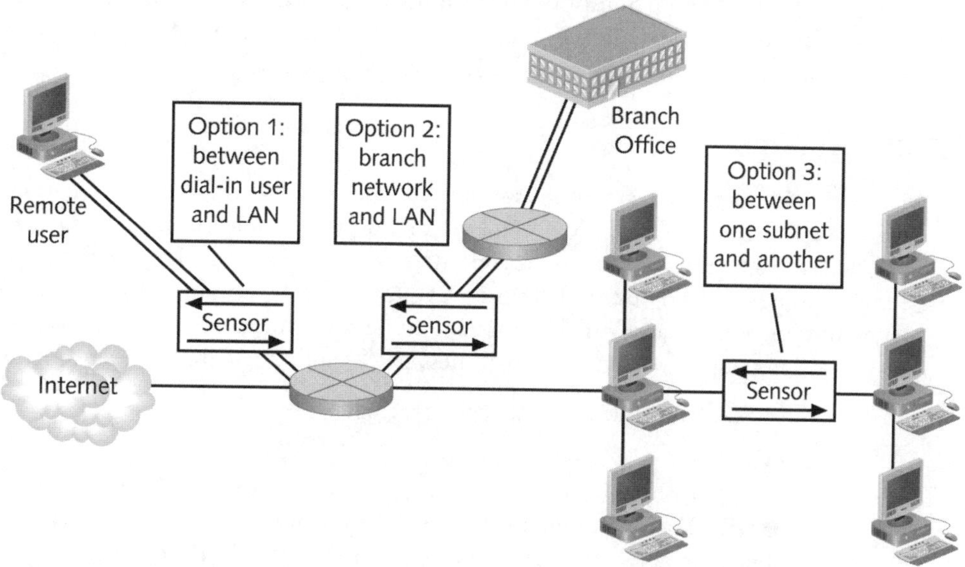

Figure 8-2 Sensors should be positioned at points of entry into the network

If a firewall is used to protect the LAN, the sensor could be positioned on either side of the firewall. However, if the sensor is placed outside the firewall at a point that is exposed to the Internet, the sensor itself could become the subject of an attack. A more secure location would be behind the firewall in the DMZ (see Figure 8-3).

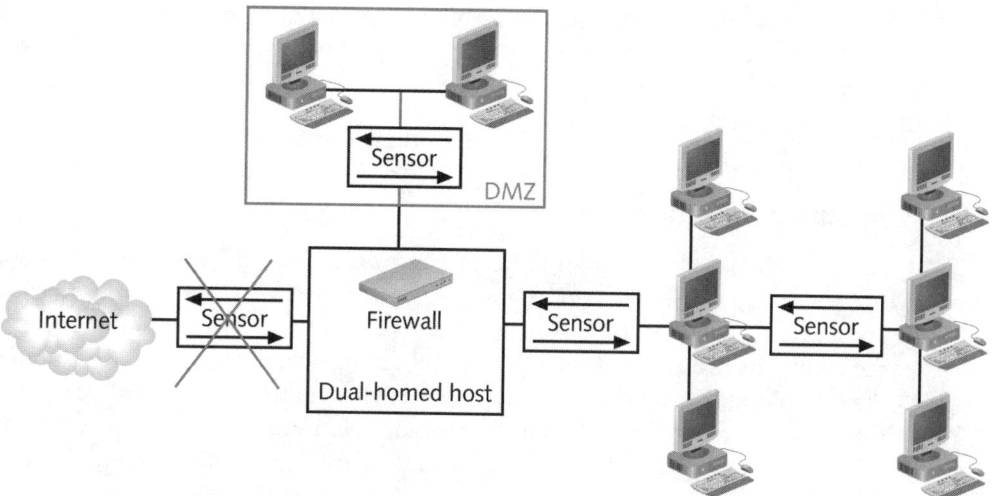

Figure 8-3 Position the sensor inside the firewall in the DMZ

The Cisco IDS Secure Sensor doesn't simply monitor traffic and detect possible intrusions. It has the ability to update access control lists in order to block future attacks. Plus, it can stop and then reset all TCP traffic if an intrusion is found to be underway.

Alert Systems

A home burglar alarm system is configured to emit an alarm sound if a particular type of event occurs, such as a window breaking or a door opening. An IDS operates in much the same way—it sounds or sends an alert when it encounters packets or traffic patterns that seem suspicious. To respond to such events, the IDS employs a **trigger** —a set of circumstances that cause an alert message to be sent. Alert messages can take many forms, such as a pop-up window, an e-mail message, a sound, or a message sent to a pager.

Alerts can result from two general types of triggers:

- *Detection of an anomaly* —The system sends an alarm when it detects an event that deviates from behavior that has been defined as "normal." This is sometimes called **profile-based detection** because it compares current network traffic to profiles of normal network usage. You might use **anomaly detection** if you are particularly concerned with misuse from inside the organization, or if you want to monitor all of the traffic heading into and out of your e-mail, Web, and FTP servers.

- *Detection of misuse* —An IDS that is configured to send an alarm in response to misuse makes use of **signatures** , which are sets of characteristics that match known examples of attacks. You might choose **misuse detection** if you have the time and ability (and perhaps the software) available to make sense of the large amounts of log file data generated by such a system. Organizations that want a basic IDS and that are primarily concerned with known attacks from hackers trying to access hosts from the Internet should choose a misuse-based system and regularly update the system's signatures.

These two triggers are discussed in the sections that follow.

Anomaly Detection

An anomaly detection system requires you to make use of **profiles** for each authorized user or group on the system. These profiles are sets of characteristics that describe the services and resources a user normally accesses on the network. Some IDS systems have the ability to create user profiles themselves during a "training period" —a period in which the IDS monitors network traffic to observe what constitutes "normal" network behavior. Otherwise, you need to create the profiles yourself. Because a large-scale corporate network might consist of hundreds or even thousands of users broken into multiple groups, profile configuration can represent a significant amount of work.

The accuracy of the profiles used by the IDS has a direct impact on the effectiveness with which it detects anomalies from those profiles. If the profiles are accurate, the IDS will send alarms only to genuine attacks. If the profiles are incomplete or inaccurate, the IDS will send alarms that turn out to be **false-positives** : alarms that are generated by legitimate network traffic rather than actual attacks. False positives cause you to waste valuable time and resources. They can also cause unnecessary alarm among your organization's staff, who might cease to take such alarms seriously should they occur often enough. You need to configure an anomaly-based IDS with sufficiently accurate profiles to minimize or even eliminate false-positives. You also need to configure the IDS accurately enough to avoid **false-negatives** : genuine attacks that occur but that are not detected by the IDS because profiles do not exist for them.

An anomaly-based detection system can also generate false-positives due to changes in user habits; individuals, after all, don't use computer systems the same way all the time. When users vary a pattern (by attempting to access a database they've never used before, for instance), a false-positive is highly likely.

Misuse Detection

In contrast to anomaly-based detection, which triggers alarms based on deviations from "normal" network behavior by users or groups within an organization, misuse detection triggers alarms based on the characteristic signatures of known attacks from outside the organization. The network engineers who configure the IDS research well-known attacks and record the rules associated with each signature. A database of such signatures is then made available to the IDS. Because the IDS comes equipped with a set of signatures, it can begin to protect the network immediately upon installation. This is in contrast to an anomaly-based IDS, which must be trained to recognize "normal" network traffic before it can begin to protect the network.

Anomaly detection and misuse detection both have their advantages and disadvantages, which are summarized in Table 8-1.

Table 8-1 IDS triggering mechanisms: advantages and disadvantages

Trigger	Advantages	Disadvantages
Anomaly detection	Because an anomaly detection system is based on profiles that the administrator creates, a hacker cannot test the IDS beforehand and cannot anticipate what will trigger an alarm.	A substantial amount of time is required to configure the IDS to use the profiles of network users and groups.
	As new users and groups are created, the IDS profiles can be changed to keep up with the new arrangements.	As new users and groups are created, the profiles available to the IDS must be updated in order to remain effective.
	Because an anomaly detection system does not rely on published signatures, it can detect new attacks.	The definition of what constitutes "normal" traffic changes constantly; the IDS must constantly be reconfigured to keep up.
	The system can effectively detect attacks from inside the network by employees or hackers who have stolen employee accounts.	After installation, the IDS must be "trained" for days or weeks at a time in order to recognize normal traffic.
Trigger	**Advantages**	**Disadvantages**
Misuse detection	This approach makes use of signatures of well-known attacks.	The database of signatures must be updated in order to maintain the effectiveness of the IDS.
	The IDS can begin working immediately after installation.	New types of attacks may not be included in the database.
	The IDS is easy to understand and is less difficult to configure than an anomaly-based system.	By making minor alterations to the attack, hackers can avoid matching one of the signatures in the database.
	Each signature in the database is assigned a number and a name so that the administrator can identify the attacks that need to set off an alarm.	Because a misuse-based system makes use of a database, a considerable amount of disk storage space might be needed.

An IDS that employs misuse detection has one other potential weakness that you should keep in mind: the need to maintain **state information** (information that pertains to a connection) about the possible attack. When a packet is received by the IDS, information about the connection between the host and the remote computers is compared to the entries in the state table. A state table maintains a record of connections between computers. Such information includes the source IP address and port, destination IP address and port, and protocol. Furthermore, the IDS needs to maintain the state information for the entire length of the attack, which is called the **event horizon** . This might require the IDS to review many packets of data; for long attacks such as those that last from user logon to user logoff, the IDS may not be able to maintain the state information for a sufficient length of time, and the attack may circumvent the system.

Besides misuse and anomaly detection, an IDS can also detect suspicious packets in other ways, including:

- *Traffic rate monitoring* —If a sudden and dramatic increase in traffic is detected of the sort that might result from a Denial of Service attack, the IDS can stop and reset all TCP traffic.
- *Protocol state tracking (i.e., stateful packet filtering)* —Some IDS systems are able to go a step beyond matching packet signatures by performing firewall-like stateful packet filtering. The IDS maintains a record of the state of a connection and only allows packets to pass through to the internal network if a connection has already been established.
- *IP packet reassembly* —IDS products like Minesweeper (*www.barbedwires.com/products/ms.htm*) are able to reassemble IP packets that have been fragmented in order to prevent individual fragments from passing through to the internal network.

Other IDS products, such as neuSecure by Guarded Net (*www.guarded.net/prod.html*), are hybrid systems that perform both anomaly and misuse detection while gathering data from many different sensors in a single interface.

Command Console

A **command console** is software that provides a network administrator with a graphical front-end interface to the IDS. The console enables administrators to receive and analyze alert messages and manage log files. In large-scale networks that may have more than one IDS deployed, a single console gives administrators a way to keep up with a large volume of events in order to respond quickly and take countermeasures.

A program such as Symantec ManHunt (*www.symantec.com*) or Cisco IDS Host Sensor provides you with a single interface to view security events that are occurring now, or look up alerts or intrusion attempts that have occurred in the recent past for comparison. An example of the command console used with Cisco IDS Host Sensor is shown in Figure 8-4. The console shown contains four icons in the toolbar that are used to classify the severity of suspicious events: High (H), Medium (M), Low (L), or Info (I). The latter designation (I) indicates that a change has been made to the system configuration that might open up a potential security hole. The System (S) icon is used to designate system events such as logoffs and logons.

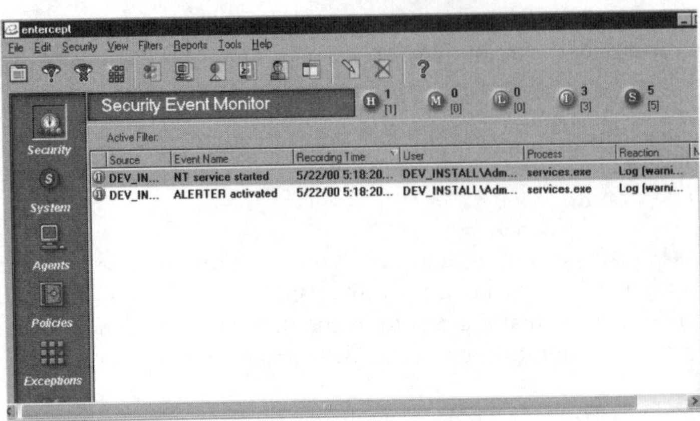

Figure 8-4 A command console consolidates events from multiple sensors

You set up a security policy for an IDS in much the same way as you would with a firewall. The IDS can collect information from security devices throughout a network, which are connected to the command console, where they can be reviewed and evaluated. The command console is typically installed on a computer that is dedicated solely to IDS in order to maximize speed of response. The command console unit should not be slow to respond because its host computer is busy backing up files or performing firewall functions when a suspicious event is detected.

Response System

As stated at the beginning of this chapter, some of the more sophisticated IDS devices can be set up to take some countermeasures such as resetting all network connections when an intrusion is detected. This should not be considered a substitute for a network administrator taking appropriate countermeasures when an attack is detected. The administrator can use his or her judgment to determine whether an alarm is being triggered by a false-positive or a genuine attack (which is sometimes called a **true-positive**). If the attack is genuine, the administrator's judgment can also be applied to gauge the severity of an attack and determine whether the response should be **escalated** —increased to a higher level. Options for responding to an intrusion are discussed in greater detail in Chapter 10.

Database of Attack Signatures or Behaviors

As was observed in the previous section, network administrators are able to exercise judgment when evaluating security alerts. Intrusion detection systems don't have the power of judgment. Rather, they need a source of information against which they can compare the traffic they monitor. Misuse-based systems call upon a database of known attack signatures; if a sensor detects a packet or a sequence of packets that matches one of the signatures, it sends an alert. The SecurityFocus online database of known vulnerabilities (shown in Figure 8-5) is frequently updated, and you can search it online for a particular type of attack in order to find out more about it. The SecurityFocus database (*http://online.securityfocus.com/bid*) is used by e-Security Advisor, an IDS system licensed by e-Security, Inc. (*www.esecurityinc.com/products/eadvisor.asp*).

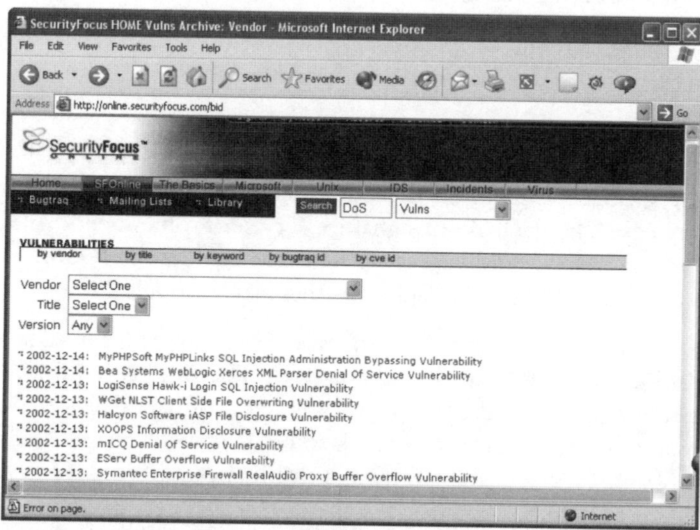

Figure 8-5 The SecurityFocus online database of known vulnerabilities

The key with attack signature databases is that they are kept up-to-date; a new type of attack that has not been added to the system's available signatures can quickly defeat an IDS. An IDS vendor that uses attack signatures should give you a way to download new entries to add them to the database. The problem with systems that depend solely on signatures is that they are passive: they monitor traffic, compare it to the database, and send alerts whenever a packet matches an available signature, which can result in numerous false-positives. Most IDS systems let administrators overcome such passivity by adding their own custom rules to the database of signatures in order to reduce the number of "false alarms."

The anomaly detection approach to IDS also makes use of a database of stored information against which network traffic is compared. For example, SecurVantage 3.0 by Securify (*www.securify.com*) takes a snapshot of network traffic over a given period of time that is considered "normal." SecurVantage develops a set of policies that describe who can normally use a network device and how the device can be used. Any deviations from the accumulated set of policies triggers an alarm.

8

Intrusion Detection Step-By-Step

IDS systems operate in different ways depending on whether they are configured to react to anomalies (deviations from normal network behavior) or signatures (characteristics of known attacks). Hybrid IDS systems can, in fact, combine aspects of both anomaly and misuse detection (see the section "Hybrid IDS Implementations" later in this chapter).

Despite differences in operation, the process of network intrusion detection can be broken into general steps that apply to virtually all IDS systems, which are illustrated in Figure 8-6. These steps are described in the subsequent sections of this chapter.

The SANS Institute maintains a useful FAQ on intrusion detection at *www.sans.org/resources/idfaq.*

Step 1: Installing the IDS Database

The first step in the process of intrusion detection occurs before the first packet is ever detected on the network. The database of signatures or user profiles needs to be installed, along with the IDS software and hardware itself. The data enables the IDS to have a set of criteria against which they can compare packets as they pass through the sensor.

In the case of an anomaly-based system, the process of installing data can take as much as a week after installation of the IDS devices themselves. The time is required so that the IDS can observe network traffic and compile a baseline set of data that describes normal network usage. Some of the data can take a week to be recorded because it occurs over a period of days—for example, a series of daily logins to the network.

In the case of a misuse-based IDS, you can install the database of attack signatures that is included with the software. Or, you can install your own custom rule base as well to account for new attacks or special situations that have caused the IDS to generate false-positives.

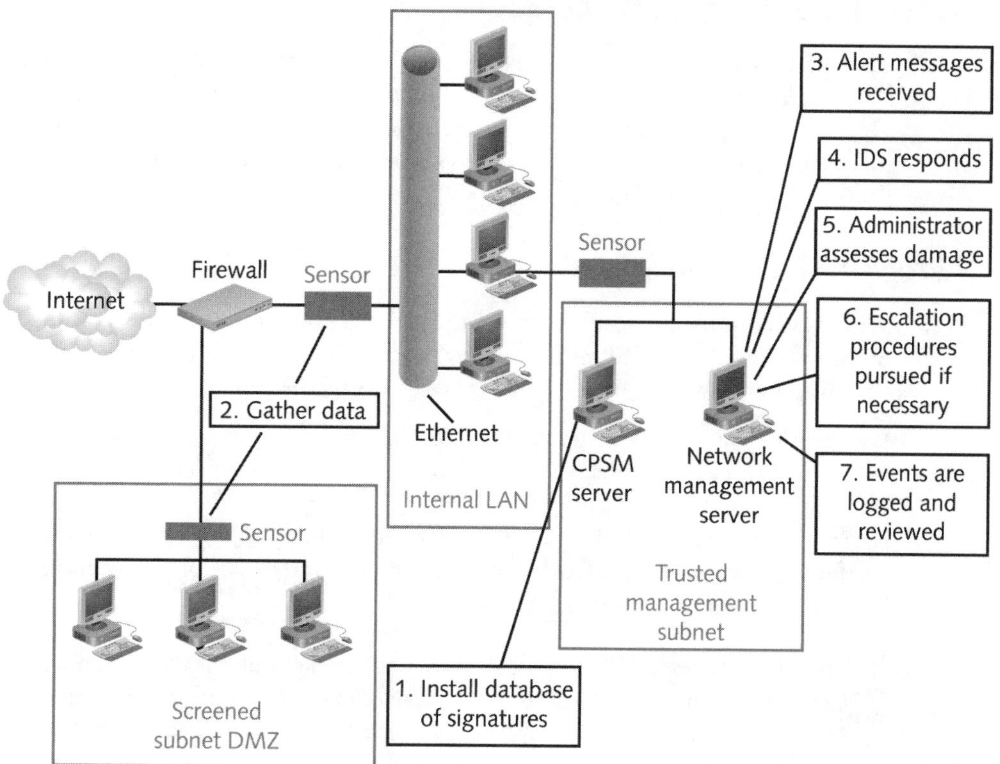

Figure 8-6 Steps involved in intrusion detection

Step 2: Gathering Data

After the IDS is installed and the database is in place, the network sensors can gather data by reading packets. Sensors that are installed on individual hosts observe packets as they enter and leave that host. Sensors that are placed on a particular network segment read packets as they pass into and out of each segment.

The sensors need to be positioned in locations where they will be able to capture all of the packets entering and leaving a host or network segment. Sensors that are placed on network segments do not always have the ability, if the traffic level becomes too heavy, to capture every packet. Repositioning the sensors on each network host will improve accuracy even though the expense of purchasing new sensors and the effort of installing them can be considerable. The important thing is to be able to capture all packets so that none can potentially circumvent the IDS.

Step 3: Sending Alert Messages

The sensor's detection software compares the packets it observes with the signatures of normal patterns of behavior stored in its database. An alert message is transmitted when a packet is observed that either matches an attack signature or deviates from normal network usage. The alert message goes to the command console of the IDS, where the network administrator can evaluate it.

Step 4: The IDS Responds

When the command console receives the alert message, it notifies the administrator in one of several ways that the administrator has configured beforehand. The console might display a pop-up window or send an e-mail message to the designated individual, for instance.

Besides the automated response sent to the command console, the IDS itself can be configured to take action at the same time that a suspicious packet is received and an alert message is sent. Typical actions are Alarm, in which an alarm is sent to the command console; Drop, in which the packet is dropped without an error message being sent to the originating computer; and Reset, which instructs the IDS to stop and restart network traffic and thus stop especially severe attacks.

The IDS stops TCP traffic by sending a TCP packet with the RST (Reset) flag set, which enables it to terminate a connection with one computer that is attempting to attack the system. Resetting TCP traffic does not affect UDP traffic, however.

Step 5: The Administrator Assesses Damage

An automated response sent by an IDS is like a call to action. It is the network administrator's responsibility to monitor such alerts and determine whether countermeasures need to be taken. When an IDS is first installed, many alerts that are actually false-positives might be received, depending on the accuracy of the information the IDS is working within its database. The administrator can anticipate having to "fine-tune" the database to account for situations that seem to the IDS to be intrusions but that are actually legitimate traffic.

In the case of an anomaly-based system, for example, an adjustment might be needed for an employee who logs on over the weekend instead of during the standard Monday through Friday workweek. In a misuse-based system, an adjustment might be made to enable traffic that might otherwise be seen by the firewall as suspicious, such as a vulnerability scan performed by a scanning device located at a particular IP address. The IDS could be configured to add a rule that changes the action performed by the IDS in response to traffic from that IP address from Alarm to Drop. The dividing line between acceptable and unacceptable use of the network is illustrated in Figure 8-7.

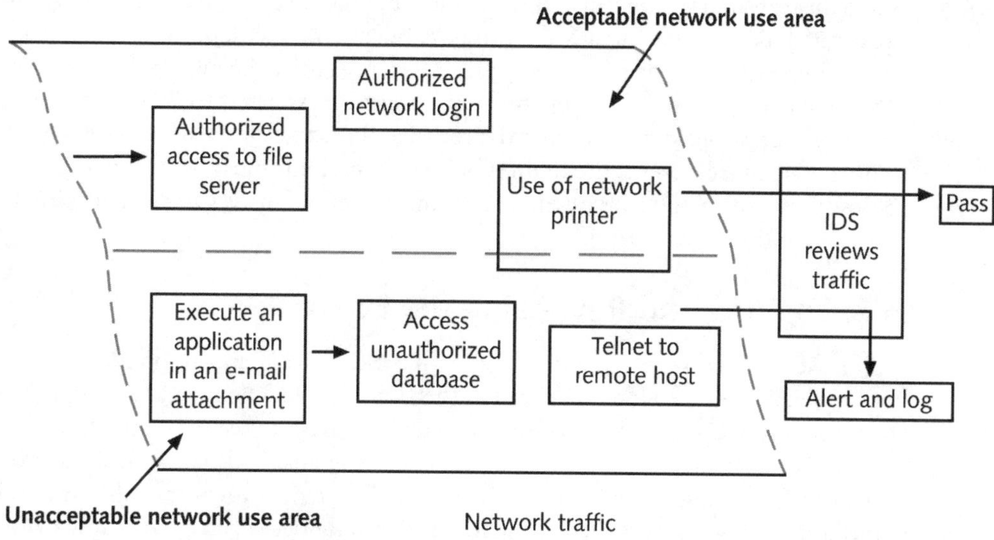

Figure 8-7 An IDS database needs to differentiate acceptable and unacceptable network usage

The line that divides acceptable from unacceptable network usage is not always clearly drawn. In Figure 8-7, for example, the box indicating the use of a network printer is shown going over the line because acceptable use of this resource depends on the purpose for which it is used. Printing office-related documents constitutes acceptable use, while printing personal photos and other personal materials probably falls onto the unacceptable side of the line.

The goal of adjusting the IDS database is not to avoid false-positives, since these will almost inevitably occur. False-positives do consume an administrator's time and energy, but they don't compromise the security of the network being protected. The goal, rather, is the avoidance of false-negatives—incidents that should cause an alarm to be sent to the command console, but do not. (These are in contrast to **true-negatives** —legitimate communications that do not set off an alarm.) False-negatives occur without anyone's knowledge and represent a potentially serious breach of security for the network. Although the individuals who configure the IDS may regard false-positives as nuisances, they are far better to have than false-negatives.

Step 6: Pursuing Escalation Procedures if Necessary

An escalation procedure is a predetermined set of procedures to be followed if a true-positive (legitimate attack) is detected by the IDS. As stated in Chapter 3, escalation procedures for security incidents should be spelled out in the organization's security policy. An escalation procedure outlines the steps that are to be taken if such a security incident occurs.

Incidents can be classified into different levels depending on how severe the threat is and how much damage has already occurred. A Level One incident might be managed quickly with only a single security professional, called a Security Analyst, being involved. A Level Two incident presents a higher threat and must be escalated to include involvement by a security professional with a higher degree of authority, called a Security Architect. A Level Three incident represents the highest degree of threat. It must be handled at once and must be escalated to include involvement by the Chief Security Officer and Chief Technical Officer for the organization.

Step 7: Logging and Reviewing the Event

After the IDS has sent an alert to the command console and responded as necessary, the event that caused the alert is entered in the IDS log file. The event can also be sent directly to a database file where it can be reviewed along with other previous alerts. Reviewing a number of alerts that are sent over a period of time enables the administrator to determine if patterns of misuse have been occurring. Such a review gives the administrator a way to view a slow attack such as a series of logins that only occur once every few days, or a series of **ping sweeps** (attempts to solicit a response from a series of IP addresses inside an internal network) that might, for example, take place once a week over a period of months.

An IDS should also provide **accountability** —the ability to track an attempted attack or intrusion back to the responsible party. Some systems have a built-in tracing feature that attempts to locate the IP address associated with an event. Although it isn't an intrusion detection system per se, Symantec Personal Firewall does give a user the ability to trace the source IP found in a log file entry. The user right-clicks the source IP address and chooses BackTrace from the context menu that appears (see Figure 8-8).

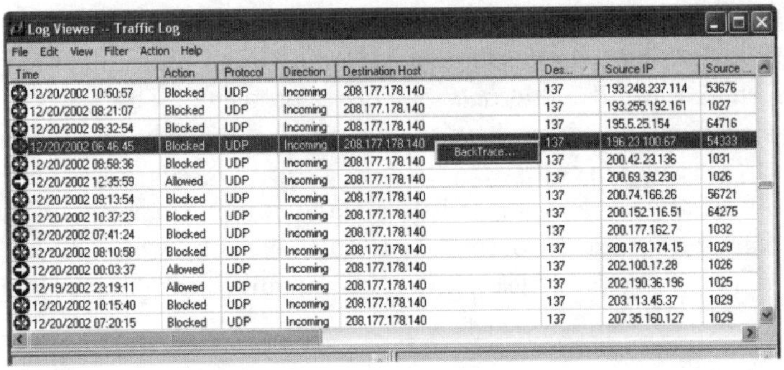

Log Viewer -- Traffic Log

File Edit View Filter Action Help

Time	Action	Protocol	Direction	Destination Host	Des...	Source IP	Source ...
12/20/2002 10:50:57	Blocked	UDP	Incoming	208.177.178.140	137	193.248.237.114	53676
12/20/2002 08:21:07	Blocked	UDP	Incoming	208.177.178.140	137	193.255.192.161	1027
12/20/2002 09:32:54	Blocked	UDP	Incoming	208.177.178.140	137	195.5.25.154	64716
12/20/2002 06:46:45	Blocked	UDP	Incoming	208.177.178.140 BackTrace...	137	196.23.100.67	54333
12/20/2002 08:58:36	Blocked	UDP	Incoming	208.177.178.140	137	200.42.23.136	1031
12/20/2002 12:35:59	Allowed	UDP	Incoming	208.177.178.140	137	200.69.39.230	1026
12/20/2002 09:13:54	Blocked	UDP	Incoming	208.177.178.140	137	200.74.166.26	56721
12/20/2002 10:37:23	Blocked	UDP	Incoming	208.177.178.140	137	200.152.116.51	64275
12/20/2002 07:41:24	Blocked	UDP	Incoming	208.177.178.140	137	200.177.162.7	1032
12/20/2002 08:10:58	Blocked	UDP	Incoming	208.177.178.140	137	200.178.174.15	1029
12/20/2002 00:03:37	Allowed	UDP	Incoming	208.177.178.140	137	202.100.17.28	1026
12/19/2002 23:19:11	Allowed	UDP	Incoming	208.177.178.140	137	202.190.36.196	1025
12/20/2002 10:15:40	Blocked	UDP	Incoming	208.177.178.140	137	203.113.45.37	1029
12/20/2002 07:20:15	Blocked	UDP	Incoming	208.177.178.140	137	207.35.160.127	1029

Figure 8-8 An IDS can trace an IP address

Notice that, in the log file shown in Figure 8-8, the IP address being traced is an anomaly: it differs dramatically from typical network traffic both in its IP address and its source port, which is in the upper reaches of the list of well-known port numbers. When the BackTrace option is chosen, a dialog box opens. It traces the address from the end user's computer back to its source (see Figure 8-9).

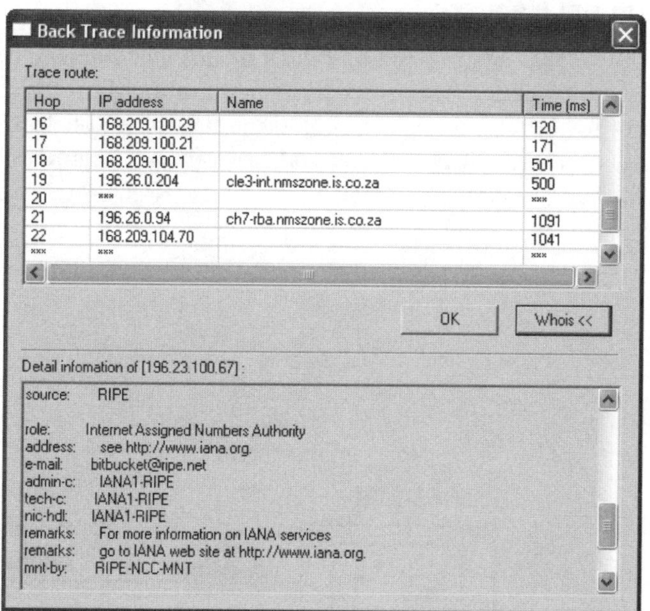

Figure 8-9 Tracing an IP address can assist with identification

It should be emphasized that the actual identification of the individual who used the source computer can be quite difficult, but a trace can at least provide a starting point for the identification of a hacker.

OPTIONS FOR IMPLEMENTING INTRUSION DETECTION SYSTEMS

The preceding sections described different types of intrusion detection systems by examining the ways in which they detect suspicious events and send alarms. In this section, you examine another way to describe intrusion detection systems: by their position on the network and how their position affects their activities. You examine network-based IDS, host-based IDS, and hybrid IDS systems.

Network-Based Intrusion Detection System (NIDS)

The following sections examine aspects of network-based intrusion detection systems (NIDS): locating them on the network; compiling known data about intruders; logging intrusion attempts; sending alert messages; and advantages and disadvantages of a NIDS configuration.

Locating the NIDS on the Network

A network-based IDS (NIDS) is a set of components that includes a command console and sensors positioned on the areas of the network where they can monitor network traffic. Three common locations for NIDS sensors are behind the firewall and before the LAN, between the firewall and the DMZ, or on any network segment (see Figure 8-10).

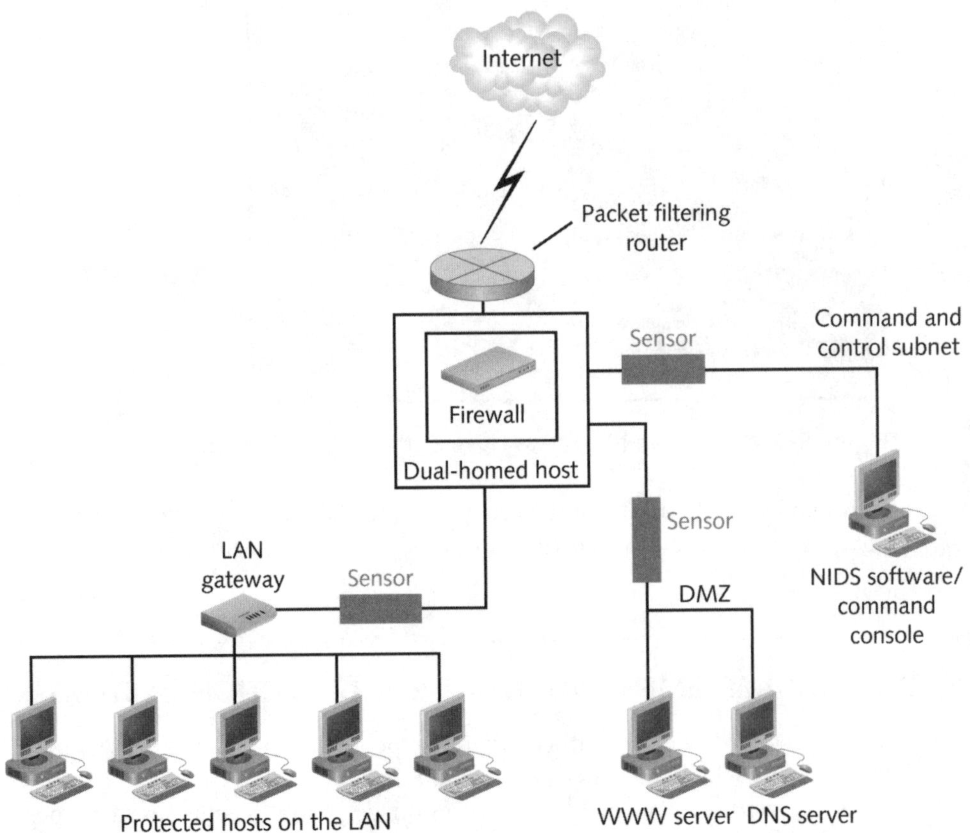

Figure 8-10 A network-based IDS monitors traffic either behind the firewall or in the DMZ

A network-based IDS typically has its primary management and analysis software installed on a **dedicated computer** (a computer that is dedicated solely to running intrusion detection software and logging traffic). The position of the sensors at the perimeter of the network is ideal for enabling the IDS to **sniff** packets—in other words, to receive and analyze packets as they pass into the network. Each IDS sensor is also equipped with its own network interface card, which gives it the ability to sniff packets in **promiscuous mode** , in which each packet is detected and analyzed in its entirety.

A network-based IDS can detect packets and transmit alerts in one of two ways. The traditional network-based configuration shown in Figure 8-1 requires the IDS host to detect the packet en route from the source to the destination computer. The following steps then occur:

1. Packets are processed in real-time by the IDS software's detection engine.
2. If necessary, an alert message is sent to the GUI command console in the LAN.
3. The command console sends a notification to the network administrator.
4. The alert message is logged and stored.
5. Analysis is performed, and countermeasures are taken to prevent future intrusions.

The other type of network-based IDS incorporates a distributed rather than a traditional design. In a distributed NIDS, the individual sensors perform the analysis of packets they monitor, and they only send alert messages to the command console.

Advantages and Disadvantages of NIDS

NIDS configurations need to be able to keep up with a large volume of network traffic because of their position. They are located at a point where all inbound traffic that has passed through the firewall passes through it. They need to be able to respond quickly to suspicious packets so network administrators can respond and prevent possible damage to files. A dedicated hardware appliance IDS makes an excellent choice in this situation.

Host-Based Intrusion Detection Systems (HIDS)

In contrast to a network-based IDS, which is positioned in a single location on the network perimeter, a **host-based intrusion detection system (HIDS)** is deployed on each host in the LAN that is protected by the firewall. Packets generated by the host itself are monitored and evaluated by the IDS. The data is gathered from operating system and application logs on the host. The host-based IDS gathers system variables such as:

- System processes
- CPU usage
- File accesses

System events that match the signatures of known attacks reach the IDS on the host computer, which sends an alert notice to the end-user or network administrator. A host-based IDS doesn't sniff packets as they enter the LAN. Rather, it monitors log file entries and user activity, and is highly effective at tracking misuse of resources by internal users.

Configuring the Host-Based IDS

A host-based IDS can have two configurations: centralized or distributed. In a centralized configuration, the host-based IDS sends all data that is gathered to a central location (the command console) for analysis. In a distributed configuration, the data analysis is distributed among the individual hosts; each analyzes the data itself and sends only alert messages to the command console.

In a centralized design, the level of performance of the host is unaffected by the IDS. However, because data is sent to the command console, where it must be analyzed, any alert messages that are generated will not occur in real time. The detection process in a centralized configuration is shown in Figure 8-11.

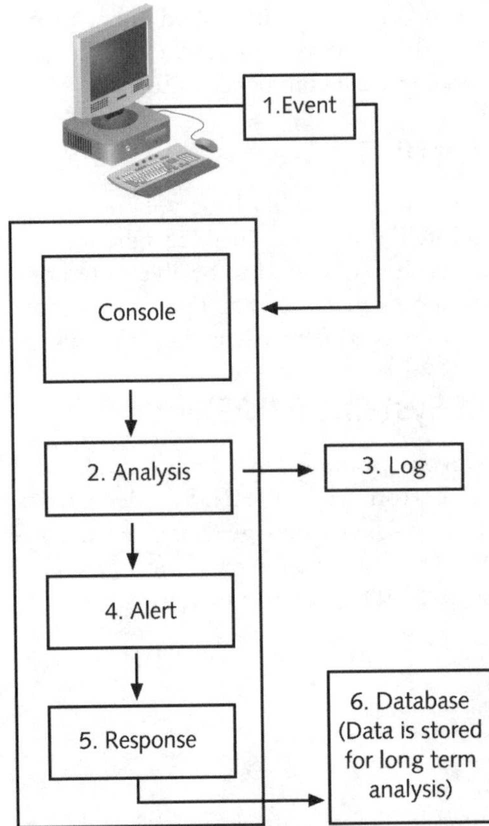

Figure 8-11 A centralized host-based IDS

As illustrated in Figure 8-11, the process is as follows:

1. The event is generated on the host.
2. The data gathered by the IDS sensor (a software program running on the host) is transmitted to the command console, where the analysis is performed.

3. A log file entry is created.
4. If necessary, an alert is generated.
5. The IDS responds.
6. Finally, the data is stored in a database where long-term analysis can be performed.

In a distributed host-based IDS configuration, the processing of event data is distributed between host and command console. The host generates the data and analyzes it in real time. As a result, the analysis can be performed without a delay, but the tradeoff is a reduction in performance on the host computer. The host processes all data, whether alerts are required or not. Data is then transmitted to the command console in the form of alert messages, as shown in Figure 8-12.

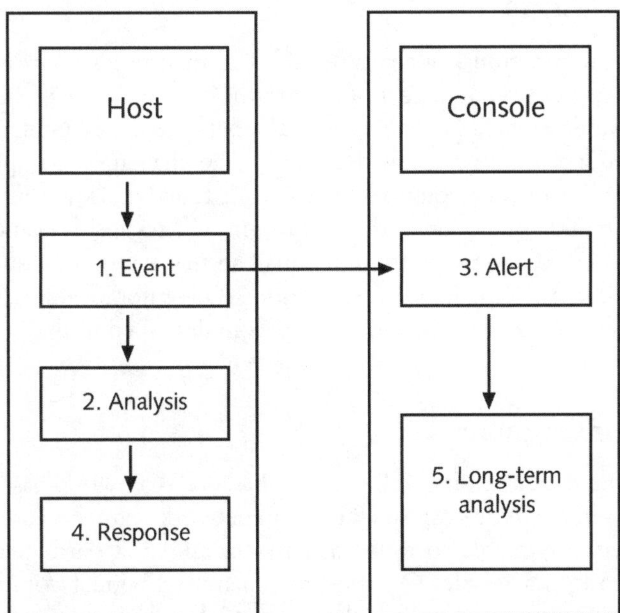

Figure 8-12 Processing event data from a host-based IDS

Choosing the Host Computer

The available RAM and hard disk memory and processor speed of the host computer depends on the type of host-based IDS that is used. In a centralized configuration, the processing is performed on the command console, so the performance requirement placed on the host in terms of IDS is minimal. However, in a distributed configuration, the host is called upon not only to gather intrusion data, but also to analyze it in real time, so the host should be equipped with the maximum memory and processor speed available. Check the IDS system requirements for recommended configurations.

Advantages and Disadvantages of HIDS

A host-based IDS can tell you whether an attack attempt on the host was actually successful. Network-based IDS provides alerts on suspicious network activity, but it doesn't tell you whether an attack attempt actually reached the targeted host and whether an intrusion actually occurred.

On the other hand, a host-based IDS only provides you with data pertaining to the host on which it has been installed and not the network as a whole. A host-based IDS can't detect an intrusion attempt that targets the entire network, such as a port scan on a range of computers in succession. If you use a host-based IDS, you need to install the IDS on every host on the network, which takes time and can be more expensive than a network-based IDS.

Hybrid IDS Implementations

A hybrid IDS combines the functionality available to more than one system in order to gain flexibility and increase security. The goal of a hybrid IDS is to achieve a higher level of security and greater flexibility than a single host-based or network-based implementation, each of which has its own advantages and disadvantages. The challenge in implementing a hybrid system is getting the various components to work together. The ultimate goals are to achieve effective intrusion detection with a minimum of false-positives and no false-negatives, and to quickly alert the appropriate individuals so that countermeasures can be taken. Varieties of hybrid IDS implementations—combined IDS sensor locations, combined IDS detection methods, shim IDS, and distributed IDS—are described in the sections that follow.

Combining IDS Sensor Locations

One type of IDS hybrid implementation combines host-based and network-based systems. The combination enables sensors to be positioned both on network segments and individual hosts. As a result, the network is able to report on attacks aimed at particular network segments or to the network as a whole. On the other hand, individual computers that contain particularly sensitive information, such as databases of job records or income-expense records, can each be protected with a host-based IDS. Having an IDS on the host (especially one that performs distributed host-based IDS) can analyze the data in real time and send an alert that notifies the administrator of a possible unauthorized access attempt at a critical resource that is immediately identifiable.

Combining IDS Detection Methods

Another IDS hybrid results from the combined use of anomaly and misuse detection. The combination helps overcome the limitations of each detection method:

- Having a database of known attack signatures in place enables the system to get up and running immediately, and effectively repels most well-known external attack methods.

- Having an anomaly-based system in place keeps the alert system flexible and able to detect internal misuse that deviates from normal usage patterns.

A hybrid IDS that combines anomaly with misuse detection can respond to the latest, previously unreported attacks. It has the capability to respond to attacks from both external and internal sources.

A drawback is that the administrator has more configuration and coordination work to do. The data from multiple sources must be collected in a location from which it can quickly be reviewed and analyzed.

Shim IDS

A **shim IDS** is a type of network-based IDS, because it involves sensors being distributed around a network and data collected from those sensors and sent to a centralized command console. However, the sensors are installed in selected hosts as well as network segments. Unlike a host-based IDS, the sensors would not have to be installed on every host in the network. They need only be installed on hosts that require special protection, such as databases that hold proprietary product information for a company.

Distributed IDS

Quick response is enhanced by a Distributed Intrusion Detection System (DID), in which multiple intrusion detection devices are deployed on a network to monitor traffic and report suspicious events. By using multiple IDSs rather than a single IDS, patterns develop that enable administrators to distinguish between harmless anomalies and genuine attacks. Two popular DID systems are myNetWatchman (*www.mynetwatchman.com*) and Dshield (*www.dshield.org*). The DShield Web site (shown in Figure 8-13) tracks attacks from all over the globe and gathers data voluntarily submitted by Internet users. The more data that is assembled, the more accurate the patterns that develop. DShield will notify you if the log files you submit contain patterns of intrusion so that you can configure the software to block the intruder.

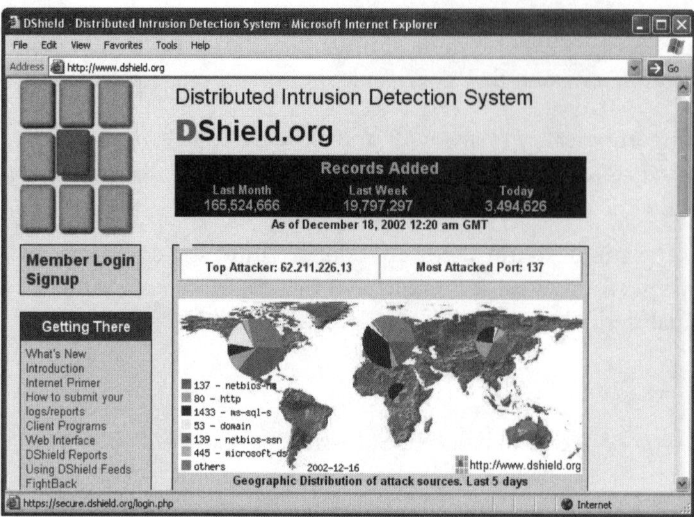

Figure 8-13 DShield provides a DIDS

Advantages and Disadvantages of Hybrid IDSs

Hybrid intrusion detection systems have the great advantage of being able to combine aspects of both network-based and host-based configurations. You are able to monitor the network as a whole with network-based sensors, and to monitor attacks that reach individual computers with host-based sensors. The drawback of a hybrid arrangement is the need to get disparate systems to work in a coordinated fashion. The data gathered from multiple systems can also be difficult to absorb and analyze easily.

EVALUATING INTRUSION DETECTION SYSTEMS

You should select an intrusion detection system (IDS) only after surveying the kinds of products that are available and matching them to your needs. Most enterprise-level IDS packages consist of multiple hardware or software components, and many cost thousands of dollars depending on the number of users.

To make an informed decision, your first step is to review the topology of your own network, paying particular attention to those parts of the network that would have direct interaction with the IDS, such as:

- The number of entry points into the network, including dial-in and VPN connections
- The use of firewalls on the network
- Whether your network consists of a single segment or is divided into separate segments, each with a distinct purpose within the organization

Evaluating IDS systems can be a time-consuming process. Many packages are not available in trial versions you can simply download and install. Some are hardware appliances that do not carry a "try before you buy" policy. The following sections aren't meant to be comprehensive, but they give you an overview of the kinds of IDS from which you can choose: freeware programs; commercial host-based programs; anomaly-based systems; network-based packages; IDS hardware appliances; and signature-based IDS. The text highlights one product per category.

Freeware Network-Based IDS: Snort

Snort (*www.snort.org*), a freeware IDS created by Martin Roesch and Brian Caswell, is a small-scale program that does not consume extensive system resources and that is ideal for monitoring traffic on a small network or an individual host. Snort is intended for installation on a computer that is positioned at the perimeter of a network. It can also function on a dedicated computer on a home or small business network.

Snort comes with a collection of rule files that are customized for individual types of network traffic and that are activated in the overall configuration file snort.conf. Separate rules exist for port scans, backdoor attacks, Web attacks, and many other kinds of potential intrusions. The rule files are text-based; you open the rule files in a text editor, and review and edit them to conform to your own network. For example, the preset rules for access attempts on the NetBIOS port 139 are shown in Figure 8-14.

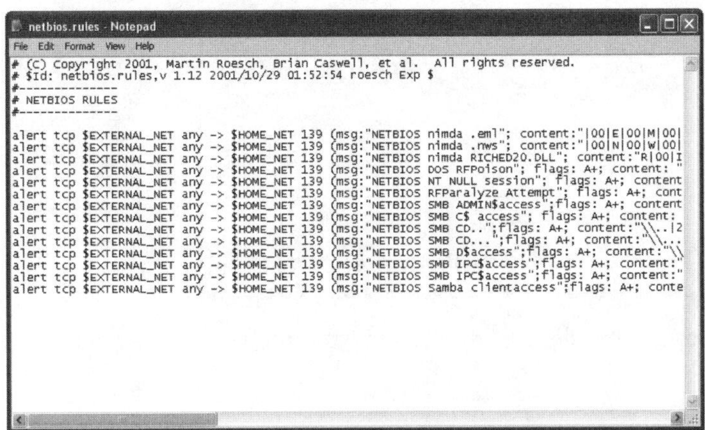

Figure 8-14 Snort comes with an extensive set of preconfigured rules

The configuration files are easy to edit and can be customized to fit a variety of other events. In addition, other configuration files contain variables that enable you to protect the SMTP, HTTP and SQL servers on your network, which can otherwise cause false alarms due to the amount of traffic that passes through them. A variety of GUI interfaces for Snort is also available. These GUIs include IDS Center or SnortSnarf.

8

Hands-On Project 2-4 describes how to install Snort, and Hands-On Project 2-5 describes the configuration of a GUI interface for Snort.

Commercial Host-Based IDS: Norton Internet Security

Norton Internet Security by Symantec Corp. is a personal firewall program designed to protect a home-based standalone computer or a computer on a small network. However, the program also contains a limited number of intrusion detection features. These features are specifically designed to block port scans as well as attack attempts on ports used by known Trojan horse programs. If an attack is detected, a feature called AutoBlock (the setup of which is shown in Figure 8-15) stops communications from the hacker to your computer for thirty seconds. In those thirty seconds, the hacker is likely to switch to another computer to attempt an attack. If the hacker attempts the same attack to your computer, communications will be blocked again.

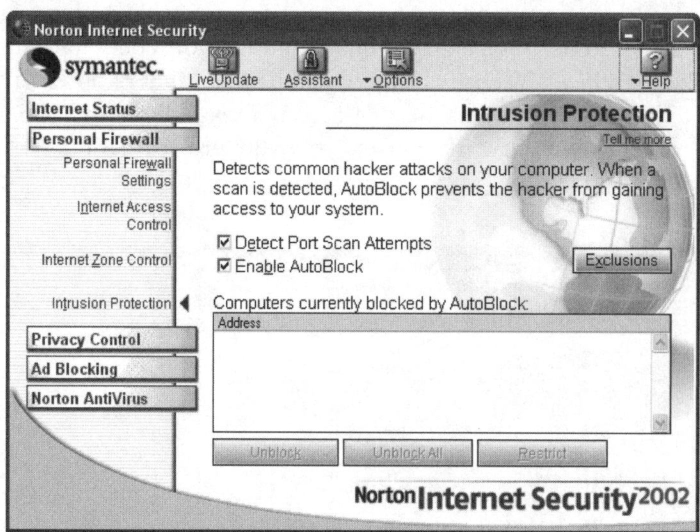

Figure 8-15 Personal firewall programs such as Norton Internet Security include intrusion detection features

Norton Internet Security, like other personal firewall programs, has the ability to "learn" what constitutes "normal" network usage and what is a deviation from that usage. It gives the user the ability to establish rules that block communications that deviate from normal usage. Pop-up alert messages appear when traffic is encountered that represents a possible intrusion. However, the program lacks the ability to set up user profiles and does not make use of a set of attack signatures other than the port scans and Trojan horse attacks mentioned earlier.

Anomaly-Based IDS: Tripwire

Tripwire, which was originally developed in 1992 at Purdue University, has long been one of the most highly regarded software IDS packages. The latest version of the program, Tripwire for Network Devices by Tripwire Inc. (*www.tripwire.com*) uses anomaly-based intrusion detection. It first establishes a baseline for normal network usage. After the baseline is established, any change in the configuration, such as a new file placed on a system or a user who accesses a server for the first time, triggers an alert message.

The software is excellent for situations in which employee activity needs to be closely monitored. Tripwire maintains a log file detailing every interaction that every user has had with network resources. In addition, any new files that have been placed on network resources since the last "good" configuration was established are noted, which enables administrators to quickly detect whether viruses or worms have been active.

Network-Based IDS: RealSecure

RealSecure by Internet Security Systems, Inc. (*www.iss.net*) is one of the most comprehensive and widely used IDS products on the market. RealSecure makes use of a distributed client-server architecture. It can implement with one or more RealSecure Network Sensor products to scan traffic on a network. In addition, OS and server sensors can monitor traffic to and from the host in order to detect any unauthorized activity. Together, the available sensors enable RealSecure to function as a hybrid IDS.

RealSecure also includes a command console called the Workgroup Manager that provides a secure channel of communications to the installed sensors. The console enables the network administrator to perform alert monitoring while making use of a database with more than two thousand known attack signatures.

IDS Hardware Appliances

IDS hardware appliances, like firewall hardware appliances, have a greater ability to handle network traffic and more scalability than software IDS packages. Plug-and-play capability counts as one of the biggest advantage of IDS hardware options. A hardware device does not have to be configured to work with a particular operating system, and does not suffer from any vulnerabilities that might be present on that operating system. Hardware IDS devices are becoming more and more common; the following are just a few examples:

- Minesweeper by Barbedwires Technologies (*www.barbedwires.com/products/ms.htm*)
- Intrusion SecureNet by Intrusion Inc. (*www.intrusion.com*)
- StealthWatch G1 by Lancope (*www.lancope.com*)

IDS hardware manufacturers sometimes claim that they only need to be plugged in to a network to begin protecting it. However, you should take the time to create a custom configuration, which prevents false-positives and blocks new attacks as they are created. In addition, hardware devices, like software programs, need to be updated periodically to remain effective. Updating the operating system and/or IDS software within the appliance is a relatively simple matter. Updating the appliance itself to keep up with a growing network can be an expensive proposition, so it pays to buy a more powerful device than you think you'll need initially.

Signature-Based IDS: Cisco Secure IDS

Cisco Secure IDS draws on a database of attack signatures to detect intrusion attempts. This network-based IDS makes use of sensors (hardware devices with their own processor, memory, and network interface cards) that are positioned around a network and that monitor traffic. Alarms are sent to one of two command consoles: the Cisco Secure Policy Manager or the Cisco Secure IDS Director for UNIX.

Signatures form the basis of Cisco Secure IDS Director, and the signatures that are available to the system are broken into various types of network traffic: IP signatures, ICMP signatures, TCP signatures, UDP signatures, Web/HTTP signatures, string-matching signatures, and so on. The system doesn't just compare traffic to its database of signatures, however. It also watches for patterns of attacks as it monitors network traffic. In addition to monitoring traffic, the sensors can be configured with rules that block all communications from untrusted IP addresses.

Chapter Summary

- This chapter presented you with an overview of intrusion detection systems (IDSs), which provide a supplementary line of defense behind firewalls and anti-virus software. You learned that, unlike a burglar alarm, some intrusion detection systems go a step beyond simply transmitting alarms. They can also reset TCP communications and block selected IP addresses, as well as provide evidence used in disciplinary actions or to prevent future attacks.
- The text examined the components of an IDS. Although some systems consist of software programs and others combine hardware devices, they all use similar elements. A network sensor should be placed at the openings to the network and individual network segments. An alert message is sent from a trigger, which can result from anomaly detection or misuse detection, or a combination of both. The alert message is sent to a command console, which provides the administrator with a single interface to the data gathered by the IDS. A response system built into the IDS instructs it to drop packets or reset traffic if attacks are detected. In order to remain accurate and avoid false-positives (false alarms) the database of signatures or user profiles used by the IDS must remain current.
- The text then discussed the process of intrusion detection step-by-step. The process begins with the installation of a set of attack signatures (if misuse detection is used) or normal network usage profiles (if anomaly detection is used). Next, the sensors monitor packets. Alert messages are sent when a packet matches an attack signature or deviates from normal network usage. An alert message is transmitted to the command console. In addition, the IDS can also respond by dropping the packets or resetting a connection. False-positives are highly likely and will require the administrator to fine-tune the system

to allow legitimate traffic to pass through without an alarm. If the intrusion is found to be a legitimate attack, escalation procedures should be pursued if necessary. The IDS also logs each alarmed event so it can be reviewed later on. Exporting the data to a database for analysis can reveal attacks that take place over a long period of time or that involve multiple events.

- After the step-by-step examination, the text discussed different ways in which an IDS can be implemented. A network-based intrusion detection system (NIDS) makes use of sensors positioned around the perimeter of the network or of network segments. A host-based intrusion detection system (HIDS) uses sensors that are deployed on each host on the LAN that needs to be protected. A HIDS uses data generated by each host. A hybrid IDS combines aspects of network-based or host-based IDS implementations. It can also combine anomaly-based and misuse-based detection. A shim IDS makes use of sensors installed both on network segments and on individual hosts. A distributed IDS collects data gathered from multiple intrusion detection systems and firewall logs in order to analyze data across a wide area.
- In the final section of the chapter, the text examined different types of intrusion detection systems you can install yourself. Only a handful of freeware or shareware IDS systems exist; the best-known is a program called Snort that makes use of a set of predetermined rules and that is designed to monitor traffic on a small-scale network. Commercial firewall programs such as Norton Internet Security include limited sets of IDS features. Anomaly-based systems like the highly regarded Tripwire for Network Devices establish a baseline for normal network usage. RealSecure is a network-based IDS that makes use of one or more network sensors and a command console. Hardware appliances can handle a higher traffic load than software programs and offer plug-and-play functionality. The Cisco Secure IDS system draws on a database of attack signatures but also monitors suspicious traffic patterns, much like a firewall.

Key Terms

accountability — The ability to track an attempted attack or intrusion back to the responsible party.

anomaly detection — A type of intrusion detection that causes an alarm to be sent when an IDS detects an event that deviates from behavior that has been defined as "normal."

command console — Software that provides a network administrator with a graphical front-end interface to an intrusion detection system.

dedicated computer — A computer that is dedicated solely to running intrusion detection software and logging traffic.

escalated — A term used to describe what happens when the response to an intrusion is increased to a higher level.

event horizon — The entire length of an attack, from the first packet received by an IDS to the last packet that is needed to complete the attack signature.

false-negatives — Attacks that occur but that are not detected by the IDS.

false-positives — Alarms that are generated by legitimate network traffic rather than attacks.

host-based intrusion detection system (HIDS) — An IDS that is deployed on each host in the LAN that is protected by the firewall.

intrusion — An attempt to gain unauthorized access to network resources and compromise the integrity and confidentiality of the data contained on the network or the privacy of its users.

intrusion detection — The process of monitoring network traffic in order to detect attempts to gain unauthorized access to a system or resource and notify the appropriate professionals so that countermeasures can be taken.

misuse detection — A type of intrusion detection in which an IDS is configured to send an alarm in response to sets of characteristics that match known examples of attacks.

ping sweeps — Attempts to solicit a response from a series of IP addresses inside an internal network.

profile-based detection — A type of intrusion detection that compares current network traffic to a profile of normal network usage.

profiles — Sets of characteristics that describe the services and resources a user normally accesses on the network.

promiscuous mode — A mode of operation in which an IDS or packet sniffer detects and analyzes each packet in its entirety.

shim IDS — A type of network-based IDS in which sensors are installed on selected hosts as well as network segments.

signatures — Sets of characteristics that match known examples of attacks.

sniff — The process of receiving and analyzing packets as they pass into and out of the network, as performed either by a packet sniffing program, a network traffic analyzer, or an IDS.

state information — Information that pertains to a network connection, which is typically kept in a state table.

trigger — A set of circumstances that causes an IDS to send an alert message.

true-negatives — Legitimate communications that do not cause the IDS to set off an alarm.

true-positive — A genuine attack detected successfully by an IDS, in contrast to a true-negative (an attack that goes undetected) or a false-positive (an attack alert generated by an event that is not an attack).

Review Questions

1. How can the data gained as a result of intrusion detection be used to improve network security? (Choose all that apply.)

    a. It can be used to prevent future attacks.

    b. It can be used to route traffic more efficiently.

    c. It can be used to shield IP addresses on the LAN.

    d. It can help determine how to respond to security incidents.

2. Name the three core activities associated with intrusion detection.

3. Which of the following are examples of multiple-session attacks? (Choose all that apply.)

    a. fragmented packets

    b. IP address spoofing

    c. port scans

    d. network scans

4. Network sensors should be positioned at what points on the network?

    a. external or internal interfaces

    b. points of entry

    c. before the firewall

    d. between the DMZ and the LAN

5. The more advanced network sensors have the ability to perform what advanced security functions?

    a. monitoring inbound and outbound traffic

    b. maintaining state information

    c. resetting TCP traffic

    d. updating access control lists

6. Anomaly-based detection makes use of what aspect of network traffic?

   a profiles

   b signatures

   c state tables

   d access control lists

7. On what feature of network traffic is misuse detection based?

   a. profiles

   b. normal traffic

   c. signatures

   d. user accounts

8. Which of the following is a way in which an anomaly-based IDS can be circumvented?

   a. new attacks

   b. changes in user habits

   c. changes in published signatures

   d. minor changes in attack methods that don't match known signatures

9. Which of the following is a way in which a misuse detection IDS can be circumvented?

   a. changes in attack methods

   b. a stolen user account

   c. making traffic appear normal

   d. attacks made during the training period of the IDS

10. Which intrusion detection approach can go online and begin protecting a network immediately after installation?

11. Which intrusion detection approach is virtually impossible for a hacker to test before attempting an attack?

12. Which activity performed by an IDS could detect a Denial of Service attack?

    a. protocol state tracking

    b. misuse detection

    c. traffic rate monitoring

    d. IP packet reassembly

13. What IDS component enables administrators to consolidate and track a large volume of events?

    a. log file analyzer

    b. database

    c. response system

    d. command console

14. Which of the following is the event with the most serious security implications?

    a. true-positive

    b. true-negative

    c. false-positive

    d. false-negative

15. Which of the following is a characteristic of a firewall rule base that is not shared by an IDS database? (Choose all that apply.)

    a. It can be custom-configured by an administrator.

    b. It should be as short and simple as possible.

    c. It starts out by blocking all traffic by default, and ends with a cleanup rule.

    d. It needs to be updated regularly.

16. Which of the following is a common location for a network sensor? (Choose all that apply.)

    a. on a network segment

    b. between a firewall and the Internet

    c. on all hosts in a LAN

    d. on both interfaces (external and internal) of a firewall

17. Which of the following is a common set of actions performed by the IDS in response to a possible attack, in the order in which they occur?

    a. Alarm, Drop, Reset

    b. Deny, Alarm, Reset

    c. Allow, Reset, Alarm

    d. Alarm, Log, Drop

18. Which of the following is almost inevitable and should be expected after an IDS is installed? (Choose all that apply.)
    a false-negatives
    b. huge log files
    c. signatures that become outdated
    d. false-positives

19. What is the value of reviewing an IDS log file, especially since you may already have a firewall log file and system log files to review?
    a. You can identify events that occur too quickly for the sensor to detect.
    b. You can identify attacks that occur over a long period of time.
    c. You can identify ranges of IP addresses that are vulnerable.
    d. You can trace IP addresses that are trying to gain unauthorized access.

20. A device that detects and analyzes each packet in its entirety is said to operate in which mode?
    a. network-based
    b. host-based
    c. promiscuous
    d. real-time

HANDS-ON PROJECTS

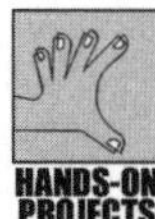

Project 8-1: Designing an IDS

Before you actually install and configure an IDS, you will probably be asked to prepare a report explaining what an IDS is and how to create one for your network. In this project you will prepare such a report. You can use any computer that is connected to the Internet to complete this project. You'll also need a word processing file or lab notebook in which to record data.

1. Describe your lab network. List the number of computers and break them into operating systems. (If you do not have access to a lab network, assume that you are working in a lab that has ten computers, eight running Windows 2000 and two running Red Hat Linux 8.0.)
2. Draw a topology map of your network.
3. List the components needed to create an IDS.

4. Position a network-based IDS in a distributed configuration in your topology map.
5. Map out the IDS process in steps that include the following:
   a. Packet detected
   b. Detection engine processes packet
   c. Alert transmitted
   d. Notification sent
   e. Alert logged
   f. Analysis and countermeasures performed

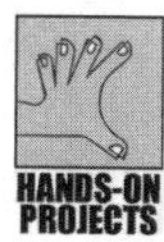

Project 8-2: Using Distributed IDS Attack Information

DShield is an organization that gathers log files from users around the world and prepares reports that those users can analyze in order to determine if their networks have encountered intrusion attempts. You can view the reports on the DShield site and apply them to your own firewall or IDS.

1. Double-click the **Internet Explorer** icon on your desktop.
2. Enter the URL for the DShield – Reports page in your Address box (**http://www.dshield.org/reports.html**), and then press **Enter**.
3. Click the **Top 10 Ports** link. The DShield – Top 10 Target Ports Web page appears.
4. Make a list of the most frequently targeted ports. (Does the list include port 137? At the time this was written, port 137 was number 1 on the list.)
5. Determine whether your computer currently has connections open on UDP port number 137 with computers that are outside your network. You have two options for determining open ports:
   a. Some firewall programs will tell you what ports are currently open. The firewall log files will tell you whether any computers have attempted to connect to UDP port 137 today. If you installed ZoneAlarm as described in Chapter 4, click **Alerts & Logs**, click **Log Viewer**, and then click the **Destination IP** column heading to sort destination IP addresses by port number.
   b. Click **Start**, point to **Programs** (**All Programs** in Windows XP), point to **Accessories**, and click **Command Prompt**. At the command prompt, enter **netstat –a** and press **Enter**. A list of open network connections should appear.

6. Note how many connections have been on destination port 137, which is used for NetBIOS traffic. How many of these are computers in your own domain? How many are not? Write down the IP addresses of any computers that are outside your domain.
7. Enter the following URL in your browser's Address box (**www.dshield.org/ipinfo.php**) to connect to the DShield IP Address page. Enter the IP address you wrote down in Step 6 in the Check another IP address box, and then click **Submit**. Where is the remote computer located?

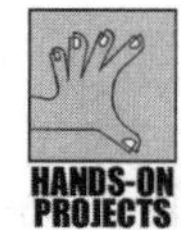

Project 8-3: Installing Distributed IDS Software

You can configure your existing firewall program to automatically submit log files to the DShield Web site. In this project, you will download and install software that works with existing firewall log files to submit log data to DShield. This project assumes that you are working on a Windows XP computer and that you have a file archiving utility such as WinZip installed. The steps that follow show how to configure software to submit logs compiled by Internet Connection Firewall (ICF), the installation of which is described in Hands-On Project 5-1.

1. Double-click the **Internet Explorer** icon on your desktop.
2. Enter the URL for the DShield – Windows Clients page in your browser's Address box: **http://www.dshield.org/windows_clients.html**. Then press **Enter**.
3. Scroll down the page and click the highlighted link **CVTWIN-SETUP.EXE**.
4. When the File Download dialog box appears, click **Save** and save the file to a location on your hard disk.
5. When download is complete, double-click the file **cvtwin-setup.exe** that you just downloaded.
6. When the DShield CVTWIN Install Files Self-Extractor dialog box appears, click **OK**.
7. If you used WinZip and a WinZip Self-Extractor dialog box appears, click **Setup**.
8. When the DShield Universal Firewall Client Setup dialog box appears, click **OK**.
9. In the next dialog box, select an installation location if necessary. Then click the computer icon button to begin setup.
10. Click **Continue** when prompted to choose a program group.
11. Click **OK** when a dialog box appears telling you that installation is complete.
12. Make sure Internet Connection Firewall is configured to create log files. Click **Start** and click **Control Panel**, then double-click **Network Connections**.

13. Right-click the icon for your Internet connection and then click **Properties**.
14. Click the **Advanced** tab.
15. Verify that the box beneath Internet Connection Firewall is clicked, and then click **Settings**.
16. Click the **Security Logging** tab, and then check the **Log dropped packets** checkbox, if necessary. Write down the location of your log file (for example, C:\WINDOWS\pfirewall.log). Then click **OK** to close Advanced Settings and **OK** to close the Properties dialog box for your Internet connection.
17. Start the CVTWIN client either by clicking **Start**, pointing to **Programs** (**All Programs** on Windows XP), clicking **DShield**, and clicking **DShield Universal Firewall Client**, or by double-clicking the program's icon in the directory where you installed it.
18. When the Dshield Universal Firewall Client program window appears, click **Edit** and click **Configure**.
19. Enter your e-mail address, your SMTP e-mail server name, and the other information required in the Configure dialog box. Be sure to choose your firewall name from the Firewall drop-down list; for this example, choose **Windows XP ICF**. Also be sure to locate the log file for Internet Connection Firewall, which you wrote down in Step 16.
20. Click **OK**. Then click **Edit** and click **Edit Source IP Filters**. The text file SourceIP.flt opens.
21. At the bottom of the list of IP addresses to exclude, enter the IP address of your own computer and any others you want the log files to ignore. Click the close box to close the text file, then click **Yes** when prompted.
22. Click **Edit** and click **Edit Target IP Filters**. In the text file that appears, enter the IP addresses of any destination computers you want the log files to ignore. Click the close box, and then click **Yes**.
23. Click **File** and then click **Convert** from the Dshield Universal Firewall Client menu bar. A set of conversion data appears in the program window.
24. Click **File**, then click **e-mail test to [your e-mail address]** to send yourself a test log file. Open the e-mail message: were any connections reported from possible intruders? Write the answer in a word processing document or lab notebook. (In order for the "e-mail test to" menu option to be available, Dshield Universal Firewall Client must have actually converted some log file data. If you had no log file data to convert, make sure Internet Connection Firewall is operating and logging data as described in Project 8-2. If it is running, your date format may be incorrect. Click **Help** and then click **Troubleshooting** from the Dshield Universal Firewall Client to troubleshoot the date conversion problem.)

25. Click **File**, then click **e-mail to report@dshield.org** to send your log file to DShield. (If the e-mail to option is not available, troubleshoot as described in Step 24.)

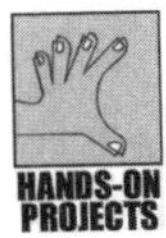

Project 8-4: Analyzing User Behavior Anomalies

Anomaly-based intrusion detection puts a burden on a network administrator to determine whether an anomaly deviates from "normal" behavior severely enough to warrant investigation. Consider the user profile in Table 8-2. The profile was created by an anomaly-based IDS system:

Table 8-2 User profile analysis

User	Behavior	Date	Time
Bob	Network Login	M-F	8:00 a.m. – 9:00 a.m.
	Login to E-mail Account	M-F	8:30 a.m. – 5:00 p.m.
	Login to File Server	M-F	8:30 a.m. – 5:00 p.m.

1. Describe how you would respond upon receiving an alert notifying you that Bob logged in at 2 p.m. on a Friday and logged off at 7 p.m.
2. Describe two possible causes (one legitimate, one suspicious) for such a series of events: You receive an alert stating that Bob had logged on at 2 a.m. on a Tuesday morning and logged off at 7 a.m., then logged on again at 8:30 a.m. and logged off at 5 p.m.
3. Describe a suitable response to the discovery that the scenario described in Step 2 was repeated every day during the previous week.
4. Explain how you could determine whether or not Bob was actually logging on at 2 a.m.

Project 8-5: Analyzing a Suspicious Signature

An IDS that depends on a database of known attack signatures is vulnerable to attacks that aren't already included in its database. Systems that enable the administrator to create custom rules depend on the administrator to analyze attack signature.

1. Observe the data in Figure 8-16. In particular, note the destination IP addresses and ports.

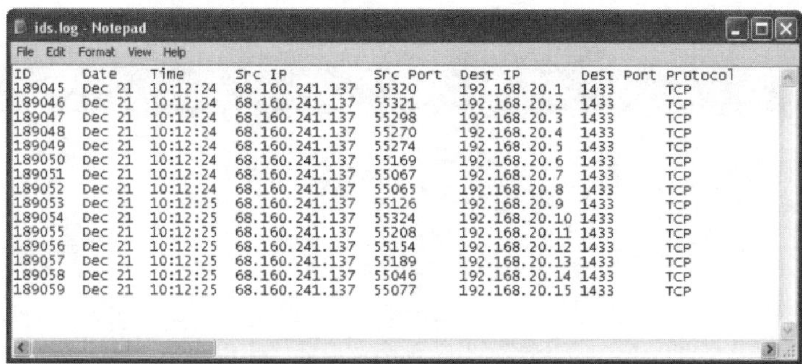

ID	Date	Time	Src IP	Src Port	Dest IP	Dest Port	Protocol
189045	Dec 21	10:12:24	68.160.241.137	55320	192.168.20.1	1433	TCP
189046	Dec 21	10:12:24	68.160.241.137	55321	192.168.20.2	1433	TCP
189047	Dec 21	10:12:24	68.160.241.137	55298	192.168.20.3	1433	TCP
189048	Dec 21	10:12:24	68.160.241.137	55270	192.168.20.4	1433	TCP
189049	Dec 21	10:12:24	68.160.241.137	55274	192.168.20.5	1433	TCP
189050	Dec 21	10:12:24	68.160.241.137	55169	192.168.20.6	1433	TCP
189051	Dec 21	10:12:24	68.160.241.137	55067	192.168.20.7	1433	TCP
189052	Dec 21	10:12:24	68.160.241.137	55065	192.168.20.8	1433	TCP
189053	Dec 21	10:12:25	68.160.241.137	55126	192.168.20.9	1433	TCP
189054	Dec 21	10:12:25	68.160.241.137	55324	192.168.20.10	1433	TCP
189055	Dec 21	10:12:25	68.160.241.137	55208	192.168.20.11	1433	TCP
189056	Dec 21	10:12:25	68.160.241.137	55154	192.168.20.12	1433	TCP
189057	Dec 21	10:12:25	68.160.241.137	55189	192.168.20.13	1433	TCP
189058	Dec 21	10:12:25	68.160.241.137	55046	192.168.20.14	1433	TCP
189059	Dec 21	10:12:25	68.160.241.137	55077	192.168.20.15	1433	TCP

Figure 8-16 Destination IP addresses and ports

8

2. Identify the possible intruder. How would you trace the intruder and determine whether or not this person has been responsible for any other attacks? (*Hint:* Review preceding Hands-On Projects in this chapter.) Write your answer in a lab notebook or word processing document.
3. Try to locate the source IP computer. Where is it located? Is the computer known to have been involved in any other attacks? Again, write your answer in a lab notebook or word processing document.
4. Describe what kind of event is happening in the example shown. Write your answer in a lab notebook or word processing document.
5. Suggest how you could prevent such intrusion attempts from succeeding in the future. Write your answer in a lab notebook or word processing document.

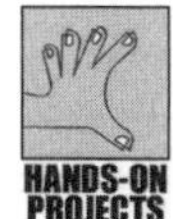

Project 8-6: Categorizing IDS Packages

You learned in this chapter that most IDS systems perform anomaly detection, misuse detection, or a combination of both. Yet, IDS systems are not always described in one of these categories, either on the manufacturer's Web site or in media reviews. On occasion, IDS packages are described as providing a "new" technology that is actually one of the aforementioned approaches. Having a firm idea of which detection methodology a product uses (anomaly, misuse, or hybrid) can help you make the right purchase for your organization. Do some online "shopping" for IDS systems and divide them into categories as shown in the following steps.

1. Read the eWeek "New IDS Tools Automate Response" at *www.eweek.com/article2/0,3959,678214,00.asp*. Pay attention to the evaluation of SecurVantage 3.0 by Securify, Inc., which is described as having a "new feature" called Automatic Policy Generation. What IDS methodology that you learned about earlier in this chapter does this system actually use?

2. Visit the Web sites of the IDS systems in Table 8-3 and categorize them as anomaly-based, misuse-based, or hybrid. Write the answers in the Method column.

Table 8-3 IDS system methodologies

IDS	URL	Method
E-Security Advisor	*www.esecurityinc.com*	
NeuSecure	*www.guardednet.com/prod/prod.html*	
StealthWatch	*www.lancope.com*	
Intrusion Management System	*www.nfrsecurity.com/products/*	
IDP	*www.netscreen.com/products/idp.html*	
Database Edition	*www.entercept.com*	

Case Projects

Case Project 8-1: Redistributing Network Sensors

You have installed a network-based IDS in a traditional design: a sensor is placed on each segment of the network, and alarms are transmitted to the command console where you can review and evaluate them. A comparison of your firewall logs to your IDS alarms indicates that the sensors are not able to capture every packet that passes into and out of the network, however. Describe how you would troubleshoot this configuration by rearranging sensors using a different configuration. What are the pros and cons of making the change?

Case Project 8-2: Handling False-Positives

You have a Cisco Host-Based IDS system installed on your network, and you use a hardware device called the Cisco Secure Scanner, located at IP address 192.168.25.101, to run periodic vulnerability checks on your network. Whenever you run such a check, however, your IDS sends alarms to the command console (in this case, the Cisco Secure IDS Director). How could you prevent false-positives from being recorded for this type of event?

Case Project 8-3: Providing Two-Tiered IDS Response

You administer a network configured with two separate subnets: 10.8.1.1/16 and 10.9.1.1/16. You add a new subnet, 10.10.1.1/16, to the network. Each of the three internal subnets now has a separate Ethernet interface on the firewall/IDS device (designated by e0, e1, and e2). The firewall IDS also has an external interface on the Internet (designated by s0) at IP address 210.10.1.1. Because your network has expanded, you need to configure the IDS. You do not want the IDS to interfere with traffic originating from the interfaces e0, e1, and e2 by resetting the TCP connections if a packet matches the database and an alarm is sent. On the other hand, you *do* want the IDS to send an alarm and reset TCP connections if a suspicious packet reaches the external interface s0. How could you accommodate both types of responses?

Case Project 8-4: Using the IDS to Trace Internal Misuse

An IDS can be used to detect and track unauthorized access attempts that come from inside the organizations' network as well as outside. For example, your SMTP server's event log files indicate that the server has been sending hundreds of e-mail messages every Monday morning at 8:00 a.m. for the past three weeks. You suspect that the company's SMTP server is being used to distribute mass e-mails by an employee who manages an e-mail newsletter. How could you verify this using the IDS?

CHAPTER

9

INTRUSION DETECTION: PREVENTIVE MEASURES

After reading this chapter and completing the exercises, you will be able to:

- Explain the benefits of the Common Vulnerabilities and Exposures (CVE) standard
- Understand why logging network traffic is an integral part of intrusion detection
- Analyze intrusion signatures so that you can block unauthorized access to resources
- Identify suspicious events when they are captured by an intrusion detection device
- Develop filters so that you can take a proactive approach to intrusion detection

At its most basic level, intrusion detection can be broken down to a simple principle: allowing the communications you want to pass through your network gateways and blocking all the traffic you don't want. The challenge is to separate the two types of network traffic. Hackers have devised hundreds of different ways to attack networks with communications that often appear to be legitimate. On the other side, the manufacturers of security hardware and software are improving and augmenting their tools to keep up with the latest vulnerabilities. It's an ongoing struggle.

This chapter examines some of the techniques used to identify what constitutes normal network traffic and what constitutes an attempt to gain unauthorized access to network resources. You'll begin by learning about a standard for recording information regarding attack signatures, the Common Vulnerabilities and Exposures (CVE). You'll then examine the connection between logging and intrusion detection. You'll analyze intrusion signatures, both normal and suspicious. Next, you'll identify a variety of suspicious events, from single-packet attacks to complex attacks. Finally, you'll learn how to develop filter rules for your IDS that can provide your network with another layer of defense.

Common Vulnerabilities and Exposures (CVE)

One of the ways to prevent attacks is to make sure your security devices are able to share information and coordinate with one another. At the perimeter of any given network, you are likely to have a variety of hardware and software devices that provide security and that need to work cooperatively with one another. You might have a router from one vendor; a firewall from another; and an IDS from a third. Unfortunately, the way they interpret signatures might well differ from one device to another. They probably address the same known attacks, but give them different names and describe their characteristics differently. The **Common Vulnerabilities and Exposures (CVE)** standard enables these devices to share information about attack signatures and other vulnerabilities so they can work together.

How the CVE Database Works

CVE enables hardware and security devices that support it to draw from the same databases of vulnerabilities, which are presented in the same standard format. For instance, a **scanner** (a device that scans a network for open ports or other potential vulnerabilities) that supports CVE compiles a report listing weak points in the system. When an alarm message is transmitted by an intrusion detection system (IDS) that also supports CVE, the attack signature can be compared to the report of current vulnerabilities to see if an attack has actually occurred (see Figure 9-1).

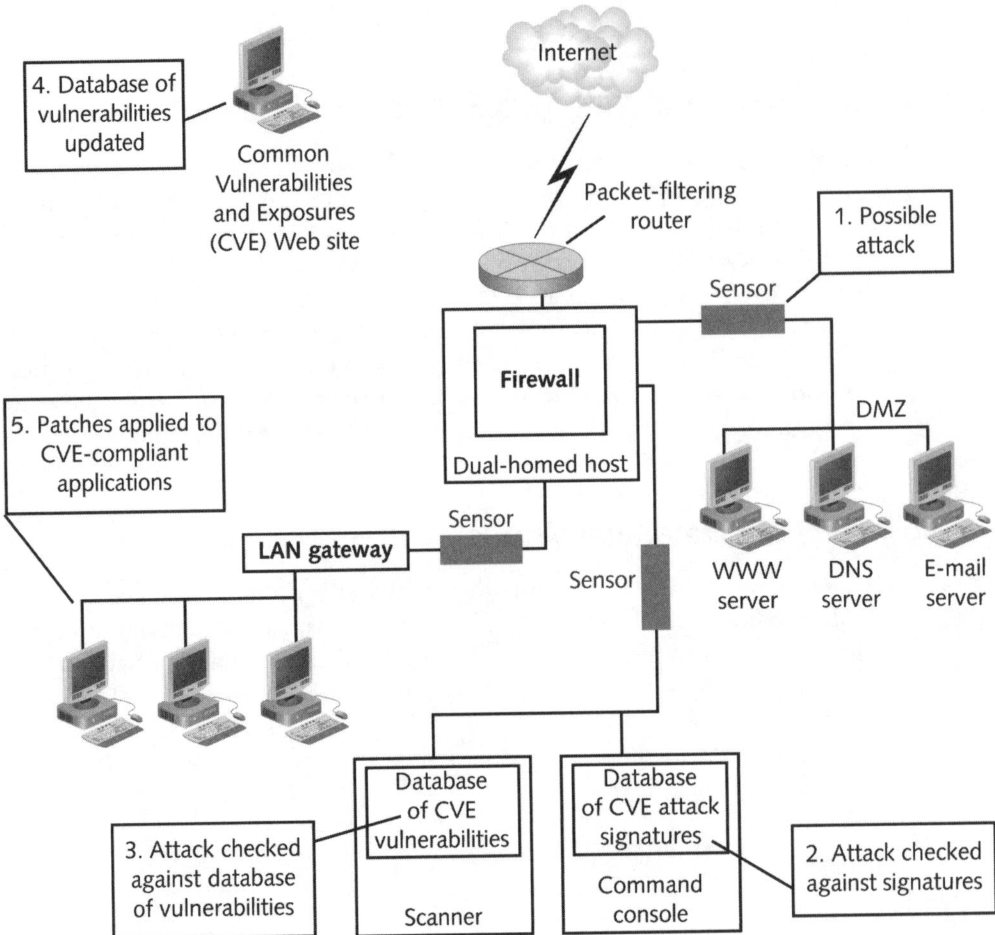

Figure 9-1 CVE enables multiple security devices to share information

In Figure 9-1, the CVE standard has an impact on many different parts of a network:

1. An attack is detected by an IDS sensor.
2. The signature of the possible attack is checked against the database of known attack signatures available to the IDS to see if a match is found. If the IDS being used is also CVE-compliant, the report on the attack contains information on known network vulnerabilities associated with the attack signature.
3. The list of vulnerabilities is compared against a database of current vulnerable points in the system that have been compiled and stored by a CVE-compliant scanner, to determine if this possible attack can have an impact on the network.
4. Periodically, the list of vulnerabilities is updated by obtaining new entries from the CVE vulnerability Web site.

5. The manufacturers of CVE-compliant applications generate patches and updates in response to vulnerabilities, and those patches can then be applied to applications on the network.

Great benefits (such as stronger security and better performance) result from all the security devices on a network understanding and using information that complies with the CVE standard. If you are in a position to be purchasing intrusion detection systems or other equipment for your organization, you should probably make sure that they support CVE.

The CVE is a cooperative effort. The database of vulnerabilities is maintained by MITRE at *www.cve.mitre.org*. Funding is provided by several U.S. government agencies as well.

Scanning CVE Vulnerability Descriptions

You can go online and view the current CVE vulnerabilities and even download the list so you can review it at your convenience. Keep in mind, however, that as MITRE points out, the CVE list is not a vulnerability database that can be used with an IDS system. It's simply an informational tool. CVE listings are brief and simply refer to listings in other databases; they don't contain IP addresses, protocol listings, or other characteristics of an event that would qualify it as a signature. When you look at a CVE reference you see:

9

- The name of the vulnerability
- A short description
- References to the event in other databases such as BUGTRAQ

The number associated with a CVE listing tells you when the listing was made. For instance, CVE-2004-0221 tells you that this listing was made in the year 2004 and was number 221 for that year. The listing shown in Figure 9-2 was the 237th for the year 2004.

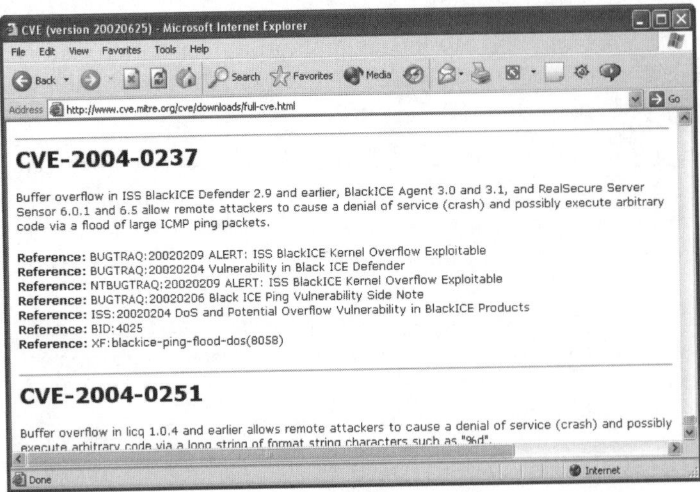

Figure 9-2 A CVE listing for a buffer overflow vulnerability that affects IDS software

The listing shown in Figure 9-2 indicates that vulnerabilities can affect IDS software as well as other types of applications.

Logging and Intrusion Detection

Over a period of time, all of the security devices on a network generate a substantial amount of log file information. Analyzing that data manually is impossible to accomplish quickly. The analysis of log file data can be automated by the installation of software programs.

A shareware program called ZoneLog is designed to analyze the log file information compiled from the firewall ZoneAlarm. The listings presented are color coded so that you can tell which ones are possible attacks from those that are routine port scans performed by your DNS server or your ISP. One such report lists the applications that scan ports on your system; as you can see from the list in Figure 9-3, many are from electronic keyboards, firewalls, and built-in applications on your own computer.

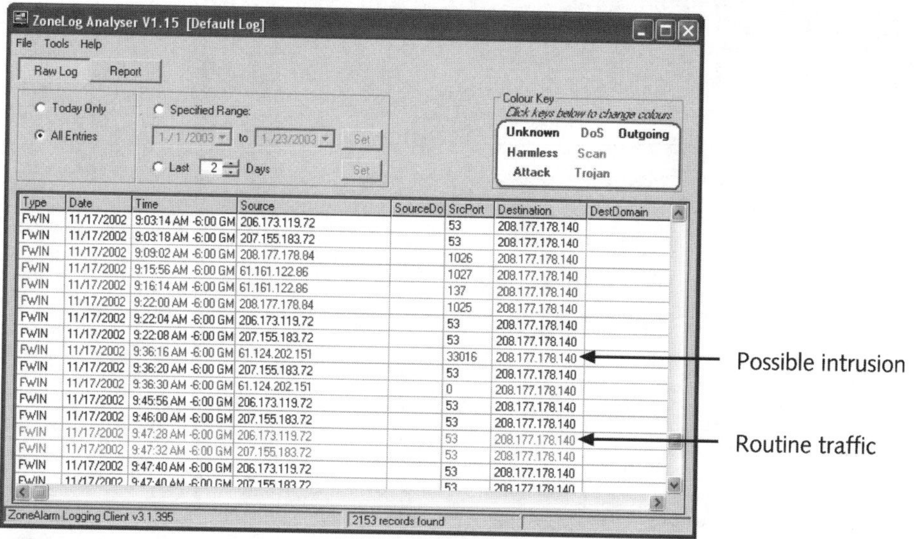

Figure 9-3 Log file analysis can help you quickly separate routine traffic from suspicious traffic

As you can see from Figure 9-3, those log file entries that are simply listed as IP addresses (and that are colored in brown, which you can't tell from this image) are possible intrusions. You can trace such events using the analysis file or using ZoneAlarm itself. The traffic that results from routine traffic can be configured to pass without being logged, which can make the analysis easier in the future.

The ZoneLog log file analysis program for use with the popular freeware program ZoneAlarm is described in Hands-On Project 9-1.

Another IDS program that is popularly used in Unix and Linux environments, Snort, creates log files that are organized by IP address. Each set of packets that originated from an IP address is contained within a folder named with that IP address (see Figure 9-4).

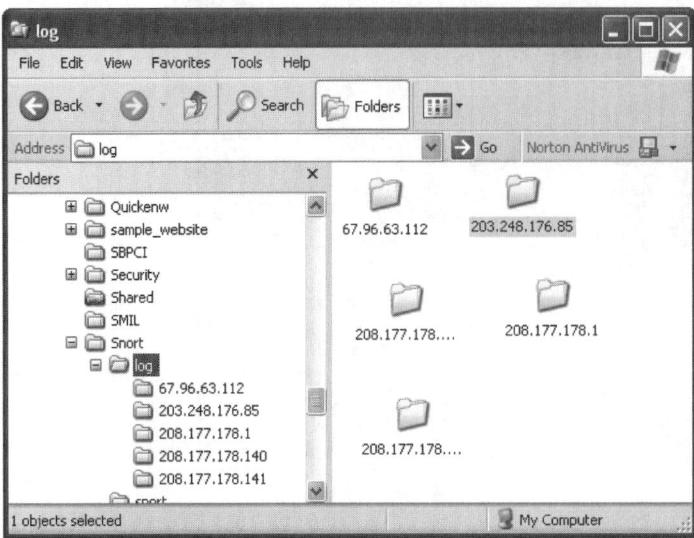

Figure 9-4 Snort arranges log files by IP address

Arranging the log files by IP address makes it easy for you if you are investigating possible attacks or intrusion attempts from a specific source. You only have to look in the folder with that source's IP address to view the data. However, once you find the data you want, you have to know how to interpret it. This is where knowledge of signatures comes in, which we discuss in the following section.

Snort, like ZoneAlarm and other security tools, can be used with a number of log file analyzers. These analyzers are available through whitehats.com: *www.whitehats.com*.

Analyzing Intrusion Signatures

A **signature** is a set of characteristics—such as IP protocol numbers and options, TCP flags and port numbers—that is used to define a type of network activity. Besides individual TCP/IP packet attributes, a signature can also consist of a sequence of packets or other events such as logons to a network.

Some intrusion detection devices assemble databases of "normal" traffic signatures. As traffic is detected, it is compared to the database, and any deviations from the normal signatures trigger an alarm. Other intrusion detection devices refer to a database of well-known attack signatures. Any traffic that matches one of the stored attack signatures triggers an alarm. Your understanding of both normal and suspicious traffic signatures enables you to configure your IDS to work more effectively—to minimize the number of false-positives (false alarms) and maximize the number of genuine attacks that are detected.

In this section of the chapter, you get an introduction to understanding signature analysis. Then you learn how to capture packets so that you can analyze them. You get an overview of some of the common normal traffic signatures you are likely to encounter. Finally, you learn about suspicious traffic signatures that indicate a possible attempt to scan and gain unauthorized access to your network.

Understanding Signature Analysis

Signature analysis is the practice of analyzing and understanding TCP/IP communications to determine whether they are legitimate or suspicious. TCP/IP packets that are sent back and forth by a host and client and that are judged to be suspicious fall into several categories: bad header information, suspicious data payload, single-packet attacks, or multiple packet attacks.

Analysis of TCP/IP packets depends on a solid foundation in the TCP/IP protocols themselves. You can find out more about this in *Guide to TCP/IP*, by Laura Chappel and Ed Tittel, published by Course Technology.

Bad Header Information

One of the more common ways in which packets can be altered is in their header information, and packet filters usually scan for such alterations (see Chapter 4). Suspicious signatures can include malformed data that affects some or all of the following:

- Source and destination IP address
- Source and destination port number
- IP options
- IP fragmentation flags, fragmentation offset, or fragment identification
- IP protocol
- IP, TCP, or UDP checksums

A **checksum** is a simple error-checking procedure used to determine whether a message has been tampered with while in transit. The number of data bits in a message is processed using a mathematical formula. A numeric value (the checksum) is then calculated. The receiving computer applies the same formula to the message; if a different checksum is found, the receiving computer determines that the message has been tampered with and drops it.

A hacker who obtains software that can be used to generate packets to specifications set by the hacker is able to forge IP addresses or a variety of other types of header information. For instance, a packet can be sent in a series of fragments. The initial packet in the fragment can be eliminated from the set, which makes the receiving computer unable to reassemble the packets and thus circumvent a packet filter. Either more or fewer packets can be sent than are indicated in the initial packet, which can disable a server that cannot process more packets than it expected to receive.

Suspicious Data Payload

The payload or data part of a packet is the actual data that is sent from one computer to an application on another. Sometimes attacks can be detected by an IDS that matches a text string to a specific set of characters in the payload. For instance, a Trojan horse called the "Hack'a'Tack" sends a UDP packet that uses both source 31790 and destination port 31789. The key is detecting the string "A" in the payload part of the packet. A graphic representation of the UDP header can be found in the arachNIDS database of IDS signatures found on the Whitehats Network Security Resource Web site (*www.whitehats.com*). The UDP header is shown in Figure 9-5.

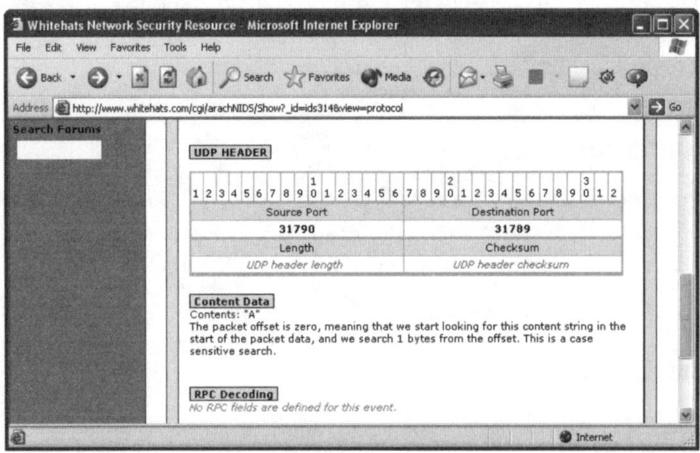

Figure 9-5 A suspicious UDP signature

In another type of attack, the UNIX sendmail program is exploited by adding codes to the content of packets. Codes such as VRFY and EXPN are used to uncover account names on the sendmail server. By adding the code EXPN DECODE in the data payload of a packet, a hacker attempts to establish a connection with an alias called decode. If a connection is made, the hacker can use it to place malicious files on the exploited system.

Single-Packet Attacks

A **single-packet attack** , also called an **atomic attack** , can be completed by sending a single network packet from client to host. Because only a single packet is needed, a connection does not need to be established between the two computers involved. Many manipulations of the IP Options settings can cause a server to freeze up because it does not know how to handle such packets. The IP Options settings are shown in Table 9-1.

Table 9-1 IP Options settings

Option Number	Name of Option
0	End of Options
1	No Operation
2	Security
3	Loose Source Route
4	Internet Timestamp
7	Record Return Route
8	Stream ID
9	Strict Source Route

As an example of IP Options processing, suppose an ICMP echo request (or "ping") packet is sent from a host to a server with Option 7 set. The echo reply response from the server might spell out the route the request takes to return from the server, thus revealing the IP addresses of hosts or routers on the network that the hacker can then target. Option 4 can be used along with Option 7 to record the time the echo reply packet spends between "hops" on the network. This information is valuable to the hacker because it indicates how many routers are on the network.

Multiple-Packet Attacks

In contrast to single-packet attacks, **multiple-packet attacks** (also called **composite attacks**) require a series of packets to be received and executed in order for the attack to be completed. Such attacks are especially difficult to detect. They require a system such as Cisco Secure IDS to have multiple attack signatures on hand to which it can refer. In addition, the sensor needs to maintain state information about a connection once it has been established, and it needs to keep that state information on hand for the entire length of an attack.

Denial of Service (DoS) attacks are obvious examples of a composite attack. A type of DoS attack called an ICMP Flood occurs when multiple ICMP packets are sent to a single host on a network. The result of this flood is that the server is so busy responding to the ICMP requests that other traffic cannot be processed. A TCP Port Sweep includes a series of connection attempts to ports on a network.

Capturing Packets

A **packet sniffer** is software or hardware that monitors traffic going into or out of a network device. A packet sniffer captures information about each TCP/IP packet it detects. By using such an application yourself, you can study packets and identify characteristic features that tell you what type of connection is underway and whether the attack is legitimate or suspicious.

Capturing packets and studying them can help you better understand signatures because the two closely resemble one another in format. Figure 9-6, for instance, shows a packet that was sent from one computer to another as part of a simple echo request.

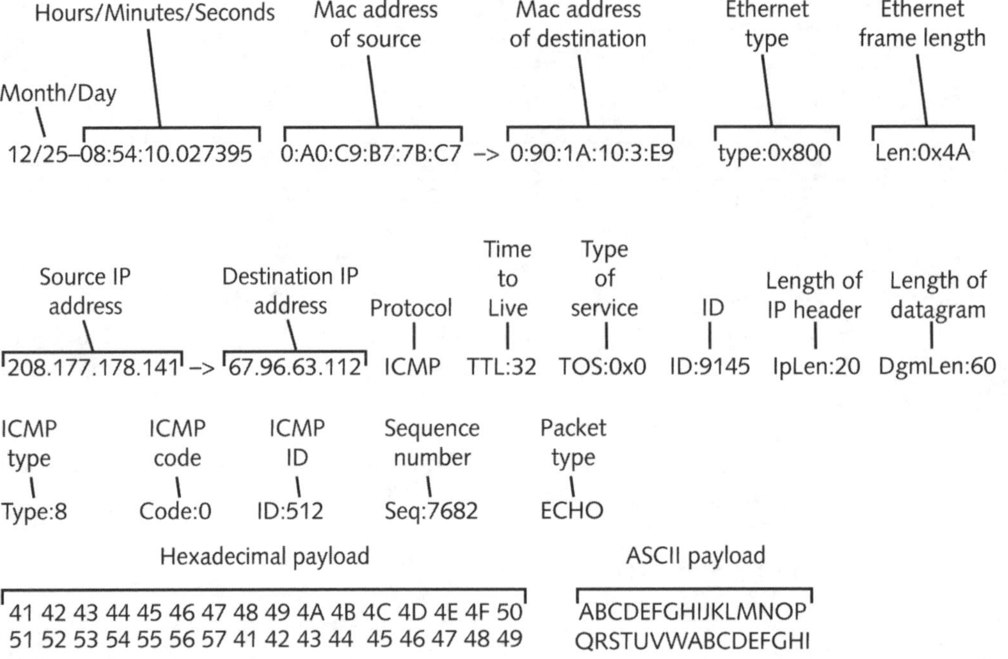

Figure 9-6 A single ICMP echo request packet capture

The lines of the packet capture have been widely separated so they are easier to read and label. Normally, they are presented very close together. The following list describes the elements in this packet:

- *12/25*—The month and date when the packet was captured.
- *08:54:10.027395*—The hour, minute and second when the packet was captured. This packet capture software (Snort) breaks the seconds down into milliseconds; not all software does so.
- *0:A0:C9:B7:7B:C7*—The Media Access Control (Mac) address of the source computer. The Mac address is used to identify a hardware device on a network.
- *0:90:1A:10:3:E9*—The Mac address of the computer being "pinged."
- *Ethernet type*—The type of Ethernet being used on this Internet connection.
- *Frame length*—Ethernet transmits data in fixed-length segments called frames. This describes the length of the frame being used on this network.

- *Source IP*—This is the IP address of the computer that makes the connection request.
- *Destination IP*—This is the IP address of the computer that is being contacted.
- *Protocol*—The protocol used: In this case, it is the Internet Control Message Protocol (ICMP), which is used to do IP error-checking and verify that computers are present on the network.
- ***Time to Live (TTL)***—In this case, 32 hops: A hop is the movement of a packet from one point on the network to another. Note that 32 and 128 are both values commonly used by Windows systems, so this indicates that the source computer is using Windows.
- ***Type of service (TOS)***—A part of the packet header that allows the sender the option to express the precedence of the packet—whether it should have low delay, whether it needs high reliability, and so on. No special precedence is being requested in this packet.
- *ID*—Every packet is assigned an identifying number when it is created. The **ID number** can be used to reassemble a packet in case it is divided into fragments. Looking at a sequence of packets to see how the ID numbers increment from one to another can indicate the type of computer being used. If the ID number moves from packet to packet in an increment of one (from 9144 to 9155), this points to a Windows computer.

- *Length of IP header*—The IP length is set at 20 bytes, a length consistent with both Linux and Windows operating systems.
- *Length of datagram*—The length of the datagram (or packet) is 60 bytes, a value consistent with Windows systems. The minimum size is 21 bytes.
- *ICMP type*—ICMP has different types of messages (Echo Request, Redirect, Source Quench, and so on). Type 8 indicates that this is an Echo Request packet.
- *ICMP code*—An 8-bit value that provides further information about some types of ICMP packets.
- *ID*—This is the ICMP ID number (as opposed to the packet ID number given earlier). It helps identify the ICMP packet so that the originating computer can make sure the response came from its original request.
- *Seq*—The ICMP Sequence number: This is used to identify the ICMP packet within a sequence of packets.
- *ECHO*—This is the type of ICMP packet being sent, based on the ICMP type number.

- ***Hexadecimal payload***—This is the actual data being communicated by the packet, expressed in hexadecimal format.
- ***ASCII payload***—This is the actual data part of the packet, given in ASCII format.

The information in a TCP packet contains elements that don't appear in an ICMP packet. The parts of a TCP packet that are different than the preceding ICMP packet are shown in Figure 9-7.

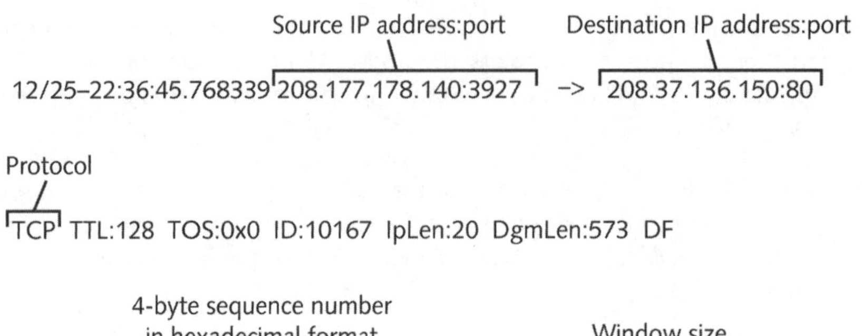

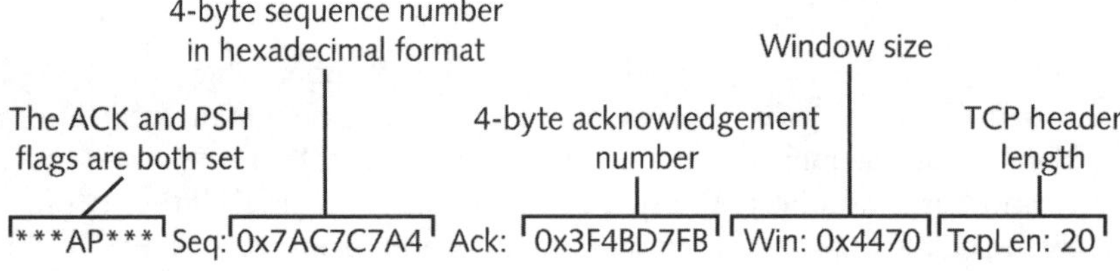

GET and HTTP used for Web traffic

```
47 45 54 20 2F 20 48 54 54 50 2F 31 2E 30 0D 0A    GET / HTTP/1.0..
41 63 63 65 70 74 3A 20 2A 2F 2A 0D 0A 41 63 63    Accept: */*..Acc
65 70 74 2D 4C 61 6E 67 75 61 67 65 3A 20 65 6E    ept-Language: en
2D 75 73 0D 0A 55 73 65 72 2D 41 67 65 6E 74 3A    -us..User-Agent:
20 4D 6F 7A 69 6C 6C 61 2F 34 2E 30 20 28 63 6F     Mozilla/4.0 <co
6D 70 61 74 69 62 6C 65 3B 20 4D 53 49 45 20 36    mpatible; MSIE 6
2E 30 3B 20 57 69 6E 64 6F 77 73 20 4E 54 20 35    .0; Windows NT 5
2E 31 3B 20 4E 4E 34 2E 32 2E 33 2E 32 29 0D 0A    .1; NN4.2.3.2>..
48 6F 73 74 3A 20 77 77 77 2E 63 6F 75 72 73 65    Host: www.course
2E 63 6F 6D 0D 0A 43 6F 6E 6E 65 63 74 69 6F 6E    .com..Connection
3A 20 4B 65 65 70 2D 41 6C 69 76 65 0D 0A 43 6F    : Keep-Alive..Co
```

Figure 9-7 A TCP packet capture

The following list describes the TCP-specific elements in the packet:

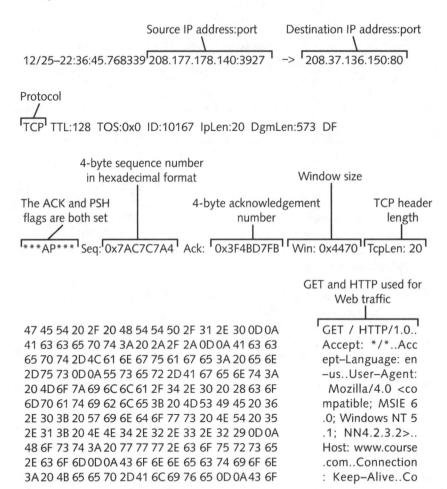

- *Source IP address:port/Destination IP address:port*—In a TCP packet, the port being used appears after the IP address, separated by a colon.
- *Protocol*—The protocol used is TCP.

- *Flags* —In the packet shown in Figure 9-7, two TCP flags, ACK and PSH, are used together. The ACK (Acknowledgement) flag indicates that a connection has been established. The PSH (Push) flag indicates that data is being sent from a memory buffer to the destination computer.
- *4-byte sequence number* —This gives the sequence number of the packet in hexadecimal format.
- *4-byte acknowledgement number* —This number acknowledges receipt of the previous packet in the sequence.
- *Window size* —This tells the recipient the size of the window on the source computer so that the recipient can determine how many packets can be sent at any one time.
- *TCP header length* —This is the overall length of the TCP packet, including header and data.
- *GET and HTTP* —The GET method and the HTTP protocol in the ASCII payload of the data indicate that a World Wide Web server is being contacted. The HTTP headers Accept-Language, User-Agent, and Host appear in the ASCII payload section as well.

The information in IDS signatures resembles the information in a packet capture. For instance, the Hack'a'Tack Trojan horse mentioned in the preceding section corresponds to the signature shown in Figure 9-8:

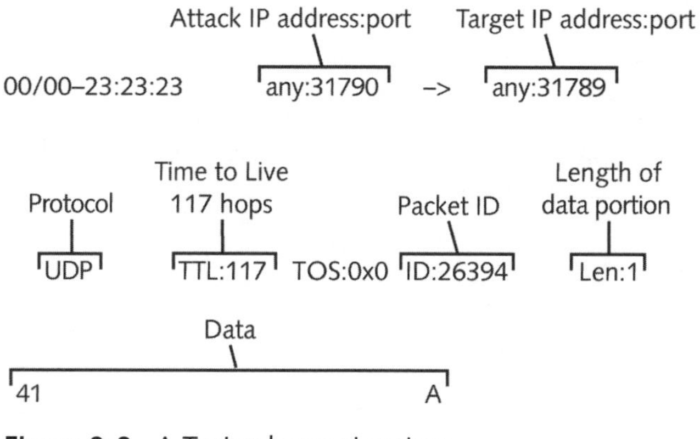

Attack IP address:port
Target IP address:port
00/00–23:23:23 any:31790 -> any:31789

Protocol
Time to Live 117 hops
Packet ID
Length of data portion
UDP TTL:117 TOS:0x0 ID:26394 Len:1

Data
41 A

Figure 9-8 A Trojan horse signature

The following list analyzes this information element-by-element:

- *00/00* —This is a generic designation of the month and date when the packet was captured.

- *23:23:23* —This is a generic designation of the hour, minute and second when the packet was captured. Additionally, some devices break the seconds down into milliseconds.
- *attacker:31790—> target 31789* —The attacker uses port 31790 and targets the port 31789 on the destination computer.
- *UDP* —This is the protocol used.
- *TTL* —This stands for Time to Live, in hops from one router or device to another.
- *TOS* —This is the type of service.
- *ID* —This is the ID number used by this packet; a hacker can manufacture an ID number along with other packet header information.
- *Len* —This is the length of the data part of the packet—only one byte.
- *The last line is the actual data part of the packet* —In this case the suspicious packet is distinguished by the presence of the character A in the payload.

A variety of software tools can be used to capture packets that pass through a computer's network interface card. In Chapter 1, you learned how to use a program called Ethereal, which is available in Windows and Linux versions. The IDS program Snort also can be used to capture packets in real time, using the following steps:

1. You open a command prompt window.
2. You start Snort by entering the path to the program file (such as C:\Snort\snort\snort.exe).
3. You add two commands, -v and –d, and press Enter.

Snort starts and begins to capture packets as they connect with your interface card. When you stop the real-time packet capture by pressing Ctrl+C, the program provides you with a brief summary of what it found, as shown in Figure 9-9.

```
Command Prompt
===============================================================================
Snort received 538 packets and dropped 0(0.000%) packets

Breakdown by protocol:                  Action Stats:
    TCP: 385        (71.561%)           ALERTS: 0
    UDP: 82         (15.242%)           LOGGED: 0
   ICMP: 59         (10.967%)           PASSED: 0
    ARP: 12         (2.230%)
   IPv6: 0          (0.000%)
    IPX: 0          (0.000%)
  OTHER: 0          (0.000%)
DISCARD: 0          (0.000%)
===============================================================================
Fragmentation Stats:
Fragmented IP Packets: 0          (0.000%)
   Rebuilt IP Packets: 0
   Frag elements used: 0
Discarded(incomplete): 0
   Discarded(timeout): 0
===============================================================================
TCP Stream Reassembly Stats:
   TCP Packets Used:      0          (0.000%)
   Reconstructed Packets: 0          (0.000%)
   Streams Reconstructed: 0
===============================================================================
pcap_loop: read error: PacketReceivePacket failed
Exiting...
pcap_stats: PacketGetStats error

C:\Documents and Settings\Greg>pingping

C:\Documents and Settings\Greg>_
```

Figure 9-9 Using Snort to capture TCP and UDP packets

One problem with using Snort as a packet-capturing tool is that it doesn't retain more than a few dozen packets at a time. The packets come across the network interface so quickly that you can easily lose your opportunity to see them and thus be unable to analyze them. Ethereal captures a far larger number of packets and stores them so you can review them. The advantage of using Snort, however, is that you can use it to set up intrusion alerts and to block network traffic.

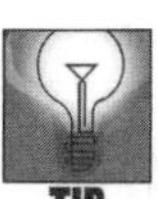

TIP

Hands-On Projects 9-2 and 9-3 lead you through the process of using Snort as a packet capture tool.

Normal Traffic Signatures

In order to recognize suspicious traffic signatures, it's important to be able to recognize normal traffic signatures as well. One aspect of normal TCP signatures that's easiest to identify is the use of flags. TCP flags are described in the following list:

- *The SYN (Synchronize) flag* —This is sent from one computer to another when a connection is initiated; the two computers are attempting to synchronize a connection.
- *The ACK (Acknowledgement) flag* —This is sent when the connection has been made.
- *The PSH (Push) flag* —This is used when data is being sent from one computer to the target application on the other, rather than being held in a storage area called a buffer.

- *The URG (Urgent) flag* —This is used when urgent data is being sent from one computer to another.
- *The RST (Reset) flag* —This is sent when one computer wants to stop the connection when there is a problem with it.
- *The FIN (Finished) flag* —This lets one computer know that the other is finished when sending data.
- *The numbers 1 and 2*— These are used for two reserved data bits.

The placement and use of these flags is very definite and strictly defined, and deviations from normal usage mean that the communication is suspicious. For instance, the SYN flag should appear at the beginning of a connection; the FIN flag should only appear at the end of a connection. If the SYN and FIN flags both appear in the same packet, it is an indication of suspicious network activity. (However, the ACK and PUSH flags can be used together when data is sent from one computer to another.)

Ping Signatures

In the previous section, a single ICMP echo request packet was analyzed. The sequence of packets shown in Figure 9-10 shows a signature of ICMP echo request packets captured by Snort when packets are sent that "ping" two different target computers.

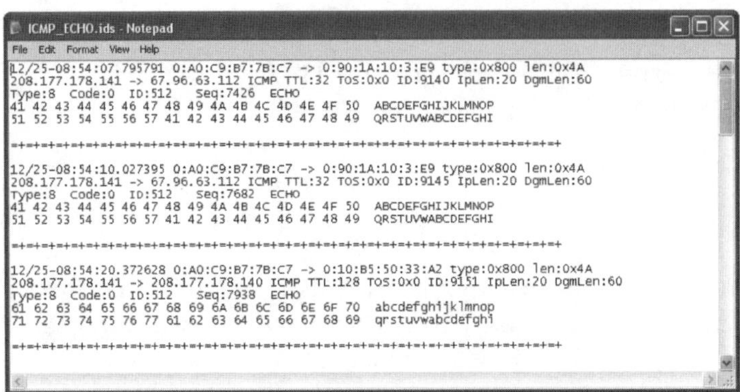

Figure 9-10 Normal signatures for ICMP echo requests

The echo request packets received did not cause a response to be sent, however. (The host computer had a firewall installed that prevented it from responding to Echo Request packets.) The packets that are exchanged when a computer does successfully respond to an echo request with echo reply packets are shown in Figure 9-11. Notice, that in Figure 9-11 each of the two computers that is exchanging packets has a unique set of sequence numbers.

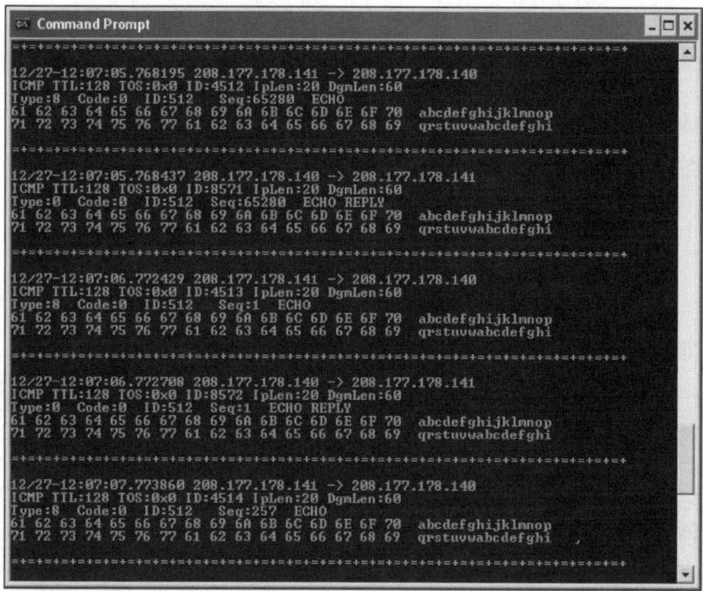

Figure 9-11 A successful exchange of ICMP Echo Request and Echo Reply packets

An analysis of each of the four packets shown reveals the following:

1. The first packet shows the computer at IP address 208.177.178.141 sending an Echo Request packet (ICMP Type 8) to 208.177.178.140 with the sequence number 4512 (shown in the figure as ID: 4512).
2. The second packet shows the computer at IP address 208.177.178.140 responding with an Echo Reply packet (ICMP Type 0) with sequence number 8571.
3. The third packet shows the computer at IP address 208.177.178.141 responding with another Echo Request packet with sequence number 4513—only one number higher than the previous packet it sent.
4. The fourth packet shows the computer at IP address 208.177.178.140 responding with another Echo Reply packet with sequence number 8572.

You can also tell from examining the packets that two Windows computers are involved, as indicated by the Time to Live (TTL) of 128, the IP length (IpLen) of 20, and the Datagram Length (DgmLen) of 60. A TTL of 64 is part of a signature of a Linux computer, as is a datagram length of 84. In addition, on a Linux computer, ICMP Echo Request packets start with a sequence number of 0.

The ASCII data payload section of an ICMP packet on a Windows computer consists of a sequence of alphabetical characters (abcdefghijklmnop and so on), while on Linux the data payload is a string of characters followed by the numerals 0 through 9 (!"#$%&'()*+,-./ 0123456789).

FTP Signatures

If your organization operates a public FTP server, you'll regularly be called upon to review the signatures of packets that attempt to access that server. You need to determine whether the computer making the connection attempt is actually allowed to access the server in accordance with your packet-filtering rules.

The signature of a normal connection between a client and an FTP server includes a three-way handshake. Three separate packets contain different TCP flags that enable you to keep track of the connection, as shown in Figure 9-12.

Figure 9-12 An FTP session's three-way handshake followed by initial data exchange packets

The packets shown in Figure 9-12 can be analyzed as follows:

1. In the first packet, the computer at IP address 208.177.178.140, port 3118 attempts to connect to the FTP server at 207.155.252.72, port 21. The third line shows that the packet has the SYN flag (S) set because a Synchronization request is being made to the remote server. In the fourth line, the TCP Option code 4 (Maximum Segment Size, or MSS) is set at 1460 bytes. This tells the FTP server the maximum IP packet size it can handle without fragmenting the packet.

2. In the second packet, the FTP server responds to the client by sending a packet with the ACK flag (A) as well as the SYN (S) set.

3. In the third packet, the client responds with a packet that has the ACK flag (A) set.

4. In the fourth packet, the ACK and PSH (A and P) flags are set and client and server identify one another. In the ASCII data payload section of the packet, the server identifies itself as ready.
5. In the fifth packet, the user's login name appears in clear text in the ASCII data payload section.
6. The FTP server responds with the ACK flag (A), and the connection is established.

The Maximum Segment Size (MSS) is only specified early in the handshake between client and server—specifically, as part of the SYN or SYN/ACK packets that are part of the three-way handshake. If the MSS option is seen in an ACK or ACK/PSH packet, that can be taken as a warning sign of a falsified packet. The NOP (No Operation) TCP option provides several bytes worth of padding (in other words, unused space) around other options. A Selective Acknowledgement OK (SackOK) message follows at the end of line 4 of the packet. This means that **selective acknowledgements** (acknowledgements that selected packets in a sequence have been received) are permitted during this connection.

When data is actually exchanged between client and FTP server, the original ports are not used. In this case, the server port 21 and client port 3118 are ports that initiate a **control connection** (an initial FTP connection). The data would be transferred over a new connection, using server port 20 and a client port such as 5005, as shown in Figure 9-13.

9

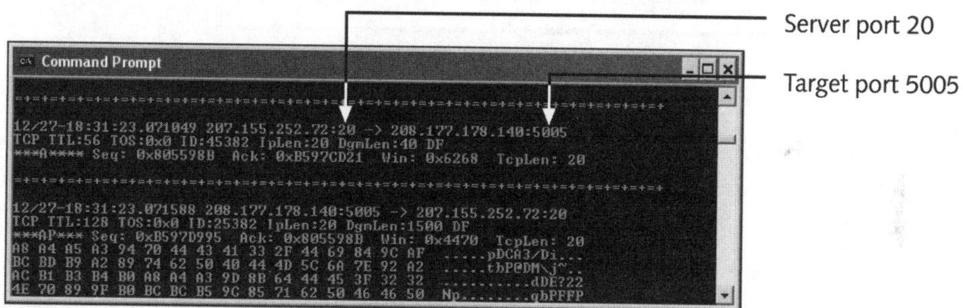

Figure 9-13 An FTP data connection

The options presented in the FTP handshake packets are the same, but they are presented in a different order. That is not, however, an indication of a malformed packet; TCP options can be presented in any order.

WWW Signatures

Most of the signatures you'll see in the log files you analyze will probably be Web-related. When a signature is Web-related, it means it consists of packets that are sent back and forth from a Web browser to a Web server as a connection is made. A signature of a normal handshake between two Web browsers consists of a sequence of packets that are distinguished by their TCP flags.

As mentioned in the preceding section, normal TCP traffic makes use of several TCP flags to control the connection. Being aware of these flags and where they are used can help you determine whether a signature is normal or part of a possible intrusion attempt.

Packets, as captured by the intrusion detection program Snort, are shown in Figure 9-14:

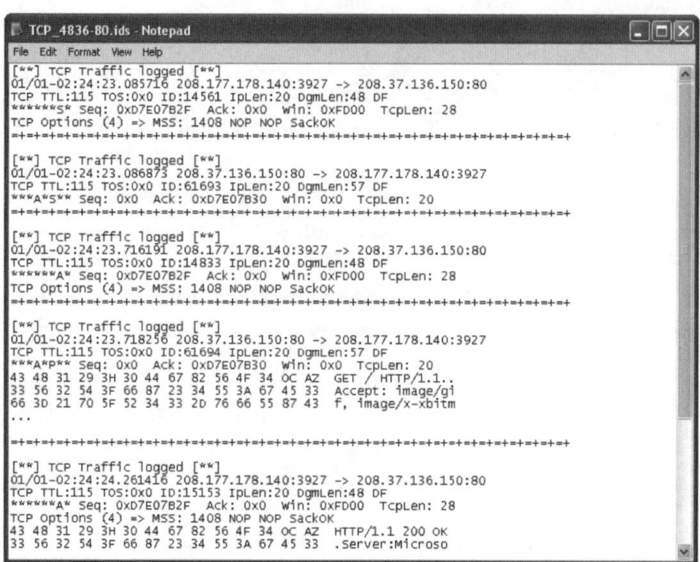

Figure 9-14 A normal exchange of packets between a Web browser and a Web server

In Figure 9-14, you see four packets that represent part of the handshake between the Web browser at IP address 208.177.178.140, using port 3927, and Web server 208.37.136.150, using HTTP port 80.

1. The first packet has the SYN flag set (as indicated by the S in the third line), as the browser asks to synchronize a session with the server.
2. The second flag has the ACK flag set, as the server acknowledges the connection with the browser. In addition, the SYN flag is sent back to the browser as the server seeks to synchronize the connection with the browser.
3. The ACK flag is exchanged to acknowledge that a connection has been made.
4. The PSH flag is used along with the ACK flag to indicate that data is going to be sent (or pushed) from memory storage areas called buffers.

Now that you know something about capturing normal traffic, you can look at analyzing more suspicious signatures.

Suspicious Traffic Signatures

As IDS becomes more widespread and sophisticated, the techniques used by hackers to circumvent them have multiplied and become more complex. Features like illegal combinations of TCP flags and private IP addresses that appear in packets are relatively easy to identify as abnormal compared with attacks that work by a range of packets.

Suspicious traffic signatures can fall into one of these categories:

- *Informational* —The traffic may not be malicious in itself, but could be used to verify whether an attack has been successful. Examples include ICMP Echo Request packets or TCP packets sent to a specific port on a specific system.
- *Reconnaissance* —Such traffic may represent an attempt by a hacker to gain information about a network as a prelude to an attack. Examples include ping sweeps and port scans.
- *Unauthorized Access* —This traffic may be caused by someone who has gained unauthorized access to a system and is attempting to retrieve data from it. Examples include the BackOrifice attack and the Internet Information Services Unicode attack.
- *Denial of Service* —Such traffic may be part of an attempt to slow or halt all connections on a network device, such as a Web server or mail server. Denial of Service examples include the Ping of Death attack and Trinoo attack.

Some of the more common examples of suspicious traffic—ping sweeps, port scans, random back door scans, and Trojan scans—are described in the sections that follow, along with their accompanying signatures.

Ping Sweeps

To gain access to specific resources on an internal network, a hacker needs to determine the location of a host. One way to do this is to conduct a **ping sweep** —to send a series of ICMP Echo Request packets in a range of IP addresses. Usually, the messages come in quick succession (multiple packets may be detected in a single second), indicating that an automated tool is being used. An example of a ping sweep is shown in Figure 9-15.

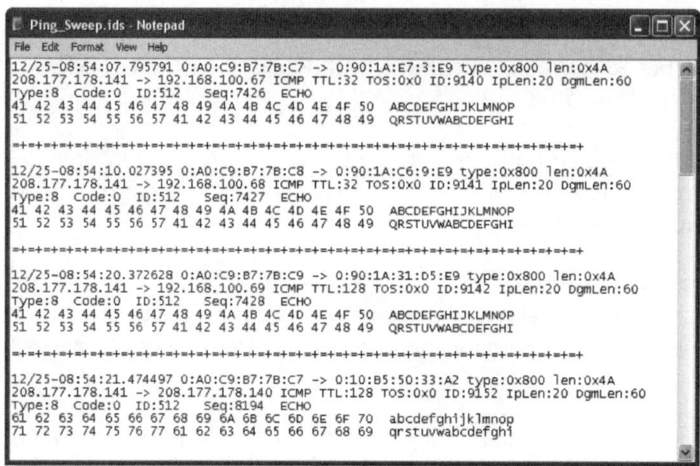


```
12/25-08:54:07.795791 0:A0:C9:B7:7B:C7 -> 0:90:1A:E7:3:E9 type:0x800 len:0x4A
208.177.178.141 -> 192.168.100.67 ICMP TTL:32 TOS:0x0 ID:9140 IpLen:20 DgmLen:60
Type:8  Code:0  ID:512   Seq:7426  ECHO
41 42 43 44 45 46 47 48 49 4A 4B 4C 4D 4E 4F 50  ABCDEFGHIJKLMNOP
51 52 53 54 55 56 57 41 42 43 44 45 46 47 48 49  QRSTUVWABCDEFGHI

=+=+=+=+=+=+=+=+=+=+=+=+=+=+=+=+=+=+=+=+=+=+=+=+=+=+=+=+=+=+=+=+=+=+=+=+=+=+

12/25-08:54:10.027395 0:A0:C9:B7:7B:C8 -> 0:90:1A:C6:9:E9 type:0x800 len:0x4A
208.177.178.141 -> 192.168.100.68 ICMP TTL:32 TOS:0x0 ID:9141 IpLen:20 DgmLen:60
Type:8  Code:0  ID:512   Seq:7427  ECHO
41 42 43 44 45 46 47 48 49 4A 4B 4C 4D 4E 4F 50  ABCDEFGHIJKLMNOP
51 52 53 54 55 56 57 41 42 43 44 45 46 47 48 49  QRSTUVWABCDEFGHI

=+=+=+=+=+=+=+=+=+=+=+=+=+=+=+=+=+=+=+=+=+=+=+=+=+=+=+=+=+=+=+=+=+=+=+=+=+=+

12/25-08:54:20.372628 0:A0:C9:B7:7B:C9 -> 0:90:1A:31:D5:E9 type:0x800 len:0x4A
208.177.178.141 -> 192.168.100.69 ICMP TTL:128 TOS:0x0 ID:9142 IpLen:20 DgmLen:60
Type:8  Code:0  ID:512   Seq:7428  ECHO
41 42 43 44 45 46 47 48 49 4A 4B 4C 4D 4E 4F 50  ABCDEFGHIJKLMNOP
51 52 53 54 55 56 57 41 42 43 44 45 46 47 48 49  QRSTUVWABCDEFGHI

=+=+=+=+=+=+=+=+=+=+=+=+=+=+=+=+=+=+=+=+=+=+=+=+=+=+=+=+=+=+=+=+=+=+=+=+=+=+

12/25-08:54:21.474497 0:A0:C9:B7:7B:C7 -> 0:10:B5:50:33:A2 type:0x800 len:0x4A
208.177.178.141 -> 208.177.178.140 ICMP TTL:128 TOS:0x0 ID:9152 IpLen:20 DgmLen:60
Type:8  Code:0  ID:512   Seq:8194  ECHO
61 62 63 64 65 66 67 68 69 6A 6B 6C 6D 6E 6F 70  abcdefghijklmnop
71 72 73 74 75 76 77 61 62 63 64 65 66 67 68 69  qrstuvwabcdefghi
```

Figure 9-15 A log file record displaying the signature of an automated ping sweep

The ping sweep, by itself, does not cause harm to the computers on your network. The prudent response would be to make note of the IP address being used in the ping sweep to track further activity. An IDS could be configured to transmit an alarm if the IP address in question attempts to connect to a specific host on the network, for instance.

Port Scans

If an attacker is able to determine any legitimate IP addresses on an internal network, the next step is to target one of those IP addresses and perform a **port scan** —an attempt to connect to a computer's ports to see if any are active and listening. The signature of a port scan typically includes a SYN packet sent to each port on an IP address, one after another, as shown in Figure 9-16.

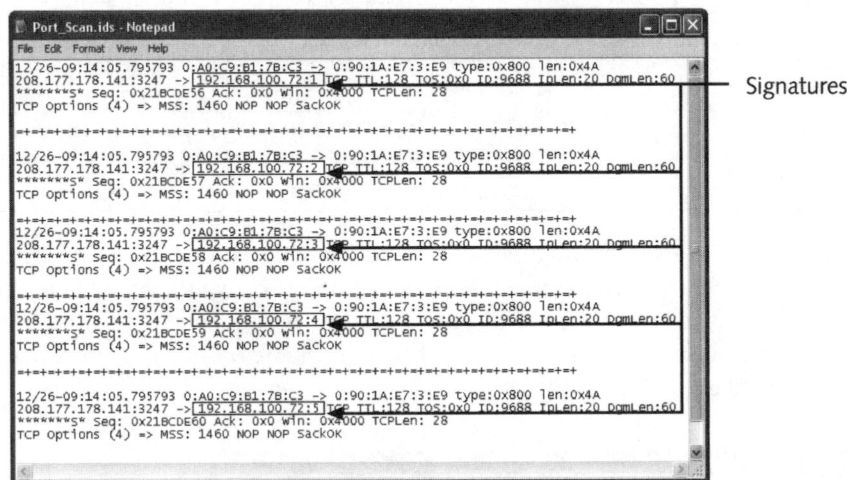

Figure 9-16 A log file record displaying the signatures of a port scan

In the example shown in Figure 9-16, the source port (3247) does not change from packet to packet. This indicates that the attacker is not expecting the target computer to establish a full three-way connection, but only to find out that the IP address is being used. In another type of port scan, the source port changes with each packet along with the destination port because a full three-way connection is expected.

Random Back Door Scans

You can think of a port as a virtual door through which data can enter and leave a computer. In that context, a **back door** can be thought of as an undocumented or unauthorized opening (such as a port) through which a computer, program, or other resource can be accessed. One type of port scan probes a computer to see if any ports are open and listening that are used by well-known **Trojan horses** —applications that seem to be harmless but that can cause harm to a computer or the files on it.

Some Trojan horses are so well-known that the "back door" ports on which they operate can be probed one after another to see if any of those applications are already present. For example, a random back door scan might target certain ports and subsequently seek to exploit the programs listed in Table 9-2.

9

Table 9-2 Well-known Trojan horse programs and ports

Trojan Horse Name	Port Used	Description
SubSeven	1243	Disables anti-virus or firewall protection
NetBus	1245	Provides Trojan horse author with remote access to the user's computer
Back Door	1999	Provides Trojan horse author with remote access to the user's computer
KeyLogger	12223	Copies user keystrokes and sends information about the user's OS and passwords back to Trojan horse's sender
Whack-a-mole	12361	Provides Trojan horse author with remote access to the user's computer
Back Orifice	31337, 31338	A scanner that records keystrokes and sends passwords back to the Trojan horse author; can also be used to run programs on a computer

A random Trojan horse scan involves an attacker searching for any Trojan horse programs that are present on a particular target computer in order to save the effort of installing such programs from scratch. Each sent SYN packet attempts to contact a different port used by a Trojan, such as the sequence of packets shown in Figure 9-17. (The ports being probed have been highlighted for clarity.)

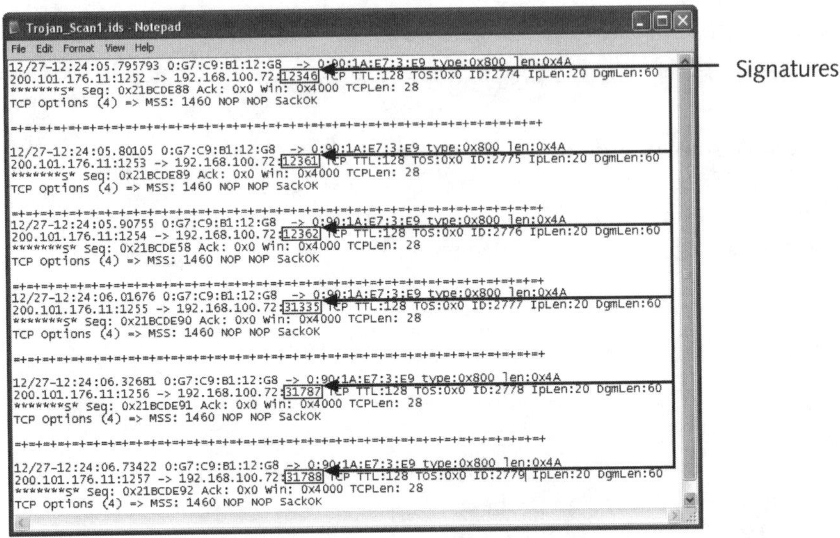

Figure 9-17 A log file record showing the signatures of a back door scan

If you see this type of scan in your log files, you need to take action quickly to block the source IP address because it is likely that specific attacks will take place in the near future.

ZoneLabs, the manufacturer of the ZoneAlarm firewall, publishes a list of well-known Trojan horses and the ports they use at *http://fwalerts.zonelabs.com/cat-mal/trojanports_num.shtml*. A more detailed list can be found at *www.simovits.com/trojans/trojans.html*.

Specific Trojan Scans

Port scans can be performed in several ways. In a **vanilla scan** , all of the ports from 0 to 65,535 are probed, one after another. In another type of scan, sometimes called a **strobe scan** , a hacker only scans ports that are commonly used by specific programs, in an attempt to see if such a program is presented and can be utilized.

One common type of strobe scan searches various IP addresses on a network for the presence of a specific Trojan horse program. If the hacker can find a Trojan horse program that has already circumvented the firewall and intrusion detection system and that is already operating, he or she can the save the time and effort installing a new Trojan horse program. For instance, in Figure 9-18, a series of IP addresses is being scanned on port 31337. This port is used by the notorious Back Orifice Trojan horse, as well as other Trojans such as ADM worm, Back Fire, and BlitzNet.

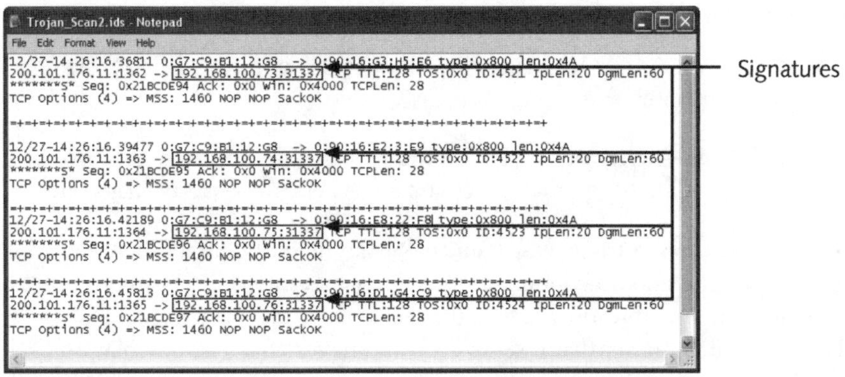

Figure 9-18 A log file record indicating a scan for the Back Orifice Trojan horse

The type of scan shown in Figure 9-18 is not necessarily dangerous. But it is worthy of serious concern because it is so specific. Hackers typically start with a general scan of IP addresses and get progressively more specific as they look for ports, back doors, or individual applications. If a hacker has received an indication from another method (such as an exchange of e-mail messages) that the Back Orifice program might be present on the network, the hacker might locate Back Orifice and an attack using the program may be imminent. You should immediately scan all computers on your network for viruses and Trojans and make sure the Trojan signatures used by your anti-virus program, firewall, or intrusion detection system are up-to-date.

Another specific Trojan scan might target port 12345, which is used by the NetBus Trojan and (like port 31337) is familiar to security professionals because it so frequently appears in security alerts and lists of frequently used Trojan ports.

Nmap Scans

A program called Nmap (an abbreviation for Network Mapper) is a popular tool for scanning networks, and you should be able to recognize the more common types of scans it enables hackers to perform. Nmap enables hackers to send packets that circumvent the normal three-way handshakes performed by two computers that establish a connection (in which 1. SYN, 2. SYN/ACK, and 3. ACK packets are exchanged). Nmap enables a hacker to send packets for which an IDS might not be configured to send an alarm. The IDS might see a combination of TCP flags that it doesn't recognize, and because no rule exists for the combination, an alarm might not be triggered. Examples include:

- *SYN scans* —The hacker sends a progression of packets with only the SYN flag set. The targeted computer will respond with packets that have the ACK flag set, but the originating computer simply keeps sending SYN packets.
- *FIN scans* —The hacker sends only packets that have the FIN flag set; a SYN flag is never sent.
- *ACK scans* —The hacker sends only packets with the ACK flag set; a SYN or FIN flag is never sent.
- *Null scans* —The hacker sends a sequence of packets that have no flags set at all. An IDS is likely to ignore such a packet because it has no flags set.

In each of these cases, a three-way handshake can never be established with the computer that is attempting to make a connection. It's likely that the hacker is attempting to determine if an application is active on a particular port: each packet has an identical source port number and a Seq number that is set to zero and never changes, in violation of the standard rules of TCP communications. An example of one of these scans—a FIN scan—is shown in Figure 9-19. The Seq numbers, source port numbers, and F (FIN) flags have been enclosed in boxes to indicate the elements you should look for in this Nmap signature.

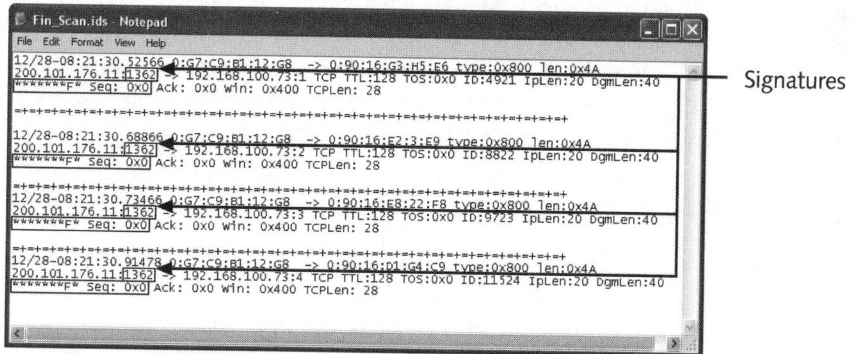

Figure 9-19 The signatures of a FIN scan conducted using Nmap

In this example, the constant source port numbers and Seq numbers and the F flag present in every packet all point to the use of Nmap in crafting these packets.

You can find out more about Nmap and how the program can be used to scan a network at *www.insecure.org/nmap*.

9

Identifying Suspicious Events

The previous section described well-known attack signatures you might encounter when inspecting your IDS log files. Unfortunately, attacks that are so widely known are often avoided by many hackers. Rather, attackers use more subtle means to try to gain unauthorized access to computers in your network. For instance, rather than the sequence of FIN packets described in the previous section, you might only see a single FIN packet sent to a port on a computer. Other "orphaned" packets might follow, but only after an interval during which a substantial number of legitimate packets have passed through. The use of the interval provides a distraction during which the different stages of the attack are separated from one another, so an analyst might not be able to realize that they are part of the same attack.

Such attacks can be extremely difficult to detect by reviewing log files manually. Rather, you need to depend on an extensive database of signatures that includes such events. Nevertheless, it's still your responsibility to respond to alarms and determine what they mean. This section describes individual events and characteristics of network communications that you need to identify as suspicious events once your IDS has responded to them by transmitting an alarm. The discussion includes packet header discrepancies, advanced IDS attacks, and remote procedure call abuses.

IDS alarms for the suspicious events described in this section may indicate that your packet filter is not working effectively (because it has let suspicious packets pass through it to reach the IDS). As a result, the packet filter's rule base needs to be revised. You can also fine-tune the way the IDS device responds to such events, as described in "Developing IDS Filter Rules" later in this chapter.

Packet Header Discrepancies

Discrepancies you see in TCP, IP, ICMP, or UDP packet headers can provide you with warning signs indicating that the packet has been **crafted** (in other words, manufactured or altered on purpose) by a hacker. However, rather than seeing such discrepancies on a well-defined and lengthy succession of packets, you might only receive a single packet with a falsified IP address, falsified port number, illegal TCP flags, TCP or IP options, or fragmentation abuses.

Falsified IP Address

Your IDS might send alarms for violations of IP header settings as specified in RFC 791, "Internet Protocol." For example, an IP address should not appear in one of the three reserved ranges (10.0.0.0 – 10.255.255.255, 172.16.0.0 – 172.31.255.255 and 192.168.0.0 – 192.168.255.255). The use of addresses in the reserved ranges is limited to private networks. If you do see one in a packet, the reason may be that a router or other device has been misconfigured or is malfunctioning. On the other hand, the packet may bear one of the private addresses because a hacker has performed **IP spoofing** (in other words, inserted a false address into the IP header to make the packet more difficult to trace back to its source).

For more information about the proper use of private IP addresses, refer to RFC 1918, "Address Allocation for Private Internets," at *www.isi.edu/in-notes/rfc1918.txt*.

The Land attack is an example of a falsified IP address that is used to cause a server to malfunction. It occurs when an IP packet is detected that has an invalid IP address setting in which the source and destination addresses are the same. Another attack that uses an invalid IP address, the Localhost Source Spoof, should trigger an alarm if the local host source address of 127.x.x.x occurs in a packet.

Falsified Port Number or Protocol

You already know that IP address information can be falsified in a packet, but protocol numbers might be altered as well to elude an IDS. TCP and UDP headers should never have the source or destination port set to 0. Protocol numbers cannot be set to 134 or greater. The use of undefined protocol numbers might indicate an attempt by an attacker to establish a proprietary communications channel, which is a channel that is known about and used only by that individual.

Illegal TCP Flags

As you saw in the section "Normal Traffic Signatures" earlier in this chapter, the TCP flags SYN and ACK are exchanged to establish a connection between two computers. The PSH flag is used when data is being sent, and the FIN flag is used when a connection is complete. Other normal TCP flag rules include:

- Every packet in a connection should have the ACK bit set except for the initial SYN packet and possibly an RST packet used to terminate a connection.
- Packets during the "conversation" portion of the connection (after the three-way handshake, but before the teardown or termination) contain just an ACK by default. Optionally, they may also contain PSH and/or URG.
- FIN/ACK and ACK are used during the graceful teardown of an existing connection. PSH/FIN/ACK may also be seen near the end of a connection.
- RST or RST/ACK can be used to immediately terminate a connection.

One of the most obvious ways to detect an abnormal packet signature is to look at the TCP flags for violations of the normal usage. A packet that has the SYN flag and the FIN flag set should not exist in normal traffic; however, a hacker may set both flags to cause the destination computer to crash or freeze because it does not know how to respond. After the server is disabled, the hacker can then attack a computer on the internal network whose IP address has earlier been detected through network scans.

The following list presents a summary of signatures of malformed packets that misuse the SYN and FIN flags:

- SYN FIN is probably the best-known illegal combination. Because SYN is used to start a connection and FIN is used to end a connection, it doesn't make sense to include both flags together in a packet. Many scanning tools use SYN FIN packets because, in the past, many intrusion detection systems were not configured to recognize or block them. However, most IDS devices are configured to catch such illegal combinations now. It's safe to assume that any SYN FIN packets you see are created by hackers.
- SYN FIN PSH, SYN FIN RST, SYN FIN RST PSH, and other variants on SYN FIN also exist, and their use is sometimes called an XMAS attack. Such packets may be used by attackers who are aware that intrusion detection systems may be looking for packets with just the SYN and FIN bits set.
- Packets should never contain a FIN flag by itself. FIN packets are frequently used for port scans, network mapping and other stealth activities.
- A SYN only packet, which should only occur when a new connection is being initiated, should not contain any data.

As mentioned in the previous section, you may also encounter **null packets** —TCP packets that have no flags set whatsoever and that could cause a server to crash. It is a violation of the TCP protocol rules to use a packet that has no flags set.

TCP or IP Options

TCP options that are present in a packet can alert you to intrusion attempts and even enable you to identify the type of operating system being used. For instance, only one MSS or Window option should appear in a packet. MSS, NOP, and SackOK should only appear in packets that have the SYN and/or ACK flag set. Additionally, TCP packets have two "reserved bits." Any packet that uses either or both of the reserved bits is probably malicious.

IP options were originally intended as ways to insert special handling instructions into packets that were not dealt with in other header fields. However, hackers mostly use IP options now for attack attempts. Because of this vulnerability, many filters simply drop all packets with IP options set.

Fragmentation Abuses

Every type of computer network (for example, Ethernet, FDDI, or Token Ring) has its own **maximum transmission unit (MTU)** —the maximum packet size that can be transmitted. Packets that are larger than the MTU must be fragmented—broken into multiple segments that are small enough for the network to handle.

After a packet is broken into fragments, each fragment receives its own IP header. However, only the initial = packet in a set includes a header for higher-level protocols. Most filters need the information in the higher-level protocol header to make the decision to allow or deny. Accordingly, attackers send only secondary fragments (any fragment other than the initial one). Such packets are often simply allowed past the IDS and filter rules are applied to first fragments only.

Fragmentation in and of itself can occur normally. However, an IDS should be configured to send an alarm if a large number of fragmented packets are encountered. Many different types of fragmentation abuses can occur. Some of the more serious ones are described briefly in the following list:

- *Overlapping fragments* —Two fragments of the same packet have the same position within the packet so the contents overlap one another. Such overlap can occur naturally in network traffic, but it can be an indication of an attack as well.

- *Fragments that are too long* —An IP packet can be no longer than 65,535 bytes in length. Packets that, when reassembled from their fragments, are more than the maximum size might cause some systems to crash and might indicate a Denial of Service attack.

- *Fragments overwrite data* —Some early fragments in a sequence are transmitted along with random data. Later fragments overwrite the random data. If the packet is not properly reassembled, the IDS is unable to detect the attack.

- *Fragments are too small* —If any fragment other than the final fragment in a sequence is less than 400 bytes in size, it has probably been intentionally crafted. Such a small fragment is probably part of a Denial of Service attack.

Yet another risk of fragmented packets is leaking of information—if you allow incoming NFS requests, but block the reply, it's still possible for fragments with sensitive information to get back to the originator of the request.

Advanced IDS Attacks

Most of the types of attacks discussed thus far have been protocol anomalies—violations of the various protocol rules described in RFC statements. Some especially complex attacks use pathnames, hexadecimal codes, and obfuscated directory names to fool the ID into letting the packet through without triggering an alarm. Some of the more advanced IDS evasion techniques include:

- *Polymorphic buffer overflow attacks* —Such attacks are as complicated as they sound. A tool called ADMutate is used to alter an attack's shell code in such a way that the code is made to differ slightly from the known signatures used by many IDS systems. After the attacking packets elude the IDS and reach their intended target, they reassemble into their original form.

- *Path obfuscation* —A directory path statement in the payload part of a packet is obfuscated through the use of multiple forward-slashes. For example /winnt/. /. /. / is essentially the same as /winnt. However, because the signatures don't match exactly, an IDS might be unable to detect this attack. Alternatively, to evade IDS systems that have been configured to trigger alarms when they encounter multiple forward-slashes, the Unicode equivalent of a forward-slash, "%co%af", is used.

- *CGI scripts* —A series of packets is sent to a series of well-known **Common Gateway Interface (CGI) scripts** (scripts used to process data submitted over the World Wide Web). Examples include such CGI scripts as Count.cgi, FormMail, AnyForm, php.cgi, TextCounter, and GuestBook. You can be certain someone is attempting to exploit your network if you do not actually have such files present but packets attempt to locate them anyway.

The only way to avoid such attacks is to keep your IDS signatures up-to-date and to watch your log files closely.

Remote Procedure Calls

Remote Procedure Call (RPC) is a standard set of communications rules that allows one computer to request a service (in other words, a remote procedure) from another computer on a network. RPC uses a program called a portmapper that maintains a record of each remotely accessible program and the port it uses. Because RPC can provide remote

9

access to applications, attackers naturally attempt to use RPC to gain unauthorized access to those applications. Some examples of RPC-related events that should trigger IDS alarms follow:

- *RPC dump*—A targeted host receives an RPC dump request—a request to report the presence and port usage of any RPC services provided by that system.
- *RPC set spoof*—A targeted host receives an RPC set request form a source IP address of 127.x.x.x.
- *RPC NFS sweep*—A target host receives a series of requests for the NFS (Network File System) program on a succession of different ports.

RPC services such as Network Information System (NIS) use a four-byte service number due to the fact that there are too many services to use a 2-byte port number. When an RPC service starts up, it allocates a random TCP or UDP port for itself. It then contacts rpcbind or portmapper and registers its service number and TCP/UDP port. Portmapper/rpcbind always runs on port 111, for example. A client wishing to talk to a server first contacts portmapper to get the port number, then continues the exchange with the server directly. A client can bypass portmapper and scan for services. There is no guarantee that a particular service will end up on a particular port.

Developing IDS Filter Rules

An intrusion detection system's effectiveness depends on how complete and up-to-date the signatures or user profiles contained in its database are. If your IDS command console receives alarms from some of the well-known intrusion signatures or suspicious events described in the preceding sections, you should respond by:

- Adjusting your packet-filtering rules
- Creating rules on the IDS

An IDS, like a firewall or packet-filtering router, can have its own rules that you should edit in response to scans and attacks. It can do more than simply reacting to undetected attacks as a second line of defense and relying upon firewalls and proxy servers to filter out packets. An IDS can be used proactively to block attacks and move from intrusion detection to intrusion prevention. This section examines the ways of configuring an IDS to filter out potentially harmful traffic: specifying rule actions, using rule options, and creating security designations.

Rule Actions

The problem with traditional IDS is its passive and reactive nature. By configuring an IDS to take actions other than simply triggering an alarm when it encounters a suspicious packet, you gain another layer of network defense. You gain more control over how attacks are recorded and handled, and you reduce false-positives. Finally, you also help the IDS in being able to handle new intrusion attempts as they are developed by ever-busy attackers.

The freeware IDS Snort gives you an idea of the kinds of actions a rule can take when it encounters a packet that matches one of its rules. The actions are set in the file snort.conf, which you can edit using a text editor. (You can also create your own custom rules file and have Snort refer to that as well.) The available actions are:

- *Alert* —This sends an alert message as you defined earlier.
- *Log* —This records the packet in the log files.
- *Pass* —This allows the packet to pass through to the internal network.
- *Activate* —This creates an alert message and also creates a dynamic rule—a rule that covers subsequent logging.
- *Dynamic* —A dynamic rule enables Snort to continue logging subsequent packets when a particular packet is detected. For instance, if a port scan packet is detected, you could call a dynamic rule that tells Snort to log the next 100 packets.

Other IDS devices also give you the option to terminate the TCP connection of the originating computer if an attack is detected.

Rule Data

After you specify the action you want Snort to perform when it encounters a match with one of its signatures, you then specify the rest of the data that applies to the rule. This includes:

- *Protocol* —Snort supports the IP, TCP, UDP, and ICMP protocols.
- *Source and destination IP addresses* —You can use the word Any to specify any IP address, or the netmask format for specifying a subnet mask. A Class A IP address uses the /8 netmask; a Class B address uses the /16 netmask; a Class C address uses the /24 netmask.
- *Port number* —You can specify an individual port or use Any.
- *Direction* —The direction from the source computer and port to the destination computer and port is specified with the -> keys. For rules that affect traffic heading in both directions, use <>.

9

For instance, a rule that logs traffic from any computer to a computer at 192.168.10.1 on port 23 would look like the following:

```
Log tcp any any -> 192.168.10.1 23
```

A rule that logs traffic in both directions from one subnet and another subnet would look like the following:

```
Log tcp 10.1.20.0/24 any <> 200.156.15.o.24 any
```

More specific attributes such as ACK flags are covered by the rule options, which follow the rule action and data.

Rule Options

Snort rules become fine-grained when you add rule options. The options are enclosed in parentheses; they come after the rule data and are separated from the data by a blank space. Each option is separated from other options enclosed within the parentheses by a semicolon and a blank space. For example:

```
Alert tcp any any -> 192.168.10.0/24 any (msg: "SYN-FIN
scan packet"; flags: SF;)
```

This rule contains two options. The msg option causes a text message to be printed along with the alert message and the data recorded in the log files. The flags option causes the rule to trigger the specified action when specified flags are detected in a packet—in this case, the SYN and FIN flags (SF) are used together.

The most useful options that Snort can implement include the following:

- *ttl* —This tells Snort to match the Time to Live (TTL) value in the IP header of a packet.
- *id* —This tells Snort to match a fragment ID number of a packet.
- *flags* —This tells Snort to match specified TCP flags set in a packet.
- *ack* —This tells Snort to match the ACK flag in a packet.
- *content* —This tells Snort to match a defined string in the packet's data payload.
- *logto* —This tells Snort to log files to a specified filename instead of the default log files.

Many more options are available for Snort rules; you'll find a complete list at *www.snort.org/docs/writing_rules/*.

The TCP flags that form an important part of signatures are usually designated in Snort rules by a single character, as shown in the following list:

- F (FIN)
- S (SYN)
- R (RST)
- P (PSH)
- A (ACK)
- U (URG)
- 2 (Reserved bit 2)
- 1 (Reserved bit 1)
- 0 (No TCP flags set)
- + ALL flag—it matches all specified flags plus any others
- * ANY flag—it matches any of the specified flags
- ! Matches all flags except the flag you specify

After you understand all of the available options, you can set up a proactive set of rules that cover many of the suspicious traffic signatures described earlier in this chapter. The rule base for an IDS is different from the packet-filtering rule base described in Chapter 4. The IDS rule base assumes that packets are already being filtered by firewalls or routers. Therefore, any traffic that gets through the packet filter and matches a signature on the IDS should be logged. That way, you can analyze what traffic is getting through the filter so you can then adjust the filter rules. The initial rules might be dramatically different than those for a packet filter.

Examine the following example rules:

```
log tcp any any -> any any (msg: "TCP traffic log";)
log udp any any -> any any (msg: "UDP traffic log";)
alert icmp any any -> any any (msg: "ICMP traffic alert";)
```

The first two rules tell Snort to log any TCP and UDP traffic that reaches the IDS. The third rule sends an alert if any ICMP Echo Request packets or other ICMP packets reach the IDS as well. Once you set up these general rules, you can create rules for specific traffic signatures such as the following:

```
alert tcp any any -> 192.168.1.0/24 any (flags: SFA; msg:
"SYN-FIN-ACK packet detected";)
```

The preceding rule sends an alert if a packet with the SYN, FIN, and ACK flags is detected. On the other hand, the following rule sends an alert if a flag is detected that does not have any flags set.

```
alert tcp any any -> 192.168.1.0/24 any (flags: 0; msg:
"null packet detected";)
```

The following two rules send an alert if any packets are detected that have the two most frequently watched-for IP options: Loose Source Routing and Strict Source Routing. (Only one IP option can be specified per rule.)

```
alert tcp any any -> 192.168.1.0/24 any (ipopts: ssrr; msg:
"strict source routing packet";)
alert tcp any any -> 192.168.1.0/24 any (ipopts: lsrr; msg:
"loose source routing packet";)
```

The following rule sends an alert if the word Password is detected in the data payload part of a packet.

```
alert tcp any any -> any any (content: "Password"; msg:
"password transmitted?";)
```

The following rule is intended to address the path obfuscation attack mentioned in "Advanced IDS Attacks" earlier in this chapter.

```
alert tcp any any -> any 80 (content: "/. /. /. /"; msg:
"possible Web URL path obfuscation";)
```

Chapter Summary

- This chapter discussed how to prevent intrusions by understanding how to interpret the signatures of both normal and abnormal network traffic. By being able to recognize the characteristics of a possible intrusion, you gain the ability to read log files and alert messages and react to them effectively. You can adjust filter rules to reduce the number of false alarms you receive from your IDS. More importantly, you are able to prevent intrusions before they occur or keep intrusions that are already underway from causing excessive damage.
- It is important to have your network security hardware and software work cooperatively by being able to share information. A standard called the Common Vulnerabilities and Exposures (CVE) enables IDS systems, firewalls, and other devices to share attack signatures and information about network vulnerabilities so they can better protect a network. A list of current vulnerabilities is maintained as an online database by MITRE, and you can use the list to update your own CVE database and learn about new attacks.
- Examination and analysis of the log files compiled by your IDS and other devices can help tell you whether remote computers are scanning your network as a prelude to an attack. However, reviewing the log files manually can be tedious and time-consuming. A log file analysis program automates the process and helps you identify which external hosts have been attempting to gain unauthorized access. The log files can also reveal patterns of access attempts that may represent intrusion attempts.
- The analysis of intrusion signatures is an integral aspect of intrusion prevention. A signature is a set of characteristics such as IP addresses, port numbers, TCP flags, and options. Normal traffic makes valid use of such settings. Note that possible intrusions are

marked by invalid settings that servers are sometimes unable to interpret and that are allowed to pass through into the internal network. Those invalid settings include bad header information, suspicious contents in the data payload of packets, IP options settings, and a succession of packets such as a Denial of Service attempt.

- You can set up the freeware IDS Snort as a packet sniffer so that you can capture packets and study their contents. You learned that parts of the packet header, such as the datagram length, can indicate whether a Windows or Linux system is being used. The TCP flags are used in sequence to create a normal three-way handshake between two computers. By learning how normal traffic signatures look, you are able to identify signatures of suspicious connection attempts. You can monitor suspicious events such as ping sweeps, port scans, random back door scans, and scans for specific Trojan horse programs. The characteristics of packets crafted with the popular network mapping tool Nmap were also discussed.
- You can identify a variety of other suspicious network events. These include "orphaned" packets, Land attacks (in which the source and destination IP addresses are the same), Localhost Source Spoofs, falsified protocol number, and illegal combinations of TCP flags such as SYN/FIN.
- Advanced IDS attacks are especially difficult to detect without a database of intrusion signatures or user behaviors. Certain complex attacks called polymorphic buffer overflow attacks can be altered so they don't match a known intrusion signature and elude the IDS. Others use confusing path names or other keywords in the data payload section of packets. Still others attempt to connect with and abuse common CGI scripts that may be present, or remote procedure calls that also enable remote users to access services on a computer.
- IDS devices can have their own set of filter rules, like packet-filtering routers and firewalls. You can configure a set of rules to send alert messages if ICMP packets or other suspicious packets pass through the packet filters on the perimeter of the network and reach the IDS. Such rules can also be configured to log events or a range of subsequent packets. Rule options such as messages that can be associated with suspicious events can greatly assist you in interpreting log files and determining how to react to attack attempts.

Key Terms

ASCII payload — The actual data part of the packet, given in ASCII format.

atomic attack — An attack that can be completed by sending a single network packet from client to host.

back door — An undocumented or unauthorized opening (such as a port) through which a computer, program, or other resource can be accessed.

checksum — A simple error-checking procedure used to determine whether a message has been tampered with in transit.

Common Gateway Interface (CGI) scripts — Scripts used to process data submitted over the World Wide Web.

Common Vulnerabilities and Exposures (CVE) — A standard that enables security devices to share information about attack signatures and other vulnerabilities so that they can work together to provide network protection.

composite attacks — Attacks that require a series of packets to be transmitted in order for the attack to be completed.

control connection — An initial FTP connection between client and server.

crafted — Manufactured or altered on purpose by a hacker.

Hexadecimal payload — The actual data being communicated by the packet expressed in hexadecimal format.

ID number — An identifying number that can be used to reassemble a packet in case it is divided into fragments.

IP spoofing — The process of inserting a false address into the IP header to make the packet more difficult to trace back to its source.

maximum transmission unit (MTU) — The maximum packet size that can be transmitted over a type of computer network such as Ethernet.

multiple-packet attacks — *See* composite attacks.

null packets — TCP packets that have no flags set whatsoever.

packet sniffer — Software or hardware that monitors traffic going into or out of a network device and that captures information about each TCP/IP packet it detects.

ping sweep — The act of sending a series of ICMP Echo Request packets in a range of IP addresses to see if any computers respond.

port scan — An attempt to connect to a computer's ports to see if any are active and listening.

Remote Procedure Call (RPC) — A standard set of communications rules that allows a program one computer to request a service from another computer on a network.

scanner — A device that scans a network for open ports or other potential vulnerabilities.

selective acknowledgements — Acknowledgements that selected packets in a sequence have been received, rather than having to acknowledge every packet.

signature — A set of characteristics—such as IP protocol numbers and options, TCP flags and port numbers—that is used to define a type of network activity.

single-packet attack — *See* atomic attack.

strobe scan — A type of port scan that probes ports that are commonly used by specific programs, in an attempt to see if such a program is presented and can be utilized.

Time to Live (TTL) — An instruction that tells a router how long a packet should remain on the network before it is discarded.

Trojan horses — Applications that seem to be harmless, but that can cause harm to a computer or the files on it.

Type of service (TOS) — The part of a packet header that allows the sender the option to express the precedence of the packet—whether it should have low delay, whether it needs high reliability, and so on.

vanilla scan — A type of port scan in which all of the ports from 0 to 65,535 are probed, one after another.

Review Questions

1. Security devices that are on a network process digital information such as text files and Web pages the same way. However, they may handle what other kind of digital information differently?

   a. protocols

   b. TCP/IP headers

   c. attack signatures

   d. port numbers

2. Which of the following is a way in which CVE can improve the coordination of intrusion information on a network?

   a. Attack signatures can be compared to the lists of vulnerabilities published on the CVE Web site.

   b. Attack signatures can be compared to current network vulnerabilities.

   c. Installing application patches can thwart an attack report.

   d. Current network vulnerabilities can be used to generate application patches.

3. What is particularly useful about the way Snort organizes its log file entries?

   a. Entries that triggered alarms are sorted in separate folders.

   b. Log files are rotated on a daily basis.

   c. Entries for one IP address are located in a single folder.

   d. Entries for suspicious connection attempts are color-coded.

4. Which of the following can be included in a network traffic signature? (Choose all that apply.)

   a. logon attempts

   b. message digest

   c. TCP options

   d. Ethernet interface number

5. What is the name of an error-checking procedure that uses a formula to calculate a numeric value?

   a. algorithm

   b. one-way hash

   c. hexadecimal code

   d. checksum

6. Which of the following is a way in which hackers use fragmentation to circumvent network defenses? (Choose all that apply.)

   a. Fragment ID numbers are falsified.

   b. The initial packet is missing.

   c. Multiple initial packets are sent.

   d. Too many fragments are sent.

7. Which of the following packets should never have a data payload?

   a. one that has the SYN/ACK flags set

   b. one that has the ACK flag set

   c. one that has the SYN flag set

   d. one that has the ACK/PSH flags set

8. Which of the following is missing from an atomic attack? (Choose all that apply.)

   a. an IP address or Mac address

   b. a TCP header

   c. two or more packets

   d. a connection

9. Which of the following is an example of a composite attack?

   a. Ping of Death

   b. ICMP flood

   c. false Internet timestamp

   d. a packet with the SYN/FIN/ACK flags set

10. Which of the following Time to Live (TTL) values is commonly used by Windows computers? (Choose all that apply.)

    a. 128

    b. 64

    c. 32

    d. 60

11. What is the purpose of the acknowledgement number in a TCP header?

    a. It acknowledges the receipt of the previous packet in the sequence.

    b. It acknowledges that a connection has been made.

    c. It verifies that the source and destination IP addresses are correct.

    d. It acknowledges the ID number being used by the packet.

12. Which of the following is the correct order in which TCP flags would appear in the course of a normal connection?

    a. SYN, ACK, FIN, RST

    b. SYN, PSH, ACK, FIN

    c. SYN, ACK, ACK/PSH, FIN

    d. SYN, PSH, ACK, FIN

13. What type of OS typically has the following as part of its signature: DgmLen 60, TTL 64, initial sequence number 0?

14. Which type of OS typically has alphabetical characters (ABCDEFGH...) in its ASCII data payload?

15. Which type of protocol uses different port numbers to establish the connection and to transfer data?

    a. TCP/IP

    b. FTP

    c. HTTP

    d. ICMP

16. Which of the following is an example of a reconnaissance traffic signature?

    a Trojan horse

    b ping sweep

    c Denial of Service

    d Ping of Death

17. A Back Orifice attack falls into what category of suspicious traffic signatures?

    a. information

    b. reconnaissance

    c. Denial of Service

    d. access

18. What is the advantage of configuring IDS filter rules if you already have packet filter rules in place? (Choose all that apply.)

    a. You can attach messages to the alerts.

    b. The filters can be configured to match TCP flag combinations.

    c. The filters can be configured to match specific ports.

    d. You gain another layer of security.

19. How do the initial rules in an IDS filter differ from the initial rules in a packet filter, which usually begin by blocking all TCP traffic?

    a. They allow all TCP traffic.

    b. They log all TCP traffic.

    c. They send an alert for any TCP traffic.

    d. They log and alert all TCP traffic.

20. What is the name of the program that keeps track of services and ports made available through Remote Procedure Calls?

    a. Network Information System

    b. Network File System

    c. Network File Sharing

    d. portmapper

HANDS-ON PROJECTS

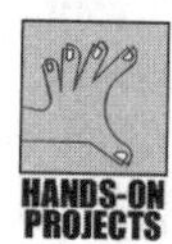

Project 9-1: Using a Log File Analysis Tool

In this project you will download and install a simple log file analyzer that is designed to work with the firewall program ZoneAlarm. This project assumes you have installed the freeware version of ZoneAlarm as described in Hands-On Project 4-4. The project can be performed on a Windows XP or 2000 computer

1. Open ZoneAlarm by double-clicking the program icon or double-clicking the **ZoneAlarm** icon in your Windows system tray.
2. Click **Alerts & Logs**, and then click **Main**, if necessary.
3. Click **On**.
4. Double-click the **Internet Explorer** icon on your desktop.
5. Enter the URL for the ZoneLog Analyser Web site (**http://zonelog.co.uk**), and then press **Enter**.
6. Click **Downloads**.
7. Click either **Site 1** or **Site 2** next to Full Install Package.
8. When the File Download dialog box appears, choose the directory where you want to download the file, click **OK**, and then click **Save**.
9. When download is complete, double-click the file you downloaded. When the Setup dialog box appears asking if you want to proceed with the installation, click **Yes**.
10. Click **Next** when the first Setup screen appears, read the license agreement, and then click **Yes**.
11. Click **Next** to save the files to a directory, and then click **Yes** to create the directory.
12. Click **Next**, click **Next**, and then click **Install**.
13. Reboot your computer when prompted to do so. When your computer has restarted, start up ZoneLog either by double-clicking its program icon or clicking **Start**, clicking **Programs** (**All Programs** on Windows XP) and then clicking **ZoneLog**.
14. If a dialog box appears asking if you want to register the software, click **Remind Me Later**. Click the **Report** button and click **Ports**, if necessary, and then click **Create** to create a report of the ports that have been probed on your computer recently. You'll notice that most of the traffic comes from your own computer or others on your network. What are the colors assigned to packets you see in the report that come from computers outside your network?

9

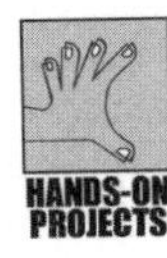

Project 9-2: Using Snort to Capture ICMP Packets

For this project you will need two computers that are connected to one another either through the same network or on the Internet. One student should sit at one computer that has Snort installed, to capture packets. The other should sit at the second computer to send echo request packets. One of the computers should have the intrusion detection program Snort installed, as described in Hands-On Project 2-4. The computers can use Linux or Windows 2000 or XP. Make sure you don't have any firewall rules set up that block ICMP traffic (such as the ICMP rules applied by Windows XP's built-in Internet Connection Firewall).

1. Both students should open a command prompt window on each of their respective computers. On Windows, click **Start**, click **Programs** (**All Programs** on Windows XP), click **Accessories**, and click **Command Prompt**. On Linux, click the **Red Hat** icon, click **System Tools**, and click **Terminal**.
2. Each student should type **ipconfig** at the command prompt, and then press **Enter**.
3. Each student should write down the IP addresses of his or her respective computer and exchange it with the other student.
4. Student 1 (the student who is working at the computer with Snort installed) should locate the snort.exe application program and write down the path leading to it. (These steps use the path C:\Snort\snort.exe as an example; replace this with your own directory path).
5. At the command prompt, student 1 should type **C:\Snort\snort.exe –v –d**, and then press **Enter**. (Substitute the path leading to snort.exe on your own computer if it is different than this example.) Be sure to leave a blank space before each hyphen.
6. Student 2 should make sure student 1 is ready and then type **ping *[IP address of student 1's computer]***, and then press **Enter**.
7. When packets begin to appear in the command prompt window, student 1 should quickly press **Ctrl+C** to stop them. Ideally, student 1 should stop the packet capture after only a few packets have crossed the network interface card so they can be reviewed from the beginning.
8. If necessary, repeat Steps 6 and 7 to stop the packet capture near the beginning of the communication. What were the sequence numbers of the packets exchanged by the two computers?

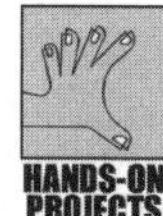

Project 9-3: Capturing a Web Site Handshake

The process of capturing the sequence of a Web site connection with Snort is one you can do yourself. It enables you to inspect the HTTP headers in each packet as well as the TCP flags that are exchanged during the handshake. You can use a Linux or Windows 2000 or XP computer; this project assumes that you have Snort installed and a Web browser as well, and that your lab computer is connected to the Internet.

1. On Windows, click **Start**, click **Programs** (**All Programs** on Windows XP), click **Accessories**, and click **Command Prompt**. On Linux, click the **Red Hat** icon, click **System Tools**, and click **Terminal**.
2. At the command prompt, type **C:\Snort\snort.exe –v –d** (substitute the path leading to snort.exe on your own computer if it is different than this example), and then press **Enter**. (Substitute the path that points to the Snort executable for C:\Snort\snort.exe. Be sure to leave a blank space before each hyphen.)
3. When a message appears stating that Snort is initializing, start up your Web browser by double-clicking the **Internet Explorer** icon on your desktop. Then enter the URL **http://www.course.com** in the browser's Address bar and press **Enter**.
4. Quickly switch back to the Command Prompt window and press **Ctrl+C** to stop the packets from being captured.
5. Snort should present a brief report of the packets captured so far. Besides TCP packets, what sorts of packets were captured? Write the answer in a lab notebook or word processing document.
6. Scroll up to the top of the packets shown in the Command Prompt window and look for the SYN, SYN/ACK, ACK three-way handshake. (If you don't see it, you may need to connect to a different Web site and repeat Steps 3 and 4.)

Project 9-4: Reviewing Suspicious Traffic Signatures

In this project you will gain familiarity with the arachNIDS database of known attack signatures that is maintained on the Whitehats Network Security Resource Web site. You'll learn how to look up specific types of attacks and review packet captures of attack attempts as well.

1. Double-click the **Internet Explorer** icon on your desktop.
2. Enter the following URL into your browser's Address bar: **http://www.whitehats.com**, and press **Enter**.
3. Click **arachNIDS Center** in the list of links on the left side of the home page.
4. First you want the database to present a list of all Web-based attacks: scroll down the page, enter **80** in the Port box (leaving all other search fields blank), and press **Enter**.

5. Scroll down the list of Web-related attack signatures and click **IDS226/http-cgi-formmail**. You can also search by using the Search for text box.
6. Read the description of the attack, then click the **Research** tab to view an actual packet capture related to this attack. Do you notice anything out of the ordinary in the packet header details? Scan the ASCII data payload part of the packet carefully. Scroll down the payload until you find indications as to how this attack takes place. What do you notice? Write your answers in a lab notebook or word processing document.
7. Click your browser's **Back** button twice to return to the list of Web-related attack signatures. Click **IDS459/probe-Synscan-microsoft**.
8. Read the description of the "PROBE-SYNSCAN-MICROSOFT" attack. Then click **Research** to view the packet capture. What clue do you see in the packet header that immediately tells you that this is an invalid packet?
9. Click **arachNIDS Center** in the links on the left side of the page.
10. In the Search all fields box, type **IP option**, and then press **Enter**.
11. Click **IDS116/source_route_icmp_lsrr**. (If you don't see this in the list, type **IDS116** in the Search for text box, and then click **Search**.)
12. Read a description of this attack, then click the **Protocol** tab.
13. A graphic depiction of the IP and ICMP headers for this packet appears. Where is the header element location that causes this attack, and what is the element called?

Project 9-5: Researching the TCP and IP RFCs

All too often, network administrators receive alerts from their IDS devices but don't know how to interpret the data. This chapter gave you some tips for analyzing both normal and abnormal traffic signatures. It's important for you to back up this knowledge with a solid foundation in the actual specifications for TCP, IP, UDP, and ICMP traffic so that you can know exactly what constitutes a possible intrusion. This exercise will have you look up the original Request for Comment (RFC) documents for this traffic, but with emphasis on possible intrusions.

1. Double-click the **Internet Explorer** icon on your desktop.
2. Enter the following URL in your browser's Address bar: **http://www.ietf.org/rfc.html**, and press **Enter**.
3. In the RFC number box, enter **793** and click **go**.
4. The original proposal for TCP packets appears. Read the RFC closely and look for an answer to the following question: The MSS size must appear only in a TCP packet that has what flag set?
5. Look at the diagram labeled Figure 6. Which flags does it indicate might appear together?

6. Read page 27 and answer the following question: What is being synchronized when a packet with the SYN flag is sent?
7. Go back to **http://www.ietf.org/rfc.html**. Enter **791** in the RFC number box and click **go**. The original specification for Internet Protocol appears.
8. Scroll down to the part of the document entitled Fragmentation and Reassembly. How big should packet fragments be, and how many can there be in a fragment?
9. Go to page 13: In the section on flags, you see an explanation of DF, which appears in many packet headers. What does DF stand for?

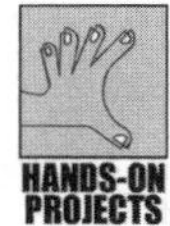

Project 9-6: Configuring Snort to Use IDS Filter Rules

In this project you will apply what you learned in this chapter about setting up IDS filter rules with Snort. You'll create your own brief set of filter rules to handle suspicious packets you learned about in this chapter. You can perform this project on a Windows 2000 or XP or a Linux computer that has the IDS program Snort installed. (You'll get best results if you have the snort.exe executable installed in C:\Snort\snort. Create a directory called log in C:\Snort. As in Project 9-3, a second computer is also needed, but it does not have to have Snort installed.)

9

1. Open up a text editor. On Windows, click **Start**, point to **Programs** (**All Programs** on Windows XP), point to **Accessories**, and click **Notepad**. On Linux, click the **Red Hat** icon, point to **Accessories**, and click **Text Editor**.
2. Type a rule that logs all TCP traffic coming in to the network.
3. Type a rule that tells Snort to send an alarm message whenever an ICMP packet from any source attempts to reach any computer on the network.
4. Write a rule that sends an alert when a SYN-FIN packet is detected.
5. Write a rule that sends the text message "Password sent" when the word "Password" appears in the data payload part of a packet.
6. Click **File** and click **Save**.
7. Type the file name **"rules.rule"** in the Save As dialog box. (Be sure to enclose the filename in quotes so that it will keep .rule as the extension rather than .txt.)
8. Save the file in the same directory where snort.exe is located, and then click **Save**.
9. On Windows, click **Start**, point to **Programs** (**All Programs** on Windows XP), point to **Accessories**, and click **Command Prompt**. On Linux, click the **Red Hat** icon, point to **Accessories**, and click **Text Editor**.

10. Enter the following at the command prompt to set up Snort to use the rules you have established: **%systemroot%\snort\snort.exe –l \ Snort\log -c \snort\rules.rule**, and then press **Enter**. (%systemroot% represents the path that leads to the snort executable file, such as C:\Program Files or C:\Snort.)

11. Go to the second lab computer and open a command prompt window as described in Step 9. At the command prompt, type **ping *[IP address of Snort computer]***. Press **Enter**.

12. Return to the first computer. Look in the log directory for a file called alerts.ids. Open the file using Notepad. Did you receive alerts for the Echo Request packets? Did you receive logs for the Echo Request packets in a file called ICMP_Echo.ids? Did you receive logs for other TCP and UDP traffic?

CASE PROJECTS

Case Project 9-1: Analyzing an Echo Request

Your firewall regularly receives a series of echo request packets from a computer at 67.118.23.141. You capture the packets with a packet-sniffing tool and notice the following characteristics: DgmLen 84, ID 0, TTL 64. What kind of computer is being used to send echo requests to your network? What other criteria could you use to identify the computer being used?

Case Project 9-2: Identifying an Nmap Scan

Normally, you review your IDS logs for intrusion attempts by having the IDS log connection attempts that were blocked or for which an alarm was issued. By mistake, someone on your IT staff sets the IDS to log connection attempts that were allowed as well. You are presented with a huge log file to review. You sort out traffic from computers on your own network and from your DNS server to reduce the file size. When you review the entries that are left, you notice by chance a series of hundreds of packets that were sent in sequence and that have no flags set. Such packets were not detected by the IDS because they are apparently of no value in making a network connection. What clues would you look for in such packets to determine that they are evidence that a hacker is attempting to gain information about open ports on your network? What should you do if you determine that such an attempt has been made?

Case Project 9-3: Filtering Out Common Scans

You have determined that an Nmap null scan has been launched against a computer on your network as described in Case 9-2. You suspect that other scans may be forthcoming. What sorts of filter rules would you establish so that your IDS can send an alarm when one is detected?

Case Project 9-4: Analyzing a Suspicious Scan Signature

You see a series of packets in your log files, as shown in Figure 9-20.

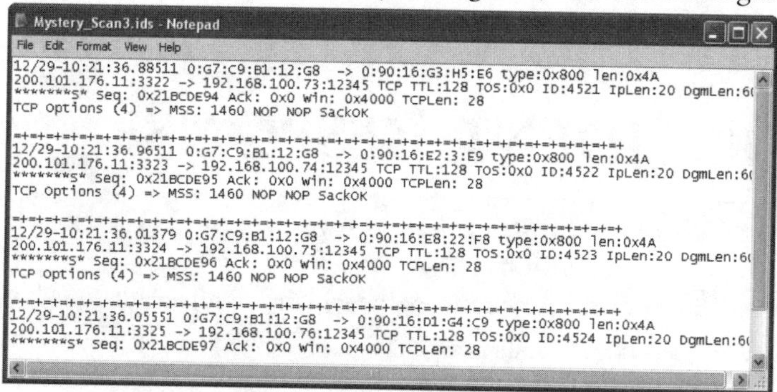

Figure 9-20 Log files

When you first look at a log file like the one shown in this figure, it can be intimidating. Discuss how you would review the sequence of packets in the figure. What would you look for?

9

What kind of scan is involved? What is the hacker attempting to locate? What is the window size of the packets that the attacker is sending? What is the source port being used by the attacker?

CHAPTER

10

Intrusion Detection: Incident Response

After reading this chapter and completing the exercises, you will be able to:

- Develop an Incident Response Team for your organization
- Follow the six-step incident response process
- Describe how to respond to false alarms to reduce reoccurrences
- Understand options for dealing with legitimate security alerts
- Describe computer forensics activities you can use to investigate hackers

In previous chapters you learned how to configure an intrusion detection system (IDS) and how to interpret signatures of both legitimate traffic and known attack attempts. Once you have installed and configured an IDS, you need to know how to respond to the alert messages it generates. Without a doubt, you will receive false alarms from the IDS, but you'll also receive legitimate attack alerts. It's essential to know how to respond to both types of events in a way that does not alarm your staff, that minimizes damage, and that prevents such intrusions from happening in the future.

Incident response is the name given to the actions taken after a computer security incident occurs in order to determine what happened and what countermeasures need to be taken to ensure the continued security of the network. Incident response is a process that follows a set of well-defined steps. In all cases, the steps need to be described clearly enough so that anyone authorized to perform security response should be able to follow them.

This chapter gives you an overview of the approaches that go into responding to intrusion alerts. You'll learn how to develop a Security Incident Response Team (SIRT), how to respond to an incident, how to respond to false alarms (otherwise known as false-positives), how to respond to legitimate alarms (true-positives), and how to conduct forensics in order to locate and, if necessary, prosecute offenders.

DEVELOPING A SECURITY INCIDENT RESPONSE TEAM (SIRT)

You can respond to a security incident in a number of different ways. Your options include countermeasures designed to block intrusions; corrections to packet-filtering rules and proxy servers to block intrusions that have been detected by an Intrusion Detection System (IDS); and alterations to security policies to cover new vulnerabilities as they are detected. By developing a Security Incident Response Team (SIRT), you give your organization the flexibility to implement any or all of these response options. The META Group research organization (*www.metagroup.com*) projects that as many as 60 percent of global 2000 companies will invest in a SIRT by 2004.

You need to establish a framework within which intrusion detection and response can take place. This section examines one aspect of that framework—the establishment of a SIRT. You'll learn how to establish goals and expectations for the SIRT; the responsibilities of the team members; when to notify public response teams; and when to consider outsourcing incident response.

Goals of a Security Incident Response Team (SIRT)

A **Security Incident Response Team (SIRT)** (also known as a Computer Incident Response Team, or CIRT) is a group of individuals who are assigned to respond effectively to security breaches. The team's primary functions can be broken down into six steps:

1. *Preparation* —Begin with a risk analysis and security policy; create the SIRT itself.
2. *Notification* —Monitor the integrity of the computing environment in order to uncover security vulnerabilities; receive notification from your intrusion detection system (IDS) or firewall.
3. *Response* —React to internal and external security breaches and policy violations; determine who to notify; determine whether the attack is legitimate or a false alarm; assess the level of damage.
4. *Countermeasures* —Contain the damage and eradicate any harmful or unauthorized files that have been introduced. These are strategies and approaches that counter threats to network security. Also, take corrective measures to prevent recurrence.
5. *Recovery* —Restore damaged files and compromised resources.
6. *Follow-up* —Record what happened; conduct forensics if necessary; decide whether to prosecute the offenders; adjust security policies as needed.

The six steps of incident response are part of a larger workflow that encompasses everything from initial risk analysis to the reevaluation of security policies and procedures after an event occurs. The incident response process does not comprise a discrete series of events, but rather an ongoing process, as indicated in Figure 10-1.

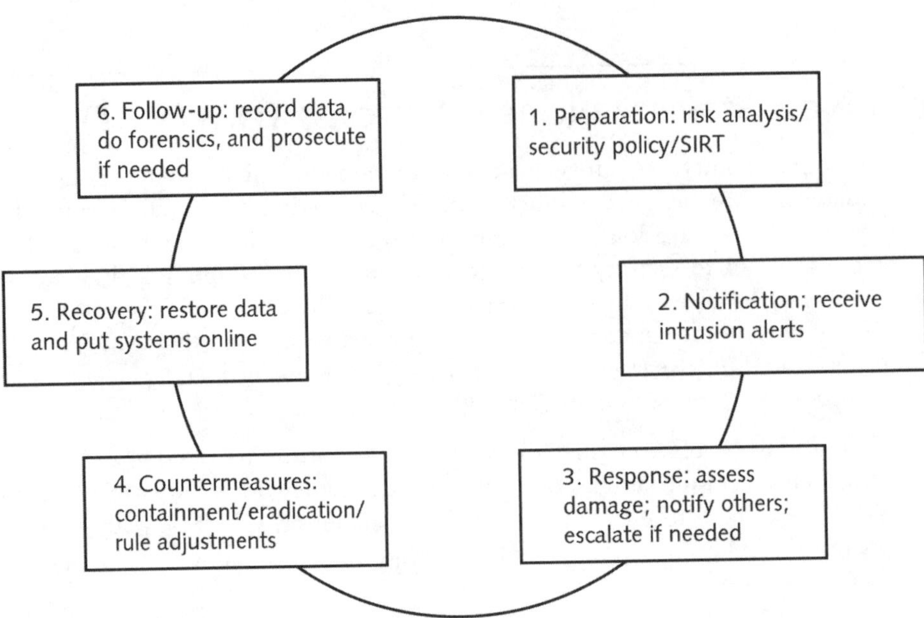

Figure 10-1 The intrusion response process

TIP

The six core response activities of the SIRT are described in greater detail in "How to Respond: The Incident Response Process" later in this chapter.

Responsibilities of the Team Members

It frequently makes sense to look within the organization for members of a SIRT. Employees who are already in-house are familiar with the personnel and the organization's procedures and rules. They have gained the trust of their fellow employees and (in organizations such as government agencies where it is applicable) obtained the level of security clearance necessary to perform their daily work.

Employees who become part of a SIRT need to have the ability to stop any work they have underway in order to respond to a security incident if it occurs. They should also be given sufficient authority to make decisions if the overall security of the organization calls for it. Such decisions might range from ordering employees to change their network passwords if one has been stolen, to shutting down the company's firewall and thus disconnecting the network from the Internet if the incident is judged to be particularly serious. The following sections discuss aspects of assembling the response team: deciding what roles members will assume, staffing and training team members, and the value of staging "fire" drills.

Deciding What Roles Team Members Will Assume

The SIRT should contain a range of different employees who represent a cross-section of the organization. This ensures that all parts of the organization will be represented in the process of responding to incidents. Each member can then report back to his or her area within the organization. They can describe any security concerns or incidents that have arisen and that might require changes in how staff people go about their daily business. Having all branches of the company represented in the SIRT reduces the chances of conflict or finger-pointing that can result if files are lost or resources damaged. Typically, the members of a SIRT are drawn from the following areas:

- *Management*— At least one member of the SIRT should be upper-level management from the organization. Decisions may need to be made that affect the entire company such as shutting down the company's Web server or e-mail service if it is attacked, taking the network offline, restricting access to sensitive resources, or other response measures. Someone with the authority to make such decisions needs to be on the SIRT.

- *Legal* —One of the attorneys in the company's Legal Department should be part of the staff in order to provide advice if the company needs to take legal action against an intruder.

- *Information Technology (IT)* —At least one member of the IT staff should be on the SIRT. IT staff will know where the affected data is located and what parts of the network should be off-limits to unauthorized users. Having several members of IT on the SIRT enables them to perform "first response" functions when incidents occur; each member can be assigned to respond on a different shift within the day.

- *Physical Security* —The staff people who physically guard a company and its resources should be involved if an incident involves physical damage to computer resources.

- *Information Security (IS)* —IS staff people are specially trained to handle computer and network-related security incidents. They will probably form the nucleus of the SIRT.

- *Human Resources (HR)* —Many security incidents originate from within the company. If employees are identified, disciplinary action will be required. HR staff may not need to be involved at every stage of an intrusion. However, if an intrusion is found to have originated from inside, HR should be notified so they can be well-informed about the incident and take appropriate disciplinary measures.

- *Public Relations (PR)* —For companies that are well-known and that have a public profile, security incidents can directly affect business. Most companies prefer to keep security breaches out of the public eye, but this isn't always possible, especially if a highly trafficked Web site goes down for a period of time due to an attack. Having a PR person on the SIRT will enable that person to convey accurate information to the media and the public.

- *Finance/Accounting* —A dollar amount on a security incident may be required for insurance purposes, and having someone from the organization's financial staff on board will make the process go more smoothly.

All of these people need not be available at any one time when an incident occurs. Because security breaches can occur any time of the day or night, you need to have at least one person on staff at all times who has been trained in responding to security incidents and who will summon members of the SIRT with a higher level of authority in the organization if decisions need to be made. The exact organization and response procedures should be worked out at an initial meeting that includes all SIRT team members.

The SIRT should, however, include one individual who is designated as the leader—who calls other members to meetings, and who communicates the activities within the SIRT to others within the organization.

You may also want to call in individuals from outside the company who can contribute to the SIRT. You may gain expertise and perspective by including outside security consultants, as well as law enforcement officers who can give advice if needed.

Serious consequence can result if you fail to include enough people in the SIRT. For instance, suppose you fail to include someone from your IT staff. You might find that after a possible attack, the IT staff simply replaces all of the data on a database with a backup copy rather than reporting it to the SIRT for proper handling. Similarly, not having a HR person on the staff can cause legal problems if staff people are accused without sufficient evidence.

Staffing and Training

A **virtual team** —a team that has other jobs to perform during regular business hours and that exists only during meetings or when an incident becomes sufficiently serious—tends to stay on top of technical issues as part of its normal activities. In contrast, a team that is devoted solely to incident response full-time can get out of touch and need to be trained. All team members will need training on a periodic basis. You can have senior staff train junior ones by mentoring them. You can encourage self-study and enable staff members to purchase subscriptions to trade publications.

Two trade publications focus solely on incident response: Responder Safety (*www.respondersafety.net*) and Homeland Protection Professional (*www.hppmag.com*).

The speed and thoroughness with which you are able to respond to security alerts depends in large measure on the number of employees involved and how many other duties they are called upon to perform within the organization. If your budget allows, you will be able to assemble a group of employees whose sole responsibility is incident response or other security-related matters such as configuring firewalls and IDS devices. But such an arrangement may be economically feasible only for large corporations. Smaller companies may find it necessary to assign people to perform incident response in addition to networking or other responsibilities. A permanent, dedicated security officer or team of individuals who perform only security tasks will give you the best level of response.

Staging "Fire Drills"

After the SIRT is in place and has held an initial organizational meeting, and when training has been completed, you need to conduct a security drill not unlike the "fire drills" conducted by public and private schools. This might take some convincing on the part of senior management because of the staff time involved. However, it can really pay off big in the long run by making response more effective and coordinated.

You don't actually need someone to attack your network. Rather, pick a time for the drill to occur, and then follow a scenario in which you assume that an attack has occurred. Such events can be scheduled beforehand or can be unscheduled. The team members should be contacted and should respond as they would to a real incident. Test the notification process: make sure all phone numbers and pager numbers are correct. Next, test the response process. Assemble the team and give them a scenario.

Such drills are intended to identify any holes in the security procedures, and to make sure everyone on the SIRT knows his or her respective duties and responsibilities. All procedures that are taken during the drill should be documented, and after the drill, a meeting should be held to discuss how the drill went, and if any procedures should be handled differently in order to respond more quickly or effectively. You may want to conduct subsequent drills on a periodic basis (such as once every quarter or twice a year) in order to reevaluate how well the response procedures work.

Public Resource Teams

A number of teams around the world have been assembled in order to publish notices and articles about serious security incidents. You can notify such a team if you encounter a significant security event in order to benefit from the group's expertise and ability to coordinate resources. Such groups also provide training for response team members. Consider contacting such groups as the CERT Coordination Center (*www.cert.org*) in the United States or DFN-CERT in Germany (*www.cert.dfn.de/eng*). You can also visit EuroCERT, the European Security Incident Coordination Service (*www.eurocert.net*).

The Forum of Incident Response and Security Teams (FIRST) holds periodic Technical Colloquia at which members exchange technical data about attacks and practical experiences with security software and hardware. Member teams are open to discussing their successes and failures dealing with security issues. To find out more about how to join FIRST, visit the organization's Web site at *www.first.org*.

Outsourcing Incident Response

Due to staff or budget constraints, you may find it necessary to outsource your incident response needs. In other words, you might need to hire a company that will monitor your network and your IDS sensors and tell you if an intrusion has occurred.

Outsourcing has its advantages and disadvantages. On one hand, you may find that hiring an outside incident response team results in lower overall costs because the team has to deal with only actual incidents rather than managing firewalls, reviewing log files, or changing passwords and user accounts. On the down side, outsourcing systems or security functions may leave your organization at a disadvantage when it comes to timely, effective incident response procedures. Your network may experience an attack at the same time as your contractor's other customers, which makes it unlikely that you'll receive priority assistance.

Be sure to obtain references from current and former customers before you hire an incident response service. Yahoo! presents a lengthy list of companies that can monitor your firewall and IDS and respond to incidents for you at *http://dir.yahoo.com/Business_and_Economy/Business_to_Business/Computers/Security_and_Encryption/Consulting*.

HOW TO RESPOND: THE INCIDENT RESPONSE PROCESS

The process of intrusion response doesn't need to be a huge undertaking. In fact, you should be able to clearly describe your own process in a short document of perhaps five or six pages that the SIRT members can refer to if an event occurs and they need to know how to proceed. The process is usually broken down into a series of steps that cover the most important motions: determining exactly what happened; notifying the appropriate individuals; and taking the appropriate countermeasures to prevent such events from happening again. This section covers the six-step intrusion response sequence described earlier: preparation; notification; response; countermeasures; recovery; and follow-up.

Step 1: Preparation

Risk analysis is the process of determining what the possibility of damage or loss is in a particular situation, environment, or pertaining to an individual object or set of objects. A **security policy** is a statement that describes how network defenses will be configured to block unauthorized access, how the organization will respond to attacks, and how employees should safely handle the organization's resources in order to discourage loss of data or damage to files. In the context of incident response, a security policy should include the following directives:

- A statement to the effect that incident response is mandatory for the organization
- The objectives of incident response
- The limits of incident response, including privacy violations and other issues that are prohibited

- The relationship of the SIRT to the law enforcement community—in other words, when law enforcement officers (LEOs) are to be brought in to the incident response process

Security policies and risk analyses are discussed in detail in Chapters 2 and 3, so they are only briefly mentioned here.

It's important to set limits to intrusion response activities in order to avoid lawsuits. Disgruntled employees or individuals who contend that they have been wrongly accused can file suit and force the company to respond in court and possibly pay damages.

Using Your Risk Analysis to Prepare Your Response

As described in Chapter 3, a risk analysis identifies an organization's logical, physical, and other assets, and assigns values to each one in order to determine the impact if that asset should be lost or damaged. The risk analysis is used to prepare a security policy, which describes how the organization should respond to intrusions—who should be on the SIRT, when incidents should be escalated, and when prosecution should be pursued. You should use this as a guideline when responding to incidents.

Active Network Monitoring

Monitoring the network for suspicious traffic is one essential activity of the Incident Response Team. Through the use of packet sniffers such as Ethereal (described in Chapter 1) and Snort (described in Chapters 2 and 9), you can scan TCP/IP traffic for suspicious activity. By taking a proactive approach to monitoring rather than the passive approach of waiting for your IDS or firewall to detect trouble, you prevent incidents from occurring. You make it more likely that the response team will be responding only to legitimate events rather than false-positives, because you have screened the possible attacks. Thus, you can be more certain that the events that actually reach the IDS are worthy of serious attention.

Monitoring involves actively testing your network to see how it reacts to scans and other events. You do this by means of a network vulnerability analyzer—software that doesn't just detect packets as they pass through a gateway, but that actively scans the network and sends packets to computers to see if vulnerabilities exist. You can download software such as SAINT (Security Administrator's Integrated Network Tool) that scans your own network much like a hacker would. By scanning your own network, you learn about any ports that are open on your network's computers or any IP addresses that respond to Echo Request packets, and thus open themselves up to attack. A convenient way to analyze a single host or a network is by using a Web-based network vulnerability scanner such as WebSaint (see Figure 10-2).

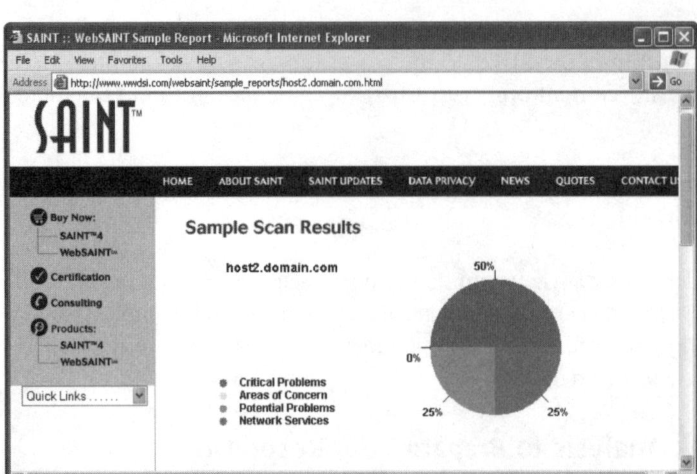

Figure 10-2 You can use WebSAINT, a Web-based service, to scan your own network

WebSAINT is available at *www.wwdsi.com/websaint/index.html*. A more in-depth examination of scanning software is provided in Chapter 11.

Step 2: Notification

Notification is the process by which the appropriate members of the SIRT receive news about security incidents. You might receive notification from your firewall or IDS, from other SIRT members, or from a network administrator who detects suspicious network activity. In addition, end users in the organization should also be instructed to notify the security team member on call when a virus is detected, oddly-named files begin appearing on the user's file system, or other signs that a security breach has occurred.

After the initial response—documenting what happened and capturing information about the event—you need to assess the level of damage, if any. Determining the scope and severity of the incident will tell you whether to **escalate** the incident (to call in a wider group of security professionals and take immediate countermeasures). Your assessment should answer such questions as the following:

- How many hosts on your network were affected?
- How many networks or subnets were involved?
- What level of privileges did the intruder gain? (If root or administrator privileges were obtained, the attack immediately becomes serious.)
- What assets were at risk?
- How many different types of attack were involved?

You don't necessarily need to call in all members of the SIRT all the time. First, you need to assess how serious the damage is. You may want to assign different levels of impact to each event. You can designate beforehand who is to be summoned if a Level 1 (not serious; probably a false alarm) incident occurs, a Level 2 (moderately serious) incident occurs, and so on. As the level of impact grows more serious, a wider range of individuals would naturally be called in to respond.

Step 3: Response

After the appropriate members of the SIRT have been notified that an incident has taken place, the measures taken in response need to be systematic, yet thorough. When an intrusion occurs, the SIRT members should keep the following principles in mind:

- Don't panic.
- Follow established procedures.

First, take time to analyze all reported events. Don't simply react to the first event you encounter. Make sure auditing is enabled so you capture the necessary data. Begin to document everything that happens.

An important aspect of response is having effective escalation procedures clearly spelled out and in place. Planning is key to efficient response. This is where risk analysis of the sort described in Chapter 3 comes in. When you perform a risk analysis, you identify the network resources that are the most critical and assign values to them. When an intrusion occurs, you check the ratings in the risk analysis to evaluate the value of the asset that has been compromised. The higher the value, the more urgent and stronger your response needs to be. In order to determine the different ways you can respond to intrusions based on the value of the assets involved, you need to answer such questions as the following:

- What are you trying to accomplish by your response? Determine whether you are primarily interested in protecting your company data, recovering lost information, or maintaining a good reputation so that consumers will have faith in your company and its products.
- How quickly can you reliably respond?
- Can you realistically call in law enforcement or take legal action against offenders without exceeding your available budget?

Establish standard procedures in the form of a flow chart that is part of a short, easy-to-read set of incident response instructions. The flow chart might look like the one shown in Figure 10-3.

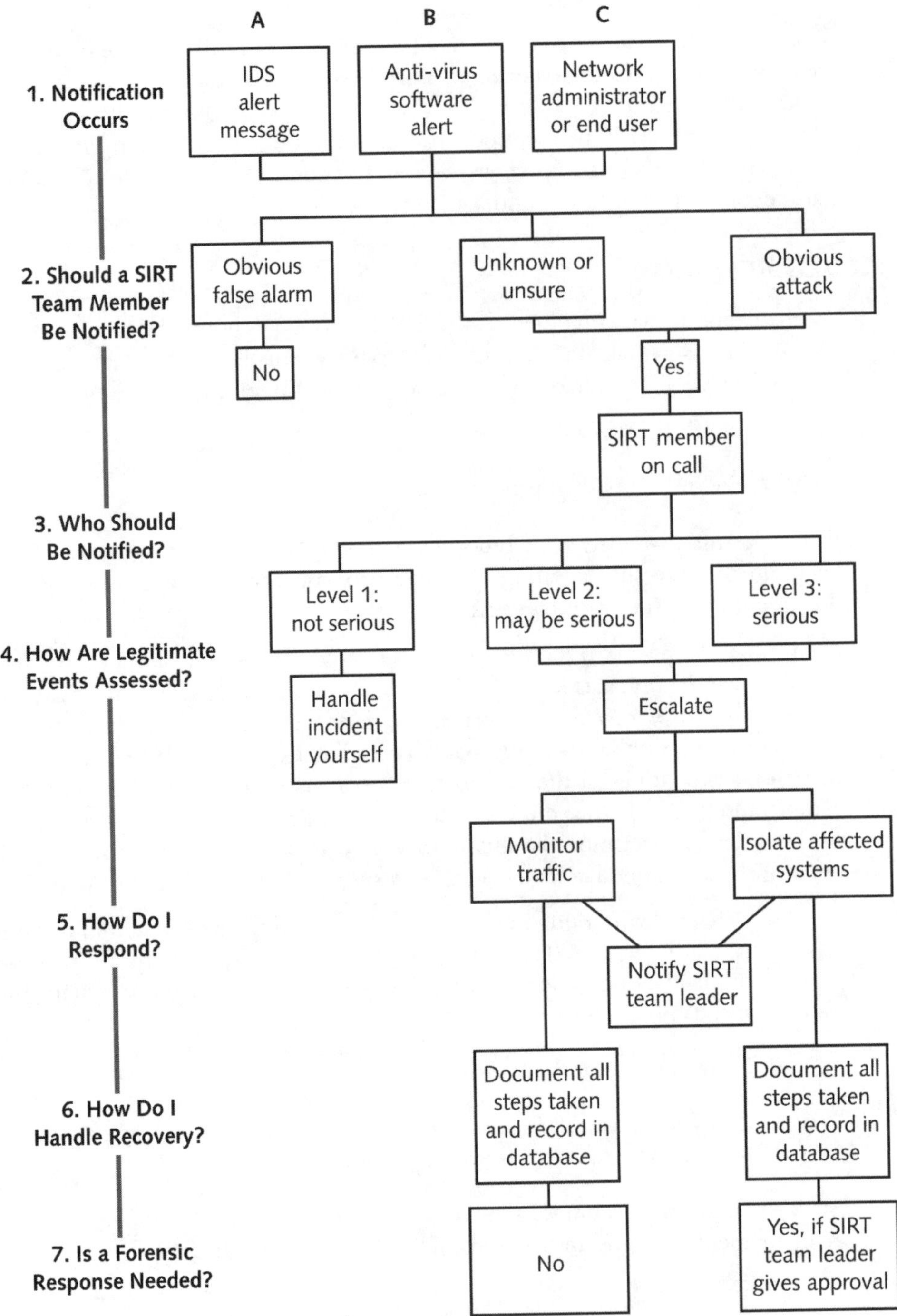

Figure 10-3 A flow chart illustrating the incident response process

Besides the flow chart, the instructions should provide such details as contact information for members of the SIRT as well as different types of incidents and their corresponding levels of severity.

Determining Who to Notify

After you have determined exactly what has happened and how severe the event is, you need to determine who else needs to be notified, or whether you can handle the incident yourself. If the incident is obviously a false alarm and no damage has occurred, you only need to analyze what happened, adjust rules and procedures to prevent such false alarms in the future, document what occurred, and move on.

If the incident is a legitimate attack, other members of the SIRT should be notified. You need to determine:

- What needs to be reported
- Who needs to know it
- How quickly you need to do the reporting

As far as what to report, you should provide the basic facts surrounding the incident—what type of event occurred, the OS involved on the affected computer, when the event took place, and whether it is still ongoing. The consequences of the attack should also be described—what systems have been accessed, what level of access privileges was used by the attacker, and any changes that have been made to the targeted system. You may want to create a form for such a report, similar to the one shown in Table 10-1.

Table 10-1 Incident reporting form

Element	Description
Incident Number	
Date	
Time	
Your Name	
Description of Event	
Origin	
Target(s)	
Data Lost	
Current Status	

You also need to figure out how people are going to be notified in case of attack: include **out-of-band notification** that occurs not on a computer network but another communications device such as a pager, cell phone, or telephone. If a natural disaster such as a flood or tornado knocks out power to your facility, you may be forced to use cell phones that don't rely on communications lines.

NOTE

If you encounter a serious security incident, consider informing the Current Activity section of the CERT Coordination Center (*www.cert.org/current/*) so that other security professionals are alerted to the possibility of similar attacks to their networks.

Following Standard Response Procedures

It's important to avoid contacting everyone by e-mail so that, if the intruder has control of your e-mail server, he or she won't be alerted to the fact that you are responding. That way, team members can be reached at any time if the need arises. You may also want to:

- *Set up a hotline* —This is a number that employees and SIRT team members can call if someone is not immediately available and an incident occurs.
- *Set up a list of people to contact* —Determine if the team leader should be contacted first, and then the leader can decide who else needs to be contacted based on the severity of the situation.

You don't want to overreact to intrusions, however. For instance, you might receive an alarm that someone has broken into the company's Web server on the DMZ. If you immediately respond by disconnecting the server from the Internet, you may be causing more problems than you are solving. You'll be taking your Web site offline and (if you operate an e-commerce site) interrupting any sales that are taking place; you'll be upsetting your employees; and the media may even find out and make inquiries, which can hurt your public relations. It's much more prudent to first determine if any files have been damaged and consult with fellow SIRT members—especially those in higher management—who have the authority to make such dramatic decisions.

On the other hand, if an intrusion is occurring and files have been compromised, you need to have procedures in place that clearly tell you to shut down a server, if necessary. The place to work out such questions is at an initial meeting of the SIRT at which such rules and procedures should be discussed. Each member should understand his or her role and know what kinds of tasks they will have to perform in case an incident arises.

Step 4: Countermeasures

After the initial assessment of the incident has taken place and the appropriate individuals have been notified, countermeasures should be taken to control any damage that has occurred. Two general types of **countermeasures** can be pursued: containment and eradication.

Containment of Damage

Containment is the process of preventing a malicious file, intruder, or compromised media from spreading to the other resources on the network. If the problem can be contained so that it only affects a single disk or computer, the hacker's efforts will be curtailed or even thwarted. You might consider doing the following:

- Shut down your system.
- Disable user and group accounts.
- Disable services that were exploited.
- Make backups of affected systems to protect the originals as evidence.

The SIRT members who are assigned to contain affected systems need to be prepared with backup media such as hard disks, removable drives, CD-ROMs, and floppy disks, so that they can make backups. They should take care to adhere to a well-defined set of containment procedures that are recorded in an incident response instruction sheet. Such instructions would tell them to keep records of who performed each task, and would remind them to perform analysis on the backup of the affected system while locking away the original media for safekeeping. Continue to record everything you do on a palm device or notebook. Advise users of the attacked system what has happened, whether data has been lost, and how long the data will be offline.

Eradication of Data Introduced by an Intrusion

Eradication involves the removal of any files or programs that resulted from the intrusion, including malicious code, registry keys, unnecessary executable files, viruses, worms, or files created by worms. Eradication usually follows containment. The process of eradicating such files can be tedious and time-consuming, but it should not be rushed. For instance, if the cause of an incident is a worm that was delivered to a computer on the network via an e-mail attachment, the SIRT members should do research on sites such as Symantec Security Response (*securityresponse.symantec.com*) to discover what files, if any, are created by such a worm. The affected systems should then be scanned and any such files should be eradicated. In addition, the SIRT members should:

- Check user accounts to make sure no additional (and unauthorized) users have been added.
- Check services.
- Check .DLL files and the registry on Windows.
- Make sure any files created during the time of the attack are legitimate.

In many cases, the affected system will simply have to be rebuilt or replaced using the most recent clean backup file. Note that removing programs that hackers installed or that viruses produce will not prevent the problem from occurring again. Any back doors that were originally exploited by the hacker to gain access to the system should be closed as well.

Step 5: Recovery

Recovery describes the process of putting media, programs, or computers that have been compromised by intrusions back in service so they can function on the network once again. Don't simply plug the machines or disk drives back in to the network and leave them to their end users, however. Rather, you need to monitor the restored devices for at least 24 hours to make sure the network is operating properly.

The SIRT member may even have the end user of the machine sign a statement agreeing to the fact that the computer has been serviced and returned, and that it is in working order. Such a statement might seem like excessive detail, but it's all part of the process of documenting every step of the intrusion response so other team members as well as management can handle similar situations that might arise in the future. Monitoring the machine closely for one or more days ensures that no undetected vulnerabilities remain. The IT staff should adjust the packet filter rules to block communications to or from any Web sites that were involved in the attack.

Step 6: Follow-Up

Follow-up is the process of documenting what took place after an intrusion was detected and a response occurred. The goal of such documentation is to prevent similar intrusions from occurring again. By recording what happened in a file such as a database, information is stored in a place where future members of the SIRT who may not have been involved with the original incident can review it.

Follow-up can be one of the most tedious parts of intrusion response. When an incident is over, your impulse is to move on to the next task. You aren't inclined to record what happened in a database. You'll see the value of such documentation if you need to refer to such a database yourself when, for instance, a Trojan horse infects a computer. Referring to the database might well reveal that another Trojan horse victimized the same machine the previous year through the same port. Following the steps that were documented when the previous incident was handled can make handling the new incident much less time consuming.

Record-keeping

Record-keeping is the process of recording all of the events associated with a security incident. Such documentation has many goals. SIRT members who encounter events similar to the ones you have encountered will benefit enormously by your notes. The organization's legal representatives can also use the information in court.

Even though you do all of your work on computers and computers are involved in the security incidents you encounter, recording the notes in electronic format may not be the best option. If the power goes out and your network is down, hand-held devices or a pad and pen provide your only option. After the incident is resolved, you may want to transfer the notes to a centralized database where all team members can access it conveniently.

Documentation is essential if you intend to prosecute offenders. In that case, your log files, hard drives, and alert messages are all parts of a trail of evidence that will play a key role in legal procedures. Something that isn't well documented can mean that hackers or employees who steal resources can go free because you cannot meet the burden of proof.

Reevaluating Policies

Any recommendations of changes in security policies or procedures that arise as a result of security incidents should be included in the follow-up database. If a hacker managed to steal a password by sending a fraudulent e-mail message pretending to be a network administrator, for instance, you should note that in the database and notify employees so they can avoid such trickery in future.

Your organization's security policy may specify that details about security incidents are for internal use only and not for public consumption. Keeping such information in-house ensures that your company won't receive bad public relations as a result of the event. It also keeps hackers from discovering that your network has fallen victim to an attack.

Dealing with False Alarms

One of the essential activities of managing an IDS is minimizing the number of false positives you receive as well as the number of false-negatives: attacks that occurred, but that did not set off an alarm.

False-positives are the bane of many IDS administrators and probably the number one complaint that people have about using IDS systems. The problem is that, as you tune the system in an effort to completely eliminate both false-positives and false-negatives, the system can become severely degraded and you can slow down the network significantly. Suppose you create a new firewall or IDS rule for every false-positive that occurs. Before long, your rule base will be so long and unwieldy that the network traffic will slow down while each rule in the rule base is checked, one after another. It's much better to adjust existing rules if needed and only create new rules if absolutely necessary.

Filtering Alerts

When you receive false alarms, you should adjust the rules used by your firewall, packet filter, or IDS to reduce them in future. Many legitimate Web sites send Echo Request packets to determine whether a client computer that is making a request is actually present on the network, for instance. You'll need to create rules that permit such traffic to pass through the filter without setting off an alarm.

One way to reduce the number of alerts is to exclude a specific signature from connecting to a selected host or IP address. If you exclude a signature, it neither generates an alarm nor creates a log record when it originates from the specified hosts or IP addresses. The addresses you exclude don't need to come from external hosts.

For instance, a command console or management computer on your own network might periodically perform a ping sweep (a series of Echo Request packets sent to each of the computers on your network in succession, to verify that they are present on the network). Such an event would obviously cause the IDS to trigger an alarm unless you exclude the management computer from a ping sweep or ICMP Echo Request signature your IDS uses. You can extend this principle to encompass an entire subnet or network. You only need to specify a host subnet mask or a range of IP addresses, such as 10.0.1.0/16.

Disabling Signatures

In some cases, you might want to disable entire signatures from triggering an alarm. If you are testing your network and doing a port scan, for instance, you want to disable any signatures that would be matched if the IDS detected a port scan. Even if a particular incident is a false alarm, you should still record it on a tracking chart that includes information, as shown in Table 10-2.

Table 10-2 Incident tracking form

Incident Number	Type of Incident	Location	Priority	Status	Last Update	Team Lead	Alternate Team Lead
28	port scan	192.168.20.1 through 255	Moderate	Inactive	5/25	JB	MK
29	Trojan horse	192.168.20.39	High	Active	5.26	JB	GH

You might also want to exclude a signature on one IDS in the interest of efficiency, if another IDS contains the same signature. By reducing the number of duplicated signatures, each device can operate more efficiently.

DEALING WITH LEGITIMATE SECURITY ALERTS

Suppose you get an alert from your IDS. How do you know the attack is legitimate? The previous section of this chapter described a six-step response process. This section examines Step 3 of that process—Response—in more detail.

Initially, you need to determine whether the attack is a false alarm (false-positive) or a legitimate intrusion (true-positive). Look for indications such as these:

- You experience system crashes.
- New user accounts suddenly appear on the network.

- Accounts that normally have only sporadic use suddenly have heavy activity.
- New files appear, often with strange file names.
- A series of unsuccessful logon attempts occurs.

Provided that the event turns out to be a legitimate intrusion attempt, you need to respond calmly and follow procedures that are already spelled out clearly in the security policy. To some extent, the way you respond to a legitimate attack depends on the size of your organization and the nature of its activities. For a small company with only a dozen employees or less, disconnecting the Web site from the Internet for a day or two might not have a big impact on sales. For a large retail company that depends on Internet sales for 10 to 20 percent of its revenues and that receives thousands of Web site visits per day, the response needs to be more measured—more people need to be involved, you should only take the Web site offline if absolutely necessary, and you should get it up and running as soon as possible.

As this book was being completed, a major hacker attack caused traffic throughout the Internet to slow and even stop in some cases. Hackers used a worm called MSSQL Slammer to infect computers running Microsoft SQL Server. The infected computers would then flood other computers with requests at UDP port 1434. The repeated requests caused a denial of service. The first defense called for the configuration of firewalls and packet filters to block all traffic to and from UDP port 1434. This attack did require affected systems to be disconnected in order for patches and service packs to be installed, if needed.

Government agencies or organizations in the public sector can call upon law enforcement personnel to handle intrusion incidents, if necessary. Companies in the private sector will find it more difficult to call in the police or other authorities. Even if law enforcement personnel are called upon to investigate, locating and prosecuting intruders can be lengthy and difficult. One of the most notorious hackers, Kevin Mitnick, was tracked by the FBI and U.S. Marshals for two years and was only apprehended in 1995 after a security expert located him. His prosecution was lengthy and he was not convicted until 1999. (You can read more about his case at *www.takedown.com*).

Assessing Impact

Once you have determined that the incident is not a false alarm, you need to find out if any of the host computers on your network were compromised. If an intruder did get into your systems, determine the extent of the damage. Many viruses and Trojan horses operate by creating files or renaming ones that already exist on an infected system. Some that infect Windows-based systems also change settings in the Registry so that they automatically start up whenever the computer is restarted. Your task is to locate any files that were added to the network computers and which ones were changed, if any. A software tool such as Tripwire by Tripwire, Inc. (*www.tripwire.com*) will enable you to document any changes to the file system since the program last ran a baseline test of the system.

Determine the scope and impact of the problem: Was one site affected or several different ones? How many computers were involved? There's no easy way to determine this other than checking each computer in turn, running virus scans, and checking firewall logs for suspicious activity such as a flood of e-mail messages sent from one machine, or tens of thousands of connection attempts from a single host to a computer located on a remote network in another country.

If your firewall itself was compromised, any computer on the network can potentially be accessed. The firewall will have to be reconstructed from scratch, which means the network will be down for a while. Then, all the host computers will need to be checked for software consistency—making sure the software on those computers has not been altered. This, however, is only the most serious kind of intrusion that can occur. The type of response you make depends on the seriousness of the event. Table 10-3 shows typical intrusion events and the level of seriousness.

Table 10-3 Intrusions and their responses

Event	Threat Level	Response
Web server hacked	Moderate	Disconnect server from Internet; check logs to determine how entry was gained; close any open ports or unnecessary services
Denial of Service (DoS) attack	Moderate	Break and restart the network connection; block all traffic from source computer
Virus infection	Low to Moderate depending on virus involved	Run anti-virus software; check published information on such attacks on virus protection Web sites; eradicate any files created by virus
Firewall accessed using stolen password	High	Immediately disconnect firewall from network and determine how entry was gained; rebuild firewall from scratch

Developing an Action Plan

Many intrusion response teams like to develop an action plan—a series of steps that need to be followed when a legitimate attack occurs. Writing out the steps to be followed might seem obvious. Individual steps like "disconnect the computer from the network" are easy to think of, after all. However, in the heat of the moment, having the list at hand can be a valuable aid to a nervous responder. The action plan might involve the following steps:

1. Assess the seriousness of the attack.
2. If a serious incident is involved, notify the team leader immediately. Determine whether a forensic investigation is required.
3. Begin to document all of your actions, including who performed them and when they occurred.
4. Contain the threat by disconnecting the computer from the network.

5. Determine the extent of the damage. Were passwords compromised? Files accessed? New files added? Are Trojans present?
6. If you plan to prosecute, make a complete bit stream backup of the media (one that includes all of the clusters on the media as well as the files) and keep the original data for evidence.
7. Eradicate the problem.
8. Restore the system or media and monitor it for integrity.
9. Record a summary of the incident. Send a memo to the CEO and Legal Department describing what occurred.

After you have determined that an attack has actually occurred, you need to understand exactly how the attack was conducted so you can configure countermeasures to prevent such an event from occurring again. For some network security analysts, the most effective tool for conducting attack analysis is one that has the ability to perform **attack visualization** . This is the process of replaying the attack so the analyst can essentially see what the hacker viewed during the attack. A program like netForensics' Security Information Manager (*www.netforensics.com*) can replay attacks and provide you with extensive documentation about what occurred.

Internal Versus External Incidents

Intrusions and security breaches frequently originate from inside an organization. When you suspect that an employee may be involved, your response needs to be more measured than if a hacker is attacking one of your computers. You may want to avoid notifying the entire staff, for instance, so as not to alert the offender.

Until you are sure who is involved, you may even want to keep the affected computers online in order to keep the intruder from knowing that you are on his or her trail. The Human Resources and Legal Departments should be made aware when you have identified the individual so that they can begin to consider disciplinary action. Only notify the entire staff when they really need to know that something serious happened, and when they need to change passwords or take active steps toward preventing future incidents.

Taking Corrective Measures to Prevent Reoccurrence

After you have contained and eradicated the problem, you need to take steps in order to prevent it from occurring again. For instance, if a password was intercepted because a hacker planted a Trojan horse on a network computer that sniffed network passwords in transit, you need to track:

- Where the Trojan came from
- Who transmitted the password

In response, you should download signatures of known Trojan horse programs that your IDS does not already include. You should also set up an intrusion rule that sends an alarm whenever a password is submitted without being encrypted.

There may be times when you need to notify others on the Internet about your attack. As stated in Chapter 9, you can upload your IDS logs to distributed IDS sites like Dshield in order to help compile reliable attack data that is drawn from around the world. Communicating the fact that you have been hit by malicious code assists everyone else in the industry by allowing them to block incoming attacks, spread the workload of definition resolution, and create patches.

Employees suspected of causing security breaches should be interviewed by trained, authorized personnel. The interviewers should explain that placing blame and administering punishment is not the ultimate purpose of the incident investigation, rather organizational security is. This tends to put employees more at ease so that they will provide information.

Working Under Pressure

In an ideal world, security incidents would occur one at a time and take place slowly enough that security professionals could respond effectively before any loss of data occurs. In the real world, incidents occur quickly, without warning, and simultaneously with other problems.

Incident response operations need to be carried out with discretion. The subject or target of the response need not know he or she is being observed. This may require you to connect a computer to a network in such a way that the computer cannot be electronically observed; sometimes it means analyzing a computer system's contents in a way that doesn't disturb the contents at all; but it always means doing things quietly, efficiently, and promptly.

When you are working under pressure, the temptation is to proceed as quickly as possible and seal off any vulnerable computers or services so that nothing will be lost. However, you also need to keep an eye on the fact that the data you collect as a result of a real intrusion may need to be presented as evidence in a court of law. The collection of the data and how you handle it can have a huge impact on how admissible it is. If the information could have been tampered with between the time it was detected and the time of the court date, it could all become invalid.

It's a good idea to fill out a response checklist such as the one shown in Table 10-4. A sample pair of entries is shown as an example.

Table 10-4 Intrusion response checklist

Date/Time	Occurrence	Response
10/20/04 07:58 a.m.	Received alert from IDS stating that an Echo Reply request had been received from IP address 62.126.0.34	Blocked request; changed firewall rules to block Echo Reply requests from 62.126.0.34
10/20/04 10:14 a.m.	Received alert from IDS stating that a series of Echo Requests had been sent from internal computer 192.168.20.38 with 200.46.101.1 as destination	Disconnected 192.108.20.4 from network. Ran anti-Trojan software. Blocked communications with 200.46.101.1

Gathering Data for Prosecution

You have to be as careful as possible when you are collecting evidence. Keep these rules of evidentiary handling in mind:

- *Make sure two people handle the data at all times* —Having one look "over the shoulder" of the other is essential; that way, no one can argue that one person alone might have fabricated or altered the data.
- *Write everything down* —Document every event that occurs and everything you do, no matter how trivial it might seem at the time. One of your team members should be designated for the task of note-taking to record exactly what was done and who did it.
- *Lock it up!* —After data is collected on hard disks, removable drives, CD-ROMs or other media, it needs to be locked away and protected so no danger of tampering can occur. Also, duplicate the media and store the duplicate in a safe location. Do your analysis off of the duplicate of the file and leave the original alone.

Early on in the process of handling a legitimate security incident, the response team members need to decide who will handle the evidence so that the **chain of custody** (the record of who handled an object to be used as evidence in court) is recorded. Each member of the SIRT needs to write down, step by step, his or her part in a response. Because some key personnel might not be present the next time you have an incident, checklists should contain the phone numbers, e-mail addresses, and URLs for that response, and should be inspected and updated on a regular basis.

You should determine before an incident occurs (ideally, it should be spelled out in your security policy) whether or not you are going to want to pursue incidents to prosecution. If you intend to prosecute offenders who successfully break into your network, you need to respond with extra care. You need to follow the data collection principles described in the following section of this chapter.

After the Attack: Computer Forensics

The term **forensics** describes events or objects that are associated with a court of law. **Computer forensics** is the set of activities associated with trying to find out who hacked into a system or who gained unauthorized access, usually with the ultimate goal of gaining enough legally admissible evidence to prosecute the person. Computer forensics can be likened to the evaluation of a physical crime scene. The goal is to determine as accurately as possible the facts of what happened. Instead of a physical crime scene such as the location where a burglary took place, computer forensics examines computers and networks where an electronic crime took place, such as Internet privacy violations or data theft.

Tracing Attacks

One of the first tasks you'll undertake when initiating a forensics investigation is the identification of the person or persons who initiated the attack. Identification can be difficult for a number of reasons. First, the offender may intentionally falsify the IP address listed as the source of the attack. Second, the hacker may have gained control of someone else's computer and used it to launch attacks against you. If you suspect that the attack originated from within your own network, there is no guarantee that the individual who normally sits at the source computer actually used it to launch the attack. Someone else might have taken the computer over for just that purpose. In this case, law enforcement officers (LEOs) may be needed to perform traditional investigative tasks such as fingerprinting in order to identify the offender.

Forensics Toolkits

Many incident handlers keep a forensics toolkit of hardware and software (sometimes called a **jump kit**) ready in order to respond to alerts. Such a kit might include a laptop computer; a cell phone; backup CD-ROMs or other disks; cables; hubs and trusted software for copying files, detecting viruses and Trojan horses, and searching for files. You should keep such a kit in a carrying case so that you can take it with you in case you need to move in a hurry to another building or office.

You don't necessarily have to scour computer retailers in order to assemble the components of your own forensics toolkit. A number of preassembled packages are on the market. Forensics Toolkit by Access Data (*www.accessdata.com/Product04_Overview.htm?ProductNum=04*) is one of the better-known packages. You can also download a set of open source tools from SourceForge.net at *http://sourceforge.net/projects/osfort*.

Forensics Software

Whether or not you assemble a toolkit, you should certainly have forensics software that can copy media or scan the files on a disk to determine how individual end users have been using their PCs. Simply copying files from one disk to another proves inadequate for forensics purposes, because deleted files can often be recovered from partitions and sectors of a disk that are hidden or unused. Rather, you need a tool that can either clone a disk or other computer media or make an image of it. **Cloning** is the process of copying the entire bit stream of a disk or removable media to a similar object. A **disk image** is a copy of an entire disk that is saved on another type of storage media. A program such as Byte Back (*www.toolsthatwork.com*) can do both disk cloning or disk imaging and can recover some files that have been deleted. DriveImage, a program by PowerQuest Corporation, enables home or office users to create a complete image of a disk or other media. The copy can then be used to restore damaged media after an attack or other disaster.

You may also want to have forensics programs like Detective by TechAssist, Inc. (*www.whitehatinc.com/techassist/detective/*) that let you search a computer for files that users on the network have downloaded from the Internet or that hackers have placed on their computers. You can search for files that contain keywords such as the word "password" or the names of sensitive files that the user has copied to his or her system, as shown in Figure 10-4.

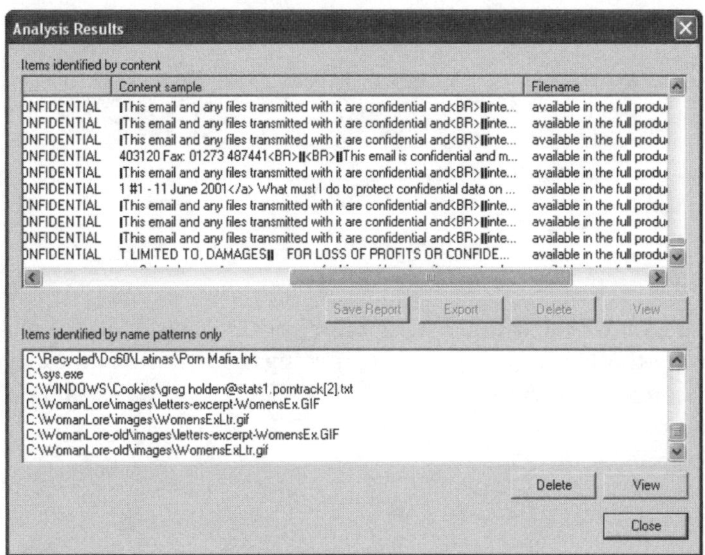

Figure 10-4 Some forensics software lets you search for keywords or specific files on users' computers

Using Data Mining to Discover Patterns

There is no reason why you need to only react passively to attacks that have already occurred. You can use your experience to prevent future attacks. For instance, if you experience a Denial of Service attack from a particular source, you can then go after that source and notify it that future attacks will be blocked. In fact, the sources of the attacks may be organizations that are unaware that their systems are being used for malicious purposes, as either wayward employees or third-party intruders using the devices as slaves are staging the attacks without permission or authorization.

Prosecuting Offenders

The SIRT will undoubtedly be confronted by the question of whether or not to prosecute computer attackers at some point during the incident response process. Forensics can identify individual computers, but not the human being sitting at that computer at the exact time an attack originated from it.

Prosecution should be considered in intrusion cases that result in financial fraud, inappropriate Web usage, theft of proprietary data, or sexual harassment. In such cases, it pays to get advice and input from other computer crime investigators. Consider contacting the following groups:

- Computer Technology Investigators Northwest (*www.ctin.org*)
- High Technology Crime Investigation Association (*www.htcia.org* or 540-937-5019)
- International Association of Computer Investigative Specialists (*www.cops.org* or 877-890-6130)

Be sure to conduct interviews with possible suspects in a timely and courteous manner. Be non-confrontational; you don't want to risk a lawsuit.

Handling Evidence

When investigating an incident within a legal framework, reliable and accurate electronic findings are critical to the success of an accurate investigation. Some of the steps involved in preparing compromised computers in order to prepare a legal case against an offender are shown in Figure 10-5.

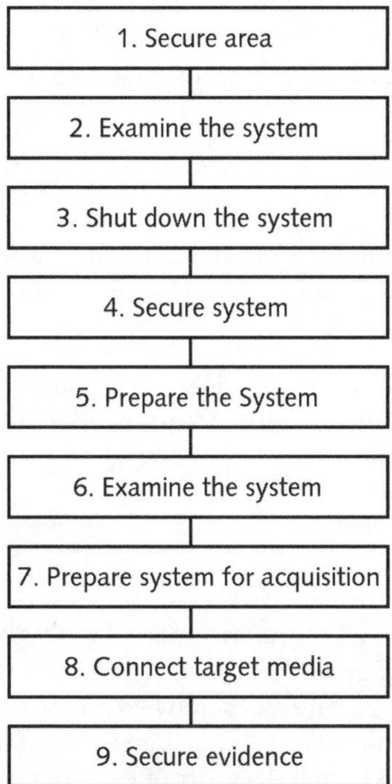

Figure 10-5 Steps involved in handling evidence for prosecution

The steps involved in handling and examining hard disks and other computer data are described in more detail below.

1. *Secure the area* —Ask all unnecessary staff people to leave the area; make sure no one disturbs you while you work.
2. *Examine the system* —You may want to examine the system while the attack is actually taking place. You may be able to identify any services that are running that the hacker is exploiting, and detect suspicious connections to other computers on your network.
3. *Shut down the system* —Disconnect the computer from the network. Note, however, that some malicious programs are configured to erase themselves when the computer is shut down.
4. *Secure the system* —After you disconnect the computer, if you plan to work on it in a lab area, place it in a plastic bag so that you can transport it. Place blank disks in any of the computer's disk drives so that the drives won't be damaged in transit.
5. *Prepare the system* —Before you begin working on the system, photograph it so you have a record of how it looked and was arranged when you started your investigation.
6. *Examine the system* —Check the current system date and time to see if it is accurate.

7. *Prepare the system for acquisition* —Boot the computer from a floppy disk that has been configured so that it will not communicate with the hard drive when the computer starts up. This preserves the hard drive in its original state so that it can be examined.

8. *Connect target media* —Place a clean disk drive in the system and copy the affected disk drive.

9. *Secure evidence* —Turn off the computer, disconnect the target media, seal the machine, and connect the target media to a lab computer so that you can begin to analyze the data.

During all of these steps, extensive notes should be recorded. The notes should keep track of when each step was performed and who performed it, in order to maintain the chain of evidence.

Chapter Summary

- The members of a SIRT should be drawn from all of the major areas within the organization. Keeping the membership wide-ranging gives the SIRT authority to take drastic measures, such as shutting down servers and requiring all employees to change their network passwords, to prevent attacks from widening. Having a member of higher management involved enables the SIRT to make such decisions. Legal staff can provide advice if prosecution is to be pursued, while Human Resources staff can handle situations involving individual employees who turn out to be the source of intrusions. Public relations staff can communicate with the press and media if a company experiences an event that is serious enough to take it off the Internet for a period of time.
- The speed and thoroughness with which the response occurs depends on the range of employees involved and how many other duties they are required to perform within the organization. Ideally, you can hire a team of individuals whose sole job is to respond to incidents full-time. Otherwise, you can assign individuals who have other tasks within the company to perform incident response on an as-needed basis. You can also outsource your incident response and security monitoring needs to one of the many contractors who provide such services.
- There are specific issues and approaches involved in responding to intrusions and security breaches that affect your network. First, the establishment of a Security Incident Response Team (SIRT), a group of individuals who are assigned to respond to alerts, assess damage, call in other team members if necessary, and take countermeasures to prevent further damage. The team's primary functions can be broken down into six steps: preparation; notification; response; countermeasures; recovery; and follow-up. Note that these six steps are also part of a larger workflow that includes an initial risk to and analysis of the reevaluation of security policies following the successful completion of incident response steps.
- The process of actually responding to security incidents should be clearly defined in a brief document to which all SIRT members can refer if an event occurs. The response should be based on principles spelled out in the company's security policy. The response

team should actively monitor and test the network in order to proactively block incidents before they actually occur.

- When notification of a security event does occur, the SIRT member on call should assess whether the incident is legitimate or a false-positive. If an incident is serious, the SIRT team leader should be summoned, as well as other members who are available. Response needs to be systematic and thorough, and may be illustrated in the form of a flow chart that all team members can follow. A list containing contact information for other team members should be available, as well as a form that members can fill out when an event occurs.
- After the initial response and assessment has taken place, countermeasures should be pursued. The two general types of countermeasures you can take are containment and eradication. Containment involves preventing the malicious file or intruder from accessing any more resources on the network than have already been accessed. After the incident has been contained, eradication should occur to eliminate any malicious files, registry keys, viruses, or other files that have been introduced.
- After eradication is complete, recovery should take place: the affected media, programs, or computers need to be put back in service so they can function on the network once again. Finally, follow-up should take place: the incident should be described fully in a database or other file where future SIRT members can access it if similar events take place.
- False alarms are almost inevitable with any intrusion detection system. If false alarms are reported, you can adjust the rules used by your firewall, packet filter, or IDS to reduce them in the future. You can exclude an IP address from attempting to access your network, or disable a signature if you need to.
- On the other hand, legitimate attacks require calm, systematic, and thorough response. Legitimate attacks can be discerned from events such as system crashes or new user accounts or new files that suddenly appear on network computers. If a legitimate attack has been detected, you need to determine how many computers have been damaged. No matter what the seriousness of the event, you should follow an action plan.
- On the other hand, external attacks by hackers you are able to identify may call for prosecution in court. In order to pursue a legal case, you need to pursue computer forensics—the practice of tracking attacks, identifying offenders, handling evidence, and developing a legal case. You need to handle evidence and document all the steps you take in order to maintain a record of the chain of custody.
- Computer forensics involves the use of special hardware and software tools used to respond to alerts and analyze data. In order to ensure that the analysis is accurate, the data should be copied completely, either by cloning or creating a disk image. The evidence gained through forensics can lead to prosecuting offenders. In order to enable prosecution to go forward, evidence should be handled carefully, and the affected computer system should be examined thoroughly in a step-by-step process.

Key Terms

attack visualization — The process of replaying the attack so the analyst can essentially see what the attacker viewed during the attack.

chain of custody — The record of who handled an object to be used as evidence in court.

cloning — The process of copying an entire disk or removable media to a similar object.

computer forensics — The set of activities associated with trying to find out who hacked into a system or who gained unauthorized access. Investigation is done through careful data retrieval and analysis, usually with the ultimate goal of gaining enough legally admissible evidence to pursue prosecution.

containment — The process of preventing a malicious file, intruder, or compromised media from spreading to the other resources on the network.

countermeasures — Strategies and approaches that counter threats to network security.

disk image — A copy of an entire disk that is saved on another type of storage media.

eradication — The process of removing any files or programs that result from an intrusion, including malicious code, registry keys, unnecessary executable files, viruses, worms, or files created by worms.

escalate — To call in a wider group of security professionals and take immediate countermeasures to handle it.

follow-up — The process of documenting what took place when an intrusion was detected and response occurred.

forensics — Pertaining to events or objects that are associated with a court of law.

incident response — The name given to the actions taken after a computer security incident in order to determine what happened and what countermeasures need to be taken in order to ensure the continued security of the network.

jump kit — A set of hardware and software tools used by incident handlers to respond to computer security events.

notification — The process by which the appropriate members of the SIRT receive news about security incidents.

out-of-band notification — Notification of a security incident that occurs not on a computer network, but on another communications device such as a pager.

recovery — The process of putting media, programs, or computers that have been compromised by intrusions back in service so that they can function on the network once again.

risk analysis — The process of determining the possibility of damage or loss is in a particular situation, environment, or pertaining to an individual object or set of objects.

Security Incident Response Team (SIRT) — A group of individuals who are assigned to respond effectively to security breaches.

security policy — A statement that describes how network defenses will be configured to block unauthorized access, how the organization will respond to attacks, and how employees should safely handle the organization's resources in order to discourage loss of data or damage to files.

virtual team — A team that has other jobs to perform during regular business hours, and that only exists during meetings or when an incident becomes sufficiently serious.

REVIEW QUESTIONS

1. What does a SIRT do when it monitors a network "actively"?

   a. captures packets as they pass into and out of the network

   b. tests the network to see how it reacts to scans

   c. continually does real-time monitoring of network activity

   d. reads active rather than archived firewall and IDS logs

2. How should the findings of a risk analysis affect the way an organization responds to an intrusion?

   a. The greater the risk of damage, the stronger the response.

   b. Physical assets require a stronger response than logical assets.

   c. The more critical the asset, the stronger the response.

   d. After intrusions, you revise your risk analysis to take the events into account.

3. Why is it important to provide for out-of-band notification of SIRT members if an intrusion occurs? (Choose all that apply.)

   a. to reach SIRT members who are traveling

   b. to prevent an intruder from intercepting the response messages

   c. Using the phone enables members to communicate the situation and receive instructions more clearly.

   d. to reach SIRT members if the computer network is down

4. What is the danger of reacting too strongly to intrusions?
   a By disconnecting servers you interrupt network communications.
   b You may frighten off intruders, thus preventing their identification.
   c You might falsely accuse staff people of causing the damage.
   d You might make decisions that higher management are only authorized to approve.

5. Why does it make sense to look in-house for members of the SIRT? (Choose all that apply.)
   a. You are able to assemble the team more quickly than by hiring outsiders.
   b. Current employees are familiar with the organization.
   c. Current employees have sufficient security clearance.
   d. Current employees are more trustworthy than contractors brought in from outside.

6. Why is it important to set limits on intrusion response activities?
   a. You may cause unnecessary alarm among your staff.
   b. You take SIRT members away from other activities.
   c. You may incur lawsuits.
   d. You don't want to spend more time than is necessary on forensics.

7. The process of determining the level of damage caused by an intrusion falls into which of the six intrusion response steps?
   a. response
   b. detection
   c. follow-up
   d. recovery

8. What is a virtual team?
   a. members who perform incident response full-time
   b. members who work in different geographical locations and only communicate electronically
   c. members who perform incident response on an as-needed basis
   d. members who assemble only when an incident actually occurs

9. Which of the following applies to "fire drills" that test intrusion response procedures?
   a. They should be unscheduled.
   b. They should be scheduled.
   c. They involve an actual "test" attack.
   d. They should follow a scenario.

10. A group that exists to help organizations with incident response is called a(n) ___________.
    a. Public Resource Team
    b. Incident Response Group
    c. Incident Coordination Center
    d. Distributed Intrusion Detection System

11. Why would you consider outsourcing your incident response needs? (Choose all that apply.)
    a. better security
    b. lower cost
    c. faster response
    d. no need for new hires

12. Which of the following is a way of reducing false alarms? (Choose all that apply.)
    a. adjusting rules
    b. decreasing network gateways
    c. excluding addresses
    d. restricting access control lists

13. What kinds of inside attackers often cause security incidents? (Choose all that apply.)
    a. upper management
    b. network administrators who are testing for security vulnerabilities
    c. employees who have access to financial and project-related information
    d. terminated employees

14. A(n) _______ is a record of who handled a compromised device and how it was handled, and it can be used as evidence in court.

    a Incident Tracking Form

    b. follow-up

    c. chain of custody

    d. audit

15. Who is likely to review the detailed information you record during follow-up after an incident?

    a. supervisors who are evaluating the performance of the SIRT

    b. public resource team members investigating reports of security breaches

    c. IT staff trying to determine whether new security hardware or software is needed

    d. future members of the SIRT who were not involved in the original incident

16. During the recovery process, what resources should be checked on a computer that has been compromised? (Choose all that apply.)

    a. user accounts

    b. the BIOS boot sequence

    c. the Windows Registry

    d. the password file

17. Why is the complete elimination of false-positives an unrealistic goal?

    a. New attack attempts are occurring all the time.

    b. As new users join the organization they may set off false alarms.

    c. Creating too many rules can slow down network performance.

    d. Firewall and IDS systems have built-in flaws that cause false alarms.

18. Why would you want to disable a signature on an IDS? (Choose all that apply.)

    a. if you are testing your network

    b. if the signature is generating too many false alarms

    c. if the signature is out-of-date

    d. if the signature is duplicated on another IDS

19. What is attack visualization?

    a. the process of describing attacks before they occur in order to prevent them

    b. the process of replaying an attack

    c. the process of documenting attacks in a follow-up database

    d. the process of matching an attack against available signatures

20. Why would you want to keep records of intrusions for internal use only? (Choose all that apply.)

    a. to prevent bad public relations

    b. to prevent disgruntled employees from attempting similar attacks

    c. to keep hackers from knowing they were successful

    d. to keep stock values from falling

HANDS-ON PROJECTS

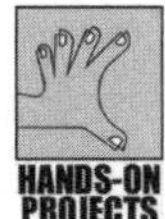

Project 10-1: Designing an Incident Response Team

Imagine that, in your school, you are going to assemble a group of six individuals who will fill the various roles of a Security Incident Response Team (SIRT). This team will be responsible for determining whether intrusions are legitimate or false-positives; they will determine how to escalate response as needed and to try to track down offenders so they can be prosecuted. Draw the members of your team from the following: IT staff member 1; IT staff member 2; IT staff member 3; Management Representative, Financial Administrator, Legal Representative, Human Resources Representative Also include an individual who is assigned to handle public relations, as well as a security staffer and a law enforcement officer (LEO) who is assigned to the school. Design a group that would be able to handle the appropriate incident response tasks by filling in the blank areas in Table 10-5 (including the heading in the right-most column).

Table 10-5 Incident response team organization

Team Member	Responsible for	When to Notify	

1. List each of the members who should be included in the SIRT.
2. Pick a leader.
3. Distribute the 24-hour initial response among the three IT staff people; each staffer should be responsible for being on call during one eight-hour period.
4. Specify the areas of responsibility for each staff person in the column labeled Responsible for.
5. In the When to Notify column, specify who should be notified for Level 1 (Minor), Level 2 (Serious), and Level 3 (Urgent) incidents, or under special circumstances such as the disconnection of the company Web server or the prosecution of an offender.
6. In the fourth column, add a piece of essential information that is missing and that is needed from each team member. Fill in fictitious sample information for each team member.

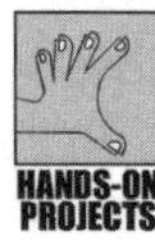

Project 10-2: Responding to an Intrusion Alert

You receive an alert from the IDS telling you that a Trojan horse attack has been detected on port 31337 of the computer at 192.168.3.33. You run an anti-virus program on the affected computer and find that the Trojan program is indeed present. While you are sitting at the computer, the e-mail program Outlook Express opens up without prompting and begins sending e-mails. Follow the steps presented below to indicate how you would respond.

1. Describe what your mental approach should be to the events just described.
2. Describe what you should do to isolate the affected computer.
3. Once the computer is isolated, describe what should be investigated next.
4. List the appropriate staff people who should be notified.
5. Describe what you would learn by a subsequent reviewing of the firewall/IDS logs?

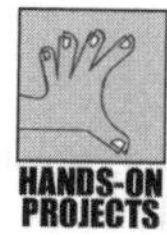

Project 10-3: Analyzing Correct Forensics Procedures

Forensics procedures have to be followed thoroughly and systematically when investigating an intrusion. In this project, you will analyze a set of steps to be followed when doing a forensic examination of computer media. You will identify problems and mistakes with the steps by referring to the published instructions on the International Association of Computer Investigative Specialists Web site (*www.cops.org*).

1. Examine the following set of steps:
   a. Secure the area.
   b. Shut down any affected computers using the Shut Down command.
   c. Secure the system.
   d. Prepare the system by writing down serial numbers and model numbers and recording the height and weight of the item.
   e. Reboot the system.
   f. Connect the target media.
   g. Secure the evidence.
2. Rewrite Step b using a better security method.
3. Rewrite Step d providing a better way of recording the characteristics of the system devices (take photos of any affected items).
4. Add a missing instruction to Step e.
5. Go to the Association of Computer Investigative Specialists Web site (*www.cops.org*), and click the button labeled **Forensic Procedures**.
6. Read the procedures under the section entitled Hard Disk Examination, and add at least three steps that you do not see in your corrected set of steps.

10

Project 10-4: Configuring a GUI Editor for the Snort Rule Base

One way to block intrusions is to update the rule base your IDS refers to in order to determine when to send alerts, drop packets, and log events. The freeware IDS Snort, which you installed in Hands-On Project 2-4, uses a set of text files with the .rules extension as its rule base. Reviewing and editing those files can be difficult using a text editor. A program called IDS Policy Manager enables you to view the rules files and edit them; in this project you will download, install, and configure IDS Policy Manager. You need a Windows 2000 or XP computer to perform this project, as well as an archiving tool such as WinZip.

1. Double-click the **Internet Explorer** icon on your desktop.
2. Enter the following URL in the browser's Address bar: **http://www.activeworx.com/idspm**. Press **Enter**.

3. Scroll down the page and click **Download** next to the final (not beta) version of the program.
4. Click one of the file names that ends with the file extension .zip under the latest final version of IDS Policy Manager listed on the IDS Downloads page.
5. When you are prompted, save the file to your hard disk.
6. When download is complete, double-click the file **IDSPolMan** that you downloaded.
7. WinZip opens. Create a directory called **IDS Policy Manager** and click **Extract**.
8. Double-click the file **IDSPM[*version number*].EXE** that you extracted. Then click **Next**. Follow through the wizard to determine where the files should be installed.
9. When the files have been extracted, either double-click the program icon **IDSPolMan.exe** to open IDS Policy Manager or click **Start**, click **Programs** (**All Programs** on Windows XP), click **ActiveWorx**, and click **IDS Policy Manager**.
10. If a dialog box appears notifying you that a "new build" of the program has been found, click **No**.
11. When the Policy Manager window opens, click the **Policy Manager** tab.
12. Right-click **Official**, and click **Open in Policy Editor**.
13. The Policy Editor opens and displays the default set of rules that comes with Snort. In addition, if a dialog box appears asking if you want to check for new rules, click **Yes**.
14. If the Add Variable dialog box appears, click **OK**. Click **OK** to each new Add Variable dialog box that appears.
15. If a dialog box appears stating how many new rules have been added to the default Snort rule base, click **OK**.
16. Click the **Settings** tab.
17. Make sure the variable **HOME_NET** matches the IP address range of your own lab network. If you are working in a lab that has its own subnet, such as 10.1.0.0/16, click the line that has the name: HOME_NET and value 10.1.1.0/24. If your network only contains one or two IP addresses, check the box next to HOME_NET that has the value (10.1.1.0,192.168.1.0/24).
18. Click **Edit**.
19. In the Edit Variable dialog box, replace the value with the IP address or addresses that apply to your network. For instance, if you are working at a two-computer network with the IP addresses 192.168.20.1 and 192.168.20.2, replace the default values in the Value box with those IP addresses. Click **OK** to close the dialog box.

20. Click **File** and click **Exit** to close IDS Policy Manager. If you are prompted to save your changes, click **Yes**.

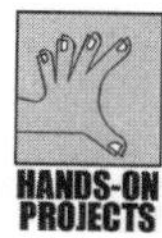

Project 10-5: Revising a Signature in Response to Incidents

In this project, you will revise the default rule base used by the IDS program Snort in response to two different security incidents—a scan of your own network by your network administrator to test for vulnerabilities, and an ICMP request packet. You will create a text-based rules file that Snort can recognize and that contains the .rules extension. You will use IDS Policy Manager, the application you installed in Project 10-4, to add the .rules file to the Snort rule base.

1. Click **Start**, point to **Programs** (**All Programs** on Windows XP), point to **Accessories**, and click **Notepad**.
2. When Notepad opens, type the following, which tells Snort not to set an alarm when you scan the network from your management console at 10.0.20.5:

   pass icmp 10.0.20.5 any -> any any

3. Press **Enter** to start a new line.
4. Next, type the following, which tells Snort to send an alert message when it encounters a type of ICMP packet called a Timestamp Request, which is denoted by Type 13 Code 0:

   alert icmp any any -> any any (itype:13; icode:0;)

5. Click **File** and then click **Save**.
6. In the Save As dialog box, double-click the directory where Snort is installed (for example, C:\Snort or C:\Program Files\Snort). In the File name box, type **"icmp-new.rules"** and then click **Save.** (Be sure to include the quotation marks so Notepad will save the file with the .rules extension.)
7. Double-click the program icon **IDSPolMan.exe** to open IDS Policy Manager. You can also start IDS Policy Manager by clicking **Start**, clicking **Programs** (**All Programs** on Windows XP), clicking **Activeworx**, and then clicking **Policy Manager** if you don't have the icon on your desktop.
8. If a dialog box appears notifying you that a "new build" of the program has been found, click **No**.
9. When the Policy Manager window opens, click the **Policy Manager** tab.
10. Right-click **Official**, and click **Open in Policy Editor**.
11. The Policy Editor opens and displays the default set of rules that come with Snort.
12. Click **Options**, and click **Add .Rules file to Policy.**

13. Click the **Look in** drop-down arrow in the Browse for File dialog box and locate the icmp-new.rules file you saved earlier. Click **icmp-new.rules**, and click **Open**. Note that the rules category icmp-new is added to the list of rules categories on the left side of the Policy Editor window.
14. Click **File** and then click **Exit**, and then click **Yes** to save your changes to close the Policy Editor.

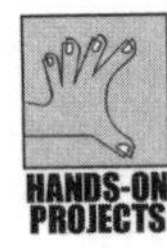

Project 10-6: Using a File Detection Tool

As part of your computer forensics toolkit, you'll probably need to have a program that can do a detailed search of all the files on a computer or disk in order to determine if security breaches have taken place. In this project you will download and install a program called Detective by TechAssist, Inc. You'll simulate a search of your own computer for a file that contains potentially sensitive content as well as a potentially harmful program. This project limits the search to a single directory on your computer to save time. If you have time and want to explore this program further, you may want to search your entire computer for files that contain links, keywords, or other types of content that Detective has been preconfigured to locate. Note, however, that such a search can take several hours depending on the number of files involved. This project can be done on a Windows 2000 or XP computer that has a file archive program such as WinZip installed.

1. Click **Start**, point to **Programs** (**All Programs** on Windows XP), point to **Accessories**, and click **Notepad**.
2. Type the following text in order to provide keywords that Detective can search for:

   Plans for New Product Under Development

   Confidential

   This company is in the process of developing a new hydrogen-powered widget. The product will be on the market in early 2007.

3. Click **File** and click **Save**.
4. In the Save dialog box, type the filename **specification.txt**, and then choose a location for the file. Then click **Save**.
5. Click **File** and click **New** to open a new blank Notepad file.
6. Click **File** and click **Save**. Type the filename " **sys.exe"** (be sure to use the quotation marks so the file will be saved with the .exe extension rather than .exe.txt), choose the same directory where you saved specification.txt, and then click **Save**.
7. Click **File** and then click **Exit** to close Notepad.
8. Double-click the **Internet Explorer** icon on your desktop to start your Web browser.

9. Enter the following address in your browser's Address bar: **http://www.toolsthatwork.com/ttw-downloads.shtml**. Then press **Enter**.
10. The Downloads page for the TechAssist Web site appears. Scroll down the page to the section that has the heading Detective Downloads.
11. Click **Proceed with Demo registration**.
12. Fill out the form on the Demo Registration page, and then click **Send**.
13. Check your e-mail for a message entitled Thank You from info@toolsthat-work.com. Click the link supplied in the body of the e-mail message in order to download the Detective demo software.
14. When your e-mail message prompts you, click **Save** to save the file to your hard disk.
15. When the download is complete, locate the file detectv.zip, and double-click the file to open it using WinZip. Click **Extract** to extract the files to a folder on your hard disk.
16. Locate the files you extracted and double-click **Detectv.exe** to start up the application.
17. Click the plus sign **(+)** next to Customize.
18. Click **Search Type**. Under Content Identification, under the heading Look for additional keywords or phrases, type **hydrogen-powered widget**, and then click **Add**.
19. Type **Confidential**, and then click **Add**.
20. Under custom name patterns, type **sys.exe**, and then click **Add**.
21. Click **Search Location**. Click **Custom Path**, and then click **Browse**.
22. Click the directory in which you placed the two files you created earlier. Then click **OK**.
23. Click **Start**. You'll have to wait several minutes while the program analyzes your computer.
24. When analysis is complete, a dialog box named Detectv appears with a note about purchasing the program. Click **OK**.
25. Scan the information presented in the Analysis Results dialog box. Did the program find the file sys.exe? What other sorts of files did it locate? If the scan took an hour or more to complete, can you examine the files that were found and suggest why it took so long?

CASE PROJECTS

Case Project 10-1: Tracking Down Internal Misuse

Your IDS sends an alert notifying you that a sensitive company file has been accessed on one of your organization's file servers. You check the server's logs, and you discover that the file was accessed by one of the computers on your internal network. You track the usage logs for that computer and find that some e-mails with sizeable attachments were mailed out around the same time to an address in Europe. The e-mail messages were entitled "Family Photos." You suspect that these were not personal photos that were being mailed out, but one or more of your company's own sensitive documents. How could you verify this?

Case Project 10-2: Locating a Virus on the Network

When you arrive at the office on Monday morning, you discover anti-virus system alerts telling you that a virus has been detected. You read about the virus on the Symantec Security Response Web site (*http://securityresponse.symantec.com*). An article about the virus states that it works by replicating itself throughout networked systems, attempting to connect to a file called cmd.exe. Given that it has had all weekend to spread through the network, how would you track the virus down?

Case Project 10-3: Tracking Down a Trojan

You receive a call at home from the member of the SIRT team on duty, informing you that someone on your internal network has logged into the firewall using an administrator (root) password. You tell the caller to disconnect the firewall from the Internet immediately; as this is a sign that someone has intercepted the password and is attempting to gain access to the firewall in order to learn about the company's network. You don't know how long the intruder has been on the firewall or whether or not the firewall logs are reliable since the intruder may have been able to alter them. What could you do in response?

Case Project 10-4: Keeping the User Community Informed

You are aware of the need to keep staff people in your organization informed about security incidents when they occur and in their aftermath. But you are also aware that all staff people should not be asked to respond to every security incident you encounter or they will either become unduly alarmed or cease to take such notifications seriously. Suppose someone gains access to your Web server, on which your Web site resides, and through which you sell goods and services to the public. You realize you will have to disconnect the Web server from the Internet while you respond. Name four different user groups within your organization who have to be notified in this case. After resolving this incident, you are faced with a situation in which a confidential password was used, apparently by someone in the company, to gain access to a file server containing financial data for the organization. Which groups of users should receive full information about the incident? What information would you convey to rank-and-file employees while you attempt to determine who is responsible for the unauthorized access to the server?

CHAPTER

11

STRENGTHENING DEFENSE THROUGH ONGOING MANAGEMENT

After reading this chapter and completing the exercises, you will be able to:

- Strengthen control by managing security events
- Heighten analysis by auditing network security procedures
- Strengthen detection by managing your intrusion detection system
- Enhance a defense by changing your Defense in Depth configuration
- Strengthen network performance by keeping pace with changing needs
- Heighten your own knowledge base by keeping on top of industry trends

Preceding chapters have presented detailed information about designing and configuring an intrusion detection system (IDS). This chapter discusses how to manage the information you receive from the IDS as well as the other security systems that provide your network defense. Through efficient management you can maximize the performance level of your IDS and other areas of your network's overall security configuration.

A growing number of organizations have created positions such as **Computer Security Manager (CSM)** to cover the ongoing management of network security systems. You may be hired for such a position one day yourself. The responsibilities of the CSM should be spelled out clearly in the organization's security policy. In this chapter you will learn about many of the managerial responsibilities. They include security event management, security auditing, managing your IDS, improving your Defense in Depth configuration, keeping pace with network needs, and maintaining your own knowledge base in order to keep up with the many fast-changing events in the field of network security.

STRENGTHENING CONTROL: SECURITY EVENT MANAGEMENT

Suppose you are hired by a large multinational corporation and given the assignment to "manage security" for that organization. Your initial tasks are likely to include cataloging the various security devices you need to manage. You might discover that the organization has already put in place a range of devices, including:

- Packet-filtering routers
- VPN appliances
- An IDS at each branch office
- One or more firewalls at each office
- Event logs or **syslogs** (system logs) for selected systems in each office

The resulting flow of information and the need to manage it efficiently is illustrated in Figure 11-1.

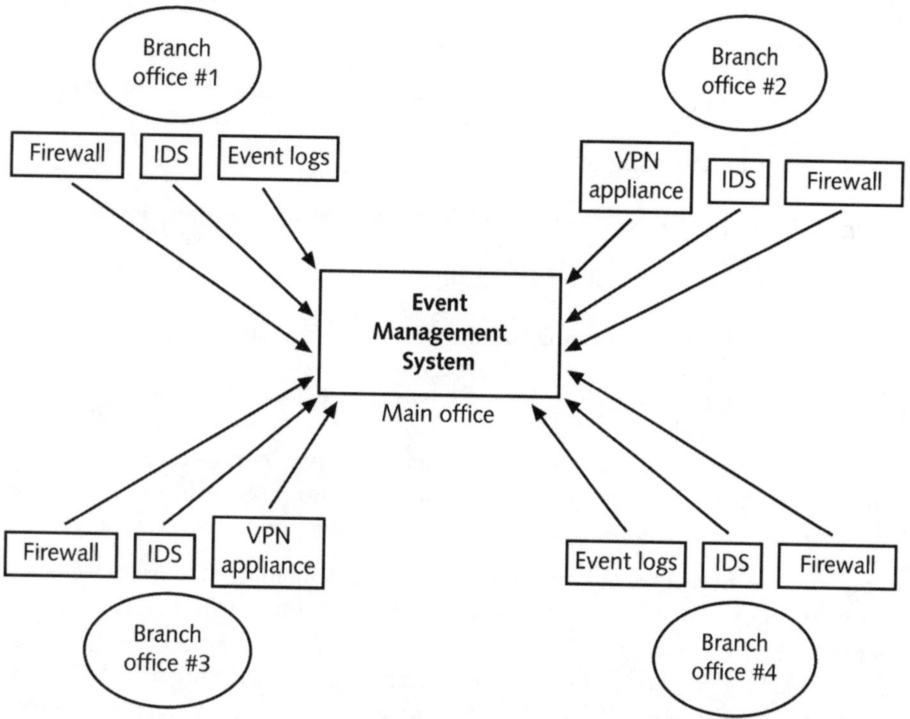

Figure 11-1 Security event management handles data from multiple sources

You could easily have 10, 20, or more separate devices sending you log file data that you need to manage. How do you keep track of all of the information and respond to legitimate security concerns without becoming overwhelmed? You need to create and manage a Security Incident Response Team (SIRT) as described in Chapter 10. You also need to establish a **security event management program** —a program that gathers and consolidates events from multiple sources so it can be analyzed and used to improve network security. The following sections discuss different aspects of such a program: the need to monitor events; the need to manage data from multiple sensors; the need to manage IDS signatures; and the need to manage change so that procedures can be improved and security strengthened in a way that maintains productivity.

Monitoring Events

Network protection needs to be conducted on an ongoing basis in order to keep up with new vulnerabilities as they appear. You need to establish a process that involves securing, monitoring, testing, and continually strengthening your level of protection. One way you can improve your defenses is through ongoing **event monitoring** —reviewing alert and event logs produced by your security devices and operating systems, and periodically testing the network to identify any weak points. The goal is to strengthen your defenses by gathering information, changing procedures, and improving the network. You need to monitor the following events:

- Logins
- Creation of user accounts and groups
- Correct handling of e-mail attachments
- Backups and other ways to maintain and protect sensitive information
- Anti-virus scanning and control
- Procedures for granting mobile users secure remote access

For example, suppose your network's database server contacts a remote host via the Internet. The IDS sends an alarm to you because you have configured such alarms beforehand; the database server is only supposed to receive incoming connections, not initiate its own outgoing connections. The port used by the database server to connect to the remote host, 40449, indicates to you immediately that the connection is a suspicious one.

You run the netstat utility by opening a command prompt window and entering the command `netstat -a` on the database server to review the current connections. The netstat utility reports that the server is listening for connections on the expected ports, such as port 1028 for NetBIOS connections. You also get a line stating that the server is listening for connections on port 40449. This information indicates that a Trojan horse application may have been installed on the database server and is initiating a connection to the remote host over port 40449. This, in turn, indicates that a hacker may have been able to log in to the database server using a legitimate password that they "cracked" or otherwise fraudulently obtained. Your response needs to go in several different directions: to block the connection; to locate and eradicate the Trojan horse application; to identify how the intrusion occurred; to change network passwords; and possibly to change the way passwords are handled by end users in the organization.

In order to be effective, such responses need to occur as close to real time as possible. Your ability to detect, in real time, intrusions into your systems and to determine the identity of the intruder may be very limited. It does not take very long to carry out an information attack, and damage can occur in an instant. You need to develop a team approach to network security and make use of automated responses, such as alarm systems that an IDS provides. You also need to coordinate data from multiple sources and keep aware of new network security threats, as described in succeeding sections.

Managing Data from Multiple Sensors

Consider a multinational organization with offices in several different countries or a national organization with branch offices in separate states. Each office network has its own firewall and IDS. Each IDS has sensors that gather data that passes through the gateway. Some of that data contains alert messages that need to be reviewed in a timely basis. How do you process all the events that occur at all of the various offices? Obviously, you need to install database software that will sort through the events and let you view them in a systematic fashion. As a security manager, you face a variety of questions including:

- Should all the data be consolidated and flow through a central security location?
- Should the data from the sensors go to security managers at each office?

The two options are described in the sections that follow.

Centralized Data Collection

When you set up a firewall or IDS, you are typically required to identify the location of a host computer that contains a management console application. Data from the security devices in both your own network and your organization's remote networks can be transmitted to that console using its IP address. Such an arrangement, in which the event data from separate offices is sent to a management console in the organization's main office, is shown in Figure 11-2.

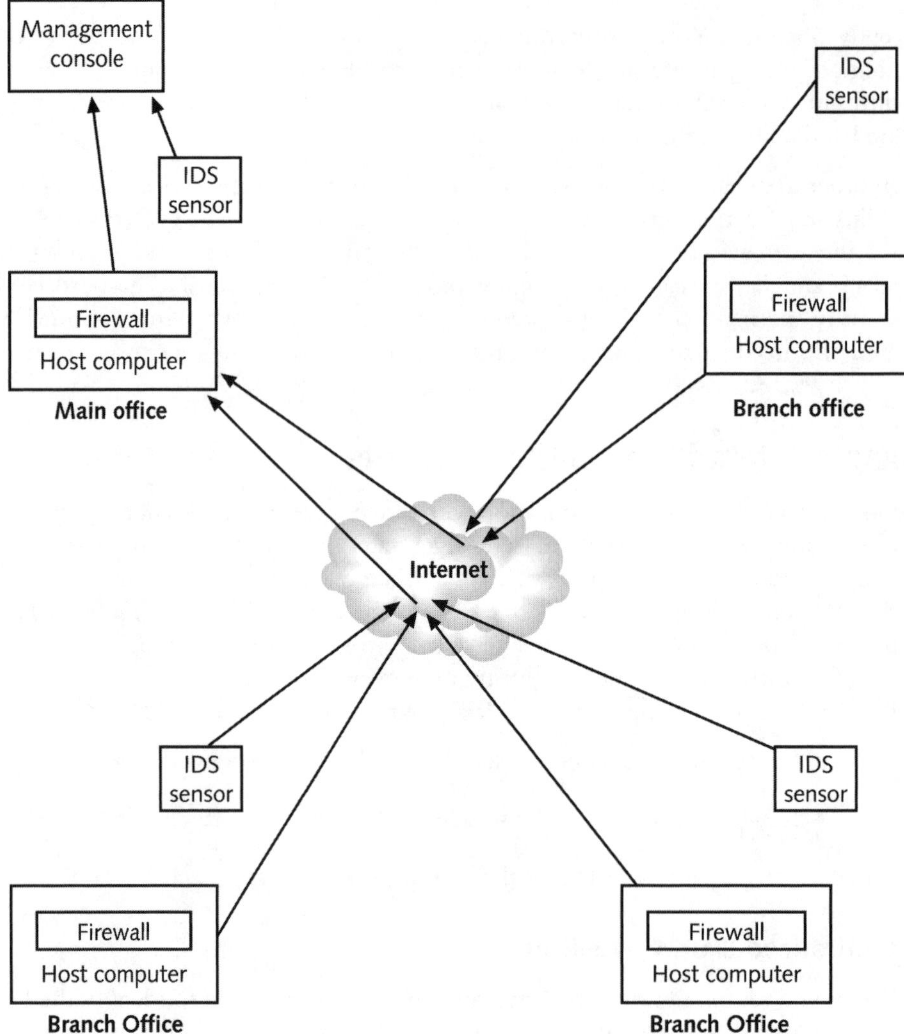

Figure 11-2 Centralized IDS data management

If centralized IDS data collection is used, you realize a number of benefits:

- Reduced cost because you have fewer systems to maintain
- Less administrative manpower required
- Greater efficiency

On the downside, you need to find a way to transmit data from each collection point back to the centralized management console. The traffic obviously needs to be protected by encryption and encapsulation; this is an ideal situation for a virtual private network (VPN) connection of the sort described in Chapter 7. However, most IDS products are able to communicate with one another using their own encrypted "handshake" mechanism, and many companies rely on this without setting up a VPN. Unfortunately, most IDS devices use standard default ports that hackers can exploit.

Distributed Data Collection

Centralized data collection results in all of an organization's event and security data being "funneled" to a centralized management console in the main office. Depending on the number of branch networks and security devices involved, the amount of data traversing the network gateways and passing through the firewall at the main office can be considerable.

The second option, distributed data collection, reduces the amount of network traffic involved. Such an arrangement is illustrated in Figure 11-3.

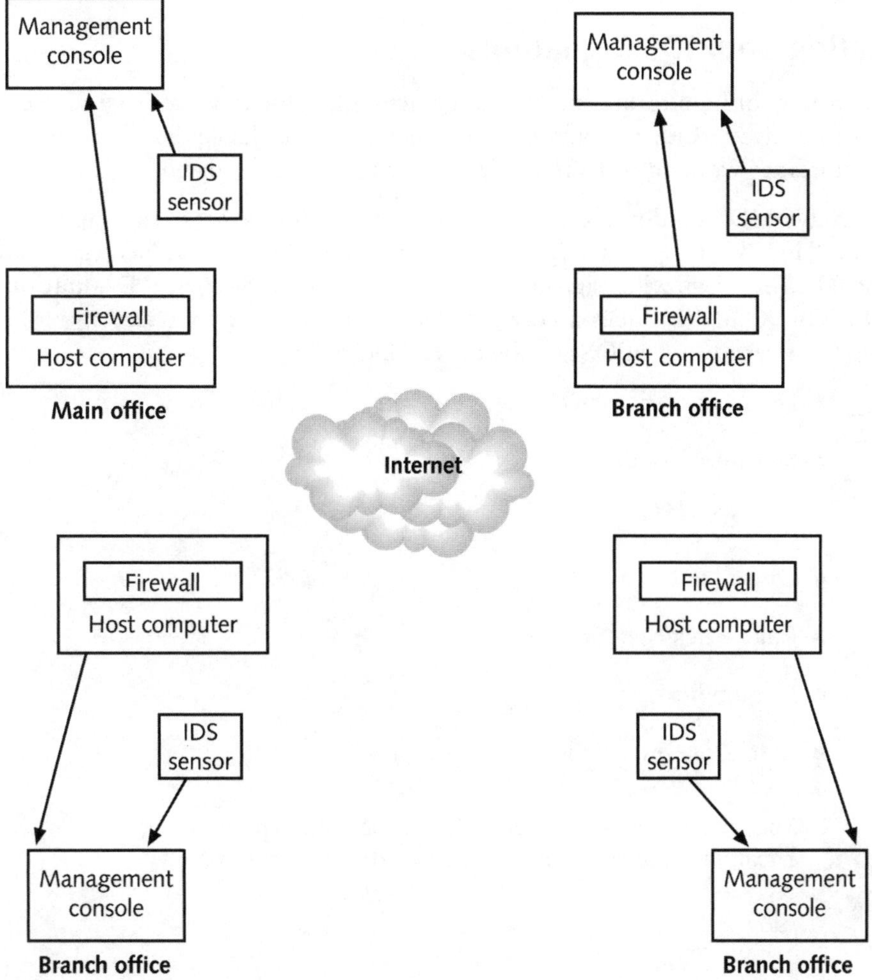

Figure 11-3 Distributed data collection

11

In a **distributed data collection** arrangement, the data from security devices such as firewalls and intrusion detection systems goes to a management console in its own local network. Security managers in each network must review the data separately and analyze and respond to events as needed. A distributed data collection setup requires the organization to maintain separate security managers in each branch office, as well as separate management console software. Such an arrangement saves bandwidth, but it still requires offices to communicate with one another about security incidents. If an event occurs at one office that could potentially affect other offices, the security manager dealing with that event should notify the other branch managers so they can proactively prevent such events from occurring in their offices.

The constant flood of log file and alert data can distract you. Don't let the need to eradicate daily security breaches distract from the bigger picture—the need to keep up with emerging security concerns as the network evolves.

Evaluating Your IDS Signatures

The reason for monitoring and evaluating network traffic is not to have a large quantity of data to analyze. Rather, you want to gather evidence that indicates whether your IDS signatures are working well enough or if they need to be updated.

A variety of IDS vendors are available, each with their own set of signatures for suspicious events. How do you evaluate signatures for each one? One vendor, Neohapsis, has proposed a standard for reviewing signatures called the **Open Security Evaluation Criteria (OSEC)** . OSEC includes a core set of tests that any network security product has to follow. In version 1.0 of OSEC, the tests include:

- Device integrity checking
- Signature baseline
- State test
- Discard test
- Engine flex
- Evasion list
- In line/tap test

You can find out more about OSEC and the test criteria at *http://osec.neohapsis.com/criteria/nids-v1/testsummary.html.*

The process of actually updating IDS signatures varies depending on the vendor. For Cisco Systems's IDS appliance, signatures can be downloaded from the Cisco Web site and installed on both the console and the network sensor. (See the instructions at *www.cisco.com/warp/public/707/ids_sigs.html.*)

It's a good idea to get in the habit of checking the IDS manufacturer's Web site for new signatures periodically. Your organization may also want to hire a security management firm on a contract basis to handle such routine tasks. For instance, the Swiss firm Celeris (*www.celeris.ch*) will perform routine signature analysis on an ongoing basis. In addition, its service agreements (*www.celeris.net/media/managed-network-ids-en.pdf*) call for the company to notify you of security incidents within 30 minutes of their detection, and to make major configuration changes in a 24 to 48 hour period, depending on the level of service you pay for.

Managing Change

The process of making a change in a procedure, network defense component, or another administrative matter doesn't necessarily have to be a drawn out and involved chain of events. However, you can run into serious problems if you abruptly make a change that has an impact on the way employees work. The impact, in fact, can be more substantial than the original problem. Suppose you determine, as a result of an alert received from one of your intrusion detection systems, that access to a database server needs to be severely restricted to selected administrative staff because a hacker nearly gained access to that server. If you make the change without assessing its impact or without properly notifying all of the staff people who will be affected by it, you're likely to be flooded with a stream of protests. Staffers will be unable to access files and send you pointed inquiries asking what has happened. You'll have to explain after the fact why the change was made. In addition, supervisory personnel may instruct you to undo the change because it occurred too abruptly and because the impact was too great.

In an administrative sense, it's best for the organization to make sure that significant changes are carried out in a systematic way so they occur smoothly. **Change management** involves the modification of equipment, systems, software, or procedures in a sequential and preplanned way. The process should include an assessment of the impact of a change, and a decision about whether the change should be made based on that impact. You might consider implementing change management in the following ways:

- Significant changes to firewall or IDS rules that will impact end users
- New VPN gateways
- Changes to access control lists
- New password systems or procedures

The full process of evaluating and making a change is illustrated in Figure 11- 4.

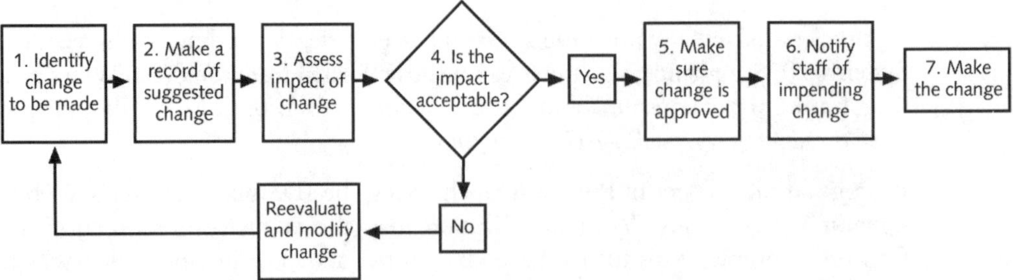

Figure 11-4 Significant changes in security procedures should be evaluated and communicated thoroughly

The process shown in Figure 11-4 may seem involved, but being systematic and thorough helps the organization run smoothly. You ensure that everyone is informed, you get the approval of the appropriate managers, and you make sure the change should take place. The following is a detailed discussion of the process from Figure 11-4:

1. Identify the change to be made. You may decide to make a change after reviewing log files, after an intrusion, or after an alert message.
2. Make a record of the suggested change. Write down the exact situation that prompted you to consider the change, and describe the change, so that you can communicate it to management and staff later on.
3. Assess the impact of the change. Will the change inconvenience staff people by making it more difficult to access the resources they need? Will the change slow down traffic on the network by creating another layer of security? Think through all the possible implications of the change.
4. Decide whether the impact of the change is acceptable. Discuss this with the head of your department or with your colleagues. You may also want to consult financial staff if the change has cost implications. If the impact is not acceptable, reevaluate it and determine whether a modification will reduce the impact. If the impact is acceptable, proceed with its implementation.
5. If the impact is acceptable, make sure the change receives the approval of the appropriate administrators. This can add a considerable amount of time to the change. If you circulate a memo describing the change and a meeting needs to be held at which the change is discussed, you may not be able to implement it for a week or more. If the change seems urgent and there is a security risk to not making the change, try to talk to individuals yourself and get approval immediately.
6. Notify staff of the impending change. After approval is given, tell all of the individual staff affected by the change that it will occur. Be sure to tell them when the change will take effect. Give people several days or even a week to prepare for the change. However, if the change needs to be made urgently, simply make the change after receiving approval, and tell people after the fact.
7. Make the change. After notifying the appropriate individuals and answering any questions they have, make the change.

You don't necessarily have to follow all of these steps for every change. For a slight change in a firewall or IDS rule, you don't need to tell the entire staff. You should follow the decision procedure only for significant changes that affect the way others in the organization do their daily business.

STRENGTHENING ANALYSIS: SECURITY AUDITING

Security auditing is the process of testing the effectiveness of a network defense system. Auditing can be performed by actively testing the network defenses by attempting break-ins. Recording and analyzing events such as logins, logouts, and file accesses can also help. In addition, an examination of the security procedures within an organization, such as the way sensitive information is handled, should be involved.

In the past, groups known as **tiger teams** were assembled in order to actively test the network. Such teams can still be used on a contract basis, but you can also do the testing yourself. You might have to put together data from many disparate sources. These include:

- Packet filters
- Application logs
- Router logs
- Firewall logs
- Event monitors
- Host-based IDS (HIDS)
- Network-based IDS (NIDS)

One way to consolidate the data generated by such devices is to transfer or "push" the information to a central database. Most IDS systems will let you do this; even the freeware IDS program Snort can be used to transmit data to a database directly. At the very least, you should store the time, data, application, OS, user, process ID, and log entry.

With multiple security components in place, you are going to accumulate so much data from log files that you need to manage it before it consumes your available storage space. Choose a time period for how long you retain detailed information from the IDS logs. Ninety days is a common target. After the data becomes older than 90 days, you can archive it to long-term storage such as on tape, DVD, or CD-ROM. Also consider paring the data down to only the most essential information.

Operational Auditing

In an **operational audit**, your own staff examines your system logs to see if you are auditing the information you need and not getting bogged down with unnecessary information. They should look for the following:

- Accounts that have weak passwords or no passwords
- Accounts assigned to employees who have left the company or user group
- New accounts that need to have validation for authorized users
- Any accounts that have recognizable words in the dictionary or other easily guessed passwords

Financial institutions regularly have to undergo security audits due to government regulations. Such audits might involve attempts at **social engineering** —attempting to fool staff people into giving out passwords or other information. Auditors who work on-site in financial institutions even look in wastepaper receptacles, attempting to determine if any sensitive information recorded in computer printouts has been discarded without shredding it. Another auditing strategy is a **Tinkerbell program** —a program in which network connections are scanned and alerts are generated when logins are attempted, or when connection attempts are made from sites that have been identified as suspicious.

Because of its highly sensitive nature (it might include passwords, for instance), information gathered as a result of a security audit should be highly protected. If an unauthorized employee or hacker would be able to gain access to the files, many network resources could be compromised. Your organization should have a clearly defined plan for handling and protecting audit data, and should follow it accordingly.

Independent Auditing

In an **independent audit**, you hire an outside firm to come in and inspect your audit logs to make sure you are getting the information you want and not gathering unnecessary information that consumes your system and network resources.

An outside firm will come in and attempt to detect any flaws or vulnerabilities in your system as well—not just in your IDS, but in other locations such as individual files or applications. Such an audit might examine where your security equipment is physically located; how well it is protected from unauthorized users or environmental disasters; and how thoroughly your data is erased when you attempt to dispose of it. Because you need to give outsiders access to your sensitive financial or other data, be sure to have the auditors sign a non-disclosure agreement (NDA), in which they state that they will not release any of your information to anyone outside their own company.

Auditing might uncover information related to your organization's employees that those employees might consider sensitive. You might need to consult the legal division so that they can review the audit information and determine if simply searching through the information constitutes an invasion of privacy. If you work for a government agency, the concern over privacy increases: the Privacy Act of 1974 requires government agencies to notify citizens when the government gathers information about them.

Strengthening Detection: Managing the IDS

As your network grows, the amount of traffic encountered by an IDS and your other security devices also increases. The amount of information generated by an IDS increases as well. In order to keep the IDS running smoothly, you may need to make adjustments to the amount of storage space available to the IDS and the rule base used by the IDS. This section briefly examines how to strengthen the IDS by maintaining the current system, by changing or adding software, or by changing or adding hardware.

Maintaining Your Current System

You don't necessarily need to add new systems or components in order to make an IDS stronger. You can also boost efficiency and strengthen detection by more efficiently maintaining the resources you currently have. The following sections discuss how to do this through backups, managing accounts, and managing disk space.

Backups

You need to back up your firewall and IDS systems in case of disaster. With a backup stored in a secure location, you can restore the systems if they become corrupted or if hackers are able to gain access to them. You should also keep backups of other security components, including:

- Routers
- Bastion hosts
- Servers
- Special-purpose devices

Automated backup software such as the Retrospect series of products by Dantz Development Corp. (*www.dantz.com*) is advisable, especially for a large-scale network.

Managing Accounts

Account management is another aspect of ongoing security maintenance. This activity involves adding new accounts, recovering old ones, and changing passwords. It is a frequently neglected task. Make sure your user accounts are reviewed every few months. You want to make sure no accounts have been added by hackers, or that no accounts belonging to employees who have been terminated are still active.

Passwords should be configured so that they expire periodically forcing you to review whether or not they are really necessary. All accounts on the firewall should be made extra secure. For instance, they should make use of one-time passwords.

Arrange to receive notices from your Human Resources department whenever someone leaves the organization (whether that person quits or is terminated) so that you can immediately delete the individual's account.

Managing IDS Rules

Scale back on the number of rules the IDS uses. Try to eliminate unnecessary rules. By reducing the amount of unnecessary processing the IDS must perform, the IDS will be able to keep up with information that passes through fast networks such as ones that use Gigabit speed interfaces.

Be sure you keep your IDS audit logs in a secure location so intruders cannot tamper with them or even erase evidence of their own intrusions.

User Management

An **awareness program** is one in which employees, contractors, and business partners all understand the company's security policy and how it should affect their behavior. Simply developing and following an awareness program can improve security by teaching employees how to use the system more securely.

You can raise employee awareness in a variety of ways. You can give a lecture on security in the organization; you can prepare booklets that need to be read and signed by employees. Signing the booklets ensures that employees have read your security policy and its associated procedures and regulations.

Changing or Adding Software

Once or twice a year, your IDS software vendor will probably release updated software. When your vendor releases an updated version of your command console software, be sure to get details of what sort of upgrade path is needed. Be sure to ask if the new version requires you to work with new data formats that you don't already use and that will require you to install new software.

Changing or Adding Hardware

It can be expensive to add hardware such as new network sensors to an IDS, but the cost is usually outweighed by the cost to the organization of lost data, erosion of customer trust, or network downtime, all of which can occur as a result of an intrusion. You may have to add a second network card for network monitoring.

You may want to add consoles in order to reduce the **target-to-console ratio** —the number of target computers on your network that is managed by a single command console. You may also want to reevaluate the placement of sensors in your network. If you are not catching all the traffic on a network segment, you might want to move a sensor to a new location or add a new sensor. Or, you may find that you have a host-based system and you want to turn it into a hybrid configuration by adding a network sensor as well.

STRENGTHENING DEFENSE: IMPROVING DEFENSE IN DEPTH

The principle of Defense in Depth should guide you as you perform ongoing maintenance of your perimeter security configuration. Defense in Depth calls for security through a variety of defensive techniques (such as those described in Chapter 2) that work together to block different attacks. On the simplest level, Defense in Depth can be the use of a personal firewall and anti-virus software to protect a single computer. Defense in Depth as it applies to network services calls for the maintenance of:

- *Availability* —Information is made available to authorized users when it is needed.
- *Integrity* —The information exchanged by network users is accurate.
- *Authentication* —Users prove their identity to other users or to computers so they can exchange information.
- *Confidentiality* —Information is kept unreadable to all but the intended recipients.
- *Non-repudiation* —Both the recipient and sender of information across the network cannot deny their participation in a business transaction.

The last item in this list—non-repudiation—requires more explanation. Repudiation sometimes occurs in business transactions, particularly those in which one business makes a purchase from, or delivers supplies to, another business. Often, due to the ease with which records can be accessed online, the transactions are initiated electronically. For instance, assume that company A orders 10,000 widgets from company B via an e-mail message. The order is placed, the goods shipped, and the payment is made electronically. However, if company A receives the bill and then denies that it ever placed the order, it is said to have repudiated the transaction. Similarly, if company B denies that it ever received the electronic payment, it is also said to have repudiated the transaction. **Non-repudiation** is the use of authentication to prevent repudiation from occurring. Through public key infrastructure, the sender as well as the receiver are authenticated through the exchange of digital certificates. Both have electronic records that the transaction actually took place, in addition to records of the date and time it occurred.

Active Defense in Depth

Active Defense in Depth is a particularly strong implementation of the Defense in Depth concept. Instead of passively waiting for attacks to occur and then reacting to incidents, security personnel expect that attacks will occur and try to anticipate them. Active Defense in Depth calls for multiple levels of protection as well as security approaches that overlap one another. It also calls for the largest and most serious network threats to be defended first. The additional layers of protection address other, less serious threats.

Active Defense in Depth requires respondents to think creatively and counter every possible threat, whether familiar or unfamiliar. In an active defensive approach, the defense changes based on the threat. Defensive approaches have the ability to "flex" and change based on where the threat occurs or what it is.

One "layer" of security is training. Security staff is constantly training and learning to keep up with attacks and their appropriate countermeasures. Efforts to improve their knowledge enable the organization to remain flexible when it comes to network defense. The process is illustrated in Figure 11-5.

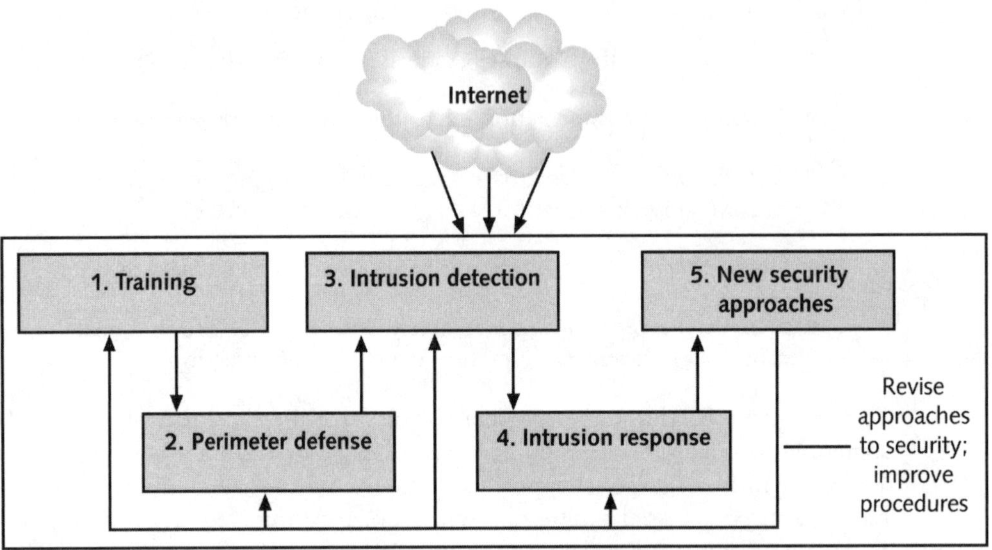

Figure 11-5 Active Defense in Depth is an ongoing process

In Figure 11-5 you see the following steps which, taken together, create a cycle that enables defenses to grow stronger:

1. *Training* —Staff people are trained in network defense configuration.

2. *Perimeter defense* —After training, security staff can establish a perimeter defense configuration for the network.
3. *Intrusion detection* —After defenses are arranged and put online, IDS systems alert the security staff to potential vulnerabilities by sending alerts.
4. *Intrusion response* —Security staff evaluates alerts and responds to block legitimate attacks.
5. *New security approaches* —Countermeasures are taken to reduce the number of false-positives as well as true-positives (legitimate attacks) encountered by the IDS, which strengthens perimeter defense and helps staff people to learn more about network vulnerabilities and defenses.

By looking at training as an ongoing process rather than something that occurs only before hiring, the organization improves its overall security stance while its staff people grow in their ability to prevent attacks.

Adding Security Layers

An Active Defense in Depth posture takes into account the fact that a single network cannot be fully protected unless all interconnecting networks are adequately protected. Your goal is to establish trust—to provide non-repudiation for your network, and to ensure the integrity and confidentiality of the information that passes into and out of it. In order to improve security, you may need to add new layers of security. For example, you may need to add an IDS to supplement your firewall and VPN. If you already have a network-based IDS (NIDS), you may want to add host-based IDS or hybrid IDS systems to strengthen detection and response.

Take the example of the U.S. Navy. In a 1998 article entitled "Defense in Depth: Security for Network-Centric Warfare," Capt. Dan Galik described the layers or "zones" of defense that were created at that time to protect one of the U.S. Navy's intranets (*www.chips.navy.mil/archives/98_apr/Galik.htm*). These layers included:

- A firewall
- Encryption
- Virus protection to filter out potentially harmful e-mail attachments
- Authentication
- Intrusion detection
- Access control
- Information integrity through Secure Sockets Layer (SSL) and Internet Protocol Security (IPSec)
- Auditing

In addition, four defensive "zones" were created to protect the end-users as well as communications between the zones. The zones enable protection to extend from the network perimeter to the end-users' individual desktops.

1. Zone 1 includes end-users' desktops, which are protected through passwords, access control lists, VPN encryption, and virus protection.
2. Zone 2 is described as a single "community of interest" or group of computers joined in a network.Routers, firewalls, virus protection, and VPN encryption protect this zone.
3. Zone 3 encompasses multiple communities of interest so that communications can be conducted smoothly between them. Protection methods include network intrusion detection, firewalls, VPN encryption, and virus protection.
4. Zone 4 is the outermost zone, which is the boundary between a Department of the Navy information system and a public network such as the Internet. Defensive mechanisms at this level include authentication for routers and Domain Name Servers (DNSs), VPN encryption, and firewalls.

By breaking its communication needs into separate systems and relying on multiple security methods, the Department of the Navy achieved effective external security. However, such a system does not always provide strong defense from vulnerabilities such as accidental misuse of resources as well as malicious attacks from insiders. Defense in Depth can often be improved by placing more emphasis on access control, user education and awareness, as well as increased higher levels of auditing.

Strengthening Performance: Keeping Pace With Network Needs

The performance of an intrusion detection system refers to its ability to capture packets and process them according to the system's rule base. Ideally, the IDS will capture all the packets that reach it, send alarms on all suspicious packets, and allow legitimate packets to pass through to the internal network. This level of performance, however, can be hampered by a number of factors. These factors—memory, available bandwidth, and storage space—are discussed in the sections that follow.

Memory

The performance of an IDS depends in large measure on the number of signatures it has to review when it receives a packet. For signatures of events that only consist of a single packet, memory requirements are virtually nonexistent. However, for signatures requiring a sequence of packets to reach the IDS, the IDS needs to maintain the state of the connection in memory. Memory is also needed to store information in cache and for any databases that contain the IDS configuration settings. The primary consideration is that the IDS has more than the minimum amount of Random Access Memory (RAM) available to it to maintain state information and thus thwart slow attacks that take place over extended periods of time.

Bandwidth

Firewalls, packet sniffers, and intrusion detection systems all need to be able to process data as fast as it moves through the network. If your network has a Gigabit Ethernet gateway but your IDS runs on a host that only has a 100MB Ethernet connection, data will pass more slowly through the IDS than it should. An IDS should be capable of handling 50 percent of bandwidth utilization without losing the capacity to detect. Intrusion detection often begins to break down if your bandwidth use exceeds 80 percent of network capacity.

Run Performance Monitor on Windows or the Top utility on UNIX/Linux to gauge how much overhead your IDS is consuming. Make sure the host computers that provide network sensors and IDS management consoles run as fast as possible. If performance lags, upgrade immediately to a faster computer or network card.

Managing Storage

Some intrusions take place over long periods of time, and the storage of a sizeable amount of historical data from the IDS log files can be essential to tracking such slow attacks. One aspect of managing an IDS is the need to provide sufficient storage space (typically, a gigabyte or more) for current IDS data, and the need to archive or securely delete data when it is no longer needed.

It's often overlooked, but the need to clear out media when it is full and the information on it is no longer needed, is an important network security consideration. You need to shred documents completely so hackers, criminals, or malicious employees cannot recover them.

For systems that contain (or contained) highly sensitive corporate information, you may want to physically remove them and degauss them. **Degaussing** is the process of magnetically erasing an electronic device such as a monitor or a disk to remove any stray data or magnetic fields from it. Simply deleting or erasing files does not completely remove all information from the disk. When you use a delete or erase command, you simply remove pointers that tell the computer what clusters are being used to store the information. That way the computer can reuse those sectors if needed. Note, however, that until the sectors are overwritten, the current information in those sectors can be recovered. Programs that can completely overwrite disk media include Mutilate File Wipe (shown in Figure 11-6), Shredder, Secure Clean and BC Wipe, as well as Norton Utilities Wipeinfo.

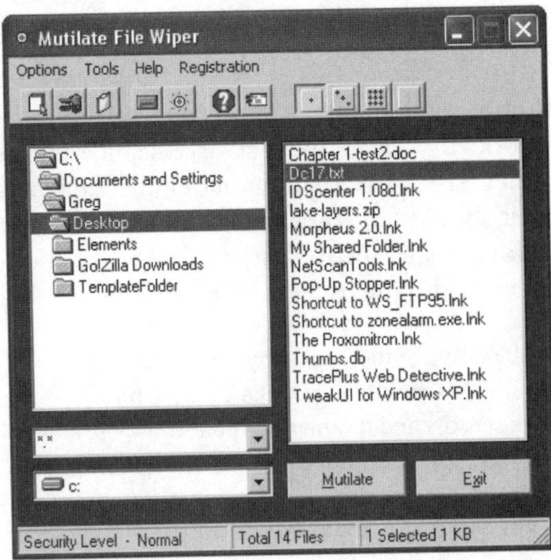

Figure 11-6 File shredder software permanently removes all traces of files from your disks

Do not allow company employees to maintain company information on their own laptop or home computers. You have no way of knowing what kind of security mechanisms are in place on a staff person's personal computer. They are, for the most part, highly vulnerable and easily attacked.

Maintaining Your Own Knowledge Base

You cannot perform ongoing security maintenance in isolation. To remain effective, you need to maintain your own knowledge and industry contacts, just as you maintain your software and hardware configurations. Visiting security-related Web sites and holding online discussions with other professionals in the field does not constitute misuse of your work time. Rather, you need to communicate to management the need to stay informed by visiting Web sites, participating in mailing lists and newsgroups, subscribing to trade publications, and taking certification tests in order to keep up with the fast-changing field of network security.

Web Sites

You'll find no shortage of Web sites that gather news headlines on virus outbreaks and security breaches that affect prominent corporations. The challenge is to choose one or two sites that you scan once a day or once every few days, looking for security issues that might affect your own network. You might visit sites such as the following:

- Center for Internet Security (*www.cisecurity.org*)
- SANS Institute (*www.sans.org*)

- CERT Coordination Center (*www.cert.org*)
- Incidents.org (*www.incidents.org*)

Establish a set of bookmarks/favorites of Web sites you visit on a regular basis (see Hands-On Project 11-5 for a suggestion of how to set up such a list). These are often good collection points for news and information about security issues.

Mailing Lists and Newsgroups

Mailing lists often provide you with more up-to-date information about security issues and vulnerabilities than Web sites or periodicals. You get firsthand information from security professionals about problems they are currently encountering as well as opinions on security-related issues. Often, you can also read about suggested solutions to those problems.

- NTBugtraq (*www.ntbugtraq.com*)
- comp.security.firewalls (*comp.security.firewalls*)
- Firewalls Mailing List (*www.isc.org/services/public/lists/firewalls.html*)
- Firewalls Mailing List Archives (*www.securityfocus.com/links/category/41*)
- SecurityFocus HOME Mailing Lists (*http://online.securityfocus.com/archive*)

Be sure to exercise caution before you post messages on newsgroups or mailing lists that describe specifics of security breaches you have experienced. You do not want hackers who may be monitoring communications in those groups to know that your network has been vulnerable.

Trade Publications

Newsletters and trade publications that cover information security often contain useful reviews of hardware and software products. These include online newsletters as well as those you receive by regular mail.

- Compsec Online (*www.compseconline.com/compsec/show*)
- Security Bytes (*www.cisco.com/warp/public/779/largeent/issues/security/sbytes*)
- SANS newsletters (*wwwserver2.sans.org/sansnews*)
- SecurityFocus ONLINE Links to security publications (*www.compseconline.com/compsec/show/*)
- Information Security News (*www.infosecnews.com*)

It can be useful to subscribe to publications you receive by e-mail or conventional mail. But be aware of privacy issues and the possibility of receiving unwanted mail. When you subscribe, give as little personal information as possible, and uncheck any boxes that are preselected to give the publisher permission to send you other publications or sell your e-mail address to other mailing lists.

Certifications

Many certifications need to be renewed periodically by retesting. Hopefully, your employer will realize that studying and certification not only benefits you personally, but improves the level of expertise that is available to the company as well. Visiting the following certification-related Web sites can help you keep up with tests you've taken or hope to take in the future.

- Global Information Assurance Certification (GIAC) (*www.giac.org*)
- International Information Systems Security Certification Consortium (*www.isc2.org*)
- CompTIA (*www.comptia.org*)
- GoCertify (*www.gocertify.com*)

Be aware of when your current certifications need to be renewed. Discuss with your supervisor whether they will help defray the cost of testing or at least give you time off so you can study and travel as needed.

Chapter Summary

- This chapter discussed aspects of conducting ongoing maintenance of network security systems, and particularly of intrusion detection systems. The text discussed the need for security event management—accumulating data from a wide range of security devices by means of a coordinated program. Such a program includes event monitoring of alert and event logs produced by security devices and operating systems. It also involves the collection of data from multiple sensors either through a centralized or a distributed system. It requires you to review the attack signatures your IDS uses to make sure they are up-to-date.
- Another aspect of event management, and one that is often overlooked, is the need to make a change in a procedure in a systematic and thought-out way. Change management describes the modification of systems or procedures in a way that includes the approval of appropriate management and that notifies staff of the impending change before it occurs.
- The text discussed the use of security auditing to test the effectiveness of network defenses after you have established them. In an operational audit your own staff examines the system logs and looks for vulnerabilities such as weak passwords or unnecessary user accounts. An independent audit is performed by an outside firm you hire to come in and inspect your logs.

- Another aspect of ongoing security maintenance is the management of the intrusion detection system to keep it running smoothly. First, you need to maintain your current IDS by making backups, managing user accounts, and cutting back on any unnecessary rules that the IDS uses. You can also strengthen overall intrusion detection by instituting an awareness program in which employees, contractors, and business partners all understand and observe your security policy. You can also strengthen the IDS by adding software or hardware as needed.
- By strengthening your network's Defense in Depth configuration, you improve network defense overall and ensure availability and integrity of information. You also provide for non-repudiation: the use of authentication to prevent the parties involved in an electronic transaction from denying that it took place in order to escape paying for goods or services. Active Defense in Depth calls for actively trying to anticipate and thwart attempts before they occur. This can be done through training or through adding layers of security.
- Next, the text discussed the importance of keeping pace with your network's needs by providing sufficient memory for the IDS to process long-term attacks by maintaining a state of a connection with a potential hacker. You also need to provide the IDS with sufficient network speed to capture and process all the packets that reach it. Finally, you need to provide the IDS with sufficient storage space for log and alert files. You also need to dispose of files thoroughly by "shredding" them electronically—in other words, overwriting them so all traces are removed from the media on which they reside.
- Finally, the text discussed the importance of maintaining your own knowledge and expertise along with your ongoing maintenance of security devices. By visiting selected Web sites, you can keep abreast of security breaches and virus outbreaks. By joining mailing lists or posting on newsgroups, you gain a resource for getting answers and opinions on issues you confront. By subscribing to online or print publications, you get reviews of new equipment as well as articles that describe how to use them. Finally, you need to keep your security certifications up-to-date in order to maintain your own level of expertise, as well as the experience level of the organization as a whole.

Key Terms

Active Defense in Depth — A particularly strong implementation of the Defense in Depth concept in which, instead of passively waiting for attacks to occur and then reacting to incidents, security personnel expect that attacks will occur and try to anticipate them.

awareness program — A program in which employees, contractors, and business partners all understand the company's security policy and how it should affect their behavior.

centralized data collection — A system in which all of an organization's event and security data is being "funneled" to a centralized management console in the main office.

change management — The process that involves the modification of equipment, systems, software, or procedures in a sequential and preplanned way.

Computer Security Manager (CSM) — Someone who is responsible for the ongoing management of network security systems.

degaussing — The process of magnetically erasing an electronic device, such as a monitor or a disk, to remove any stray data or magnetic fields from it.

distributed data collection — A system in which the data from security devices such as firewalls and intrusion detection systems goes to a management console in its own local network.

event monitoring — Reviewing alert and event logs produced by your security devices and operating systems, and periodically testing the network to identify any weak points.

independent audit — An audit in which you hire an outside firm to come in and inspect your audit logs to make sure you are getting the information you want and not gathering unnecessary information that consumes system and network resources.

non-repudiation — The use of authentication to prevent organizations involved in an electronic transaction from denying that it occurred.

Open Security Evaluation Criteria (OSEC) — A standard set of criteria used for reviewing intrusion detection signatures.

operational audit — An audit in which an organization's own staff examines their system logs and security logs to accumulate and analyze information about intrusions and other unauthorized accesses.

security auditing — The process of testing the effectiveness of a network defense system by testing the system, analyzing event logs, or observing procedures.

security event management program — A program that gathers and consolidates events from multiple sources so it can be analyzed and used to improve network security.

social engineering — The act of fooling staff people into giving out passwords or other information.

syslogs — System logs created in a Unix environment.

target-to-console ratio — The number of target computers on your network that is managed by a single command console.

tiger teams — Assembled in order to actively test the network.

Tinkerbell program — A program in which network connections are scanned and alerts are generated when logins are attempted or when connection attempts are made from sites that have been identified as suspicious.

Review Questions

1. Which of the following is a type of security audit? (Choose all that apply.)
   a. automated
   b. independent
   c. centralized
   d. operational
2. Why is it important to protect the information you gather through auditing? (Choose all that apply.)
   a. Employees' privacy could be compromised.
   b. It might become corrupted when you store it.
   c. Hackers could discover passwords.
   d. Viruses could infect it.
3. When should you follow the elaborate procedure for implementing changes that is illustrated in Figure 11-3?
   a. when many staff people will be affected by the change
   b. when the change needs to be made urgently
   c. whenever a change needs to be made to security configurations
   d. when the change will have a substantial impact
4. If the impact of a security or procedural change in your organization seems too great, what should you do?
   a. forget about making the change
   b. document the fact that you considered the change and move on
   c. reevaluate and modify the change
   d. discuss the situation with your supervisors

5. How much time should you give staff people to prepare for a significant change in your organization's security-related processes? (Choose all that apply.)

   a several weeks

   b several days to a week

   c no time at all, if the change needs to be made immediately

   d several hours

6. What is the name given to an auditing program in which current connections are scanned and alerts are generated when logins are attempted?

   a. social engineering

   b. port scan

   c. event monitoring

   d. Tinkerbell program

7. A staff person whose primary responsibilities include maintaining and strengthening network defenses is called a ___________.

   a. Security Incident Response Team leader

   b. Computer Security Manager

   c. Chief Information Officer

   d. Security Auditor

8. What is a realistic goal of ongoing security management? (Choose all that apply.)

   a. block all suspicious packets

   b. trace all attacks

   c. trace as many intrusion attempts as possible

   d. continually strengthen and modify defenses

9. Which of the following describes a goal of a security event management program?

   a. consolidate events from multiple sources

   b. respond to events as quickly as possible

   c. conduct forensics to trace and prosecute offenders

   d. manage IDS signatures

10. How can you gather information on a variety of security events and respond to them in near-real time?
    a. assemble a large response team
    b. perform distributed data collection
    c. automate collection and analysis
    d. outsource security management

11. Which of the following is an advantage of centralized data collection? (Choose all that apply.)
    a. reduced traffic through network gateways
    b. reduced administrative costs
    c. reduced software/hardware costs
    d. only one person is needed to review the data

12. Why would you choose distributed rather than centralized data collection?
    a. to reduce traffic through the gateways
    b. to reduce the load on security managers
    c. to reduce cost
    d. to reduce hardware/software costs

13. What is a potential security risk that arises with a centralized data collection system?
    a. More time is required to respond to alerts.
    b. There are more gateways for hackers to attack.
    c. There is dependence on remote network hosts that might fail.
    d. There is the need to encrypt data as it passes through the Internet.

14. Before installing new signatures for an IDS, what do you need to do?
    a. back up the IDS
    b. stop the IDS
    c. change passwords
    d. double-check to verify whether new signatures are really needed

15. What can happen if you make a change in security configurations too abruptly and without proper authorization? (Choose all that apply.)

    a Staff people may ignore the change.

    b. The change may surprise other security managers.

    c. You may be flooded by protests.

    d. You could face disciplinary action.

16. The change management process might apply when which of the following occurs?

    a. New password login procedures are needed.

    b. You need to block access to the DMZ servers.

    c. A new VPN gateway is installed.

    d. You need to change a fragmentation packet rule in a packet filter.

17. If your assessment of the impact of a change is that the impact is too great to justify the change, what should you do?

    a. don't make the change

    b. modify the change and reassess the impact

    c. modify the impact but make the change

    d. seek approval from managerial staff

18. Security auditing involves which of the following? (Choose all that apply.)

    a. reviewing log files

    b. reviewing hardware and software costs

    c. testing defenses

    d. rotating firewall logs

19. Why should you review your user accounts on a regular basis? (Choose all that apply.)

    a. to make sure passwords have not expired

    b. to eliminate accounts introduced by hackers

    c. to reduce disk space

    d. to delete accounts of ex-employees

20. What is non-repudiation?

   a. the ability of a system to authenticate users

   b. the ability to rely on information gained through a security audit

   c. a legal defense used by employees whose privacy has allegedly been violated

   d. the ability to validate transactions through electronic documentation

HANDS-ON PROJECTS

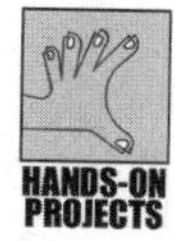

Project 11-1: Testing IDS Performance

One aspect of ongoing security maintenance is monitoring the performance of your IDS software and other security devices. You can do this simply using the Windows XP or 2000 Task Manager, as well as the freeware IDS Snort, to determine how much of your available system resources it costs to run Snort. This project assumes that you installed Snort as described in Hands-On Project 2-4.

1. Open the Task Manager by pressing **Ctrl+Alt+Delete**.
2. Click **Performance**.
3. Write down the total kernel memory. Also write down the handles, threads, and processes.
4. Click **Start**, point to **Programs** (**All Programs** on Windows XP), point to **Accessories**, and click **Command Prompt**.
5. Make sure you have Snort installed and that you have a directory within the top-level Snort directory named "log" in which you will store your log files. For instance, if Snort is installed in C:\Snort\snort.exe, create the directory C:\Snort\log.
6. Enter the following at the command prompt to set up Snort to use the rules you have established: ***[%systemroot%]* \snort.exe–1\Snort\log–c\snort \rules.rule**, and then press **Enter**. (*[%sysytmroot%]* is only a placeholder—it represents the path that leads to the snort executable file, such as C:Program Files or C:\Snort.) Also, remember that you are entering a single blank space before –1 and –c.
7. After Snort is up and running, click the **Task Manager** taskbar button. Now write down the total kernel memory. Also write down the handles, threads, and processes.
8. Calculate how much memory Snort is using by subtracting the memory before you started Snort to the available memory after Snort was running. The memory changes constantly; just pick one average and write it down.
9. Calculate the handles, threads, and processes as well. How many is Snort using?

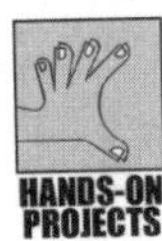

Project 11-2: Making IDS Alert Files Easier to Analyze

The freeware Intrusion Detection System Snort is relatively easy to set up (as described in Hands-On Project 2-4) and configure filter rules (as described in Hands-On Project 9-6). However, its log files can be hard to read because they are in raw text format. A tool called WinSnort2HTML takes Snort's alert messages and converts them to Web page HTML format so that it's easy to read. The program can sort listings as well. You need any Windows 2000 or XP computer to perform this project. You also need a file archive utility such as WinZip.

1. Double-click the **Internet Explorer** icon on your desktop.
2. Enter the URL **http://home.earthlink.net/~ckoutras/**, and then press **Enter**.
3. When the Windows Utilities for Snort Web page appears, click the file name **ws2h[** ***version number*** **].zip**.
4. When the File Download dialog box appears, click **Save**.
5. When the file has downloaded, double-click it to open it in an archiving utility such as WinZip.
6. When WinZip opens, click **Extract** and choose a directory on your computer where you want to extract the files.
7. Double-click the file **Setup.exe** to install the program.
8. When setup is complete, double-click the file icon to start up WinSnort2HTML (or click **Start**, click **Programs** (**All Programs** on Windows XP), and click **WinSnort2HTML**).
9. Click **Alert File**.
10. When the Select a Snort alert file dialog box appears, click the **Look in** drop-down list. Double-click the directory where your Snort log files are located. (See Step 5 of Project 11-1 for the location of the log file directory.)
11. Click the file **alert.ids**. Then click **Open**.
12. In the box next to HTML File, click to position the text cursor. Type the path leading to the HTML file you want to create. This file should probably be located in the same directory where the log files are located as well. (If the log files are located in C:\Snort\log\alert.ids, enter **C:\Snort\log\alert.html** for the HTML version of the alert file.)
13. Click **Make HTML File**. You'll probably have to wait several minutes while the conversion proceeds.
14. When conversion is complete, click the **Internet Explorer** button in the Windows taskbar.
15. Click **File** and click **Open**.

16. In the Open dialog box, click **Browse**.
17. Locate the **alert.hmtl** file you just created. Click the file, and then click **Open**.
18. Click **OK**.
19. The alert file opens in your Web browser in HTML format.

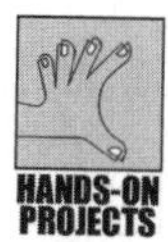

Project 11-3: ™Deleting a File and then Recovering It

One aspect of ongoing security management is the management of files on your network's computer systems. You need to delete files that contain sensitive information about your organization. However, conventionally deleting a file by throwing it in your operating system's trash can or Recycle Bin doesn't mean it's gone forever. Hackers or criminals can still manage to recover it, as you'll discover in this project. It can be performed on any Windows 2000 or XP computer that has WinZip or another file archiving utility installed.

1. Click **Start**, point to **Programs** (**All Programs** on **Windows XP**), point to **Accessories**, and click **Notepad**.
2. When Notepad opens displaying a blank file, type some text that is meant to represent that this is a sensitive document: ™**Sensitive– Top Secret– Plans for Upcoming Product Line.** .
3. Click **File** and click **Save**.
4. In the Save in drop-down list of the Save As dialog box, click **Desktop**.
5. Type the name **SensitiveFile.txt** in the File name box. Then click **Save**.
6. Click **File** and click **Exit** to close Notepad.
7. Go to the Windows desktop, right-click the **SensitiveFile.txt** file, and then click **Delete**.
8. When prompted to verify whether you want to delete the file, click **Yes**.
9. Right-click **Recycle Bin** and click **Empty Recycle Bin**.
10. When prompted to verify whether you want to empty the Recycle Bin, click **Yes**.
11. Double-click the **Internet Explorer** icon on your desktop.
12. Enter the following URL in your browser's Address bar: **http://www.webattack.com/download/dlpcinspector.shtml**. Press **Enter**.
13. When the File Download dialog box appears, click **Save**. Select a location on your computer where you want to save the file, then click **Save**.
14. When download is complete, double-click the file **PCIFR** ***X*** **.exe** (where *X* is a placeholder that stands for the current version number).

15. When the Choose Setup Language dialog box appears, verify that **English** is chosen, and click **OK**.
16. When the InstallShield wizard opens, click **Next**. Follow the instructions presented on subsequent screens in order to install PC Inspector File Recovery on your computer.
17. When installation is complete, locate the program file PC Inspector File Recovery and double-click the file to start up the program.
18. When the Choose Language dialog box appears, verify that **English** is chosen, and click **OK**.
19. When the Welcome to Drive Rescue dialog box appears, click the icon next to the heading Recover deleted files.
20. When the Select drive dialog box appears, in the Logical drive tab, select your hard disk, and click **OK**.
21. A list of folders appears under the heading Deleted. (If it does not, click the plus sign next to Deleted to view the folders.) Scroll down the list and click the **Recycled** folder.
22. Locate the file you just created. You are looking for a small file with the file extension .txt that was created on today's date. Right-click the file and click **View as text** from the popup menu.
23. When the Select FAT dialog box appears, verify that **noFAT** is selected, and click **OK**.
24. What can you view when you choose **View as text**? Scan through the list of other files located in the Desktop folder. In the condition column, look for any files that are described as good. Right-click the files and choose View as text, then verify that **noFAT** is selected, and click **OK**. Can you read the contents of these files?

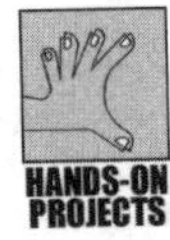

Project 11-4: Shredding a File Permanently

You are probably familiar with the use of paper shredding hardware devices to shred printed documents. For electronic files, you can perform a similar operation using a file shredding application. You need a Windows 2000 or XP computer to complete this project. This project assumes that you have created and recovered a file as described in Project 11-3.

1. Open a browser. Go to **http://simplythebest.net/file_shredders.html**.
2. Click **Mutilate File Wiper**.
3. Click **Download Mutilate File Wiper *[version number]***.
4. Click **Download Mutilate File Wiper *[version number]* Full Version Including all Required Runtime Files**. When a dialog box appears asking you if you want to continue, click **Save**.

5. Follow the steps shown in the Setup wizard to install the program. When a dialog box appears telling you that Mutilate File Wiper was installed successfully, click **OK**.
6. Double-click the program file **Mutilate.exe** and double-click the file to start Mutilate File Wiper (or click **Start**, click **Programs** (**All Programs** on Windows XP), and click **Mutilate File Wiper**.
7. When a dialog box appears, click **Free Trial**.
8. Locate the file you created in Project 11-3 by navigating through your folders as displayed in the left-hand side of the Mutilate File Wiper window. (If you don't have such a file or can't locate it, select a file you are sure you don't need any longer.) Click the file to highlight its name in the right-hand side of the window.
9. Click **Mutilate**.
10. A dialog box appears stating that the file is about to be destroyed and deleted. Click **OK**. The file is removed from the Mutilate File Wiper window.
11. Check your desktop to see if the file exists. Open the Recycle Bin to look for the file.
12. Open PC Inspector File Recovery (the application described in Project 11-3) by either double-clicking its desktop icon or the program icon in the directory where you installed it.
13. Verify that English is selected, and click **OK**.
14. Click the **Recover deleted files** icon.
15. Click the logical drive where the file was located, and then click **OK**.
16. Locate the same directory where the file you deleted was located. Is the file present?
17. Click **Object** and then **Exit** to close PC Inspector File Recovery.
18. Click **Options** and then **Exit** to close Mutilate File Wiper and return to the Windows desktop.

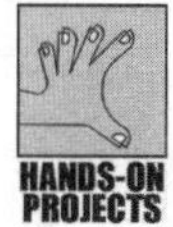

Project 11-5: Assembling Security-Related Bookmarks

As part of your ongoing security management program, you need to regularly visit some of the primary Web sites and other resources devoted to network defense issues. One way to ensure that you will visit the resources on a periodic basis (for example, once a week) is to assemble a list of bookmarks that you can access quickly. You can then set up an e-mail reminder notifying you that you need to check for updated software and other security-related news. This project can be performed on any computer that is connected to the Internet and that has Internet Explorer installed.

1. Double-click the **Internet Explorer** icon on your desktop.

2. Enter the URL for the Security Focus Online home page in your browser's Address bar (**http://online.securityfocus.com**), and then press **Enter**.
3. Click **Favorites**, and then click **Organize Favorites**.
4. Click **Create Folder**.
5. When the new folder appears, type the name **Security**, and then press **Enter**.
6. Click **Create Folder**.
7. When the new folder appears, type the name **News**, and then press **Enter**.
8. Click **Move Folder**.
9. In the Browse for Folder dialog box, click the **Security** folder, and then click **OK**.
10. Repeat Steps 6 through 9 for two more new folders, named **Discussions** and **Other Resources**, respectively.
11. Click **Close**.
12. Add the SecurityFocus Online home page to the News folder by clicking **Favorites**, clicking **Add to Favorites**, clicking **Create in**, clicking **News**, and then clicking **OK**.
13. Look around the SecurityFocus Online home page for a security-related resource that isn't a news source or a discussion group; click the link for the resource, click **Favorites** and click **Add Favorites**, and add the resource to the **Other Resources** folder. What resource(s) did you find? Write the answer in a lab notebook or word processing document.
14. Click the **Mailing Lists** link.
15. Scan the list of mailing lists and choose three that seem relevant to the subjects covered throughout this book. Add them to the Discussions folder. Record the mailing lists you added in a lab notebook or word processing document.
16. As an optional, final step, add the URLs listed in the section "Maintaining Your Own Knowledge Base" to the appropriate folders in your Security favorites folder.

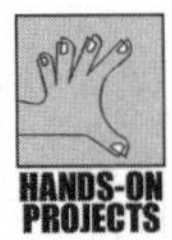

Project 11-6: Developing Test Criteria

In this project, you will develop a set of test criteria for your own network, using the OSEC criteria developed by the security organization Neohapsis, Inc. as a starting point. You can use any computer that has an Internet connection and a Web browser installed in order to complete this project.

1. Double-click the **Internet Explorer** icon on your desktop.

2. Enter the URL for the Neohapsis OSEC – Test Criteria Web page (**http://osec.neohapsis.com/criteria**) in your browser's Address bar, and then press **Enter**.
3. Click **Test Descriptions**. Scroll down the Test Details page to view the descriptions of the various tests included in the current version of OSEC.
4. Under Section D, Discard Tests, write down a type of attack that targets particular ports that you should test for.
5. Scroll down to Section F, Evasion Tests. What are two types of attacks described in this section that you should test for yourself?
6. Scroll down the list and look for an attack that involves 100,000 separate connection attempts followed by an attack attempt. Write down the name of this type of attack.
7. Write down three types of HTTP obfuscation tests that involve mangled or malformed URLs or URIs that are listed under Baseline Attacks and that you should perform on your own servers.

CASE PROJECTS

Case Project 11-1: Analyzing an Intrusion

You receive an alert stating that one of your database servers makes a connection to a remote computer. You open a command prompt window. You start up the nestat utility by entering the command **netstat –a** and then pressing **Enter**. Netstat returns the information shown in Table 11-1.

Table 11-1 Network connections

Protocol	Foreign Address	State
TCP websrv:web	*websrv:0*	*LISTENING*
TCP websrv:ssl	*websrv:0*	*LISTENING*
TCP websrv:epnap	*websrv:0*	*LISTENING*
TCP websrv:microsoft-ds	*websrv:0*	*LISTENING*
TCP websrv:1028	*websrv:0*	*LISTENING*
TCP websrv:1030	*websrv:0*	*LISTENING*
TCP websrv:1031	*websrv:0*	*LISTENING*
TCP websrv:2000	*websrv:0*	*LISTENING*
TCP websrv:41499	*websrv:0*	*LISTENING*
UDP websrv:1028	*websrv:0*	*LISTENING*
UDP websrv:1030	*websrv:0*	*LISTENING*

Analyze this data and identify a probable intrusion event that is taking place. What kind of operating system is this server using?

Case Project 11-2: Deciding When to Communicate Change

As a result of security evaluations, your IDS sends you a series of alerts. One requires you to change a rule to block traffic to a server from the firewall. Another requires you to block access to a server that contains job records that employees use. How would you handle these two changes?

Case Project 11-3: Evaluating a Data Collection System

Your organization has a security team in each of four branch offices, so you have established a distributed data collection system. If serious alerts or successful intrusions are detected in a branch network, the team member on duty is required to e-mail the other members. One of the networks receives an e-mail attachment that is downloaded by an employee. The employee's e-mail program sends a mail message with the same attachment to others in the organization. The team member, upon learning of the event, e-mails other team members. By that time the original e-mail message bearing the potentially harmful attachment has already reached the e-mail server at the other branch networks. Name two alternatives to the current system that would overcome this problem.

Case Project 11-4: Strengthening Centralized Data Collection

Your small organization only has a few security specialists at its main office, so a centralized data collection system is established for the main office and two branch offices. You find that, with only three staff people available, an alert of a SYN-FIN packet being sent to an application server on the network is not received for two hours. Name two solutions that would provide more timely response, but that don't involve switching to a distributed data collection system (which, due to lack of personnel, is impractical).

SC0-402 OBJECTIVES

Table A-1 maps the Network Defense and Countermeasures objectives specified in Security Certified Professional's (SCP's) SC0-402 course to the corresponding chapter and section title where the objectives are covered in this book. Because the SCP exams undergo periodic updating and revising, you should check the SCP Web site for the latest developments at *www.securitycertified.net*.

Titles of subsections are enclosed in parentheses.

Table A-1 Objectives to chapter mapping

Objective	Chapter and Section(s)
Domain 1.0: Network Defense Fundamentals	
1.1: Examine Network Defense Fundamentals	Chapter 1: Foundations of Network Security (**Understanding TCP/IP Networking**, **Securing Individual Workstations**, and **Web and Internet-Based Security Concerns**) Chapter 2: Designing a Network Defense (**Common Attack Threats**)
1.2: Identify Network Defense Technologies	Chapter 2: Designing a Network Defense (**Providing Layers of Network Defense** and **Integrating Intrusion Detection Systems (IDSs)**)
1.3: Examine Access Control Methods	Chapter 1: Foundations of Network Security (**Routing and Access Control**)
1.4: Define the Principles of Network Auditing	Chapter 2: Designing a Network Defense (**Essential Network Security Activities**) Chapter 3: Risk Analysis and Security Policy Design (**Formulating a Security Policy**)
1.5: Identify the Impact of Defense	Chapter 1: Foundations of Network Security (**Goals of Network Security**)

Objective	Chapter and Section(s)
Domain 2.0: Security Policy Design and Implementation	
2.1: Examine the Concepts of Risk Analysis	Chapter 3: Risk Analysis and Security Policy Design (**Getting Started with Risk Analysis**)
2.2: Define the Methods of Risk Analysis	Chapter 3: Risk Analysis and Security Policy Design (**Getting Started with Risk Analysis**)
2.3: Describe the Process of Risk Analysis	Chapter 3: Risk Analysis and Security Policy Design (**Getting Started with Risk Analysis**)
2.4: Examine Techniques to Minimize Risk	Chapter 3: Risk Analysis and Security Policy Design (**Deciding How to Minimize Risk**)
2.5: Examine the Concepts of Security Policies	Chapter 3: Risk Analysis and Security Policy Design (**What Makes a Good Security Policy?**)
2.6: Identify Security Policy Categories	Chapter 3: **Risk Analysis and Security Policy Design** (**Formulating a Security Policy**)
2.7: Define Incident Handling Procedures	Chapter 3: **Risk Analysis and Security Policy Design** (**Performing Ongoing Risk Analysis**) Chapter 10: Intrusion Detection: Incident Response (**How to Respond: The Incident Response Process**)
Domain 3.0: Network Traffic Signatures	
3.1: Describe the Concepts of Signature Analysis	Chapter 9: Intrusion Detection: Preventive Measures (**Analyzing Intrusion Signatures**)
3.2: Examine the Common Vulnerabilities and Exposures (CVE)	Chapter 9: Intrusion Detection: Preventive Measures (**Common Vulnerabilities and Exposures (CVE)**)
3.3: Examine Normal Network Traffic Signatures	Chapter 9: Intrusion Detection: Preventive Measures (**Analyzing Intrusion Signatures**)
3.4: Examine Abnormal Network Traffic Signatures	Chapter 9: Intrusion Detection: Preventive Measures (**Analyzing Intrusion Signatures**)
Domain 4.0: VPN Concepts and Implementation	
4.1: Identify Concepts of VPNs	Chapter 7: Setting up a Virtual Private Network (**Exploring VPNs: What, Why, and How**)
4.2: Describe IP Security Protocol (IPSec)	Chapter 7: Setting up a Virtual Private Network (**Understanding Tunneling Protocols**)
4.3: Examine VPN Design and Architecture	Chapter 7: Setting up a Virtual Private Network (**Exploring VPNs: What, Why, and How**)
4.4: Describe the process of VPN Configuration	Chapter 7: Setting up a Virtual Private Network (**Exploring VPNs: What, Why, and How**)

Objective	Chapter and Section(s)
Domain 5.0: IDS Concepts and Implementation	
5.1: Identify the goals of IDS	Chapter 8: Intrusion Detection: An Overview (**Intrusion Detection System Components** and **Intrusion Detection Step-By-Step**)
5.2: Examine Host-Based Intrusion Detection	Chapter 8: Intrusion Detection: An Overview (**Options for Implementing Intrusion Detection Systems**)
5.3: Examine Network-Based Intrusion Detection	Chapter 8: Intrusion Detection: An Overview (**Options for Implementing Intrusion Detection Systems**)
5.4: Describe IDS Log Analysis	Chapter 8: Intrusion Detection: An Overview (**Intrusion Detection Step-By-Step**) Chapter 9: Intrusion Detection: Preventive Measures (**Logging and Intrusion Detection**)
5.5: Describe Methods of using an IDS	Chapter 9: Intrusion Detection: Preventive Measures (**Developing IDS Filter Rules**)
5.6: Configure an Intrusion Detection System	Chapter 10: Intrusion Detection: Incident Response (**Dealing with False Alarms**) Chapter 11: Strengthening Defense through Ongoing Management (**Strengthening Control: Security Event Management**)
Domain 6.0: Firewall Concepts and Implementation	
6.1: Recognize Firewall Components	Chapter 2: Designing a Network Defense (**Essential Network Security Activities**) Chapter 4: Choosing and Designing Firewalls (**Firewall Software and Hardware**)
6.2: Create a Firewall Policy	Chapter 4: Choosing and Designing Firewalls (**Establishing Rules and Restrictions**) Chapter 6: Strengthening and Managing Firewalls (**Managing Firewalls to Improve Security**)
6.3: Define Firewall Rule Sets and Packet Filters	Chapter 4: Choosing and Designing Firewalls (**Establishing Rules and Restrictions**) Chapter 5: Configuring Firewalls (**Approaches to Packet Filtering** and **Creating Packet Filter Rules**)
6.4: Examine the Proxy Server	Chapter 6: Strengthening and Managing Firewalls (**Working with Proxy Servers**)
6.5: Examine the Bastion Host	Chapter 4: Choosing and Designing Firewalls (**Choosing a Bastion Host**)

Objective	Chapter and Section(s)
6.6: Describe a Honeypot	Chapter 4: Choosing and Designing Firewalls (**Choosing a Bastion Host**)
6.7: Install and Configure Firewall-1	Chapter 6: Strengthening and Managing Firewalls (**Installing and Configuring Check Point NG**)
6.8: Install and Configure ISA Server	Chapter 6: Strengthening and Managing Firewalls (**Installing and Configuring Microsoft ISA Server 2000**)
6.9: Install and Configure IPChains	Chapter 6: Strengthening and Managing Firewalls (**Managing and Configuring iptables**)

APPENDIX

B

Security Resources

Intrusion detection and network security are all constantly evolving fields these days. In order to keep up with the latest developments in the field, you should visit the Web sites and other resources mentioned in this section. Many of the sites contain information not only about incident response, but they also present white papers, research papers, and other background information on topics such as firewalls, packet filtering, authentication, and encryption. In addition, and more importantly, you should visit these sites to learn about the latest threats against which you need to defend. Bugs, security holes, and the patches to plug them will be available online before you read about them in a book.

Security Standards

In order for network defense systems to work, a variety of different hardware and software resources need to work with one another. Standard criteria and settings enable devices manufactured by different companies to share information so that they can protect your network more effectively. The following Web sites give you more information about such standards.

Open Security Evaluation Criteria (*http://osec.neohapsis.com*)

The Open Security Evaluation Criteria (OSEC) is a standard for reviewing intrusion detection systems prepared by Neohapsis, Inc. OSEC enables intrusion detection hardware and software to be evaluated using the same criteria.

Common Vulnerabilities and Exposures (*www.cve.mitre.org*)

The Common Vulnerabilities and Exposures (CVE) standard enables security devices to share information about attack signatures and other vulnerabilities so that they can work together. Through this Web site, you can also find out how to create SQL queries designed to test for vulnerabilities on local computer systems using a new standard called the Open Vulnerability Assessment Language (OVAL) that was derived from CVE.

Viruses and Security Incidents

The following Web sites specialize in information about intrusion detection and how to respond to security incidents if they occur. If you encounter an intrusion attempt, a virus, or a worm, go to one of these sites to see if other systems have been affected, and to read about countermeasures you should take.

Symantec Security Response (*http://securityresponse.symantec.com*)

If you are looking for information about viruses, Trojan horses, and other malicious code, this is the place to go. You'll find an extensive database of viruses that have been reported to Symantec and that have been accounted for in the company's anti-virus software. You'll also find information about security incidents, but the emphasis is on protecting against and eliminating viruses and other harmful code.

Whitehats Network Security Resource (*www.whitehats.com*)

Whitehats is a community of network and computer professionals dedicated to the open-source and free software approaches. This Web site gathers recent security incident and news headlines on its home page. The site is also notable for the arachNIDS database (*www.whitehats.com/ids*) of intrusion detection signatures.

Incidents.org (*www.incidents.org*)

This site, which is also affiliated with SANS, specializes in intrusions, incidents, security alerts, and how to respond to all of the foregoing. The organization's Web site is called the "Internet Storm Center." The site presents a map of the world that illustrates the kinds of security breaches that have been reported by geographic region. You'll also find a list of current attack trends, such as ports that have been attacked most often, and malicious software that has been reported.

Dshield.org (*www.dshield.org*)

This site is the home of the Distributed Intrusion Detection System, in which network administrators from around the world share firewall and intrusion detection log information in an effort to track attack patterns. You'll find lists of the Top 10 ports that have been attacked recently, as well as the Top 10 computers from which attacks have originated.

Security Organizations on the Web

The following Web sites provide you with general information about Internet and network security.

The Center for Internet Security (*www.cisecurity.org*)

The Center for Internet Security is a nonprofit organization devoted to the development of security standards it calls "benchmarks." For instance, the group recently published a set of benchmarks establishing the secure operation of a Windows 2000 computer. Benchmarks are available for Linux, HP-UX, and other operating systems as well.

SANS Institute (*www.sans.org*)

The System Administration, Networking and Security (SANS) Institute is a research and education organization that focuses on network security. SANS conducts seminars and workshops in security around the country, and offers tests to prepare for important certifications like the CISSP. The SANS Web site (*www.sans.org*) includes links to important resources such as a list of the Twenty Most Critical Internet Security Vulnerabilities (*www.sans.org/top20.htm*) and the SANS Security Policy Project (*www.sans.org/newlook/resources/policies/policies.htm*), which contains sample security policies plus guidelines for producing them.

The Cert Coordination Center (*www.cert.org*)

The Cert Coordination Center, a group affiliated with the Carnegie-Mellon Institute, contains lists of security alerts, incident notes, and vulnerabilities on its home page. CERT also offers tips and articles about aspects of network security, plus training courses. Contents are oriented not only toward corporate and educational users, but also toward home users who need to know about security.

FIRST (*www.first.org*)

The Forum of Incident Response and Security Teams (FIRST) is a coalition of security incident response teams working in government, commercial, and academic organizations that seeks to promote rapid reaction to security incidents by coordinating communication and sharing information among its members. If you're a member of an incident response team, you should strongly consider joining FIRST.

MAILING LISTS AND NEWSLETTERS

It can be difficult to remember to visit sites like Incidents.org to find out about the latest security alerts. Sometimes, it's easier to absorb current information if it's sent to your e-mail inbox. Here are a couple of suggested mailing lists and newsletters you can subscribe to in order to keep up with the threats you need to combat.

Mailing Lists

Mailing lists provide security professionals with up-to-the-minute news and views from other professionals. By discussing issues and problems through an e-mail list, you gain an instant source of support in case you run into trouble or have questions about an incident.

NTBugtraq (*www.ntbugtraq.com*)

The name refers to Windows NT, but this mailing list covers security issues pertaining to Windows 2000 and XP as well. Its goal is to share information about security exploits and bugs that affect Windows systems. The group is well-known and highly regarded.

Firewall-Wizards Mailing List (*http://honor.trusecure.com/mailman/listinfo/firewall-wizards*)

This closely moderated mailing list deals with security issues in general, as well as firewall-related issues in particular. You can subscribe to a regular (one e-mail message at a time) or digest (one consolidated e-mail message per day) version of the list. Searchable archives are also available so you can investigate specific topics that have already been discussed.

SecurityFocus HOME Mailing Lists (*http://online.securityfocus.com/archive*)

SecurityFocus operates a variety of security-related mailing lists on topics ranging from intrusion detection to firewalls to honeypots. One of the best features of the lists is the ability to search archived messages by topic—in other words, you can investigate specific issues and topics without actually having to subscribe. However, if you do want to join a list, you can get current news and views on a daily basis.

Newsletters and Trade Publications

Online newsletters and trade publications give you up-to-date news and views on specific topics related to network security. Usually, you can either visit a newsletter's Web site on a regular basis, or subscribe so that you can receive the newsletter by e-mail each time a new edition appears.

Compsec Online (*www.compseconline.com/compsec/show*)

Computer Security Online is a Web site devoted to news and reports for computer security professionals. Some news headlines and an archive of news items and feature stories are available to everyone. However, other content can be accessed only by paid subscribers. Titles of available publications include "Computer Law and Security Reports," "Computers & Security," and "Computer Fraud & Security."

Information Security News (*www.infosecnews.com*)

This site provides a news service that you can view either on the Web or in the form of an e-mail newsletter. News items are taken from around the world rather than focusing on any one region.

SANS Newsletters (*http://server2.sans.org/sansnews*)

The set of newsletters published by the SANS Institute includes a weekly News Bites publication as well as a weekly Security Alert Consensus listing current security threats and their available countermeasures.

Security Certification Sites

The following sites offer certification through exams that can be invaluable for obtaining employment in the field of network security.

Global Information Assurance Certification (GIAC) (*www.giac.org*)

The GIAC Web site provides information about the certification exams and deadlines offered by the SANS Institute. Programs range from the entry-level Basic Information Security Officer to more specialized certifications such as the GIAC Certified Firewall Analyst (GCFW).

The International Information Systems Security Certification Consortium (ISC)2 (*www.isc2.org*)

ISC2 is an international nonprofit organization dedicated to maintaining a common body of knowledge that is pertinent to information security, and to certifying industrials. ISC2 prepares and administers two of the most highly prized certifications in the field of network security: the Certified Information Systems Security Professional (CISSP) and the System Security Certified Practitioner (SSCP).

CompTIA Certification (*www.comptia.org/certification/default.asp*)

The Computing Technology Industry Association is best known for the A+ series of certifications. The CompTIA Security+ Certification exam is also available to establish fundamental security competency related to firewalls, encryption, and intrusion detection.

Glossary

Access Control List (ACL) — A list of the users and groups that are authorized to use network resources, and the details about what level of authorization each user has.

accountability — The ability to track an attempted attack or intrusion back to the responsible party.

Acknowledgement (ACK) Flag — If the ACK Flag is set to 1 rather than to 0, the destination computer has received the packets.

Active Defense in Depth — A particularly strong implementation of the Defense in Depth concept in which, instead of passively waiting for attacks to occur and then reacting to incidents, security personnel expect that attacks will occur and try to anticipate them.

anomaly detection — A type of intrusion detection that causes an alarm to be sent when an IDS detects an event that deviates from behavior that has been defined as "normal."

ASCII payload — The actual data part of the packet, given in ASCII format.

assets — The hardware, software, and informational resources you need to protect through the development and implementation of a comprehensive security policy.

asymmetric cryptography — A type of encryption in which two different keys are used. A private key is kept by the certificate holder and never shared, while a public key is shared among users to encrypt and decrypt communications.

atomic attack — An attack that can be completed by sending a single network packet from client to host.

attack visualization — The process of replaying the attack so that the analyst can essentially see what the attacker viewed during the attack.

auditing — The process of keeping records of the activities of computers on the network; these include who is connecting to a computer, what resources are being requested, and whether access was granted or blocked.

authentication — The process of determining the identity of an authorized user through the matching of a username and password or by other means.

Authentication Header (AH) — A method provided as an option with Internet Protocol Security (IPSec), in which an encrypted header is added to a packet in order to authenticate its source.

awareness program — A program in which employees, contractors, and business partners all understand the company's security policy and how it should affect their behavior.

back door — An undocumented or unauthorized opening (such as a port) through which a computer, program, or other resource can be accessed.

basic authentication — Authentication system in which a user submits a username/password pair to a server that maintains a local file of usernames and passwords.

bastion host — A computer that sits on the perimeter of a network and that has been specially protected through operating system patches, authentication, and encryption.

buffer overflow — A type of attack in which a program or process attempts to store more data than can be held in a temporary disk storage area called a buffer; the host computer is being flooded with more information than it can handle.

cache — Store data on a disk so that files can be retrieved later on if needed; an area of a hard disk where files are stored.

centralized data collection — A system in which all of an organization's event and security data is being "funneled" to a centralized management console in the main office.

certificate authority (CA) — A trusted organization that issues digital certificates that can be used to generate keys.

chain of custody — The record of who handled an object to be used as evidence in court.

chains — Sets of packet filtering rules used by the Linux tool iptables.

challenge/response authentication — Authentication system in which a computer or firewall generates a random code or number (the challenge) and sends it to the user who wishes to be authenticated. The user re-submits the number or code and adds his or her secret PIN or password (the response).

change management — The process that involves the modification of equipment, systems, software, or procedures in a sequential and preplanned way.

checksum — A simple error-checking procedure used to determine whether a message has been tampered with in transit.

chkconfig — Short for *configuration state checker*, a UNIX utility that provides configuration listings for services being run on the computer.

ciphertext — Ordinary text that has been rendered unreadable as a result of encryption.

cleanup rule — A packet-filtering rule that comes last in a rule base and that covers any other packets that haven't been covered in preceding rules.

client authentication — The process of granting access to network resources based on a source IP address rather than user information.

client sets — Groups of client computers that you can group together by IP address so that you can identify them by name when you create rules.

client-to-site VPN — A type of VPN connection that makes a network accessible to remote users requiring dial-in access.

cloning — The process of copying an entire disk or removable media to a similar object.

command console — Software that provides a network administrator with a graphical front-end interface to an intrusion detection system.

Common Gateway Interface (CGI) scripts — Scripts used to process data submitted over the World Wide Web.

Common Vulnerabilities and Exposures (CVE) — A standard that enables security devices to share information about attack signatures and other vulnerabilities so that they can work together to provide network protection.

composite attacks — Attacks that require a series of packets to be transmitted in order for the attack to be completed.

computer forensics — The set of activities associated with trying to find out who hacked into a system or who gained unauthorized access. Investigation is done through careful data retrieval and analysis, usually with the ultimate goal of gaining enough legally admissible evidence to pursue prosecution.

Computer Security Manager (CSM) — Someone who is responsible for the ongoing management of network security systems.

connectionless — A feature of the UDP protocol, which does not depend on a connection actually having been established between a host and client for a UDP packet to be sent from host to client.

containment — The process of preventing a malicious file, intruder, or compromised media from spreading to the other resources on the network.

control connection — An initial FTP connection between client and server.

countermeasures — Strategies and approaches that counter threats to network security.

counters — Utilities that keep track of the number of active TCP, UDP or other connections currently forwarding data on the network.

covert channel — A communications channel, such as a port on a computer or a network connection, that can be exploited in a way that compromises the security of a computer.

crackers — Individuals who are attracted to the challenge of detecting passwords and removing copy protection from software.

crafted — Manufactured or altered on purpose by a hacker.

customize access — Identify criteria under which a connection request would be allowed by a firewall, rather than allowing the firewall to automatically deny all or allow all instances of such requests.

Cyclical Redundancy Check (CRC) — An error-checking procedure sometimes appended to the end of a TCP/IP packet.

data — The part of a datagram that contains the actual data being sent from client to server.

data encapsulation — The process of protecting a packet of digital information by enclosing it within another packet.

Data Encryption Standard (DES) — An encryption scheme developed by IBM in the mid-1970s that was adopted as an encryption standard in 1977.

data warehouses — Central repositories where data is stored so that it can be accessed and analyzed as needed.

datagrams — *See* packets.

dedicated computer — A computer that is dedicated solely to running intrusion detection software and logging traffic.

deface — The hacker's act of breaking into a Web site and leaving publicly visible messages on the site's Web pages so that friends of the hacker can see the hacker was there.

default gateway — The router or hub that the computers on a network use by default in order to gain access to resources either within or outside the network.

defended networks — Networks that put an emphasis on defensive measures and restricted access.

Defense in Depth (DiD) — A set of security layers that protect a network at many different levels using a variety of strategies and methodologies.

degaussing — The process of magnetically erasing an electronic device, such as a monitor or a disk, to remove any stray data or magnetic fields from it.

Demilitarized Zone (DMZ) — A subnetwork of publicly accessible Web, e-mail, and other servers that is outside the LAN but still protected by the firewall.

dependency services — Services that an operating system needs to function correctly.

destination port — The port at which the data is received by a computer from another computer.

destination sets — Groups of destination computers that can be named and handled together to make rules easier to configure.

digital certificate — An electronic document issued by a certificate authority that contains information about the certificate holder and that can be used to exchange public and private keys.

digital signature — A series of numerals and characters generated by an encryption process that is easily transportable, can be time-stamped, and is commonly used to authenticate the identity of the person who possesses it.

disk image — A copy of an entire disk that is saved on another type of storage media.

distributed data collection — A system in which the data from security devices such as firewalls and intrusion detection systems goes to a management console in its own local network.

Distributed Denial of Service (DDoS) attack — An attack in which hundreds or thousands of hijacked computers are used to launch an attack against a computer such as a Web site server.

DNS poisoning — *See* DNS spoofing.

DNS spoofing — A type of attack against a DNS server that enables a hacker to gain control over it; the hacker submits false information that causes a DNS server to behave as if a domain has a different IP address range than it actually does have.

Domain Name Server (DNS) — A server that resolves IP addresses into easy-to-remember domain names.

domain objects — Objects that exist within your organization's own domain.

dual-homed host — A computer that has been configured with more than one network interface.

dynamic port numbers — Numbers that applications assume for the length of a communications session and that are in the range 49152 through 65535.

Encapsulating Security Payload (ESP) — An encryption method provided as an option with Internet Protocol Security (IPSec), in which the data payload of a TCP/IP packet is encrypted.

encapsulation — The process of enclosing a packet within another one that has different IP source and destination information to provide a high degree of protection.

encryption — The process of concealing information to render it unreadable to all but the intended recipients.

eradication — The process of removing any files or programs that result from an intrusion, including malicious code, registry keys, unnecessary executable files, viruses, worms, or files created by worms.

escalate — To call in a wider group of security professionals and take immediate countermeasures to handle a problem.

escalated — A term used to describe what happens when the response to an intrusion is increased to a higher level.

escalation procedure — A set of roles, responsibilities, and measures taken in response to a security incident.

event horizon — The entire length of an attack, from the first packet received by an IDS to the last packet that is needed to complete the attack signature.

event monitoring — Reviewing alert and event logs produced by your security devices and operating systems, and periodically testing the network to identify any weak points.

extranet — A network that uses Internet technologies and consists of one or more networks connected to one another.

false-negatives — Attacks that occur but that are not detected by the IDS.

false-positives — Alarms that are generated by legitimate network traffic rather than attacks.

fault tolerance — The ability of an object or system to continue operations despite a fault in its makeup or environment.

firewall appliances — Hardware devices that have firewall functionality.

follow-up — The process of documenting what took place when an intrusion was detected and response occurred.

footer — *See* trailer.

forensics — Pertaining to events or objects that are associated with a court of law.

fragment — One packet within a sequence of TCP/IP packets that makes up a whole communication.

fragmentation — The division of a single IP packet into multiple packets, each of which is a fragment.

fully qualified domain name (FQDN) — The complete DNS name of a computer, including the computer name, domain name, and domain name extension, such as *www.course.com*.

gateway-to-gateway VPN connection — A VPN that uses hardware devices such as routers to connect two networks.

granular — A very fine level of control that you need to limit the amount of traffic through a firewall as much as possible.

hacker — An individual who attempts to gain access to unauthorized resources on a network, usually by finding a way to circumvent passwords, firewalls, or other protective measures.

half-open session — A connection that is initiated, but not completed, between client and server.

hardened — A term that describes a computer that is made more secure than any others on the network by eliminating all unnecessary software, closing potential openings, and protecting the information on it with encryption and authentication.

hash function — A mathematical function (such as MD4 or MD5) that creates a digest version of a message.

header — The part of a datagram that contains source and destination information and general information about that datagram.

hexadecimal payload — The actual data being communicated by the packet expressed in hexadecimal format.

hide-mode mapping — The process of hiding multiple private IP addresses behind one public IP address.

hide-mode NAT — A form of NAT in which the actual IP addresses are turned into addresses in one of the three ranges of non-routable IP addresses, such as 10.0.0.1/8.

honeypot — A computer that is placed on the perimeter of the network in order to attract hackers.

host-based intrusion detection system (HIDS) — An IDS that is deployed on each host in the LAN that is protected by the firewall.

HTTP cookies — Short segments of HTML code that a Web server places on a visitor's Web browser to identify that browser on subsequent visits.

hybrid firewall — A product that combines aspects of both firewall appliances and software firewalls in one package.

Hypertext Transport Protocol (HTTP) — A protocol used by Web services that communicates via a computer's TCP/IP port 80.

ID number — An identifying number that can be used to reassemble a packet in case it is divided into fragments.

incident response — The name given to the actions taken after a computer security incident occurs in order to determine what happened and what countermeasures need to be taken to ensure the continued security of the network.

independent audit — An audit in which you hire an outside firm to come in and inspect your audit logs to make sure you are getting the information you want and not gathering unnecessary information that consumes system and network resources.

interface — The plug or socket that a device uses to connect with another device or with a network.

Internet Control Message Protocol (IMCP) — A protocol that functions as a housekeeping protocol for TCP/IP, helping networks to cope with various communication problems.

Internet Group Management Protocol (IGMP) — A protocol that allows computers to identify their multicast group membership to routers on the network.

Internet Key Exchange (IKE) — A form of key exchange used to encrypt and decrypt data as it passes through a VPN tunnel. IKE uses tunnel method encryption to encrypt and then encapsulate packets for extra security.

Internet Protocol Security (IPSec) — A system of encrypting communications at the TCP/IP level rather than the communications produced by a specific program such as a Web browser or Web server.

Internet Protocol version 4 (IPv4) — The addressing system currently in widespread use on the Internet, in which addresses are created with 32 bits or 4 bytes of data.

Internet Protocol version 6 (IPv6) — A new version of IP that is gaining support among software and hardware manufacturers and that will eventually replace IPv4; it calls for 128-bit IP addresses.

Internet Security Association Key Management Protocol (ISAKMP) — A component protocol used by Internet Protocol Security (IPSec) that enables two computers to reach agreed-upon security settings and securely exchange security keys so that they can encrypt communications.

intrusion — An attempt to gain unauthorized access to network resources and compromise the integrity and confidentiality of the data contained on the network or the privacy of its users.

intrusion detection — The process of monitoring network traffic in order to detect attempts to gain unauthorized access to a system or resource and notify the appropriate professionals so that countermeasures can be taken.

intrusion detection system (IDS) — Software or hardware that detects whether a network or server has experienced an unauthorized access attempt and sends notification to the appropriate network administrators.

IP spoofing — The process of inserting a false address into the IP header to make the packet more difficult to trace back to its source.

IPSec driver — Software that handles the actual tasks of encrypting, authenticating, decrypting, and checking packets in an IPSec connection.

iptables — A packet filtering program that comes with version 2.4.x or later of the Linux kernel; also called Netfilter.

jump kit — A set of hardware and software tools used by incident handlers to respond to computer security events.

key — A long block of code that is generated by means of a mathematical formula called an algorithm. The longer the key, the harder it is to crack and the stronger the level of encryption involved.

keys — Values that can be processed by an algorithm to encrypt text, or to decrypt text that has already been encrypted.

leased lines — Point-to-point frame relay or other connections established by the telecommunications companies that own the lines involved in making the connection.

load balancing software — Software that prioritizes and schedules requests and distributes them to a group of servers based on each machine's current load and processing power.

load sharing — The practice of configuring two or more firewalls to share the total traffic load.

Local Address Table — A set of IP addresses that defines the internal addressing scheme of your network for a firewall or proxy server.

log files — Records detailing who accessed resources on the server and when the access attempts occurred.

logical assets — The word processing, spreadsheet, Web page, and other documents contained on your network computers.

man-in-the-middle attack — A type of attack in which an individual intercepts part of an encrypted data session in order to gain control over the data being exchanged.

maximum transmission unit (MTU) — The maximum packet size that can be transmitted over a type of computer network such as Ethernet.

mesh — A configuration in which all participants in the VPN are connected to one another.

message digest — A code that results from processing a message or other input through a mathematical function, usually resulting in a shortened version of the original input.

misuse detection — A type of intrusion detection in which an IDS is configured to send an alarm in response to sets of characteristics that match known examples of attacks.

Monte Carlo simulation — An analytical method meant to simulate a real-life system by randomly generating values for variables.

multicasting — The process of sending packets to all of the IP addresses on a subnet rather than to a single IP address.

multiple-entry point configuration — A type of VPN configuration in which multiple gateways are used, each with a VPN tunnel connecting a different location.

multiple-packet attacks — *See* composite attacks.

network address — The part of an IP address that a computer has in common with other computers in its subdomain.

Network Address Translation (NAT) — The process of concealing the IP addresses on a network by translating them into another IP address used by a router, firewall, or system software that performs NAT.

network assets — The routers, cables, bastion hosts, servers, and firewall hardware and software that enable those within your organization to communicate with one another and other computers on the Internet.

network interface cards (NICs) — Cards that connect a computer to a network and that enable the computer to communicate on a network.

network uptime — The amount of time you are connected to a network, such as the Internet.

node — A single workstation, a VPN appliance, a gateway, a host, or any combination of these.

non-repudiation — The ability to prevent one participant in an electronic transaction from denying that it performed an action.

notification — The process by which the appropriate members of the SIRT receive news about security incidents.

null packets — TCP packets that have no flags set whatsoever.

one-to-one NAT — A form of NAT in which each workstation that has a private IP address is assigned an external IP address on an individual basis.

one-way hash — *See* message digest.

Open Platform for Security (OPSEC) — A protocol developed by Check Point Technologies that enables its firewall products to integrate with software that provides anti-virus protection, intrusion detection, and other solutions.

Open Security Evaluation Criteria (OSEC) — A standard set of criteria used for reviewing intrusion detection signatures.

operational audit — An audit in which an organization's own staff examines their system logs and security logs to accumulate and analyze information about intrusions and other unauthorized accesses.

out of band — A term that describes the practice of locating computers outside the internal network, on a protected subnet of their own.

out-of-band notification — Notification of a security incident that occurs not on a computer network, but on another communications device such as a pager.

packet monkey — A hacker who is primarily interested in blocking the activities of a Web site through a Distributed Denial of Service attack.

packet sniffer — Software or hardware that monitors traffic going into or out of a network device and that captures information about each TCP/IP packet it detects.

packets — Segments of digital information that are of uniform length and that contain header information as well as a data payload; also called datagrams.

perimeter network — The subnet that's attached to the firewall and contained in an organization's DMZ. *See* Demilitarized Zone (DMZ).

ping sweep — The act of sending a series of ICMP Echo Request packets in a range of IP addresses to see if any computers respond.

Point-to-Point Tunneling Protocol (PPTP) — A tunneling protocol that is used for dial-in access to a remote server.

port filtering — The process of filtering packets of digital information by reviewing their TCP or UDP port numbers.

port scan — An attempt to connect to a computer's ports to see if any are active and listening.

private key — A key that you generate after obtaining it from a Certificate Authority (CA) and that you never exchange with anyone else; rather, you use the private key to generate public keys.

profile-based detection — A type of intrusion detection that compares current network traffic to a profile of normal network usage.

profiles — Sets of characteristics that describe the services and resources a user normally accesses on the network.

promiscuous mode — A mode of operation in which an IDS or packet sniffer detects and analyzes each packet in its entirety.

protocol filtering — *See* port filtering.

proxy server — A program that provides Web browsing, e-mail, and other services on behalf of networked users in order to conceal their identity from those outside the network.

public key — A key that you create with your private key and that you issue to individuals with whom you want to conduct secure communications.

public key cryptography — A form of network authentication that identifies individuals through the exchange of public and private keys.

Public-Key Infrastructure (PKI) — A system used to store, distribute, and manage public and private keys within an organization.

quarantine — An area of disk storage where viruses are placed when they cannot be deleted, and where they cannot replicate themselves or do harm to other files.

recovery — The process of putting media, programs, or computers that have been compromised by intrusions back in service so that they can function on the network once again.

redundancy — Back up systems that ensure that databases and other stores of information remain accessible if the primary systems go offline.

Remote Authentication Dial-In User Service (RADIUS) — An authentication method used to identify and verify the authorization of users who dial in to a central server in order to gain access to networked resources.

Remote Procedure Call (RPC) — A standard set of communications rules that allows a program on one computer to request a service from another computer on a network.

report — An analysis of a set of firewall data that is then presented in a format that is easy to read and interpret, such as a graph.

reverse firewall — A device that monitors information going out of a network rather than trying to block what's coming in.

risk — The possibility of incurring damage or loss.

risk analysis — The analysis of the primary security risks faced by a network.

risk management — The process of identifying, choosing, and setting up countermeasures justified by the risks you identify.

role-based authentication — A type of authentication that gives users limited access based on what role they play in the company and what applications they need to use.

rotate — The process of moving the current log file to a storage area and opening up a new log file.

router — A device that connects and directs traffic between networks.

routing table — A list of network addresses and corresponding gateway IP addresses that a router uses to direct traffic.

rule base — A set of rules maintained by a packet filter to determine whether packets should be allowed to pass through or be dropped.

safeguards — Measures, such as installing firewalls and intrusion detection systems, locking doors, and using passwords and/or encryption, that you can take to reduce threats.

scalable — A term that describes the ability of hardware or software to handle an increasing amount of throughput.

scanner — A device that scans a network for open ports or other potential vulnerabilities.

screened subnet — A network of servers or other computers that's shielded (or screened) by a router or firewall.

script kiddies — Individuals who spread viruses and other malicious scripts and use techniques to exploit weaknesses in computer systems.

Secure Shell (SSH) — A VPN authentication that works with UNIX-based systems that creates a secure Transport layer connection between participating computers and makes use of public key cryptography.

Security Association (SA) — A designation used to describe users, computers, or gateways that can participate in a VPN and encrypt and decrypt data using keys.

security auditing — The process of testing the effectiveness of a network defense system by testing the system, analyzing event logs, or observing procedures.

security event management program — A program that gathers and consolidates events from multiple sources so that they can be analyzed and used to improve network security.

Security Incident Response Team (SIRT) — A group of staff people designated to take countermeasures when an incident is reported.

security policy — A statement that spells out exactly what defenses will be configured to block unauthorized access, what constitutes acceptable use of network resources, how the organization will respond to attacks, and how employees should safely handle the organization's resources in order to discourage loss of data or damage to files.

Security User Awareness program — A program in which employees are formally instructed about the organization's security strategy.

security workstation — A dedicated computer that deploys a security policy through a centralized firewall to other firewalls that protect branch offices or other networks within the organization.

seed — A random string that will be used to generate a one-time password.

selective acknowledgements — Acknowledgements that selected packets in a sequence have been received, rather than having to acknowledge every packet.

server — A computer that provides Web pages, e-mail, or other services to individuals both inside and outside the network being protected.

server farm — A group of servers that are connected together in their own subnet and that work together to receive a large number of requests; the load is distributed among all of the servers in the "farm."

service network — *See* perimeter network.

session authentication — The process of authorizing a user or computer on a per-connection basis using special authentication software installed on the client computer that exchanges information with the firewall.

shim IDS — A type of network-based IDS in which sensors are installed on selected hosts as well as network segments.

signatures — The characteristics that identify a particular type of network traffic, such as source or destination IP address, protocol, or a combination of features.

single entry point configuration — A VPN configuration in which all traffic to and from the network passes through a single gateway such as a router or firewall.

single-packet attack — *See* atomic attack.

sniff — The process of receiving and analyzing packets as they pass into and out of the network, as performed either by a packet sniffing program, a network traffic analyzer, or an IDS.

social engineering — The act of fooling staff people into giving out passwords or other information.

socket — A network connection that uses a TCP/IP port number combined with a computer's IP address.

Socks — A communications protocol that provides proxy services for applications that don't normally support proxying and that enables applications to set up a secure tunnel using encryption and authentication.

softspot component — A network component that is both essential and at risk of being compromised.

source port — The port from which data is sent out to another computer.

source routing — The process of specifying the precise route a packet must take between computers to reach its destination.

spoofed address — An address that contains falsified information intended either to confuse or fool a server.

spoofing — Entering false information into the packets of data that travel along the Internet or on any network that uses TCP/IP.

star — A VPN configuration in which a single gateway is the "hub" and other networks that participate in the VPN are considered "rim" networks.

state information — Information that pertains to a network connection, which is typically kept in a state table.

state table — A file maintained by a firewall or other software that contains a record of all current connections or processes.

stateless packet filtering — Filtering that examines TCP/IP header information and blocks or allows packets based on that criteria, regardless of whether a connection has been established between server and client.

station address — The part of an IP address that is unique to computers in its subdomain.

strobe scan — A type of port scan that probes ports that are commonly used by specific programs, in an attempt to see if such a program is present and can be utilized.

subdomain — A set of IP addresses within a domain.

subnet mask — A value that tells another computer which part of a computer's IP address is its network address and which part represents the station address.

survivability — The ability to continue functioning in the presence of attacks or disasters.

survivability wrappers — Message filters applied at the OS interface level through authentication or other means.

Survivable Network Analysis (SNA) — A security process that starts with the assumption that a computer system will be attacked and follows a set of steps to build a system that can survive such an attack.

symmetric cryptography — A type of encryption in which the same key is exchanged by the sender and the recipient.

syslog daemon — A UNIX utility that runs in the background, receiving, logging, and displaying messages from routers, switches, and other devices on the network.

syslogs — System logs created in a Unix environment.

target — In the Linux packet filtering application iptables, this term denotes the action (such as drop, accept, queue, or reject) associated with a rule.

target-to-console ratio — The number of target computers on your network that is managed by a single command console.

threads — Processes used on operating systems such as Windows that respond to requests for documents.

Threat and Risk Assessment (TRA) — An approach to risk analysis that starts from the standpoint of the threats and accounts for risks that confront an organization's assets, and the consequences of those threats and risks should they occur.

threats — Events and conditions that have not yet occurred but that can potentially occur, the presence of which increases risk.

three-pronged firewall — A firewall that has three separate interfaces—for example, one to a DMZ, one to the Internet, and one to the internal LAN.

tiger teams — These are assembled in order to actively test the network.

Time to Live (TTL) — An instruction that tells a router how long a packet should remain on the network before it is discarded.

Tinkerbell program — A program that scans network connections and generates alerts when logins are attempted or when connection attempts are made from sites that have been identified as suspicious.

token — A small electronic device that generates a random number or password that can be used in authentication.

topology — The way in which the participants in a network are connected to one another.

trailer — An additional section that is added to a TCP/IP packet and that tells a computer that this is the end of the packet.

Transport Control Protocol/Internet Protocol (TCP/IP) — The combination of two protocols, Transport Control Protocol and Internet Protocol, that allow information to be transmitted from point to point on a network.

transport method encryption — A type of VPN encryption in which only the data portion of a packet is encrypted, not the header.

trigger — A set of circumstances that causes an IDS to send an alert message.

Trojan horse — A harmful computer program that initially appears to be something useful, but that creates an opening through which a hacker can potentially gain control of a computer.

true-negatives — Legitimate communications that do not cause the IDS to set off an alarm.

true-positive — A genuine attack detected successfully by an IDS, in contrast to a true-negative (an attack that goes undetected) or a false-positive (an attack alert generated by an event that is not an attack).

trusted networks — Networks that permit access to trusted users whose identities they can reliably verify.

tunnel — The connection between two endpoints in a VPN.

tunnel method encryption — A method of key exchange that encrypts both the header and data parts of a packet and encapsulates the packet within a new packet that has a different header.

two-factor authentication — A form of authentication that combines a password or PIN number (something the user knows) with something the user physically possesses, such as a smart card or token.

Type of service (TOS) — The part of a packet header that allows the sender the option to express the precedence of the packet—whether it should have low delay, whether it needs high reliability, and so on.

user authentication — The process of identifying an individual who has been authorized to access network resources.

vanilla scan — A type of port scan in which all of the ports from 0 to 65,535 are probed, one after another.

variable-length subnet masking (VLSM) — A way of applying multiple masks of varying sizes to the same network.

virtual private network (VPN) — A relatively low-cost and secure connection between organizations that use the public Internet as well as sophisticated encryption and authentication methods.

virtual team — A team that has other jobs to perform during regular business hours, and that only exists during meetings or when an incident becomes sufficiently serious.

virus — Computer code that copies itself from one place to another surreptitiously and performs actions that range from creating files to damaging information on a hard disk.

VPN appliance — A hardware device specially designed to terminate VPNs and join multiple LANs.

VPN client — A router or operating system that initiates a connection to a VPN server.

VPN domain — A set of one or more computers that is handled by the VPN hardware and software as a single entity, and that uses the VPN to communicate with another domain.

VPN protocols — Sets of standardized communication settings that computer software and hardware use to encrypt data that is sent along a VPN.

VPN server — A computer that is configured to accept VPN connections from clients.

vulnerabilities — Situations or conditions that increase threat and that, in turn, increase risk.

well-known ports — Ports that have been reserved for use by common TCP/IP services.

worm — A type of virus that creates files that copy themselves over and over and take up disk space.

worst-case scenarios — Descriptions of the worst consequences that befall an organization if a threat is realized.

Index

C

D

G

H

J

K

L

M

N

O

P

W

Z